UITGAVEN VAN HET
NEDERLANDS INSTITUUT VOOR HET NABIJE OOSTEN TE LEIDEN

voorheen Publications de L'Institut historique-archéologique néerlandais de Stamboul
sous la direction de
Machteld J. MELLINK, J. de ROOS,
J.J. ROODENBERG et K.R. VEENHOF

XCV

ELUSIVE SILVER

G. van Driel

Elusive silver. In search of a role for a market in an agrarian environment.
Aspects of Mesopotamia's society.
Uitgave: Nederlands Instituut voor het Nabije Oosten te Leiden (*voorheen* Uitgave van het Nederlands Historisch-Archeologisch Instituut te Istanbul, ISSN 0926-9568; 95)

ISBN 90-6258-096-3

Printed in Belgium

INTRODUCTION

The three studies presented here describe a variable orbit around one question which can be asked, but not effectively answered. It is that of what made the ancient Mesopotamian economy function as it did in the periods which were high points in its cyclic development. In a sense that question has occupied me often during the time I was privileged to spend at the Leiden Assyriological Institute, now practically of fond memory. It is the question how to find a market for what are basically agricultural bulk products, which ultimately results in payments in silver, which itself had to be earned through foreign trade. Study one suggests that already on the turn of the Third Millennium suitable circumstances existed, even though the backgrounds remain unclear.

That the Mesopotamian economy was agrarian can be no point of discussion. That it was cyclic will perhaps be accepted after some thought. If we look at the archaeological map, restricting ourselves to the proto-historic and historic periods and using our imagination, we notice a first period of growth into the ED I period, followed by a relative but notable decline. A new period of growth with political ups and downs starting somewhere early in the second half of the Third Millennium, or somewhat earlier, ending about the middle of the Old Babylonian period forms the next stage. After what seems to represent a sharp decline, but possibly nevertheless a happy period of ruralisation, slow growth starts again in the second quarter of the First Millennium, which quickens in the Chaldean and Achaemenid period and lasts at least until well into the Parthian period. In this we forget about regional differences, unequal intensity, faltering documentation and the problems caused by the unmistakable influence of increase in political scale, for that is, with the position of the non-sedentaries, another basic element of the Mesopotamian equation. An essential marker of the periods of growth is the existence of a four tiered settlement system, which has much of its basis in the structure of agricultural management. The status of the four-tiered system of settlement is a benchmark of the stage in the cycle attained in a given period.

The four tiered system manifests itself in different ways, as it has to adapt to the political situation, which can cause considerable strain to the system. Mesopotamian institutional management of agriculture easily translates into a four-tiered system, it can adapt to a society of small political units and it is equally compatible with a larger centralised monarchy where decisions are taken in one -sometimes moving- political centre, which can grow out of all proportions, at the costs of many a smaller centre. Perhaps that is a main reason why political centralisation in the later Early Dynastic period, and again in the middle Old Babylonian period was such a difficult, and often harmful, process. It is not the intention to elaborate on this point here, we want to contribute at this stage, especially through the third study, to the understanding of the situation found in the period of new prosperity which had begun by the middle of the First Millennium. Study three deals especially with policies influencing the prosperity of agriculture and, much more hesitatingly, with the results of increasing production.

The Babylonian solution we can perceive in the First Millennium lies in the role played in the settlement system by the regional religious centres with their considerable practical share in agricultural management. The second of the three studies presented here attempts to reconstruct a system which enabled a local elite to make the local sanctuary a viable basis for economic interests resulting from developments which found, as far as we can see for the moment, their origin in not strictly economic developments in the Ur III to Old-Babylonian period. Essential in this was that the lower clergy obtained a fixed share in the perks of religion. The sanctuaries came for practical purposes into the hands of a relatively broad based group, a system which survived the decline of the second half of the Second and the first quarter of the First Millennium. Though the clergy acted primarily out of its own interest, indirectly it constituted a pressure group for urban renewal. Those involved developed into a recognisable urban core population, of which the adoption of family names, with the prebend-related names standing out, is a sign. Seen from below, the towns with the old sanctuaries thus could function as an effective third layer under the monarchical capitals with their sometimes exorbitant growth. The third study suggests in passing that the presence of a tax office was probably one of the marks which singled out settlements -the second layer- which were more than a group of dwellings of ploughmen, important though this basic layer of simple villages was in the agricultural system. What is not studied in the second study, but what is of importance, is that if the prebendaries may have been the intelligentsia of their period, they also were, like other elements of the urban population, businessmen.

The third study deals with an aspect of the new growth of the First Millennium, in which taxation and stimulation of the agrarian production worked in tandem. The central question, with which it is difficult to come to grips, remains that of the market in which the silver was earned, basically through the sale of the agricultural products, whatever the form in which this occurred may have been. For the moment only analogy can help us, but the first study suggests that already in the Ur III period silver circulated in Mesopotamia. The additional problem of the later period, at any rate in the years of Achaemenid rule, is that much of the silver was taken out of circulation through payments to the, in essence foreign, king, which made replenishment of the stock a necessity. That silver had to be earned. But we cannot simply see the Persian period as one in which Mesopotamia was exploited. The Persians forged greater political unity and thus peace. Labour and silver went to Elam, but there it was used in part for constructive purposes. We need not assume that public works came to a halt in Babylonia itself. The general economic situation was one of expansion.

The broader overall analogies which suggest themselves are the export of textiles and the transit trade in tin in the Old Assyrian period, as studied by K.R. Veenhof, and the lucrative participation in internal trade in foreign parts as studied by J.G. Dercksen. A possible external trade in bulk products on the Persian Gulf and with Elam cannot be effectively studied for the moment. The internal trade in agricultural bulk products in the form of what F.R. Kraus dubbed the "Palastgeschäft" is being restudied by F. van Koppen, a fact which directly inspired the first study here. The role of the monarchy, on which studies two and three insist, is, as far as the Ur III period is concerned, R. de Maaijer's concern. We must await whether the monarchic form of government will be confirmed as an essential element in the management of the economy. The structure of all Mesopotamian states in our period was monarchical, to the degree that the four tiered settlement system had to adapt to that political reality, in which growth in scale meant increasing centralisation and, consequentially a reduction of the number of settlements in the top tier, whether this caused problems or not. The structure of the elite of the not too successful Neo-Babylonian temple in Sippar was H. Bongenaar's contribution, which the second study here exploits. In this manner what is presented here fits well in the partial obituary of what has been our institute.

I also want to mention in a general context the publications of the real Neo-Babylonians, especially M. Jursa, F. Joannès, J. MacGinnis and C. Wunsch as sources of inspiration and help. For the later Achaemenid period the contributions by M.W. Stolper tower above all else. Their work has been ransacked, but not exhausted.

The three studies presented here should be seen as dealing with elements of the structure that, with other factors, carried Ancient Mesopotamian society. As such they cannot be more than another down payment in what is a matter of ongoing concern.

Acknowledgements

These studies could not have been written without the MOS project, which was financed by NWO, and enabled my three colleagues, doctores H. Bongenaar, J.G. Dercksen and R. Jas to work for four years on studies which have not, as yet, been completed, but which I expect them to bring to fruition, just as they expect me to write down what they surmise hidden in a by now worn, bald skull. The weekly discussions we used to have, have marked the considerations put on paper here considerably, as they will be even more aware than I am. The two principal supervisors of the MOS project, Prof. Dr. M. Stol and Prof. Dr. K.R. Veenhof will know themselves associated in these thanks. Without their willingness to accept responsibility, of which the hazards are all too clear, the project would not have been possible. Actually the third study published here was intended for the Festschrift for K.R. Veenhof, but rapid growth entailed its disqualification for the purpose. The MOS project had the effect that a number of participants and active supporters made available much raw material, texts, transcriptions, notes, to others, on condition that they should be willing to contribute themselves. This material has been drawn upon here without it always being possible to thank a specific person. It is regrettable that the changes in structure which the university has imposed upon the shrinking Leiden Assyriology mean that the risk exists that it is no longer a suitable place where such material can be kept.

Several individual colleagues helped with advise in their specific fields of study. Th. Krispijn, as always and permanently, helped with all matters Sumerian. I have disturbed him countless times with inopportune questions. The first contribution could not have been written without R. de Maaijer and his extensive knowledge of the Ur III world. The many Friday afternoons we spent in trying to understand bureaucratic niceties are as much remembered with fondness, as regretted as a thing of the past. The importance of the subject of the first study dawned upon me when F. van Koppen proposed the Old Babylonian "Palastgeschäft" as the subject of his research project: the phenomenon occurs in other periods and we must continuously re-read the evidence before us. Something comparable will have existed in the Neo-Babylonian period. M. Stol is in sense directly responsible for the second study in urging me to tackle the subject for RLA, where it can find only limited space, and where much of the speculation presented and certainly the purpose offered here, must be regarded as out of place. The Neo-Babylonian texts dealing with taxation I read initially on several occasions with students interested in the Neo-Babylonian period, most recently with W. Meinhold and F. Weiershäuser. Afterwards I tried to turn the subject into an article, put it aside and reworked it in a different direction, making stimulation of land use an equally important factor as the simple gathering of income by the government.

Special thanks are due to H. Bongenaar for the considerable number of unpublished texts of which he made transcriptions, notes and occasional copies available, the texts often containing essential information. F. van Koppen helped especially with information on Old Babylonian Sippar, handing me notes and transcriptions and discussing matters of mutual interest. M. Stol also contributed unpublished material. I must thank W. van Soldt and K.R. Veenhof for answering more questions than they will realise. C. Waerzeggers, Gent, gave me insight in the material of her dissertation, she will hardly have noticed how much a sleepy head can absorb when it mulls over the consequences of what was said.

Study one was read by practically everybody in Leiden and commented upon by many. Number two was read in various early stages by C. Waerzeggers, H. Bongenaar, F. van Koppen and Th. Krispijn, in this order. All provided me with their notes and remarks. The last one benefited from hasty scrutiny by F. van Koppen. M. Stol read all, provided notes and discussed many points of mutual interest in the later stages of preparation. In extremis R. Jas provided a number of useful notes. All should be assured of my gratitude.

This comes at the end of a stay in an institute that has meant much for me. By "institute" I mean especially the informal structure that made Leiden Assyriology an excellent place to work, which it owed, and for the moment still owes, above everything else, to its library, and to those persons who have made that what it still is. Which will be, soon perhaps, has been, so excellent, because it did not belong to the University, which has not been such a pleasant place to work in for the last twenty years. The less said, the better, even great institutions go through periods of bad management, deplorable administration and financial problems.

I must thank my wife, Dr. C. van Driel-Murray, first for her critical scepticism concerning all Assyriological attempts to obfuscate the obvious, and secondly because she found the time to look at what is called English in Holland.

All faults are mine, not in the least degree those on this final point.[1]

Leiderdorp, April 2002

[1] The lists of literature appended to each of the studies contain only those publications which are of general importance for the subject concerned, much other literature is quoted in the footnotes. The excerpts of texts quoted in the third study are intended to urge the reader to study the evidence him- or herself, complete quotation is impossible, and what is given is a not always happy compromise between the essential and brevity. Special abbreviations used can be found at the end of the list of literature.

TABLE OF CONTENTS

PART I

MERCHANTS AND THE PROBLEMATIC MARKET IN TEXTS FROM UR III UMMA AND NIPPUR

CHAPTER I
THE UMMA MERCHANTS

1. Introduction: the problem

There are two groups of texts which, though strictly spoken unrelated, yet bear on the same question: was late Third Millennium Mesopotamian society completely dominated by its institutions, temple and palace, or was there a place for market forces, supply and demand, working, at least partially, outside these institutions and influencing their functioning? Perhaps we must exclude from our considerations times of scarcity, when people would be willing to give up anything. But what is the definition of scarcity? There is always "demand"., but the question is whether it can afford "supply"?

Elsewhere I have tried to argue that the institutions did not have the economic size to dominate society in all respects, though I would not deny their importance as repositories of economic power or as tools of governance. Here I want to (re-)discuss two groups of texts on the assumption that they throw light on the fact that the late Third Millennium institutions functioned in a society in which a market of some sort for agricultural products operated, with a special role for silver. The text groups are the Umma balanced damkar accounts, and the texts documenting small scale credit in Nippur and to a lesser degree in Umma in the same period.[1] The importance of the subject is the role attributed to silver: it had to be earned in a market of which the operation is difficult for us to reconstruct.[2]

2. The material

Reading the literature on the balanced accounts dealing with the affairs of the Ur III damkars from Umma conjures a uniform, consistent picture. Yet it is difficult to retrieve an answer to certain important questions from an already sizeable number of publications, of which the contributions by Hallo and Curtis, Snell and Neumann must be singled out as especially pertinent.[3] The procedure behind the texts is generally known and easily explained: a limited group of persons is made responsible by the institutions for commodities, preponderantly agricultural bulk goods, but also silver. On principle all the goods are valued in silver. In response those made accountable deliver other goods and, notably, silver to the institutions. The persons concerned, indicated with the term DAM.KAR$_3$, are, we can assume, personally accountable in the usual Ur III manner. The texts concerned balance the value in silver of the goods received against that of the goods returned. In case the damkar has received more than he has returned, as is generally the case, the surplus is indicated in silver with the added term LA$_2$.NI, if the opposite occurs and more has been returned than received, it is called DIRI. The (negative) SI.I$_3$.TUM returns at the head of the next account, for an exact balance is rare. Normally we are dealing with current accounts which are settled at certain intervals,

---

1 Similar texts from other places, especially Lagaš and Ur, are not numerous and pose their own problems. They need not be considered here.

2 Please note: (in Part I) g = GIN$_2$; š = ŠE (=1/180 GIN$_2$).

3 Curtis and Hallo, 1959; Snell, 1982; Neumann, 1979; Neumann, 1992a; Neumann 1992b; Neumann, 1993.

though there is one case in the corpus in which an account is closed down because the person concerned had died.[4] If goods of equal value were exchanged there is no reason why they should (re-)appear in a balanced account, though at any rate the institutional partner would have to account for the transaction in his own accounts. A simple receipt would be sufficient for the damkar in such a case, however. The upshot is that the balanced accounts in silver do not of necessity provide the complete picture of the transactions between the institution and the damkar, all the more so because there were other, commodity specific, accounts. The silver accounts are, however, of special significance.

In the relevant text corpus the term damkar is used in two different types of texts. The first one has a colophon NIG_2.KAS_7 AK PN DAM.KAR_3, in which the word DAM.KAR_3 can be skipped, though it is clearly intended, as it is evident for prosopographical reasons that the person concerned belonged to this category. The institutions regarded these persons as damkars. Whether a person could be, or under circumstances had to be, a damkar outside the context of the institutions is a question which cannot be answered, though it is possibly of some importance: does the term indicate a form of institutional accreditation, or could a person act as a damkar did, without requiring, or being permitted, to bear the "title", or without occupying the "function"? The matter is perhaps of importance for the question of the relation between the two groups of texts referred to at the outset.[5]

In a second group of related Umma texts the colophon NIG_2.KAS_7 AK DAM.KAR_3(.NE) plus an additional remark, sometimes consisting of a personal name, but not necessarily so, is found. Sometimes the remark reads ŠA_3.BALA.[6] The two relevant accounts share the fact that an intermediary (GIR_3) is mentioned, respectively Agu, probably the well-known Umma manager/keeper of the reed-account and Irmu, the KA.GUR_7, the keeper of the grain store, together with an Ur-Numušda, about whose status we will not speculate. These are accounts with a very specific background, as comparison with SNAT 490 (ŠS 4, but with items from yr. 3) explains, where the additional remark reads: ŠA_3 URI_5^{KI}.MA GIR_3 Abbagina,[7] through whom a direct link with YNER 8, 14 (ŠS 6) exists, where the remark is restricted to the name. In these accounts the term DAM.KAR_3 is positioned before the personal name, and not behind it, it can therefore not refer to that name. In this way SNAT 504 (ŠS 6) and 518 (ŠS 7) mentioning Lu-Ḫaia become comparable. The most important account of this type is, however, AO 6037 (ŠS

---

[4] I will avoid all terminology which could suggest that we are dealing with a form of double entry book keeping, Ur III, and indeed all institutional book keeping in Mesopotamia is something completely different, the word balanced merely refers to the relation between the value of what is received and what is handed back.

[5] Formerly it was suggested that only a damkar could or was allowed to handle silver (as a form of currency). I will not follow this way of reasoning on account of the role of silver in institutional accounting in general and especially because of the implication involved: anybody noted handling silver (as a form of currency) should be a damkar, which is definitely untrue.

[6] AAS 65 (AS 8 Š.B.) and Nik 403 (AS 9 Š.B.), in which ŠA_3.BALA functions as a kind of date and indicates an account.

[7] In texts from Umma we find this man regularly in connection with business in Ur and nearby Gaeš, where Umma had to contribute to the building of a sanctuary. Abbagina is mentioned in the balanced account of the damkar Šeškalla Ist UM 910 (AS 9), in YNER 8, 9 (XI AS 6), account of Ur-Dumuzida, he is in Gaeš. YNER 8, 14 (ŠS 6), is an account of Abbagina with damkars in general, mentioning his own institutional account. Important is also D. Frayne ARRIM 7, 1989, McGill 12 (AS 7), a LA_2.NI/DIRI account of commodities of a certain Duggagina, sealed by Abbagina.

6), mentioning Lukalla, the Umma keeper of the central silver account. None of these persons was a damkar, they were "officials".[8]

The question is: are these persons, at any rate those of the first group of accounts really involved in "trade"? Did they supply the market with goods, did they respond to a general demand for goods, especially for the locally produced bulk goods? Reading Neumann's contribution in AoF 6 suggests a notable difference between the damkars of Umma and the GA.EŠ$_8$s of Ur, sea-going traders, however marginally these may be documented. The Umma damkars operated completely, that is according to the balanced accounts, within the sphere of institutional requirements and obligations, the marker "(institutional) exchange-agent" would seem to be to the point in this respect. But did they also function outside the institutions, notably in what could be regarded as a market, where supply and demand played a role?

This is where our other main text group becomes relevant. Especially in Nippur a group of texts has turned up which is much less explicitly institutional, rather even, a rare phenomenon in the Ur III period, preferably to be regarded as originating in a private context. It is not so much that in this text group persons occur who are, perhaps sporadically, indicated as damkars, but rather that these persons provide credit against interest, to avoid the perhaps applicable "were involved in usury". In Umma such persons were not completely absent, but the number of texts available is much smaller, though the dates of the texts are of some interest. It is the amount of the Nippur material which constitutes its importance. Credit was mainly provided in the form of barley or silver. Dates, fats (sesame oil, lard) and wool are generally of lesser importance.[9] Anyhow the credit activities involve the agrarian bulk products and silver, the main liquid asset.[10]

The question of the link between the damkar of the institutional accounts and the providers of credit is of considerable importance, for the institution supplied the damkar with the agrarian bulk products and the form of credit provided suggests demand, the existence of a local market for bulk goods, even though these goods were the staple products of local agriculture.[11]

3. The situation in institutional Umma

The personal background of the damkars of the Umma balanced accounts is not easily explored. That is the logical result of the restricted background of the material available. Ur-Dumuzida, who has left the greatest number of relevant texts, is styled "damkar of Šara",[12] the

---

[8] That is, they were responsible for specific internal institutional accounts. The damkars were of course also responsible for their specific account, but that is not the point, unless the term damkar indicates exactly that fact. It is not clear to me whether the mentioning of an intermediary, GIR$_3$, in these texts is a period indicator. It is clear that accounts with special purposes for specific commodities existed, for instance someone's silver or wool account and it is also clear that accounts, or exerpts from accounts, dealing with others were made. Lukalla appears for instance as a GIR$_3$ in the (exerpted) comprehensive grain-account of the ENSI of Umma YNER 8, 13, which was to all likelihood composed after the death of the governor concerned and which belongs to the final settling of his accounts.

[9] That (small quantities) of wool occur in one text group is of some interest, this is a commodity not generally intended for immediate consumption, it involves a kind of "investment".

[10] Garfinkle 2000, which arrived too late in Leiden to be properly digested, contains many useful observations.

[11] This idea is far from original, it is found, for instance in Lutzmann's conclusion (1976) , cf. also Englund 1990, p. 199f. points in the same direction as that explored here.

[12] Neumann, AoF 20, p. 77, seal on MVN 13, 860, that of son Ur-Šulpae. (An Ur-TAR SUKKAL DAM.KAR$_3$ is a mere slip. We must regard Ur-TAR.LUḪ as a PN.)

main deity of Umma, but how the "House of Šara" operated remains in the dark.[13] In this case there must at least be question of some kind of appointment or accreditation, but in isolation it does not mean that all damkars were in a similar position. But if a damkar held a "title" of this type it is likely that he received rations or was assigned sustenance holdings by the relevant institution. In turn that would imply that the damkar would be directly involved in agricultural production. Ur-Dumuzida's activities do not notably differ in the texts available from those of the other Umma damkars.

The Umma archive is that of the central provincial administration under the responsibility of the local ENSI. In the balanced accounts the named individual damkars are accountable, but the party to which they are in that position is not specified, there was no need for that. The institution remains hidden behind the individuals who provided the capital, even if they certainly did not act in that capacity as private persons. Amongst these providers of capital figure the ENSI and prominently Lukalla, son of the important official Ur-e_{11}-e, who was, as mentioned already, during practically the whole period for which we have the balanced accounts keeper of the silver account.[14] This is a simplification, for there was not only his NIG_2.KAS_7 KU_3.GA[15] but also at least a NIG_2.KAS_7 SIKI.[16] These are accounts of a specific high ranking person, let us assume Lukalla, who was in turn accountable directly to the ENSI. The balance of his accounts had to be included in the final account of the ENSI to the king.

If this is correct TCL 5, AO 6037 (ŠS 6) must be regarded as a crucial document, it is not the account of a named damkar but of transactions with the damkars for which Lukalla was accountable, it functions at the same level as his silver or wool accounts.[17] The text is directly comparable to those accounts bearing the remark $ŠA_3$.BALA ("during the BALA", in Nippur) or "in Ur". These too belong to the segment of the administration for which Lukalla was responsible at a central provincial level. This is preferable to an interpretation which would turn "the damkar" into some collective body or which would change the phenomenon into a separate institution.[18]

---

[13] I can only mention YOS 18, 123 IV 10, account of Ur-Dumuzida, AS 9, also AO 5680 V 35, ŠS2, cf. furthermore Snell YNER 8 p. 88-9. The relevant receivers of goods must be identified, but it is at least clear that not all (trade) goods destined for (the E_2) Šara went through Ur-Dumuzida.

[14] It could therefore be suggested that the documents available are the remnants of the justificatory documents belonging to his account.

[15] e.g. TCL 5, AO 6037 I 4 ; SNAT 502 1-2. Silver account of the (absent) ENSI: YNER 8, 13, YBC 16607.

[16] TCL 5, AO 6037 I 4 en X 4.

[17] No individual persons/damkars are mentioned, but for the important official Šara-kam in VI 15 and 19 and Lu-Ḫaia, who should not be seen as a damkar, but rather fulfilled an important role in the local district administration of Apisal.

[18] This does not imply an explication of the reasons why AO 6037 should be called "the damkars' account of Lukalla". Amounts are transferred from one account to another, but those who supply "capital" no more than those who take delivery of goods are known to us as damkars. In so far as they can be identified they are institutional managers in Umma, but as said commodities pass from one account to another -all under Lukalla's responsibility? Similar considerations apply to other documents of the same type, like SNAT 504, Lu-Ḫaia, and YNER 8, 14, Abbagina. Possibly these documents derive their name from the fact that the goods in the expenditure section were provided by damkars. Or: possibly we still do not understand the word "damkar", which refers to a very specific form of activity.

Occasionally the persons on whose accounts the goods are booked are indeed damkars, for instance in BM 105345 (AS 1),[19] dealing with locally produced horticultural products.[20] In other instances the colophon uses the term damkar in a collective sense, though including others, not known as damkars. NATN 805 (AS 7) dealing with wool, mentions a number of known damkars, but also Lu-Enlila, to all probability the known foundry manager/accountant and Ur-Šulpae, who is explicitly called a KU_3.DIM_2, "goldsmith".[21] In what is called someone damkars' account more than one strain in the accounting process come together, the person accountable does not deal only with damkars, the various LU_2.NIG_2.DAB_5.BA, possibly, here, "accountable managers", are also implied, especially as receivers of goods, and not everybody who supplied the institution was a damkar. TCL 5 AO 6045, an account of Ur-e_{11}-e deals with goods as occurring in the damkar accounts, comparable are also the accounts of Ur-Šulpae, no doubt the same person who occurs in our damkar balanced accounts as "customer" for a variety of (minor) edible products.[22]

As generally accepted, this form of accountability was a typical internal affair of the institution even if the end result was destined for scrutiny at a higher central level. The texts tell us only something about the role of the damkar within the institutional accounting pyramid. It is possible that Ur-Dumuzida was an intermediary in the process of exchange of goods present in the "House of Šara" which were required for specific cult-related purposes, but that is only a possibility, for he definitely works also for Lukalla's account, that is for the provincial central organisation of the ENSI. The damkar was not exclusively tied to one type or level of institution or to a specific department.

The central provincial administration of the ENSI had many external obligations, deliveries for the BALA, mainly for the cult in Nippur, for Ur and for Uruk and for building projects undertaken by the central government. This is exactly where the damkars play a role. They provide in Nippur, Ur and Uruk specified commodities for specified requirements, for the king and for the cult, which had to be delivered by the province for the account of which the particular damkar acted. Perhaps BM 105345, referred to above, shows the manner in which the delivery of such goods was divided over those who were in the position to provide them for the institution. On the other hand the best interpretation of TCL 5, AO 6046 (AS 4), with the colophon SAG.NIG_2.GA.RA DAM.GAR_3.NE, "capital in relation to the damkars" is possibly that it is a schedule for the apportioning of the available capital over the various damkars, from which, however, other expenditure had to be deducted already at the outset.[23]

---

[19] The text was kindly made available by B. Jagersma.

[20] The structure of the text is particular. As far as I can see the products concerned are "never" booked on the capital side of the accounts, they are always delivered by the damkars. Here they appear as LA_2.NIs of named damkars, implying that we are dealing with backlogs in the delivery.

[21] We find this person for instance in connection with Babati, the noted pluralist, and the acquisition of gold in Ur in MVN 2, 23 III 11-15 (ŠS 6). Especially in connection with precious metals the goldsmith plays a role comparable to that of the damkar. This is not only understandable on account of the expertise required, but it also has to do with resources.

[22] Cf. in this respect his own accounts STA 11 (AS 1, GIR_3 Lukalla), AAICAB I Ash 1911-220 (A/Š/IS 1), YNER 8, 18 (AS 4), MVN 15, 127 (AS 9, sealed by a son of the PISAN.DUB.BA), IstUm 685 (ŠS 2, with commodities delivered by the damkar Lugal-nilagare), MVN 1, 151 (ŠS 5, outgoing, with for instance as GIR_3s Lukalla, and Ur-Dumuzida damkar). Probably there is much more.

[23] If my interpretation of his views is correct, Englund (Fischerei) is inclined to regard the damkars as indebted to the institutions. AO 6046 seems to indicate that the institutions had to scrape together the required capital and could not even earmark it properly. The planned assignations of lard in the capital sections, on which below, but paid in reality in barley, point in the same direction. Note in AO 6046 the leather products, which appear only in AS 5, and the beginning of yr. 6, in the accounts.

4. Products: local or not?

The products involved are probably the best indicators for the role of the damkar. Even if import products might seem to be more interesting at first sight, local products are of greater importance for our purpose. Surplus production of these products will theoretically have been concentrated in the institutions, but that does not seem to be a fact in general terms: products which could be produced locally are definitely acquired by the institutional administration through the damkars.[24]

The main question is that of the of the nature of the goods: what was produced locally, what can be qualified as an import product and how do these products end up in the hands of the damkar? Lexical problems cause considerable difficulties in this respect. It is preferable to start with the commodities the damkar received from the institution as his working capital, which must be regarded as the credit provided to him by the institution.

In the main[25] the list contains cereals (barley, exceptionally wheat), dates, fish, wool and silver, but we leave that last commodity aside for the moment. This list of the basic bulk products, provided by the institutions from their surplus production and possibly from their rent and taxation income, suggests a link with something much better known in the Old Babylonian period: the so-called Palast- or Tempelgeschäft (PTG), the process through which institutions changed their surplus income into (liquid) silver by allowing a certain rebate to the merchant acting as an agent.[26] But the question has an extension: does the PTG presuppose a local market for the commodities? Of the products mentioned wool was perhaps the only commodity which was readily saleable,[27] but what occurred with the other bulk products? Is the fact that the damkar took delivery of them sufficient for the supposition that a market existed?

In relation to the institutional craft industry in general it is clear that the damkars provided mainly basic raw materials. This applies especially to the production of metal objects. Not even bronze,[28] but only tin, copper and the not properly identified flux SU.GAN (and perhaps lead,) occur.[29] These are imports from outside Mesopotamia and we have little inkling how the local Umma merchants acquired these goods. These commodities were taken delivery of by the "smith", more properly the "foundry-accountant", Lu-Enlila.[30]

Other basic products for the crafts industries are in my opinion NAGA, "alkali" supplied as SI.E$_3$ "sprouted" and GAZ/KUM "crushed", A$_2$.DAR, "(ibex) horn", *eš-ku-ru-um*, "wax",

---

24 An escape for those who are convinced of the general predominance of the institutions could be to reason that for instance the House of Šara produced goods which did not go directly to the central institution of the ENSI, but through an "exchange agent", for instance because the imposed obligations had already been fulfilled and something could be demanded in return.

25 On leather, or craft products in general, see below; fruit occurs in YNER 8 no. 8, account of KUD.DA (AS 6), other commodities are even less important in the capital section.

26 Kraus, 1958, esp. Chapters 6 and 7.

27 It could be exported by the Ur seafaring merchants. Strikingly enough the Umma damkars did not receive textiles from the institutions. Textiles constituted Mesopotamia's assumed main export product, at any rate in the Old Assyrian period. Both wool and textiles belong to the commodities exported by the Ur gaeš's. The only craft product provided, and that may have been only a temporary question, were leather products, cf. TCL 5, AO 6052 en 6056, YNER 8, nos. 4, 7 and 8.

28 But cf. HUCA 30, Šeškalla As 3, 29 where some silver is given for the buying of an unspecified amount of bronze.

29 And, of course, gold, but that belongs to another sphere, see below.

30 Lexical problems prevent a similar apodictic statement concerning the aromatics, for the possibility exists that such products had already undergone some processing, which would imply that we are dealing with half-products. Cedar, supplied by weight, might for instance have the shape of shavings or of a powder.

PA.MUŠEN, "feathers", SIG_4.BA, possibly to be regarded as "turtle shell", and the chemicals IM.BABBAR (KUM), *a-la-ḫa-ru* and IM.GUŠKIN. There is no reason to assume that these products had to come from outside Mesopotamia, some may have been produced in Umma itself. To this the bitumen products can be added: ESIR, of the varieties A.BA.AL, E_3.A, $ḪAD_2$ and IGI.ESIR. These are presumably Mesopotamian products, but from outside Umma.

All types of fat included in the texts had undergone some processing: I_3, specified as DUG_3.NUN.NA, so *ḫimētu* and an animal product, GIŠ, thus vegetal, and KU_6, fishoil. I_3.UDU, if it really represents tallow should also belong here. To all likelihood these are local products, possibly produced by specialists. The damkar could act as an intermediary, but that would imply local specialised production outside the institutions. Very important is I_3.ŠAḪ, "lard", occurring both in the capital and in the expenditure sections of the accounts. But as we will see, it is in practice often replaced in the capital section by barley. Still in the Old Babylonian period it occurs in texts as a bulk product supplied to soldiers.

Timber for construction purposes or for furniture occurs rarely, where such is the case specified local products are involved: $ASAL_x$/*ṣarbatu*, "poplar", U_3.$ŠUḪ_3$/*ašūḫu*, "pine", but not, for instance, cedar.[31] Important is that, again, the damkar takes up a position between the local producer and the customer, the institution, though we are dealing with products also produced by the institutions themselves.

Among the lesser agricultural products it is notable that the damkars certainly supply the locally produced onion-family products to the institutions.

Umma animal husbandry takes place almost totally outside the documented sphere of activity of the institutional damkars. Only sheep and goat occur sparingly, rather accidentally, certainly when compared to the volumes occurring in other types of text. KUŠ.UDU, "sheep skin" and surprisingly KUŠ.ŠAḪ, "pig skin", are also mentioned incidentally in the Umma texts, these are supplied by the damkars.[32] Wool is the only animal product supplied as capital. This is not enough to suggest that the documented Umma damkar occupied an important central position in animal husbandry.[33]

An import product is possibly LAL_3, *dišpu*, "honey".[34] The absence of beverages is notable, if we skip the occasional reference to ŠIM.GAR, BAPPIR. There is also no local wine, GEŠTIN.$ḪAD_2$, "dried grapes" is therefore presumably an import from the North. Fruit occurring as both $DURU_5$ "fresh" and $ḪAD_2$ "dried" is of local origin (ḪAŠḪUR, "apple" and $PEŠ_3$, "fig"), $ḪAD_2$ without complementary $DURU_5$ is therefore probably an import. It is again the locally produced fruit which is of real interest for us: it supports the idea that the damkar occupies a position between the home producer and the home buyer.

Difficult are the flavourings. The origins of something simple like MUN, "salt", in Umma and the South in general remains an open question, local production is a rather obvious choice. GAZI, *kasû*, "mustard" will have been planted locally. But what with KU.MUL?, ZA_3.ḪI.LI, *saḫlû*, "cress" and ŠE.LU_2, *kisibirru*, "coriander", are also local, but ŠE.LI, *kikkirânu*, if really the seeds of the juniperus, will come from "the West", therefore also ZA.BA.LUM,

---

[31] Wood supplied in weighed amounts should be counted amongst the aromatics.

[32] Cf. above *ḫimētu* and tallow.

[33] The possibility that in animal husbandry the *nāqidu*, as a "chief-shepherd", plays a comparable role could be considered in the light of S.J. Garfinkle's study of the SI.A-a archive, though animal husbandry does not play a notable role in the texts available. Garfinkle 2000 p. 45ff. On the other hand any "keeper of an account" would usually be in the position to provide credit.

[34] Or are there *ḫumbubēti* in the South? Whether LAL_3 really is (always) honey and not rather anything sweet and sticky, i.e. some date product, is becomming a communis opinio. Th. Krispijn stresses that LAL_3 generally occurs together with GEŠTIN and dates. On that basis LAL_3 is a local product, and GEŠTIN is, at least, not always wine.

supalu.[35] I do not venture an attempt concerning the various types of ŠIM, but for noting that ŠIM.GIG, *kanaktu* is said to be a mountain product acclimatised in the lowland.

Disregarding the many, especially lexical, problems, two important facts remain: the damkars receive bulk products produced by local agriculture, and deliver both for internal use and to implement the local obligations at an interregional level both local and imported commodities. The fact that they supply ordinary local products is of considerable importance when we attempt to understand the role of the damkar: even locally he is situated between production and market, represented in this case by the institutions. His role is not only to provide imported goods from Mesopotamia itself or from the outside.

5. The core of the matter: bulk products and silver

The institutions supplied the damkars with agrarian bulk products on which the institution itself put a value in silver. Therefore they must have been able to pay that silver back if it exceded in value the commodities they were asked to supply. This implies two things: the existence of a market for the bulk products and the circulation of silver. At least a part of the volume of the goods supplied was exchanged for silver. For practical purposes this mainly refers to barley. Wool was probably less of a problem. The volume of the other products involved is limited.[36]

To a certain degree the damkars could obtain local craft products and more importantly local agricultural products. It is certainly too risky to assert that they occupied an intermediary position which enabled them to use the agricultural bulk products received from the institutions as wages for the producers of the specialised products mentioned. These producers would work in that case for the market and the damkar would be a classic example of an entrepreneur of a type we find for instance in the Neo-Babylonian period. Onions were part of the basis of the Egibi fortune, but though the Umma damkars also dealt in onions, we would already have gone a step beyond the PTG-theory in supposing that they arranged for the production of onions in order to market them, though the possibility can be left open.

Remains the fact that exactly the local agricultural non-bulk products tell us most concerning the position of this group of persons: though a local phenomenon these accounts betray especially at a local level a certain degree of production of bulk products[37] not intended for use by the institutions themselves, but which were partially used to acquire also locally produced special products.[38]

Participation in the flow of goods from the province to the political nerve centres Ur, Uruk, Nippur, would have meant access to places where imported goods were present. In later periods Babylon was the place where this type of products was available. The institutions had interlocal obligations, in order to fulfil their obligations regarding a number of special products they engaged the damkars, who in this way obtained better access to non-local goods. This would apply especially to the ordinary base metals and luxury goods like aromatics and gold. Bitumen is also interesting, but the way in which this was exploited in this period is as yet

---

35 Not assured, Joannès, MARI 7, 1993, p. 255.

36 This information derives mainly from the balanced accounts. There are some additional texts informing us on other aspects of the matter, for instance direct payment in silver by a known damkar for fish products.

37 This includes rents and taxation.

38 Remarkably enough not textiles in Umma. But if the Ur gaeš was able to export textiles that implies that somewhere in Southern Mesopotamia there existed a textile "industry" which worked for an external market.

unknown.[39] Someone must have gathered it and have made it transportable in standard amounts. In excavated material the impressions of the mats in which the bitumen was packed are occasionally visible. In the Neo-Babylonian period it is notable that there were specialists who were able to deliver this material over long periods of time.

The only damkar about whose background something more is known was, it would seem, a damkar of Šara. This could mean that his activities belonged completely to the institutional sphere, but if we observe that he received bulk products and delivered required special products, that becomes fairly dubious.

Strictly spoken nothing remarkable, but the local trade in products is here of more theoretical importance than the long distance trade, even though that probably produced, at least relatively, greater gain, if the general theory applies. More importantly: it provided the essential silver.

6. Bulk products: was the damkar charged a favourable price?

A possible approach to the problem "role and position of the damkar" is a detailed study of prices, as carried out by Snell. The PTG-theory presupposes that the damkar received a rabat and enjoyed credit. The credit is fairly obvious in Umma, certainly if we assume that the "capital" was made available at the outset, but this is not completely certain as is it possible that the accounts are no more than the periodic -but at irregular intervals- settling of outstanding matters, whereas many transactions were settled *ad hoc* and need not appear in the accounts, as at least a text from the Ermitage suggests.

We must especially look for deviations from the institutional "notional prices", and on which side of the balance these can be found. In making the attempt we must take the ancient measures mentioned by the texts at face value, even if we know that this was certainly not always a fact in this complex of texts.[40]

Regrettably Snell's lists are no longer complete and his arrangement of the facts is often difficult to use. A first requirement is to establish what the status of a text in which a certain price occurs is. The price for a bulk product charged to a damkar, that is the amount in silver in the section of the text dealing with the credit provided to him, is not necessarily identical with the price in an account of for instance the ENSI or Lukalla, and potentially even less is it equal to the hypothetical market value. The potential differences are the core of the matter. The amount of useful information available is therefore restricted. What follows is directly derived from the accounts.

a. Barley[41]

Barley in the capital section of balanced merchants' accounts

publication	date	name	barley	silver	pro kor
Bromski 1-2	XIII AS 2	Ur-TAR.LUḪ	49.0.0.0	65g60š	1.33g
3-4			2.2.3.0	3g22.5š	1.25g
YNER 8 7 3-4	AS 5	Lu-Inanna	40.0.0.0.	33g60š	0.833g
YNER 8 8 2-3	AS 6	Kudda	90.0.0.0	75g	0.833g
YNER 8 11 8-9	IX AS 7	Padda	15.0.0.0	15g108š	1.04g
10-11			5.0.0.0	5g	1g

[39] For technical aspects M. Stol refers to M. Schwartz and D. Hollander, Annealing, Distilling, Reheating and Recycling: Bitumen Processing in the Ancient Near East, Paléorient 26/2, 2000, p. 83-91.

[40] YNER 8 13: 1-2, (YBC 16607, ŠS1-5).

[41] In the following sections first the evidence from the accounts of named damkars is given, it is followed by that from the "general" damkar accounts of officials, named or not, after that comparable material can be quoted.

HUCA 30 2-3	AS 3	Šeškalla	30.0.0.0	30g	1g
AO 6056 1-2	AS 5	Šeškalla	60.0.0.0	60g	1g
IstUm 910 6-7	AS 9	Šeškalla	5.0.0.0	5g	1g
AOAT 203 I12-3	I AS 3	Ur-Dumuzida	180.0.0.0	225 g	1.25g
15-6			7.4.0.0	9g135š	1.25g
Erm 14969[42] 13-4 X	AS 3	Ur-Dumuzida	60.0.0.0	65g	1.08g
MVN I 240 I 8-9 XII	AS 8	Ur-Dumuzida	30.0.0.0	40g	1.33g
YOS 18 23 1-6	AS 9	Ur-Dumuzida	360.0.0.0	360g	1g
8-9			60.0.0.0	60g	1g
AO 5680 7'-8'	ŠS 2	Ur-Dumuzida	95.0.0.0	83g150š	0.88g
10'-11'			91.3.0.0	81g90š	0.89g
YNER 8 15 1-2	ŠS 7	Aakalla	60.0.0.0	85g130š	1.425g
			6.0.0.0	6g(10š?)	1.(027)g
Expenditure section balanced damkar account					
STA 23 III 23 XI	AS 6	Padda	0.1.0.0	36š	1g
Damkar account					
AO 6046 IV 1-2;	AS 4	general	55.0.0.0	37g90š	0.683g
Damkar accounts of Abbagina					
SNAT 490 1-4;	ŠS 4		15.0.0.0	20g	1.33g
YNER 8 14 1-2	ŠS 6		38.3.1.3	27g107.5š	0.71g.
Damkar account of Lukalla					
AO 6037	ŠS 6		400.0.0.0	285g129š	0.71g
			60.0.0.0		
			420.0.0.0		
			262.2.5.9		
			742.2.5.9	530g77š	0.714g
Account of (deceased?) ENSI compiled by Lukalla					
YNER 8 13	ŠS 1		180.0.0.0*	157g9.5š	0.872g
	ŠS 2		70.0.0.0	70g	1g
	ŠS 3		134.0.0.0	157g90š	1.157g
Silver account (of Lukalla?)					
HSM 911-5-23[43]	ŠS 2 price accepted (/obtained?) by Urša-kidug and Ḫašaša:				
			<720.0.0>	600g	0.833

* This amount consists of 70 kor measured by a 1.0.5 kor measure and of 110 kor measured by a 1.0.4 kor, if this is recalculated according to the 300 $SILA_3$ kor the price is only 0.545g per kor, by far the lowest value for barley assigned. This must caution us.
Note: 0.833g = 150 ŠE; 0.71 g = 130 ŠE.

The interpretation of this set of dates is not easy. The notional price of 1 g per kor occurs, it is especially notable in Šeškalla's accounts for the reign of Amar-Sin, but in general the damkar is charged more, 25% or even 33.33%[44] (still more once in the Aakalla account ŠS 7), though 5/6 g also occurs. Notably the 1 GIN_2 equivalent appears in the one outgoing occurrence noted, but it cannot be compared with an incoming post in this same year. Why in the same year one damkar is charged more than another requires explanation. Moreover the

42 N. Koslova, SANTAK 6 no. 119.

43 See below.

44 Accidentally or not the normal interest for respectively silver and barley? 25% might suggest a silver-related transaction.

question of annual or seasonal variations needs consideration. The lowest values occur in internal accounts for ŠS 6, but they cannot be compared with other estimates for this year for the moment. In ŠS 2 Ur-Dumuzida is charged less than the ENSI, but it is slightly more than other damkars, Urša-kidug and Ḫašaša, see below, accept. There is thus no firm basis for the supposition that the damkar is uniformly charged a favourable price by the institution when dealing with cereals.

b. Dates

Dates in the capital section of balanced merchants' accounts

Text	Date	Name	amount	price	pro kor
AO 6052	AS 5	Inimmanizi	24.4.2.0	16g109š	0.665g
			97.0.0.0	64g120š	0.666g
YNER 8 8	II AS 6	Kudda	120.2.3.4	80g61.5še	0.666g
SNAT 365	AS 6	KA.UR.ša	30.0.0.0	20g	0.666g
YNER 8 2	AS 3	Padda	12.0.0.0	12g	1g
			18.0.0.0	12g154š	0.714g
YNER 8 4	AS 5	Padda	63.0.3.2	42g16š	0.666g
			60.0.0.0	40g	0.666g
STA 23	XI AS 6	Padda	74.0.5.0	49g140š	0.662g
YNER 8 11	IX AS 7	Padda	40.0.0.0	33g 60š	0.83g
AO 6056 12-3	AS 5	Šeškalla	64.0.0.0	42g 120š	0.666g
15-6			50.0.0.0	33g60š	0.666g
(YNER 8 6 1-2	AS 5	Šeškalla	30+	25+g	---)
JRAS 1939 9-10	XI AS 6	Šeškalla	90.0.0.0	60g	0.666g
IstUm 910 9-10	AS 9	Šeškalla	12.0.0.0	10g	0.83g
YOS 18 122 I 2-4	AS 4	Ur-Dumuzida	219.0.5.0	156g100š	0.714g
YNER 8 9 I 5-6	XI AS 6	Ur-Dumuzida	96.0.0.0	60g	0.625g
7-8			27.0.0.0	16g120š	0.617g
13-14			?	5g110š	---
YNER 8 10 I13-4	VII AS 7	Ur-Dumuzida	30.0.0.0	25g	0.83g
STA 1 I 3-4	VII AS 8	Ur-Dumuzida	121.1.0.0	93g45š	0.679g
MVN I 290 I 5-6	XII AS 8	Ur-Dumuzida	72.0.0.0	60g	0.83g
IstUm 3187 I 4-5	XIII ŠS 1	Ur-Dumuzida	3.1.0.6	2g86š	0.82g
Damkar account					
AO 6046	AS 4		175.0.0.0	116g40š	0.664g
Damkar account of Lukalla					
AO 6037	ŠS 6		589.4.0.2	294g20š	0.498g

Note: 0.666g is 120 ŠE, 0.714g is 130 ŠE and 0.83g is 150 ŠE.

In Ur III Umma dates seem to have been cheaper per kor than barley when they are assigned a value in the accounts of named damkars. They have definitely not reached the interchangeability with barley which was administratively accepted in the NB period, but probably also there did not constitute a reality in the market, as barley remained more expensive. 1 kor equals 1 g seems to occur only once, and irrespective of the amount two thirds of a GIN_2 was common in AS 5 and 6, with 0.83 (= 5/6 GIN_2) being "normal" in AS 7-9. The value put on dates in Lukalla's damkar account for ŠS 6 is strikingly low. Compare what seems suggested concerning barley: values tend to be lower than in the named damkar accounts, but not always.

Snell, YNER 8 p. 137 boldly stated that 1 GIN_2 of silver buys 1 kor of dates, but he can only quote a number of Ur III texts from Ur for this equation. If we are bold we find here some proof for the theory that the damkars are charged favourable prices by the administration. This is, however not supported by the values assigned by the two administrative accounts available. The evidence is too limited, though it is fairly consistent as to time. Annual fluctuations do seem to play a role.

c. Wool

Wool in the capital section of balanced merchants' accounts

Text	Date	Name	amount	price	per GIN_2
AO 6052 I 8-9	AS 5	Inimmanizi	360m	40g	9m
SNAT 365 I 1-2	AS 6	KA.UR	600m (GI)	60g	10m
3-5			300m	33g.60š	9m
YNER 8 4 I 1-2	AS 5	Padda	360mg	40g	9m
AAICAB# I 3-5	XI AS 5	Padda	780m	83g60š	9.36m
6-7			420m (n.)	33g60 š	12.6m
STA 23 I 9-10	XI AS 6	Padda	480m	53g.60š	9m
11-12			1200m	120g	10m
			1m	20š	9m
YNER 8 11 I 5-6	IX AS 7	Padda	567m	57g126š	9.8m
YNER 8 12 I 3-4	ŠS 5	Padda	20m (GI)	1g120š	12m
AO 6056 I 6-7	AS 5	Šeškalla	120m	40g	3m*
YNER 8 6 I 6	AS 5	Šeškalla	360m	40g	9m
BM 106064 I 4	XI AS 6	Šeškalla	300m	33g60š	9m
6-7			420m	42g	10m
AOAT 203 I 9-10	I AS 3	Ur-Dumuzida	600m	60g	10m
19-II 1			1920m	192g	10m
YOS 18 122 I 7-8	AS 4	Ur-Dumuzida	976m	108g80š	9m
I 10-11			1200m	130g	9.23m
YNER 8 9 I 3-4	XI AS 6	Ur-Dumuzida	2280m	228g	10m
YNER 8 10 I 3	VII AS 7	Ur-Dumuzida	630 m	63g	10m
I 4-5			580m	58g	10m
I 8-9			300m(s)	30g**	10m
STA 1 I 6-7	VII AS 8	Ur-Dumuzida	1153m	96g	12m
YOS 18 123 I 12-3	AS 9	Ur-Dumuzida	2160m	180g	12m
16-8			1800m	150g	12m
20-21			7m	45š	12m
IstUm 3187 I 10[45]		Ur-Dumuzida	50m	5g30š	9.67m
AO 5680 I 4-5	ŠS 2	Ur-Dumuzida	300m	25g	12m
Damkar account					
AO 6046	AS 4		2700m	300g	9m
Damkar account of Lukalla					
AO 6037 IX 39-41	ŠS 6		400m	120g	3.33m
X 2-4			865m40g	72g25š	c 12m

45 Emendation of GAZI into SIKI is suggested by the fact that a weights measure is used and that wool commonly occurs in capital sections.

[#] Stands in the summaries for AAICAB I 1924-667
* Text states ŠA$_3$.DUB.BA, possibly meaning "only this amount is included in this account"?
** Additional remark.

Out of 28 useful occurences eight have 9 mina of wool for one GIN$_2$ of silver, three offer between 9 and 10, nine show 10 mina and six have 12 mina. Exceptional is AO 6056 (AS 5, Šeškalla) I 6-7 with 1 GIN$_2$ equalling 3 mina, but the wool is accompanied by the ununderstood remark ŠA$_3$.DUB.BA, which possibly could mean that only a part of the price is included in the account in question. It is notable, however that the damkars are charged in the course of the period of the accounts a notably lower price for wool, a decrease of 25% is considerable. But what does it mean: overproduction, diminishing demand or a favourable price for the damkar, possibly because other prices developed less attractively? Especially regarding wool quality will influence the price in an institutional context.

d. Fish in the capital section of balanced merchants' accounts
A= KU$_6$.GIR$_2$.US$_2$; B= KU$_6$.ŠE$_3$.BAR; C= KU6.SAG.KUR$_2$; D= KU$_6$.SEG$_6$; E= KU$_6$.GAM.GAM; F= B+ ERIN$_2$; G= C+ ERIN$_2$; H= KU$_6$.SAG.KEŠ$_3$ BU; I= KU$_6$ GANA$_2$.MAḪ.

			number	silver	per item
AO 6052	AS 5	Inimmanizi	A 12570	16g20š	0.23š
			B 1380	3g84š	0.45š
			C 1980	2g36š	0.2š
			D 3.1.2.4 gur	1g105š	1 kor = 61.1š
			B 600 (sig)	69š	0.115š
			C 660 (sig)	76š	0.115š
			E 660	1g12š	0.29š
YNER 8 8	II AS 6	Kudda	A 11970	15g48š	0.22š
			B 1380	3g84š	0.45š
			C 1980	2g36š	0.2š
			F 600	69š	0.115š
			D 4.0.0.0	1g	1 kor = 45š
			E 720	144š	0.2š
		I$_3$.KU$_6$	0.1.0.0	2g	1 kor = 10g
YNER 8 4	AS 5	Padda	A 8640	11g22.5š	0.23š
			B 600 (+BU)	69š	0.115š
			H ?	+76š	---
			E 1980	2g24š	0.193š
			C 2190	2g77š	0.1995
		I$_3$.KU$_6$	0.2.0.0	4g	1 kor = 10g
(Erm 7724	AS 3	Šeškalla	D 26.0.0.0	15g162š	1 kor =108.69š)
AO 6056	AS 5	Šeškalla	C 1980	2g36š	0.2š
			B 720	2g	0.5š
			A 3300	4g50š	0.23š
			C 2190	2g78š	0.2š
		I$_3$.KU$_6$	0.2.0.0	4g	1 kor = 10g
STA 22	AS 4	Ur-Dumuzida	D 28.3.0.0	12g55š	1 kor = 77.4š
			I ?	3g60š	---

Damkar account

AO 6046	AS 4		A 27600	35g99š	0.231š
			A 6540	5g63š	0.147š

	B 900	2g	0.4š
	B 3000	8g60š	0.5š
	C 4380	4g156š	0.2š
	A 16200	20g135š	0.2305š
	B 1740	1g168š	0.2š
	E 4560	5g12š	0.2š
	D 17.3.0.0	8g 144š	1 kor = 90 še
	B 3000	1g170š	0.1166š
	C 3300	2g11š	0.1124š
	C 9900	11g	0.2
I_3.KU_6	1.4.0.0	18g	1 kor = 10g

NB: 1 for 0.115š means ca. 1565 for 1 GIN_2; 1 for 0.2š means 900 for 1 GIN_2; 1 for 0.23š means c.780 for 1 GIN_2; 1 for 0.45š means 400 for 1 GIN_2;

It is notable that fish only seems to occur in the accounts of AS 3-6. Erm 7724, the only AS 3 text, Šeškalla, is (on top of that) a separate fish account. The text is of considerable importance in that it seems to represent a straightforward conversion of a bulk commodity into silver by a damkar.[46]

In general the prices of AO 6046 agree with those of the accounts of the named damkars. Only category D is strikingly erratic.

e. "Leather" in the capital section of balanced merchants' accounts
A= ^{KUŠ}UMMUD; B= $^{KUŠ}A_2.GA_2.LA_2$ (*mâš-li-um*); C= ^{KUŠ}E.SIR_2.E_2.BA.AN; D= ditto with ŠU.SU.UB and E= ditto with ŠU.LI.LA,[47] in both these last instances E_2.BA.AN can be left out.

AO 6052	AS 5	Inimmanizi	420 KUŠ.UDU UG_7	4g120š	1 = 2š
			A 25	1g 70š	1 = 10š
			B 65	1g145š	1 = 5š
			C 40 + E 5(?)	2g165š	(C = 12š, and E = 9š)
YNER 8 7	AS 5	Lu_2-Inanna	A 10	100š	1 = 10š
			B 40	160š	1 = 4.71š
			? 24	1g150š	---
			D 5(?)	45š	1 = 9š
YNER 8 8	II AS 6	Kudda	A 25	1g 70š	1 = 6š
			B 70	1g150š	1 = 4.71š
			420 KUŠ.UDU	4g120š	1 = 2 š
			C 40 + D 5	2g165š	C = 12š and D = 9š
YNER 8 4	AS 5	Padda	420 KUŠ.UDU.UG7	4g120š	1 = 2š
			A 20	1g 20š	1 = 10š
			C 48	3g 36š	1 = 12š
			D 5	45š	1 = 9š

---

46 The absence of fish from accounts does not mean in itself that the damkars were not involved in the disposal of surplus fish, only that the commodity was not included in the balanced acount.

47 Duely registered A. Salonen, Fussbekleidung der alten Mesopotamier, Helsinki 1969, p. 20-21. We can only note that the terms ŠU.SU.UB and ŠU.LI.LA are complementary in this small text group and that the value is the same.

			B 40	1g 20š	1 = 5 š
AO 6056	AS 5	Šeškalla	A 10	101?š	1 = 10š
			C 10	120š	1 = 12š
Damkar account					
AO 6046	AS 4		C 198	13g	1= 11.818š
			E 30	1g 90š	1 = 9š
			A 160	16g	1 = 10š
			B 300	7g 90š	1 = 4.2
			2400 KUŠ.UDU	40g	1 = 3š

The limited time range has been remarked upon already. This may or may not have the same background as noted in the case of fish. Notable is the difference in price for the KUŠ.UDU between AO 6046 and the other texts. For the general question of the meaning of this group of accounts these commodities are of limited value, though the texts indicate that institutional craft products occasionally were provided to the damkars

f. I_3.ŠAḪ, *nāḫu*, "lard"

Lard is of special interest in that it on the one hand belongs to the bulk goods which the institutions at least planned to provide to the damkars. But in reality they always had to exchange the product for barley or silver as passages containing the phrases ŠE I_3.ŠAḪ or KU_3 I_3.ŠAḪ, "barley/silver in lieu of lard", indicate. On the other the interest is, that it was in reality a commodity provided by the damkar to the institution, albeit in small quantities. This suggests that the institutions intended to produce more, but consistendly failed to deliver what they had intended. The damkar had to make good the shortfalls in production.

In the capital section of accounts of individual damkars:

AO 6052 1-2	AS 5	Inimmmanizi	I_3.ŠAḪ	silver?	pro kor
YNER 8 8	II AS 6	Kudda	(ŠE for I_3.ŠAḪ?	75g)	
AAICAB	XI AS 5	Padda	(ŠE for I_3.ŠAḪ	60g)	
YOS 18 123	AS 9	Ur-Dumuzida	(ŠE for I_3.ŠAḪ	360g)	
In the expenditure section of accounts of individual damkars					
YNER 8 11	XI AS 7	Padda	3.4.2.9,33	77g172š	20g
HUCA 30	AS 3	Šeškalla	0.0.5.1	3g174š	23.33g
Orient 21	XI AS 6	Šeškalla	0.0.3.3,66	1g 120š	15g
STA 22	AS 4	Ur-Dumuzida	1.3.3.4	39g176še	23(+)g
YNER 8 9	XI AS 6	Ur-Dumuzida	3.3.3.2	45g108še	12.3g
YOS 18 123	AS 9	Ur-Dumuzida	0.4.5.2,5	22g135še	23.33g
			10.0.0.0	250g	25 g
Damkar account					
AO 6046	AS 4		226.0.0.0 ŠE for I_3.ŠAḪ	188g60š	150 š
Damkar account Lukalla, expenditure section					
AO 6037	ŠS6		10.2.0.7	208g84š	20g
			0.1.0.0	4g	20g
			0.0.0.7	80š	19g
			0.0.2.9	1g81š	15g

The prices for I$_3$.ŠAḪ are not very informative, only the discrepancy between intended delivery of surplus material to the damkar and the need to acquire it (in modest quantities) from him is of some interest. This is a local product, which could be provided by the damkar.

g. Various other goods in the capital section

Accounts of individual damkars

Bromski 7-9 XIII AS 2	Ur-TAR.LUḪ	22 ^{GIŠ}PEŠ$_3$ ŠE.ER.GU x	
		0.0.2.6 ^{GIŠ}PEŠ$_3$.x	147.5š[48]
YNER 8 8 II AS 6	Kudda	0.3.0.0 ^{GIŠ}PEŠ$_3$.DURU$_5$	90š (1.0.0 = 150š)
STA 23 IX AS 5	Padda	0.3.3.0 ^{GIŠ}UR$_2$*gunû*	105š
(YNER 8 11 IX AS 7	Padda	MA$_2$ SU.A	20š)
JRAS 1939 II AS 6	Šeškalla	? ŠIM$_3$.AM$_3$ KU.MUL	70š
YNER 8 9 XI AS 6	Ur-Dumuzida	0.2.0.0 ^{GIŠ}[x}	60š
Damkar account at Ur			
SNAT 490 ŠS 4		0.0.0.4.5 LI	13g90š

No useful information can be distilled from this disparate set of figures.

7. Turning commodities into silver[49]

The accounts are phrased in silver. All outstanding amounts, LA$_2$.NIs,[50] from previous accounts are calculated in this metal and (rare) DIRIs are withdrawn in it, but these amounts are in reality the outcome of adding and subtracting the equivalents of the commodities received or delivered in the previous account, and the amounts need not represent silver actually present. More important are the amounts of silver listed as actually receipted by the institutions on the delivery side of the accounts.[51]

For a start it should be noticed, however, that the authorities regularly provided silver to the damkars, but those actually transferring silver included other damkars.[52] The more important text is AOAT 203 (Ur-Dumuzida I AS 3) where Lukalla provided one mina, the damkar Ur-Ninsu double that amount, and the official Ur-e$_{11}$-e another 40 GIN$_2$. But note, table below, that this text also mentions repayments in silver. In YOS 18, 13 (Ur-Dumuzida, AS 9) Lukalla provided 118 GIN$_2$ 145 ŠE, and in AO 6680 (again Ur-Dumuzida, ŠS 2) 63 GIN$_2$. These are not strikingly high amounts, in general small additions to the capital already available are intended or provided otherwise in the form of commodities. Only in AO 6162, Sag.ku$_5$ (AS 4) the complete capital (58g 60š) is provided in silver by the ENSI both through Lukalla and

[48] Reading of x is problematic, cf. Englund 1990, p. 38 with note 132. Neither LIBIR, "old' or HUL "destroyed", for figs (PEŠ$_3$), or possibly for ḪAŠḪUR, "apples", for (limited amounts of) fodder is attractive for a merchandise.

[49] The phenomenon is illustrated by LB 3119 in the unpublished master's thesis of R. de Maaijer: 4 mina 19$^1/_2$ GIN$_2$ minus 5 ŠE of silver are said to be NIG$_2$.ŠAM$_3$.MA.TA SA$_{10}$.A KI DAM.GAR$_3$.NE.TA, bought with merchandise and received from the damkars.

[50] Exceptionally phrased: YNER 8, 12 (Padda, ŠS 5) were an amount in silver occurs as LA$_2$.NI SU.GA Padda, cf. also Šeškalla, IstUM 910, AS 9: LA$_2$.NI SU.GA ŠA$_3$ SI.I$_3$.TUM KI Š.TA.

[51] The "Bromski" account of Ur-TAR.LUḪ (XIII AS 2) deals with the final accounting after his death and the payment section is thus in silver. These are exceptional circumstances and they cannot be considered to be particularly relevant here.

[52] Small amounts from Lukalla occur in SNAT 356 (Lu-Inanna, AS 5, 3 GIN2), YNER 8, 11 (Padda, AS 3, 5 GIN$_2$, more comes directly from the ENSI: 102.5 GIN$_2$), ASJ 14 (Padda, VII ŠS 1, 5 GIN$_2$ 150 š), HUCA 30 (Šeškalla, AS 3, 12 GIN$_2$ 101 š, IstUm 3187 (Ur-Dumuzida XIII ŠS 1, where also a Lugal-nesage delivers a small amount of silver.)

Lugalkuzu and personally.[53] In the other account in which only silver constitutes the capital, SNAT 356, Lu-Inanna (AS 5), that silver is identical with the (previous) SI.I$_3$.TUM with a minimal additional 3 GIN$_2$ being provided by Lukalla.[54]

It is, however, not the crediting of silver to the damkars in the capital section of their accounts which is of interest here. Much more important is the frequency and size of (re-) payments in silver from the accounts of named damkars, compared to the total amount of the credit provided to them, both in the initial capital and in the final LA$_3$.NI sections. DIRI outcomes are strikingly rare, though not completely unknown. The question is whether the general outcome suggests comparison with what is known as the Old Babylonian Palast-/Tempelgeschäft, defined above as the changing of agricultural bulk products into silver, with special concessory rates for the damgars.

In considering the facts available some attention must be paid to the additional role of gold in these accounts, as the buying of gold seems to absorbe notable amounts of silver. Not that gold should be considered as a type of currency, as silver was, but it deserves some special attention. In general it will have disappeared into the various treasuries in the shape of valuable objects, or it was used for gilding in a cultic or ceremonial context.[55]

The following table lists the (re)payments in silver by the damkar's. Attention should be drawn to the fact that a realistic picture of the relative importance of these repayments is obtained only by comparing the total capital minus the amount not spent (LA$_2$.NI) with the payments.

Text	Date	Damkar	SI.I$_3$.TUM	Capital	Payment(s)	LA$_2$.NI
AO 6162	AS 4	Sag.ku5	---	58g60š	---	not given
(MVN I 238 IXAS5 balanced barley/reed account of Ur-Ištaran)						
AO 6052	AS 5	Inimmanizi	---	208g57š	74.5g	120g152š
SNAT 356	AS 5	Lu-Inanna	13g130š	16g130š	---	3g87š
YNER 7	AS 5	Lu-Inanna	3g87š	40g33š	15g	13g10š
YNER 8*	IIAS6	Kudda	--	233g68š	120g	78g28š
SNAT 365	AS 6	KA.UR.ša	--	113g69š	25g	32g55š
YNER 2	AS 3	Padda	--	112g64š	---	1g132š
YNER 4	AS 5	Padda	--	155g90š	59g15š	93g61š
AAICAB	XIAS5	Padda	93g61š	267g1š	121g75š	96g87š
YNER 19	AS 5	Padda	96g78š	96g78š	38g	47g107š*
STA 23	XIAS6	Padda	47g117š	271g12š	---(?)**	147g152š
YNER 11	IXAS7	Padda	31g	251g120+š	---(?)**	97g 10.5š

---

[53] This text, account of Sag.ku$_5$ DAM.KAR$_3$, is the only one of the group which repeats in an at first sight somewhat redundant manner the individual value in silver of the different commodities delivered, and not just the amount of silver to be withdrawn from the account. Though the amount to be withdrawn can be calculated, the LA$_2$.NI is erased. As Sag.ku$_5$ is the name of an Umma damkar and not simply an accounting term, the text demonstrates something of the manner in which the determination of the value in silver of the commodities is registered during the accounting procedure. Line I 6, in the capital section, is also exceptional: DUB Sag.ku$_5$ NU ZI.IR. We are almost certainly dealing with an intermediate stage in the accounting procedure.

[54] In SNAT 504 1 mina 35 GIN$_2$ 145.5 ŠE come from "the silver account", but this text is, as stated, not a "normal" balanced account of a merchant, it is the "merchants' account" of Lu-Ḫaia and it is not even stated to be balanced, though it is in practice.

[55] It disappeared, so to say, out of the economy. No doubt some of it was released again at the fall of the Ur III kingdom when the king had to deliver considerable tributes to his enemies. The economic consequences belong to the imponderables. In a sense gold was hoarded.

ASJ 14 VI ŠS 1	Padda	81g20š	(86g80š)	---	64g13š
YNER 12 SS5	Padda	5g150š	13g60š	---	---
HUCA 30 AS 3	Šeškalla	---	42g101š	20g60š	57š*
YNER 6 AS 5	Šeškalla	?	76g94š	30g	4g102š
AO 6056 AS 5	Šeškalla	4g102š	201g76š	89g76š	61g32š
Orient 21 XI AS 6	Šeškalla	61g32š	196g132š	40g	69g70.5š
IstUm 910 AS 9	Šeškalla	23g66.5š	43g36.5š	---	---
AOAT 203 I AS 3	Ur-D.	211g41š	927g83š	240g	271g135š+
(Erm 14969 XAS3	Ur-D.	?	742g122š	240g	60g)+
STA 22 I AS 4	Ur-D.	145g74š	163g8š	30g	17g125.5š+
YOS 122 AS 4	Ur-D.	17g125.5š	412g45š	--(?**?)	14g57š+
YNER 9 XI AS 6	Ur-D.	52g150š	389g80š+	121g120š	79g97š?[56]
YNER 10 VIIAS7	Ur-D.	79g97š	264g90š	---	135g29.5š
STA 1 VII AS 8	Ur-D.	68g60š	297g120š	149g175š?[57]	144g90š
MVNI240 XIIAS8	Ur-D.	--	310g+	---[58]	38g30š
YOS 123 AS 9	Ur-D.	--	869g70š	?[59]	---
IstUM 3187	Ur-D.	21g144.5š	59g105.5š	---	3g104š
AO 5680 ŠS 2	Ur-D.	?	335g114.5š	?[60]	(diri 14g163š)
YNER 15 ŠS 7	Aakalla[61]	--	91g130š	60g[62]	

Erm 5624, Koslova, MVN 21, 332, ŠS 1 is a balanced barley account of Ur-Dumuzida, but called "accounting (for) barley (by) damkar".

YNER is always YNER 8 and YOS stands here for YOS 18. * means: needs further calculation, the number of še cannot be corect. + means: text contains expenditure in silver on gold

** text damaged at crucial place: withdrawals by Lukalla.

Two additional balanced silver accounts throw light on the role of persons who to all likelihood were damkars. Both happen to mention Urša-kidug, whom we will discuss as a provider of credit and as the origin of a number of small texts mentioning the value in silver of various commodities. The two texts are HSM 911-5-23 (ŠS 2)[63] and the very damaged Museon 85546b[64], date lost. The accounts are from Umma but anonymous, which makes the assumption that they derive from the highest levels of the administration reasonable, they are probably accounts of Lukalla. In HSM 911-5-23 silver is provided by Urša-kidug and by Ḫaḫasa, who

---

56 Uncertain, mainly based on the ŠI.I$_3$.TUM of YNER 8, 10.

57 Rev III 36 + 39, both belong ultimately to the Lukalla withdrawals.

58 53g 100.5š is withdrawn for a rare DIRI and 126g is spent on the entertainment of the NIN, 30g goes into gold.

59 Passage damaged IV 25, 27 and 32, where in total three persons, including Lukalla receive silver. IV 29 and 31 deal with the buying of gold, amounts of silver similarly lost. The text is in many respects "difficult". It is the only account of this type with colophon NIG$_2$.KAŠ$_7$ AK NIG$_2$.ŠAM$_2$.MA PN DAM.KAR$_3$.

60 Possibly VI 1, but 3; a small expenditure in silver on/in the DU$_6$.KU$_3$.GA is mentioned IV 25: 6 g.

61 Son of (the?) Ur-Dumuzida.

62 This 60g is received for MAŠ$_2$.DA.RI.A; 3g172.5š is withdrawn for DIRI of an earlier account. By this time Gududu had taken over the silver account from Lukalla. It is possible that MVN 5, 92 is another balanced damkar account, here Gududu received 4 g from the capital provided.

63 OA 22, 203.

64 R. de Maaijer, JEOL 34, 27-9: 1.

elsewhere occurs as a damkar. They pay this silver because they have both sold or accepted barley at a rate of 1.1.0 kor per GIN_2. As they pay in together 10 mina of silver the transaction must have involved 720 kor of barley,. The purpose of the account is to justify the expenditure of the silver which is handed to some of the highest personalities in the land, including the king and queen or used for the most solemn occasions. A considerable amount of barley[65] is changed into no more than pocket money for top people. But the silver was actually available to the two persons mentioned.

The damaged Museon text is much more run of the mill and deals with the expenditure of small sums against the silver and barley received. One of the two persons paying in silver is Urša-kidug. The special importance of this text is that it indicates that the institutions play a certain role in bringing small amounts of silver into circulation.

In considering the position of the damkars it is probably not helpful to state that they were indebted, even though they were generally in arrears. For there is no indication that they paid interest on what was still due from them, that is at any rate not before their account was settled.[66] At least in this respect their position was favourable, what was credited to them was interest free, at least for a certain period. That they were capable of providing payment in silver is made clear by the table mentioned. As it indicates, it is not uncommon that silver was withdrawn from the account of the damkar, a fact normally indicated by KIŠIB Lukalla or simply Lukalla ŠU.BA.TI. In relation to the capital provided the withdrawals could equal a third to a half of that amount, though there does not appear to exist a rule. Where there are no withdrawals in silver the capital provided is often very small or (other) expenditure (virtually) equals the capital. ASJ 14, Padda and YNER 8 10 I 15-7, (VII AS 7), Ur-Dumuzida, are possible, but not very significant, exceptions.

The overall impression must be that the damkars were capable of transferring silver to the institutional accounts. This seems to fulfil an essential requirement in relation to the question of "Palastgeschäft or not".

The question of the gold bought for silver in the damkar accounts needs some further discussion as it further illustrates the importance of payments in precious metals by the damkars. Not all gold was obtained through the damkars, especially Ur-Dumuzida, for, as we have seen, KU_3.DIM_2s were also directly involved.[67] Sometimes silver for the buying of gold was being made available in the capital section, especially in the damaged passage YNER 8, 9, Ur-Dumuzida, XI AS 6, but how this functioned in the expenditure section remains unclear.[68] On occasion sums spent on gold were very modest, e.g. 5 g in HUCA 30 line 27 (Šeškalla AS 3). For more important withdrawals we must turn to a number of accounts of Ur-Dumuzida, notably those of AS 3 and 4, which could suggest requirements relating to some special project. The expenditure on gold should be compared and added to the other amounts paid in silver mentioned in the previous table:

---

65 Plus, presumably, the 10 kor of line 2, which cannot be understood, but probably refers to that amount being loaded or filled into something, the sign cannot be identified with certainty. Possibly this constitutes a premium for Urša-kidug, as no silver for this amount is mentioned

66 Payments of interest on the SI.I_3.TUM of accounts is especially attested in a number of cases in Nippur and it is not completely unknown elsewhere either.

67 In YOS 4 ,47 (III ŠS 1) the damkar Ur-Dumuzida and the KU_3.DIM_2 Ur-Šulpae received together an amount of silver for the buying of gold.

68 I expect this to be the case in YNER 8, 11 I 16-18, Padda IX AS 7, a passage which makes no sense in the way it seems to stand, especially as "losses" are mentioned. The expenditure section of the text is very incomplete.

AOAT 203	(Ur-Dumuzida I AS 3)	total 73g68š in silver,
(Erm 14969	(Ur-Dumuzida X AS 3)	total 205g+80g+16g112š=301g112š)
STA 22	(Ur-Dumuzida AS 4)	total 50g
YOS 18 122	(Ur-Dumizida AS 4)	total 300g.

At least two of these withdrawals are substantial, 5 mina of silver or slightly more.[69]

8. From the provincial to the central bureaucratic level

In the Palastgeschäft the damkar also played a role in the transfer of provincial wealth to the central administration. That the Umma damkar played an important role in the Ur III BALA is evident. The BALA was (one of) the means by which regional wealth was made subservient to the over-all religious and political system of the Ur III monarchy. The Umma damkar was in a somewhat different position from that of his OB Sippar counterpart. Though both belonged to the province, the Umma damkar worked -in the accounts- primarily for his own provincial administration, the Sippar damkar was in direct, accountable, contact with the central palace in Babylon. But both groups played a role in the transfer of local wealth to central institutions.

The (Umma) damkar had the opportunity to exchange the locally produced bulk goods for specially required rarer commodities. Special BALA accounts with silver as capital are AAS 65 (AS 8) and Nik 403 (AS 9), SNAT 490 (ŠS 4) is a comparable account of the DAM.GAR$_3$ ŠA$_3$ URI$_5$^{KI}.MA. All these documents end with GIR$_3$ PN (and PN2) before the date. Nik 403 mentions Abbagina, as he can be associated with the Umma obligations in Ur and neighbourhood, this text too belongs to all likelihood to the group dealing with BALA-type obligations. These also turn up in Lukalla's damkars' account AO 6037 (ŠS 6), in both the capital section (I 10) and in the expenditure section (II 19, where a special BALA-account is mentioned).

Padda and Ur-Dumuzida were involved in expenditure on the BALA[70] and in connection with the king and his entourage, but with Šeškalla especially a relation to Ur is mentioned, cf. BM 106064, ZI.GA BAL.A. MVN 1, 238 (IX AS 5) is an account of the damkar Ur-Ištaran ŠA$_3$ BALA which balances barley against bundles of reeds. Directly linked to expenditure of special commodities on the BALA or at Ur are the many other posts which can be related to the person of the king or his entourage: this too represents expenditure subservient to central purposes.

Essential is that the damkar travelled and had contacts in the centres of power where the more rare commodities were available -as in later periods.

Locally the Umma damkar played another essential role in providing local crafts industries, represented by their administrators, with essential materials. Lu-Enlila is obviously provided with metal and related material for his foundry, but also Agu, the reed accountant and Akalla the AŠGAB, thus the manager of the leatherworkers, are much in evidence. One of the important "withdrawers" of "small commodities", often the rarer foodstuffs, is Ur-Šulpae, whose title and position is not completely clear to me. He crops up in nearly all the accounts. It should be realised that these "resort-administrators" were themselves directly involved in provisioning the BALA, deliveries figure in their own accounts. How "local" deliveries by damkars were therefore needs further scrutiny, much of the goods provided by the damkars in the end actually may have left the local economy.

---

[69] Cf. also NATN 805 (AS 7), lines 10 and 11, and, no doubt, 12, wool for the buying of gold by damkars, LU$_2$.NIG$_2$.DAB$_5$.BAs and the KU$_3$.DIM$_2$ Ur-Šulpae.

[70] This is sometimes a special section in the accounts, e.g. STA 23 IV 23.

The accounts of the Umma damkars indicate that at a provincial level the role of the institutional damkar was much wider than what "Palace Geschäft" would imply. That means that not the whole sum of his account was available in silver: other commodities were required not only centrally but also locally. Remains the fact that bulk commodities were exchanged for silver. That inevitably means that there was a market for such goods somewhere. "Somewhere" probably means "(also) locally".

9. Interim balance: the Umma balanced accounts

The Umma balanced accounts suggest the existence of a damkar who knew how and where to change agricultural local bulk products into silver, and who could deliver both locally produced and imported commodities to local institutions, often for use by central authorities in localities with a central function. For at least some commodities the damkar was situated between the local producer and the local institutional customer. In itself this suggests the existence of a kind of market, some system of supply and demand which required the intervention of specialists already at a provincial level in the Ur III period. This cannot be claimed to represent an important discovery, but in a general assembling of arguments when dealing with the economy of Third Millennium Mesopotamia this is not without importance when questions of the existence of a market economy or not are involved. The existence of a market in itself does not create a market economy where supply and demand dominate all housekeeping. Nothing sensible can be said regarding the size of this market. Its scope was, inevitably, limited, and its existence cannot be disconnected from the fact that the provincial centres had been independent not too long ago. Centres which have lost part of their political function as a consequence of political unification run the risk of loosing more functions, especially the exchange of rare commodities will move to other localities which retain or acquire a central political function.

Supply and demand are also related to the question of the existence of credit. There is always demand, but it has to have the wherewithal to avail itself of the supply. Much of the credit in an agricultural society is consumptive. There are signs that there was a demand for credit, even if that was mainly consumptive and the direct result of a personal or general stress situation, it often operated at the level of simple usury. Yet the small scale credit on which we will focus here, suggests at a simple level the workings of "supply and demand". Absolute lack of credit in the end often simply means starvation. Not everybody led an "embedded existence". The occurrence of usury is an obvious indicator of that fact. Here the texts from Nippur must play their role with some Umma support: they again suggest a role for a, perhaps limited, internal market for agricultural bulk products.

CHAPTER II
"PRIVATE CREDIT" IN NIPPUR AND UMMA

1. The role of the Nippur "private credit" texts[1]

We are dealing with a core group of 376 texts from Nippur directly or indirectly belonging to text groups which can be considered as "private", but of these texts 24 are useless because an essential element of the contents is lost. A number of mainly agricultural text groups is not included, nor is the Dusabara group, as it is, though found in Nippur, not Nippurian. These text groups suggest however, that it would be possible to enlarge the number of texts even more. The texts from the Innana temple are also excluded because "private and not so private" are especially difficult to separate in this case, though there are exactly here a few texts from the immediate post-Ur III period, which indicate the continuing provision of "small-credit".[2] The credit provided was in barley or in silver.

The core of the text group we are dealing with consists of files centring on a specific person, among which there are not only debt notes and receipts, but also contracts or court documents, in fact these are texts from small "private archives".[3] Determining what is really a debt note and what represents a deferred payment connected which the buying of some commodit, is sometimes rather difficult, though one might expect that such an object would be mentioned. In theory there are under normal circumstances no documents dealing with cash payments for goods other than real estate or slaves and sometimes animals, in short "capital goods". "Credit documents" in silver payable after harvest represent sometimes explicit cases of usury, in other instances they are examples of a futures transaction: future delivery of a commodity is arranged against a credit to the producer, who in this way runs the risk of getting into the grips of his creditor. Interpretation is a question of the point of view selected. Some 250 texts out of the number mentioned belong to "small archives". A silent criterion is that the core texts come from publications which mainly or to a considerable degree contain texts purportedly excavated in Nippur. That this is a problematic assumption needs no elaboration here. Texts of similar nature, comparable to those included through belonging to discrete Nippur groups from the same publications have also been included, even though they remain for practical purposes isolated documents. This concerns about 100 texts out of the 376. In this manner the prosopographically possible is strained to a degree.

Exclusion of the small agrarian archive groups from Nippur is deliberate. Some of these groups contain texts indicating the providing of (small) credit by superiors to subalterns. This is very important for our understanding of the functioning of institutional

---

[1] For the general type of text on which the following is based cf. Lutzmann, 1976.

[2] Not included is also the Ur-Nuska "archive", but it does not contribute much to our subject, only some five texts are relevant. (All texts are re-edited Garfinkle 2000 p. 402ff.)

[3] Core personalities include: Adda; Addakalla; Alala; Azida; Lugalazida; Lugalmedugga; Lubalšaga; Ludingira; Ur-Damu; Ur-Dukuga; Ur-Enlil; Ur-Suen; Ur-sukkal; Ur-Šulpae and some others with fewer texts.

agriculture and it requires separate investigation.[4] In view of our limited understanding of the prosopgraphical background of the Nippur texts, there is a reasonable possibility that some of the texts which have been included in the 376 used actually belong to the agriculture-related groups which have been formally excluded. Accepting that 350-odd texts can be used here is thus to an important degree a matter of faith.

What is counted are those texts mentioning a sum in silver or in barley, rarely wheat, emmer or dates and which contain some clause concerning interest,[5] either in a positive or in a negative sense.[6] Not included are texts which only register a receipt (ŠU.BA.TI) of which there are (additionally) 73 in the same ill-circumscribed groups. Some of these are, especially in view of the wording of the seals impressed on them of an administrative nature, even if witnesses are mentioned.[7]

Not included in the 376 texts gathered, are also those texts which only mention the obligation to repay, that is a phrase including the terms SU.SU or GI$_4$.GI$_4$, sometimes merely LA$_2$ or AG$_2$ or even SE$_3$, but which contain no statement concerning interest. There are some 30 of these, but the longer texts are, the greater the risk of damage becomes. The occasional occurrence of a term like EGIR.EBUR AG$_2$.E.DAM indicates that we are dealing at least sometimes with loans intended to bridge the harvest period, some other texts of this type are clearly administrative, like EHE 268 (XII IS 1) mentioning no less than 40 kor of barley and sealed by a NU.BANDA$_3$/EGIR GIR$_3$.NITA$_2$. Some of these texts deal clearly with protracted affairs, which may have a long previous history: a time limit is imposed after which a fine becomes payable.[8]

After some hesitation also those texts which contain an explicit remark concerning interest, but also state that the amount mentioned is the SI.I$_3$.TUM of an account, have been excluded, for these texts have no real bearing on the question of "small-credit". There are minimally nine of these texts among the Nippur group we are dealing with. The background of the accounts concerned is not known, they indicate that this institutional type of "credit" in the end was not interest free, though perhaps only after the account was finally closed down or at least settled. We do not know. Texts with this type of phrase are perhaps primarily institutional, but that is no more than an assumption. The amounts are, in general, considerable.

The texts included in the "corpus" have been split into two groups, interest bearing and -explicitly, whatever that may mean- free of interest. Further gradation is based on the volume of the transaction. "Notionally" 1 GIN$_2$ of silver is equated with 1 kor of barley as a kind of basic price equivalent. For our purpose there are both for silver and for barley

---

[4] Especially if the position of the DUB.SAR GU$_4$ and the NU.BANDA$_3$ GUD and even the simple ENGARs is important for the degree to which a local agricultural system is "institutional" or "entrepreneurial".

[5] A slight problem is posed by those texts which contain reference to two transactions, for instance involving a small amount of barley and some silver. These texts have been counted for one in the overall count, but below they figure twice, under each separate commodity. This is problematic, because two small transactions together constitute a bigger one. This is not considered further.

[6] The special problem posed by the phrase UR$_5$.ŠE$_3$ MAŠ$_2$ NU.TUK is solved in the sense that the texts are counted with the interest free texts.

[7] Not included in the 73 are for instance comparable texts dealing, like some texts in the Lugalazida-file, with commodities like fats or oil, though these could belong to the "small-credit" sphere.

[8] BE 3, 13 (III ŠS 8, Ur-sukkal file), dealing with 1 mine 10 GIN$_2$, a SI.I$_3$.TUM payable up to 7 IV (SUM.MU.DAM) otherwise the double amount is due: [IB.]TAP.PE. In NATN 403, ŠS 6, Adda file, a normal interest of 20% starts precisely after a month. Sometimes there is a longer term, e.g. in NRVN I 117 (ŠS 2) from VI to III, but doubled after <NU?>.GI$_4$. Especially notable is NRVN I 176 (IS 2) SAG.BI GI$_4$.GI$_4$.DAM after the harvest, but in Ešnunna.

three relevant subgroups: S 1 or B 1, up to and including 1 GIN_2/kor, similarly 2 GIN_2 and 2 kor is the limit for S2 and B2 and for S3 and B3 it is 5 GIN_2 or 5 kor, above these limits everything constitutes a major amount, above the limits of the "small credit", which is not considered here. The level of interest is here also not of real importance,[9] for silver it is universally 20%, with barley it is normally 33$^{1}/_{3}$%, 0.1.4.0 per kor, but 0.1.3 occurs too often to regard it as a mere copying mistake. Rarely 0.1.0, or 20% occurs for barley, but a closer look often indicates that silver is involved in these cases. The "notional" equation which makes 1 kor of barley equal 1 GIN_2 of silver is at the basis of all further considerations.

A count (disregarding texts over the 5 GIN_2/5 kor limit) results in the following:
No interest ($MAŠ_2$.NU.TUK):
Barley 1: 13 texts, B 2: 7, B: 3: 5, total 25, (over 5 kor: 2);
Silver 1: 10 texts, S 2: 5, S 3: 3, total 18, (over 5 GIN_2: 3);
Interest bearing:
Barley 1: 35 texts, B 2: 25, B 3: 32, total 92;
Silver 1: 45 texts, S 2: 31, S 3: 35, total 111.

Other: dates BE 3, 31 with 2 kor "class D 2", interest 20%, and NATN 789 where 1 GIN_2 of silver ("S1") is equated with 2.2.3 of dates ("D 3") which smacks of usury.
But these matters are complicated. In the archive of the Inanna temple there are two (immediate) post-Ur III texts giving a one to one equation for dates and barley, but if dates are really regarded as less valuable than barley, repayment of dates in the form of an equal amount of barley includes in reality a mark up.[10]
Oil: NATN 111: 0.0.1 I_3.GIŠ, ŠE.BI 1.1.0(?), confirmed TuM 107 (I IS 2, Lugalazida file; 0.1.0 I_3 = 6.0.0 of barley, therefore "oil": barley = 1:30
AUCT 3 451: 0.1.0 in oil is 5 GIN_2 K.B. (= 1:25)
Wool plays a very limited role: only in NATN 273 recalculated, 1 GIN_2 of silver equals 9 mina, NATN 2 (Dr? IS 2) 1 GIN_2 equals 15 mina. Prices not only fluctuate, but the effect of quality remains an imponderable.

We must conclude that "small credit" was obtainable in Nippur, there are nearly 250 texts dealing with credits under the 5 GIN_2/5 kor limit, of which some 170 remain below the 3 GIN_2/3 kor limit. We can assume that generally we are dealing with consumptive credit. But anyhow, even this indicates a market for at least barley. The fact that a very high proportion of the texts comes from the last years of Ur III domination in Nippur is possibly of some importance, for we can assume a period of scarcity.

In general the evidence is not strong enough to connect the credit activities in Nippur with the Nippur damkars. There was a market for cereals in Nippur, but whether damkars supplied that market, and whether they supplied it with barley provided by the institutions remains prosopographically weak.

2. Similar texts from Umma: a note

The texts from Umma are fewer in number, that means that the possibility that we are dealing with several different persons bearing the same names and not with one and the same person increases, as the groups of texts become less dense. This is especially the case when dealing with ordinary names like Lu_2-dingir.ra or Lu_2-dug_3.ga, but Ur-Si_4.an.na is

[9] On the period for which the interest mentioned is valid cf. the explicit Umma text Utah 55 (ASJ 19, 1997, p. 162): 1 g of silver, interest 0.1.0 in barley (= "notionally" 20%) for the period I to IV inclusive. The interest specified is valid not for a complete year, bur for a(ny) segment of a year, possibly especially "from before until after the harvest". (This matter is studied Garfinkle 2000.)

[10] R. Zettler, The Ur III temple of Inanna at Nippur, Berlin 1992, 5 NT77 and 5NT656.

perhaps slightly less common and more important is the Ur_4.ša$_3$-ki.dug$_3$ who provided credit, occasionally against interest. In some of his texts a value in silver is given for wool or dates. We have already discussed two balanced silver accounts which mention presumably this same person when discussing the role of damkars in the conversion of commodities into silver.

Umma institutional texts are often sealed on the tablet itself. It is thus often clear that a text does not really belong to a private context, as it bears the impression of the seal of a third person authorising the expenditure. Such a text is institutional. Ist Um 1455 (IX AS 6) ŠE.UR$_5$.RA provided by Dingira is, for instance, sealed by Lu-Ḫaia.[11] As there are more texts with the same date it is better to disregard the whole group as not "private", but as somehow "administrative". Others are suspect because the taker bears an official title. This makes all the texts naming Lu$_2$-dug$_3$.ga as the "creditor" of dubious value for our purposes,[12] even if there are small loans among these texts.[13] Though many of the barley loans given by Ludugga bear interest, they probably belong to the institutional sphere as typical bridging loans towards the end of AS 7 and 8 and ŠS 1 and 2, with some scattered texts from other years. Some of the amounts provided are considerable, others are smaller and could represent an unofficial sideline. It is better to leave also this group outside our considerations.[14]

These text groups share the fact that they contain no witnessed texts.[15] Possibly this is more or less typical for the texts from Umma, for also the texts mentioning Urša-kidug are rarely witnessed. But witnesses are found in general on the texts which were published in YOS 4 and which have Ur-Sianna as the creditor. These 12 texts deal, but for one, with amounts under the 3 g/3 kor limit we used to define the small loans in Nippur, this is perhaps the only group which can be compared directly.[16] But there are clear signs that these texts also come from the shadowy area between private and institutional. It is possible that the worsening economic situation resulting from and causing the decline of the Ur III monarchy stimulated these credit activities.

---

[11] I regard it as a coincidence that Adda is the name of both the taker of the loan and the father of the scribe Lu-Ḫaia. In the comparable Ist UM 1548 we do not find this complication. Princeton 282, Ist Um 1385, 1506 and 1550 are sealed by the respective receivers of the ŠE.UR$_5$.RA. I disregard the texts mentioning Dingira and also those mentioning Atu, generally simple receipts, but also MVN 10, 175, with a scribal seal.

[12] In AUCT 2, 246 (XI AS 7) a NU.BANDA$_3$ receives an interest bearing loan of 66 kor, cf. 248-249 and 404-405 for other NU.BANDA$_3$'s and further considerable amounts. Cf. also AUCT 1, 166.

[13] Interesting 0.2.0 ŠE.UR$_5$.RA from Ḫaḫaša MU Lu$_2$-dug$_3$.ga.ŠE$_3$ Ab.ba-ša$_6$.ga.KE$_4$ ŠU.BA.TI which would normally be interpreted as A has received for L from Ḫ (who is probably the same as the damkar Ḫ), but probably means that Ḫ acts for L in handing to A, as in the AUCT texts Ludugga generally is the creditor, and Ḫašaša hardly occurs. All the more so as in AUCT I 200 (IX ŠS 1) he acts as an intermediary (GIR$_3$) in a loan given by Ludugga.

[14] Though many of the debtors have simple two lined seal inscriptions.

[15] Lu-Šara texts, Šeš-kalla texts, Ur-Lisi texts.

[16] No witnesses are found in YOS 4, 39, where the interest bearing barley is said to be intended for workers and the barley is to be returned to the silo from which it was taken. The same stipulations occur in YOS 4, 27, where the interest amounts to 50% and which is also unwitnessed. The silo clause also occurs in YOS 4, 48 and in YOS 4, 40, respectively witnessed and not witnessed. MVN 13, 686 may belong to this group, it is undated and without witnesses. Interest: MAŠ$_2$.NU.TUK YOS 4, 52; 55; 51; 5 (silver); MAŠ$_2$.GA$_2$.GA$_2$: YOS 4, 24; (silver) 33; $33^1/_3$%: YOS 4, 39 and 40, all barley unless specified otherwise; 1 g of silver repayable as 1,5 kor of barley YOS 4, 20 and 27, perhaps also 49 i.e. "notionally" 50%, comparably silver into barley 40% in YOS 4, 48. The high rates of interest are found in yrs IS 2, 3 and 4, possibly a clear sign of the worsening economic situation.

The net result is that only the texts of Urša-kidug remain as really comparable to the Nippur groups, even though the texts are very simply formulated and unwitnessed. I cannot provide proof that he really was the known damkar, but his activities strongly suggest the fact. All transactions documented are small scale and dated between I AS 7 and V ŠS 3, that is when the political situation was "normal".[17] None contains a remark regarding the moment of (re-)payment, which could tempt us to suppose that we are concerning ourselves "in some cases" with written documents dealing with transactions involving payment on the spot. This would be exceptional and for the moment I assume that the moment of repayment is simply not mentioned as it was "traditional". Urša-kidug converts small amounts of dates, up to 1 kor, into barley at a premium of 20% of the volume, occasionally at 16.66%. Only once a value in silver is given.[18] Barley is given out at the rate of $33^1/_3$ %, rarely at 20% and occasionally there is just ŠU.BA.TI.[19] The other important bulk product, wool, figures prominently in these texts, it is valued in silver, usually at a rate of 10 or 8 mina for a GIN_2.[20] Other commodities occur only occasionally,[21] but just often enough to suggest that this man traded not only in agricultural bulk products but also in imported goods.

Though the material is not rich enough for more than a few remarks, it cannot be regarded as detracting from the conclusions to be drawn from the Nippur material. Perhaps it could even be said that the Umma evidence suggests that the need for credit is shared by the institutional and the non-institutional sectors of the economy, which is again in itself far from shocking.

3. Conclusion

This conclusion is based more on the Nippur than on the Umma material, which is a natural effect of the composition of the two groups of texts. In Umma the institutional dominates, and known credit activities take place at the margins of the institutions. The subject of the private aspects in the management practices of Ur III institutions has hardly been touched upon by Ur III studies in general, but one of its traits is the giving and taking of interest bearing credit by people in management positions. Such interest bearing credits were occasionally given by people in the highest administrative ranks in Umma. Similar phenomena occur in the small, generally much less well-known (lower management level) Nippur agricultural archives, but this is not the place to discuss the matter further. In Nippur

---

[17] Whether AUCT 3, 247 belongs here is not clear, nor is it of importance.

[18] The texts are mentioned in chronological order. At the rate of 20% AUTC 3, 279; 446; 1, 631; 3, 352; 1, 963, at the higher rate I 260, 201, exceptionally a price of 1 g of silver per kor is found in AUCT 3, 378.

[19] $33^1/_3$% AUCT 3, 293; 385; 20% occurs in AUCT 3, 491; ŠU.BA.TI in AUCT 3, 332 and 331 and Utah 54; I do not understand the transaction in AUCT 1, 330 where 5.1.3 in barley fetches 10 g 54 ŠE of silver. This is the only transaction of the group in which the value exceeds the 3 g/3 kor limit for small credit we used in Nippur. AUCT 1, 534 is seriously damaged but probably does not contain an interest clause. The texts dealing with barley are somewhat difficult to isolate as there is also a brewer called Urša-kidug, for instance AUCT 1, 306 is probably to be assigned to him.

[20] No attention is paid here to remarks concerning the quality of the wool. 10 mina for 1 GIN_2 AUCT 3, 251; 313; 373; CST 595 only 8: AUCT 3, 350; AAICAB 1, Ashm 1911-212; in AUCT 2, 292 it is 8.5 mina. In PTS 300 $10^2/_3$ mina is valued at 1 g 45 ŠE; exceptional is MVN 15, 171, sealed by Urša-kidug s Baša, scribe, where he *receives* 8 mina for $1^1/_3$ g out of a store. The same seal occurs on AUCT 3, 393, an administrative text in the sphere of animal husbandry. This is probably after all not our Urša-kidug.

[21] Wengler 45 (Or SP 6 p. 59) values (the) 2 mina (of an?) IG.GUL at 45 ŠE of silver; in Heisserer 12 4 mina of copper(?) have a value of 1/2 g of silver.

credit specialists, to use this euphemism, are easier to isolate, but it is not so easy to convict them of having been damkars, who also operated in an institutional context. That is, however, a strong suspicion with Urša-kidug from Umma, who anyhow acted occasionally in the company of known damkars.

This is postponing a real conclusion. In my opinion the possibility existed to obtain "small-scale credit", even if that type of credit will have been predominantly consumptive, in both Nippur and Umma, and therefore no doubt elsewhere. Such credits were possible in both institutional and private contexts, in institutional context they could assume considerable proportions. What looks like an interest bearing credit can represent, however, the outstanding backlog of an institutional account on which interest is due.

But not always. We have arrived at a situation we could suspect to have existed all along: the institutions disposed of their bulk goods through the damkars, perhaps cheaply, but circumstances could develop in such a manner that they were obliged to reaquire the selfsame products at a considerable premium. Whatever may have been the case, the net result is that there could develop a real market, in which supply and demand had a role, at any rate regarding barley.

Many texts are late Šu-Sin or early Ibbi-Sin. It is therefore not difficult to propose at least two solutions: a crisis is announcing itself or the situation is not yet really abnormal, but on account of the political and economic problems of these years an exceptional number of debts remained unpaid. That could be the reason why our documentation is good, even though locally, especially in Nippur, affairs continued pretty much unhindered after Ur III had ended for practical purposes. There are just more texts preserved than is normally the case. But at any rate in IS 3 in Nippur people took loans from the moment of the harvest onwards, as is documented by the Ur-Šulpae-file, and also in that of Lugal-azida and in some smaller files. Therefore: golden times for hoarders of grain, in the classical manner: the situation created their market.

There is demand in IS 3, though in Nippur the rate of interest does not rise, as it did in Umma. But look back at IS 2 and at the later years of Šu-Sin: there is already a clear demand for barley. It is not only scarcity which is the cause, there are other reasons why people incur "debts", for instance through accepting pre-payment for services to be rendered at a future date, especially during the harvest. That does not invalidate the idea that a market for grain can not only be supposed to have existed, but it can really be demonstrated. The existence of a supply of grain stimulated the existence of a labour market. The embeddedness of human existence is occasionally already the riskier one of the market.

In short: in a town like Nippur there was a market for grain. Was supply controlled by damkars operating in a Palastgeschäft-type structure? Possibly, but prosopographically the fact is not completely established. Remains, however, that there is both supply and demand.

MERCHANTS LITERATURE

Curtis - Hallo 1959	J.B. Curtis and W.W. Hallo, Money and merchants in Ur III, HUCA 30, 1959, p. 103-139.
Englund 1990	R.K. Englund, Organisation und Verwaltung der Ur III-Fischerei, Berlin, 1990.
Garfinkle 2000	S.J. Garfinkle, Private enterprise in Babylonia at the end of the Third Millennium BC, Diss. Columbia University, New York, 2000.
Kraus 1958	F.R. Kraus, Ein Edikt des Königs Ammi-ṣaduqa von Babylon, Leiden 1958.
Lutzmann 1976	H. Lutzmann, Die neusumerischen Schuldurkunden, Teil I, Erlangen,1976.
Neumann 1979	H. Neumann, Handel und Händler in der Zeit der III. Dynastie von Ur, AoF 6, 1979, p. 15-67.
Neumann 1992	H. Neumann, Zur privaten Geschäftstätigkeit in Nippur in der Ur-III Zeit, CRRAI 35, 1992, p. 161-175.
Neumann 1992a	H. Neumann, Nochmals zum Kaufmann in Neusumerischer Zeit: die Geschäfte des Ur-dun und andere Kaufleute aus Nippur, CRRAI 38, 1992, p. 83-94.
Neumann 1992b	H. Neumann, Zu den Geschäften des Kaufmanns Ur-Dumuzida aus Umma, AoF 20, 1993, p.69-86.
Snell 1982	D.C. Snell, Ledgers and Prices, Early Mesopotamian Merchant Accounts, YNER 8, New Haven and London, 1982.

PART II

MESOPOTAMIAN PREBENDS
FINANCING THE CLERGY

CHAPTER I
INTRODUCTION: THE SUBJECT AND THE EVIDENCE

1. The Subject
a. A definition

The term "prebend" belongs to Western European ecclesiastical history and is therefore, when applied to Ancient Mesopotamia, an anachronism.[1] It can, however, play a meaningful role in a Mesopotamian context when properly defined. This is not to imply that "prebend" was a proper Mesopotamian concept, from which in turn follows that no modern definition can cover the subject adequately.[2] Nor can use of the term suggest that

---

[1] Nolet-Boeren 1951 p. 185: *praebenda* is "that, what has to be given", and translated from the Dutch: "a fixed allowance paid out of the income of the Chapter or resulting from specific goods, rents or tithes assigned to a specific person". The structure of the mediaeval western European priesthood made inheritance by descendants of these rights and the connected tasks formally impossible, but p. 354 in discussing *beneficia*, mentions *beneficia patrimonialia*, which only could be enjoyed by those who fulfilled certain requirements, one of which could be belonging to a specific family. There is a certain justification for the use of the term prebend in Mesopotamian circumstances, though the venality accepted there was, at any rate at a theoretical level, anathema in an ecclesiastical context. Whether allowed or not, accumulation of functions occurred and execution of tasks by others through the creation of minor functions was normal. These had to be funded somehow.

[2] The fractiousness of the terminology can perhaps be made somewhat clearer by looking at some relevant Old Babylonian ("Sippar") texts dealing with *isqu*. In his comment to AbB 13 no. 114 W.H. van Soldt confronts us, as he remarks, with a new concept: (barley *ša qāti*) *na-aš is-qí-im*, translated: "(barley, the share of) the one who brings the allotment". The context is uninformative beyond the fact that the *nāš isqim* was entitled to receive barley. It is perhaps possible to regard this *nāš isqim* as a person who fulfilled a certain function and was therefore entitled to a remuneration, or to consider the possibility that the barley was required by him for fulfilling his obligations. In both instances the function may be prebendal, but it was not so of necessity. That *isqu* regularly indicates a prebend needs no arguing, it happens to be used for GALAs: C. Janssen, CRRAI 36, 1991 p. 103, D 586: 11; D. Charpin RA 82, 1988 p. 29: 17. But the question is whether a function indicated in this manner is automatically prebendal in the sense of our definition: not all *kalû*s were prebendaries later on. CBS 414, date lost, made available with collations by E. Woestenburg by M. Stol is a mere scrap of a text, presumably from Sippar, suggesting that even in the context of sanctuaries the term *isqu* is used in a much wider sense than the word "prebend" will be here. Not much context remains, we only quote two the relevant passages briefly: 3') [*i-s*]*i-iq mu-ša-ki-l*[*u-tim*] 4') [*ù*] *si-ra-šu-tim* 5') [E]Š$_3$-EŠ$_3$.ḪA$_2$ U$_4$ 20 KAM x etc. 11) [*a-n*]*a i-si-iq pa-ši-šu-tim*. Without speculating about the nature of the transaction we note that *isqu* is used for *mušākilūtu*, the function of "fattener of animals", probably comparable to the Ur III institutional KURUŠDA, perhaps, but at a lower level (?) OB ^{LU_2}KU$_7$, and thus certainly an important official providing -also- for the cult. *isqu* is used also in combination with the function of brewer, *sirasūtu*, and for *pāšišūtu*, which is certainly a function of a priestly nature, even if the contents of that function are virtually unknown. The brewer was one of the purveyors of the cult whom we will have to discuss, but CBS 414 would be, for the moment, the only occasion the *mušākilu* would be a prebendary. A role in the actual cult would, however, be difficult to imagine. A certain amount of arbitrariness in defining the subject is inevitable, but it seems to be assured that *isqu* and "prebend", as used here, are not exactly the same.

the terminology used by the Ancient Mesopotamians in a context we could regard as prebendal, was reserved for the specific segment of Mesopotamian society we will be dealing with. All elements of the terminology used in a prebendal context could be used and were used at some moment in time not only in a much wider context, but also in a much looser sense. We must, however, limit our subject.

GARZA/MARZA, *parṣu*, GIŠ.ŠUB.BA, *isqu*, BALA(.GUB.BA), *manzaltu*, NAM+function, or even function in *-ūtu,* generally terms which can only be translated approximately, partially cover the concept "prebend", but these terms also include much that is not prebendal in the sense used here, which excludes strictly administrative functions. This is not a study of these terms. Here the question of how those directly involved in the institutional cult of the Mesopotamian gods were funded and which functions were practically involved, must be central. It must be considered as unlikely that all functions involved are documented, however. The letter of the definition kills, but we will anyhow only consider functions which have some link with sanctuaries. Functions which had a cultic task often also played a role outside the cult proper.

A prebend is defined here as a right to income deriving from the fulfilling of a function in the cult of the gods which involved contact with the divine and which was from the outset hereditary, or became so in the course of its development. In the remuneration the remains of the offerings placed before the gods concerned were of importance, but they were not reserved exclusively for those whom we will regard as prebendaries. Gender played a predominant role in the eligibility to office for the functions we will be concerned with.[3]

b. "Priests"

We will not deal specifically with the thorny question of what constituted a Mesopotamian priest, not even in an institutional sense. It will become clear who must be included on the basis of the available documentation concerning prebends and what the arguments for inclusion are. These are sometimes of dubious value and leave room for dissent. Not all relevant functions are documented, or even known, however, and some functions are of greater importance for our subject than others. The assumption will be that some form of consecration or dedication was an essential precondition, and that the

---

A comparable type of difficulty is found in CT 2, 43 (25 III Si 25) a dispute between a brother and a sister which mentions income 10) *ša ša-ta-mu-ti-šu šá* E_2 ^{d}UTU, "of his function as a *šatammu* in the Šamaš temple". In the Neo-Babylonian period the *šatammu* is the highest internal functionary in the most important sanctuaries, we will have to include him in that period in the "clergy", but in the Old Babylonian period he is still a relatively modest member of the hierarchy, whose ranking can be more or less figured out from the material collected Harris 1975 p. 154 note 5. He is to be situated somewhere in the region of the *gudapsûs* and the *ērib bītis*. But the real question is whether he can be classed amongst the "priests", or is he still merely an administrator in this period? If we compare M. Gallery, AfO 27, 1980, p. 1-36, esp. p. 21 we are confronted by doubts concerning the existence of a *šatammūtu* "benefice". Again we cannot escape from arbitrariness.

The choice of a definition does not dispense us of the need to make choices, for we are dealing with concepts which do not overlap completely, and often we simply do not know. In CT 45, 24 *isqu* and SUKU in the temples of Šamaš and Išḫara are shared without specification. Only prosopographic investigations can perhaps help in establishing the nature of the income and the nature of the function involved, if circumstances are favourable.

[3] The text published by Borger (Borger 1973), lines 9-10 makes it inevitable that women could never be allowed to accomplish (certain) priestly tasks. Physical inspection was an element of the initiation rites, these are evidently gender determined. Cf. also the Enmeduranki text edited by Lambert, 1998, which formally excludes women. On physical requirements in general H. Holma, Or NS 14, 1945, p. 242ff.

function involved direct, regular, contact with the divine, but that function and remuneration were not always intimately connected in all their aspects. We are dealing with an institutional phenomenon, not with "priests" in general. Those whom we can regard as prebendaries were also involved in other aspects of institutional life. But that does not help us much in a practical sense, for the perceived degree of the directness of the contact with the gods required for inclusion -by us-, remains an open question. We must accept that the various degrees of the intensity of the contact created differences in status. There were non-consecrated members of what we would regard as "priestly", or rather "ritualistic" occupations, as well as consecrated members of what we would regard as "trades" or "crafts" who were initiated to the same level as the "ritualists" because they indeed participated in the same rites.[4] The term "clergy" is in all periods of history ill-circumscribed, but nevertheless effective in a practical sense.[5] The margins of the subject are therefore fluid.

For being included amongst our institutional prebendaries some form of consecration is essential, and a precondition for consecration was, in turn, being of the right descent, at any rate in what we will call the later period. We will assume that those in receipt of income which we will identify as prebendal belonged to those consecrated, but with the proviso that rights to prebendal income could be in the hands of persons who could not fulfil the obligations, for instance for gender reasons, or simply because they were (young) minors. Bodily or mental impediments will also have been grounds for disqualification. We will have to look closer. A first rough sorting of those involved suggests a division according to status and occupation, in which the manner of remuneration can serve as the basis for further subdivision. Details will be discussed later on, often with uncertain effect, and we will also have to concern ourselves with the higher functions which are often left out of the discussion concerning our subject.

On account of status we must certainly include $GUDU_4$s, ŠITAs and *ērib bītis*. The actual function of these groups of prebendaries, "priests", is far from clear and constitutes a main problem. Ritual specialists to be incorporated are the *kalû*, "lamentation reciter" and,

---

4 This implies that I do not subscribe to the theory of the existence of craft (and other) guilds in the Mesopotamian institutions, which has been proposed for the Neo-Babylonian period. I suppose that there were at least three, perhaps four, social tiers among the "craftsmen" active in an institutional context: 1) prebendaries, consecrated and deriving in the Neo-Babylonian period from the *mār banī* class, recognisable in this period by having and using family names; 2) members of the *mār banī* class, including not consecrated members of prebendal families, but possessing their "family skills"; 3) *širkus*, having only a father's name in addition to their given name, and, possibly, 4) slaves, with a given name and indication of their master, performing tasks incumbent on those masters. I assume that the craftsmen involved in Weisberg, YNER 1, Text 1 had prebendal status, and that the injunction put upon them according to this text, was intended to prevent property belonging to Eanna from being used on other sanctuaries, many prebendaries equally having functions there.

For the earlier periods the evidence for different social layers among institutional craftsmen has not been investigated. The documentation is not promising, but we must assume that also in the Ur III/Old Babylonian period craftsmen's tasks had to be executed in the sanctuaries, even though there are only limited signs of the existence of crafts' prebends. Especially during the Old Babylonian period there exists a dearth of information in this respect. An additional question is that of the status of the *ummānu* as a group in rituals. Collectively they occur in the Babylon New Year's ritual RAcc p. 141, line 367, but it is not stated explicitly that they have *ērib bīti* status. It is clear that they must leave the ceremony at a given moment (384). Çağirgan - Lambert, 1991-93 (73-80) involves a DUMU.SAG *ummān*. The position is not clear, but that is the case also with other participants, for instance with the boatmen in the same ritual (94-105), who even play a central role at a certain stage of the proceedings.

5 As Charpin 1986 has shown. Ecclesiastical history in Western Europe can illustrate how difficult, and opportunistic, matters of "benefit of clergy" could be.

perhaps, already with some doubt concerning his proper status, the *nâru,* "singer", but often clearly (also) an instrumentalist. Also the *āšipu,* "exorcist", in various guises, may belong here,[6] but the *bārû,* "haruspex", is already more problematical: does he have a role in the actual cult? Next in succession we have those "tradesmen" whom we will call "purveyors": brewers, bakers, oil pressers, slaughterers probably, and the like. That there were prebendal craftsmen is certain, at any rate in the late period. Certainly on the basis of VS 15, 1, a text which is of crucial importance for our subject, but of uncertain background, there were among them persons who had *ērib bīti* status, therefore were "allowed to enter the sanctuary". But at this point problems begin in earnest, for is *ērib bīti* in itself a separate "function" and not merely a "status"? Not all specialists, even in otherwise ritualist occupations, associated with the sanctuaries were initiated.

We will have to consider regularly whether a certain function, by acting its role in the presence of the gods might belong to the *ērib bīti*s or not. In the First Millennium high officials prided themselves in being *ērib bīti*s, the title implied status. But is this the case, for instance, with the various "performers", *kurgarrû*s and the like, however tainted their reputation in a section of Assyriological literature may be?[7] This fact is, of course, in itself actually irrelevant: these people had a specific cultic role, especially relating to Ištar, which included ritualised fighting.[8] The role in the cult may be a ground for inclusion.

With the evidence available it is difficult to make a case for a special group of "lower prebendaries", virtually acting under those involved in the regular cult. In such a group we might classify, possibly with the performers alluded to already, the *kisalluḫḫu*s, "courtyard sweepers",[9] (at least some of) the *atû*s, the gate keepers and also the GIR$_3$.SE$_3$.GA, "(lower) personnel", "servants", with, as so often, a for us unspecified task. It should be stressed that some of these functions occur especially in the early period, like that of *kisalluḫḫu,* and that others belong to both the early and the late period, though their prebendal status becomes clear only in the later of the two.[10] Participation in the actual cult is often problematic in these cases, essential though the function may have been. There were also functions of which very few representatives, for instance only one, may have belonged to prebendal circles. Demarcation of what was prebendal, and what not, is difficult, especially at the lower end of the scala of functions. Words belonging to the prebendal

---

[6] The gods did not need the *asû*, a mere medical practitioner, it would seem, but that does not mean that there were no prebendaries who were interested in medical texts. We must await the publication of the relevant material from the Bēl-rēmanni archive and can only mention the wide ranging interests displayed by the texts from the Acquisition Barbora where the Šaṭir texts in every sense indicate a convergence of different backgrounds. Cf. F. Joannès, Les archives de Ninurta-aḫḫê-bulliṭ, in ed. M. deJ. Ellis, Nippur at the Centennial, CRRAI 35, Philadelphia 1992, p. 87-100.

[7] From the Old Babylonian Mari ritual we can add the *ākilu*, who is suggested to have been a "fire eater" or a "sword swallower", cf. CAD A/1 p. 266-7. Reasons are not given.

[8] I must thank Th. Krispijn for especially pointing out this aspect of their activities to me.

[9] Also occurring in an (Old Babylonian) palatial context, F. van Koppen, in W. van Soldt and others eds. Veenhof Anniversary Volume, Leiden, 2000, p. 211ff.

[10] GIR$_3$.SE$_3$.GA, *girsequtu*, was a saleable prebend in Hellenistic Uruk, cf. Doty, 1977, p. 128, Funk 1984 p. 199-207, McEwan 1981. Doty, 1977, p. 410-11 has edited the fragmentary text Oppert 4 which strikingly enough combines an *ērib bīti* prebend with a *girseqû* prebend in a transaction of which the nature cannot be made out anymore. But GIR$_3$.SE$_3$.GA already occur in an unmistakable cultic context in an Old Babylonian text, Kingsbury 1963, "152", where they, on a par with others, receive oil in connection with their presence during the execution of a ritual. In the late ritual fragment Falkenstein 1959 p. 40, 9 they are dressed like the unconsecrated *kalû*s, as other non-*ērib bīti*s were. Neither of the two last texts implies prebendal status for these people, but this is always problematic at the lower end of the scala.

terminology may be used, for instance *manzaltu*, without the function concerned being properly covered by our definition. Cult related perks of a fixed nature in an institution serving the gods constituted prebends, even if the perks were only available once or twice per annum, on special, but regular, occasions during the cultic year. Often only new evidence can clarify the situation.

Particularly the question of what an *ērib bīti* was, will occupy us continuously. We assume that an *ērib bīti* was a relatively high ranking prebendary in the late period and that there existed a link between being an *ērib bīti* and appearing in the presence of the gods, as the term implies. But can we also assume that someone who appears directly before the god in a role in the cult therefore had to be an *ērib bīti*? We will have to consider the consequences of such an assumption.

c. Remuneration

Our prebendaries operated in an institutional context and enjoyed a status deriving from their role in the cult, which they often exercised in combination with other functions, from which they drew additional income. One of the manners in which this status was given expression was through the assignment of land,[11] at least occasionally in combination with the personnel to till it. Though the indications are rather limited, we must accept that many prebendaries held institutional land. In this they did not differ from other functionaries and employees. Land could also be granted directly to these persons or to their families by the king. The second manner of remunerating the prebendaries was through assigning them a share in the remnants of the offerings, to be separated into a non-bloody and a bloody category. This type of grants was assigned by the king. But this manner of remuneration was again not specifically destined for the prebendaries either. A third method, which we will call the *maššartu*[12]*-pappasu*-system, can only be identified securely in the Neo-Babylonian period, though there are perhaps earlier indications. This method was peculiar to the purveying trades, who were assigned additional allowances from the bloody offerings if they did not belong to the butchers.[13] Remnants of bloody and of non-bloody offerings functioned differently in the system of remuneration regarding this group, some prebendaries participating in the one, but not in the other, for which they were compensated by other mechanisms, though these are not always clear. Assigning material against delivery of an *iškaru* was a common method of having goods produced in normal everyday life. This is to a degree comparable to the prebendal *maššartu-pappasu* system. The term *iškaru* plays a certain role near the lower fringes of the prebendal system. In the late period there were also certain institutional accounts which were used to reward specific prebendaries, possibly such accounts also existed within the larger local organisation for payments due to the personnel of the smaller sanctuaries belonging to same the local system. These accounts are not well documented. Normal assignment of *kurummatu*, "sustenance", or even *idū*,

---

[11] Land grants to clerical personnel go back far, but that stands to reason if we assume that prebendal personnel gained a special status only later on. Th. Krispijn tells me that he interprets the Ancient Kudurru no. 18, the "figure aux plumes", as a land grant to a person with priestly status.

[12] The word, probably basically indicating disbursement of material intended for a specific use, occurs, of course, earlier, here we must restrict ourselves to the Neo-Babylonian transfers to people like brewers and bakers who provided their products for the (non-bloody) offerings to the gods. Especially the MB texts from Nippur use *maššartu* in a way comparable with, but more general than, NB usage, but we can notice there too the presence of brewers.

[13] We assume that the non-bloody part of the remuneration of the butchers resembled that of the *ērib bīti*.

"wages", always remains another, fourth, possibility, and occasionally prebendal income of the other types mentioned can even be indicated by such a term.[14]

The smaller sanctuaries operated in an organisation supervised by the local main sanctuary, in which specific gods had their own personnel rather than that this belonged to the temple, or its main deity, in general. But also inanimate constructions or objects could have their prebendaries. The ziqqurrat seems to have enjoyed a cult of its own, and equally the chariot of certain gods. Especially in Babylon where Marduk had a ziqqurrat, which must have been separate from Esagil, the situation will have been of special interest, but we are utterly uninformed on the personnel involved. An *ērib bīti* of the ziqqurrat in Sippar is known, and the same archive also knows of a right to income related to the chariot of Šamaš.[15] We can probably expect that in Sippar, where in the late period a statue of Sargon of Akkad enjoyed veneration, this too would have had its personnel.

A rapid overview of the texts preserved will suggest that some elements of the system of remuneration over time retained a stronger link with the prebendal functions than others. Especially land was not strongly linked to function in the case of the prebendaries, but there were other elements of the system which could loose much of the connection they had with the functions to which they originally belonged. This is probably especially the case with meat portions, with income deriving from special cultic occasions or income related to the manipulation of certain specific objects. We assume, however, that originally the income was always linked to some cult related act. We could regard this as the "vertical splitting" of cultic functions, "horizontal splitting" being the division of functions into blocks of time within the (same) cultic year. We must stress that none of the manners of remuneration identified was really specific to our prebendaries, which again contributes to the fluidity of the system.

Not strictly prebendal was the type of income found in the so-called Edict of Belsazzar, of which the contents must not be discussed here,[16] but which allowed the EN.NAM, the UMBISAG.MEŠ,[17] the *man-di-du*.MEŠ and the I_3.DU_8.ME, *atûs*, a share in the produce of the land the temple leased, in the period of Nabonidus, in the form of a rent farm, to larger or smaller entrepreneurs. Such payments existed already much earlier, however, at least from the early reign of Nebuchadnezzar onwards. This *bēl pīḫāti*, EN.NAM, was probably not the provincial governor,[18] and the others mentioned were certainly institutional officials of whom the *atû* , I_3.DU_8, "gate keeper" and the *mādidu* , "measurer", occupied -at least sometimes- prebendary-type positions, without the nature of

[14] In VS 5, 72 (21 III Dar 9) barley is stated to constitute the value ($ŠAM_2$) of the bread, beer, meat and *makkasu* ŠUG.$ḪA_2$ GIŠ.ŠUB.BA, the *kurummatu*, "sustenance" of the prebend. This is directly comparable, as F. Joannès noted, to RA 74, no. 3, p. 147-8 (= Charpin-Durand, Strasbourg no. 132,) 3[+] IX Dar [6]?: barley counter value of *kurummatu* (consisting of) beer [bread? or meat?] and *makkasu* before the statue of Bēl in the Ninurta Temple. In both cases the nature of the prebendal income, bread and beer, could be suggestive of an *ērib bīti* prebend, which is a distinct possibility in VS 5, 72. In VS 5, 124 (29 x [Dar] 13, from Borsippa) we find *i-di šá maš-šar-t*[*u*$_4$] in what is presumably an account concerning the execution of *naptanus*, BUR. Cf. VS 5, 97, 2 VII Dar 25. On *makkasu*, "off-cuts", after meat portions see below.

[15] Waerzeggers 2001, ziqqurrat text no. 8, chariot nos. 14 and 15.

[16] For a translation see the contribution on Taxation, below.

[17] We will see that the appropriation attributed to a person as a temple scribe occasionally was assigned at the same moment as he received prebendal functions and income.

[18] The identity of this official, according to my conviction not a tax farmer or someone comparable, is discussed in the contribution on Taxation, Chapter II, note 31. There is a distinct possibility that "secular" titles of this type were used in a temple context.

their participation in the actual cult being clear. Here we must inevitably relax the rules imposed by our definition. The scribes, UMBISAGs, though not prebendaries as a consequence of their function, often belonged to this group as possessors of other, prebendal, functions. The functions mentioned by the Edict were paid, or paid in part, from what were the specific accounts mentioned already. We can do little more than consider the possibility that such accounts were especially fed by Edict-type income. A certain degree of overlap existed between the prebendal and non-prebendal income of certain functionaries, all the more so as also this type of income was ultimately assigned by the king. The question is complicated by the fact that there are indications that an Edict-type form of income was used to pay the *qēpu*, who was in the Neo-Babylonian period the foremost of the royal representatives in the main sanctuaries, and who was never one of the prebendaries. Again we must not expect that the margins will be clear-cut. Meat portions always have come from the bloody offerings for all categories of prebendaries, but we may expect that the slaughterer occupied a special position in this respect.

Our definition deliberately excludes a more general link between the term "prebend" and the simple possession of a sustenance field, which is occasionally being referred to as someone's prebend in Assyriological literature. Only if such fields are mentioned in the context of prebendal functions as defined here, they can play a role in the following discussion. Receiving income deriving from the offerings presented to the gods can not be regarded as typically prebendal either, as we noted already, even though the leftovers of the offerings played an essential, probably status linked, role in remunerating the clergy. Such income could be granted by the king, probably as the (formal) provider of the sacrificial material offered to the gods, but to anybody he thought fit.

That the term "prebend" often refers one-sidedly to the income aspect of the system probably reinforces the impression that, in any period, tasks and income tended to become increasingly divorced from one another. Inheritance and sale documents concentrate on the income, not on the tasks. The conclusion that in these cases the income did not represent obligations is, however, probably wrong.

d. Inheritable functions

Though there is a small number of texts assigning ostensibly newly funded prebendal functions to individuals, none of them explicitly states that the function could be transferred to descendants. Yet this was a universal fact for many functions. The hereditary character of the exclusively male prebendal functions and their income inevitably created problems. There comes a moment in the development of society at which it no longer accepts that functions, even when gender determined,[19] are under circumstances only inheritable in the wider family, when that results in loss of income to the direct -in our case: female- heirs.[20] Inheritance by members of the other gender and both fragmentation and concentration of functions put the system under strain, already a minority caused problems. The strain had to be reduced by allowing transfer of tasks and income.[21] Whether prebends

19 It will become evident that we will be dealing with the male clergy only. Especially if we give the *nadītu*s "benefit of clergy", the decline in the numbers of the female clergy, already during the Old Babylonian period, is dramatic. This is in itself an important question, though it does not affect us here. But note that, for instance, a *nadītu* still "officiates" in Çağirgan and Lambert, 1991-93, p. 98 line 101. Someone must have fulfilled this role, Th. Krispijn suggests that the queen might fit the position of LUKUR in this case. EREŠ.DINGIR, GAL and TUR, but otherwise unspecified, survived in Kassite Nippur.

20 This is, again, not specific to prebends, it also applies to military holdings.

21 There is a practical difference between ownership shared by several persons, especially members of one family and the practical execution coming into the hands of several owners. In the case the execution

could be sold freely or not is a difficult problem, which is linked to the problem whether anybody, of the right gender, could be consecrated. Not all, or rather very few, family connections are known to us. Our knowledge of the relevant prosopography will always be limited.

The fragmentation of many functions caused by inheritance divisions and partial sales, already evident in the early period, the fact that women owned functions which they could not fulfil, the possibility that there were also male owners in the same position on account of impediments, with the additional complication of persons owning functions in different towns, or combined in their person various functions of different nature, asked for special measures. Not too long ago K. Kessler argued on the basis of a considerable group of texts dealing with Neo-Babylonian baker's prebends in Eanna in Uruk, that there are practical reasons for the proposition that not all owners of shares in the purveying functions could participate in the practical execution of the tasks, which was probably the most lucrative aspect of the prebend, or at any rate of this type of prebend.[22] Only detailed prosopgraphical studies can verify this thesis.

Though it is difficult not to assume that elements of the remuneration of the clergy, for instance the land or the meat portions,[23] could be sold separately, it goes too far to assume that the prebendal functions themselves could be sold freely, if only because there are -but explicitly only in the Neo-Babylonian period- indications that formally tasks could only be undertaken by those of the right descent -and gender-, not only in the male but specifically also in the female line.[24] If taken seriously such requirements make absolute freedom to sell unlikely.

e. The higher functions

Though at first sight the definition would seem to be fairly strict, it solves an essential problem raised by Charpin by extending the subject rather than by limiting it.[25] Many Assyriologists only regard those who possessed the lower, dividable and sellable functions as prebendaries. We must accept that there is little sense in attempting a strict

---

became divided the shares had to be split, if only ownership was shared this was perhaps not imperative, only the proceeds required division. This is probably the case in VS 5, 37, (Borsippa, Ilija A, 13 IX Cyr 2) where someone sells his share in an undivided (line 10: *la i-zu-zu*) gate keeper's prebend amounting to 1,5 days. As the buyer was a co-owner we can speculate whether or not the text is no more than a realignment of ownership after an inheritance division, intended to limit fragmentation. We can reasonably do so, as the payment of the price is phrased as a gift. The gate keeper's prebend involved Edict-type income, line 3. Cf. also TuM 2/3, 4 (same, date virtually lost) where a gate keeper's position will have been shared for some time by two persons.

22 Kessler 1991 p. 72. We will return to the question.

23 It is difficult to come to grips with this type of fragmentation. We can assume that it involves not only land and tradable commodities like meat portions, which were difficult to standardise and thus had to be assigned specifically. Pinches, Peek no. 7 (15 VII Dar 22) is a good example of the treatment of meat portions separately from the obligations undoubtedly connected to their assignment. We know little about prebendal rights to textiles, but a similar severance between obligations and appropriations can be expected. Textiles are mentioned explicitly as an element in the allowance pertaining to the *šangû* in BBSt 36. Special allowances on festive occasions are possibly also an element of the remunerations which could be alienated, for instance the *muttāqu* on occasion of the *eššešus*. For Bongenaar 1997 p. 265 the *muttāqūtu* of the thirteen *šalām bīti*s constituted a separate prebend. Perhaps we must consider the obligation as an element of a *ṣaḫit-ginê* prebend which was in the process of becoming detached from the main occupation. See Chapter IV.

24 Cf. particularly San Nicolò 1934, 1935.

25 Charpin 1986 p. 251.

separation of the personnel employed in the Mesopotamian sanctuaries into those engaged in cultic, administrative and menial tasks, because all those tasks had to be fulfilled at several levels. The cult of the Mesopotamian gods served their very human needs, which required a specialised personnel, but their sanctuaries also had to fulfil a range of tasks in the field of administration and production which were not directly cult-related. Many occupations functioned with their own separate personnel in the cult and for administration and production, but some of the higher officials had tasks in all the fields mentioned. Potentially the role of all the cultic practitioners meets our definition of prebendaries, but they also include certain high-ranking officials, beginning with the SANGA/*šangû* and at least occasionally, possibly, the ŠABRA in the earlier period and at any rate later on the *šatammu*, who was at first only an administrator, not to mention specifically cultic functionaries like the ŠEŠ.GAL/*aḫu rabû*[26] and the *kalamaḫḫu*, who was also a (cultic) administrator.

It is certainly wrong to regard the appropriation for these higher functions as on principle different from that of the lower personnel, which according to texts from private archives was transferable. The appropriation for both types of functions was, on principle not different from that of other, non-prebendal, tasks, even, as stated, as to the remnants of the offerings. Essential is therefore that the function was exercised in a context where it had cultic implications. In archival texts, especially the higher institutional officials appear primarily in their administrative roles, internally they will have had invariably some task in the cult, though the information, culled mainly from ritual texts, is practically limited to the later period. On the other hand some essentially "ritualist" functions, like the Neo-Babylonian *aḫu rabû*, hardly figure at all in administrative texts or in material from private archives, yet it would be folly to underestimate the importance of their status or their prebendal background.

In the Neo-Babylonian period, when the hereditary principle for the higher functions had lost much of its meaning under the influence of the politics of the day, the possession of one of the lower functions was probably, if not required, at least helpful in order to make a person eligible for the higher functions. In the higher functions, the succession of one member of a family by another is far from unknown in the later period, but it was not so regular as Charpin's studies suggest it was in Old Babylonian Ur, and we can add, in Ur III times, at any rate in Nippur[27] and Lagaš[28]. But already there the political implications of occupying the higher functions in the temples, both male and female, can occasionally be observed. "Succession" is in these cases perhaps a better word than "inheritance". The higher clergy fulfilled a political role, which made it vulnerable to political changes.

---

[26] I venture no opinion regarding the reading of the name of this function, *aḫu rabû* or *šešgallu*, but suppose, like others, that he was the first of the *ērib bītis*. Note that the Anu ritual AO 6460 obv. 33 (RAcc p. 119) has a ^{LU_2}KU$_4$.E$_2$ GAL-*ú*, "head *e.b.*".

[27] On the Ur-Meme family in Nippur cf. R.L. Zettler, The Genealogy of the House of Ur-Me-me, a second look, AfO 31, 1984, p. 1-9, with further literature. Cf. also Zettler 1992, p. 235 on the intensity of the family's interest in the Inanna temple.

[28] The progeny of the ENSI Ur-Baba occupied many of the higher functions in the "temples" of the province, a concentration of power which doubtlessly contributed to their joint downfall, cf. K. Maekawa, ASJ 18, 1996, p.107-122. The crucial point here is not the real or assumed "confiscation of private property", but the elimination of a whole number of related high ranking (male and female) functionaries, involving the resumption of their appropriations.

f. A difference between higher and lower functions?

The distinction between functions which could be split up between several persons according to period of service and which could be sold or divided further through inheritance, -those that are often regarded as "prebendal" in a narrow sense-, and functions which -especially in an Old Babylonian perspective- could be transmitted in an undivided form only, and which could not be sold at all,[29] constitutes a problem. Indivisible seem to have been the highest functions in the organisation of the sanctuaries, where the fulfilling of priestly tasks was doubled by essential administrative obligations. We must stress however, that the manner of funding of the indivisible functions did not essentially differ from that of the divisible ones.[30]

In my opinion it is not a prerequisite for the qualification "prebendal" that many of those functioning in the prebendal system exercised their functions in an alternating manner for a limited period in the course of the year or on certain days of the month. The occurrence of earlier alternating functions, possibly originally indicated by use of the term BALA, is not a core feature of the system if it was merely a result of the fragmentation of functions through inheritance or sale. The alternating execution of (later) functions observable in the texts is certainly mainly caused by an ever increasing horizontal splitting up of individual tasks and their remuneration. Both early and late there is evidence that functions which could be split up were held or granted in an undivided manner at a specific moment in time, though there remains the possibility that for certain functions the term BALA genuinely implied a rotation of their occupants in the earlier period. There is some limited lexical support for this point of view which will be discussed below.

The granting of date plantations with the obligation to provide dates for the table of the gods on a specific day of the calendar is a special aspect of the *rab banî* prebend at least observable in the late period. Alternate functioning thus would seem to be certain in this case, at least in theory. In reality the products required were gathered in the same manner as dates produced by ordinary gardeners were, so this should not be regarded as an effective example of a "Wechselamt". BALA is in our case in general "the specific period in which a certain person has the right and duty to serve", for whatever reason. Especially here the general inability to calculate the number of full places reserved for a specific cultic occupation makes itself felt. There were, or came into existence, of course also functions

---

29 In the Neo-Babylonian period the type of higher function intended here is not generally regarded as inheritable by those who have studied the matter. Political interference in this period can be assumed to be one of the major reasons for the changeover from one family to another for the higher appointments. Essential seems to be that the higher functions were not as a rule split up among several different persons. The replacement of the temple scribe (DUB.SAR E_2.DN) by (some) four others, sometimes also entitled "scribe of the temple of DN" is an exception, but these were possibly strictly spoken not prebendaries. We will return to this matter. A major difference between the earlier and the later, Neo-Babylonian, period, is the much more pronounced presence of royal supervisory personnel in the temple organisations. These persons stand, as far as we can see, outside the prebendal system, which encompasses functions entailing contact with the godhead within the circle of those belonging to the institution. Such functions sometimes imply other, especially administrative tasks. Or must we rather pose the question whether for certain "internal" administrative tasks the possession of some form of prebendal status was required or at least desirable? It should be noted on the other hand that at any rate in Sippar the *qêpu*, the main royal representative, actually received Edict-type income, even though he is not listed among the functionaries mentioned by the Edict. (J. van Dijk's remark on a document referring to the sale of "das Amt des Urigallu", meaning that of *aḫu rabû*, UVB 18, 1962, p. 41, belonging to the NB Uruk Nabû-supê-muḫur archive, will have to be regarded as a slip, as there is no such text among those published by Kessler, 1991.)

30 Perhaps it would have been better if Assyriology had preferred the term *beneficia* over prebends.

and tasks linked to specific, though infrequent, cultic occasions. Such functions may have been a result of the sale of specific elements of a certain function or of a specific grant answering a specific need perceived.

g. Importance

We are dealing with a stabilising factor in Mesopotamian society and must stress the permanent features of the system.[31] The endurance and toughness of the temple as one of Ancient Mesopotamia's essential institutions cannot be dissociated from the existence of a group of people who managed it both from a cultic point of view and as a source of income. Here the latter rather than the former is of importance.[32] Yet there are inevitably changes in emphasis in the prebendal system in the course of its history and it was, like the economic role of the Mesopotamian temple, a tool of governance. It could be used as a means for creating a following. When outside control slackened the risks of internal divisions increased.[33]

It must be clear that many aspects of the inheritable and other functions of the Mesopotamian clergy can only be studied on the basis of extensive prosopographic investigations. These require concentration on the material from one specific locality in a specific period in the manner of Charpin's Clergé. Such studies are not intended here, we must concentrate on the general outlines of the system and on what seem to be changes in emphasis through time. Systematic disregard for the prosopographic links between those involved therefore seriously limits the scope of this study. Some attempt at condensation of the evidence is inevitable, however.

If the accomplishment of cult related tasks implied, for instance, the utterance of specified prayers or other formulae during the preparation of food -as well as other goods-, as appears to be confirmed by at least one late ritual prescription text,[34] it could be imagined that such tasks could hardly be transferred to persons without the proper consecration or training. Teaching or even showing tablets containing material with cultic implications to

---

31 This differs in purpose from Renger's point of departure in Renger 1967 p. 110-111, but it is in no manner intended to deny important changes in the course of time, or, for that matter, local differences.

32 Of the former Charpin 1986 gives some, of necessity incomplete, idea for Ur in the Old Babylonian period. Harris 1975 p. 142ff. differs considerably when looking at Sippar somewhat later in the same period: our documentation is blatantly incomplete.

33 This is the situation in Borsippa described in the text re-edited by W.G. Lambert, JAOS 88, 1968, p. 124-130, describing events during the reign of Nabû-šum-iškun, the author of which had accumulated the functions of *nešakku*, *ērib bīt Nabû* and *šākin ṭēmi* of Borsippa (Ib 11 and repetitions) which remains a notable combination of clerical and secular charges, all the more so as his antagonist (Ib 22) is another *ērib bīt Nabû* , who was the *šatammu* of Ezida. That high ranking clerics became provincial governors later in their career is later also attested in the case of certain *šangû*s of Sippar, and VS 1, 35 betrays that a *šākin ṭēmi* of Dilbat could provide for a younger son with temple functions which were, we can assume, his personal property. In Nippur the combination of high temple and administrative functions was, as is well known, the rule.

34 RAcc p. 76ff. AO 6451. Line 45 registers a *naqbītu* by the *ṭēnu*, line 45-6 by the *nuḫatimmu* and rev. 9-12 by the *ṭābiḫu*: the miller, the cook and the slaughterer. There are no indications that a miller could be a prebendary beyond a case in Hellenistic Uruk, where the function is a kind of "specialisation belonging to a baker's prebend", see below. Thus, after all, also the other utterances could probably be spoken by uninitiated persons. It would not be unthinkable that a small prayer-like phrase would be uttered anyhow on commencing tasks like those mentioned here.

širku's, or un-initiated persons in general, was punishable or at least frowned upon.[35] This is a common theme in the colophons of tablets with religious implications. But if exclusion of the un-initiated was theoretically required, it was practically impossible to apply such an injunction rigorously. There is something contradictory in the system, which probably hides some serious misunderstanding on our part: on the one hand access to functions was limited, on the other slaves could be employed for the practical chores. But this is probably a problem of our making: at least already in the Ur III period ordinary workers controlled by the temple prepared the ingredients for the meals of the gods. Some types of work were simply not done by people of means and status.[36]

The circle of those admitted to the service of the gods concerned was probably always restricted locally, even though there are clear signs that belonging to the prebendal circles attached to one local sanctuary made it easier to penetrate another. In the Neo-Babylonian period there were clear links between Babylon and Sippar and between Uruk and Larsa, to mention only the most conspicuous cases.[37] This is not the same as the migration of "priestly" families from Eridu to Ur or from Uruk to Kiš as discussed by Charpin,[38] though the results will have been comparable in the long run: though titles vary, we are dealing with fundamentally a single class of people. In the Old Babylonian period the links were reinforced by the institutional contraction we can observe, in Neo-Babylonian times the recollection of previous contraction[39] plays an obvious role in answering to the possibilities offered by fresh expansion.

The occupation of functions based on the principle of heredity in the family group, combined with a fixed source of income, together with the transfer of specialist knowledge within the family, made the prebendaries a separate social group, even though that did not automatically imply complete cohesion. We can assume that at least in the Neo-Babylonian period there existed an inner circle consisting of the *ērib bīti*, those who had the right to enter into the presence of the gods and who formed together with the heads of the non-*ērib bīti* prebendaries a kind of council[40] acting under an administrative top containing on the

---

[35] Beaulieu 1992. The text published by Beaulieu indicates better than others that reserved knowledge had to be kept secret, an impression also provided in a totally different manner by Borger 1973, lines 23-6, difficult though the text may be.

[36] My colleague B. Haring tells me that the situation in Egypt did not differ essentially in this respect.

[37] In the Neo-Assyrian North STT 44 is relevant: when a new temple (for Zababa and Baba in Ḫuzirina?) was endowed by Sanherib, the *šangû* of Adad in Aššur was transferred/appointed as a *šangû*, with his family, cf. J.N. Postgate NRGD no. 40 p. 78ff. The question is to be connected to Sanherib's attempts to upgrade Aššur by seeking grounds for promoting Zababa as Aššur's son. In this improving the status of Zababa through pronouncements by Sin of Ḫarran serves the same purpose as the building of a temple in Aššur. H. Galter, ARIM 2, 1984, p. 1-2 and K. Deller and V. Donbaz, BaM 18 p. 221-228. Enhancing the status of Sin of Ḫarran probably lies behind the facts mentioned by colophon 500 in Hunger 1968: according to which a copy of a text was made by PN *áš-ta-lu-ú* of Sin, a son of a *kalamaḫḫu* of Sin of Ḫarran who was a descendant of a *kalamaḫḫu* of Esagil (in Babylon). The *lē'u* copied came from Babylon. The *e/aštalu* was possibly a kind of entertainer. Consecration and dedication are qualities enhanced by an inherited background, also in Mesopotamia.

[38] Charpin 1986 p. 342ff., esp. p. 379ff. and p. 403ff.

[39] Probably to be dated after the second dynasty of Isin. Kassite reconstructions are attested in at least Ur, Uruk and Larsa. A Kassite endowment for Ištar of Uruk has been preserved, see below.

[40] I will avoid here the subject of the *kiništu* and of *mār banē* acting as a collective. Much of the relevant material and literature can be found in M. Dandamayev, The Composition of the Citizens in First Millennium Babylonia, AoF 24, 1997, p. 135-147, but I am not sure whether I can follow all the arguments and conclusions, though I will accept that assisting as a witness or assessor at a formal discussion of institutional matters is a sign of a certain status. The question is what confers the status.

one hand an inner, institutional element and on the other royal agents. The importance which the group of prebendaries as a whole inevitably attached to its material prerogatives is probably one of the main reasons for the tenacity with which, especially, the Uruk temples maintained their existence into the Hellenistic period.[41] The prebendal system with its privileged material basis was thus rather a source of strength for Mesopotamian institutional religion than a mark of its decline, as some students of the Babylonian institutions have suggested.

2. The Evidence

We depend on the documentation available, but we know that it is insufficient. Yet we must attempt to see the remuneration of the Mesopotamian clergy as a system. What is the nature of the material that can help us? We will attempt to avoid repetition of the vital factual lists of relevant material already effectively provided by others,[42] but will try to generalise and to condense the evidence in order to concentrate on what seems to be essential.

a. Administrative files[43]

If the endowment of the clergy is the core question when dealing with prebends, the problem is as old as the Mesopotamian sanctuaries in general. Our overall understanding of the texts and the survival of material make it impractical to consider the period before Ur III. The practical possibilities even for the Ur III period are limited, not withstanding the huge amount of material containing information on especially the sacrificial aspect of the cult, which is directly related to the remuneration of prebendaries.[44] It remains a fact that our knowledge concerning the ("clerical") personnel of the cult in the Ur III period is rather limited, though the availability of texts from the Inanna temple in Nippur has improved the situation.

Of importance is that Maekawa has proposed a reform introduced by Šulgi, initiating in "Lagaš" a formal division of the institutional personnel into a cultic and an agricultural section.[45] For Nippur the texts which are particularly relevant in a prebendal context have been published very selectively.[46] In summary for the Third Millennium: the administrative archives in general, though containing much on expenditure in a cultic setting, are not very informative on organisational aspects of the personnel responsible for the execution of the cult. We can notice, certainly already in the Ur III period, that entering upon a function we would regard as at least potentially cultic, involved some form of "ceremony".

From administrative text groups we need those files which demonstrate expenditure on the cult and its personnel. We often have difficulty in recognising that expenditure on the cult may reappear as expenditure on personnel. To all probability what was spent on offerings and the product of these offerings, which were handed on to others would both be

---

Being juridically free is important, but probably not enough. I will continue to avoid the term "citizen", even for this group of persons.

41 For a maximum opinion on the longevity of the Babylon temples cf. Boiy 2000 p. 181.

42 Such as Renger, 1967a, 1969 and 1967b; CAD I/J p. 201; Bongenaar 1997 in essence p. 141-2.

43 For brevity's sake I will call (Ur III plus) Old Babylonian "early" and Neo-Babylonian (with "Hellenistic") "late".

44 This is the material on which Sallaberger 1993 is based. Texts like UET 3, 1126, dealing in a balanced manner with incoming and outgoing remnants of offerings are rare.

45 Maekawa 1999.

46 Zettler, 1992.

booked as outgoing posts in different types of texts. Linking the two directly is often only possible if they are connected by texts from a specific file. Often prosopgraphical difficulties will prevent recognition of the individuals concerned. That there were special files which were particularly relevant for our subject has been demonstrated by the one from Old Babylonian Nippur reassembled by Sigrist, which in its structure has unmistakable "Ur III traits".[47] The texts list cultic expenditure on the obverse and transmission of some of it for earthly purposes on the reverse. It is, however, somewhat difficult to use this material effectively owing to its fragmentary state and the schematic manner of publication. From Neo-Babylonian Uruk we have the SWU texts,[48] which, fragmentary though they are, inform us particularly on the organisation of the bakers and brewers in Eanna and the *maššartu-pappasu* system, which provided them with the means to deliver the products required from them and with the remuneration that was due to them. In Sippar evidence on this type of expenditure must usually be culled from documents dealing with expenditure in general, where the prebendal is often difficult to separate from the non-prebendal.

That we are informed on questions like that of the suitability of a certain person for prebendal status and the correctness of the application of certain ritual actions in which prebendaries took part, is in a number of cases a result of the circumstance that the Uruk Eanna archive contains, generally, a notable number of texts dealing with administrative responses to abuses, disagreements and problems. Such texts usually provide relevant background information which is not found in administrative lists or in contracts dealing with the transfer of property.

Recognising scattered and isolated analogous material from other administrations than those in Nippur, Uruk or Sippar helps in understanding the range of the prebendal system[49] and it extends the possibility of recognising its workings in earlier periods. That there existed registers of holders of rights in the Neo-Babylonian period is certain, but as these registers were primarily kept on wooden boards, their loss is inevitable. Comparable material, presumably on clay, must have existed in earlier periods.

b. The Old Babylonian period and earlier: private archives

The scarce Third Millennium private files do not appear to be relevant for our subject. There is, however, the odd private dedicatory inscription which suggests a link with prebendal funding. Such a document would, of course, belong to an institutional "archive", but its importance is that it hints at a certain role of private persons in the development of the prebendal system. A good example is the text published by M. Civil (1989). Not all funding came from the king. Rare and significant are also two juridical texts suggesting that lower, inheritable, prebendal functions already existed in the Ur III period and that prebendaries had their sustenance land.

For the moment there are no reasons for assuming that the beginning of the Old Babylonian period meant a fundamental change in the structure of the manning of the cult. The fact that during the (middle) Old Babylonian period (Ḫammurabi, Samsu-iluna) cultic functions together with the income pertaining to them, were not only being inherited, as had normally occurred previously, but that they were or had also become transferable through sale, has been regarded as a sign of the increasing secularisation of society in the course of the Old Babylonian period.[50] There are no relevant texts from the early Isin-Larsa

---

[47] Sigrist 1984.

[48] Freydank 1971.

[49] Charpin 1986.

[50] Edzard, 1957, p. 6, where the sale, donation and inheritance of prebends, as a sign of the secularisation of the temples, is regarded as an indication of a fundamental change in the Mesopotamian state.

period, and only the later contracts confront us in an unmistakable manner with prebends as private property. This documentation dates predominately from the later Isin and Larsa kings and from the reigns of Ḫammurabi and Samsu-iluna in the South. This does not exclude earlier occurrence of the phenomenon and some caution is advisable in another respect, for, as remarked, the question which should be answered first should be: "was the circle of those to whom cultic functions could be sold limited or not?" An answer would require better prosopographic insights than are at present available.

In Nippur the documents deal with the sale and the inheritance division of prebendal functions belonging to several local sanctuaries. This evidence is not easily linked to the administrative material published as "the *sattukku* texts from Ešumesu" by Sigrist. Whether or not certain persons or functions mentioned there belonged to the prebendal clergy remains a guess if there is no corroboration, minimally as to the function concerned, by texts from the private archives.[51] The texts from private archives from Isin do add details to the Nippur material, but on principle the information is of a similar nature. The Nippur private archives involved are principally those of Attā, the Enlil-zimu group and the Mannu-mêšu-liṣṣur texts, supplemented by the texts from Isin attributable to the Dadā-archive. There is also some material which cannot be assigned to a specific file.

In Ur the information is patchy and difficult to handle, but it has benefited from Charpin's sense for order and precision and thus constitutes one of the major sources on the context in which the prebendal system functioned in what is for us the earlier phase of its existence. Material from elsewhere consists essentially of isolated texts. In Sippar the few texts from the later Old Babylonian period, after the reign of Samsuiluna, deal mainly with court cases and so reinforce the impression that the income aspects of the prebends prevailed for those involved over the tasks they imposed.[52]

c. The Middle-Babylonian Period

The Middle-Babylonian period in its widest sense constitutes a gap, but primarily in the documentation, not in the development of the phenomenon under discussion. We cannot be absolutely certain whether all cultic activity in sanctuaries like those of Ur, Uruk or Larsa, or even Nippur, really stopped. If it stopped, it was certainly resumed periodically. Kassite building activities are known from all localities mentioned, and that implies at least resumption of the cult and presence of some sort of clergy. We know that in certain cases the clergy moved to safer places, probably, as seems to have been the case in the Neo-Babylonian period, awaiting the possibility of a return. We can probably regard the brewers documented at the EM-site in Ur as potential prebendaries. A handful of *kudurrus* is witness to the presence at various locations of people with priestly status. Nippur is better documented, but only a more complete publication of the Kassite archival material can provide the certainty that there is no direct information on prebendaries in what is preserved. There is, however, no reason for assuming an absolute break in the cultic tradition there.[53]

---

51 Asking confirmation as to the person concerned would be too much. This leaves open the possibility that a specific person, though occupying a function which can be prebendal, yet received the remnants of the offerings without being a prebendary proper.

52 Possibly the publication of the Ur-Utu archive will change the situation, the *kalamaḫḫu* being in the late Old Babylonian period potentially an important prebendary.

53 Sassmannshausen, 2001, p. 61ff. contains a section on the available information from the (later) Kassite period on priests and related functionaries and p. 157ff. one on the temple and the cult. Whether there is some connection between the considerable amount of material on the processing of grain and especially the activities of brewers and bakers with a possible prebendal system (in Nippur) needs perhaps

d. Private archives: Neo-Babylonian and Hellenistic-Parthian

The Neo-Babylonian private archives demonstrate that possessing prebendal rights was not a general phenomenon amongst urban families. In an archive like that of the Egibi, with all its ramifications, there is no sign of an interest of any substance in prebendal rights. Texts dealing with prebends occur only in a number of specific family archives. These families are otherwise fully engaged in the exploitation of their land holdings, generally leased to tenants, and other normal business activities, which were, for instance like brewing, sometimes directly related to the prebendal obligations. The ownership of slaves was normal and these were also involved in the prebend related activities of their owners. The prebendal families constituted a special group within the well-to-do urban population. In the Hellenistic-Parthian[54] period virtually all private archival material stems from prebendal families, at any rate in Uruk.[55]

Especially in Sippar it seems to be clear that private documents were often kept in places where the excavations of the last century could easily have mixed up material with a private origin and material from institutional administrations. The fact that such private material clusters in certain sections of specific accession numbers in the British Museum collections sometimes suggests a distinct, possibly even a separate origin. There could, however, be several reasons for the close association. It may be storage with official documents, either for safe keeping or on account of involvement in some official procedure. But this is less likely than the simpler explanation that prebendaries owned storerooms in the temple precincts, presumably primarily in connection with execution of their prebendal tasks, which were also used for the safekeeping of their private documents. In Uruk such storerooms were inherited and bought or sold, especially in the Hellenistic period with fairly precise descriptions of their situation, which makes it perfectly clear that they were situated within the enclosure of the temple. It is regrettable that, particularly in Sippar, the find spots of the private tablets are not known. Some explanation is required for the mixed occurrence of private and official texts from the reign of Darius in several of the text groups originating from Sippar. Especially if such private documents are regarded as remnants which have been selected from much larger archives.[56]

In Borsippa files we do find information on the storerooms, but it is not precise enough to make location on an archaeological plan feasible. Though the god owned his temple, parts of it were for practical purpose private property, the ultimate divine ownership having become in fact a kind of juridical encumbrance. That several of the "later" Borsippa

---

some investigation, but such a link is not obvious. The Middle-Babylonian Nippur archival material as such does not, it would seem, strike a (cursory) reader as being temple-related, but that does not mean that prebendal phenomena were absent.

[54] I will omit the "Parthian", from now on, the term "Hellenistic" must cover the whole period. Needless to say Neo-Babylonian (when used in a narrower sense) also covers the early Achaemenid period up to the early years of Xerxes when all information, including that on prebends, was interrupted.

[55] For the material from Babylon Boiy 2000, p. 227ff. At least some of these people will have had prebendal status but administrative documents often skip family names which are a first indication of status, and without private documents there is no corroboration. The presence of *rāsinus*, "executors (of prebendal tasks)" in the late Babylon texts is at least suggestive.

[56] See for the moment especially C. Waerzeggers 2001 p. 2ff. The problem is that with the administrative material from Ebabbar we have tablets which are stated to have been rejected from the Marduk-rēmanni archive, thus not what was kept. Possibly we must conclude that all material represents discards.

text groups are linked, seems, however, to be fairly obvious. Here a private background is likely, however, for institutional administrative material is poorly represented.[57]

That private archives were kept and discarded in private houses stands, of course, to reason, and is now especially well-attested in Uruk.[58] Such archives have been published by Hunger (1970) and especially Kessler (1991), with wide ranging discussion of the backgrounds.

The early Neo-Babylonian *kudurrus*, which are of considerable interest for the question of prebendal funding, are basically transcripts of private documents, royal grants to individuals, possibly with additional flattery at the address of the grantor and curses for those who would rescind the grants. BBSt 36, with its Nabopolassar box, was possibly formally laid to rest after the interest of the particular Šangû-Šamaš branch[59] had lapsed or, perhaps, was brought to an end, for whatever reason. These are only scattered reflections of royal documents regulating and renovating the cult. We can assume that there were many more documents of this type. When, for instance, Esarhaddon restored the cult of Marduk he will have had to reinstate the complete apparatus serving that god and his entourage, which will inevitably have been expanded by the Chaldeans. A fragment of a document confirming prebendal income by Šamaš-šum-ukīn, notably *ki-i* $^{LU_2}KU_4.E_2$-*ma*, "corresponding to what of an *ērib bīti* is used to enjoy", resulting from a renovation of the cult of Bēlit-Ninua in Babylon under Aššur-nādin-šumi, before Sanheribs hard hand made itself felt, has been published recently.[60] Similar measures will have been repeated regularly almost everywhere. Little is available to us.

All the evidence from private archives comes from archives of holders of relatively small shares in fairly minor functions. There is, as yet, no archive which illustrates the role of the holders of the major functions in the institutional hierarchy, "temporal or spiritual": was it in the late period a requirement to possess some office on a hereditary basis in order to be able to fulfil such a function?[61] Not, of course, if the function was hereditary in itself, but it may have been of importance when for political reasons someone from another family had to be selected. Direct information on political interference in the staffing of the more important functions would be important. For the moment we only have the dates of the changes in the higher personnel which suggest political interference, e.g. the changes at the beginning of the rule of Nabonidus. The importance of the higher clergy, who had of course considerable administrative responsibility in local economic affairs, transpires from the fact that in Borsippa the *šatammu* married a daughter of Neriglissar immediately after

---

57 A further reason for the spread of "private documents" in general may be their use as study material for the training as scribes of young members of the family.

58 A special case is the "archive" of Bēl-supē-muḫur, published Kessler 1991, which obviously constitutes the rejects from his private archive which had lost practical meaning and were buried separately in a jar.

59 If that family was really involved.

60 Da Riva and Frahm 2000, line 3. The text sums up in lines 5-7 a whole range of prebendal rights which had been granted to the father of the beneficiary.

61 The texts are also suggestive as to the manner in which administrators from these circles behaved as persons. Waerzeggers 2001 p. 113-4 deals with a murky affair in which Marduk-rēmanni had to settle by paying a hefty fine in order keep his hand and to escape from being beaten up. Some form of personal violence belongs to the milieu, as also a Nappāḫu family text attests: C. Wunsch, Die Jugendsünden eines Babyloniers aus gutem Hause, AoF 24, 1997, p. 231-241. Though these matters are not dealt with here, they are just as important to notice as the intellectual proclivities and the business activities of this group of people.

his usurpation.[62] Political interference disturbed the basic pattern of transmission through inheritance, and if interference occurred often enough, the pattern tended to disappear.[63]

Though there is Neo-Babylonian material on the sale and the use as a collateral of prebends, there is much more on arrangements regarding the execution of obligations. Inheritance documents are relatively rare in this period, but that does not put the principle in jeopardy.

There are some important clusters of information. From Babylon we have primarily that of the Nappāḫu family[64], with relevant texts from Nabonidus 12 to Xerxes 1. Otherwise there is only scattered information on prebends in Babylon. A minor exception is the small archive of a branch of the Ea-eppeš-ili family edited by Joannès (1980). These texts are exclusively focused on the income, especially the meat portions deriving from rights related to a divine Ṣalam-Bēl in the Ninurta-temple.

Particularly rich is the material on prebendal families from Borsippa. Here we find an, as yet mainly indirect, link between holding *ḫanšû*-land and belonging to a prebendal family. Transfer and use of prebends as a collateral occurs in the archives of the families Iliia (A and B), Ilšu-abušu and Rē'u-alpi. Borsippa is especially important on account of the material related to the practical arrangements made by members of these families both at a contractual level for the mutual execution of obligations and at a practical level for the actual production of the foodstuffs, especially beer, that had to be delivered. Such texts occur in the archives or files of nearly all known families: Atkuppu,[65] Bēliau, Ea-ilūta-bani, Ḫuṣābu, Iliia (B and unassigned), Ilšu-abušu, Lakuppuru, Mannu-gērûšu and Rē'u-alpi. It may be assumed that close links exist between several of these files. Our elementary list indicates the importance of the Borsippa archives for the practical aspects of prebend ownership.[66] There is, of course, a whole range of texts of which the archival context remains uncertain. These include a small file which can best be regarded as belonging to mutual arrangements regarding the execution of service obligations. These will be dealt with separately.

A considerable expansion of the information on prebendal families may be expected from Zadok's forthcoming publication of new material from the British Museum, especially from Dilbat. For the moment we have a group of texts, dating late in the reign of Darius I, from VS 3 and 5 concerning the holdings of a woman called Amat-Bau and concerned with the exploitation of a *ḫallatu*-plantation which was being leased as ordinary date plantations were, without the obligation to provide for the table of the god on a certain day appearing once. This seems to confirm what we can observe in Sippar: the gardens held by the *rab banî* were exploited as ordinary date plantations were. Some other documents on prebends can be associated with this file.

---

62 Ner 13, the date is significant: 1 I Ner 1.

63 Boiy, 2000 p.193-5 has listed the evidence for the succession of the *šatammu* of Esagil in the Hellenistic period, the evidence for the hereditary nature of the function is impressive , especially in view of the limited amount of information on the function in general. See also R.J. van der Spek, Fs. Oelsner, AOAT 252, Münster 2000, p. 437-446.

64 The Oxford dissertation of H.D. Baker deals with this subject. Some details must, however, be listed below. We will not discuss the general economic activities of this family, which is possibly the best documented of all prebendaries.

65 Regrettably VS 6, 37, (13 IX Nbk 33), regulating the responsibility for five days of an *atkuppu*-prebend held by a member of the Atkuppu family contains no specification of the obligations.

66 On the Borsippa archives especially Joannès 1989. Cf. for the terminology used in indicating the text groups mentioned, Van Driel 1992. It remains a matter of regret that Pinches' copies of the material from the former Amherst collection published in excerpts by Ungnad 1959/60 have not surfaced.

There are some Dilbat documents involving *mādidu*-prebend shares, which are of special interest in that they link this prebend, explicitly connected with the cella of Uraš, to what can be regarded as income deriving from taxation.

Nippur managed to retain some of its old particularity, if we can trust our texts. There is, however, not much material on prebends available from this town. Up to now it is the only place where a Neo-Babylonian NU.EŠ$_3$ (of Ninurta) is attested in a care-adoption document benefiting a brother's son: ROMCT 2, 37, reign of Nebuchadnezzar. Like other material from Nippur from this period, the text is virtually unique.

Some of the Nippur texts indicate, that, as in the Old Babylonian period, and as was the case in at least Babylon, Sippar and Uruk and no doubt elsewhere in the Neo-Babylonian period, many, or even all, sanctuaries in a town were incorporated into one integrated system controlling the provisioning of the temples and their personnel. These systems were supervised by the administrative top of the main local sanctuary. It is of some importance that this is clearly demonstrated by the private archives and not only transpires from the administrative material.

As stated above, most of the Sippar private archives or files must be disentangled from the Ebabbar archive, whether the mix-up occurred during the old excavations or much earlier. Much information on individuals, whether from administrative or from private archives, can be found in Bongenaar 1997. On Bēl-rēmanni from the Šangû-Šamaš family see Jursa 1999 and on Marduk-rēmanni Ṣāḫit-ginê Waerzeggers 2001, which together with the Babylon Nappāḫu texts, are the only Neo-Babylonian private archives which can be compared effectively to the Uruk material.

Other localities have left only dispersed and isolated information, for instance Larsa and Marad, which does, however fit the general pattern obtained elsewhere.

Of particular interest is Joannès' publication of the so-called Šaṭir group in TÉBR. The importance is not just that this group contains scarce relevant material from the later Achaemenid period, but particularly that the persons concerned were not only involved with the prebends of their local Bēl-Šaṭir, but also with the local military *ḫadru*-structure, thus illustrating that in this period people were clearly combining elements of several different local social structures. We are poorly informed on the sources of the funding of local cults, but we can hardly assume that the king played a practical role in matters at this level.

It is possible that somewhere behind the linkage of the various social spheres of influence there was a deliberate policy on the part of the Achaemenid rulers aiming at putting all subjects under one taxable system, though it is clear that already in the Chaldean period prebendal families were included in urban systems linking property and service obligations. A comparable fusion of differing strands may perhaps also be observed in another important text group which contains material from the later Achaemenid period, the long-running Ur archive of the Gallābu family, where at a private level in the end a heiress of a prebendal family married a presumably Babylonian servant of a Persian and adopted his children. That occurred in the reign of Artaxerxes III: UET 4, 1-2.

More likely is that there were earlier links between the prebendal system in the larger urban sanctuaries which were -nominally- funded by the king and earlier systems of land for service. A suggestive later example is provided by VS 6, 169 (reign of Darius), a badly damaged *ēpišānūtu* contract for a slaughterer's prebend in the Eulmaš temple of Bēlet-Akkade in Sippar. In lines 10-11 it contains clauses on the yield of the prebend and the *ilku* of the *ṣāb šarri*.[67] Whether connected directly or not, the fragment suggests that prebendaries had already been drawn into the structures through which military and civil projects were financed. We can safely expect earlier indications.[68]

The relevant Hellenistic private archives all come from Uruk. Some of the illegally excavated material can be traced to its origins through related excavated texts: many texts were stored in the temple precinct. The main studies are Doty 1977, Funck 1984, and McEwan 1981. The Hellenistic material from Babylon is not really helpful, cf. Boiy 2000.

Though there is much material from Neo-Babylonian private archives, it remains haphazard in nature and it is insufficient for a balanced overview. In private and in administrative archives the "purveying trades", bakers, brewers and butchers, are reasonably represented, but other aspects, including the *ērib bīti*s in the widest sense of the term, are less so. Especially information on craftsmen-prebendaries remains notably scarce.

e. Assyria

Nearly all documentation available derives from Babylonia and there is only limited information from Assyria. All that is known on the cultic personnel has been collected by B. Menzel.[69] There will have been differences, an even greater dependence -at least in the documentation- on the person of the king probably being the root cause, but there are distinct signs that structures similar to those in the South were not unknown in the North. The most suggestive information is perhaps provided by the Maganuba-document[70] relating to the acquisition by Sargon II of the terrain on which Dūr-Šarrukīn was to rise: he had to acquire the hereditary land of the bakers of Aššur, originally granted by Adad-nirari III. In Assyria, as in Babylonia, the temples were dependent on royal grants for much of the elaborateness of their personnel structure.[71] A vineyard of the *ginē* of Aššur and Mulissu is mentioned in ADD 363 (rev. 6'). A possible remnant of a sale of a prebend in Aššur is the fragment StAT 2, 106.

Originally from the later Middle Assyrian period, reign of Tiglathpileser I, we have Ebeling 1954 no. IV, p. 12ff,[72] which deals in detail with sacrificial material and its distribution, in particular with the meat portions.

---

67 Lines 10 ff. (the executor is responsible for interruptions in the delivery) 11) ... *ebūr* GIŠ.[ŠUB.BA]-*šú* LU MU *il-ki šá* ^{LU}ERIN$_2$.MEŠ LUGAL x x (=*il-lak*?). I cannot reconstruct the passage with any confidence.

68 The question will be studied elsewhere.

69 B. Menzel, Assyrische Tempel, Bd I, Rome 1981 p. 130-299.

70 SAA 12, no. 10.

71 The Assur archive N 33, O. Pedersén, Archives and Libraries in the City of Assur II, Uppsala 1986, p. 131ff., edited by K. Radner, Ein neuassyrisches Privatarchiv der Tempelgoldschmiede, StAT I, Saarbrücken 1999, does not contain information on prebendal matters, but it derives from what could be regarded as the "right milieu" of craftsmen and purveyors: goldsmiths, bakers and brewers, with some presumably somewhat lower personnel, for instance that of the chariot of Aššur. Some additional texts can be found in StAT 2.

72 Cf. Frankena, OLZ 1956 cols. 134-5 and Postgate, NRGD p. 118ff. Ebeling 1954 V, p. 18ff. is comparable, but it refers to the cult accorded to the dead kings. Personnel attached to the cult of dead persons, especially kings, would belong to prebendal circles, but outside Assyria there is little information. Though the cult of dead kings and ENSIs is attested in the Ur III and earlier periods and *kispu* is relatively well documented in the Old Babylonian period, the personnel, which would interest us here, is virtually unknown. It is not difficult to imagine that special personnel could be attached to the royal palace and even to various local palaces, as for instance, the Lagaš ENSIs enjoyed a mortuary cult under the Ur III kings, though offerings to ancestors always will have retained a family aspect. Endowment of personnel with clerical tasks outside the ("specialised") sanctuaries of the gods is a distinct

The Ebeling text and the Maganuba case will not have been the isolated phenomena the scant documentation suggests, but we will not discuss Assyrian matters, assuming wide ranging similarities with Babylonia, which, however, does not imply strict conformity. We can assume that the mausoleum of the Assyrian kings in Aššur had its own special prebendal personnel. On this point we are a trifle better informed in Assyria than in Babylonia. Occasionally direct transfer of prebendal personnel from Babylonia to Assyria in its widest sense, notably Ḫarran, is attested, and together with the presence of typically Babylonian cultic textual material, speaks for a strong Babylonian cultural influence also in this field in Assyria.

f. Cultic rituals

The actual cultic role of the clergy as participants in the rites can be observed best in the preserved rituals, even though it is not always easy to establish whether we are dealing with consecrated personnel or with persons only fulfilling a specific task in a certain, equally specific, context. Participation in a cultic ritual is regarded as indicating priestly status, but it cannot be denied that the rituals themselves occasionally explicitly mention the presence of non-consecrated persons. Relevant documents mainly come from Uruk and Babylon from what is called here the Hellenistic period, but at least some texts are older or pretend to be so. It is of special importance that the initiation text published by R. Borger (1973) was preserved in both an Assyrian and a Babylonian context. Even though the offices mentioned tend to be rare or even obsolete in the late period, the text is of great importance on account of the information it provides on some essential, basic aspects of the Mesopotamian (cultic) priesthood.

For the Old Babylonian period we are limited to the Ištar ritual from Mari, originally published by Dossin (1938) and restudied by Durand and Guichard (1997).

The importance of correct execution of cultic requirements is underlined by a number of Neo-Babylonian administrative protocols from Uruk, mentioned already. That cultic matters were taken seriously is not remarkable, but the texts are especially of importance because they underline the special status of the prebendaries. Insistence on the maintaining of secrecy regarding cultic practices will have stressed this importance of status among the prebendal families.

We will concentrate on the Old and Neo-Babylonian periods in Babylonia, and, marginally, on the material mainly from Uruk from the Hellenistic period, as that is easily accessed through the studies published by Doty, McEwan and Funck. Special attention must be paid to the early Neo-Babylonian *kudurrus*. Though in general nothing essentially new can be said, there is some use in rephrasing the problems and regrouping the evidence. The documentation determines the subjects which can be broached: funding, personnel and organisation. Whether the question of the relative economic value of the prebendal system can be tackled with any effect is dubious and we will not attempt to discuss prizes.[73]

---

possibility. The existence of a palatial clergy is not completely unthinkable. A (Neo-Babylonian god) Sin of the *bīt ridūti* is attested in BM 42408: 4, Jursa 1999, p. 177.

[73] Cf. in this respect MacGinnis 1991-2 p. 76, with Jursa 1999 p. 82, for Neo-Babylonian prices of prebends. It is difficult to generalise from the scant useful material available, as special circumstances are all too evident, especially regarding the *edil bābi* texts from Uruk. We will restrict ourselves to specifying as far as possible the basic sums mentioned by the texts and make a rare comparison of prebendal income with that from a different source, but we will not explore the matter systematically. Jursa 1999 p. 57-9 gives useful information on the value of the *pappasu* of the Sippar bakers, cf. p. 62-3 for the brewers.

CHAPTER II
THE PREBENDAL SYSTEM

1. Introduction

Discussing prebends primarily means a study of the endowment of the core personnel of the Mesopotamian sanctuaries. Charpin uses the term "clergé", but in a wider sense than we will here study prebendaries, as we will not include the administrators. The funding of the clergy can only be studied with some success if relevant material from both private and administrative archives is available. The private archives, in general, indicate that far from all families that can be regarded as reasonably well-off had a share in the prebendal functions: families possessing prebendal interests constituted a special sub-group of the better-off element of the urban population. This is possibly valid for both the "early" and the "late" period. The nature of the functions and their remuneration in general is much better illustrated by the private documents than by the administrative evidence available, but that informs much better on matters dealing with practical expenditure.

The available archives were left by urban families. We have every reason to assume that these families were juridically spoken of free status. But perhaps we must be cautious in this respect when we use Third Millennium texts, for there is a distinct possibility that certain cultic tasks were fulfilled by the ordinary unfree institutional personnel. There is also no compelling reason to assume that there were no prebendaries in small countryside sanctuaries. Their status will not have differed much from that of other villagers and in Šaṭir in the late period they belonged to the milieu of the military fief holders and were interested in what we could call "intellectual pursuits". This should warn us against the assumption of a watertight division in cultic respect between the free, the unfree and also the military with their often special ethnic background. The little evidence available is just sufficient to suggest this.

Though there were in the late period notable differences between Sippar and Uruk, the only sanctuaries about which we have a reasonable amount of information, the relevant structures were basically similar and additional information from Babylon, Borsippa or Dilbat easily fits the pattern suggested. Partially the differences are those of scale and administrative habit, Eanna being as an institution considerably larger than Ebabbar. Of importance is that the Marduk temple in Babylon was clearly regarded as exemplary. In the Old Babylonian period old local traditions were stronger, as is best illustrated by Charpin's discussion of the survival of the Eridu priesthood in Ur.[1] Though comparable transfers of traditions, possibly partially fictional, are not unknown in the Neo-Babylonian period, where BBSt 36 is an important witness, structures were much more uniform in that period. We assume that the prebendal system developed from something with very particular local traits into something predominantly uniform in nature.

2. The roots of the system, a question for the future: the Third Millennium

If the question of the remuneration of cultic functions is as old as the Mesopotamian sanctuaries, a coherent picture of the early stages can only be created in the future with a

---

[1] Charpin 1986, p. 343ff.

better understanding of more relevant material.[2] The prebendal solution for the remuneration of the clergy meant that specialised functions received specific forms of income linked to specific persons who were enabled to hand on function and income. It meant that a separate element of the population had to come into being. The earliest secure signs date back to the Ur III period, but for the higher functions an earlier date is easily possible.

The origins of the prebendal system are virtually unknown. Even if it can be regarded as a system of remuneration of the cultic personnel applied in some manner or another in all sanctuaries known, we cannot adduct reasons for an assumption that it was consciously created at a specific moment in time. Rather we must suppose that it arose in various places in somewhat differing local forms with a terminology of its own, interacting in the successful cases with the increasing importance of the pertinent local sacrificial cult. Increased importance of a sanctuary meant increased offerings, which in turn would make an increase in the personnel feasible. As the king, under whatever title, was, at least in name,[3] in Mesopotamia the most important provider of offerings, the matter had political aspects, all the more so as the *reḫātu* could be used for non-cult-related purposes, just as in Babylonia in general the temple was one of the means with which the government managed a particular sector of agriculture. Continuously the king intervened actively in cult related matters.[4]

Perhaps we must, on principle, regard the main Mesopotamian sanctuaries in a sense as "royal particulars", as a kind of Chapels Royal in which the king had to play in person, or in effigy, an essential role in the ritual at certain crucial events of the ritual calendar. In such circumstances the prebendaries had not only access to the god but also to the person of the king. This will have enhanced the status of the prebendal class. We know that the king shared in the prebendal income and could use his share for the funding and refunding of functions. This is probably an underestimated aspect of the matter. The system had the built

---

2 Stol suggests that mention should be made of the "mythical explanations" of the origin of Mesopotamian prebends. First there is the story of Enlil and Namzitarra, published by M. Civil, AfO 25, 1974-77, which does not help us in a practical sense. Namzitarra is perhaps freed from his masters, the GUDUs in order to serve Enlil directly. Which type of split in functions this represents remains unspecified. Th. Krispijn refers to PBS 1, 135, edited by Van Dijk, La Sagesse, 1953, p. 128ff. He was so kind as to provide his edition of the damaged text, which possibly takes the guise of a dialogue between two dogs. Line 16 definitely deals with a temple function, and line 23 mentions that of SUSBU, a kind of *ramku*, "purification-priest". The verdict by Sin (lines 43ff.) is not interpretable in a practical sense. Perhaps the Letter of Ugudulbi (F.A. Ali, Sumerian Letters: two collections from the Old Babylonian schools, 1964, no. B 14) should also be mentioned in this context. For the moment not too much meaning can be attached to the fact that the "stories" are preserved in an Old Babylonian version. Almost all Sumerian literature is preserved in texts from this period, the fact should not be used to date the prebendal phenomenon, which certainly changed during the Old Babylonian period.

3 The *niqê šarri* are much more important, at any rate in the documentation, than the *niqê kāribi*, "offerings by (ordinary) believers", of which it is uncertain whether they constituted a dependable form of income.

4 Bongenaar, 1997 p. 235 mentions the existence of a PA E_2.KUR.MEŠ, reading not completely certain, probably *šāpir ekurāte*, whom he dubs "minister of temple affairs", and who had precedence over the *šangû* (in Sippar). Possibly he was in the royal household a kind of embryonic "Kultusminister". In YOS 6, 10 (Eanna archive, 28 I Nbn 1) the *rab unqāti* handed out summary orders to the royal representative in Eanna. In this context we can also refer to the *zazakku*, on whom F. Joannès, NABU 1994/103 and for more literature cf. J. MacGinnis, NABU 1996/19. The cult was an object of a "persistent solicitude", to translate a Dutch phrase used in another context for a certain permanent involvement on the part of the central government. We need not mention royal intervention in purely economic matters.

in means to renew itself. There is additionally some evidence that private persons could fund a priestly function, in which there is in itself nothing historically remarkable. It is often a manner of safeguarding a part of the family capital, not only in Ancient Mesopotamia.

We can note in the later Third Millennium that persons with what are in clearer Old Babylonian contexts priestly titles occur in ordinary wage lists, along with (other) ordinary labourers. This is especially the case with the GALA. In the pre-Sargonic Lagaš $E_2.MI_2$ archive, both male and female GALAs occur in wage lists,[5] but the status of such a GALA was probably low and they were, or could be, unfree.[6] As in the late period not all *kalûs* will have been consecrated,[7] we probably must not assume automatically that Pre-Sargonic GALAs -all- had priestly status or were of necessity employed in the cult of the gods.[8] Sometimes they are numerous, notably in DP 159. $GUDU_4$s do occur less often in the

---

5 This is not the place to list all occurrences, we can only note that persons indicated as GALA or $GUDU_4$ occur. What their function was remains uncertain and their status is definitely not very elevated. On the early male and female GALAs we can refer to H. Hartmann, Die Musik der sumerischen Kultur, Frankfurt/Main, 1960, 129ff., where also material on the NAR is collected. They occur predominantly as ordinary workers. Occasionally a GALA receives half the wages of a NAR, Selz, AWAS 119, 12: 1-2. DP 159 mentions numerous GALA. $GUDU_4$s occur occasionally, AWAS 75 (BIN 8 347) 5: 1-2, 6: 5-9. That these people appear in ordinary wage lists is the fact to stress.

6 Mentioning Edzard SR nos. 44 and 45 should be sufficient. On the other hand GALAs figured as witnesses in land and house sales, which suggests a certain status. We have little idea of what these free or unfree male or female GALAs did, and the same is valid for the contemporary $GUDU_4$s. Until better information is available the hypothesis has to be that people in possession of the skills of the lower "ritualists", served as ordinary labourers and received the ordinary wages of the groups of workers to which they were assigned, but that they could be employed additionally in the cultic contexts for which they possessed the appropriate skills. If employed so, they obtained the appropriate perks in a manner the (later) Kingsbury text could suggest.

7 This consecration meant obtaining the status of being admitted to a particular sanctuary. We do not know, strictly spoken, what made e.g. a GALA a GALA, whether he, or in the early period at least, also she, had to graduate in some way, the family serving probably as the school. The skills would thus come before the initiation. It could be imagined that in the late period a person could own a *kalû* prebend, but not possess the relevant skills, thus being obliged to engage an executor, but this remains hypothetical. Whether an early GALA functioned in a manner comparable to a later *kalû* can not be considered, but an early GALA was perhaps not in every respect a person of status. Even in the reign of Ammiṣaduqa we find in CT 6, 23b (lines 7-9) an $A.U_5$, a NAR and a GUDA amongst harvest workers, together with a Kassite (line 17). In the late period the prohibition to divulge secret material would prevent study of that material before initiation, but it is perhaps dubious whether the prohibition was valid within the families of the traditional functionaries.

8 We must avoid the "reform texts" of Uruinimgina, even though they deal with fees paid to "priests". The texts indicate that already at this time -and not surprisingly so-, there existed sources of income outside the daily cult of the gods for "ritual practitioners", notably on the occasion of funerals, and as J. Bauer, WO 9, 1977, p. 6ff. has noticed, on at least one other occasion. Whether what Bauer dubs "Aktion B" could be regarded as referring to some sort of tariff for the costs of engaging a "cultic practitioner" should be left open. Of some importance is, however, that, not unexpectedly, the status of the officiant and the size of his remuneration are obviously linked. This text deals, however, with matters which should fall outside our definition, as the rites concerned do not belong to the ordinary cult of the gods for which the prebendaries were remunerated. We are essentially badly informed concerning similar opportunities in later periods, but there were possibilities for institutionally uninitiated "ritualists" to earn a living. Where applicable their skills somehow will have had to be recognised, that taking up the function implied some formality will be noted below. Their occasional presence in institutional texts is therefore also not a matter of surprise.

material from this period, though, occasionally, they held land.[9] The E_2.MI_2 archive, though ostensibly posing as the household of the goddess Baba for at least part of the time, is not informative on its clerical personnel.

The same must be admitted concerning the bulk of the Ur III archival material, with that from the Nippur Inanna temple as the sole exception.[10] Maekawa has suggested that a reform carried through by Šulgi implied that the institutions were split up into an agricultural section ultimately under a central provincial administration led by the ENSI, from which most of our archival material derives, and the "house of the god" proper, which appears only marginally in the texts.[11] Of the 23 texts dealing with institutional personnel from "Lagaš" discussed by Maekawa only three include possible clerical sections.[12] Whether the split between agricultural and household personnel -in a restricted sense- was really so absolute as Maekawa suggests, would need more investigation. The colophons of several of the texts explicitly refer to agricultural work only, for which the house personnel would only be called up under specific circumstances. I would suppose that as in Charpin's Old Babylonian Ur the higher administrative officials of a "temple", certainly the SANGA, would double as higher clerical functionaries. We can only note than certain "priestly" functions occur in considerable numbers and that their position was evidently not very elevated. This seems to be valid for the GALA, the $GUDU_4$ and also the IŠIB. Especially Maekawa's text 22 suggests that the proposed division into two sections was perhaps not so complete as he wants us to assume, but that there certainly were ritual specialists, to mention here only the GALA.MAḪ.[13] The difficulty is that texts have their purposes and conclusions are only valid in so far as this purpose can be assessed in relation to the subject in hand. But even if Maekawa's proposed split in the divine households was less absolute than suggested and

---

[9] HSS 3, 40+AWAS 39, 10: 4-5, a lease by a $GUDU_4$. Cf. VS 25, 4625 12: 2 which mentions the/a GALA.MAḪ of Girsu.

[10] And, perhaps, a few texts from Ur, including the important UET 3, 1126.

[11] Maekawa 1999, especially p. 87, end of section X.1.

[12] No. 18, MVN 17, 3, of which Maekawa includes a copy, where seven $GUDU_4$ appear in a balanced personnel account. No. 19, AAS 186, lists "additional personnel" including $GUDU_4$. No. 22, BM 19724, published by Maekawa deals with flour shared out to personnel in Guabba and includes a ŠITA.AB.BA (III 19), a GALA.MAḪ (III 22) and no fewer than 31 $GUDU_4$. In L 7037 (Š 42/AS 6) we find 25 $GUDU_4$ as a complement in a group of labourers belonging to the "temple" of Ningirsu. Numerous though these $GUDU_4$ may have been, the functionary does not figure in the wage lists available from the Nippur Inanna temple, nor is there a PA_4.ŠEŠ to be found. Numerous IŠIBs can be found occasionally in the Akkad period: RTC 120. An unpublished Ur III text from Lagaš suggests that a (single) ENGIZ earned twice what the 19 $GUDU_4$ and an unknown number of NARs received: 0.2.0 against 0.1.0 (each) per month, 120 against 60 $SILA_3$, The first amount seems to have been normal for a GALA.MAḪ, a local ^{LU_2}MAḪ and a minor EREŠ.DINGIR, an EREŠ.DINGIR of a slightly more important god like Nindara might receive 0.3.0. All these functionaries occur in ordinary wage lists, there are no signs of special endowments or of payments in which remuneration and ingredients for food to be delivered are combined.

[13] Especially in Umma the administration headed by the ENSI was clearly responsible for providing for the sanctuaries, goods are receipted regularly by specific persons, explicitly including clerics, but this falls outside our subject. As a matter of principle the "temple" must still be regarded as essentially one "service" in this period, at least involved in the cult and in agriculture. The splitting up of many Lagaš temples into a section under a SANGA and one under a ŠABRA is intriguing from the point of view of the cult when the fact is taken into account that the Inanna temple in Nippur operated under a ŠABRA/PA.E_2, which function can on the one hand be found amongst Old Babylonian Nippur prebendaries and on the other, in Sippar, where there were at least two at a time, amongst the administrators, Harris 1975, p. 161-2. Perhaps a case of local particularities, or an indication that the higher "internal" administrative functions always imply some cultic task.

even if clerical personnel could on occasion still be used for agricultural work, the fact that an important segment of the personnel was used exclusively for agricultural purposes is in itself sufficient to indicate that the clerical personnel was achieving a special position.

If we accept that Maekawa's text no. 22 combines clerical and agricultural personnel, we must also accept that the clerical personnel was (still) included in ordinary wage lists and did not enjoy a fixed separate special remuneration, i.e. a prebend. But that does not exclude the possibility that such personnel had claims to special remuneration on occasions on which its special capabilities were required. According to the texts from the Nippur Inanna archive clerical and other personnel shared the remnants of the offerings. These must have been assigned to them on an individual basis, as is indeed suggested by two, incidentally non-prebendal, texts ultimately deriving from the same archive. That a person's assignment to a certain "service" meant attribution of a share in the wages available for disbursement to that service requires no discussion for the Ur III period.

This situation persists in the Sigrist *sattukku* texts, also from Nippur, which reach the middle Old Babylonian period. The situation found in the Kingsbury text[14] where cultic personnel receives all sorts of "gifts", obviously related to their functioning on a specific occasion, dates from the same period. In this period we also find in private archives inheritable and saleable prebends of the type which were from then on normal, even though the overlap with the functions mentioned in the contemporary administrative texts is limited. As comparable material from earlier periods is very restricted in scope, this should not convince us that such functions did not exist earlier. The fractionating of prebends in the texts from private archives alone is a sufficient argument, as it suggests a certain amount of development, which required time. We must, however, accept that we are dealing with different aspects of one and the same phenomenon: person, function and also remuneration had become linked.

The remuneration of clerical personnel in the Ur III period and earlier was not yet a matter completely separate from the payment of wages to the institutional personnel in general. On top of these wages came extras related to participation in the cult, in the manner suggested by the Old Babylonian Kingsbury text. When the perks connected to an *ad hoc* functioning in a cultic context became included in a fixed system of remuneration the prebendal system had come into being. But that does not exclude that even then there remained other perks, for instance, as may be specifically the case in the Kingsbury text, on visiting and officiating in other sanctuaries. The prebendal system seems to retain during its whole existence traces of a link between special cultic occasions and special remuneration. Such proceeds could, it would seem, be treated as separate elements of the system. Theoretical though this may seem, we are not dealing, again, with something with sharp, clear-cut demarcations.

As an early example of the type of prebend we will be dealing with, the Lagaš Ur III text Falkenstein, NSGU no. 112, ITT 3, 6575, might be regarded as particularly relevant, especially as the affair seems to deal with something of a routine character. It is a (repeated) court case between two brothers, according to Falkenstein both GUDU$_4$s, though that is not completely certain for the loosing party, regarding what is stated to be 19) A.ŠA$_3$.KURU$_6$ U$_3$ BALA PN GUDU$_4$.E E$_2$-^{d}BA.BA$_6$ I$_3$.DIB$_2$.BA, "the sustenance field and the function which PN (their father), GUDU$_4$ of the Baba-temple, held".[15] Though it might seem to be attractive to

14 Kingsbury 1963.

15 A good example of the fact that the function of GUDU$_4$ was inheritable in this period. The exact meaning of BALA is a moot question here: a "Wechselamt", a shared function, or even, in reality, a function on specific occasions? The all-important question is how the function was instituted.

combine the two objects of litigation into one linked phenomenon, that is not completely certain, as the land, which is placed before the "prebend" is not explicitly tied to the function, even though a connection can be assumed. Whatever may be the case, there is a link between a function, and the claims by a person. That this deals with an inheritance question involving a function may be noted in passing: these functions were inheritable, on principle.

Already in this period certain functions clearly implied a special status, requiring initiation. That some ceremony was involved in becoming a GALA in the Ur III period is underlined by a number of texts, of which MVN 15, 142 is one: V 22-23: 3 $MAŠ_3$ Tu-ra-nu-um MAR.[TU?] U_4 NAM.GALA.$ŠE_3$ I_3.IN.KU_4.[RA], "three goats for the Amorite Turanum when he became a GALA", quoted by d'Agostino, MVN 20, 173 in support of a somewhat less explicit, but probably comparable case.[16] The question is, perhaps, whether or not this refers to an institutional occasion, admission to a specific sanctuary, or whether the ceremony merely meant recognition of skills acquired. The second alternative is the likeliest, no god or temple being named.

That there were also developments towards special forms of remuneration for other services in a cultic context than that of $GUDU_4$ or GALA is suggested by the statue inscription published originally by Civil.[17] Owing to the incomplete preservation the structure of the text is not clear in every respect. It fully merits the classification "difficult" used by the later editors. I assume that a certain form of remuneration is preceded twice by an obligation, both relating to a group of persons indicated by the collective term GAŠAM, "craftsmen", though the obligations imposed are not easily related to the tasks specifically executed by this category of workers. The purpose of the statue plus inscription would be to publicise the funding of the recompensation due for the accomplishment of certain tasks which had not been properly assigned and funded previously: III 23.[18]

Column III 8 mentions NIG_2.BA GAŠAM.[KA]M, which though in itself an equivocal formulation, presumably constitutes income, perks, for the craftsmen, related to an obligation registered in the partially damaged lines II 6-13. It would seem to be logical to assume other obligations in III 9-III 24 (or IV 3?), which are followed in column IV by a list of provisions concluded by line 13, NIG_2.DAB_5 GAŠAM.KAM, "receipts of the craftsmen", presumably again the remuneration made available to them after a task was mentioned. This is followed by fields (IV 14-18), possibly the principal source of the income, and by a possible summary formulation of the tasks, in three rather enigmatic lines (IV 19-21), after which line IV 13 is repeated, with an, according to Civil, different slant: what is assigned first is paralleled by a charge later, using the same words, but this is not accepted by Steible or Frayne. As prebendal income is held against specific obligations, nominal or not, and as the inscription must have been addressed primarily to the god, the obligations should be as important as the benefices granted. The phrase used, NIG_2.DAB_5.BA, is strictly spoken neutral, it can refer to both income or perks and obligations or responsibilities, a double

---

[16] More instances are quoted by H. Hartmann, Die Musik der sumerischen Kultur, Frankfurt/Main 1960 p. 141, were the ordinary/former occupations of those concerned are sometimes mentioned.

[17] Civil 1989, cf. H. Steible, NSBW 2, no. Šulgi 26 p. 178-83. D.R. Frayne, RIM Vol. 3/2, Ur III Period no. 2031. As known, the inscriptions on certain statues and *kudurru*-type inscriptions are sometimes closely related.

[18] Note the interpretations given by Steible and Frayne respectively.

sense is probably intentional. As long as the cultic context of the occurrences referred to remains virtually unknown, much in the inscription will remain un-understood.[19]

Civil's interpretation, followed in its core by both later editors, is that the text bears witness to the institution of prebends, rights to income, for craftsmen of the/a Nindara temple in the Lagaš area as a pious foundation by an official for the life of Šulgi, if we follow in this respect the reconstruction of the beginning of the inscription by both Steible and Frayne.[20] The basic endowment will have consisted of the land mentioned towards the end of the inscription, whatever GIR_3.GIN.NA of the craftsmen (IV 19) may have meant in concreto. We seem to have here a case of non-royal endowment of particular functions and also an instance of prebendal endowment for craftsmen, though perhaps for a ritual role not primarily related to their basic skills. Perks are attached to cultic occasions and both are assigned in combination to "performers". We will encounter more examples. The basic endowment should generate the income required for remunerating the task imposed. During the whole period we are dealing with that means primarily land.

The information from the Ur III Nippur Inanna temple is best treated together with the comparable Old Babylonian material from the Sigrist *šattukku* texts when individual functions are discussed in Chapter IV.

3. The Old Babylonian ritualists in action in a cultic context and the likely implications

The use of the word "ritualist" must be qualified by the remark that the cultic action should belong to the normal rites belonging to the cult of the gods proper. Tanret and Van Lerberghe (1993) have listed a number of partially gender specific rites (*parṣu*) (p. 440ff.) which were executed on the orders of a person indicated by the term "protector", sometimes acting through a "commissioner", who seems to have guaranteed the payments required, by a "performer" through the galamaḫ, acting as the organiser. Whatever the case, the "performer" is presumably financially responsible and is to be seen primarily as the person who finances the rite in question, makes the material available for use during the rite and ultimately for consumption, but he or she is not strictly the executor of the rites. The article quoted, possibly the material itself, leaves perhaps doubt on this point, which probably means that the actual execution of the rites is in the hands of the personnel serving under the galamaḫ, and not, that is at least in non-cultic rites, that the males and females mentioned actually acted.[21] That the goddess, Annunītum, on occasion actively solicits the execution of a rite, does not need to mean that the ritual belongs to her cult proper, but it involved various cereal products, and if the final payment, generally a debt, to the fatteners is taken

---

19 It is probably not warranted to connect this term with the somewhat later Nippur prebendal term NAM.LU_2.NIG_2.DAB_5.BA, on which below in a discussion of Old Babylonian prebends from that town.

20 If dedication of the statue implies belonging to the personnel of Nindara, this could perhaps conform in an ideal manner, much better than is the case with the Ur-Meme family as documented at present, to a waqf-type arrangement of the type proposed by Zettler (1992, p. 211). The official concerned bears the typical, basically unfree courtier's name of Šulgi.ki.ur_5.sag_9.kalam.ma and he was ^{LU_2}GIŠ.TAG.GA.NI, so probably, it is especially stressed, his "man in charge (of his, the king's,) offerings". This probably betrays that the means available to this man for his endowment came from his appropriation on the part of the king. Such appropriations were at the king's pleasure, so it is reasonable to suppose that we are dealing with an attempt at safeguarding in the manner Zettler proposed. Note that Zettler quotes other statue inscriptions. The question would be whether we can link the person of the fundator to the group benefiting.

21 If *muqabbirūtum* is a burial rite, the "performer" can hardly have undergone the rite, it must have been performed for someone else, and this will anyhow not have been a rite belonging to the actual cult of the gods, which may also have been the case concerning the other rites mentioned.

into consideration, also bloody offerings, which had to be paid for by those who commissioned the rites. This meant income for the underlings of the galamaḫ. We assume that these texts, which are still unpublished, do not deal with activities by prebendaries, or if they do, that the actual performers act outside the cult of the god in a narrow sense.[22]

The administrative text published by Kingsbury[23] mentions a whole range of participants in cultic activities who received remuneration on account of their presence at and their role in the proceedings. The status of the text is not completely clear. If it were an ordinary accounting text it should have ended with a summation of all expenditure, which is not the case. On the other hand it is properly dated to 24 VIII (RS 2?), after the proceedings had begun on 15 VIII (line 112). The text thus can be assumed to represent a list of expenditure. As there is no (preserved) heading or a summation, it is possibly not the final document. As Kingsbury has stressed, identification of the occasion poses its own problems. Let us assume that we are dealing with expenditure on the successive visits of a number of gods to a specific sanctuary.[24] The question is of importance as it determines the nature of the perks handed out to the participants, who included not only "clerics", but also "personnel", $GIR_3.SE_3.GA$.[25] There is a direct link between rites executed and personnel receiving "remuneration", which differs somewhat according to the divinity involved. This suggests that the personnel receiving the "perks" is that of the visiting god,[26] with a possible exception for the collective groups of NARs, ŠU.Is and $GUDU_4s$ who figure in all main passages,[27] and who possibly could be "at home", though that is not absolutely certain. If the perks were distributed to the visitors, we are dealing with extras, if the personnel was "at home", we might conclude that we are concerned with occasional prebendal income, whether included or not in the regular remuneration of the functions concerned.

We must assume that the material shared out had two functions: it was required on the one hand for the proper execution of the rites[28] and it had on the other to serve as a remuneration for specific individuals who participated and who are being mentioned by name occasionally. I assume that there is a certain difference between passages like lines 82ff. where, for instance, each individual participant mentioned singly or as member of a

---

22 The payment of *nēbiḫ kezirti*, a payment for the services, whatever their nature, of a *kezirtu*, who was, or could be, the unfree property of a lady of some social standing, also belongs to the *parṣu* related payments. The matter has been restudied by N. Yoffee, JESHO 41, 1998, p. 323ff. The payment is, perhaps, better not seen as a tax on the keeping of a *kezirtu*, it rather belongs to possibilities open to "ritualists", in this case in the Old Babylonian periods inevitably female, to practise their trade. That the "palace" had an interest in all these activities, is, however, also clear.

23 Kingsbury 1963. Collectively we find NARs, ŠU.Is, $GUDU_4s$, BAPPIRs, $ḪUB_2$.BI.MEŠ (once), (male and female) KISAL.LUḪs, (female) NAR.LUKUR.MEŠ, $GIR_3.SE_3.GA$, individually, on one specific day, an EN Enki, a NAR.GAL, a NESAG, a GUB.BA (*maḫḫu*), a ŠITA, an EGIR ŠITA, a DIM_2, $I_3.DU_8s$, (an?) *ararru* and named individuals, often with a "title". As in Nippur there is only a limited correspondence between these charges in an administrative text and what is found in the private documents dealing with prebendal functions from the Larsa kingdom.

24 Not counting the preliminary lines 101-113 and the tailpiece 952-8. As the passage lines 902-951 differs from the other central passages, possibly visits to (line 951) the temple of Sin are intended. He possibly was the god of the locality visited.

25 223, 347, 507, where also $MI_2.UR_5$ are mentioned, (625), 753, (859).

26 Line 210 specifically mentions the EN of Enki, a ŠITA and his coadjutor occur only in connection with Šamaš, lines 329, 330, cf. 358.

27 As Kingsbury remarked, a comparable group of GALAs occurs only in relation to certain gods in connection with a rite called *kinūnu*: (303), 430, 722 and (822).

28 Here we find a potential precursor for the later *maššartu-pappasu* system.

group received one $SILA_3$ of sesame oil, which I would regard as a personal "gift" and passages closing with phrases like ŠU.TI.A NAR.MEŠ (129), etc. which constitute collective assignments intended for cultic use, with the possible implication that the material was retained, in so far as it was not "consumed" during the actual rite, in the end, by those mentioned. Where such passages start is not always clear. Line 128 with beer and bread certainly belongs to 129, but it is equally possible that the passage goes back to perhaps 125. What belongs to 138, ŠU.TI.A ŠU.I.MEŠ, is less clear, we must go back probably to 131, all from 139 to 142 being intended for the $GUDU_4$s. Such collective attributions are listed in all main passages for NARs, ŠU.Is, $GUDU_4$s and, as remarked upon already, sometimes, for the GALAs. These collective attributions are connected to specific, named rites.

It is highly unlikely that the rites[29] which occasioned the expenditure were unique, though that may be the case with their application to the occasion. Remuneration was linked to the specific ritual executed, not all rituals were required for all gods all the time.[30] The question is up to what degree we can attempt to generalise regarding the material used or perks distributed on the occasion of the ceremonies. The participants received remuneration both in relation to their ritual task and in the form of individual "gifts", just as the gods received "gifts", presumably also as participants. The theory being developed proposes that in the early period those involved in the cult received the ordinary wages due to all institutional personnel according to rank and status, including the use of sustenance fields, but that they were over and above this, also in receipt of other, much more valuable goods or goods ready for consumption, when participating in ritual tasks.

It is possible to envisage a double development. With some functions the perks and the function became intimately linked, in which the function, from the point of view of the person who fulfilled the tasks, tended to become more circumscribed by the nature of the perks than by the contents, in other words developed into the prebends of the private documents, where "rights" are being inherited or sold, etc. That process had in fact already come to a certain conclusion by the time of Rim-Sin, as the documents from private archives indicate. In the slightly later Sippar process documents the litigation concerns especially the income. The Kingsbury text illustrates the nature of the perks, probably referring to a specific occasion, but mentions rites normally forming part of the ordinary cult and therefore implying ordinary remuneration.

Expanding the hypothesis might suggest that other functionaries were to assume responsibilities for certain deliveries and received the ingredients required in such a manner that production costs and remuneration were included. The link between perks and function is not difficult to make in the Kingsbury text. That the attribution of material required for the cult included remuneration, of which the later *maššartu-pappasu* system is a special, expanded, development, as it involves the processing of the material, can only be inferred. Of the (later) purveying trades there is only positive proof of the presence of the brewer

---

[29] Some may have been more basic than others, others may have been no more than elements of more complicated proceedings, but the gods do seem to have been hungry all the time. We could mention the following occasions: ZAG.GAR.GA.RA/*ina bītišu/ša*(?), *ana urim*/A_2.GU_2.ZI.GA, *pīt bītim, iptinum, nindabûm, ana rešāti,* possibly belonging to *tazziztum*, *ana paššuri, ana pit(t)im*, NIG_2.GI_6, *ana šarāpim*, *ana kinūnim*, A_2.U_4.TE.NA *ina erēbišu/ša*, of which some may exclude others or involve participation of different sets of ritualists. This is not the place for elaboration, but the matter requires further study.

[30] This brings us no nearer to what the tasks of the $GUDU_4$s were, the occupations registered by Kingsbury 1963, p. 7 note 28 are hardly all-encompassing or particularly relevant for us. The practical tasks of the $GUDU_4$, and the ŠITA, are as difficult to grasp as those of the (later) *ērib bīti*, but that would be all the more understandable if the terms refer more to a status than to a task.

(lines 83, and 90, also!). But beer, like bread, is present as such, and the sheep and oxen are certainly being sacrificed and cooked, by whom is not deemed worthy of explanation, though the E_2.MUḪALDIM clearly functions. That there existed administrative practises which could lead to the later *maššartu-pappasu* system would seem to be acceptable, but the existence of the system as such in this period is not evident. Of the later prebendal purveying trades the brewer had obviously a special position in the Old Babylonian period, not only here, but for instance, also in Ur, Nippur and Isin, as we will see. The baker occurs in a prebendal context in Isin and we will speculate about his occurrence in Ur.

The specific value of the Kingsbury text for our subject is that, even though the status of the text is somewhat uncertain, it explicitly links the participation of the various executors of the rituals to a share in the materials provided by the organiser of the ceremonies. As such it can hardly have been unique.[31] At any rate the providing of material for ritual purposes to groups consisting of persons sharing a specific function or status was known. The root of the later *maššartu-pappasu* system can be sought in such practises.

OLA 21 no. 4 (25 III Ae 28) represents a further step. The text directly links specified income to participation in a specific rite: 1) *u_4-mi ša te-re-tim ša i-na e-re-eb il-tim* 2) *a-na* $GUDA_4$.MEŠ *ú e-ri-ib* E_2 *^{d}An-nu-ni-tum in-na-di-nu*, ("on) the day notified(?)[32] on the entry of the goddess (the following) is given to the gudas and the enterers of the temple of Annunītum" (which PN s PN2 gave). The list which follows contains the handing out of two types of bread and of beer to named persons and others indicated by title or as a group only. Two deviating lines (14 and 31), which do not fit the heading and suggest the availability of two, and not one, type of beer, mark a caesura in the text and make the structure understandable: lines 9-14, indicate the presence of six *erīb biti*s and 16-31 of fourteen $GUDU_4$s, of whom the first four seem to be of higher rank, therefore probably represent the *gudapsûs*.[33] All of these are individually named, receive their bread separately, but their beer collectively. Before these groups are registered, the list is fittingly opened by the GALAMAḪ followed by the UGULA of the *kulmašītu*s, conventionally translated "female devotees", the NAR.SAs and the GALAs. At the end, after the $GUDU_4$s, we find a range of other persons with various cultic, administrative and menial tasks, beginning with the brewer and the barber.[34] We again are dealing with a specific cultic occurrence during which the participants are especially remunerated. One and the same list contains persons we would regard as potential prebendaries and other higher and lower ranking temple personnel.

We could propose that the prebendal system came into existence through a linkage of the ordinary wage- and sustenance-type institutional income and the perks occasioned by the execution of ritual tasks. We assume that each local system had its own particularities, but that political unification meant uniformisation, in which process interruption of the existence and restoration of local sanctuaries played an important role.

---

31 Cf. OLA 21, text 4, from Sippar.

32 This translation is tentative. The possibility that *têrtu* has a technical meaning in connection with prebends should be left open.

33 On a "college" of four *gudapsûs* cf. Van Lerberghe and Voet, AoF 24, 1997, p. 157, where the context suggests the *gudapsûs* of the temple of Šamaš, in OLA 21, 4 we are dealing with the personnel of Annunītum.

34 Van Lerberghe suggests in 43 Su-pé<-ša> SANGA, amongst the least remunerated. Is that correct?

4. Changes in the system

For practical purposes a long term view of the development of the system after it had come into being, or rather had become visible for us, by the middle Old Babylonian period can be obtained by contrasting this "early" evidence with what is known about the Neo-Babylonian, "late" situation. The most striking differences concern the female clergy, but there changes are so fundamental that comparison of early and late becomes purposeless: there is not any more a female clergy that deserves the name in the late period.[35] But also the male clergy changed.

What certainly disappeared in the course of long term developments are the pronounced local differences which make themselves felt in the differently named sets of functionaries in, for instance, Nippur and Ur, which persist in the Old Babylonian period.[36] Behind the differences lies a development of religious institutions on a local basis which had to acquire a degree of similarity in structure under the influence of the increase in scale of the political structures in which the sanctuaries had to function. This process was not finished in the Old Babylonian period, to the contrary, the disappearance of the unity created by Ur III will have slowed down uniformisation. We can assume, however, that interruptions in the cult in the southern towns greatly contributed to the process, many of the higher southern functions being unknown in the North of Babylonia, which served, to all likelihood, as a refuge.[37]

Who reads the lists of the prebendal occupations in Old Babylonian Ur or Nippur and compares them with those found in Neo-Babylonian Uruk and Sippar notices a distinct change. In the earlier period the emphasis, certainly when the number of occurrences of functions is taken into account,[38] in naming the occupations is on the quality acquired through initiation,[39] in the later it is on skills and down to earth jobs, with only the title *ērib bīti* indicating a status acquired through initiation.[40] In Old Babylonian Ur the brewer, a rare down to earth clerical job in this period, is paired with the NAM.ŠITA$_4$[41] and in Isin with the

---

35 Virtually no female clergy remains recognisable in the later period, it would seem. Nabonidus' appointment of his daughter in Ur can be regarded as completely aberrant, though H. Bongenaar refers us to the problematic Kaššā, *rabītu ša* Bīt-Šarrat-Sippar, discussed Bongenaar 1997 p. 249 amongst the Sippar prebendaries; Stol *apud* Bongenaar identifies her with the princess of the same name. At least one late ritual mentions a *nadītu*. We are also unable to compare even the Third Millennium and (middle) Old Babylonian structures, with the undetermined EREŠ.DINGIRs in Nippur, on this point.

36 On this subject see J. Renger, Örtliche und zeitliche Differenzen in der Struktur der Priesterschaft babylonischer Tempel, CCRAI 20, 1975, p.108-115.

37 We must not, however, dismiss a possible role of the Sealand dynasty, and thus a longer maintenance of southern traditions, too automatically. Gulkišar is mentioned as a benefactor by one of the for us relevant later kudurrus: BE 1, 83.

38 The number of GUDU$_4$s mentioned more or less equals that of all other male clergy together, cf. the list provided by Renger 1969, p.144-158.

39 That is: basing oneself on the Akkadian "translations", the Sumerian terms are completely opaque for me from an etymological point of view and the authorities available are at odds with one another regarding the question which term is the real equivalent of which other. Th. Krispijn suggests for GUDUG <*GU$_3$.DUG$_4$, "he who calls/prays loudly" and ŠITA < *ŠID "to recite" or <*ŠUD(U)$_3$+A "*orans*". Neither of the tittles represents in this manner a "status" in Sumerian, but the meaning remains general and unspecific.

40 I assume that the title/status is Akkadian and that the writing KU$_4$.E$_2$ is artificial Sumerian.

41 YOS 5, 19, Charpin 1986 p. 234, cf. p. 259 where there are two statements concerning the NAM.ŠITA$_4$: a) "pourrait avoir trait à la préparation de la nouriture" and b) "semblent avoir appartenu au groupe des purificateurs".

MUHALDIM, in Neo-Babylonian sanctuaries we find brewers, bakers, butchers and even an occasional fisherman and provider of cow milk, and not only that, there is a whole range of specific craftsmen of prebendal status. This does not imply a denial of the fact that these people, when engaged in preparing their special products for cultic use, were not obliged to submit to special regulations, had not to enunciate the appropriate utterances or had not undergone initiation. But there is a difference: in the earlier period suitability in a ritualistic sense comes first, in the later period that is in a considerably increased number of cases hidden behind the earthly skill required from the specialist in the appropriate craft, even though that does not in any way mean that rituals loose their importance, or implies that the person concerned fulfils the tasks himself. Diversification of personnel takes place in the spheres of the artisans and of the purveyors, but notably enough some of these functions retained or acquired *ērib bīti* status.[42]

The second half of the Second Millennium and much of the first half of the next constitute a blank in our information concerning prebends. But in this period something important took place: the rise in the old towns of Southern Mesopotamia of groups of families sporting a family name, either deriving from the name of an ancestor or from some trade or function. Some of these, first of all those of the type Šangû-DN/GN/TN, emphatically belong to the sphere of the temples, but at a humbler level we have more importantly the Ṣāḫit-ginê/sattukki family, which has a name which is explicitly cult related and not simply *ṣāḫit(u/-šamni)*, or something comparable, "oil-presser". Others take their name from occupations which were both prebendal and non-prebendal: baker or brewer, but which obtained their special cachet through the association with the sanctuary, which is perhaps especially relevant for still other occupations like that of the *kurgarrû*. Still others, known to us by an ancestral name only, cf. VS 15, 1, may have been linked to a prebendal task in which there was room for more than one executor, which made use of the employment as a family name insufficiently distinctive. Notably enough, *ērib bīti* itself does not occur as a family name, as far as can be seen. Some trades, like Ša-ṭabtišu, "Provider of salt", and others of this type, never made the step to prebendal status as far as we know, but yet may have possessed a link with the temple. We can venture to propose the theory that hypothetically the hereditary position of a family possessing one of the functions mentioned in the cult of one of the old sanctuaries played a specific role in the process of adoption of family names in Babylonia.[43]

---

42 Not all special functions resulting from diversification were strictly spoken artisanal. Not, for instance, the *ṭupsar enūma-Anu-Enlil*, "astrologer", who is attested already in the Assyrian period, Iraq 34, 1972 p. 22, 19-25, reference R. Jas. This function did not become, as far as can be seen, a family name. Its prebendal status requires further discussion.

43 That does not mean that of necessity all names had to derive from the temple milieu. Names like *dēkû*, "mobiliser" or Miṣirāia, "Egyptian" are at any rate not directly suggestive of a temple background. The proposition of a link between the adoption of family names and functions in "temples", not of necessity all being or becoming prebendal, could be used to explain the relatively limited number of family names. They had their origins among a limited group of autochtone families in the old cultic centres. This possibly solves some of the difficulties felt by M. van de Mieroop, The Ancient Mesopotamian City, Oxford, 1997, p. 107-8. That unrelated families with the same occupation in different centres could adopt the same family name is not a problem, tough we must realise that mobility was probably greater than might be expected. That there are no Aramaic family names, at any rate obviously not strikingly so, is also explained in this way. That certain families do not belong to the prebendaries of the town where they resided is easily explained by migration or by the junior status of certain branches of families. That more names were adopted once the phenomenon of the family name had established itself, also stands to reason. A name like Miṣirāia is probably a good example. Whether the adoption of family names by urban families is to be dissociated from the confrontation with tribal traditions regarding ancestral

The occurrence of these names illustrates the fact that a change from a more initiation oriented nomenclature for the prebendaries to a more "vocational" terminology had already taken place when these family names became common. It was a feature of the badly documented period between "early" and "late".

A small number of monumental copies of royal grants from the early phase of the Neo-Babylonian period underlines the fact emphatically. These documents are of a special importance for our subject. We will not discuss here the role of these families as land holders, having a share in the land divisions initiated by kings like Erība-Adad and Marduk-apal-iddina II, though, if we regard their role in the sanctuaries as vital, their hold on land will also have had its effect on their position as a distinctive social elite, especially in those cases where agricultural personnel went with the land.[44]

In general we can observe the outcome of a long term process in which on the one hand many of the earlier high ranking titles disappeared from the roster of priestly ranks and on the other, lower down, a diversification into a range of very varied occupations with an in the sanctuaries special task took place. Whether this implied a rise in status of a certain groups of urban families after the Old Babylonian period must remain a matter of speculation, likely though it might seem. On the one hand the major sanctuaries were firmly linked to the monarchy, on the other they were the preserve of a local elite, recognisable by its prebendal status. These people inevitably had to take up a political position and in the case the monarchy was contested, this elite inexorably became involved in the problems: it had a role of its own.

The theory proposed suggests that from the Third Millennium onwards certain groups of institutional personnel acquired status and income by performing a specific role in the cult. Their ultimate successors were the prebendal elite of the Neo-Babylonian towns of the First Millennium.

---

lineages is another matter. The use of family names by the prebendal families in our late period is an undeniable fact, even if the family name is remarkably often skipped in administrative texts.

44 The link between *ḫanšû*-land and family names in Borsippa will be re-discussed in the contribution on taxation, Chapter VII.

CHAPTER III
ENDOWMENT

1. Introduction

It is not easy to form a balanced opinion on the question of the funding of the institutions. However rich an institution might have been, its means were never unlimited and it is not clear whether it could institute prebendal functions on its own account. The presence of many prebendal functions can be registered, but the problem that it is hardly ever possible to calculate how many full places of each separate function were available in one sanctuary needs to be addressed.[1] Several, even many, persons may have been active in the same function in a given period, but that tells us little about the number of full-time equivalents funded. The early Neo-Babylonian *kudurru*s suggest that the posts of several prebendaries could be created by the king, as a group, and as *ērib bīti*s, but it is also clear, from texts like BBSt 36, that the means made available could then be used to finance a better paid higher ranking functionary, thus presumably reducing the actual number of those appointed. It is also clear that from the moment finance was made available different functions were intentionally being combined in the hands of one and the same person.

The texts available, whether from private archives or from administrative sources, tell us little about the obligations of the prebendaries, but in the later periods they are increasingly restricted to dealing with the emoluments, especially the meat portions. It is clear that here at least, land plays a subsidiary role. But not only shares in the meat of the animals sacrificed were an important element in the remuneration of the prebendaries. Even before the Old Babylonian period other food is more in evidence, and in the *kudurru*s the amount of bread and beer assigned seems to be the clearest indicator of rank. Especially the bread which "came back from the temple" is a recognisable element in the system of remuneration. The few royal grants from the early Neo-Babylonian period are of special interest, both because they clarify a more complete scala of assignments, and because they suggest the existence of standards of remuneration, which were, no doubt, time, place and status related.

The endowment texts do not inform us on the method of remunerating certain prebendaries through the *maššartu-pappasu* system. It is not mentioned either in private documents dealing with the sale or division of for instance baker's or brewer's prebends, where it applied. In the case of the butchers it is even uncertain how they were involved. This is understandable, as none of these texts contains a specification of what had to be spent on a particular, specific rite, or by whom it had to be performed, though occasionally passages in royal inscriptions suggest such a link. The amount and the nature of the food to be produced depended on the nature of the rite and number of the divine and, probably, human participants. As the *maššartu-pappasu* assignments contained elements for both costs and remuneration, the arrangements will often have been of an internal, administrative, nature, requiring regular adaptation, as is suggested by the SWU texts. This was not a purely local affair, also in this field the central administration intervened, using Babylon customs as a standard.

---

[1] For an attempt to draw (partial) conclusions from the degree of fragmentation see Charpin 1986, p. 261. Some direct evidence for Sippar is, however, available.

We will not follow a strictly chronological order, but will attempt to isolate in a global manner the various elements of the income the prebendaries enjoyed and the question of the source and origin of that income. There is, not unexpectedly, a clear relationship between the importance of the institution and the status in that institution of the god served by the particular prebendary and the size of the prebendal income enjoyed by the person concerned. There can also be little doubt that there is a link between royal interference, that is primarily funding, and the importance of the sanctuary. A rich god could afford more personnel and a greater differentiation in functions. In a large sanctuary a small chapel of a minor god had a restricted number of officiants. In a small local sanctuary all functions may have been in one hand and the king may not have been involved at all. Both contents and remuneration of a function indicated by the same term will therefore have differed from sanctuary to sanctuary.

It is clear that some families retained their interest in small local cults, presumably in their places of origin. In the Neo-Babylonian archive of the Nappāḫu family three texts have been preserved dealing with rights to income in the *papāḫu*[2] of a local god called Bēl-Ālia *ša* (Āl)Šarrabānu without the prebendal function concerned being specified: VS 6, 89 (25 IV Nbn 17),[3] 117 (27 IV Barz 1) and VS 5, 57-8 (30 V Barz 1). In this last, most explicit document, the relation who looses his claims to the prebend in the earliest text, is given the right of being informed in the case the prebend should be leased or sold, even after it had changed hands through adoption in the wider family. VS 6, 117 is probably an execution arrangement, but the text is damaged in the crucial place. In this text and somewhat more elaborately in VS 5, 57-8 the rights involved were minimal, though the period is not specified: half a SILA$_3$ of beer and bread each per day, a one-fourth share in the *ḫarmil-* meat of oxen and an unspecified share in what is called the *paššūru*, "table". This is the smallest standard amount of bread and beer mentioned in texts dealing with prebends, nevertheless those involved at a distance were keen to safeguard even potential rights.

For the Old Babylonian period rights to similar interests in small sanctuaries of local importance are documented by CT 6, 36a, no date, dealing with the *šangūtu* of Ḫaniš-Šullat in Sippar pertaining to a private foundation. This was obviously a minor post, but important enough for the *šangû* to have his rights formally confirmed against possible claims by the founder. The presumption must be that this *šangû* fulfilled all cultic functions for his god in this small sanctuary. On principle the street corner chapels like those in Old Babylonian Ur will have been a source of some sort of income for the officiant. Being involved in the cult of a god brought in income and it was tied to the family, possibly even funded by it. These are the real *beneficia patrimonialia*.

In all the main religious centres, both in the Old and in the Neo-Babylonian period some central administrative structure can be recognised, which manages the provision of the offerings and the prebendal income. A question which we cannot answer is at what stage of development small "private cult installations" were drawn into these centralised organisations. Though not abundant, and avoiding archaeological evidence of the type hollowed out by Charpin,[4] there is with CT 6, 36a, the Nappāḫu texts dealing with Bēl-Ālia and also in the Šaṭir material published by Joannès, just enough textual evidence to suggest the existence of small scale sanctuaries at what might be regarded as a private level. Increasing importance of such a chapel would presumably attract funding from the local central temple organisation, which could ultimately involve the king.

---

[2] In VS 6, 117 the *papāḫu* bears the grand Nippur name E$_2$.ŠU.ME.ŠU, which might suggest some connection with Ninurta.

[3] Cf. VS 5, 27.

[4] Charpin 1986 p. 268-9.

The staffing of the cult depended on its income, and that in turn was to an important degree the result of what had been granted by the king, who retained the right to dispose of the *reḫātu*,[5] all that remained after food offerings had been made. Probably this also concerned other material like textiles which had been offered to the gods or used during the ceremonies. This may be considered to represent the *zitti* or the *makkūr šarri* of some texts, which may also cover income from prebendal posts in the possession of the king.[6] The king, it must be repeated, could spend this income, even though it resulted from offerings to the gods, in the manner he thought fit. Some of it was granted to the cultic personnel of the sanctuary as prebendal income, but not all.

In general the texts suggest a differentiation in treatment between food in general, especially bread and beer,[7] and cuts of meat, between non-bloody and bloody offerings.[8] They required different sets of purveyors and also occasioned differing approaches to the remuneration of those concerned. The cuts of meat due to the king were at least occasionally disposed of by those having rights to other cuts of the same offerings. They had to pay others, who to all likelihood acted as the representatives of royal interests, even though the fact is not indicated explicitly. It is not unlikely that they leased the rights to sell from the king, possibly through his *ša muḫḫi quppi*, or they acted for him.[9] The possibility that certain prebendaries played some role in supplying the towns with a part of their food requirements cannot be discussed for want of documentation on the marketing aspect, though it is certain that cuts of meat were obtainable. Especially some texts from the Babylon Nappāḫu archive are suggestive,

---

5 Hence the delivery of the *reḫātu* by the clergy was tantamount to recognising someone as the legitimate king.

6 That the possessions of the king were neither stable, or even well-circumscribed, appears from YOS 7, 79 (Uruk, Eanna archive, 12 III Cyr 8) where eight months of a prebend which had to provide milk had been added ("counted with", *manû*) to the *makkūr šarri*. In TCL 12, 57 (Uruk, 13 VIII Nbk 41) a person ostensibly eager to help the administration of Eanna to fulfil financial claims made by the king, promises to uncover hidden prebendal rights illegally held by others and duly pertaining to the *quppu* of king (and to that of the *šatammu*), if he was granted the lease of their rights, in which case he also promised to provide additional sweeteners. The eagerness will have had its reasons.

7 The beer poses a problem: meat portions and bread clearly "return from the house", were therefore available for human consumption, but the beer offered is generally supposed to have been offered as a libation. If the temple provided it to its prebendaries, as it did sometimes to other personnel, it will have had to brew more than what was required for the offerings. Sigrist, SAT II, no. 310 (Š 42) lists amounts of bread and beer with the gods to whom it was assigned. Lines 17 and 18 totalize respectively the bread and the beer provided and the text concludes, before the date, with NINDA.DAG.TA GUR.RA, "the bread that has come back from the DAG", the DAG being probably some smaller sanctuary mentioned in lines 1 and 3. The beer, simply KAŠ, did not come back, it would seem. It is also not completely convincing to reason that in a (late) text like AO 6459, RAcc p. 89f. line 9 the KAŠ.U$_2$.SA SIG$_5$ and KAŠ.U$_2$.SA *rib-ku* would be presented as solid *billatu*, if only for the simple reason that they were put on the table together with wine and milk, which were certainly in a liquid state. If solid *billatu* really was put before the gods that would have been done with the intention of having it available for later distribution. I know of no certain instance. On the principle of food "returning from the house" see Sigrist 1977.

8 For "einen sehr hübschen Beleg" regarding meat removed from the offering table and made available cf. Jursa 1999 p.48, BM 43146: 10.

9 In Sippar the *ša kurummat šarri* officials expedited at least a part of what pertained to the king, either left-overs or a special *kurummat šarri*, which probably represents the same, to him. Whether this represented more than a token amount probably depended on the practicalities. Cf. Bongenaar 1999, 168, note 27. We will have to pay closer attention to some aspects of this document.

though not really informative on this aspect.[10] In endowment documents bread and beer are assigned separately from meat portions, the practical result was probably that it was not difficult to alienate through sale or through use as a collateral meat portions separately from the other prebendal income belonging to the same function.

Being involved as a purveyor in providing the temple with prepared food created other economic opportunities. The production apparatus required and the products handled could both be exploited.

2. The early Neo-Babylonian grants

The early Neo-Babylonian grants are of special importance as they provide an idea of what holding a complete prebendal function meant from the point of view of income, even if these texts are syntactically sometimes difficult to interpret on this point.[11]

The change in circumstances which had taken place before the beginning of the Neo-Babylonian period is illustrated, but by no means initiated, by a small group of "*kudurrus*" from the second quarter of the First Millennium, with a place of honour, however dubious some of the details related may sound, for the Sippar Šamaš stone tablet, BBSt 36.[12] It betrays the tenacity by which a family clung to "traditions" and managed to benefit from this persistence. The fact that these and other receivers of royal munificence thought a stone copy, possibly for special deposition in the sanctuary concerned, desirable, indicates the importance attached to the grant. Disregarding the special backgrounds of BBSt 36, these assignments took place in structures which already existed. The Sippar document is possibly an element in a program of complete refurbishment of the cult of Šamaš in Sippar, based at least partially on traditions which had survived in Babylon.[13] This may have found a later, but virtually undocumented parallel in the re-establishment of that of the same god in Larsa, to all likelihood with Uruk as a basis.[14]

The Sippar document, BBSt 36, was not so much intended to record what was granted to Šamaš by successive kings, as to fix what was assigned by them in increasing quantities to the successive members of a family which ostensibly had aspirations to the function of *šangû* of Šamaš.[15] It is the nature of these grants which interests us here. The first, by Simbar-Šiḫu (I

---

[10] That it was possible to buy separate cuts of meat is illustrated by Nbk 402, (Nbk yr. 42, C. Wunsch, Iddina-Marduk, 1993, no. 47) from the Nūr-Sin files of the Egibi archive, but, of course, nothing indicates explicitly that these ultimately derived from a temple. What is certain, is that meat could be bought on occasion.

[11] It is often particularly difficult to recognise when elements of remunerations are summed up, whether one is dealing with an apposition or not.

[12] The document has been discussed anew by H. Bongenaar in Bongenaar 2000, p. 77-8, but attention must be drawn in a wider context to certain aspects not discussed there.

[13] There is some slight evidence for a similar link between Babylon and Marad, especially in the involvement of the Šangû-Ištar-Bābili family: cf. JRAS Cent. Supp., 1924, Pl. 4-5 (=BR no. 35), found in Marad but written in Babylon and perhaps CT 51, 56 (11 VII Dar x) written in Marad but with clear Babylon links, though the name E$_2$.KAR.ZA.GIN$_2$.NA may possibly have indicated any temple of Ea.

[14] Cf. VaB 4, Nabonidus no. 3, which states that the earlier foundations were noticed only in the reign of Nebukadnezzar II, creating the opportunity for restoration. There is, of course, some archaeological evidence for the existence of a late Middle-Babylonian continuation of the cult.

[15] The members of the family importuning successive kings are consistently called by the writer of the document *šangû* (E$_2$.BAR) Šamaš ^{LU_2}ḪAL. We are probably supposed to regard in this "Šangû-Šamaš" as a family name, but the, likely hereditary, occupation was probably that of a *bārû*, possibly during the period in which the cult of Šamaš was in abeyance. It is conceivable that the conceit is in reality to hide the fact that the family managed to obtain the position of *šangû* of Šamaš only in the course of the proceedings described. The for a family name normal A/DUMU ^{LU_2}SANGA is avoided, just as it is for ^{LU_2}ḪAL. H. Bongenaar discusses the question Bongenaar 2000 p. 78. The matter is complicated further by

20ff.), is treated cursorily, but not therefore uninterestingly: the king assigned *sattukku* to the god and allowed the beneficiary to take possession of what was granted. This reflects the *sattukku*-procedure we find in the Old Babylonian texts from Nippur as proposed by Sigrist, and thus what seems to have been the ordinary sequence of events: offerings were assigned to the gods and the left-overs used to remunerate the personnel, the size of the offerings possibly being related to the requirements of the personnel intended, if Sigrist's proposal is correct. After the lapse of this grant the next stage is reached in II 4, where we find, though phrased differently, virtually the same proceedings: one $SILA_3$ of bread and one of good beer, belonging to the sustenance (*kurummatu*) of a functionary called the *šaknu* of Esagil, which derived from the regular offerings (*ginê,* the same as *sattukku*) of Bēl, were assigned to Šamaš (*kunnu*) and granted (*râmu*) to the beneficiary. At the same time a garden in the (eastern) New-Town "within Babylon" was given to Šamaš (*nadānu*), but entrusted to our beneficiary (*pan* PN *šudgulu*). Normally prebendal endowment included land, not only in this text. Šamaš was still in exile at this moment.

The next stage took place after the well-known remaking of the image of Šamaš (III 19ff.) which could signify reinstitution of the cult at its proper location. After a re-listing of the earlier benefices the king freshly established unspecified amounts of bread, beer, *mirsu* (a sweet confection containing dates), beef, mutton, fish and vegetables for Šamaš, and only after that the text comes to the point (IV 54) and fixes the share of the *šangû*, which demonstrates that this high functionary was recompensed, as other lower ranking prebendaries were, from the various types of offerings. The *kurummatu* of the *šangû* equalled (or was identical with?)[16] half the share of the king from the offerings assigned. From the sheep sacrificed during the whole year on behalf of the king (*niqê šarri šá kal šatti*, "all royal sacrifices of the whole year", this will have represented the normal daily offerings), the share included the $^{UZU}UR_2$ ("upper leg"), ^{UZU}KUŠ ("hide"), ^{UZU}EGIR ("rump") , ^{UZU}SA.MEŠ ("tendons") with half the stomach and the intestines plus two ^{UZU}*kur-sin-nu* ("lower leg") and a vessel containing bouillon (A.MEŠ UZU), with a similar share in the oxen and sheep offered by ordinary believers (*kāribus*). But this did not constitute the complete portion of the *šangû*, these represented only a specified, so to say additional, share in the bloody offerings. For from the five *ērib bīti* prebends established, we must assume when the king re-endowed the god, two were assigned to the *šangû* in bread, beer, *mirsu*, beef, mutton, fish and vegetables of (that is: representing or with?)[17] a butcher('s prebend) with the *unāt libbi*, "(better quality?) internal organs", of two *ērib bīti* places. In all regular offerings belonging to rites of the town, the roasted flour offerings of the believers and in all that entered Ebabbar half the royal share and that of two *ērib bīti*s were for the *šangû*. An *ērib bīti* prebend was thus something of a known, specified, size, serving as a kind of standard in the organisation concerned. Additionally there was a specified share in the textiles presented to Šamaš, Aja and Bunene on six equally specified days, with again a comparable share in the offerings made by the *kāribus*. The registration of this endowment of the post of *šangû* of Sippar by Nabû-apal-iddina undoubtedly constituted the core of the contents of the text.[18] There is a clear link between the standard set by the income of an *ērib bīti* and that of a *šangû* -in this case.

---

the occurrence of a *šatammu* of Sippar in the early Neo-Babylonian period. The affair is somewhat suspicious.

[16] The phrasing is ambiguous, but suggests anyhow that the king retained a considerable share of the offerings, even if half of that was ceded to the *šangû*.

[17] The formulation is not clear, the possible intention is that with a share equalling that of two *ērib bīti*'s in the non-bloody offerings also a similar share in the slaughtered animals was granted. Cf. the translation provided by CAD E p. 292.

[18] The text, if it were necessary, also confirms that the normal daily offerings were formally regarded as those of the king, to which those of others are irregular additions.

The partial copy on the terracotta box from the time of Nabopolassar indicates that the text was regarded as (partially) normative.

VS 1, 36, dated 12 III Nabû-šum-iškun 8, indicates the size of an *ērib bīti* prebend in the sanctuary of Nabû in Borsippa in this period: daily one *sūtu* of bread and beer each, *mirsu*, NINDA.DU.DU,[19] beef, mutton, fish and fowl, and vegetables (the basket) in the *sattukku*, the slaughtered offerings of the king and the believers and various extras, from whatever came into Ezida. As much as was due to an *ērib bīti* was assigned (by the king) to the beneficiary in an already existing organisation encompassing several separate sanctuaries, as additionally indicated by the witnesses present.

In RA 16, 1919, p. 117ff. Thureau-Dangin published a comparable text from the time of Marduk-zākir-šumi listing the endowment granted to a person who was perhaps primarily a *kalû* of Ištar (III 9), but who accumulated a whole number of functions, including that of *ṭupšar Eanna*. Here we find presented first a piece of land of 12 kor, with, notably, a family from the Amukanu tribe, with its house and garden, probably to till the land. There follows one SILA$_3$ of bread and beer each before Nanāia, Kanišurra and Anu with Enlil -thus probably three separate prebends- and bread, beer, *mirsu*, meat, fish and vegetables forming the share of (these?) three *ērib bīti*s at *šalām bīti* ceremonies. An additional meat assignment comprised one sheep "before the various gods" and the *tikku*, "neck", of an ox and a sheep belonging to the ordinary offerings and the *guqqû* offerings of the king (and) the believers. Presumably all this income constituted that of three *ērib bīti* functions,[20] possibly one before each of three the gods mentioned at the start of the passage. Furthermore there is 0.2 of barley per month from the income of the temple scribe, and a syntactically unclear passage could signify a claim to 1/30th per kor in cereals entering the temple, with "a fist full" of twelve loaves from what was booked off.[21] Finally there is one SILA$_3$ of bread and of beer each as income for a *kalûtu*-function in the sanctuary of Sin "in the courtyard", also without specification as to time or frequency. Line II 12 could possibly be regarded as meaning that all this constituted the endowment of the *kalûtu*, lamentation-reciter's prebend, settled by the king on Ibni-Ištar of the Ḫunzu family, who was also (already?) a *kalû* of Ištar, (and now became an) *ērib-bīti* of Nanāia and (was already) the *šangû* of Uṣur-amassu in combination with *ṭupšar Eanna*, a function which he had possibly acquired only now. This last fact could explain the passage concerning the scribe's income with the unclear passage following, which probably represents the right to a payment from the *gimru* due to scribes, best known from the so-called Edict of Belsazzar. The titles of the beneficiary at least partially refer to rights not listed in the document, which must therefore represent earlier possessions. Other rights granted only now were not covered by the final list of titles of the beneficiary of the document, this is not his full list of honours.

VS I, 35 is likewise a *kudurru*, but it is the monumental version of several documents among which there is one in which the *šākin ṭēmi* of Dilbat established the share of a younger son in his inheritance. The "share" (*isqu*), which figures here, is thus an unspecified prebend in

---

19 M. Stol suggests a reading KU$_7$.KU$_7$, *matqu*, "sweet", which occurs in combination with bread in Dreambook p. 316 IV x+4-6.

20 P.A. Beaulieu, AOAT 252, Fs. Oelsner, Munster 2000, p. 10-11 stresses the link between the function of *kalû* and the *tikku*. Perhaps we are dealing with a generally phrased passage also including rights belonging to the *kalūtu* prebend before Sin mentioned after the rights belonging to the function of *ṭupšar bīti*.

21 Quoted CAD K 259L as a "fistful per 12 loafs", which does not really make sense. Is a "portion consisting of 12 loafs" completely excluded? An *upnu* was an Hittite measure, and it occurs in other NB texts in a comparable context. AHw. p. 1424L.

the temple of Lagamal consisting of all that came in and was expended (*urbu u tēlītu*)[22] and of a sheep (any sheep sacrificed?) the breast and an upper leg, or rather those cuts "as father received them"?

Three other documents of comparable nature are less well preserved: BBSt 35, from the time of Marduk-apal-iddina II, VA 3614[23] and the tiny fragment VS I 57.[24] Of these the first is possibly an endowment of a *šangû* (rev. 11)[25] in which again the income of an *ērib bīti* (rev. 14) figures as a standard. The practical contents were registered in lines rev. 8 to 15, but these are too damaged to be of use, though the person who benefited from the grant was possibly (also?) a singer of Nabû (Edge 2). VA 3614 dates from the reign of Šamaš-šum-ukīn and was intended for a *kutimmu* of Ebabbar in Sippar. The elements of the prebendal income, deriving again from the offerings of the king and the unspecified believers are listed rev. 2-6, in a list starting with the tell-tale one *sūtu* of bread and one of beer, as in Borsippa, and again taking, rev. 5, the share of an *ērib bīti* as a standard. The document is important, for it confirms not only that craftsmen *ērib bītis* existed at this time, but that they were funded on purpose. VS 1, 57 does not contain any longer useful additional information.

The overall importance of these texts is that they provide an impression of the practical size of the allowances of the various functionaries, that they do not refer to fragmentation of tasks by granting the same function to different persons or to specific periods of service and that they indicate the existence of standard allowances within local organisations which encompassed the sanctuaries of several gods. They do not refer to members of the purveying trades, but only to persons with *ērib bīti* status amongst whom we must include the *kalû* and probably the *kutimmu*, whereas also at least one higher ranking functionary is included in the same system of remuneration. As is to be expected, the size, and thus the value of the recompensation varied according to the local importance of the god concerned. The source of the endowment consisted of the material made available by the king (and his predecessors) for both ordinary and additional offerings on regular but special occasions of the cultic year, generally on a monthly basis, increased by the special offerings made by the ordinary believers on unspecified occasions. Possibly the assignment of portions equalling, or more precisely, constituting *ērib bīti* prebends (BBSt 36 V 19f.), indicates that the official concerned, the *šangû*, automatically became or had to be one of them. Differentiating between the higher functions and the lower ones is not warranted. They belong to one and the same prebendal system.

The application of fixed, this time country-wide, standards is also implied by YOS 6, 10 (28 I Nbn 1), from Uruk, according to which an official of the central administration, the *rab unqāti*, ordered, no doubt on behalf of the new king, to provide the brewers and bakers with (material for) the regular offerings like (those of) Esagil and Ezida, and to assign land like those of Bēl and Nabû held, to the *rab banîs* of Bēlet-ša-Uruk. That the *maššartu-pappasu*-system existed by this time is not new, but it is of importance that the central administration intervened in its implementation. "Give six ^{UZU}GAB.ME ("breasts") and flour of the *sattukkus* to the *ērib bīti*" is the next requirement. There follow some other specific orders not relevant here. *ērib bītis*

---

22 This can hardly be taken literally and illustrates a general difficulty in this group of texts, that of the proper linking of income and function. What is meant is probably that the unspecified functionary receives a right to the customary share attached to his function from what is listed. This may have been called "(receiving) incoming and outgoing".

23 F.X. Steinmetzer, AnOr 7, 1935, p. 314-7; copy AnOr 12, p. 314-8.

24 Cf. J. A. Brinkman and S. Dalley, ZA 78 p. 97-8.

25 The text possibly contains a reference to income of the type called *gimru* in the Edict of Belsazzar pertaining to a *šangû* in the form of what is phrased as *irbi tēlīt šurubti ekuri*. This matter will be discussed here in the study on taxation.

did not receive cereals only in the shape of bread and beer. That standards set by Esagil were regarded as applicable to other main sanctuaries was not only the case in prebendal matters, but as the "Edict" of Belsazzar suggests, also regarding agriculture and the remuneration of officials, which, incidentally, can be linked to our prebendaries, as we will see.

3. A note on some earlier *kudurrus*

Six Kassite and Post-Kassite *kudurrus* are relevant for the question of the funding of the cult of the gods. Q 2.1.1[26] dates to the reign of Kurigalzu, son of Kadašman-Ḫarbe. It deals with a grant of land and daily 3 kor of bread and beer, with 0.2.0 of *mirsu* and a *ṣimdu* (0.0.3) of *asnê*, "Dilmun dates", and of *šamnu ḫalṣu* , "(pressed) oil", each, with three sheep for Ištar, presumably of Uruk. The grant can be deemed sufficient for a reasonably varied complement of clerical personnel: at one *sūtu* each per *ērib bīti*, and ignoring for the moment the fact that the higher ranks received several times the *ērib bīti* remuneration, it would suffice for 90 persons. But not all would be available for that one purpose, of course.[27] The text seems to constitute the only basic grant funding an institution that is available at the moment.

U 2.18 was excavated in Larsa and dates from the reign of Nazimaruttaš. It is a grant to the *nargallu* of Ebabbar consisting of land, referring to an earlier grant by Burnaburiaš. Other documents referring to grants of land are (PKB) 4.2.8 for a *nešakku* of Enlil who was also a *gudapsû* of Nusku and a *ḫazannu* of Nippur.[28] 4.2.8 was intended for a priestly father and his son who had fled from Elam, which is not relevant here, unless it is regarded as an indication that kings could be persuaded to care for clerics who had lost their livings. 5.2.2 constitutes a grant for the goddess Nanše, referring to an earlier endowment by the Sealand king Gulkišar. In none of the texts there is a direct, explicit link between the granting of the land and prebends, yet the two were inevitably connected in that they were included in the same grant. The endowment granted to the god enabled that god to maintain personnel, and the personnel received occasionally directly additional land. It is clear that the Kassite and Post-Kassite periods did not constitute a break in the prebendal system, only our documentation is even more limited than either before or after. There is at least one direct reference to measures relating to prebends taken by a Sealand king.

4. The inclusion of land in prebendal endowments[29]

In two cases the endowments discussed already mention land: in BBSt 36 a garden in Babylon was granted and in RA 16 p. 117ff. land and a family with a garden in Uruk. In neither case is the nature of the link between the (other) prebendal income and this land spelled out specifically: it is an element of the grant but the other, specifically prebendal, elements of the same grant are not directly dependent on it.[30] The prebendaries held land, possibly on the basis

---

[26] The numbers refer to Brinkman's catalogues, Material and Studies for Kassite History Vol. I, Chicago, 1976, and Political History of Post-Kassite Babylonia, AnOr 43, Rome, 1968 p. 323ff. Additionally there is J 2.19.1, damaged but mentioning a *nešakku* of Enlil as the beneficiary.

[27] Assuming the use of a kor of 180 SILA$_3$.

[28] Note the use of "old" terminology in Nippur.

[29] On this subject MacGinnis 1991-2 p. 75 note 7; in relation to the Bēl-rēmanni texts cf. Jursa 1998 p. 91 with the literature in note 370. The use of *kurummatu* in a prebendal context should be noted. On the role of land in a prebendal context also MacGinnis 1999 p. 4-5.

[30] This is, it should be stressed, something different from the question of the *ḫallatu*-garden of the *rab banîs*, the land is here an additional source of income, it is not the direct basis for the fulfilling of obligations as was the case with the *ḫallatu* plantations.

of an original endowment, but this was in the late period not usually inherited or sold as an integral part of the prebend.

The question of the *ḫanšû*-land assigned by the early Neo-Babylonian kings to specific families in "old towns" like Babylon, Borsippa, Dilbat, Sippar or Uruk will not be discussed here.[31] If there was a general link between the Neo-Babylonian family names and the fact that the status of these families in the old towns derived at least in part from their occupation of positions which can be associated with the sanctuaries, the status of these families was inevitably also linked to the *ḫanšû*-type of land holding. This is perhaps best demonstrated in Borsippa.[32] The endowment of a number of named prebendaries documented by the early Neo-Babylonian *kudurrus* mentioned took place in the same general period in which certain kings, notably Erība-Marduk and Marduk-apal-iddina II granted the *ḫanšû*-land in what seems to have been a general share-out of rights, from which also the temples as institutions profited.

A link between land and prebendal rights is not something of the Neo-Babylonian period alone. SAOC 44 no. 88, Old Babylonian Nippur, date lost, could suggest a link between NAM.I$_3$.DU$_8$ (line 1), "the function of a doorkeeper" and A.ŠA$_3$ SUKU$_6$.BI, "its sustenance lot" (line 4), but the text is not very well preserved, and the status of a door keeper is perhaps in the Old Babylonian period not always that of a full-blown prebendary, see below. A much better case for prebendal land can be made out with ARN 23 (IV Sumuel 28), cf. PBS 8/2, 169, where we find 1.0.0 of A.ŠA$_3$.SUKU$_6$ (line 6') between the NAM.GUDU$_4$ of Ninlil and the various NAM.BUR.ŠU.MA listed, thus suggesting a direct link between the NAM.GUDU$_4$ and the sustenance land mentioned. For more comparable Old Babylonian examples from Nippur see the remarks on the various prebends in that town below.

Even if the direct link between land and prebends in inheritance or sale documents in both our periods was weak, it can be assumed that endowments generally meant an assignment of both land and other forms of income. It was, however, not the habit to treat the two as insolubly linked.

5. The shares in the bloody and non-bloody offerings in other texts: Uruk

Here again the information from the later texts is much more ample than that from the earlier ones. The most explicit text, which mentions two instances of a specific grant to a named individual by king Nabû-apal-iddina and which is a copy of an older exemplar dating presumably to the reign of that king, was re-edited by McEwan[33]. This is not the place to re-open the discussion of this important text, but a number of structural aspects are vital enough for our subject to be repeated here, even though it is obviously a text which would have needed regular updating. It can be split up into a number of sections which find certain structural parallels in other, later, texts dealing with rights to sacrificial material in Uruk, though the interpretation is hampered by the fact that the essential "headings" of the various sections into which the text can be divided are damaged.[34] In texts dealing with offerings we generally find a fixed succession of *ginê*, "regular", *guqqû*, "special, (but regular)", and "festive", for instance *eššešu*. The text mentions towards the end *šalām bīti* and (*taḫlipti*) *ḫarê*. In the late period especially the *eššešu*, the *baiātu* and the *šalām-bīti*-offerings[35] are mentioned as recurring

---

[31] The question will be reconsidered in the contribution on taxation, Chapter VII.

[32] There is for instance a link between land and occupations occurring as family names such as Kurgarrû and Mubannû, functions we can regard as potentially prebendal, see below. Many families to which prebendaries belonged held *ḫanšû* land.

[33] Langdon OECT I Pl. 20-21, McEwan 1983.

[34] Lines 1, 25, 48-50 and 74-75 in McEwan's counting.

[35] So Peiser, Verträge 107, 2 x Dar 26, Babylon see MacGinnis 1991-2, p. 88-9 no. 7: 5, Nappāḫu archive.

special occasions, but there will have been more special monthly rites.[36] In general a differentiation between the offerings *ša šarri* and *ša kāribi* can be applied. As already stressed offerings made, at least in name, by the king can be regarded as resulting in secure income for the prebendaries, those added by "believers" must be regarded as additional and uncertain.[37]

Prime position in the Uruk meat text is taken by the *ginê* of Ištar of Uruk and Nanāia, which occur twice, respectively from line 1 and line 26 onwards. The second passage deals explicitly with sheep and at the beginning of the first line of the text only one short sign is damaged. It is reasonable that it must be restored as GU_4, "ox", the more expensive animal thus preceding the more common sheep. A third, damaged, section of daily offerings begins with line 50. McEwan's reconstruction is based on parallelism with the previous sections. There is no clear reading for line 50. We can only assume that the section refers to both oxen and sheep, and in view of lines 58-60 to offerings to the lesser goddesses of Eanna (line 74): Bēlet-[ša-Rēš] (58), Uṣur-amassu (59) and (here) Annunītu (60).[38] In line with what can be expected the next passages deal with *guqqû*, first oxen, then sheep (75-84). After that special cultic occasions follow which result in the slaughter of young male animals (line 85) and, remarkably enough, female animals (line 86), the shares in which are established in respectively 87-92 and 93-97. It is notable that the king has no share in the section mentioning the female animals, but otherwise he comes first in each of the further subdivisions which can be made within the major sections of the text, those according to the rank order of the various cuts of meat. The king's share is indicated here as his *kurummatu*. The question of those entitled to the other cuts will be discussed below, if relevant. In general we can note that both in the early and in the late period general terms are used attributing unspecified "portions" of meat to those entitled, the specific cuts were possibly assigned in separate documents, possibly of the type discussed here.

---

36 The most "complete" list of such "rites" I know of is RAcc p.79, AO 6451 rev. 35-39, in a somewhat halting sentence. It mentions sheep of the *ginê* and oxen and sheep *ana guqqāne*, after that follow the *eššešu*, the *petê bābi*, the *lubušātu*, the *egubbû*, the *baiātānu*, the *kinūnu*, the *parṣe ḫašādu*, to finish with *kāribi* and *tardītu šarri*, which two terms possibly refer back in shorthand manner to the rites already mentioned for the (royal) sacrifices belonging to *ginê* and *guqqāne*, intending the same shares as listed, but now from offerings presented by ordinary believers and by the king on exceptional occasions. The list can be compared with Peiser, Verträge 107: *niqê šarri*, *niqê kāribi*, *ginû*, *guqqû*, *eššešu*, *baiātānu*, and *šalām bīti*. The list is certainly not complete in this way for it does not mention, for instance, the *ḫarê* of the Uruk meat text. Certain terms may, however, be subsumed in those already mentioned, like *nubattu*. *rimku* is possibly not attested in the cult in the Neo-Babylonian period, unlikely though it might seem. *kispu* belongs probably especially to the ancestral cult of which we virtually know nothing in the Neo-Babylonian period. Possibly it belonged -in the context of the ordinary cult- to the *eššešu*, the same is the case with *nabrû*. But the summing up in AO 6451 includes both *eššešu* and *lubuštu*s, whether one rite implies another seems of no importance there, it being, like *lubuštu*, a precondition? Much may have been subsumed by *guqqû*. What the rites involved is not of immediate importance here, but all of these occasions will have generated special income for specific ritualists, and this special income may have become a separate, negotiable, element of the prebendal system. Already the much older Kingsbury text suggests a link between a specific rite (for a specific god), a specific performer and specific material for offerings made available.

37 With the *niqê šarri* and the *niqê kāribi* the opposition is between *šarru* and *kāribu* and not between the god who received the offerings from the king and a divine Kāribu, as I once mistakenly suggested as a possibility.

38 Ištar/Bēlet-ša-Uruk, Nanāia, Bēlet-ša-Rēš and Uṣur-amassu constituted the core group of goddesses of Eanna, but they are not the only ones provided for by the institution, cf. already the remarks made on the "*kudurru*" RA 16 p. 117f. above. As in Ebabbar in Sippar there were the "minor sanctuaries" which occupied a special position and had their own prebendal personnel, cf. Bongenaar 1997 p. 229ff., though they were supplied by the (local) central organisation.

The Uruk document is a list of specified entitlements. Though there may have been "supernatural" reasons why specific cuts of meat were assigned to specific office holders, those reasons are not being made explicit. Nabû-apal-iddina had assigned a lower leg of beef[39] to one *āšipu* (line 6) but retained a piece called EGIR[40] which seems to have gone with it regularly, and on two days of the month the hide (*šiḫtu*), plus parts of the intestines to another exorcist (lines 17 and 19). This arrangement does not support the idea of the existence of a fixed system of specific shares for specific prebendal functions.[41] The assumption must be that the meat shares were allocated on an *ad hoc* basis, there being no direct link between meat portion and function, though the status of the cut played a role. The result would be that, as with land, the link between prebendal meat portions and prebendal obligations was not absolute. A separate arrangement established the exact nature of the cut. Income and obligation could be dissociated from one another, with the result that prebendal rights to cuts of meat could be transferred on their own. A transfer of meat portions does also not refer automatically to a *ṭābiḫūtu*, "slaughterer's", prebend.

A rare text in which rights to bread and beer are directly combined with those to meat constitutes the last partially preserved passage in SWU 117, with an unspecified date in the reign of Nabopolassar as terminus post quem: 3 SILA$_3$ of beer and of bread with one *imittu*, "shoulder" and unspecified *ba-me-e* of an/the ox(en) or sheep?[42] constitute the *isqu* of the *ērib bītis* of Uṣur-amassu and Urukītu according to this text.

This text is of further interest in that the preceding passage deals with the *ginê* of Šamaš, Aja, Bunene and Lugal-x-x.[43] In this passage the prebendaries receive bread and beer on an individual basis, but their assignment of meat is not specified as to person.[44] The text is one of

---

39 On the assumption that the first passage of the text indeed deals with oxen.

40 Discussed by McEwan 1983 p. 196 and regarded as a cut "in the lower back region". But "rump" being one of the prime cuts I find it difficult to accept that it was classified in the second group. The *rapaštu* belongs definitely to the first category.

41 An immediate objection might be that the granting of a right to sacrificial material, even to an *āšipu*, by a king does not mean that the beneficiary becomes automatically a member of what we might call the clergy of an institution. The text also refers to a grant to another *āšipu* which had been regranted to a son of the king. There is no indication that he was appointed to some clerical function.

42 In his note to the line on p. 117 H. Freydank hesitatingly compares *bamtu*.

43 Line 19'. This is presumably during Nabopolassar and therefore before the wind showed the outlines of the foundations of Ebabbar of Larsa to Nebuchadnezzar: this Šamaš was obviously venerated in Uruk, but he may represent the Larsa Šamaš having found refuge in Uruk. The passage is remarkable because it mentions after a number of named persons who receive either daily three SILA$_3$ of both bread and beer or half that amount, all, but for the last, "before Šamaš", some others: 12' ^{LU_2}EN.NAM (followed by a difficult to explain *u*), then, before Bunene 13' ^{LU_2}ZABAR, thus an *āšipu*, 14' ^{LU_2}KAŠ.ŠEMxX [(x)].ME (= erasure?, one SILA$_3$ would be very little for more than one person, note that this is not qualified as *pappasu*, which would be expected with a brewer), 15' the ^{LU_2}*mu-ban*!-*ne*-e (with 2 SILA$_3$), 16' the ^{LU_2}ŠITIM, and 17' an unexplained ^{LU_2}NU.x.PAP, followed by 18' an unspecified SILA$_3$ for *pi-qid bīti*. Why some persons are not mentioned by name, while the others are, is not spelled out, for instance by a statement that those who are being mentioned by name represent the *ērib bītis*. As far as the titles of the others are understandable we will encounter these functionaries again. Incidentally ^{LU_2}ŠITIM occurs together with *mubannû* in this text, the term cannot indicate the same functionary.

Kessler 1991, p. 32 regards the Šamaš prebend in his text 89 (lines 7-18, 28 X Nbk 3) as referring to rights in Larsa, which is not specified, but not altogether impossible.

44 In line 20' we must read *ina* ITI 4 (and not *šá*, 3 is normally being written with three juxtaposed vertical wedges in this text) UDU.BAR.GAL, "per month four lambs having a coat of wool", animals in their later first year, a number which, together with more bread and beer, Nabopolassar instituted. These sheep will have been part of the sacrifices.

the rare cases in which "non-bloody" and "bloody" entitlements are directly combined in one administrative document. But it does not constitute a real disclaimer for the proposed relative weakness of the link between the meat portions and the service obligations we proposed: the text notes the rights, but the entitlements were distributed separately. We can also assume that this passage deals with the total assignments from the main local sanctuary to one of the minor temples belonging to its entourage. The last line of the first passage cannot be explained in a satisfactory manner, but the text, of deviating format amongst the SWU texts, is possibly a record of rights to income deriving from offerings as established by the king, as named persons are listed, at a specific moment in time, probably by Nabopolassar.[45]

We must perhaps conclude that rights to income consisting of certain types of cuts of meat were assigned to a group of persons with a specific function, but that rights to individual pieces could be alienated at an individual level.[46]

6. Practical aspects: prebendal texts from three Neo-Babylonian private archives

We will briefly discuss three groups of prebendal texts from private archives. They illustrate the limited nature of the evidence regarding our subject contained in even the more informative private archives. The owners of these archives did not belong to the prominent collectors of prebendal functions, but they are probably typical for the rank and file prebendaries, different though their holdings may have been. No private archive deals with the main prebends of one of the central sanctuaries of the local set-up in one of the main towns. The presence of an inheritance division in two of the cases studied is important, as it provides some certainty that at least the initial holdings of the person concerned are known, which provides an idea about the families' position. The same is more or less ensured by the minority of the owner of the third group of texts.

There are, of course, other private archives in which prebendal holdings are an important element in determining the status of the persons concerned, like the Ur Gallābu archive, and archives which are important because they throw light on one special aspect of the prebendal system, like the Kessler's Uruk Bēl-supê-muḫur archive for the baker's prebend.

The three cases chosen are, however, especially important, because in the first place the prebendal holdings concerned are varied and in two cases seem to illustrate how various separate prebends seem to originate from what was originally one and the same, all encompassing function.[47] In the second place the texts are, or will soon be available, together with the other material from the archive in studies which indicate how the prebendal affairs of the family were only one aspect of much wider economic interests. These are important for the elite role of the prebendaries, but will not be discussed here: the prebends constituted for those involved only a segment of their activities, which, however, opened up access to other economic opportunities. The third archive selected indicates especially what occurred when an owner was not capable of executing the functions himself. In this manner the three archives touch upon matters which are central to what occupies us.

a. The Babylon Nappāḫu texts

The Babylon Nappāḫu archive is informative because it contains material on the variety of small prebends available in a local organisation and on the disintegration, especially

---

45 See Freydank's comments on the text p. 15.

46 Another administrative text from Uruk dealing with prebendal income combining in some sense "bloody" and "non-bloody" material is VS 20, 99, probably an accounting document on the period of the succession of Neriglissar by, ultimately, Nabonidus, cf. line rev. 10'. Compare also, indirectly, VS 20, 105.

47 Perhaps called *šangû* or *ērib bīti*.

"vertically", of a "small sanctuaries prebend". It provides some insight into what the function of an *ērib bīti* could mean and the economic role of the prebendaries in general. Texts from private archives only rarely specify the exact contents of the benefices involved, if such information is included, it is welcome, even though practical problems abound.

The Nappāḫu interest in the local Bēl-Ālia prebend at Šarrabanu has already been mentioned above.

The first text to be discussed here is MacGinnis 1991-2 no. 9 (= Peiser, Verträge 91), 16 VIII Nbn 12, where two brothers belonging to the family share *ērib bīti* prebends. The division seems to avoid fragmentation, though that was not completely feasible. At any rate not all functions were split, which is normal under comparable circumstances. One prebend before Sin of Egišnugal amounted to 4 $SILA_3$ of bread and beer each and a sheep on the occasion of an eclipse. Unspecified remains the nature or duration of an *isqu* before a divine Kāribu of the cult room of Marduk, which was divided into two parts of $^5/_6$ and $^1/_6$ respectively, the smaller part going to the younger brother. Separately there was also a tun of beer before the god Zāriqu. This does not look impressive, though the equal amounts of bread and beer characterising a particular set of emoluments must retain our attention.

More important are the prebendal rights in the Išḫara temple, which must represent one of the "small sanctuaries" belonging to the local central organisation supervised in Babylon by Esagil. Three $SILA_3$ of beer and bread each belonged to the holdings divided. It constituted the core of the share of the younger brother and it again constitutes a type of remuneration which suggests an *ērib bīti* position.

There are two additional stipulations: whoever of the brothers (holds/fulfils?) the $^{LU_2}E_2$.BAR-*ú-tu,* "the function of *šangû*", enjoys his/its(?) right to income (called here *isqu*), and, additionally, according to their share the brothers will accomplish the *kīnaiātu*, the "regular obligations", of their father.[48] How or where this *šangûtu* was exercised, is not explained, but there is perhaps some additional information. Explanation could be sought in VS 6, 273+325, an order given by the *šatammu* of Esagil to (a) person(s) called $^{LU_2}E_2$.BAR. This possibly recalls the E_2.BAR-*ú-tu* which the two brothers of the original inheritance division were to exercise on the basis that the one carrying out the function also enjoyed the income. The(se) *šangû*(s) "of a small sanctuary" was/were subject in Babylon to the authority of the *šatammu* of Esagil. Speculation would suggest that the *šangūtu* of the Išḫara temple, or a fraction of it, was possibly in the hands of the Nappāḫus. The text is a remnant of an order to provide 3 *sūtu* of bread and beer, with dates (*makkasu*) and flour (*maṣḫatu*) from the food/meal (*naptanu*) brought from Esagil to the temple of Išḫara to various persons entitled to respectively the income belonging to twice five days and twice ten days. The first person mentioned, for the 1st to the 5th of the month, is the one who left us what we call the Nappāḫu family archive. The question might be whether this *šangūtu* was held only by the Nappāḫu brothers, or whether also the others mentioned had their share. The possibility that *šangūtu* represented occasionally a prebend which could be split seems to suggest itself, it was clearly a subaltern position. This serves to confirm what Bongenaar has elucidated for the Gula temple in Sippar, a "small sanctuary" belonging to the Ebbabar circle.[49] The evidence underlines again that the function of *šangû* belonged to the prebendal system in the Neo-Babylonian period, and certainly so in the context of the "small sanctuaries". The 3 $SILA_3$ mentioned equals the amount assigned to the younger brother in the inheritance division. Could we speculate, in the line of the *kudurrus* discussed, that this *šangû* received an *ērib bīti* share?

---

[48] 11) PN1 and PN2 *man-nu* $^{LU_2}E_2$.BAR-*ú-tu* 12) *pa-na-at* GIŠ.ŠUB.BA-*šú ik-ka-al.*

[49] Bongenaar 1997 p. 239, referring to CT 57, 155: SANGA.MEŠ *ša* ^{d}Gula, note also the reference to Uruk.

Without discussing the adoption and inheritance affairs of the Nappāḫu family the Išḫara prebend(s) pose(s) its/their own problems, of which we have already encountered one. Nbk 247 (29 IV Nbk 32) is a retroact belonging to the archive. It concerns the transfer of two *ṭābiḫu*-prebends. One is that of the 2) ... ^{LU_2}GIR$_2$.LA$_2$-*ú-tu šá* GU$_4$ UDU.NITA$_2$ *niqê šarri* 3) *niqê ka-ri-bi gi-nu-ú guq-ú šá kal* MU.AN.NA, "the function of slaughterer of the oxen and sheep of the royal offerings, the offerings of the ordinary believers (pertaining to the) ordinary and (regular) special offerings of the complete year". It yielded seven specified cuts of meat and annually seven skins of sheep before Išḫara. The stress put on the fact that the prebend concerned the whole year is of importance: the right, in so far as positively formulated is undivided and presumably includes all special occasions. But that does not mean that all the meat portions belonging to the function were included, for lines 8-9 stipulate that "he will not cut off other specified pieces" (*ul i-qa-ra-aš*). We can assume that rights to these pieces were kept by the holder. The sale therefore means a breaking up of directly related rights. The other slaughterer's prebend in Nbk 247 concerns a minor right before Papsukkal on the 8th of Nisan. The document is a retroact with Kohler-Peiser Rechtsleben II p. 20-1 (16 IV Nbn 14), which separates the two slaughterer's prebends, and it can be directly related to the sale document Peiser, Verträge 107, re-edited MacGinnis 1991-2 no. 7 (Dar yr. 26), which quotes the *ul i-qa-ra-aš* passage found in Nbk 247. The later text further increases the scatter of the elements of the full prebend's remuneration by selling off the rights mentioned in Nbk 247 in so far as they refer to the *eššešu*, *baiātānu* and *šalām bīti* ceremonies. Here we have a good example in which a prebend is not so much split "horizontally", as to the number of days for which it was valid, but as to its fund of assets, "vertically", in a period lasting from Nebuchadnezzar 32 to Darius 26. None of the texts refers to the duties involved.

The question of the claims of Kabtia dr. Damqia[50] on this prebend would not be of importance had not Peiser Verträge 118 indicated this butcher's prebend as a GIŠ.ŠUB.BA KU$_4$.E$_2$ ^{d}*Iš-ḫa-ra*,[51] an "*ērib bīti* prebend of Išḫara". If we could accept this literally, possession of a slaughterer's prebend could convey *ērib bīti* status, but a mix-up is easily possible.[52] The prebend meant could, after all, be identical with the one assigned to the younger brother on 16 VIII Nbn 12 by Verträge 91, for as we noted a tell-tale similar amount of bread and beer was involved, a typical aspect of *ērib bīti* prebends. As in VS 6, 96 (19 II Cyr 2) the owner would deliver barley for the *naptanu* of Išḫara and as VS 6, 85 (4 XIIb Nbn 12) mentions barley in exchange for beer, there is a good possibility that there was also a brewers or purveyors prebend. The brewing was executed, as so often, by others. VS 6, 324, a *maššartu* document, confirms that we are indeed dealing with such a prebend.

There was still another Išḫara prebend in the same hands since I Dar 18, that of *nâru*, "singer", which yielded meat portions on 8 I.[53] Whether we must really conclude that this meat constituted the only form of remuneration is perhaps too rash a conclusion, elements like bread and beer could be included automatically, while meat had to be defined more precisely. This is little more than speculation. Much more attractive is to assume that all the Išḫara prebends originally constituted one entity, what Bongenaar calls a "small-sanctuary prebend", which was

---

50 Verträge 108, 118, 113 and 114.

51 Line 3'; in Peiser's reading there is no LU$_2$.

52 There is also Verträge 109, where Peiser's restitution of the relevant passage suggests the existence of two prebends before Išḫara: GIŠ.ŠUB.BA ^{LU_2}[GIR$_3$.LA$_2$-*ú-tu*] *u* KU$_4$.E$_2$ ^{d}Iš-ḫa-ra. This requires collation. H. Bongenaar suggests the possibility that the family possessed originally an all-encompassing prebend, possibly called "the *ērib bīti* prebend before Išḫara", which was split into various separate elements, of which the butcher's prebend was one. This is a most helpful idea. Old habits of speech would have persisted.

53 MacGinnis 1991-2 no. 5 = Verträge 97 and Dar 463, cf. 487 and Verträge 96 with 123.

in a process of disintegration which had not reached that final stage in which the elements had become completely separate. We can imagine that in such a process the supervising body, led by the officials of Esagil, had to play a regulatory role.

VS 6, 129[54] (7 XII Dar 12) indicates that the rights of the brothers, which they clearly exercised together, consisted of -or included on- 17 days of every month *takkasû* before the divine Kāribu already mentioned. The contract stipulates that a third party would bring as an executor five *takkasû* on these seventeen days from 1 XII onwards. This is not easily reconciled with VS 5, 87-8 (28 II Dar 19) where in a similar document the younger brother is said to obtain every month four *rab-bu-ú šá tak-ka-su-ú*, with AHw 934R, "four big *takkasû*-cakes". This should represent 1/6 of the common share, which therefore amounted in total to 24 units.[55] In VS 6, 129 we found 85 units, but these were possibly smaller. *takkasû* is used in prebendal context for what the *nuḫatimmu* delivered in bakery products for the meal of the gods. Receiving *takkasû* does, however, not imply with absolute certainty that the receiver in this particular text had made arrangements concerning a baker's prebend, the nature of the function remains unspecified.

The Nappāḫu archive merits a special study. Here we are only interested in prebendal matters. The meat portions were obviously of special importance, and not only through the butcher's prebend, but also through the access to the share of the king, mentioned before, it provided. The fact that a butcher's prebend known from a whole range of texts can suddenly be indicated as an *ērib bīti* prebend without further specification suggests that there are aspects to that type of prebend which we do not understand properly. A slaughterer's prebend possibly entailed standard allocations of bread and beer which needed no specification, an aspect which it would share with an *ērib bīti* prebend,[56] whereas the meat portions were function specific. The original close link between all functions in small sanctuaries in the form of Bongenaar's "small sanctuaries prebend" probably explains the situation best: the prebend originally encompassing all tasks[57] and income, it was being expanded and split into a number of different functions, which might themselves be further split into time related portions. This may have affected the rights to income in a very erratic manner. We assume that the status of Išḫara had grown in importance in the period mentioned, especially under the Chaldean kings.

b) From Sippar: Bēl-rēmanni s Mušebši-Marduk Šangû-Šamaš[58]

All essential information on this text group is to be found in Jursa's monograph on the archive, but as the group is one of the most illustrative on a family of minor owners of purveying prebends it is useful to summarise the evidence here. Any study inevitably suffers

---

54 On the readings cf. Ungnad NRVU no. 592.

55 The text is obviously an execution contract, as line 9 indicates.

56 If the purveying prebendaries received remuneration out of the material they prepared for use, the bakers and brewers received barley and dates, but they were also assigned a meat portion. The slaughterer received a share in the animal slaughtered, but did he receive barley and dates or bread and beer as his cereal allocation? If the second was the case it would, at least outwardly, constitute a link with the *ērib bītis*. For equal bread and beer portions for slaughterers see BM 74550, below, and for the fact that they probably were not *ērib bītis* the remarks on their "non-initiated" attire. But especially here we should be aware of the likelihood of local differences in status.

57 Possibly excepting those requiring special ritualistic skills, like *kalûtu*, for which, if relevant, help had to be engaged on an *ad hoc* basis.

58 Jursa 1999, where the prebends and their backgrounds are discussed in Chapter V, p. 40-86. The texts are edited in the book in the order of their BM numbers, which must serve to indicate them here. Additional texts belonging to this group can be found in I. Spar and E. von Dassow, CTMMA 3 as archive F (by E. von Dassow), p.182-194.

from the regrettable effects of the fact that the documents have become dispersed, which entails considerable loss of context. It is not easy to separate this text group from other files, especially those of certain branches of the Ṣāḫit-ginê, the Ilē'i-Marduk and the Isināia families.[59] We cannot enter into the specifically significant question that the archive, with its "medical" component, contains information not only on the social and economic background of those involved, but also on the intellectual climate in which its owners operated. In this it does not stand alone, however, as the texts from Šaṭir indicate. In the present context those texts are important which suggest the existence of basic standard prebendal incomes, inform on the question of the status of the *ērib bītis* compared to that of other prebendaries, and contain the information on the practicalities of the service.

The Bēl-rēmanni after whom this group of texts has been called, dealt in agricultural products and he held land in Til-Gubbu, where prebendal land holding can be found, as did the other protagonist, Nidinti-Marduk s Šamaš-šum-līšir of the Ilē'i-Marduk family. The question of the land must remain in the background here, like the question of the civil and military obligations of the prebendaries as members of *eširtus*, on which primarily Jursa's monograph should be consulted.

Bēl-rēmanni was obviously a younger son, the affairs of the elder brother were not completely separate, but our insight in the family's prebends is inevitably limited. A number of texts published with the archive by Jursa obviously belongs to the administrative files of Ebabbar, but throws valuable light on the activities of the persons concerned.[60]

The earliest text of the group, or rather a copy of that text, BM 43146+, [x] I (Npb/early Nbk) deals with a "small sanctuary" *ērib bīti* prebend in the temple of Adad and Šala in Sippar.[61] The text is incomplete in the for us crucial passage, lines 1-13, which deprives us of some of the for our subject essential information. It starts with a heading which at any rate mentions an *ērib bīti*-position before Adad and Šala. The problem is that the position is mentioned again in line 7 and that we find thereafter a list of animals consisting of oxen, sheep, fowl and a lamb,[62] belonging to the normal offerings of the king plus other meat (line 10) pertaining to half the post of brewer, baker and slaughterer, possibly, therefore again a kind of combined post in certain small sanctuaries. That we are indeed dealing with more than one prebend[63] could, however, be suggested by line 5, which mentions lambs, indicating that the share in animals belonging to the *ērib bīti*-status was listed there separately. Important is that for the *ērib bīti* we have again a standard amount of bread and beer: one *sūtu* of each.[64] Of further interest is also that for the "purveying trades" only the claim to a share in the meat is mentioned. Having a share in the *maššartu* is presumably an automatic result of owning the (half) share in

---

59 This is especially valid for the later BM accession numbers in which Bēl-rēmanni related material occurs.

60 It is often difficult to decide whether a text belongs to the Bēl-rēmanni archive or not, and the exact link with the Nidinti-Marduk group is also problematic, no less than the connection with the texts around Marduk-rēmanni family Ṣāḫit-ginê, which is in turn linked with material from the related Isināia group, and there is more.

61 Bongenaar 1997 p. 240ff.

62 Support for SILA_4 can be found in BM 42343+ (reign of Darius) where a slaughterer's prebend is sold to Bēl-rēmanni and SILA_4 seems to be evident. The order of the animals is distinctly remarkable, though it is, as Jursa remarks, not uncommon in the context.

63 The first line may have conveyed that information, listing (on the original?) the functions of lines 11 and 12 after the *ērib bītūtu*, with in line 2 *ina* IGI DN.

64 This is not only based on the general parallelism with other texts, but it also conforms to the traces in line 3.

the purveying function mentioned.[65] *maššartu* shares are never stated to be inherited or sold, they constituted probably the core of the purveying functions to which they were implicitly assigned.

Unspecified remains the background of the meat portion before Bunene acquired by Bēl-rēmanni in BM 42425 (4 VIII Dar x)[66]. Bēl-rēmanni pledged a right to 3 SILA$_3$ of bread and of beer on 17 I Dar 13 for a debt originally incurred by his brother Šamaš-nāṣir according to CTMMA 3, 90. Equal amounts of bread and beer could suggest an *ērib bīti* post, but that of slaughterer cannot be excluded.

ēpišānūtu is in Sippar definitely the term (also) used when the execution of prebendal tasks is temporarily transferred by one holder of rights to another, that is between colleagues.[67] In BM 42572 (22 I Dar 4) we find a double transfer, both using the term *epišānūtu*, between members of the wider Šangû-Šamaš family. BM 42568 (26 IV Dar 8) not only indicates the relative stability of such arrangements, but also that the *pappasu* payments due from the executor to the owner could be transmuted into silver, which means that the executor had a -probably profitable- purpose for the barley involved.[68] In BM 42365 (3 I Dar 33) the execution of a brewer's prebend belonging to a woman is transferred by a man (her husband?), to Bēl-rēmanni. From BM 42363 (x IV Dar 30) we can only conclude that the executor carries off the *sattukku* and that the owner does the same with the *pappasu*, in dates,[69] but that the owner also receives an additional payment of one kor of barley. Similar is VS 4, 109 (23 XII Dar 35). The executor pays a rent of one kor of barley and the owner "carries" the *pappasu* (himself) from the store. Such a prebend obviously yielded the owner more than just the *pappasu*.[70] The days concerned are the same as in BM 42363, but there was a change in ownership.

The nature of the remuneration obtained by the executor is not specified in these cases.[71] It is remarkable that Bēl-rēmanni fulfilled these brokerage activities after he had ceased his official activities as head of the bakers.[72] This might be seen as a confirmation in Sippar of Kessler's suggestion for Uruk of the existence of an inner circle which virtually monopolised the practical activities. Yet the occurrence of the additional payment should be regard as primarily betraying an economic motive, as the executor pays the owner in Sippar more than just the *pappasu*, which suggests that he could not be pressurised by the executor, who would, according to Kessler's theory, be in a monopoly position. More generally this also means that part of the

---

65 This is not completely true, for in BM 43178+ (21 III Dar x) 7,5 days of a baker's prebend in E$_2$-Babbar are specified as belonging to the *maššartu* of the second half of month IX. In this case the term *maššartu* serves, however, rather to specify the period of service than the income. The transfer is qualified as a free gift (*rēmūtu*) not withstanding a, presumably modest, payment.

66 In line 6 Jursa reads *maš-šá-kát-tu$_4$-šú*. Is this an aberrant writing for *maššaktu*, which is to all likelihood the general term for a prebendal meat appropriation?

67 That is the proposed Uruk *rāsinūtu*.

68 On BM 42402 (26 VII Dar 19) with the related 42551, and 42299 (11 VII Dar x) see below under bakers. Of interest is Jursa's (implied) proposition, cf. Jursa 1999 p. 77, that Bēl-rēmanni acts in this case during a number of years on the orders (42551 line 6) of the acting head of the prebendal bakers. This would perhaps serve to explain the mutual payments.

69 The text is, again, damaged in the decisive places, ends of lines 8 and 10.

70 The importance for the value of the prebend of this additional payment on top of the *pappasu* was duly stressed by Jursa.

71 Handing on *epišānūtu* obligations is normal in this archive, cf. also BM 42613, date lost.

72 Bongenaar 1997 p. 449-50. Direct possession of a brewers prebend before Šamaš seems, as yet, unattested, but that is a result of the nature of the documentation. Ownership of a shared brewer's prebend together with his brothers is at least indirectly attested.

sattukku destined for the god disappeared into the owner's pocket and that it is the *sattukku* and not the *pappasu* which contained an element for costs. There was even enough for middlemen.

BM 43309+ (x VI Dar x) confirms that the actual brewing for a brewer's prebend could be done by the slave of another person. Normal was possibly that the actual brewing was done by one's own slaves, where documentation was less of a necessity.

Prebendal income as a collateral, to be seen as a likely step towards a loosening of the link between tasks and income, occurs in BM 43098+ (11 XI Dar 18), where half-monthly brewer's and baker's prebends for the second order Sippar deity Annunītu are mentioned, but the document virtually amounts to a sale after the fixed term for the payment of the debt would have passed. Possibly, however, this represents a case of recuperation of old family holdings.

A mixed debt and prebend document is BM 42434 with parallels including VS 4, 400 (20 VIII Dar x). The net result is that Bēl-rēmanni as a debtor and an executor had to pay interest and had to deliver a number of *dannus* of beer. Something similar is possibly the case in BM 42405, (16 I Dar x), damaged and unusually phrased, where a number of brewer's days belonging to one member of the Šangû-Šamaš family are due to or the responsibility of someone else, with Bēl-rēmanni standing security.[73] The combination of the two tasks suggests again that in this "small sanctuary" the vertical splitting up of prebendal tasks was not yet complete.

Jursa's Bēl-rēmanni seems to have been a not too successful business man.

c) From Sippar: Nidintu-Marduk s Šamaš-šum-līšir Ilē'i-Marduk

Bēl-rēmanni was deeply involved in the affairs of the minor Nidintu-Marduk s Šamaš-šum-līšir Ilē'i-Marduk,[74] whose activities were managed by his mother during a long minority which lasted at least from Dar 8 until Dar 19.

In such a situation execution contracts were inevitable. Some, as is always to be expected in exceptional circumstances, contain unique, specified information. In the *epišānūtu* contract BM 42424 (11 III Dar 8) for in toto 10 days of a brewers prebend the executor had to deliver to the owner a specified, and for ten days considerable, *pappasu* of 8 kor of dates and 2.2.3 kor of barley. Of special interest is line 12: the executor is also responsible for the *šu-gar-ru-ú šá* ^{LU_2}SANGA *Sip-par*^{KI}. This suggests an obligation of a prebendary towards the *šangû* as the head of his institution, but whether this was a standard obligation is questionable. The *šugarrû* seems to have consisted of dates,[75] and dates were not the basic raw material required by a prebendal brewer, though they could be included in his *pappasu*.

Especially when prebends were used as collaterals in antichretic transactions the income aspect prevailed over the obligations. The father of Nidinti-Marduk had already given a brewer's prebend in the Šamaš temple as an antichretic security, BM 42354, date lost. Characteristically the debt incurred by Nidintu-Marduk himself in BM 42302 (x x Dar 19) was the consequence of an *ilku* obligation resulting in service in Elam.[76] The nature of the prebend in Ebabbar involved is not even specified, only its income amounting to (lines 4-5) 3 SILA$_3$ "sustenance" (SUKU$_6$.ḪA$_2$), 12 *takkasû*-cakes, 3 SILA$_3$ of beer, with monthly two portions (*pi-i-ri*) of meat and (directly linked to them) two pieces/shares of *makkasu* being mentioned.

---

[73] Possible explanation Jursa 1999 p. 79.

[74] On his prebends especially Jursa 1999 p. 85.

[75] CAD Š/3 p. 197-8, where *šugarrû* is a "a type or processed form of dates", specified in the discussion as a sweet product made from dates. Perhaps the meaning of *š.* could be expanded to indicate a "sweetener" in a wider sense. It could be paid in silver.

[76] For other service obligations in the same year see BM 79128, 2 IV Dar 19. Taxation obligations of the prebendaries will be discussed in Part III, Taxation, Chapter VI.

This poses the problem of what the (three) $SILA_3$ $SUKU_6$.$ḪA_2$, which appear especially in Sippar texts, represented.[77] If these are parallel to the three $SILA_3$ of beer they could specifically indicate the standard amount of bread, which for me together with the beer constitute the basic indicator of the value of the prebend, especially that of *ērib bīti* status. Could this mean that the three $SILA_3$ was delivered in the form of the twelve *takkasû* mentioned next? One *takkasû* would represent a quarter of a "litre".[78] Expanded by $^{UZU}UR_3$ a similar set of income from an unspecified prebend occurs in BM 42348 (22 IV Dar 34) as a security for the *nudunnu* of a wife. Line 8 could read [3 $SILA_3$ NINDA/$SUKU_6$].$ḪA_2$ *ù* 3 $SILA_3$ KAŠ.SAG 2 *pi-ra-a-ni šá* UZU *ù ma-ak-ka-su*,[79] followed by (one?) $^{UZU}UR_3$. This would again be a standard amount, and such standard amounts strongly suggest *ērib bīti* status. It is sometimes difficult to understand the exact nature of the antichretic arrangement: if the tasks are included we are dealing with a particular type of execution agreement, if not, the income has become, at least in this instance, separated from the tasks. It is, however, not difficult to imagine that transferring the tasks of a purveying prebend would be easier than those of a prebend requiring special skills of an intellectual nature, and special initiation, though such temporary transfers occurred in practice.

This is the case in another rather special prebendal execution contract involving Nidintu-Marduk: BM 42408 (27 XIIb Dar 13). It concerns, following Jursa's translation: "the income of the function of incantation-prebendary (*zabarūtu*, written phonetically) and of observation of the liver[80] of the sheep belonging to the regular offerings and the *guqqû* of the *akītu* and the monthly *kiskirru*(?)-assignments of Šamaš of the *bit ridūti*, with the vegetables and the *gi-pu-ú*[81] and sheep offered by the ordinary believers". The yield amounted to 5 *š*. Though the text is not without its problems, we can be certain that though prebendal execution agreements other than those for the "purveying trades" are rare, this is one. The occasions mentioned do, possibly, not belong to the daily cult, the *akītu* and a special account, *kiskirru*, associated with a god Sin of the *bīt ridūti*[82] being mentioned.

7. Other cases of standard specification of prebendal income

The Nappāḫu inheritance division discussed above mentioned two instances of standard prebendal income: four $SILA_3$ of bread and beer (and a sheep) on the occasion of an eclipse,

---

77 H. Bongenaar suggests the possibility that the use of $SUKU_6$ intends to leave open the possibility of payment in either barley or dates, or "any food". This seems reasonable, though beer is paralleled by bread when standard *ērib bīti* emoluments are involved. Paying in the form of an equal amount of dates would imply a reduction of the value of the income, the actual value of comparable amounts of dates being lower than of barley, even though the commodities are regularly treated as equivalent in administrative texts.

78 A constant difficulty with texts summing up prebendal income is the permanent uncertainty whether the list is merely summing up or also contains specifications of what is listed in the form of an apposition to a previous term.

79 The combination of 2 *pi-ri šá* UZU and 2 *ma-ak-ka-su* as a collateral also occurs in BM 42508 (date lost, month III) line 18', another case of use of income as an antichretic security. For the meaning of the correspondence of the numbers see below.

80 For this problematic translation cf. Jursa's comments. This occurrence of *kiskirru* is rather uncertain. Note that the partial payment is still received by the mother, and not by the son. In contracts the person who obliges himself to do or to deliver something regularly acts as a scribe. This is not wholly excluded in this case, especially as the document is also a partial receipt. But that makes it unlikely that the text belonged to the holdings of the scribe. There is a minor problem in this.

81 Possibly refers to dates.

82 This would possibly represent a rare instance of a prebendal right in connection with a palace god, but, as stated, the reading of *kiskirru* is not completely certain.

presumably of the moon, before Sin, and three SILA$_3$ of bread and beer before Išḫara, presumably on principle on a daily basis. Comparable standard amounts occur in the Bēl-rēmanni and Nidintu-Marduk texts, where NINDA, bread, is sometimes replaced by SUKU$_6$, *kurummatu*, "sustenance". In neither of the Nappāḫu cases the function exercised is specified, though there is the possibility that the Išḫara prebend intended was a brewery one. This is one of the purveying trades, where usually *pappasu* is given as a remuneration and not the bread and beer, primarily indicative of *ērib bīti* status. This is a problem, but it may be a result of, again, what is developing into several separate prebends in a small sanctuaries context still being subsumed under one term.

The question is whether an income, consisting of a fixed, possibly standard, amount of bread and beer, is to be regarded as the basic allowance of an *ērib bīti*. In a number of cases private documents specify the amount of bread and beer due as that of an *ērib bīti*, as we will see, and in the early Neo-Babylonian *kudurrus* the income assigned in a similar manner is related to that of a (basic) *ērib bīti*. Perhaps we could consider the possibility that for bread and beer deriving from the offerings, functions were graded according to the number of basic *ērib bīti* portions they received. Such a procedure was, of course, less feasible for meat portions, as these are less easily standardised and were handed out according to the prestige attached to the piece, although there existed terms like *mākālu* and *pīru*, which are likely to refer to meat portions which were obviously considered to be equivalent without the cut being specified.[83] There are a number of texts mentioning such "standards". Some of the texts containing these statements date to the earlier Neo-Babylonian period, others come from late in the reign of Darius.

The publication by C. Waerzeggers of the Ṣāḫit-ginê/Marduk-rēmanni archive increases the number of examples from Sippar. There are several *ērib bīti* prebends represented by the equal income in bread and beer we are inquiring after. There is 6 SILA$_3$ of each for the ziqqurrat in text no. 8, which possibly represents a complete prebend, also as it had been assigned in the past to Marduk-rēmanni's grandmother as equivalent to no less than 10 minas of silver. In text no. 121, together with a separate meat portion from a doorkeepers prebend (cf. also no. 155), an *ērib bīti* prebend for Šarrat-Sippar is rated at 3 SILA$_3$ and mentioned as a security for 4 mina 20 *š* of silver, but the amounts mentioned are qualified as (7) ḪA.LA *is-qu*, and represent therefore inevitably not the complete income. The same amount with two portion of meat before Šamaš is mentioned in a lease document (no. 157) mentioning a sub-lease for 16 š per annum plus 0.0.3 in dates.

From Dilbat we have JCS 36 no. 19, (14 I Kand 18, identical with OECT 10, 398), a sale which restored old family property to the family of the original owners. In this case the bread and the beer are the only specified elements of a long list: *isqu* ^{LU_2}KU$_4$.E$_2$-*ú-tu ina* E$_2$ Imbianum, the sanctuary of Uraš and Bēlet-Ekalli: 0.0.1 NINDA.ḪA$_2$ 0.0.1 KAŠ.ḪA$_2$ 3) NINDA.<I$_3$.>DE$_2$.A *ku-šip-pe-ti* KAŠ.<U$_2$.>SA$_2$ SIG$_5$-*ti* UZU KU$_6$ 4) *ár-qa šu-gar-ru-ú gi-nu-ú šà-gi-guru$_6$-ú* 5) *par-ṣe* E$_2$.A.NI *ir-bi šu-ru-ub-ti* E$_2$.KUR *ma-la ba-šu-ú*[84] 6) SUKU$_6$.ḪA$_2$ *maš-ša-ak-ti ù mim-ma* ḪA.LA ^{LU_2}KU$_4$-*ú-tu*, "one *sūtu* of bread and one *sūtu* of beer, *mirsu*, "flat bread", good *billatu*,

[83] According to CAD M/1 p. 387 *maššaktu* is "a kind of payment as income from a prebend". That *maššaktu* refers to income in the form of meat portions was already suggested by MacGinnis 1991-2 p. 75, by Bongenaar, 1997 p. 104 in connection with the king's share, and by Jursa, Iraq 59, 1997 p. 122 *ad* Birmingham no. 39. Note that the text quoted here differs from other occurrences in suggesting that *m.* refers to pieces of beef only, but this is not confirmed by other occurrences, least of all Gordon, Smith College, 90, where the term includes meat of oxen and sheep and also fowl.

[84] This phrase could suggest a tax based form of income, of the type called *gimir* in the Edict of Belsazzar for a "governor", for measurers, gate keepers or scribes. We will not pursue the matter in detail, but see below.

meat and fish, vegetables, (processed) dates, of the ordinary and voluntary ritual offerings in the temple and of what comes or is brought into the sanctuary,[85] as much as there is, sustenance and *maššaktu*, any share pertaining to the status of being an *ērib bīti*". This can be compared directly with what is found in the *kudurrus*. As befits the importance of the temple of Uraš the basic rate is one *sūtu*.

Much later, but also from Dilbat, is VS 5, 108, (11 VI Dar 35), an exchange carried out by the *šatammu* in which a prebend belonging to the sanctuary of Bēlet-Ekalli amounting to the share of one *ērib bīti*, (15) returned to the temple, formed an element. It amounted to two $SILA_3$ of bread and of beer, the status of the goddess, though the wife of Uraš, being rated lower than is the case in JCS 36 no. 19 with her spouce.

In Sippar we can refer to CT 55, 70 (7 X Dar 32!), where Bēl-uballiṭ s Iqīša Eppeš-ili, a known *kutimmu*[86], leased his rights of, significantly, 0.0.1 of bread and beer plus five *pi-i-ri šá* UZU!, "five cuts of meat" *ù ma-ak-ka-su* per month before Šamaš to another person for 33 *š* of silver per annum. I understand lines 12-5 in such a manner that the owner guaranteed the lessee the delivery by the temple of the food listed, if that stopped the lessee would inform the lessor, who had to indemnify the lessee.[87] Note that in line 19 the food is characterised as $SUKU_6$.ḪA_2, *kurummatu*, which is not the usual prebendal term. This Eppeš-ili branch was, however, certainly a prebendal family. The standard amounts of bread and beer suggest, if the theory proposed here is correct, *ērib bīti* status, which is not impossible on the basis of the available evidence on the *kutimmu*.[88]

BM 74550, Bertin 2720-1 (12 VI Dar 33) is quoted Jursa 1999 p. 66. It is a combined antichretic lease of a slaughterer's and a gatekeeper's prebend of respectively 21 and 20 days before Šamaš and of an unspecified function in the temple of Gula. Before both Šamaš and Gula there are rights to bread and beer, in total nine $SILA_3$ of each[89] before Šamaš, with 6 *pi-i-ri* of meat and *makkasu*[90] plus two specified cuts per annum and also three $SILA_3$ of bread(!) and beer

---

[85] This clause could suggest a connection with the *māditu*-prebend, discussed below, Chapter IV.

[86] Bongenaar, 1997 p. 386.

[87] In lines 12-3 perhaps *pu-ut ba-aṭ-lu šá ši-*[*-i-ri*?] 13) *ù*(!) *tak-ka-su-ú*, but I cannot find an exact parallel. Note that line 3 mentions *makkasu* and line 13 has *takkasû*, "bakery products", after an incomplete *ù*? (text: ŠI). The writing with long u of *takkasû* discourages emendation. After *pīru* in line 3 *makkasu* will indicate off-cuts of meat. This is a minor problem. I have no solution for line 11, which must describe another obligation.

[88] Uncertain in several respects is BM 77929, Bertin 2187, (17 IX Dar 19). It is an *epišānūtu* contract for a prebend in Ebabbar, according to Jursa 1999 p. 50 note 178 that of slaughterer, belonging to Iqīša s Marduk-šum-uṣur, presumably the father of our Bēl-uballiṭ. Tentatively I would suggest that MacGinnis 1991-2 no. 10 (x XII Dar x) also refers to our Iqīša-Marduk s [Marduk-šum-uṣur] Eppeš-ili, father of, in this case Bēl-bulissu, who was adopted by [Bēl-uballiṭ] s [x x-]DU Rabā-ša-Ninurta and received an *ērib bīti* prebend before Šamaš of which the income was specified in lines 6-8, with the stipulation that he was not liable for debts of the adopter (lines 10-11). There may be talk of land and *kurummatu* granted by Iqīša-Marduk to Bēl-uballiṭ.

[89] This might suggest a division into one share of a *sūtu* and another of half a *sūtu*, five and four or seven and two $SILA_3$ being unlikely, as five and seven $SILA_3$ do not seem to occur as appropriations. The *šūtu* with its six $SILA_3$s might correspond to the meat portions, but this is speculation. The doorkeeper's prebend was probably the least important.

[90] Jursa suggests attractively that a cut of meat is intended in this context, and proposes that it represents the ("vulgar continental") Austrian "Schnitzel", taken, if I am well-informed, from the rump. I do not want to follow him in this respect, as the rump will be one of the prime *pīrus*, but think rather of unspecified off-cuts, belonging to the equally unspecified main cut indicated by the term *pīru*. But in proposing this I must eliminate BE 8/1 153:4 with its 1-*en ma-ak-ka-su*. This difficulty can be transferred easily to the *makkasu* of dates, which are combinable with *kusipētu*. Possibly *pīru* and *makkasu* constitute a fixed

before Gula, plus unspecified meat, cooked or not. If our theory concerning fixed daily rations in bread were correct this would again mean that these prebends had *ērib bīti* status, which is not strictly attested otherwise. The slaughter's prebend possibly had a special status regarding bread and beer. The possibility of local particularities must, of course, remain open.

From Uruk, and again early in the period, we have von Weiher, SpBT IV 221 (AUWE 12, 6 IX Nbp 0, as "King of Akkad"). The text involves again an *ērib bīti* prebend, this time explicitly belonging to E_2 (family of) Ea-kurbanni, in the sanctuary of Inanna-Uruk and Nanāia. It amounts to 3 $SILA_3$ of bread and 3 $SILA_3$ of beer, vegetables, *makkasu*-dates, the regular and (regular-) additional offerings of the king and the believers *ki-i pi-i* 1-*en* $^{LU_2}KU_4.E_2$ Eanna, "as pertains to one *ērib bīti* of Eanna" (lines 1-6). The explicit link to a specific family must have had a meaning, to all likelihood related to the modalities of the institution of the function, but this family is not among those belonging to the *ērib bīti* group listed in VS 15, 1. The passage can at any rate serve to strengthen the idea that there is a link between a family -and thus probably also certain types of land holding- and prebendal status. The early date of the text may be significant.

8. The problem of the Neo-Babylonian *ērib bīti*

Especially OLA 21 no. 4. suggests that in the Old Babylonian period the *ērib bīti*s formed, at any rate in the Anunnītu sanctuary in Sippar, one of the groups of prebendaries which had, it would seem, like the GALAs and the $GUDU_4$s, a fixed number of members. Their tasks remain, however, unspecified.

Though the texts quoted in the previous section are not numerous, it is notable that in some cases they refer in a rather neutral fashion to the status of an *ērib bīti, what* the function implies is not specified. What exactly an *ērib bīti* was, has regularly come under discussion: "someone who was allowed to enter (all parts of) the temple" is now generally accepted. That this right of entry was the core of the function, is not the problem, but whether this "right" existed independently from a specific task and proficiency, which, at least some of the bearers of the title definitely possessed, has not been considered adequately. It is at any rate certain that not all who belonged to the institutions and carried out work of the type certain *ērib bīti*s executed, were *ērib bīti*s. Distinguishing those who were from those who were not, therefore anyhow made sense. That the distinctions appropriate to the function were of a visible nature transpires from a fragment dating to the Hellenistic period dealing with clothing prescriptions. We might assume that the *kalû*, the "lamentation-reciter" belonged to the cultic functionaries who had to enter the sanctuary. The text makes clear, however, for this "cultic" profession, that those who were *gullubu*, "shaven/initiated", possibly in itself something permanently visible, were dressed differently from those who were not.[91]

Bongenaar has formulated his ideas on *ērib bīti*s in the following manner[92]: the term does not mean more than that the person concerned owned an *ērib bīti* prebend which implied duties of a cultic nature and that he was eligible for the higher functions reserved for those

---

sequence, with equal numbers of both, for which *pīru* can stand on its own. Whether the (meat) *makkasu* can, is another question.

91 Falkenstein 1959, p. 40 lines 10'-11'. It is of some importance that brewers, bakers and slaughterers, together with persons indicated as $^{LU_2}SIG_2$.BAR.RA, ^{LU_2}ŠU.BAR.RA and $^{LU_2}GIR_3.SE_3$-*qí* were dressed similarly to the uninitiated *kalû*'s, probably indicating, again, that they did not belong to the *ērib bīti*s. Who are intended by SIG_2.BAR.RA and ŠU.BAR.RA is not clear, translating ŠU.BAR.RA with "freedmen" does not help, for this category of people as such does not play a role of any note in the Neo-Babylonian period texts. Especially for the position of the slaughterers their mention in this context is probably decisive: they do not normally belong to the *ērib bīti*s.

92 Bongenaar 1997 p. 158-9.

working within the institution. At least some *ērib bītis* were craftsmen with cult related tasks, while other ritualists played prominent roles in cultic acts without being called explicitly an *ērib bīti*, for example, some *kalû*s or the *kurgarrû*s in the cult of Ištar. This does not answer the question whether a person could be an *ērib bīti* with only a(n unspecified) cult related (so to say "unskilled") function, although it seems that anybody exercising a specific, skilled, cultic function and being an *ērib bīti* could be indicated by that title only. The question whether one had to exercise some specific occupation with a meaning in the cult in order to be an *ērib bīti* remains.

Kümmel[93] did not even dedicate a separate section to the *ērib bīti*, but proposed the general translation "Kultpersonal", which might suggest that he was confronted with similar problems. Texts like the Uruk meat text,[94] mention the *ērib bītis* as a group as receivers generally several times per specific type of sacrificial animal, e.g. lines 4, 5, 8 and 18 in the section dealing with the assumed ox. But next to them occur special categories of prebendaries whom we might expect to have been of *ērib bīti* status, e.g. the *kalû* (line 12) and perhaps the *mubannû* (line 9). In the end this type of text does not decide in favour of the existence of *ērib bītis* without a special occupation, if only because a specified cut of meat could always have been assigned to a particular section of persons or to an individual.[95] The meat text mentions none of the craft sections of which we know with reasonable certainty that specific members could belong to the *ērib bītis*, thus exactly they are likely to have been covered by the term *ērib bīti* used by the text. Whether VS 15, no. 1[96] goes back to an earlier original or represents only later speculation on the "original" prebendal families must remain an open question, but there are no "mere" *ērib bīti* families listed in this text, all exercise some specific function besides belonging to the category being discussed. But the E_2 of Ea-kurbanni of SpBT IV 221 is not included, as noted already.

The tentative conclusion could be that an *ērib bīti* always exercised some (other) specific function which was regarded as essential for the execution of the immediate cult of the gods, and that the title represented primarily a status, not an occupation. The status was the result of an initiation of the type described by the text published by Borger, which allowed entry to the presence of the gods.[97] We can assume that it included "ritualists" like the *āšipu* and the *kalû*, various craftsmen who had to maintain the sanctuary and the trappings needed for the cult, and perhaps those who placed their meal before the gods, but only those who had been specifically initiated. It is almost inevitable that the higher ranks of the institutional personnel had to belong to this group. In this, the "small sanctuary prebend" plays a role of its own. It comprised a range of practical tasks, of which a number could be hived off, and it could possibly be called *ērib bīti* DN, though *šangû* equally seems to be possible. The term could be used in a general, unspecified, manner.

Yet this is not completely satisfactory. TCL 9 137, a letter of Belsazzar to Nabû-šar-uṣur, the *qêpu* of Eanna, gives the following order: 8) 10 $ERIN_2$.MEŠ KU_4.E_2 9) ^{LU_2}AB.BA.MEŠ 10) *šá mil-ki*[98] 11) *šá la man-zal-ti-šú-nu* 12) *it-ti-ka* 13) *ab-ka*, "(come,) bring with you ten *ērib*

---

93 Kümmel 1979 p.164.

94 McEwan 1983, see above.

95 There are more functions in the same position: *šešgallu/aḫu rabû*, *šatammu*, *kalû*, *narû*. They almost inevitably were of *ērib bīti* status. On *mubannû* cf. the remarks below, mainly based on BM 79116, Jursa 1999, p. 250-1.

96 Cf. Bongenaar 1997, p. 158, with note 181 on previous literature, cf. especially Kümmel 1979 p.157-8.

97 Borger 1973.

98 The problem would change in nature if we could read *iš-qí* in stead of the rather insipid *mil-ki* (obviously accepted CAD M/1 p 229 R) and translate: "elderly men who have a prebendal share but no

bītis, older men with experience who have no position". This could suggest that it was possible to have undergone the initiation but not to possess a position in the cult. Perhaps we have here an example of the problem of clergy without benefice, not unknown in the European Middle Ages. But we must also consider the possibility that Belsazzar simply did not want to risk interruption to the cult and asked for people who were not required for actual service at the moment intended. *manzaltu* indicates after all the practical obligation to perform service.

Concerning the earlier Old Babylonian *ērib bīti* little more can be said than that the function existed as the title of a specific group of people belonging to the clergy, that it is a title assigned to witnesses and that as an inheritable function it occurs in one document. That text indicates fragmentation of the function and thus a sharing of one position of this status by a number of persons. In itself that could suggest that it was a separate function.

9. Rights to income and their relation to tasks

A number of documents suggests that rights to meat portions on occasion had a particular status which made them salable, loose from further obligations. A loosening of the ties between income and tasks is suggested by texts in which the *ebūru* of prebends was used as a mere right to income, which could, for instance, be handed over as a collateral,[99] and by a small group of Hellenistic texts phrased like prebend sales in which rights to *kurummatu* were sold without any reference to the tasks for which the income had been granted originally.[100] But we must constantly remind ourselves that even if a certain type of income derives from material belonging to the offerings to the gods, that does not imply that it was prebendal income in the sense in which that is defined here.

This is definitely to be considered in the case of a group of texts informing us on a branch of the Ea-eppeš-ili family edited by Joannès[101]. VS 4, 89 (22 X Dar 1) is obviously an antichretic lease of cuts of meat before the statue of Bēl in the temple of Ninurta on three specified days: 8) .... *ebūr is-qu* 9) *ù* UR_5.RA *kaspi iānu*. The use of the word *isqu* suggests the prebendal nature of the income, which seems to be completely divorced from its obligations in this case. What matters is only the income. But Joannès no. 13 (13 II Dar I 32) is a receipt for 8 *maš-šak-tu*$_4$ GU_4 110 UZU.UDU.ḪA_2 between IV yr. 30 and III yr. 32 which constituted the $SUKU_6$.ḪA_2 *šarri* before the same statue, to which we probably can connect also VS 6, 162 (5 V Dar 34), another receipt for meat belonging to the *kurummat šarri* 1) *šá* UDU.$NITA_2$ 2) *šá gu-uq-qa-ni-e* UZU *šá* GU_4 3) x[102] to end IV yr. 34. In these cases the meat portions were tradable goods not belonging to the prebendal income of the family, the king probably selling his meat portions through the givers of the receipts, who acted as intermediaries. The receivers of the receipts, probably prebendaries belonging to the Ea-eppeš-ili family, were the direct dealers.

Yet Joannès no. 3 (3+ IX Dar 9?) illustrates that there was no complete division of the various types of prebendal income even in the case of this family. It is a receipt for barley

---

part in the execution of the cult", *išqu* for *isqu* is, however, Assyrian, and as such unacceptable in this letter.

99 Further examples of prebends used as collaterals, see already above under Bēl-rēmanni and Nidintu-Marduk, and e.g. VS 4, 101 (25 VI Dar 5, Borsippa, Iliya A); Lee, JCS 39 p. 49 (10 X Camb 6, Iliya B); TCL 12, 15 (9 VI Šmšk 5, Nippur).

100 In a case like MacGinnis AfO 1991-2 p. 69 no. 11 (21 VI Dar 18?) a payment in silver called $BURU_{14}$ *isqišu*, "yield of his prebend", we probably have an example of a payment by one member of a wider family to another through a third person also belonging to this family, for prebendal income which was held jointly. Only further prosopographic details can help.

101 Joannès 1980. To the here relevant texts of this group belong also VS 4, 89 and 6, 162.

102 A reading u GEŠTIN of this sign or these two signs makes no sense and we must be dealing with meat portions.

representing the value of the bread,[103] the beer, the meat and the *makkasu* going with it, the SUKU$_6$.ḪA$_2$ *isqi* of PN1 and PN2 before the statue already mentioned between III yr. 4 and VII yr. 6. The payment was made by the holders of the prebend to someone who is called a *sepīru*, but the barley paid came from the grain store of Esagil. The explanation is possibly that the *sepīru* somehow acted as the executor of the obligations. That would be problematic, for the *sepīrus* are even less prebendal than the ordinary scribes.

MacGinnis 1991-2 no. 11 (21 VI Dar 19[+]) is a payment in silver for the yield,[104] of "his" prebend. It is received by the son of the owner from what must be an executor. The arrangement had run for over two and a half years, and there is no trace of the obligations, but this is rather a matter of execution than of dissociating obligation and income.

The Hellenistic prebend-type sales of *kurummatu* without reference to obligations have been discussed by McEwan.[105] At most these texts suggest that it was possible to treat obligations and income as if these were separate entities, but the total evidence is after all not impressive. Obligations remained generally attached to rights.

10. Rights to income in the earlier period

References to meat portions belonging to prebendal income before the Neo-Babylonian period are rare, as McEwan has noted.[106] This is partially the result of the fact that the Old Babylonian private documents never specify the emoluments pertaining to the prebendal functions and that there is no set of contemporary documents for meat-portions comparable to Sigrist's *sattukku* texts on bread. There is, however no reason to assume that in the earlier period all meat from offerings was destroyed and thus was not available for consumption. Edzard, Tell ed-Dēr 104 and, less so, 105,[107] should at least be sufficient in this respect.[108]

Luckily we are somewhat better informed on what happened to the non-bloody offerings in the earlier periods. Sigrist (1984) has made available evidence from the Old Babylonian texts found in the area of the Ištar temple in Nippur which probably originated in the Ninurta temple and which were removed with surrounding material during Parthian levelling operations. The correctness of the assumption is supported by a small text published by Civil as OIC 22 no. 9, which states that respectively from 1 III and 1 IV Ḫ 34 onwards 5 SILA$_3$ of bread was assigned as sustenance to two potters. According to lines 3-4 and 11 this was KU$_5$.DA/ SA$_2$.DUG$_4$ NINDA ^{d}NIN.URTA.KE$_4$ "cut off from the *sattukku* bread of Ninurta". This is no doubt a kind of standing arrangement through which sustenance for individual workers was arranged. Sigrist's *sattukku* texts are, as to their reverse, which deals with the reapportioning of bread from offerings, the gross lists summarising such individual assignments.[109] The OIC text and Sigrist's texts underline that being provided with material from offerings is not a prebendal privilege. Only

---

103 Preferring the reading NINDA over SUKU$_6$ with the comparable VS 5, 72, against Strasbourg 132.

104 BURU$_{14}$, MacGinnis explains "usufruct", but in a case in which an owner would have pledged his prebend he would not have received the income.

105 McEwan 1981 p. 136ff.

106 McEwan 1983 p. 187.

107 F. van Koppen refers me to the more relevant CT 2, 43: 9) 2 *mi-še-er-tim* UZU ŠU.TI.A PN 10) *ša ša-ta-mu-ti-šu ša* E$_2$.^{d}UTU. Cf. CAD M/2 p.119. Like *malaku*, *mišertu* represents a standard sized portion of meat in the Old Babylonian period, comparable to *maššaktu* or *pīru* in the Neo-Babylonian period. These are not specific cuts, but portions deemed to be of a standard value.

108 For Assyria, and much later, cf. Ebeling 1954 text IV.

109 OIC 22 no. 10, referring to work for Ninurta, has probably a similar background, but deals with an occasional task. It is of interest, as it not only assigns bread but also two *ma-la-kum* UDU per day for a specific period. On the implications of the text cf. Charpin 1986, p. 323: this is to all probability also material deriving from sacrifices.

other texts explicit on this point can determine the prebendal status of someone receiving the bread or otherwise. Such documents are the prebendal sale and inheritance documents of the Old Babylonian period, in particular those from Nippur to be discussed below. But these texts cannot be regarded as guaranteeing that the functionaries in *sattukku* texts were prebendaries.

Two other important texts from Nippur, both from the 21st year of Rim-Sin,[110] do also not differentiate between what were to become our prebendaries and other personnel of rank. The tabulated texts deal with cattle, and sparingly, sometimes with beef,[111] and sheep assigned to persons of rank. We can suppose that the central organisation in Nippur provided animals and meat, and that, as in the *sattukku* texts, there is as yet no differentiation between prebendaries and others.

Strictly spoken we have no means of deciding whether comparable material from earlier periods, specifically Ur III, really refers to prebendaries proper, but if general circumstances are comparable, texts on the allocation of foodstuffs within sanctuaries can possibly indicate the existence or the coming into being of a comparable group of people. That "clerical"[112] functions were on principle transmitted from father to son is plausible, if not actually certain. The case of the Inanna temple in Nippur is the best example available. Among the texts from the temple there is a highly suggestive document[113] dealing with the allocation of bread and beer. As bread, and not barley or even flour are distributed by the ŠABRA of Inanna, the assumption that this bread constitutes "left-overs" of the cult seems reasonable. We can only compare the functions of the receivers with known Old Babylonian prebendal functions in Nippur, but the overlap is limited. At least the GALA,[114] the NU.EŠ$_3$.BUR.ŠU.MA, the SANGA, and the brewer would probably qualify immediately, but the A.U$_3$.A, almost certainly a type of singer, the ^{LU_2}MAḪ, "exstatic", perhaps the MUŠ.LAḪ$_4$, "snake charmer", and the GAL.NAR, "chief singer", can be added with some confidence to this group. There are amongst them people whom we can consider as (potential) prebendaries.

11. The Neo-Babylonian *maššartu-pappasu* system

In the Neo-Babylonian period a system of remuneration of certain prebendaries is attested which is not easily paralleled by earlier texts: it is widely accepted that especially bakers and brewers were, at least partially, remunerated by providing them with the raw material for the ingredients they required for their obligatory deliveries of prepared foodstuffs, in such a manner that they found the recompensation they required in the form of surplus ingredients, from which also costs had to be paid. We call this the "*maššartu-pappasu*-system" of remuneration. Its existence is demonstrated by administrative material from both Uruk and Sippar, but it is not found in private documents other than in arrangements regarding the execution of duties by others than the holder of the rights. There the terms *sattukku* and *pappasu* occur regularly, but *maššartu* is notably rare even there.

The matter has been formulated succinctly by Bongenaar[115] : *sattukku* + *pappasu* = *maššartu*, in which *sattukku* is the raw material required for the preparation of the offerings and the *pappasu* the additional remuneration. The two together were often supplied as one amount

---

110 Copies were published by M. Çiğ in Fs. S. Alp, Ankara 1992, p. 93ff. I could use notes on these texts by F.R. Kraus and M. Stol.

111 Ni 2436 uses *ma-la-kum* GUD UDU, cuts/portions of beef and mutton in the heading.

112 In the sense of Charpin's "clergé".

113 Zettler 1992 6 NT 364, 17 VI IS 6. This is a one day routine document of which several parallels remain unpublished, cf. p. 194 of Zettler's text.

114 On evidence for some form of initiation in the early period see above.

115 Bongenaar 1997 p. 143. That this formula is sometimes a little too simplistic has been argued by Jursa, 1999, p. 48.

called *maššartu*.[116] That *pappasu* had a purpose differing from *sattukku* is especially clear in those cases where the *pappasu* consists of material which could not be used by the receiver to fulfil his obligations, e.g. dates handed over to prebendal brewers, who were only allowed to provide beer brewed from cereals for the gods. That *pappasu* was treated in a different manner from *sattukku* when provided to prebendaries is beyond doubt, but one of the two had to contain an element covering the costs. It is clear that a part of the *sattukku* also ultimately ended up in the pockets of the owner of the prebend.

Perhaps we underrate the problems involved in turning the raw material provided into ready ingredients: that entailed especially labour costs, which could be expressed in food. Time and again prebendal bakers were supplied with, especially, barley. Before they could bake their bread milling was necessary, a laborious process, unlikely to be undertaken by the prebendary himself. The unease about the matter is fuelled by the fact that earlier on, notably in the Ur III Nippur Inanna archive, that is in the only archive which deals with the internal workings of a not too big institution, there is a special category of personnel indicated as *sattukku*-millers, or in a wider sense as "personnel for preparing ingredients for the *sattukkus*, the *guqqûs* and the feasts.[117] The possibility that *pappasu* was being handed out partially for wage costs deserves consideration.[118] On the other hand persons accepting the lease of the type of prebend concerned were willing to hand over the *pappasu* with an additional amount, for instance one kor, of barley to the owner, a clear sign that additional gain derived from the *sattukku* part of the *maššartu*, which in consequence had to contain additional material, for instance for covering the costs.

The question is whether a baker or a brewer, to mention only the most important receivers of *pappasu*, received other income similar to that what, especially, the *ērib bītis* received. In the case of the meat portions that fact is easily established, the Uruk meat portion text confirms the fact.[119] But for the (other) non-bloody offerings this is less easy to decide, negative facts being more difficult to establish. It would certainly be too rash to propose that non-*ērib bītis* could never receive equal amounts of bread and beer. We can mention the slaughterers in BM 74550.[120] Possibly a trade which involved no handling of cereals could, like the *ērib bītis*, receive a standard amount of bread and beer. Not all the remnants of offerings in the end went to prebendaries, that a non-*ērib bīti* prebendary could have a share is therefore not strange. Receiving bread and beer is thus not an unmistakable sign of belonging to the *ērib bītis*. There is also the question of the "special accounts" of certain occupations and smaller sanctuaries, which possibly look forward to what can be observed dimly in later Babylon, the administration by the *bēl mindis* of what was due to certain (prebendal) occupations.

---

[116] In some SWU texts *ginû* is used for *sattukku* and combined with *guqqû*, cf. nos. 53 and 91a, *pappasu* is added in no. 34, where *maššartu* occurs to indicate the complete allowance. The importance of the SWU texts is also that, generally at the end of the texts, they explicitly register additional amounts for, for instance, *eššešu* days e.g. no. 32 or 118, *bāiatanu*, no. 35, or the *lilissu* ZABAR, nos. 65, 101 or 104. These special allocations must have been put at the disposal of those having rights to the days concerned.

[117] Zettler 1992, as examples: 6 NT 199+ V 16, $AR_3.AR_3.SA_2.DUG_4.ME$, with female millers in II 21; 6 NT 190+ I 28 $^{GEME}{}_2AR_3.AR_3$ $SA_2.DUG_4$ SIZKUR *ù* EZEN.DIDLI, cf. 6 NT 195 III 10'. In 4 NT 213 II 5 more comprehensively $GIR_3.SE_3.GA$ $SA_2.DUG_4$ GUG.GA.NA *ù* EZEN.DIDLI.ME, incidentally the same sequence of occasions which in later texts indicates the occasions resulting in entitlements of prebendaries. Female millers also occur in sections of the Kingsbury text.

[118] As Bongenaar suggested already in relation to the textile craftsmen, 1997 p. 311.

[119] McEwan 1983, lines 14, 16, cf. 38 and 39, 64-65, and 81, only the brewers.

[120] We must also mention SWU 117, 14', where it is acceptable that we are dealing with a brewer. Whether a *mubannû* was a "purveyor" or not, will be discussed below.

12. Trends in income[121]

We cannot usefully establish the prices of prebends, but the practical value of the ordinary functions can up to a degree be discussed, as far as the basic amounts issued are concerned. It is not possible to compare complete remunerations, as only basic amounts of barley (relevant for the Third Millennium and non-prebendal functions suitable for comparison with those of the prebendaries) or bread (Ur III, sometimes in combination with beer, and OB), or bread and beer (Neo-Babylonian) are known as a kind of "standard", to which, we may suppose, other elements were linked pro rata, according to availability. They were not listed in, for instance, documents dealing with funding, as the amounts were related to standards set in barley or bread and beer. Many of the relevant functions were part time only and for the early period prebendal status is often uncertain.

In the Ur III period in "Lagaš" a $GUDU_4$ or a NAR received 2 $SILA_3$ of barley daily, with an EREŠ.DINGIR and a GALA.MAḪ of a minor, let us say "tertiary" god possibly reaching double that amount, a rate which could also be obtained by someone like an *engiṣu* (EN.ME.GI), "cook".

In the Inanna temple in Nippur the GALA received towards the end of the Ur III period one *sūtu* of bread and beer each, we assume per day, in this period 10 $SILA_3$. This will have had a special background, for the ^{LU_2}MAḪ got only two $SILA_3$ of each, the MUŠ.$LAḪ_4$, and for instance the LUNGA, if we may regard him as a prebendary, only one $SILA_3$ of each.[122] This represents, compared to earlier periods an increase in so far as processed food in stead of barley is concerned, but it is nevertheless an increase.

The Nippur *sattukku* texts, which must stand for the Old Babylonian period as a whole, only deal with bread which was shared out according to the relevant $ŠA_3$.BI.TA-sections of the texts. The evidence has been discussed by Sigrist. In practice the useful information on wages is minimal.[123] There are merely fourteen texts with useful information from a period stretching from Lipit-Enlil to Dāmiq-ilišu out of an administrative routine which should have yielded one text per day. This fact is rather important, for it allows us to accept that on certain days of, for whatever reason, greater cultic importance, assignments will have been more substantial. The only Sin-iddinam text available, with its exceptionally high amounts, should therefore be treated with caution.[124] It is also not always completely clear to members of which institution these payments were awarded, but we assume that we are dealing with an institution which was close to the prebendal world, though of the functions mentioned none is explicitly indicated as prebendal. The link with the occupations which we can regard as prebendal with certainty, which in practice means that they occur as prebendal in the texts from the private archives, is not strong. We know that personal factors played also a role.

2 $SILA_3$ is paid to the MUŠ.$LAḪ_4$, the GIR_3.SE_3.GA and the craftsmen, the I_3.DU_8 and the KISAL.LUḪ received 1 or 2 $SILA_3$. For the GALA.MAḪ and the PA.E_2, whom we would regard

[121] As stated, it is not the intention to discuss the question of the value of prebends. For the late period the references given to MacGinnis and Jursa must suffice, at any rate for the moment.

[122] Zettler 1992, 6 NT 364. The Nippur GALA was notably well paid, elsewhere in this period he was a lowly person.

[123] Sigrist 1984, Chapter 5, pp. 155-172, especially relevant are the tables on p. 165 and, less so, p. 168 for the remunerations, p. 158 lists all personnel mentioned and p. 160 contains a proposal on the manner in which to separate the cultic personnel from the administrative and the menial functionaries. A complete synopsis of wages and functions can be found on p. 173. It is sometimes difficult to compare the information contained in the various tables. Of the personnel qualified as cultic the *kalû* and the *narû* occur as prebendaries in the Nippur private documents and the IŠIB does so outside Nippur. Otherwise $PA.E_2$ is a prebendal title in Nippur. The *atû* and the *kisalluḫu* sometimes are prebendaries.

[124] As Sigrist 1984 p. 165 indicates, the Sin-iddinam text is exceptional on this account.

at first sight as much more important, there is 3 $SILA_3$. The higher wages suggested by the limited information from the reigns of Sin-iddinam and Sin-iqišam can be ignored, as under Damiq-ilišu normal levels returned. In general 6 or 7 $SILA_3$ was attained by IŠIBs, EREŠ.DINGIRs (of not too important gods) and we can perhaps put here the $MAŠ_2$.ŠU.GID_2.GID_2, who occurs with 5 $SILA_3$, but only under Damiq-ilišu. The one *sūtu* mark, or at this moment 10 $SILA_3$, is only available for people like the $ŠA_3$.TAM, still primarily an administrator in this period. Higher paid functionaries have no counterparts in other periods, who can be readily compared.

This is somewhat rough and ready, but it indicates that in the Isin-Larsa period even what could be regarded as relatively important prebendal occupations, like that of GALA.MAḪ, received in bread 1.5 times what in the Ur III period lower ranking "Lagaš" personnel earned in barley, which, however, still makes a difference. The six $SILA_3$ which becomes -in bread plus beer- standard later on for the more important *ērib bītis* is reserved for the few.

In the Neo-Babylonian period the best paid *ērib bīti* received as a kind of standard remuneration one *sūtu* of both bread and beer per day, thus six $SILA_3$ in this period, but lower amounts of four $SILA_3$ and less occur also, as stated already. The amounts are linked to the importance of the sanctuary or god, in the case of a small local establishment an *ērib bīti* could get as little as half a $SILA_3$ of both bread and beer. But the basic remuneration always consisted of both commodities.

If we pass by the problem of the differing status of the various institutions, which influenced the level of "wages" paid, there is a suggestion of relative stability. In the Ur III period persons at $GUDU_4$ level in Lagaš earned no more than an average labourer, $ERIN_2$, some of whom even got more. We can note a difference in the Ur III period between Lagaš and Nippur, and conclude that there is a certain amount of stability from Ur III to Old Babylonian in Nippur, which is not remarkable. Only a Neo-Babylonian prebendary, if he had a complete function, which as a rule he had not, could be much better off, if be belonged to one of the more important sanctuaries. The fact that we do not know what an Old Babylonian $GUDU_4$ or ŠITA, on whom the Sigrist *sattukku* texts are remarkably silent, earned, makes real comparisons difficult, but a *kalamaḫḫu* received no more than two or three $SILA_3$, which is perhaps indicative of a generally low level of remuneration. We must add that a Neo-Babylonian institutional labourer, when working for the *qêpu*, that is presumably on relatively urgent business, earned a kor of barley per month, that is six $SILA_3$ per day, but of unprocessed barley, which had to serve for both his bread and his beer.[125] Of necessity all this remains a low level of comparison.

Yet differences are of a limited nature, there is not an exorbitant rise in income. This is perhaps to be expected in a milieu which basically receives its remuneration in goods which are locally produced and intended for immediate consumption by the receiver. The prebendal income is ostensibly not exposed to the workings of a market.[126]

---

[125] We can ask ourselves whether the six $SILA_3$ of barley constituted the real net wage, for there are texts which indicate that actual food was at least occasionally provided. J. MacGinnis, in a forthcoming article will argue that the workers concerned were predominantly agrarian temple personnel, who would under normal circumstances have received wages or held a sustenance plot. The question of the economic situation of agrarian temple personnel in Sippar is complicated by the fact that Sippar heads of plough teams (often/regularly) had tenancy contracts with the temple. There is a reasonable chance that the wages paid for work on projects came on top of other income.

[126] The growing influence of silver in every day practice is perhaps not so much visible in sale documents as in "leases" of prebends, in which the "owner", regularly a sub-lessor, is paid in silver, though even there the ordinary naturalia remain in evidence. For Sippar cf. Jursa 1999 table on p. 50, where modest sums are involved, but Waerzeggers 2001 includes some texts indicating that silver plays a more important role: no. 80, and less so no. 157. This is a point to be watched.

13. A conclusion regarding remunerations

The use of the words "prebend" and "prebendal" implies here a direct link between a function exercised by an individual and the remuneration he received. As said, especially in the Neo-Babylonian period there is in a number of cases a direct link between the type of remuneration received and the function exercised. This is especially the case with the prebendal bakers and brewers, if, as seems to be the fact, the *maššartu-pappasu*-system contained an element of remuneration. But the functions mentioned do not seem to have been alone in this. The prebendal herdsman who provided milk in Uruk received from the temple cows, with their calves -otherwise the cows would run dry rapidly- as the means of production, in combination with a *širku* for the herding. The direct remuneration also included a cow every four months.[127] We can expect that in other occupations practical arrangements were of a similar order: fulfilling a function implied receiving relevant perks.

Prebendal remuneration probably included, at least, basically, land, but the link between land and the prebendal occupation seems to have become weaker with the passing of time. Documents from private archives do not, as a rule, combine land and function as being both prebendal.

Normal for persons with *ērib bīti* status in the Neo-Babylonian period seems to have been a share in the left-overs of the non-bloody offerings, in which bread and beer (-if the latter really was a left-over and was nor brewed especially-) were specified and constituted a clear sign of status. A *sūtu*, six "litres" in the late period, of both bread and beer was a kind of daily maximum, which was multiplied, in the form of so and so many *ērib bīti* shares for the higher functions. In itself that amount is relatively modest, but it should not be compared in a one to one relation with, for instance, the unprocessed barley in which a journeyman would be paid: that would represent his complete wages.[128] For the prebendaries there was also a share in the bloody offerings, in which the prestige of the piece assigned will have corresponded to the rank of the receiver, even though it would be indicated by a general word like *pīru* and its associated *makkasu*, and it would have to be specified in a separate document sharing out the sacrificial animals in the manner the Uruk text did.

Prebendaries belonging to the "purveying trades" also received a share from the sacrificial animals, the pieces and occasions involved are sometimes specified, but their remuneration in non-bloody foodstuffs was regulated otherwise than for the *ērib bīti*s, especially through the *maššartu-pappasu* system. The remuneration of those not involved with cereals may have been comparable to what the *ērib bīti*s received. Probably for certain functions other sources of remuneration were used, the terms *kiskirru* and *kallānu* being applied, but beyond the fact that these terms imply allocations drawn from some special account, their workings cannot be elucidated with confidence, though we will return to the question.

The sharp outlines suggested initially by an attempt to differentiate between the various categories of prebendaries are in reality blurred and that not only through the combination in one and the same person of rights to income from a range of sources belonging to different categories of functions and by the transfer of rights and tasks to others. The royal endowments found in the *kudurru*s imply that it was the avowed intention that various functions were

---

[127] YOS 7, 79 (12 III Cyr 8).

[128] Some indication of the practical value is provided by a text like Nbn 113 (17 VI Nbn 13) from Sippar where a man is made to promise that he would provide his wife and son with four SILA$_3$ of bread and three of beer daily and annually with 15 minas of wool, 0.1.0 of both sesame and salt and 0.0.5 of cress. Comparable is CT 55, 133 (reign of Cyrus?) for wife (alone?), amount of bread lost, 4 SILA$_3$ of beer, and annually 3 SILA$_3$ of oil, 0.0.2 of salt and 0.0.1 of cress, with a difficult passage on festive days, cf. CAD Š/3 p. 219, *šukkammu*. This could indicate what an ordinary, reasonably well-off family expected.

exercised concurrently by the same person. It would be illogic to assume that such functions would be granted only with the intention to have them turned over at once to privileged specialist executors. All features of the prebendal system conspire to keep outlines blurred.

We will have to accept that the terminology was not used in a sharply defined manner. Prebendal terminology is basically ordinary terminology applied to specific circumstances.

CHAPTER IV
THE PERSONNEL: THOSE INVOLVED

1. Introduction

If we could assume, which we cannot, that the documentation available is at all representative, it would seem that many of the earlier higher functions disappeared, while lower charges were differentiated and assumed a notably "specialist" aspect. This seems to be the case across the whole range of prebendal functions, whether they were of a ritualistic nature, belonged to the purveying trades, or can be regarded as craft specialisations. The first and the last group belonged on principle to those with *ērib bīti* status, the purveying trades had a special position. A kind of intellectual specialisation also played a role in the process. Whether the *ṭupšar enūma-Anu-Enlil*, "astrologer" was, had become, or could be a prebendary in the Hellenistic period remains dubious, though there are indications, notably the existence of a special *bēl mindi* for this occupation, which suggests that the process of funding new specialisations continued into this late period. "Astrologer" was at any rate an inherited function operating within the administrative structure of a sanctuary.[1]

We can assume that the higher clerical functions always implied *ērib bīti* status, if that is taken as a general term for "having access to the sanctuary". The higher clerical titles occur, up to a degree, and intermittently, in royal titles, but whether that had a practical cultic meaning is another question, though it is clear that the kings came regularly into direct ritual contact with the gods, who were in a special sense "their gods".[2] The lexical

---

1 The occupation of astrologer was long a honourable one, and we need not be sensitive about applying the term to Babylonians. The status of the astrologer in Hellenistic Babylon is discussed by Boiy (2000, p. 251), with the conclusion that prebendal status cannot be attributed with complete certainty. The term "prebend" is also avoided in this context by others who use "guild", probably is a loose manner. Their position was at least comparable to that of prebendaries, whom we know of for practical purposes only in Uruk in this period. Especially the existence in Babylon of a *bēl mindi* responsible for their remuneration could be pointed out, parallel to a similar official for, for instance, the brewers. Note also that the astrologers had special allotments, a question already discussed by R. J. van der Spek, Grondbezit in het Seleucidische Rijk, Amsterdam, 1986, p. 99 and Van der Spek 1981 esp. cols. 548ff. There is a "link" of the astrologers with Esagil in the Arsacid period and it had a material basis. Of general interest is Van der Spek's suggestion that "money", silver, became of increasing importance in remunerating these functionaries. Boiy's study makes clear that prebends in Babylon are next to undocumented, but existed, see esp. p. 235. F. Rochberg has restudied the question of the status of the astrologers (Rochberg 2000). On p. 370 she characterises the "link" between temple and astrologer by saying that the astrologer was being "hired" and on p. 371 she considers the meaning for the cult of his contribution and questions priestly status, with a negative conclusion: their lore belongs to "civilisation" in general, as a result of which it entailed remuneration, which I would deem to be a relatively modern, though now sadly rather obsolete, idea. To be remunerated learning will have had to have a perceived practical purpose. So no proof that the *ṭupšar enūma-Anu-Enlil* really was a prebendary, though his remuneration by the temple seems certain.

2 Whether there ever existed a conscious royal long term policy of eliminating or assuming the higher clerical titulature is unlikely, as also functions which are not found at all in royal titulature disappear and *pašīšu* was used as a title by the kings of Akkad long before its "elimination". The titles assumed by kings are: EN, *išippu*, *pašīšu*, *šatammu*, ŠABRA and *šangû*, which occur occasionally, compare Seux

tradition, which will not be discussed, has preserved traces of the titles of the clergy in various old cult centres. Charpin (1986) has described, as far as the material permits, the workings of the local clergy in Ur in the Ḫammurabi era. Some of the functions discussed were administrative, others were primarily status related and indicate "ritual aptness". That means that the actual task was only indicated in a broad manner, GALA and NAR being more easily circumscribed in this respect than ŠITA or $GUDU_4$, for which not for nothing the Akkadian equivalents encompass more Sumerian functions.[3] The focusing on a special task, like brewing, is rare in this period. The limitations of the documentation available must, however, be kept in mind and the conclusion, mainly based on very limited material from Sippar, that a number of the old higher functionaries were no longer active towards the middle Old Babylonian period[4] is probably premature, especially in the light of the Kingsbury text, which indicates a fully active role of functionaries not found any longer in the following sub-period. Not unexpectedly so in view of the scant information available. In the reduction in the variety of higher clerical titles known to us, the disruption of the southern cults in the later Old Babylonian period almost certainly played a predominant role. The real disappearance of many functions will have taken place in the second half of the millennium.

In Nippur the *nešakku* was a rare survival in the Middle-Babylonian period,[5] though the title occurs occasionally later on and elsewhere. Perhaps Nippur retained some of its particularities longer than other towns, though relevant Neo-Babylonian material is scarce.[6] In Neo-Babylonian times some major sanctuaries retained a *šatammu*, an official whose relative importance had obviously increased since the Old Babylonian period, but others, notably Ebabbar in Sippar, were reduced in status by having their *šatammu* replaced by a *šangû*. Here the disappearance of a high ranking function can actually be observed.[7] Where we find a *šatammu* of the main local sanctuary, the function of *šangû* of some of the smaller sanctuaries could be divided among several persons in a manner comparable to

---

1967. But the matter is problematic, cf. the comment in CAD N/1, p. 191R, on Sargon II calling himself $NU.EŠ_3$ Aššur. *šatammu* and *šangû* anyway retained a practical role. The function of EN perhaps survived in some form or another in the late rituals, but not as a special function, as far as we can see. The rituals had probably a multi-layered structure resulting from a long history and the practice of execution knew its own traditions. There is at present not enough material to attempt an historical analysis of the available cultic rituals, but tasks carried out by functionaries of whom the titles disappeared will have been taken over by specific other functionaries. Someone will have acted as the *nadītu* mentioned in the late ritual Çağirgan-Lambert 1991-3, 101.

[3] Cf. AHw. This requires no discussion in the context of the documented prebends.

[4] The later years of Ḫammurabi and the early ones of Samsuiluna, before the information from the South stops and we become virtually dependent on Sippar, as Nippur with its notable variety of titles also ends.

[5] In the Isin II Hinke *kudurru* the *ḫazannu* of Nippur is styled *nešakku* of Enlil and *gudapsû* of Nusku, II 14.

[6] In Nippur in ROMCT II, 37 (15 x Nbn x) there is still a GIŠ.ŠUB.BA $^{LU_2}NU.EŠ_3$-*ú-tú pa-pa-ḫi* ^{d}Ninurta which was transferred to an adopted brother's son. In Borsippa the title occurs in the accumulation of functions listed for one of the protagonists in the text republished by W.G. Lambert JAOS 88, 1968, p. 124-130, preferring a reading *ni-šak-ku* over *ì-šak-ku* in Ib 11 with CAD N/2 p.191L, where other occurrences in earlier *kudurrus* and in inscriptions. Perhaps our documentation on later occurrences of this function is exceptionally restricted.

[7] Bongenaar 1997 p. 6ff. Note that the question also raises that of the relative status of the *šangû* and the royal *qêpu*. Involved are matters of religious policy at the beginning of the reign of Nabopolassar which we do not understand. The loss of the *šatammu* represented a degradation of Sippar in relation to Babylon. On the other hand the earlier BBSt 36 represents itself as the endowment in Sippar of a *šangû* and not as that of a *šatammu*. The question may be more complicated than it seems to be.

what occurred with other, lower, prebendal functions. In Sippar the same was the case under a *šangû* as the head of the main sanctuary.[8] Both earlier and later the local sanctuaries of a town constituted one administrative entity with the principal divine household and its staff at the head, but under the constant supervision of royal officials.[9]

In the late period, excepting *šatammu* or *šangû*,[10] the upper ranks of the later clergy consisted as far as we know only of the *aḫu rabû*[11] and the *kalamaḫḫu*.[12] But these two important clerics, who, though they were present occasionally as witnesses, do not seem to have played a notable administrative role in the late period. They have not left any known private archival material, nor have *šatammu* or *šangû*, but for rare, isolated documents.[13] Neither do we have access to the private archive of a major owner of prebendal functions. What is available stresses the fragmentation of a system, which yet practically and administratively managed to fulfil its task. The question of the actual reconciliation of private fragmentation and the administrative need for an adequate, unified, fulfilment of duties is reserved for the next chapter.

Excepting again the *šatammu* or the *šangû* with their double tasks, the temples had also exchanged their titled administrators of the Ḫammurabi period[14] for just a DUP.SAR E_2-DN. He was replaced, at any rate in Sippar and Uruk, in the course of the Neo-Babylonian

---

[8] We will not deal with the question of high ranking clerical dignitaries occupying important positions in the royal administration outside the temples, for instance that of *šākin ṭēmi*, either in combination with a clerical position or after a career in the "clergy". There is not much material, but the phenomenon is an aspect of the relationship between the king and the upper tier of the urban population, which kings not only had to humour, but also employed.

[9] Whether the temple of Marduk in Babylon constituted, in the later period, a kind of supreme sanctuary for Babylonia could be considered. Together with its immediate satellites, Borsippa, Dilbat, Kiš, Kuta, it served as a kind of paradigm, not only in the "Edict of Belsazzar", but also, for instance, as mentioned, in YOS 6, 10 regarding prebendal payments. The same is valid for the conditions under which outsiders could lease land which the institutional *ikkarus* could not manage, see below. The possibility that gods of other sanctuaries paid a kind of tax to Marduk will be considered elsewhere.

[10] I regard Nabonidus' dedication of his daughter in Ur (YOS I 45 and parallels) as *entu*, or rather as an EREŠ.DINGIR.RA, as something completely anachronistic, as lines 26ff. of the text demonstrate: the king had little idea of what he was doing. The partially archaic terminology used for the accompanying clergy, lines 25-30, covers probably the normal Neo-Babylonian complement. The case should be regarded as a-typical.

[11] According to the colophon of BRM 4, 7 the ŠEŠ.GAL who owned the exemplar copied was both a *mašmaššu* and a *ṭupšar enūma-Anu-Enlil*, Hunger, 1968 sub *urigallu*. BRM 4, 7 is formulated in such a manner that all functions listed must be in one hand, as is, of course, the case in the other comparable colophons where the formulation could be regarded as somewhat ambiguous.

[12] Both were active according to the late (cultic) ritual texts, the *aḫu rabû* regularly, if not daily. For the *kalamaḫḫu* see Falkenstein 1959, obv. 13'. In the same text 5' we also find a ^{LU_2}*mu-uk-kal*, cf. CAD M/2 p. 187, otherwise known there only as an epithet of Nabû. There is every reason not to believe that we know the full complement of the late "ritualists". What is clear, is that in the late period (some) "artisans" had prebendal, even *ērib bīti*, status. But what was the status of those who fulfilled their tasks in the Old Babylonian period and earlier? Did they belong to the $GUDU_4$s? That would seem to be unlikely, for the inscription for Šulgi mentioned above, though strictly spoken uninformative on this point, shows artisans directly in what could be considered to be prebendal positions, without another more comprehensive title being used.

[13] That in the Old Babylonian period the *kalamaḫḫu* Ur-Utu played an important economic role in Sippar in its widest sense seems to be certain, but we remain uncertain whether this concerned private or official undertakings.

[14] Charpin 1986 passim.

period by a group of often four, and rarely more, scribes for whom we must invent a phrase like "college scribe" in order to differentiate them from others. Occasionally they are singled out individually as scribes of, for instance, Ebabbar, but as a group they have no special title.[15] They were supplemented by the *sepīru*, the "Aramaic scribe", though his origins probably must be sought in the entourage of the *qêpu*, that is among the king's men. There arises in our later period a whole number of supervisors appointed by the king, where there was, perhaps, no more than the ZABAR.DAB$_5$ in the Ḫammurabi period.[16] But even he was not a complete outsider in this period, as he could acquire prebendal functions,[17] which is unattested, perhaps unthinkable, for the later *qêpu*s and *bēl piqitti*s, who often had *ša rēš šarri* status, in the Neo-Babylonian sense, and were thus explicitly "the king's men". We can, however, assume that they were paid by the sanctuary to which they were posted, though only for the *qêpu* this can be shown to be actually the case. Though not mentioned in the Edict of Belsazzar itself, it is reasonable to assume that he received payments comparable to those of the functionaries mentioned there.[18] None of these administrators belonged on account of their function to the prebendaries, even though their income derived at least in part from Edict-type income, which also provided for functions we can regard as in a sense prebendal.

Though I would hesitate to regard this development as an unmistakable sign of increased royal influence, as already at least during the Ur III period the king dominated the temple, certainly in an economic sense, it is clear that many earlier high ranking functions disappeared. There was no longer room or a need for the old ENs and EREŠ.DINGIRs. The result is a sign of a change in cultic purpose, which had as a consequence a situation in which the "specialist-artisanal" aspect of the prebendal functions is emphasised. This must not be seen as a decline in the importance of ritual. The reasons need not bother us here. Perhaps the fact that the number of people involved increased also played a role, it will have stimulated differentiation.

2. The Old Babylonian evidence on saleable, inheritable prebends in private archives

The Old Babylonian evidence on these functions predominantly derives from private archives from Ur, Isin and Nippur, other places merely add details. They are in the main contemporary, and date in general from the time of the last kings of Isin and Larsa and from that of Ḫammurabi and Samsuiluna as rulers of a unified alluvial Mesopotamia. There is thus no evidence from the early Isin-Larsa period. With the proviso that the transmission is haphazard at best, the material available suggests that the prebendal system had clear local features in the Old Babylonian period, especially when an attempt is made to

---

15 It is a task for the future to investigate whether or not these scribes were in charge of specific accounts and in which manner they acted as a check on one another.

16 The function survives as important, but marginally documented, within the later households. But it is, again, striking that Nabonidus selected this function for the entourage of his daughter on her installation in Ur.

17 Charpin 1986 p. 158ff. on financial aspects, acquisition of a prebend p. 160, YOS 12, 297 (16 IV Si 8), on the status of an official with this title cf. also p. 236ff., where a ZABAR.DAB$_5$ is shown to belong to the internal personnel of the sanctuary.

18 For Sippar we can refer especially to Jursa, AfO Beih. 25 no. 46 (25 x Cyr 5), a lease containing an Edict related phrase which adds the *qêpu* to those entitled to payments. In CT 56, 460 (<Nbk> yr. 16), Jursa p. 139, we are probably dealing with an obligation imposed on institutional plough teams to supply the *qêpu* with 10 kor of barley each. Both outsiders and the institutional personnel had to contribute, but possibly the *qêpu* made costs for which he had to be reimbursed. Note also that in Sippar the *qêpu* when supervising "public works" received double the wages of all the others involved: two kor of barley against one kor per month for all others, whether they had a minor supervisory function or not.

condense the evidence. Though the later Old Babylonian clergy of Sippar can be reconstructed to a degree from lists of witnesses, and some administrative documents, the prebendal aspect of the functions there is virtually undocumented at present, though some prebends occur in a limited number of court cases.

a. Ur

Charpin[19] provides the short list of the relevant Old Babylonian prebends in Ur, from which place there is also valuable information from administrative documents. The $GUDU_4$[20] (with a prebend called NAM.$GUDU_4$ or rather, often in a neutral manner, merely MAR.ZA[21]) is attached to a god (or a statue or a cultic object, but that does not seem to be fundamental), with, as of special stature the $GUDU_4$.DUB.LA_2.MAḪ and, more importantly, the $GUDU_4$.ABSU.[22] The Akkadian term *pašīšu* used for $GUDU_4$ does not refer to a specific function but to a status, that of having been anointed.[23] There is no evidence through which

---

[19] Charpin 1986 p. 252-260.

[20] Charpin 1986 p. 252-6: a long list of Ur $GUDU_4$s, which includes, it should be stressed, unspecified MAR.ZA, fewer $GUDU_4$.ABSUs, not many NAM.ŠITA_4 cum brewers (so no ŠITA_4 sec), scarce gate keepers, a rare *kisalluḫḫu*. The restricted panorama is perhaps less an "illusion due à les lacunes de nôtre documentation", real though they are, as a witness to the fact that in Ur the various functions hide even more than in Nippur or Isin behind the omni-presence of the $GUDU_4$. The status of this $GUDU_4$ was certainly upgraded compared to that of his Ur III predecessor, especially in comparison with the Lagaš variant. In Old Babylonian Sippar $GUDU_4$ (sec) is rare in private texts, yet he is certainly a persistent and numerically important element of the personnel of the sanctuaries.

[21] Whether MAR.ZA always and automatically stands for $GUDU_4$ is not completely certain, though the two terms are not often used together in the same text, I can only refer to TS 14 (XII RS 9, Charpin, Archives familiales, 1980, p. 45 and p. 209), where we find $3^2/_3$ day of a MAR.ZA E_2 ^{d}NIN.GUBLAM, $1^1/_2$ day NAM.ŠITA_4 E_2 ^{d}NANNA and a whole year $GUDU_4$ E_2 ^{d}NIN.LIL_2, which suggests, if it has any meaning at all, that $GUDU_4$ and MAR.ZA do not have the same contents, which is not remarkable, as the first term stresses the (priestly) status and the second the fact that a *parṣu*, a function entailing income, is involved. But the terms are not mutually exclusive either. UET 5, 274 (X Se 7) is a care adoption in which a MAR.ZA E_2-^{d}Nammu is an element of the grant to the adopted son. In UET 5, 90 (II ṢA 1) we happen to have a comparable case, where we must probably (also) read $GUDU_4$ ^{d}Nammu with Charpin 1986 p. 254. This could suggest that GUDU4 is the common, general term for "consecrated member of the clergy", whose position can be represented by the even more general MAR.ZA, perhaps especially when the stress is on the income aspect of the function. Similar alternations in Charpin's list 1986 p. 253ff. for Baba, Gula, or Inanna, which is probably the reason why MAR.ZA in general is automatically equated with $GUDU_4$, which in turn could again suggests that $GUDU_4$ is primarily a status and not a function. Whether the automatic equation of MAR.ZA with $GUDU_4$ is (always) justified should be subject to confirmation. We will note, however, that in Nippur sale documents of prebendal functions nearly always the list of functions specified commences with NAM.$GUDU_4$. Such a list of functions, often of minor nature, might perhaps be represented by MAR.ZA.

[22] The $GUDU_4$.ABSU ranks above the ordinary $GUDU_4$. Whether the $GUDU_4$.DUB.LA_2.MAḪ functioned in court proceedings is here no more than a matter of speculation, a link between "ritual" and court proceedings is not difficult to construct. On the spread of the title *gudapsû* cf. CAD G p. 119.

[23] This statement is bound to be controversial. I.J. Gelb, MAD 3, p. 219, though listing *pašišu* under a root *pšš* yet adds "Apparently a lw. from Sum.", i.e. from PA_4.ŠEŠ, which will be argued again by Th. Krispijn in a forthcoming article, stressing, on Eblaite grounds, that the š-s are not proper š-s. Von Soden AHw 845 unhesitatingly translates "Gesalbter", though quoting MAD 3 p. 219. Deriving *pašīšu* from *pašāšu* may be a question of popular etymology, even though PA_4.ŠIŠ = *pašīšu* is "niemals belegt" according to A.W. Sjöberg, HSAO 1, p. 216 note 25, and even though having an early *aḫu rabû* parallel for the Neo-Babylonian dignitary of that title would have its own attraction. Borger 1973 p. 174 points out the limited basis for connecting *pašišu* and *pašāšu*. It should be noted that in the Mari ritual Durand-

the practical tasks of the *pašīšu* or $GUDU_4$ can be determined, in this he is paralleled by the rarer contemporary *ramku*, or ŠITA,[24] and the in the documentation of the period equally scarce *ērib bīti*, whose namesakes will play such an important role in our later period.

These assumed "general" functions could, to propose a theory, from the outset, either encompass various specialisms, or there may have taken place a process of specialisation which led to a situation in which "ritualist" and "artisan" specialists remained in an inner circle as *ērib bīti*s and the "purveying trades" developed into prebendaries of the outer circle. An original combination of the two is perhaps not wholly impossible, the first giving rise to the second, as another kind of specialisation.[25] Such a development would be analogous to the vertical splitting up of the later "small sanctuary prebend", which provides a kind of "model" for the development of prebendal functions. In the early period the higher ritual functions would be the first to be absolved from humdrum daily obligations, they would be followed by a select group of lower ritualists, including specialists (GALA, NAR, types of *āšipu*). Perhaps only towards the middle Old Babylonian period the purveying trades would reach this stage of being freed from ordinary tasks, possibly beginning with the brewers. The important fact is that the sanctuaries obtained in this manner a socially more broadly based personnel, with a for them essential economic interest in their institution.

We also find a NAM.$ŠITA_4$,[26] mentioned sparingly in association with the brewer. In Ur the NAM.$ŠITA_4$ seems to be attested only in relation to the cult of Nanna, where the function, as the material listed by Charpin indicates, was dividable and saleable.[27]

Guichard 1997, no. 2, Dossin 1938 IV 20ff. a number of DUMU.MEŠ *pa-ši-ši-im* figure under a *ša-gu-ú*, *šangû*, which perhaps militates against a basic meaning "elder brother", which on principle would allow the presence of just one. Durand translates "*oints*". It may sound paradoxical but the matter is only of secondary importance, being an "anointed (priest)" or an "elder brother" is both primarily a question of "status" and not of actual tasks. Th. Jacobsen's note in PAPS 107, 6, 1963, p. 477 footnote 11 should be mentioned, but the etymology remains difficult to comment upon.

24 The Akkadian equivalents of both $GUDU_4$ and ŠITA in the lexical material are unstable and involve other titles. This is not investigated here, nor is the question of the relationship of a possible PA_4.ŠEŠ with *pašišu* and either $GUDU_4$ or ŠITA.

25 We need more information on the origins of the "later" *maššartu-pappasu* system. We have noted, however, already a case in which a Nippur Ur III LUNGA received both bread and beer, which we regard as a trait characteristic of the later *ērib bīti*s. The fact that in Nippur purveying trades occur in strings of functions starting with NAM.$GUDU_4$ could be an argument supporting the theory of the vertically splitting off, to an "outsider position", of the purveyors,

26 $ŠITA_4$ as such does not play a role, it would seem. NAM.$ŠITA_4$ cannot be a high ranking position, its existence is thus possibly an indication of a proliferation of functions already in the Old Babylonian period in connection with the cult of the most important local gods. We must separate ŠITA and NAM.$ŠITA_4$. Still different was the ŠITA.$EŠ_3$, who was a much more important cultic functionary, as was the ŠITA.AB.BA whom we find in Ur III Lagaš sanctuaries, cf. Maekawa 1999, for instance text 22, in Guabba, together with one GALA.MAḪ and 31 $GUDU_4$.

27 Charpin 1986, material on p. 258, with on p. 259 the suggestion that NAM.$ŠITA_4$ could be a recent innovation. The texts listed on p. 258 link NAM.$ŠITA_4$ with the temple of Nanna, but UET 5, 518 has an amount NAM.$ŠITA_4$ NINDA of day x, and in TCL 10, 59 NAM.$ŠITA_4$ [temple x] is differentiated from ^{LU_2}LUNGA temple [x (or y?)]. TCL 10, 52 could be the sale of 1) 2 ^{LU_2}LUNGA.MEŠ 2) 1 NAM.$ŠITA_4$ NINDA of the Sin temple of three months duration (each, so three separate jobs), putting the NAM.$ŠITA_4$ job next to the brewers functions and linking it with NINDA, bread. Reading NINDA is, of course, rather arbitrary. In his edition of TCL 10, 52 Charpin (1986 p. 178) preferred NI_3 plus temple name as indicating that the prebend belonged to the temple, but such a fact is not normally indicated in this manner, the GAR must tell something about the function, though UET 5, 518 could be misleading if

Importantly enough it also occurs in connection with Inanna-Zabalam,[28] where it equally was dividable and that together with the only case of a similarly treated IŠIB-prebend.[29] I would suggest that the function is a sign of a differentiation which makes not only the function of a brewer but also that of a cook a separate prebendal charge, as seems to be indicated also by material from Isin mentioning a prebendary called MUḪALDIM, "cook", "baker", usually in a list of functions beginning with NAM.GUDU$_4$. In Ur, duly registered by Charpin, YOS 5, 163 mentions fifteen ERIM$_2$ NAM.ŠITA$_4$ ù ^{LU_2}LUNGA and in UET 5, 790 the NAM.ŠITA$_4$ and the GUDU$_4$.MEŠ separately receive flour, both indications in favour of a differentiation in function, but not against a task in the purveying sphere for the NAM.ŠITA$_4$.[30]

Finally there were in Ur the *atû* and the KISAL.LUḪ, whose practical functions do seem to be unproblematic. KISAL.LUḪ, "courtyard sweeper", can only have been a very modest occupation. With a share of twelve days per annum in the case attested, it was, notwithstanding its modesty, extremely fragmented.[31] We must expect that also other prebendal functions had a modest economic basis.[32]

b. Isin

In Isin, in roughly the same period, someone's prebend was his BAL.GUB.BA +(NAM.)function, which could be shortened into BAL.NAM+function or simply BAL+function, which always happens to pertain to a temple rather than to a specific god[33],

---

regarded as a parallel. NINDA might be, as Charpin suggests, the material delivered, though its place in the sentence is unusual, which is possibly caused by a direct link between NAM.ŠITA$_4$ and NINDA. Charpin makes a back link with ŠITA, *ramku*, which would put the NAM.ŠITA$_4$ in the ranks of the "purificateurs". NAM.ŠITA$_4$ occurs now earlier, notably in the inscription for Šulgi published by Civil in a context which is not without problems either: IV 1 (visible on photo), where the function possibly could be the responsibility of the craftsmen favoured. The formulation using numbers before the functions in TCL 10, 52 is remarkable. Over all ^{LU_2}LUNGA and NAM.ŠITA$_4$ seem to represent comparable types of employment.

28 Also attested with Nindara in the Ur III inscription published by Civil.

29 Riftin 2, (RS 18), why not from Zabalam itself? On the IŠIB-prebend cf. Renger 1969 p. 123, note 622, considering emendation. Also Charpin 1986, p. 258 note 1, as from Larsa.

30 This confronts us reluctantly with the question of ŠITA.EŠ$_3$, "*ramku*". That ŠITA.EŠ$_3$ and NAM.ŠITA$_4$ are different functions is evident from comparing YOS 5, 163 lines 11 and 19. The matter is discussed under ŠITA$_x$.UNU by Renger 1969 p. 129, and compare Borger 1973 p. 174. In the Kingsbury text the ŠITA.EŠ$_3$, just one, belongs to the following of Utu, in which case there occurs an under-ŠITA, lines 329-330, which suggests a certain importance. For Charpin the ŠITA.EŠ$_3$ was an administrative official, 1986 p. 215. (Reason given: ŠITA.EŠ$_3$ could be a *gudapsû*, and could be compared with the AGRIG.) Th. Krispijn identified for me Ni 4485, quoted by Renger from Van Dijk SG 2 p. 127, as a part of the Nanše hymn, W. Heimpel, JCS 33 p. 117, where we have a ŠITA.EŠ$_3$.A BALA.GUB.BA.NI, a "ŠITA.EŠ$_3$ who fulfils his turn in the temple". This concerns definitely a ritualistic task, even if fulfilling a BALA is for us not in itself proof of fulfilling a prebendal function, but there can be little doubt that he belonged to the right milieu. We must probably separate ŠITA(.EŠ$_3$) which is comparable to *ramku* and/or *pasīšu* and NAM.ŠITA$_4$, even though NAM.ŠITA$_4$ can possibly be linked with Asalluḫi (Charpin 1986 p. 259), by which exorcist connotations can be suggested. NAM.ŠITA$_4$ is a rather humble function.

31 Charpin 1986 p. 260.

32 The other Ur functions discussed by Charpin were administrative and do not appear to have been saleable, though they were passed on in the family regularly, as all such functions were in this period.

33 BIN 7, 193, 16 IV Si 19, has only BAL.GUB.BA E$_2$-^{d}A-ra-li. This is completely unspecified as to the nature of the function. YOS 14, 328 (reign of Sin-māgir) is comparable for E$_2$-^{d}Damu.

for instance BAL.GUB.BA $GUDU_4$ E_2-^{d}Damu.[34] The same applies to (BAL.)NAM.^{LU_2}LUNGA E_2 (^{d}Nin-Insina)[35], only NAM.I_3.DU_8 was linked to a gate, not to a temple.[36]

Of some special interest is BIN 7, 66: BAL.NAM.$GUDU_4$ MUḪALDIM *ù* NAM.^{LU_2}LUNGA E_2-^{d}Damu, also found RA 26 p. 101, AO 11152, as BAL.NAM.$GUDU_4$ NAM.^{LU_2}LUNGA 2) *ù* NAM.$^{[LU_2]}$MUḪALDIM E_2 ^{d}Damu, to be compared with BIN 7, 214 where the order is 11) BAL.GUB.BA $GUDU_4$ NAM.MUḪALDIM *ù* ^{LU_2}LUNGA. The prebendal baker therefore certainly occurs (as a MUḪALDIM) in the early period in his own right in Isin, though in combination with the function of brewer, contrary to what seems to be the case in both Ur and Nippur, where he seems to fail to appear, though the brewer is present.[37] Whether this evidence is enough to conclude that the prebendal baker and brewer had to be a $GUDU_4$ is not certain, but the possibility must be considered, just as it could be possible that baker and brewer were combined functions in a cultic context at a certain stage. Perhaps RA 26 p. 102 AO 11153 is significant in a double respect, as it does not mention a BAL.NAM.$GUDU_4$ but only a BAL.GUB.BA.^{LU_2}LUNGA <*ù*> MUḪALDIM E_2-^{d}Damu in female hands, which were transferred to an other person. Baker and brewer are associated here again, but, perhaps, in what is locally only a sanctuary of the second order, for Nin-Insina has a separate brewer, also without NAM.$GUDU_4$.[38] Is this a sign that functional specialisation at prebendal level had begun to be indicated in an explicit manner and that combinations of functions persisted longer in smaller sanctuaries?

The lease of prebends, execution by others, was possible in this period: in BIN 7, 193 it is simply called BAL.GUB.BA E_2-^{d}Arali and the remuneration is half a shekel in silver, which is not much, but yet in a small sanctuary possibly this could indicate "all functions". In AO 11153, mentioned already, a prebend in female hands was sold.

c. Nippur

The richer material from Nippur private archives is summarised less easily, its range in time is slightly wider, but it is yet essentially contemporary with that from Ur and Isin. The notable differences are therefore not a result of temporal disparity. SAOC 44 no. 81, one out a whole number of in this respect identically phrased texts from the reign of Samsu-iluna, gives a list consisting of NAM.$GUDU_4$ NAM.PA.E_2 NAM.^{LU_2}LUNGA NAM.I_3.DU_8[39] NAM.KISAL.LUḪ NAM.PUR.ŠU.MA E_2-^{d}Utu.kam, with occasional changes in the order of the functions. This seems to contain all the elements which also occur in less encompassing combinations in the Attā-file,[40] where such functions are subsumed as GARZA(.BI.ŠE_3),

---

34 YOS 14, 328.

35 RA 73, 1979 p. 77, AO 11139 and RA 45, 1951, p. 106, MAH 15881, etc.

36 BIN 7, 175, this "prebend" is not resumed in the text as BAL.GUB.BA PN, but NAM.I_3.DU_8 is repeated, which may or may not have a meaning, all the more so as the same occurs in BIN 7, 167, where the gate keeper's position is, however, one of a temple. A complete, unfragmented, function might be intended. There is also always the possibility that though gate keeper is a temple function, it is not automatically always a prebend in our sense.

37 A possible preference for calling this function EN.ME.GI_4, ENGIZ, *engiṣu*, for instance in Ur in connection with the cult of Ea, is only a very partial explanation for the scarcity of the prebendal cook/baker in "early" texts. It could be noted that Nabonidus in providing for his daughter indicated the baker by this term, YOS 1, 45, II 46.

38 BIN 7, 65 (I Damiqilišu 6) and AO 11139, RA 73 p. 77, same reign, also Sollberger, RA 45 p. 106, MAH 15881, etc.

39 NAM.EN.NU.UN occasionally occurs in lists of NAM.NI.DU_8, PBS 8/2 133, 25 Si 13, lines 6-10 and 15-19.

40 Cf. A. Goetze, JCS 18, 1964, p. 102-113, texts also in SAOC 44.

"(relevant) rites/functions". The list occurs in the same manner in PBS 13, 66+BE 6/2, 66 (5 XII Si 24) in the temple of Enki and Damgalnuna. In BE 6/2, 36 the same list occurs again, this time in the E$_2$-^{d}MAR.TU and in BE 6/2, 39 with the E$_2$-^{d}Kù.sud, in both cases summarised as BAL.GUB.BA. For less complete lists we can mention for E$_2$-Lugal.ab.a SAOC 44, no. 83, and for ^{d}Lulal TIM 4, 13, where ^{LU_2}LUNGA is not present. The type of accumulation found in the texts is in this manner probably typical for a small Nippur sanctuary. Reduced by one or more elements it occurs for more small temples, possibly the combination of functions represents all the prebendal tasks in such a small temple. Note in passing that to begin with these prebendaries again were GUDU$_4$s. There is no reference to a separate baker's prebend in these texts. NAM.BUR.ŠU.MA, "elder", we might expect to be a matter of status, but the other functions are "practical", PA.E$_2$, "*šāpiru*", probably having not only administrative implications, but possibly also fulfilling the other *šangû*-type tasks.[41] This would be in direct succession of the PA.E$_2$/*šāpirus* of the type we find in the Ur III Inanna temple in Nippur, where administrative and cultic responsibilities were combined.[42] This function could be sold in the Old Babylonian period, it would seem, but possibly only regarding the smaller sanctuaries, for which we will find a later parallel in the case of the *šangû* of smaller sanctuaries operating under the head of the local centralised temple organisation.

It is not likely that a similar representative list can be reconstructed for the more important Nippur temples. A NAM.NU.EŠ$_3$ of Enlil figures in BE 6/2, 43 (XII Si 13).[43] Texts like ARN 20/21 and ARN 23 from the Enlil-zimu group have respectively GUDU$_4$'s of Enlil and Ninlil, thus not of temples, and that seems to be common and in line with the expected greater differentiation in the main sanctuaries, which required, and could afford, separate parallel officiants for the various cult localities and gods within the same complex.

Both texts specify another function in the same hand as a NAM.BUR.ŠU.MA and that, respectively, of the DUMU.NIBRU^{KI} DUMU.I-si-in^{KI}-na *ù* DUMU.$^{(KUR)}$MAR.TU A.NA.ME.A.BI, references to the ethnic background of a function of which we cannot circumscribe the ritual contents.[44] In its phrasing the text twice strongly suggests a link between land and the prebends, which is made explicit in ARN 46 where the A.ŠA$_3$ SUKU$_6$.NAM.GUDU$_4$ (^{d}Nin.líl.lá) is mentioned twice. Other texts are less explicit but can be considered as analogous in content.

The term NAM.BUR.ŠU.MA, of course, comes directly from the Akkadian. But on all occasions NAM.GUDU$_4$ comes first. The NAM.BUR.ŠU.MAs in ARN 23 are a Nippur affair, in PBS 8/2, 146+ (16 VI Si 27) 2f. (cf. 16) we are confronted by NAM.GUDU$_4$ NAM.BUR.ŠU.MA ^{d}NIN.<TIN.>UG5.GA.x /ŠA$_3$ NIBRU^{KI} *ù* ŠA$_3$ BAL.A.RI *ù* ŠA$_3$ I$_3$[.SI.IN^{KI}], for 12 days per annum, with which in line 16 other gods are associated. This is formulated

---

41 It can occur alone: PBS 8/2, 166 III 15.

42 Cf. Zettler 1992, p. 177 note 1.

43 CBS 7075, published by K. van Lerberghe, eds. M. Lebeau et Ph. Talon, Mélanges A. Finet, Leuven, 1989, p. 177-9 is a balanced account concerning BALA.GUB.BA NU.EŠ.E.NE over 13 months in Si 27-8 (lines 26 and, restored, 35) in the Enlil temple in Nippur. The income in barley listed is place and time related, but the nature of the three posts constituting the expenditure is not so clear. Perhaps 14 talents of wool is bought and 7 pieces of textile. Could we conclude that seven *nešakku* officiated together and that BALA.GUB.BA, though placed at the beginning of the line, and certain only in line 26 in the section of the text listing the income, and thus possibly not identical with line 35 in the expenditure section, where the nature of that expenditure might be explained, indicates that these were not always the same persons?

44 Nothing can be added to Renger 1969 p. 201. But note perhaps that Zettler 1992, 6 NT 364 (17 VI IS 6), a standard Ur III list of personnel receiving amounts of beer and bread, includes a NU.EŠ$_3$ BUR.ŠU.MA receiving the lowest amount distributed of 1 SILA$_3$ of both.

as explicitly referring to different localities. PBS 8/2, 182: 6-7 (18 II Si 13) deserves separate mention: NAM.GUDU$_4$ NAM.LUNGA(?) ^{d}INANNA ^{d}NA.NA.A.BI MU.A ITI.2.KAM A.ŠA$_3$ SUKU$_6$.BI *ù* NAM.BUR.ŠU.MA. This is not the complete list of functions, but again we find a clear reference to prebendal land[45] as well as a probable reference to a cult with Uruk connections.

In the Lú-Inanna or Mannu-mêšu-liṣṣur-group of texts we encounter regularly a group of prebends consisting of some NAM.I$_3$.DU$_8$ of specific gates[46] and a prebend called NAM.E$_2$.DA.DI,[47] which remains sometimes unspecified, but which is in other texts more fully represented by the NAM.E$_2$.DA.DI[48] of Enlil and Ninlil combined.[49]

In the temple of Nusku, a sanctuary of the third order in Nippur,[50] we do find not only a NAM.PA.E$_2$ but also a NAM.LU$_2$.NIG$_2$.DAB$_5$.BA (E$_2$ ^{d}Nusku).[51] A NAR-prebend, not combined with NAM.GUDU$_4$, of a range of minor divinities is known[52] and the *kalû*[53] occurs also. The Nippur texts show some particularities not occurring in what is available from elsewhere. The functions can be traced back sometimes to Ur III period precedents, but as information is restricted, it remains uncertain whether we are dealing with uniquely Nippur phenomena.

For an example of a prebend, and notably that of a GUDU$_4$, in female hands we can refer to PBS 8/2, 182: 9. This means that the absence of NAM.GUDU$_4$ in the Isin text RA 26 p. 103 AO 11153 probably means that a LUNGA and a MUḪALDIM, possibly in combination, not of necessity had to be GUDU$_4$s. In turn that would mean that brewers and bakers, the "providing trades", possibly were already becoming a group of prebendaries with a separate status. Or does it mean that the fact that any prebendary had to be a GUDU$_4$ was so automatic that this function, or rather status, could be skipped?

45 Lines 1 and 2 refer to a NAM.GUDU$_4$ of Ninurta and another function which is lost, for three months, its sustenance land and probably a NAM.[BUR.ŠU].MA. For a NAM.GUDU$_4$ of Nin-urta and land cf. also PBS 8/2, 146.

46 e.g. OECT 8, 2; 18; Stone-Owen no. 26; no. 51, etc.

47 Stone-Owen no. 26.

48 Somewhat deviating in formulation BIN 7, 19, RS II "b". For NAM.E$_2$.DA.DI cf. perhaps E$_2$.DA.SA$_2$.a quoted by Charpin 1986 p. 247 in relation to UET 5, 506, with reference to W.W. Hallo and B. Levine, HUCA 38, 1967 were a reading GAN$_2$.DA.DI.a is discussed; also Charpin p. 316 note 1, E$_2$.DA.SA$_2$.a should be a special manner of presentation of flour. Could this represent a prebendal right attached to a special cultic occasion? Such rights are not otherwise unknown in later periods. Both reading and contents must remain problematic.

49 These functions are not preceded by NAM.GUDU$_4$. OECT 8, 9 (21 IV Si 12) from this same group of texts mentions a NAM.EN.NUN ALAM E$_2$.KUR, therefore to be associated with the Enlil temple, also Stone-Owen no. 51, etc.

50 If Ekur was the most prestigious sanctuary, Ešumešu, the temple of Ninurta, seems to have played the administratively more important role, for which there may have been historical reasons. A temple as that of Nusku takes third position.

51 BE 6/2, 37 with PBS 8/2, 131 (6 XI Si 11), cf. also PBS 8/2, 135 (5 IV Si 12) and 138 (18 X Si 28). The term could suggest a link with the role of the craftsmen in the Ur III inscription published by Civil, mentioned above. But there is probably a better equation with the lexical *ša nindabî* or ^{LU_2}NIG$_2$.DA.AB.BA, CAD N/2 p 238, based on OB Lu A 427, understood as "a person in charge of *nindabû* offerings", -so possibly a term for (one of) the purveying trades?

52 Cf. JCS 3, 184f.

53 BE 6/2 26: II 20 and III 7, E$_2$.^{d}Nin-sun, 42:2; 57:3.

d. Other

Other texts come as isolated documents from various places. Riftin 2 (RS 18) is the division of an inheritance. Lines 1-2 mention six months of the NAM.ŠITA$_4$ and six days of IŠIB[54] in the temple of Inanna-Zabalam as one share, both lines 7-8 and 14-13 register 3 months and 6 days each of the same two prebends. In view of the obvious fragmentation it will be accidental that this seems to be the only private text mentioning the inheritance of the position of an IŠIB. The function is supposed to have been that of a fairly high ranking prebendary,[55] etymologically of the *āšipu*-type and relatively well represented in Nippur in the Sigrist *sattukku* texts in connection with several gods, but absent in the private archives. On the possible meaning of NAM.ŠITA$_4$ see above under Ur. This function was completely in one hand in Riftin 2 before this inheritance document split it up. There is a possibility that the text comes from Zabalam itself.

TCL 11, 224 (RS 51), from Larsa(?), is an inheritance division mainly dealing with real estate, which mentions three portions of eight days of ^{LU_2}KU$_4$.E$_2$ ^{d}Nanna (II 73, II 92 and rev. III 83) and one of nine days before Šamaš (rev. III 18), each time, rather unusually, as the last element in the division. This is the only occurrence known to me of *ērib bīti* in an "early" practical document, but it again indicates fragmentation of the function and thus also its under-representation in the texts. *ērib bīti* occurs, of course, as an epithet of witnesses, especially in Old Babylonian Sippar, therefore later in the Old Babylonian period, which may have some meaning for the development of the function, though GUDU$_4$ is also known there.[56]

YOS 12, 353 (10 X Si 11) has an unknown provenance, but it will come from Southern Mesopotamia. In it a person buys back, as belonging to his paternal estate ([E$_2$ *a*]-*bi-šu*, line 14) 55 days of MAR.ZA NAM.K[ISAL.LUḪ] 2) *ša* E$_2$ ^{d}Nin.šubur, which had been sold previously to someone who fulfilled the charge of *ababdû*,[57] a good Old Babylonian example of someone of a higher rank buying what to all likelihood was a lowly employment. The Kingsbury text mentions special remuneration of *kisalluḫḫus*, but it can be regarded as dubious whether a high ranking official would act himself as a courtyard sweep. This could represent an investment.

The available relevant documents from private archives from Sippar are few in number, they date from Ḫammurabi onwards, are thus in general slightly later than the material from the South. But they deal primarily with prebendal income, not with the tasks involved. and they do not inform us on structural matters either.[58] Only HG 96 (after Aṣ 5) seems to have referred directly to a prebendal function, according to the editor of the text, D. Charpin, that of a "lamentateur". A NAR.SA(*-tum*), a “position of string-instrument-

---

[54] CAD I/J p 243 expects NAM.IŠIB.

[55] Cf. CAD I/J p. 242-3. It is one of the “priestly” titles which passed into the royal titulature. In the *sattukku* texts IŠIBs are moderately well remunerated with generally 7 SILA$_3$ of bread per day, Sigrist 1984 p. 165.

[56] F. van Koppen kindly refers me to CT 45, 109. The title also occurs on seals, CT 47, 15a and 69a (no copies of these seals, I assume that GUDU$_4$ is intended). Cf. also K. van Lerberghe and G. Voet, AoF 24, 1997, p.157.

[57] Charpin 1986 p. 241-3, an administrative function.

[58] Special thanks are due to F. van Koppen for pointing out several of the Sippar texts and for providing me with his transcriptions. For HG 96 see D. Charpin, RA 82, 1988, p. 29-33. The text is an example of the fact that often only prosopgraphic studies can explain contexts. Other relevant texts from Sippar are CT 2, 43; 4, 11a; 6, 28a and 45, 24, cf. Harris 1975, p. 360, where the relevance of not all the material listed is, however, directly clear to me.

player",[59] in a temple of two gods, no doubt of minor status, was together with a house the object of a courtcase.[60] Sippar *ērib bītis* as witnesses have been mentioned, but of especial importance is the administrative list OLA 21, 4, mentioned already, as the text enables us to establish the strength of some of the priestly groups serving Annunītum:[61] six *ērib bītis*, 14 $GUDU_4$s, of whom the four better paid ones were to all likelihood the *gudapsûs*. There were thus ten ordinary $GUDU_4$s.[62] The GALAs and the NAR.SAs are only mentioned as a group, of which the size cannot be calculated. These "round" numbers do not suggest that they are the

---

59 BE 6/2, 86 (1 II Si 30) edited by C. Wilcke, ZA 73, 1983, p. 59-66. The prebend is indicated as 2) NA[R].SA-*tim is-qí-im ù te-e*[*r-tim* (...)]) E_2 DN1 *ù* D[N2] (which was 4) *uk-la-at* PN and had been handed on together with the house to a(n adoptive) son. Of some importance is that the witnesses include after the judges first a *gudapsû* and then four (other) NAR.SA. (The function also occurs, as we saw in OLA 21 no. 4, but it is perhaps too much to conclude that there where therefore always "colleges" of four NAR.SAs in the "Sippar" sanctuaries.) It is not clear whether these men shared the same post or occupied separate parallel functions, no time limit being indicated, but it would be known to those concerned. Wilcke interprets *isqu* and *têrtu* as respectively indicating the income and the function, in which he is followed by K. van Lerberghe and G. Voet, AoF 24, 1997, p.152, where the total possessions in a case in which an adopted person is disinherited are indicated as: (he will not claim:) 15) *is-qí-im te-re-tim* 16) *bu-ši-im ù ba-ši-tim* "the income (nor) the office, the property nor the possessions". This sounds rather formulaic and means "nothing". It is artificial to differentiate between *bāšītu* "immovables, and *būšu* "movables", we can speculate that likewise the combination *isqu* and *têrtu* refers to (all) prebendal rights. The *u₄-mi ša te-re-tim* of OLA 21, 4: 1 belongs in this context, practically the text lists allowances payable on a special religious occasion. (A minor problem is the *uk-la-at* PN in BE 6/2 86: 4, which Wilcke translates by "Lebensunterhalt", with which one must agree notwithstanding Stol's remarks in eds. M. Stol and S.P. Vleeming, The Care of the Elderly in the Ancient Near East, Leiden 1998, p. 66, for whom the term refers to prebends only. The meaning of the word is wider.).

60 Probably from Sippar is CBS 414, as already mentioned, made available by M. Stol and quoted CAD S p. 310 as referring to an [*i-s*]*i-iq mu-ša-ki-l*[*u-tim*] [*ù*] *si-ra-šu-tim*. CAD M/2 p. 254 mentions *mušākilu* in the Old Babylonian period and interprets rather blandly as a "purveyor (as title of an official)". In the Neo-Babylonian period the *mušākilu* is in an institutional context a "fattener of animals", especially of fowl, but there are no signs that he should be regarded as a prebendary. In the Old Babylonian period the in itself logical connection between brewing and fattening of animals seems to be attested in CT 6, 23c, quoted CAD S p. 309-10, where a fattener of animals has a father who is overseer of the *manzaz sirašūtim*. Even if the *mušākilūtu* is qualified as an *isqu* in CBS 414 that does not imply that it represented a prebend in our sense, even though the possibility must be considered. *mušākilūtu* is mentioned in CBS 414 before *sirašūtu*, one of the attested purveying trades. Especially if responsibility for sacrificial animals is involved, a prebendal position is not to be excluded completely, but some connection with the cult would be required in accordance with our definition. Words like *isqu* or *manzaltu* do not automatically imply prebendal status in the sense it is used here. The possibility that a *mušākilu* in an Old Babylonian institutional context is not strictly a "fattener of animals" could perhaps be left open, but such a person (also?) seems to have been called *mārû* or $^{LU}2KU_7$, cf. Tanret and Van Lerberghe 1993, p. 444.

61 The text refers also to an UGULA NU.BAR, ranking directly after the *kalamaḫḫu*. Stol provided a transliteration of the unpublished text BM 16546 (8 XI Aṣ 12), listed in Sigrist, Figulla and Walker CBT BM 2 p. 42. Ibbatum son of Warad-Ulmašītum, UGULA NU.BAR hires Iddatum son of U-ṣe-e-bi-tim, from himself, for a wage (A_2-di) of halve a *š* for three days per month of (*a-na*) *ši-pi-ir pa-ši-šu-tim*. No wages, *i-di*(*-šu*), in case of default. The simplest explanation is probably that the three days were the property of Ibbatum, but it cannot be excluded completely that he acted in an official capacity. The three seal impressions cannot be read, Šamaš and Aja are witnesses.

62 On comparable numbers of the personnel of the Šamaš temple cf. Van Lerberghe and Voet, AoF 24, 1997, p. 157.

result of an arbitrary splitting up of a task, they may represent "complete functions". The problem is how this relates to the divisions in ownership found in the private documents.[63]

e. Conclusions regarding the early prebends

There are unmistakable signs of an incipient prebendal system in the Ur III period. That clerical functions were already inheritable, on principle, is not to be regarded as abnormal. Such functions belonged to the normal institutional personnel and the persons concerned will have enjoyed additional remuneration on fulfilling clerical tasks on top of what they earned as a result of their daily chores. The prebendal nature of the function came to the fore when tasks and remuneration, so to say, solidified in the hands of a specific group of people who had been assigned a task of a clerical nature. This presupposes a development in which people were "delegated" to fulfil certain tasks, a process which will always begin at the top. The making available of special remuneration seems to be illustrated by the inscription for Šulgi published by Civil (1989). When this development started is not known.

The documentation on prebends is restricted and far from representative for the Old Babylonian clergy in general, even in the probably still incomplete manner in which it can be reconstructed from the considerable amount of material collected by Renger.[64] The number of functions we can study in relation to prebends is far more restricted. There are considerable problems concerning the specific tasks fulfilled by documented functionaries and their colleagues, who happen not to be represented in the private texts mentioned. We can let rest this question in general, the matter is of interest for us only in so far as that we must compare the "earlier" functions with the "later" ones. We cannot simply presume that missing functions were of such a rank or importance[65] that they could not be divided and that, though transmission virtually was through inheritance, the mechanism for handing the function down differed from what occurred in the limited number of inheritance documents we possess.[66]

---

63 CBS 8550, published by R.M. Sigrist, JCS 29, 1977, p. 169-183, concerning offerings in the Nusku temple in Nippur also contains some information on groups of personnel with the same rank serving together. In Col VIII: 5 (indented) we find 5 GUDU$_4$.BAL.A, and in line 20 there are 6 EREŠ.DINGIR. We could tentatively assume that BALA refers to the fact that the payments were intended for the actually serving GUDU$_4$s, which would confirm that certain groups of functionaries indeed served together, here five, and that the fact that each of the five persons serving did not possess a complete function was simply a matter of routine, as might be expected. Also mentioned are a MUŠ.LAḪ$_4$, two different gate keepers, one or more NAR.SAs and a female person indicated only as a daughter of her named father.

64 Renger 1967/1969, 1967 and 1975, for our type of documents see especially 1969.

65 It would be of some interest to scrutinise administrative texts for payments to people who are indicated by terms like "brother" or "son of the *šangû*" or some similar phrase, especially if their given name is not mentioned. Such payments could indicate that though (higher) positions could not be split and shared formally, members of the relevant families could have a claim to a certain income and possibly may have provided certain services in exchange. The lack of insight in the relevant prosopography will generally hide the fact. In the Ur III personnel lists the "sons of the *šangû*" have clearly a position differing from that of the "(additional) sons of plough men". As always status is inherited up to a degree even without the function. MVN 17, 3 is a good example.

66 Kings regularly mention the designation or appointment, preferably of their offspring, to high ranking clerical functions before from the Ur III period, but we do not have any protocol establishing the fact. The custom is no doubt older. There inevitably will have been some form of warrant which confirmed someone's appointment to or designation for the higher clerical functions, probably in combination with the assignment of an income, but nothing seems to remain. The appointment to functions is anyhow badly documented. That the habit of appointing members of the royal family to important clerical

Of the better attested prebendal functions in the documents the LUNGA, "brewer" and the *atû*, "gate keeper", survived into the late period. The MUḪALDIM occurred already in the early period, at least in Isin.[67] The status or function of an *ērib bīti*[68] is attested and was extremely fractionated in the documented prebendal instance in Larsa. But perhaps this is not the complete picture as to this function, for in AbB 2 65:32 the *ērib bīti*(s),[69] rank before the *gudapsû*s, and that function is generally being regarded as not saleable.[70] So a function may possibly have existed at various levels of importance in different places. The *kalû* and the *narû* are explicitly attested in our type of prebendal functions in Nippur, they both occur to all likelihood also in a broken text from Sippar. The *gallābu* may be assumed to have functioned in rituals, but there are no private documents. That is not so problematic as the prebendal nature of the function in the late period is also not well-illustrated. At least four ritualists and three purveying functions thus persist from "early" to "late", but these numbers are definitely much too low. Prebendary craftsmen are not much in evidence, but there is just enough in the early period to accept the fact of their existence.

An explanation is required for the disappearance of the early omni-present $GUDU_4$, together with the much rarer ŠITA. We can only venture the suggestion that they somehow amalgamated with the later -equally- frequent *ērib bīti*, which indicates a similarly vague function of a "general nature". It is striking that the Nippur administrative texts on income consulted do not use the general term $GUDU_4$, whereas in the private texts NAM.$GUDU_4$ is almost the standard first function listed. The earlier private texts as a type are much closer to the later private texts in recording the prebendary phenomenon than the earlier administrative texts are to the later in terminology. Substitution or rather replacement of $GUDU_4$ by *ērib bīti* might explain much of the later frequency of the *ērib bīti*. The process may have begun already in the Old Babylonian period, but caution is required for $GUDU_4$ and *ērib bīti* occur together in later Old Babylonian Sippar, even though $GUDU_4$ is relatively rare in the documentation available. Especially the Nippur material seems to suggest, however, that it was virtually impossible to occupy a function of the type studied without being a $GUDU_4$.

3. The saleable and inheritable functions in the later period

The CAD provides under *isqu* a list of the relevant functions.[71] It can be compared to Bongenaar's list for Ebabbar,[72] Kümmel's discussion for Eanna[73] and the systematic

---

functions must have had consequences for the development of the prebendal system stands to reason: these people required a proper entourage. But again nothing is documented.

[67] If we forget about the *engiṣu* in the ambiance of Enki and the explanation suggested for NAM.$ŠITA_4$.

[68] Cf. simply CAD E p.290-292, *ērib bīti* discussion.

[69] In his edition Frankena translated a singular, but *ērib bīti* can equally be intended to represent a plural, which, perhaps, must be preferred, as the preceding and following functions are represented by plurals.

[70] CAD G p. 119, discussion, but the argument is perhaps not conclusive as the sample is small and even contradictory if we compare Harris 1975, p. 154 note 5.

[71] CAD I/J p. 201. I have no solution for the $^{LU_2}NIG_2$.KAL.ŠEN-*ú-tu* in the hands of the king of TCL 12, 57:6 mentioned there.

[72] Bongenaar 1997 p. 141-2.

[73] Kümmel 1979, p.148. This concerns, however, exclusively the "purveying trades", not the craftsmen, who are discussed on p. 20ff. For a possible prebendal status of individual craftsmen in Uruk Kümmel's remarks on family names, and on occurrence of such a name in VS 15, 1 must be followed up. Whether a person occurs with a family name is important, but it is to all likelihood in itself not enough for being a prebendary, if only for the reason that not all persons with an ancestral name belonged to the prebendal groups. Cf. also Kümmels's remarks on herdsmen, fishermen and the *rāb banī*. Kümmel was especially

treatment of relevant functions in the Hellenistic period in Uruk by both McEwan and Funck in their respective books.[74] In that period virtually all information derives from private archival documents dealing with the transmission of prebendal functions and rights, which were extremely fragmented.[75] For the Neo-Babylonian period we can assume that there were many functions at the level intended here, while information on transmission is rather thin. We will concentrate mainly on the private archives which, however, provide, rather unexpectedly, only limited information.

If *ērib bīti* really is a kind of catch-all title for those in one way or another occupied in the actual cult, there remains a group of prebendaries not covered by that title who are relatively well-documented. Here belong at any rate the bakers[76] and the brewers.[77] That they did not belong to the inner group of prebendaries has long been obvious, only their *šāpirus* joined the *ērib bītis* and the higher administrators in cases in which administrative problems had to be solved.[78] In VS 15, 1 bakers and brewers are not included amongst the *ērib bītis*.[79] Important for the position of non-*ērib bīti* prebendaries is probably whether they were included in the *maššartu-pappasu* system[80] or received something called *kiskirru*, possibly comparable with *kallānu*. These terms probably indicate a kind of account from which the payments concerned were made.[81] Information on this point remains virtually restricted to Sippar, our knowledge on both *kiskirru* and *kallānu* being rather limited. We can only remark that especially in the Hellenistic period, but possibly earlier on, there were officials called *bēl mindi* who held accounts dealing with specific prebendal (and other?) occupations. That scribes were responsible for specific accounts is known earlier.

a. Some *ērib bītis* and presumed *ērib bītis*: "ritualists"

It is unlikely that like the *aḫu rabû* and the *kalamaḫḫu* the *šangû*, and with him the *šatammu*, was not of *ērib bīti* status in the sense of being allowed to enter the sanctuary. All the principal executors of cultic rituals will have been. But not all rituals belonged to the cult of the gods or were necessarily executed in a cultic context, and there will have been

---

interested in the connection between family (name) and (the/a particular) trade. In administrative documents prebendaries often occur with their father's name only, and that not only in Uruk.

[74] McEwan 1981 and Funck 1984, cf. the respective tables of contents.

[75] Relevant material from Babylon is scarce, cf. Boiy 2000 p. 227ff. for confirmation.

[76] On the bakers especially Bongenaar 1997 p. 166ff. and Kessler 1991 with the for the subject important Bēl-supê-muḫur texts, p. 71ff.

[77] Cf. Bongenaar 1997 p. 200ff.

[78] A good example from Uruk is AnOr 8, 48 (15 III Cyr 5).

[79] Nor are the slaughterers as occasionally proposed, cf. Kümmel 1979 p. 27, note 34 for KAB.SAR and not $GIR_2.LA_2$ in VS 15, 1. Cf., already, Renger 1971, p. 497R.

[80] Bongenaar 1997 p. 290 attested in Sippar for prebendal bakers, brewers, oil pressers and weavers.

[81] For Bongenaar 1997 p. 289-290 *kiskirru* is attested in Sippar for boatmen, measurers, gate keepers, potters and for the "small-sanctuary prebend". Cf. Bongenaar also for probably related payments indicated by the term *kallānu*. *kiskirru* is qualified CAD K p. 424 as a special manner of registration of income, mentioning that for *atûs*, *mādidus*, *paḫārus* and *malāḫus*, cf. AHw p.486. For *kallānu* CAD K p.78-9 indicates that it is a technical administrative term, and mentions its use in relation to measurers and boatmen. This mention of *atûs* and *mādidus* could suggest a -strictly spoken unproved- link with the payments due to the officials mentioned in the Edict of Belsazzar. Far from all retained there went to those mentioned. We have already seen that the *qêpu*, not mentioned by the Edict, received Edict-type payments, so why not still others? The *gimru* of the Edict might involve the boatmen. But it would perhaps be difficult to put the "small sanctuaries prebend" in this category. Or was that maintained from still another special account dealing with material made over by the -local- central cultic organisation? What is known about the prebends belonging to the Išḫara temple in Babylon would fit this rather well.

-in a cultic respect- unconsecrated "practitioners". For the *kalûs*[82] this is absolutely certain, and the same must have been the case for comparable "occupations" such as that of *āšipu*,[83] in rituals generally called *mašmaššu*, and perhaps also the *bārû* and the *narû* and the like.[84] Both consecrated and unconsecrated status can be assumed to have existed for the "entertainers", of whom some were certainly prebendaries. I am inclined to class those who belonged to these groups and were consecrated, with the *ērib bīti*s, on the assumption that they performed before the gods, and thus came in contact with them. Whether this direct contact is an actual reason to promote those involved to *ērib bīti* stature is for the future to confirm or falsify, there is no actual proof beyond the occasional private document which treats a function of this type like other generally accepted prebends.

In many respects it remains problematic whether all those participating in rituals which made the gods more visible than normal, e.g. processions and visits to other gods, had to be consecrated. On principle we assume that contact with the god required consecration, though it is evident that also unconsecrated ritualists, notably *kalûs*, could participate in certain rites. The matter requires future attention and better documentation. One could be a *kalû* without having been consecrated, which suggests that there existed means by which a person could be recognised as an unconsecrated *kalû*, that is as someone technically capable of carrying out the tasks involved, but not allowed to enter the temple. Who recognised someone as a technically competent practitioner? Was it a matter of family reputation?

One of the functionaries undertaking the corporal inspection of the candidate for the priestly function in the text published by Borger[85] was the *gallābu*, "barber". We have very limited information on this prebendal function.[86] Only UET 4, 57 and 58 (21 IV Art II 9) mention five persons as ^{LU_2}ŠU.I.MEŠ ^{LU_2}GIŠ.ŠUB.BA ^{LU_2}ŠU.I-*ú-tu u*[87] ^{LU_2}*šá ba-nu-ú-tu it-*<*ti*> *a-ḫa-meš ip-pu-šu* (lines 5-7), "the barbers who will execute together the prebendal tasks of the barber and of (the inspector of) physical suitability."[88] Even though the scope of the prebendal system remains relatively unknown, the *gallābu* of Borger's text would almost inevitably have to belong to the *ērib bīti*.

In private archives prebendal functions of a specifically "ritualistic" type are rare. BM 42408 was already quoted in the context of the Bēl-rēmanni/Nidinti-Marduk group published by Jursa. The *zabarūtu*-prebend leased, "given against *ebūru*", has been

---

[82] On a Seleucid family of *kalûs* and its intellectual milieu, cf. P.A. Beaulieu, Fs. Oelsner, AOAT 252, Münster, 2000, esp. p. 8-15.

[83] It is perhaps of interest that the function could be exercised by women in the late period: CT 49, 140, but whether they became prebendaries by being allowed to belong to the professional group is something else. The fact deserves our attention.

[84] Perhaps the rare *maḫḫu*, ^{LU_2}GUB.BA, "ecstatic" who, though not in private archival texts, yet seems to survive from the early to the late period, could be included here, but he is marginalised by a general lack of information, even though he occurs in late cultic rituals, cf. CAD M/1 p. 90-1.

[85] Borger 1973 line I 7-13. The importance of the *gallābu* in a ritual context is probably underlined by what is suggested by AO 6479, obv. 24-5, RAcc p. 36, where we can assume that the person of the king is subject to his attentions.

[86] It seems to have occurred on a (later on) damaged (and now) lost tablet from Babylon.

[87] The repetition of the line replaces this "*u*" by *ša*. We thus either have a double function or a specialisation of the barber's prebend, "the barber who inspects".

[88] Following (reference M. Stol) F. Joannès NABU 1995/20, who also explains the reasons for the solidarity stressed by the document. A small problem would be that other prebendaries, and not the institution, would have to pay the barber. But this is not impossible, we encountered already the *šugarrû* for the *šangû*. Does the passage imply the recurrence of both shaving and physical inspection? That might imply even more cases in which execution of tasks had to be transferred to others.

extensively discussed by Jursa.[89] The ^{LU_2}ZABAR represents an *āšipu*. This is an addition to the already ample terminology indicating the exorcists. The *mašmaššu* occurs at any rate in the late rituals in a position which makes an *ērib bīti* status possible.[90] This is certain in VS 15, 1, where seven out of the 21 *ērib bīti* families listed are classified as *āšipu* families.[91] IŠIB is no longer a normal term in this period. That BM 42408 is a rare example of an execution contract for a non-purveying function has been stressed already.

A special and problematic class of ritualists is probably that constituted by the so-called "performers/entertainers". They occur already in the early period, but their prebendal status is, of course, nearly always questionable. One of these curiosities is the *kurgarrūtu*, which according to VS 5, 54 (26 II Camb 7, Borsippa) a woman[92] transferred back to her mother, together with other possessions which she had received and which originally belonged to her father. The function in question is indicated as 6) (*u*) *put zitti šá babtu* ^{LU_2}*kur-gar-ru-tu*, "the share in the balance of the performership", 7) *ša* PN, her father, which was held jointly with his brother and later on with a son of his. That the *kurgarrû* played a role in the cult is obvious.[93] The consequence could be that the *kurgarrû* was a "ritualist" and thus possibly an *ērib bīti*. Some form of prebendal status is more or less assured by the Uruk meat text.[94]

There is the possibility that the actual tasks had to be executed by specially trained persons. Berens 103 (18 I Kand 19) is a contract dealing with the training of a *kurgarrû* who was to become also a *ḫuppû*, "acrobat", an employment already mentioned in a cultic context by the Old Babylonian Mari ritual.[95] Such contracts were usually concluded for persons who were placed in training by their owner or father, who intended to profit from the schooling received by the pupil. This would of necessity imply a lowly status. But on the other hand there was also land *šá* E_2-^{LU_2}KUR.GAR.RA.MEŠ *ina* 50-*e šá* ŠE.NUMUN-*šú*, "belonging to the Kurgarrû family estate in the *ḫanšû* where its arable is situated(?)", which suggests that the Kurgarrûs, as a family, participated in an earlier Borsippa land division,

---

89 Jursa 1999 p. 72-75, cf. Bongenaar 1997 p. 288. Camb 236 links the status of *ērib bīti* and that of ^{LU_2}ZABAR-*ú-tu*. Also in Dar 162: 5 we find a ^{LU_2}ZABAR. In both Camb 236 and Dar 162 the functionaries mentioned share (rests of) *ma-la-a-ta/tu*$_4$. Another occurrence can be found in the Šamaš section of SWU 117, discussed above in the context of the meat portions.

90 In Uruk in the Tešrit ritual for Anu, in the nightly ceremony for him AO 6460, also in BRM 4, 7. KAR 132 for Ištar to the Akītu, in Babylon in the New Year's ritual (line 340 and following).

91 Lines I 8 and II 2.

92 With VS 5, 143. It is perhaps of some interest for the milieu in which the transaction takes place to point out that the woman concerned was qualified as a ^{MI_2}*nārtu* in the marriage document VS 6, 95, where she marries a father's brother's son, thus seemingly unifying the family's prebendal interests. Marriage contracts mentioning *nārtu*s, unless the *nārtu* brings a sufficient dowry, often contain an additional clause regarding adultery. I must thank C. Waerzeggers for reminding me of some of the ins and outs of the case.

93 Cf. CAD K pp. 557-9, esp. the reference to Lackenbacher 1977 rev. 25' is relevant. Cf. for *kurgarrû* in Uruk also LKU 51, 18', again in a cultic context. In Babylon this cultic role is especially documented in relation to Bēlet-Bābili alias Ištar of Babylon, cf. recently A. George 2000, p. 270 ff. with the literature mentioned there. The *kurgarrû* operated with the *asinnu*, on whom there is no relevant information from private archives. For the general context cf. S.M. Maul, *kurgarrû* und *assinnu* und ihr Stand in der babylonischen Gesellschaft, in ed. V. Haas, Aussenseiter und Randgruppen, Konstanzer althistorische Vorträge und Forschungen Heft 32, 1992, p. 159-171.

94 McEwan 1983, line 96, the only case of sacrifice of female animals in the text.

95 Dossin 1938 III 21, cf. the Kingsbury (1963) text line 332. (Not in 211!)

implying a certain status.[96] There can be no doubt that entertainers took part in rituals, but that does not mean that all entertainers inevitably had clerical status.

VS 15, 1, as is well known, qualifies families belonging to certain types of craftsmen explicitly as *ērib bītis*: after the here less relevant *āšipus*[97] we find *naggārus*, *kabšarrus*, *purkullus*, *gurgurrus* (obsolete for *nappāḫus*?) and *kutimmus* included in this category. Only the *kutimmus* are otherwise known as prebendaries. An *ērib bīti* is not exclusively a "ritualist", he can ostensibly also be a craftsman with a task in the ritual. The cultic employment of certain craftsmen is explicit in the Babylon New Year's ritual and also implied by the role of the *bīt pirišti* in the Hellenistic text from Uruk of which the dress prescriptions are preserved.[98] The *bīt pirišti* and the *kutimmu* are especially associated in a prebendal context in this period.[99] *ērib bīt pirišti* will not have been the same as *ērib bīti* sec.

Though the *ērib bīti* is in a number of cases with reasonable certainty someone who plies a specific trade either of a ritualistic or of an artisanal type,[100] the problem remains that such a specific task cannot be established in all cases. In the *kudurrus* reference to the title *ērib bīti* offers a standard of remuneration without specification of a particular occupation, and as a term typifying a source of income the qualification also occurs in private documents other than texts mentioning the tell-tale standard amounts for bread and beer. For instance in the inheritance division Gordon, Smith College 90 (Borsippa 21 VII Dar 15), where it is not combined with any other prebendal function, though the specific *maššaktu*, share in meat portions, is stressed.[101] With the standard equal amounts of bread and beer it can occur in various types of document, as we have seen.

Perhaps the approach to the problem selected is fundamentally wrong, as appearance in a private document has been chosen as the point of departure. Any prebendal function consisted of a combination of specific (ritual) tasks and income of (basically) ration type, often deriving from offerings, plus additional perks. The perks were often the result of performance of or participation in a specific rite or the performance of specific tasks. Some tasks, those of, for instance, the baker or the brewer, could be executed without participating in the direct cult. Other functions implied execution of specific ritual acts which could take place both within and outside a cultic context, for instance the activities of the *āšipu* or the *bārû,* who would demand remuneration on practising their skills outside the

96 M.T. Roth, Babylonian Marriage Agreements, 7th-3rd Centuries B.C. AOAT 222, 1989, no. 22 (19 XI Dar 1). In line 5 read 50-*e* instead of TIR.

97 That is: for us, for the writer of the text it may have signified that being an *āšipu* indicated possessing a skill comparable to that of the other trades, of which there had to be a supply as *ērib bītis*.

98 Falkenstein 1959 p. 40 ff., lines 3'-4', cf. rev. 3'. Rites also took place in the *bīt ummi,* ibid. p. 37, colophon. Possibly the *bīt pirišti* and the *bīt ummi* workshops were identical or related. Cf. also the eclipse ritual published by D. Brown and M. Linssen, RA 91, 1997, p. 157, rev. 6', where the E_2 *pirišti* occurs towards the end between the *akītu* house and the *ubšukkinnakku* in what is intended to be a comprehensive list of consecrated buildings or loci.

99 On this fixed combination McEwan 1981 p. 80. See also Doty, 1993, for OECT 9, 50 which specifies the perks of the goldsmith's prebend in detail and illustrates that such perks were related to the specific rites in which the functionary participated, as was already the case in the Old Babylonian Kingsbury text. For *ērib bīt pirišti* in Neo-Babylonian Sippar cf. Bongenaar 1987 p. 306 nt. 323, with p. 149 nt. 165, where the link with goldsmiths is obvious.

100 The case rests especially on VS 15, 1; but note that Borger 1973 stresses the fact that the person to be consecrated is to enter the sanctuary for the first time.

101 BM 67216, J. MacGinnis, AfO 38/9, 1991-2, no. 10 (p. 94-6), an adoption involving an *ērib bīti* prebend before Šamaš in Ebabbar in Sippar, which contained a detailed specification of the income, lines 6-8, but it is too damaged for reconstruction.

cult for private clients. Acting within a cultic context required additional appropriate consecration on top of proper training which was possibly combined with special initiation into the secrets of the specific trade. If we want to understand who were the cult related prebendaries, we must know who performed which particular type of rite in a cultic context,[102] for the execution of which the appropriate material they required had to be provided, in the manner certain occupations received the requirements for the execution of a particular rite in the Kingsbury text. We must leave open the possibility that in certain rites more than one occupation participated, like the *mašmaššu* and the *ṭābiḫu* acting together in a purification rite in the New-Year's ritual.

The question is whether there were rites reserved for *ērib bītis*, just as there seem to have been rites for (mainly) *kalamaḫḫus*. The possibility exists.[103] Performing those tasks constituted the function of *ērib bīti* and entailed the related remuneration. Other specialist functionaries received the same initiation in order to be able to function within the sanctuary and could (also) be called *ērib bīti*. It has perhaps always looked unproblematic, but the specific rites of the *ērib bīti* are strictly spoken unidentified as far as I can see. One of the keys to the prebendal system might be the link between the function or title and the specific cultic task which generated the income, with the proviso that new specialisations resulted in fresh vertical fractionating of existing functions.[104]

What an *ērib bīti* had to do probably also depended on the scale of the institution to which he was attached. The ultimate specialisation in a top ranking sanctuary might thus be "being just an *ērib bīti*", but equally the status might imply “all functions” in a smaller temple. For our understanding it would be of importance if an *ērib bīti* prebend could be leased, used as a collateral or sold without specification of a special task or without combination with one of the purveying prebends. Sale is unequivocally attested in Uruk,[105] lease in the Sippar Marduk-rēmanni texts.[106] That it could be transferred through adoption, specifically in the wider family, is less of a problem, the skill required would in such cases also be transmitted in that way.[107]

---

[102] Cf. lists of the type found RAcc p. 79 AO 6451 rev. 35-39, but there was more.

[103] For instance the unnamed ritual acts undertaken, possibly every morning, after the *aḫu rabû* had opened the doors, parallel to, it would seem, those performed by *kalûs* and *nārus*, as mentioned as a routine for the various days for which the Babylon Newyear’s Ritual is preserved. Had the *ērib bīti* a special ritual task at the opening -and closing- of the temple? A study of the specific performers of the various rites would seem to be required, on the principle that any cultic rite generates income and thus has to play a role in the prebendal system. The RA 16 Marduk-zākir-šumi *kudurru* poses a number of problems when we must assign specific forms of income to equally specific functions for which the king provides. If we assume that I 28 to II 2 are an extension of lines I 25-27, the *šalām bīti* of line 28 belong to the rites in which *ērib bītis* participate. In the Anu ritual AO 6460, RAcc p. 120, "all *ērib bītis*" are involved in the *šalām bīti* ceremony. Whether *malītu* is more than a term for a form of offering and income is not clear to me, but at any rate in Camb 236 rests of the *malītus* are destined for the *ērib bītis* in conjunction with the ^{LU}2ZABAR, whom we now know to be an *āšipu*, as remarked already. They are also associated with *malītus* in Dar 162.

[104] Many cultic rituals are, it would seem, function specific, they do therefore only help up to a degree, as is sometimes clear from the colophon of a text. The Babylon Newyear’s ritual seems to concentrate on what the *aḫu rabû* had to do, or, sometimes, had not to see.

[105] E. von Weiher, SpBT IV 221 (AUWE 12), 6 IX Nbp 0.

[106] Waerzeggers 2001 texts M.r. 76 and 157, it involved, rather exceptionally, payments in silver.

[107] A secure case of an adoption is MacGinnis 1991-2 no. 10. Adoption by a woman, tablet damaged, relation between adoptee and adoptrix unclear. Rechtsleben I p. 10 is the adoption by a grandfather of a daughter's son, cf. eds. M. Stol and S.P. Vleeming, The Care of the Elderly in the Ancient Near East,

A curiosity is that the Borsippa prebendary Zēr-Bābili s Šumā (Ea-)ilūta-bani was qualified as "(the) *ērib bīti* of Nabû" with a certain regularity in situations where use of the title has little obvious sense, for instance in date *imittu* texts where the delivery was due to him. Possibly it only served to differentiate him from a namesake. Or was he simply proud of his title? That might be a factor of some importance.

b. Presumed non-*ērib bīti* prebends: the "purveying trades"

If the position of the bakers[108] and brewers is to be seen primarily as that of providers of the foodstuffs required for the meals placed before the gods,[109] a range of other occupations should fall in the same category: the butchers (GIR$_2$.LA$_2$, *ṭābiḫu*), the fishermen (ŠU.ḪA, *bā'iru*), the date gardeners (GAL.DU$_3$, *rab banî*), the various (prebendal) herdsmen, i.e. those who delivered cattle or sheep for the sacrifices, that is those who were engaged in the preliminary fattening of these animals, and those who were responsible for the delivery of dairy products. The oil pressers (*ṣāḫit sattukki* or *ginê*) probably also belonged to this category. The position of makers, repairers and cleaners of divine clothing needs consideration in this context, though classification with the craftsmen could be considered, especially if they were personally involved in dressing the gods, which would imply direct contact. Otherwise these are the "purveying trades". We assume that as a rule they were not *ērib bītis* but received prebendal income, which put them apart from others who exercised the same trades within the institutions without possessing the qualifications required for consecration or having access to prebendal posts.

Notwithstanding the efforts of Bongenaar, Jursa, Kessler and Kümmel the information on the "purveying" prebendaries in Sippar and Uruk in the Neo-Babylonian period remains limited to a restricted number of functions, in many cases based on few texts or on more frequent repetitive documents, which are therefore not very informative. This is unlikely to be truly representative of the system, though there is now some additional information.[110]

The problem is partially that individually members of all these occupational groups could be *ērib bītis*, at least because they also possessed other prebends to which this status was attached. This was certainly the case with many of the so-called "college-scribes" and also with others. Single members of other occupations for one reason or another may have had to belong to this group.

When discussing the texts of the Nappāḫu family it transpired that a prebend, in this case that of a slaughterer, which had never been indicated by the term of *ērib bīti* in the

---

Leiden 1998, p. 162 note 1. AnOr 8, 48 has been mentioned in relation to the question of the admission to prebendal occupations.

108 We must reckon with the effects of differences in size. TÉBR 35 (4 IX <Art II> 2 deals with a baker's prebend in the local temple of Bēl-Šaṭir. Line 10 uses, in indicating the tasks to be fulfilled, the verbs *ṭēḫû* and *sanāqu*: does this imply that the *nuḫatimmu* concerned did place his products before the god himself? *ṭēḫû* occurs probably earlier in the baking process, *sanāqu* may indicate delivery, which occurs, of course, later. Cf. RAcc p. 77, 46 *ṭa-ḫu-ú ša im-me-e-ti*, translated "serving of the hot (loaves)", CAD E p. 151L. None of this is compelling. TÉBR 35 deals, of course, with a small local sanctuary, an *ērib bīti* in such a context inevitably will have carried out many jobs. In a non-prebendal context, and thus perhaps also when dealing with prebendaries, the skills of a slaughterer and a baker/cook could be combined. Revillout, BOR 2, 1887-8, p. 119-120 (8 X Dar 8) is a contract according to which someone's slave was to be trained in both trades combined.

109 This group of prebendaries has been treated for Uruk by Kümmel 1979, p. 148ff.

110 Needless to say, what follows is not a complete list of texts from private archives dealing with this type of prebends.

documents, was apparently suddenly referred to by that term.[111] This opens the further possibility that, though not all prebendaries belonging to the "purveying trades" were *ērib bītis*, at least some members of these "trades" were, in the Nappāḫu case possibly not only because they also possessed an(other) *ērib bīti* prebend. It is, however, more probable that the Nappāḫu text uses the terminology loosely, which might become more likely if the Nappāḫus had originally possessed a complete minor sanctuary prebend for Išḫara. The prebendal world would not stand alone in imprecise use, since technical terminology always derives from terms originally occurring in a much wider context.

For practical purposes use of the term *pappasu* implies remuneration with the same material as that used for the preparation of the food that was to be delivered for the divine table. The term is not used in connection with animals for slaughter, but in the case of the slaughterers the granting of a complete sheep or a special share in sacrificial animals could be regarded as comparable to that what seems to be attested for bakers and brewers, as it is a remuneration in the line of the trade itself. As we saw, like the bakers and the brewers, the slaughterer dressed like the un-initiated *kalû* in the text published by Falkenstein. The position of the slaughterers differed from that of other providers of food in that they alone were directly concerned with bloody offerings.[112] It is of course not very likely that slaughter took place in the immediate presence of the gods.[113] In JCS 36 no. 6 (27 I Kand 6), excavated in Babylon, *na-ka-su* UDU.NITA$_2$, "the butchering of sheep", is especially mentioned as the task of the *ṭābiḫūtu*-prebendary concerned (lines 2-3).[114] But on the other hand the *bārû*,[115] whom we would probably regard as a "ritualist", though he is, perhaps, better classified as a "technician", would have had to inspect the entrails of any sacrificed animal as a matter of routine. There would have been, however, no need for his presence before the gods either. A specialist of this type would probably be available in a major sanctuary, though not necessarily in every temple. In the course of the New-Year's" ritual in Babylon a *mašmaššu* and a *ṭābiḫu* became ritually tainted after a purification rite involving the killing of a sheep. Both had to leave the town for the duration of the rites concerned.[116] But this concerns a purification rite and not a sacrifice belonging to the repast of the gods, which is definitely something different.

The *mubannû*, if indeed a "layer of the table", could be regarded as a person who had to enter the sanctuary, in particular if he really had to display the food before the god concerned. If our theory is correct, the basic allowance for *ērib bītis* was expressed in fixed

---

[111] In Peiser Verträge 94 there are clearly two prebends of which the second is that of an *ērib bīti*, the phrase indicating the first is lost, but it was to all likelihood that of a slaughterer.

[112] The "baker" had to cook the meat, of course.

[113] Though the interpretation of buildings like the Red and the Grey "temples" on Jebel Aruda as sanctuaries is subject to doubt, it remains a fact that already in the Late-Uruk period these buildings in their various building phases can be associated with "kitchens", which were each time relocated in a position where they were more or less out of sight from the main buildings. In this respect "temples" differ from ordinary houses.

[114] That a slaughterer does the butchering himself, is, perhaps, not so remarkable, the purport of the statement is that he slaughtered sheep and not cattle. A sign of specialisation? Peiser Verträge 107 (2 x Dar 26, Nappāḫu archive) states that the *ṭābiḫūtu* of that text includes that of both cattle and sheep and that on a whole range of occasions. On *nākisu/nēkisu* as a term for slaughterer cf. Bongenaar 1997 p. 294.

[115] On this function we can practically refer only to the remarks made by Jursa 1999 p. 177 *ad* 2f., on the problematic passage in BM 42408.

[116] RAcc p. 141, 360.

amounts of bread and beer, related to the importance of the deity involved. BM 79116[117] is an antichretic loan involving a prebend consisting of ten days of *mubannūtu* in Ebabbar in Sippar. In an antichretic arrangement the direct income from the collateral replaces the interest on the capital concerned. The income is strikingly specified as the flour (line 10) and dates (line 12) for ten days and is thus not in the shape of the bread and beer we tentatively assumed to have been characteristic for an *ērib bīti* prebend. This suggests that the *mubannû* was after all not an *ērib bīti*, even though he had a ritual role in an Uruk ritual.[118] C. Waerzeggers[119] in her study of the Ṣāḫit-ginê family texts has added more material to the two *epišānūtu* texts mentioning *mubannūtu* in conjunction with the two linked prebends of oil presser and *muttaqūtu* already edited MacGinnis 1999. The texts suggest an involvement with food, such as dates, some, just one *ṣibtu*[120] of *takkasû*, beer and vegetables. The *mubannūtu* is thus probably just another of the purveying trades, as CAD M/2 suggests, perhaps the arranger of the dishes, and thus not an *ērib bīti* after all.[121] We can add that in Borsippa there was a *ḫanšû* of a Mubannû family.[122] I assume that the *muttāqūtu* prebend was a specialisation split off from that of the *ṣaḫit ginê*, as both handled sesame and are clearly linked in M.-r. text no. 156:5-6 in *šalām bīti* ceremonies.[123]

Bakers:[124] Some texts illustrate that this prebendal occupation entailed specific costs, which had to be covered. TuM 2/3, 209 (23 XIIb Nbn 13) from Nippur is regrettably damaged, but still contains some interesting information regarding the execution of the prebendal obligations: the owner seems to hire an executor for the tasks, who is responsible for the *manzaltu*, the actual prebendal obligations. The owner was to provide him with the means to heat the oven[125] and he pays the monthly *idū*, wages, 0.1.2 in barley, to the

---

117 Jursa, 1999, but, as stated there, not related to the Bēl-rēmanni archive, p. 250-1. Other texts relating to *mubannû* have been (re-)edited in MacGinnis 1999.

118 KAR 132 III 16, cf. RAcc p. 99.

119 Waerzeggers 2001 p. 141 discusses a group of related relevant texts, nos. 156, 161, 179, 180 and 181, tabulated on p. I 151, all dealing with the lease of an oil pressers prebend, a *mubannu* prebend and a *muttāqūtu* prebend. In relation to these prebends only income in foodstuffs is mentioned, which is obviously related to the functions and not of *ērib bīti* type. All three definitely belong to the purveying trades, and the oil pressers and *muttāqūtu* prebends are clearly linked.

120 *ṣibtu* is a "general purpose word" which is used in "prebendal texts" for amounts of bread and *takkasû*. Cf. CAD Ṣ p. 158 "(a type of bread)" with p.162-2, the discussion suggesting a link with *aṣābu*, "to increase in size", which could possibly be imagined for textiles and even for bread, but only with difficulty for dates. AHw p. 1099 gives "Brotfladen". The word must represent a known, fixed amount, but we cannot calculate how much, as the information contained in the material quoted by the CAD seems to be irreconcilable. The word *ṣibtu* is a general quagmire. No better interpretation than "helping" can be suggested in a number of cases.

121 T. Boiy, 2000 p. 235, has reopened the question whether ^{LU_2}ŠITIM represents Babylonian *mubannû*, as a reading *itinnu* is not attested in a prebendal context, which is in itself not compelling. SWU 117 lines 15' and 16' had already decided the issue, as *mubannû* and *itinnu* occur next to one another in the same text.

122 M.T. Roth 1991, AOAT 222, App C 12 (1 XI Dar 5), cf. also BE 8/1, 108 (28 XII Dar 6). See the contribution on taxation sub *ḫanšū*.

123 Cf. the table Waerzeggers 2001 I p. 151. Some doubt whether this set of documents realistically represents the situation of the tree prebends occurring in them is perhaps warranted, as these may be scribal exercises. The obvious manipulation of the witnesses, and perhaps the considerable detail presented, invite caution.

124 Especially important is Kessler 1991, p. 65ff.

125 Line 7, *ḫuṣābu* and NU[-x x]?

executor from the *mi-in-[du?]*[126] of the MUḪALDIM-*ú-tu*, by which possibly the same as the *maššartu* was meant, line 9-10, "his" *pappasu* being mentioned in line 8; line 12 mentions a delivery of 0.1.0 in barley and 0.0.3 in flour to the executor. *pappasu* being the prebendal income, costs, the conclusion seems inevitable, again, would have to be paid from the *sattukku*, nominally provided for the god. The text is too damaged for a valid conclusion and perhaps we must again not expect that terminology in general is that precise.

In BM 42551+[127] Bēl-rēmanni had fulfilled obligations pertaining to four days of a baker's prebend belonging to a member of the Isināja family called Šuma-iddina, during a period of six months. The text is best characterised as a receipt given by Bēl-rēmanni. This makes it somewhat problematic to assign the document to his archive, but on the other hand it also specifies what remained due to him, thus giving him an interest in the document. Bēl-rēmanni had received *uppuntu*-flour, fuel and *mu(ḫ)ḫ(u)ru*[128] and monthly 6.0.0 of barley and 0.3.2 of emmer-wheat "for serving(?)" (*a-na qe-er-re-bi*), and he had given the *paḫīdu*-flour for the four days to Šuma-iddina. Barley, emmer, [x, y etc.?] and dates, the/his *pappasu*, and emmer Bēl-rēmanni had not received from Šum-iddina. Remarkably enough the *pappasu* seems to go to the executor in this case, who delivers *paḫīdu*-flour to the owner: perhaps we are dealing with arrangements in which parties take over only certain specified tasks from each other, but not the complete charge involved.[129] The exact meaning of *qerēbu* is not clear either. We do not have the contract between these parties, *epišānūtu* is perhaps not always a simple straightforward affair. It looks in this case like a kind of *ḫarrānu*, a joint venture, a word not apparently used in prebendal context.

Also BM 42299 (11 VII Dar x) from the same archive contains additional information on the nature of baker's prebends. It concerns a dispute between the elder brother of Bēl-rēmanni and members of the Isināia family centring on specified days of a baker's prebend and additionally 2,5 days of a special obligation of cultic nature called *sel-le-e sa-mu-tu*[130] (lines 11 etc.) which were (line 22) an element of the baker's prebend to be delivered for both morning and evening meals (line 13). What these "red baskets" were, is not specified, but the phenomenon is for us of a more general interest, in that it again indicates that a prebend could be subdivided "vertically" into specific smaller elements, which could be regarded as separate tasks and sources of income.[131] The splitting up of

---

[126] Line 10. *mindu* could indicate the total material measured out for the function, cf. CAD M/2 p. 85R, where this possible occurrence is not registered. It would be much earlier than the others. In the Hellenistic period the *bēl mindi* of various occupations were responsible for payments to the individual members of the group. By that time having a *bēl mindi* possibly could indicate that an occupation had prebendal status. This is especially of importance in relation to the status of the function of the *ṭupšar enūma-Anu-Enlil*.

[127] Jursa 1999 p. 198-9, with p. 56, with pertinent comments on the text also p. 77: Šumu-iddina acts as the *šāpiru* of the bakers. Jursa bases his ingenious reconstruction of lines 17-18 on BM 42402 (ibid. p. 175), but though the text refers to the same affair two years later, that text refers to specific amounts, not to generalities as here. I therefore prefer to read the sign interpreted as m[a as Z[IZ$_2$, but must accept that line 16 has to contain in that case other commodities.

[128] Text: *mu-ḫur*MEŠ. Jursa 1999 p. 199 ad line 9 and p. 56, "material for the *muḫru/miḫru*(?) offerings". This remains an embarrassment.

[129] The passage is damaged, but Jursa's reading is confirmed by related BM 42402, which deals with a part of the following two years.

[130] Jursa 1999 p. 56.

[131] The only reference known to me to a miller's prebend is best interpreted as vertical split of a baker's prebend. OECT 9, 62, McEwan 1981, p. 68ff, combines a baker's and a miller's prebend (^{LU_2}ḪAR-*ú-tú*, *ararrūtu*) in an execution (*rēsinūtu*) arrangement intended to last for ten years. The text underlines the fact that the baker was responsible for grinding the cereals he used and that is mentioned separately by the

prebends into various periods of service is well-attested, but they also could be divided according to the various obligations entailing income.[132] In general the splitting up of functions in their constituent elements may have been a marked feature of the late period.[133] It is perhaps a general phenomenon in all organisations, related to their innate need to enhance the importance of the minutiae of their workings.

Brewers: That the brewer had to undergo some form of initiation, even if he did not, in general, belong to the *ērib bītis*, is clear from YOS 7, 167 (Eanna archive, 9 XII Camb 4), where the term *gullubu* is used. We can assume that this equally applies to the other "purveying trades". Note that the brewers had to carry the god on certain occasions.[134]

For the practical implications of the tasks of the brewer TuM 2/3, 79, Nippur, date lost, not attributed to a specific file, is important. The text indicates that the Nippur brewers operated in an organisation which comprised both the (main) E_2.KUR and other local sanctuaries, E_2.KUR.MEŠ *gabbi ša* NIBRU^{KI}, as was the case elsewhere. They were to carry out their tasks *itti* ^{LU_2}UN.IL_2.MEŠ-*šú-nu* ^{LU_2}LUNGA.MEŠ TUR.MEŠ, with, an obsolete term, their "underlings" and the "junior brewers", a welcome confirmation of the fact that the entitled belonging to the "purveying trades" employed others, who did the actual work.

Brewing was probably the most "commercialised" of the purveying trades. Especially from Borsippa there is much information on the subject, which cannot be listed in full here. VS 6, 182 (x XI Xer 0?) is an *epišānūtu* contract for 300 *dannu* of beer[135] per annum for the *naptanu* of Nabû which seems to have run since IX Dar 36 between Rēmūt-Bēl s Iddina-Nabû of the Ilšabušu family and Nabû-ušallim s Nabû-apal-iddina of the Lakuppuru family, who acted as a brewer.[136] The "customer" also acted on behalf of

---

text. That the development had gone further than a simple separate listing, might be concluded from line 10 if McEwan's interpretation is followed. The food portions consisting of meat and a volume of an unspecified commodity, possibly barley, payable for the baker's prebend, is separated by McEwan from the ^{UZU}ḪAR.MEŠ, which he interprets as intended for the miller, even though only the baker's prebend is mentioned at the end of the phrase, strictly spoken. The alternative in McEwan 1981, p. 70 note 70, "lungs", deserves reconsideration.

132 *In margine,* and without discussion, we can mention here the question of the *isqu šá(-)qa-a-a-tu*$_4$, understood by Doty 1977 p. 135-6, with McEwan 1981 p. 99, as referring to "hulled barley", but accepted CAD I/J p. 201 as a (separate) *šaqqaja* prebend. The text concerned is BRM 2, 36. Not found CAD Q p. 54, where there is a reference to Neo-Babylonian use of *qajātu*, "parched barley" in a ritual context. On the institutional craftsman *šaqqaja*, "sack maker", Bongenaar 1997, p. 313-4, without any reference to a possible prebendal status. BRM 2, 36 refers to all likelihood to a sub-specialisation of a purveying occupation.

133 But not only in the late period. F. van Koppen has drawn my attention to CT 4, 11a, Old Babylonian from Sippar. In view of the witnesses the text certainly belongs to a temple environment, and whatever the *ne-pi*$_2$*-a-tum* may signify, (*nēpītu* is a baker's trough), they had financial implications and were inherited by Nidnat-Suen from three persons, after which he transferred three to his brothers. The possibility that this refers to some element of the ritual-related work of the baker could be considered.

134 Uruk, BRM 4, 7, F. Thureau-Dangin, RA 20 p. 107f. In the Old Babylonian Mari ritual they take up position with the craftsmen, Durand-Guichard 1997, no. 2, = Dossin 1938, line I 17'.

135 As argued already KAŠ.U_2.SA, *billatu/biltu*, is almost inevitably delivered in a fluid state in this period, as it should be ready for consumption at the *naptanu* of the god.

136 For each *dannu* of KAŠ.U_2.SA the "customer" would provide the executor with 0.2.1 of barley and 0.0.1 of kasia. On the assumption that 3 volumes of barley produces 1 volume of beer (Freydank 1971 p. 50) we could assume that the contract amounts to 300 tuns of 26 $SILA_3$ of beer for the unspecified *manzaltus* of the two persons mentioned in line 7. Such a tun would be remarkably small. It differs considerably from Freydank's calculation which equates a *dannu* with 1,5 kor, 270 $SILA_3$. It is of some interest that the customer owned the tools (lines 23-5) and provided his *šutummu*, but it is not completely

another person, but both were obviously prebendaries. For practical purposes we might regard this again as a *ḫarrānu* lacking the term. On BRM I 82 (3+ VIII Dar 27) see below.

Herdsmen: TÉBR 84 (II Dar 25, Borsippa, Rē'u-alpi) differentiates between an *isqu rē'u* $GU_4.AB_2$.MEŠ of four months and an *isqu rē'u* GU_4-*ú-tu* of 10 days, a cowherd's and an ox-herd's prebend respectively, belonging to Ezida, for which the holder had a right to *pappasu* for four months and ten days with the additional qualification of *ša ku-tal-la*.[137] These were clearly separate tasks, the first to all likelihood to be related to the delivery of milk[138], for which in Uruk the prebendal *rē'u šizbi* was responsible. The ox herd was probably responsible for the delivery of specially fattened male animals for sacrificial use.[139] The fragmentation of this function should be noted. That these special herdsmen needed fodder for their animals and therefore incurred costs, goes without saying. They probably received that fodder with the additional *pappasu*. Payment of *pappasu* suggests, not-unexpectedly in these cases, a non-*ērib-bīti* status.

Important is YOS 7, 79 (12 III Cyr 8, Uruk),[140] on the position of the milk-herdsman's prebend, the *isqu* DUMU ^{LU_2}SIPAD-*ú-tu ši-zib*, which was, appropriately enough, in the hands of the Uruk Rē'u-alpi family, not only because the text indicates that prebendal rights could revert to the king, but also because it contains details on the practical execution of tasks and the remuneration. The institution provided a *širku* for the actual herding of the cows and their calves and handed on a regular basis the means of production over to the prebendary, who was remunerated, again regularly, with a head of cattle. But again: the actual work was done by others of lower status. That will also have been the case elsewhere.

BM 26518 (19 XIIb Nbp 7) is an arrangement between two parties concerning a shepherd's prebend of the Nabû temple in Borsippa which one of them had bought and transferred partially to the other. This would not be remarkable were it not for its notable phrasing: 9)... GIŠ.ŠUB.BA *it-ti a-ḫa-meš* 10) *i-šaq-qu u i-šap-pa-l[u]*: "they will share gains and losses resulting from the prebend", which sounds eminently commercial.[141]

The function of *rē'u ginê/sattukki* occurred in both Uruk and Sippar, but it was clearly not prebendal in Sippar.[142] The function had given rise to a family name in Uruk, but I can find no clear indication that it was prebendal there. This could perhaps be a direct result of the fact that it was in the hands of only one family, which reduced the need for

---

certain that the actual brewing took place there. As the *manzaltu* of the two customers will have fallen on certain specific days there will have been available a considerable spare brewing capacity on other days, which can hardly be assumed to have been lying idle. These persons were businessmen, even if, or rather, especially because, they left the work to others.

137 The same prebendal rights occur in VS 5, 102 (14 VI Dar 29). This use of *kutallu* does not occur in CAD K it would seem. A possible explanation, without proof, could be that this indicates the secondary repast following the main meal, thus representing another term for *tardennu* or *qallu*, which were actually used in this context. This is, however, no more than a council of despair. Perhaps we must rather think of keeping animals which could be used as a replacement or for extra sacrifices at short notice.

138 Female animals are not usually required for offerings, but cf. the Uruk meat text, McEwan 1983, lines 86 and 93.

139 And thus comparable to Ur III and OB institutional KURUŠDAs, who were certainly not prebendaries, though there is a possibility that the Old Babylonian *mušākilu*, in CBS 414, discussed above, was one, on occasion.

140 Kümmel 1979 p. 83.

141 S. Zawadski, AfO 42/3, 1995-96 p. 210.

142 Explicit on this question Bongenaar 1997, p. 416: these people appear in the ordinary wage lists.

written contracts.[143] This functionary dealt especially with sheep. There are clear signs that the function was inheritable, it went at any rate from father to son, as in Sippar, without being prebendal in that place.

It is of some importance to note that "prebendal aspects" are shared by functions which do not attain that status. This can draw a whole range of other, often humble, occupational family names into the institutional orbit, even though such families did not attain prebendal rank.[144] This is important for the theory that institutional occupations played an important role in the rise of the Neo-Babylonian family names from the second half of the second millennium onward. The possibility that especially on this point there were local differences must be kept open. In one location a function may give rise to a family name, in another such a development may have been stunted. The name also might become that of a prebendal family or not, even if its members belonged to the personnel of the sanctuary.

Fisherman: ŠU.ḪA, *bā'iru*, on whom there is evidence from Uruk, will be dealt with below, when the workings of the system are discussed. The potential financial importance of this prebend, if it represents a real prebend, is suggested by the Borsippa contract TuM 2/3, 206 (x II Nbn x+2).

The GAL/GAN$_2$.DU$_3$,[145] as a holder of a *ḫallatu*-orchard intended for the production of dates for the table of the gods during a specified period, also will not necessarily have had to enter the sanctuary. Generally the garden concerned had to provide for a specified day of the month, according to the Dilbat and Uruk evidence. But the strict attribution of a specific plot to a specific day was probably largely fictional, for the gardens were commonly sold or leased to gardeners, in which there is as a rule no reference to the obligations towards the temple, not even in Dilbat[146] and they were subject, at any rate in Sippar, to the ordinary *imittu* procedure followed by delivery at harvest: the *rab banî* did not deliver, as far as can be seen, the specific dates for his fixed day, but, perhaps, he had to present the dates for that day from a general store.

c. Craftsmen *ērib bītis*

VS 15, 1, as mentioned, explicitly qualifies certain families of craft prebendaries as *ērib bītis*. The link between function and family requires no further discussion. Here too local particularities can be expected. Though already in the Old Babylonian Mari ritual craftsmen participated in a cultic ritual,[147] information on craftsmen's prebends from private archives is limited. With the *kutimmu* prebend of *ērib bīti* status only the builder's prebend in the Hellenistic period has received separate treatment, but the function is not included in VS 15, 1.[148]

---

[143] Kümmel 1979 p. 86.

[144] Especially for instance the family names of the *ša* x-*šu*-type.

[145] Useful observations in Waerzeggers 2001 p. 137-140.

[146] Coquerillat 1973/4, on the link with specific days p. 101, 105 and 117 for Borsippa. Especially in the case of the Dilbat woman Amat-Bau: VS 5, 105, VS 3, 152, 153 etc. As an element of a *nudunnu* VS 5, 104. For Sippar cf. especially Jursa, AfO Beih. 25, 1995, p. 57ff., where it is difficult to find any link between garden and day.

[147] Durand-Guichard 1997, no. 2, identical with Dossin 1938, lines 17-9, listing after ^{LU_2}LUNGA: ^{LU_2}NAGAR, ^{LU_2}AŠGAB, ^{LU_2}TUG$_2$.DU$_8$, ^{LU_2}TUG$_2$. They are summarised as DUMU.MEŠ *ú/um-me-ni*.

[148] Funck 1984, p. 214-239. Note that a ŠITIM has to be present on a specific day according to AnOr 8, 44.

Reed worker, *atkuppu*: YOS 6, 135 (16 IV Nbn 10), from Uruk, is probably an arrangement imposed by the institutional authorities,[149] in which PN1 transfers the *maš-šak-ti*, the "meat portions", of the *ginê* and the *guqqû*, belonging to the reed worker's prebend of Eanna to three persons against a payment of 7 *š* per annum. The term is mentioned without specification. PN1 will give (line 12) the x x ^{LU_2}AD.KID from the NIG$_2$.GA, the institutional store. What this exactly represents cannot be read, but we may reasonably expect that it is the material required for performing the job. Notable is that the three persons will pay the 7 *š* to Eanna. The backgrounds are far from certain, but this is certainly a prebendal function. VS 6, 37 (13 IX Nbk 33) is a contract regulating the execution of *atkuppu*-duties during a five day period in the first month in obviously a one-time short term contract between members of the Atkuppu family. This is the second execution contract for a non-purveying prebend known. The Uruk and Sippar *atkuppu*s known to respectively Kümmel and Bongenaar were for all practical purposes ordinary workmen, not prebendaries, but that is a matter of documentation only. Whether the prebendal *atkuppu* really should be a craftsman *ērib bīti* should be left open, but this function is at any rate not found in VS 15, 1.

On the prebendal weavers in Sippar cf. Bongenaar 1997 p. 310ff. with comments on their *pappasu*, out of which personnel costs had to be paid. On the basis of *pappasu* indicating a "purveying trade", the prebendal weaver was not an *ērib bīti*, but a purveyor. The TUG$_2$.BABBAR (Bongenaar 1997 p. 313) received *kiskirru*-type payments, which could also suggest prebendal status.[150]

d. The Edict of Belsazzar and the gate keepers, measurers and scribes

This brings us to the special position in the prebendal system which was taken up by the measurers and probably also the gate keepers,[151] as they enjoyed income from an external source. This position was shared by the institutional scribes, who are not usually regarded as belonging to the prebendal system proper. The extend of these rights is best illustrated by the so-called Edict of Belsazzar, but there is a distinct possibility that similar entitlements were spread even wider.

Gate keepers/porters: For the *atû*[152] the claim to payments as meant in the Edict of Belsazzar, which lists these special payments as *gimru* to be paid by institutional tenants[153] is perhaps reflected in the Uruk text Nbk 129 (15 VII Nbk 21, file of the family Atû) where 1-*it* ^{GIŠ}IG *šá* ^{LU_2}I$_3$.DU$_8$-*ú-tu šá bāb sa-li-mu u mim-mu-šú šá* URU *u* EDIN serves as a collateral, but the "all in town and country" probably refers to the other possession of the person who pawns his right to income, and not to rights connected specifically to the doorkeepership, though other texts leave the possibility open.

A much better witness to this fact is VS 5, 37 (Borsippa, Iliya A, 13 IX Cyr 2) concerning the function of gatekeeper of the Bab-nīribi-Nabû of Ezida: 3) ... *a-di ir-bi ṣi-i-*

149 Discussed Kümmel 1979 p. 43 with information on the persons involved.

150 Cf. also Waerzeggers 2001 p. I 131, where only weaving of textile for a *lubuštu* is mentioned and not the function. S. Zawadski will publish additional material.

151 Often called "porters" in the literature.

152 Kümmel 1997 p. 44-45, not treated in Bongenaar 1997; cf. also, Esagil, Babylon, JCS 36 no. 6 (27 I Kand 6) line 5 ff., which attests to the fragmentation of both the *ṭābiḫūtu* and the *atūtu* prebends in this period: two days of both are sold for two minas of silver. Marad: CT 51, 56 (11 VII Dar x), Ea temple, or does this refer to a temple in Babylon and is the transaction only dated in Marad? For a butcher's prebend in Marad see G.R. Driver, JRAS 1924, Cent. Supp. (20 VIb Šmšk 2).

153 The question will be dealt with here in the separate contribution on taxation. Cf. for Uruk Kümmel 1979 p. 45. On a possible link with *kiskirru* and/or *kallānu* see above.

ti, "with what enters and goes out", mentioning meat portions of the *bīt ka-re-e*, held in an undivided state with others, which was sold by the partial owner concerned. Cf., perhaps, also TCL 13, 182 (13 IV Dar 2). The tasks are described in TCL 12, 80. That these were not always attractive transpires from YOS 7, 89 (date lost), where the function of gatekeeper of the *akītu*-house in Uruk appears to have been difficult to fulfil after the flight of its previous occupant. It was reassigned to a member of the family to which the original holder belonged. He was provided with food, but this is possibly not a case of a prebendal gatekeeper. Note that the unspecific term *kurummatu* is used. From the Borsippa Ilšabušu archive we have VS 5, 100 (15 IV Dar 28) in which a woman entrusted a gatekeeper's prebend in the temple of Nabû consisting of six days per annum to someone else against a payment in silver, incidentally also an execution contract dealing with a non-purveying function.

Measurers: For the *mādidūtu*, measurer's prebend, a number of texts from Dilbat is of particular importance. Some, but not all, of these texts belong to the Amat-Bau-file. The position of the *mādidu* is set out in VS 5, 21 (10 XI Nbn 2), an old-age maintenance contract between a father and his daughter: 8): *isqa* ^{LU_2}*man-di-di-ú-tu* 9) *ina* E_2.Imbianum *papāḫu* ^{d}Uraš *u* ^{d}Bēlet-ekalli 10) *ù ina ṣēri* ^{LU_2}*man-di-di-ú-tu gabbi aki* 11) ^{LU_2}*man-di-di*.MEŠ *šá* ^{d}Uraš, a two-thirds share of etc., "measurer's prebend in Eimbianum, the sanctuary of U. and B., and out-off-town, a measurer's function like that of the measurers of Uraš". The intention is to summarise the fact that the measurer had an *isqu*, prebend, which encompassed income not only deriving from activities in the temple itself, but also from participation in the managing of tasks on institutional land. This refers to all likelihood to income of the type assigned to the measurers and others in the "Edict of Belsazzar". This type of income is taxation related when seen from the point of view of the institutional tenant, but seen from the point of view of the measurer it would have been inseparable from the income from the measurer's prebend in general. VS 5, 76[154] (28 VI Dar 3) refers to the same rights as *kiṣir šá ṣēri*, perhaps translatable as "taxation-rights outside the town".[155] The text is also important because it mentions ŠE.BAR *šá maš-šar-ra-a-tú*, barley of the *maššartu*-assignments, a rare occasion in which that term turns up in a private document, suggesting that the *mādidu* received emoluments linked to the *maššartu-pappasu* system, even though he will not have produced products required for the cult. According to lines 2-3[156] he also received 2 $SILA_3$ of barley daily(?), *makkasu* and 0.0.3 of flour on the occasion of *šalām bīti* ceremonies. The same 2 $SILA_3$ of barley for a $^1/_6$ *mādidu*-prebend can also be found in the lease VS 5, 107 from the Amat-Bau-file (Dar 34).[157] Directly comparable is VS 5, 76 (28 VI Dar 3) where the *šalām bīti* income is listed more completely as consisting of barley, emmer, *makkasu* and flour, but remains unspecified as to amount. This text, line 6, also refers to *i-ri-ib* and *a-ṣi-tu₄ šá* E_2.KUR, which provides a link with income of the scribes. If we are allowed to interpret the texts one step further, the *mādidu* did not receive bread and beer, like the *ērib bīti*, but what he received included cereals,

---

154 But we must not forget that the early Neo-Babylonian *kudurrus* mention similar rights in connection with "ordinary" *ērib bītis*, or functionaries, compare VS 1, 36 II 11; VA 3614, 4; BBSt 36, III 31-33, also VS 1, 35, 4. This type of "right" may have been spread much more widely than the Edict suggests.

155 Cf. VS 5, 74-5 (24 I Dar 11) line 11. A *kiṣru* payment in wool to measurers in Sippar is found in Nbn 898.

156 Line 2 is to be understood through comparison with VS 5, 107 where also a $^1/_6$ share in a *mādidūtu*-prebend is described.

157 VS 5, 107 (x x Dar 34) a lease of a fraction of measurer's prebend expressed as 2 $SILA_3$ ŠE.BAR 6-*šú* ḪA.LA 2) ^{LU_2}*man-di-di-ú-tu* in the temple of Uraš. The text is quoted in Chapter V under Leases and in Taxation Chapter II in the discussion of the functionaries entitled to Edict-type payments.

dates and ingredients. If he participated in the *maššartu-pappasu* system that fact in itself suggests that he made costs, probably especially on personnel.

Additionally the scribes. The scribe of the temple, DUB.SAR E_2 DN, like the later "college scribes" is not usually regarded as occupying a prebendal function.[158] If the income received by the measurer from Edict-type payments is regarded as inseparable from his (other) prebendal income, the income that scribes, and for that matter, the higher ranking officials within the institution, enjoyed from the same source can hardly be regarded differently. For Dilbat we can refer again to VS 5, 107 (Dar 34), mentioned already in connection with the *mādidus*.

Another link with a source of *mādidu*-type income is found in VS 6, 331 (1 VI Bēl-šimanni 0) which contains the settlement of what could be regarded as a demarcation dispute between two scribes, one of whom declares, after ordered to do so by the *šatammu* 5) .... *dul-lu par-si* 6) *dul-lu ṭup-sar-ru-ú-tu ul ep-pu-šú*, "I will not exercise the functions attached to the *pa/irsu*[159] (and) the function of scribe". Thereafter the contestants came to an agreement, resulting in the arrangement that one of them would keep the register (^{GIŠ}DA) of the *irbu*, "the incoming (goods)" and the other that of the *tēlītu*, "the expenditure". There is another, incompletely preserved, clause on the periods concerned. The core of the matter will have been that keeping a certain type of account meant a right to a special type of income. It may be assumed that a due had to be paid when something had to be added to the register concerned.

e. A tentative conclusion on the status of the ordinary prebendaries

There would appear to be an important difference between “early” and “late” as far as personnel was concerned, but if the $GUDU_4$, with the ŠITA, was indeed replaced or superseded by *ērib bīti* that may perhaps be more a question of words than of substance, these terms could be regarded principally as referring to status,[160] and thus encompass various actual functions. Possibly there is the implication that on principle these people could fulfil all ordinary cultic tasks for which no specialist knowledge was required, even if, especially in Sippar, *ērib bīti*s were a group clearly separate from the $GUDU_4$s. Some "small-sanctuary prebends" of the late period seem to illustrate that (such) an all encompassing prebend could split up both "horizontally", as to time and occasion, and “vertically”, as to functional elements. Perhaps we can regard what was observed in connection with the "small sanctuary prebends" as a general phenomenon explaining the development of the Mesopotamian prebends we are studying.

In the later prebendal system the main difference seems to have consisted in being a “ritualist”, which included certain craftsmen, or a “purveyor”, in which the type of task determined the degree of initiation and the manner of recompensation. The question of status was, it would seem, not always directly linked to the remuneration and emoluments involved. That there were, in general, degrees of initiation, seems likely, but the question is largely beyond our grasp. Proficiency, requiring its own test, and admission to participation

---

158 On the development of the situation in Sippar and a comparison with Uruk cf. Bongenaar 1997 p. 56-8, where also the problem of interpreting the writing ^{LU_2}ŠID is treated. The SANGA, *šangû*, certainly enjoyed an appropriation comparable to that of other prebends, a "*beneficium*", though the function was not saleable, at least not as to the more important posts.

159 What is intended by *parsu* in this context is not clear to me, the preceding word cannot be read. AHw p. 835 suggests *par-si*, "Arbeit (eines Schreibers)", but quotes no relevant similarly phrased parallel.

160 This refers more to the Akkadian version of the titles than to the Sumerian, where the etymology suggests a connection with "praying", but even that is hardly a "function" in Mesopotamian prebendal context.

in the cult were probably different matters. Important is, that as a result of the initial granting of various functions and of the combined workings of fractionation and concentration several types of prebends could be combined in one hand: the difference in status between the three main prebendal groups could therefore never become a problem.

The (late) purveying prebends were of a special nature, which made them suitable for some degree of commercialisation. It can be concluded that the formula *maššartu* equals *sattukku* plus *pappasu* also implies a solution for the costs involved in producing the product required, which could be taken from both the *sattukku* and the *pappasu*. Not all included in the *sattukku* went to the gods, through the costs the prebendary had an additional interest in his *maššartu*-share as a whole. This conclusion is supported by the texts mentioned already, according to which the owners obtained more than just the *pappasu* from their executors, which suggests a form of bargaining between parties.

The income related to some other functions remains less clear. The words *kiskirru* and *kallānu* are used in relation to certain functions and we know that some of these functions are mentioned in the Edict of Belsazzar.[161] Hypothetically we can link the two and extend speculation to include the *bēl mindi*, who in the Hellenistic period managed income and expenditure in relation to certain functions, possibly of prebendal status, which might draw the *ṭupšar enūma*-Anu-Enlil as a latecomer into the circle of the prebendaries. This involved an account regarding the payment of the functionaries concerned, and that account would have to be fed. Edict-type income might be regarded as especially suitable. All accounts required someone to keep them and keeping an account seems to have been in itself a source of income.

We can summarise in the following manner. Providing for the gods and the remuneration of the higher cultic and administrative personnel of the Mesopotamian sanctuaries was centrally organised and supervised in each cultic centre. There were three main sources of income: 1. The remnants of the offerings and sacrifices to the gods; 2. The raw material to be prepared for the offerings, which was assigned inclusive of costs and remuneration to those responsible for the preparatory work and 3. Elements of taxation imposed upon underlings and tenants of the institution, which were used to feed particular personnel accounts. To all probability the importance of silver increased in the course of time, especially in the Hellenistic period.

Society had allowed the development of a system which freed a group of people from ordinary tasks, in which the ritual concentrating on the well-being of the gods played a central role. Locally this system managed to maintain itself notwithstanding considerable political and social changes. A tribute to the resilience of institutionalised private interest, but also a phenomenon of non-negligible importance for southern Mesopotamia as an urbanised society.

---

161 BM 42408, quoted in the section on Nidinti-Marduk s Šamaš-šum-līšir Ilē'i-Marduk knows perhaps of *kiskirru* assignments of Šamaš of the *bīt ridūti* in the context of a *zabarūtu* prebend, and we would expect that this *āšipu* had a cult-related function.

CHAPTER V
SOME ASPECTS OF THE PRACTICAL OPERATION OF THE SYSTEM

1. Did a prebendal function constitute a "Wechselamt"?

If the higher offices are included amongst the prebendal functions the "Wechselamt" cannot constitute a basic element, since such functions were in one hand for all the time. "Wechselamt" implies an intentional "horizontal" split in the execution of a function, that is as to time, at the moment funding was instituted. In the early period the relevant periods of functioning were indicated as NAM.x or MAR.ZA generally of either a god or of a temple. The difference may be linked to the degree of complexity of the structure in which a functionary operated: if a temple (of a god) is mentioned the organisation can be supposed to have been relatively simple, the personnel served one god, if a god is being referred to personally, that could indicate a differentiation regarding similar functions, according to the status of the particular god within the sanctuary to which they were allocated. A person's (share in a) function was his, occasionally her, BALA or BAL.GUB.BA, "period of service", implying the combination of tasks and income we call a prebend. In themselves the use of these phrases do probably not mean that the period of service was restricted. Already in the early period, as intended here, there were cases of considerable fragmentation, but there were also instances where a function which was split later on still encompassed the complete year, e.g. NAM.ŠITA$_4$ in Riftin 2. There are also cases in which a number of persons with the same title functioned together, OLA 21 no. 4 is a clear example.

In itself the use of BAL(.GUB.BA)[1] should not be regarded as indicating that on principle people fulfilled the tasks concerned in a rotating fashion, according to a roster. The rosters we know of are primarily arrangements obviating the results of fragmentation and not of the fact that several persons had been appointed to the same function for limited alternating periods. "Wechselamt" should on principle refer to a function in which a number of persons were appointed for limited periods and took turns in executing a function. The only practical support for such an interpretation in the early period which I can find lies in the fact that the lexical tradition concerning GUDU$_4$s differentiates between GUDU$_4$s who, as the CAD suggests, alternated in their office (GUDU$_4$.BAL.LA, which means, rather: "in function"?), or left it (BAL.LA.TA.E$_3$.A), which is certainly to the point.[2]

---

1 BAL.GUB.BA PN means primarily "the specific period which is the property/task of PN".

2 CAD G p. 120L. There is also a lexical GUDU$_4$ who is said to be a BAL.LA.TUR.RA/TU.RA, but this *guduballaturru* according to the principles applied to the interpretation of lexical texts must be a junior-GUDU$_4$, and not a GUDU$_4$ BAL.LA.KU$_4$.RA, one "who enters upon his function". Does the lexical junior GUDU$_4$ imply the existence of various degrees of initiation? Or is not TUR.RA yet a mistake for KU$_4$.RA, opposite to BALA.TA.E$_3$.A? On the other hand there was a GALA.MAḪ, a GALA and a GALA.TUR, and the same diversification existed for the NAR, so why not a GUDU$_4$.TUR? Possibly in the Third Millennium only the seniors of each profession were employed full-time in the cult and they sometimes remained in later periods: *kalamaḫḫu, nargallu.* Cf. perhaps also the ŠITA.AB.BA, and the *gudapsû* who disappeared. Juniors, with limited, perhaps especially "trade related" initiation, were perhaps only called in on special occasions.

Looking closer these matters are far from clear-cut, certainly not in the late period, as Kessler's discussion of the later terms *bēl manzalti* and *bēl ūmi* indicates.[3] Do these terms refer to "owners" or "executors", and do all executors have a comparable status, i.e. is, rephrasing Bongenaar's formulation of the question,[4] an Uruk *rāsinu* a Sippar *ēpišānu*, whereas an Uruk *ēpišānu* was only a lower type of Sippar *ēpišānu*, an executor who only fulfilled subordinate tasks related to the prebendal obligations, for instance providing ingredients, though still possibly occasionally a fully entitled colleague of the (purveying) prebendary?[5]

I regard the alternation observed in the execution of prebendal functions as primarily the practical result of the fragmentation of these functions. The supposition is that the original funding will have been intended for a complete function. That does not imply that not more than one place for a person with a certain function may have been created. Especially from both Old Babylonian Sippars there are indications that certain functions were fulfilled by groups of colleagues. This seems to be valid at least for *ērib bītis*, *gudapsûs* and $GUDU_4$s, and is probable for the NAR.SAs, and can be assumed for the GALAs. The round numbers, 4, 6 or 10, cf. OLA 21, 4, suggests that these numbers are not the result of a haphazard splitting of functions, but represent a proper "college". Why some functions could be split up and sold, and others not, is not clear from the outset. Perhaps the succession was left for some functions, the lower ones, to the individuals concerned, whereas for the higher functions, which also were transmitted in the (wider) family, additional forms of approval or registration were required.[6] If the lower functions were on principle remunerated at the level of ordinary workers, labour shortage may have played a role in attempts at keeping clerical numbers at an acceptable level, it being

---

3 Discussed Kessler 1991 p. 92f. If I understand the argument, the *bēl ūmi* is for Kessler the person responsible for the execution of the tasks required, not the owner. He acts for persons who can not fulfil the tasks themselves on account of his inherited right to do so. Kessler is against terms like "leasing" when dealing with prebends, he prefers "Pfründendienstvertrag" and assumes that the owner is often compelled to leave the execution of the tasks to others. I find it very difficult to establish which of the two parties in such contracts is "compelled" to act. There are a number of cases in which one party has accepted an obligation and transfers that selfsame obligation to a third party. Kessler wants to see this type of transaction as a sign of the existence of an intermediate group within the purveying trades, basing himself on what can be seen among the Uruk fishermen, some of whom assume greater responsibility than others. I prefer to assume a more "economic" motive. These people have spare production capacity or personnel, and want to use that. Bēl-supê-muḫur, though a member of the core group, had possibly little spare capacity. (Kessler 1991, p. 116.) He at any rate hands the execution of his own prebends over to others (p. 103). The situation of the Uruk bakers was complicated. In the main sanctuary there were four goddesses, each with their separate baking house, so at least 1440 prebendal days per annum and there were still more gods requiring services. The number of days in one hand seems to have been limited, Kessler's Bēl-supê-muḫur being supposed to have owned some 30 days (p. 102) in total, for possibly three out of the four goddesses. Regrouping of rights by execution contracts was for practical reasons inevitable under the circumstances, and it had consequences for the income drawn from the function by the owner, as Kessler has underlined on p. 104. Brokerage may in itself have been lucrative, as may be suggested by the contracts in which leased rights are passed on. Many of those entitled had other interests, and it was possible, as the Sippar Bēl-rēmanni texts suggest, to obtain from the executor more than the *pappasu* normally accruing to the owner. In the Bēl-supê-muḫur archive the specified payments by the executor to the owner, discussed Kessler 1991 p.83, possibly could be linked to this fact, cf. what is said about VS 5, 109 on p. 123.

4 Bongenaar 1997 p. 167.

5 If I may understand Kessler 1991 p. 113 in that way.

6 Renger 1969 and Charpin 1986 give many practical Old-Babylonian examples of inheritance or at least succession by members of a family in functions at all levels, which would, no doubt, increase in number if the prosopographies of the relevant families were better known.

normal, as in other occupations, that in such functions a son followed a father, but this remains largely speculative.

The general term for the ordinary prebend in the late period is *isqu* or GIŠ.ŠUB.BA, but the actual period of service, with the obligations, is indicated by *manzaltu*, a term which probably primarily refers to the obligations attached to actual service, possibly irrespective of the question of who was the owner. The term thus more or less replaces the earlier BALA.GUB.BA. The early Neo-Babylonian *kudurru*s suggest that though parallel functions were being funded occasionally, these functions were intended to be "complete". That many of the functions went through a process of increasing fragmentation is clear, in the Hellenistic period shares of less than one tenth of a day were common, and even further fragmentation is attested to under 1/60th of a day. But fragmentation took place already in the Old Babylonian period. That this could create an unworkable situation is evident: some practical solution for the execution of service obligations must already have existed. If Kessler is right at any rate in the late period these arrangements would have created inequality between those who were allowed to practice the trade and those who had no option but to engage someone who had that right, - even though they fulfilled all requirements themselves. For the moment I prefer regarding the fractionation as creating opportunities for those willing to take them, and I regard the fishermen, to be mentioned, not as representative for the purveying trades as a whole. In practice, however, much of the practical work will have been done by unfree personnel, which also makes the question of "rights" somewhat questionable.

2. Prebendaries and non-prebendaries, the role of slaves

In general, a certain group of prebendal functions implied regular, perhaps daily, contact with the divinity concerned. Some of the contact may, however, have involved only the occasional presence of the beneficiary, for instance on the occasion of special festivities, like the procession to the *akîtu*-house.[7] In the case of daily contact these people could be expected to have had prebendal, especially, *ērib bīti* status. In the case of occasional contact the matter is perhaps not so clear cut, as the intentions of, for instance, a procession anyhow include that of being seen. Perhaps there existed a whole range of functions, fishermen and boatmen being the ones actually identifiable, which operated as an occupational group within an institution, out of which only one or a few had, for cultic reasons, a status comparable to the prebendaries, possibly even with *ērib bīti* rank. This remains problematic. In AnOr 8, 44 a fisher appears with others who without any doubt were prebendaries, mainly, but not exclusively, purveyors. Those belonging to the purveying trades are not supposed to have been *ērib bīti*s automatically, though they regularly will have occupied that status through the possession of another function.[8] In the Neo-Babylonian period the Mesopotamian sanctuaries had a plethora of personnel of varying status, but there remains often the question of who did the practical work.

All those in regular contact with the godhead will have undergone some form of initiation, in which an act indicated by the verb *gullubu* seems to have constituted an essential element in the Neo-Babylonian period. Those who underwent initiation will have been made

---

[7] The prebendal boatman is probably the best example, Bongenaar 1997 p. 288-9. It would seem to be reasonable to suppose that he belonged to the *ērib bīti*s as his boat will have been relatively small, implying direct contact with the god. Cyr 304 (x II Cyr 8) is an *ēpišānūtu* arrangement between members of the same wider family.

[8] If prebendaries were recognisable on account of haircut and dress the question of which rank or function prevailed can be asked but not answered. We can also expect that being an *ērib bīti* was valid for one specific god or sanctuary.

recognisable,[9] and this includes the purveyors, just as the unfree *širkus* were recognisable through bearing a mark. There is no reason why something similar was not the case in earlier times.

We know explicitly that in Uruk, but also elsewhere,[10] the "milk-herdsman" could call upon the services of a *širku* for the practical herding, and, probably, for the actual milking. An incomplete Nippur text informed us of the fact that the brewers had their UN.IL$_2$s, (reading, equivalent?), an overtly archaic term by this time, and their "junior brewers".[11] In the Ur III and presumably also the Old Babylonian periods milling for the repasts of the gods was undertaken by specialised institutional labour,[12] and the same seems to have been valid up to a degree for the Neo-Babylonian and the Hellenistic periods,[13] when there were millers in the "house of the bakers" in Uruk.[14] It is notable that Nabonidus included the millers among those freed from *ilku* obligations in the provisions for his daughter in Ur. That unfree persons owned by the institutions, even prisoners, were involved in providing ingredients for the cult is certain, but unfree persons belonging to the prebendaries themselves also played a role.

The difficulty in separating prebendal and non-prebendal craftsmen is most obvious in the interpretation of the administrative documents of the Neo-Babylonian period, when prebendal status was attached to all sorts of occupations which were obviously deemed necessary for the proper execution of the cult. The problem is exacerbated by the practical arrangements for the fulfilling of obligations, which often entailed the simplest forms of menial work, like the grinding of flour, which hardly can be supposed to have been carried out by the holders of the rights and for which others, slaves of the prebendaries or persons specially engaged, were probably employed. In the New-Year's ritual from Babylon craftsmen play a role, they are indicated by their occupation as *gurgurru*[15], "metalworker", *naggāru*, "carpenter" and *kutimmu,* "jeweller"[16] or they appear in general as *ummânus* "master-craftsmen". We can reasonably assume that *ērib bīti*-craftsmen were intended here, but when an administrative text

---

[9] Borger 1973 deals with the personal requirements and the incantations prescribed when a NU.EŠ$_3$ or a NAM.ŠITA, appearing in the Akkadian translation as *nešakku* and *pašīšu,* entered the house of the god for the first time. The text is preserved in several Assyrian and one late Babylonian versions, but the functions mentioned are distinctly "archaic" by this time. Perhaps we must assume that the proceedings could be applied with suitable changes in comparable circumstances to other functions. The barber, called *šuginakku*, for *šuiginakku*, line 5, plays a prominent role. For the special clothing of prebendaries cf. Falkenstein 1959, p. 40ff.

[10] For Borsippa cf. BE 8/1, 106 (1 XI Dar 5) in which the owner of an ox-herd prebend transfers, probably within the wider family, his prebend against a *qištu* in silver and is promised periodical deliveries of food as long as he lives. Included in the transfer is a slave who bears the mark of the god: *marru u qanṭuppu*, line 9. He had been made available to all likelihood, as in Uruk, for the practical work, he constituted a perk.

[11] TuM 2/3 211, date lost.

[12] Note the presence of *ararrû* among those remunerated on the occasion of the divine visits listed by the Kingsbury text, 1993, lines 336, personnel of Utu, and, suggested by Kingsbury 747, personnel of Bēlet-ekallim. Should these have been female? A(?) female miller occurs in line 614 with Nanāia. The presence of these ordinary workers once again poses the question of the status of those participating in ritual acts, as there is no clear indication that a miller could be a prebendary, at any rate not in our sense.

[13] That the institutional prisons delivered flour for cultic purposes is certain, cf. Bongenaar 1997 p. 115-6.

[14] According to RAcc p. 6, AO 6451, obv. 21ff. Cf. the "house of the millers" in Sippar, mentioned Bongenaar 1997, p. 123, note 138.

[15] Not in daily use as a term for metal workers in the late period, though it occurs to indicate the relevant families in VS 15, 1.

[16] RAcc p.132, DT 15+ 190ff.

registers delivery of material or when payments to a *naggāru* or an *ummânu*, in general, are made, the status of these persons often must remain undecided, all the more so as there seem to have been craftsmen who were prebendaries, but not of necessity *ērib bītis*. That there were special arrangements through which such craftsmen received the raw materials they needed from the institution is evident in the case of the *atkuppus*, who were possibly non-*ērib bīti* craftsmen-prebendaries.[17]

A policy of restoring the religious establishments to former standards, as pursued by the Chaldean kings inevitably meant expansion of the cultic and the non-cultic personnel.[18] Especially Nebuchadnezzar II regularly mentions his pious increases in the offerings granted to certain gods, which were particularly appropriate on the execution of new building projects.[19] Relevant for our subject is VaB 4, Nbk no. 19, V 11, where he also expanded the numbers of the fishermen of Marduk by an additional group of twenty. The passage is regrettably damaged. These persons will certainly not have belonged to our prebendaries, though a fisherman could at least on occasion attain that status.[20]

The employment of one's own slaves is occasionally attested. From Babylon we can mention TuM 2/3, 205 (=BE 8/1, 8, 15 VII Nbp 8) resulting from an arrangement between someone and his *qallu* concerning 1) month VIII, ITI *ma-ṣar-ti šá* E_2-^{d}Nin.ezen 2) *šá* PN 3) *a-di-i* PN2 ^{LU_2}*qal-la-šú* 4) *ú-šá-az-za-zu*, that is: of which they assume the responsibilities jointly, but for which the owner of the slave, who, incidentally, bears the same given name, Mušezib-Bēl, pays a third party annually the sum of $1^1/_2$ *š* in silver.[21] In BM 43309+[22] Bēl-rēmanni employs someone else's slave for the practical brewing for nine days of a brewer's prebend in Ebabbar. The remuneration will have been contained in the amount of barley that will be made available to the executor. In the comparable BM 42525 the executor seems to be free, but there is nothing on the manner in which he will be paid. This is a matter which is left open in many documents stipulating only what is due from the person engaged.

Also elsewhere the involvement of slaves in prebendal work is evident. The Borsippa text VAT 18499[23] (16 I Nbk x) represents the contracting for the delivery of beer destined for the *naptanu* of Nabû between a certain Nabû-šum-ēreš s Balāṭu Kudurānu, who will deliver to Nabû-eṭiranni, slave of Nurea, family Ilija for prebendal obligations (*manzaltu*) of -explicitly-Nabû-eṭiranni in month IV, as beer had been delivered for the prebendal obligations of Nabû-

---

[17] See previous chapter under *atkuppu*.

[18] A good example is Nabonidus' installation of his daughter in Ur, with its suggested harking back to outdated practices, which would also have included the appointment of prebendaries. Of these there is, by the way, no trace in the after all limited number of practical texts in UET 4. The archaic *engiṣu* would be a normal *nuḫatimmu*.

[19] Cf. VaB 4 Nbk no. 19 A IV 28 on the daily offerings to Marduk and Ṣarpanitum: a considerable fund for prebendal emoluments. The clergy of Marduk is virtually unknown, however.

[20] A text which deals with the division of a fisherman's prebend of the Nabû temple in Borsippa, is TuM 2/3, 206, from the reign of Nabopolassar. This was a valuable asset. In Uruk, however, *manzaltu* when used to indicate obligations of fishermen obviously not always means a prebendal position, it rather indicates a much humbler hereditary position, which entailed the obligation to deliver an *iškaru*, that is, here, a kind of *mandattu*, payable by unfree persons, like those given to Marduk by Nebuchadnezzar.

[21] The assumption is that the master and not the homonymous slave engages the additional person. Whether the affair is prebendal or not, is perhaps not completely certain, but I assume that some gatekeeper's task is involved.

[22] Jursa 1999 p. 234. BM 42525 on p. 193. In BM 42404 the executor seems to be obliged to provide Bēl-rēmanni with beer to the value of eight kor of barley, but the amount of barley the executor is to receive is lost (lines 15-18.).

[23] Or NS 54, 1985, p. 73-4.

šum-ēreš in month I. Here the prebendal obligation rests directly on a slave. The transaction is a kind of exchange of delivery dates. In BRM 1, 82 (3+ VIII Dar 27) we find the customer of VS 6, 182, mentioned above, transferring his *dul-lu* LUNGA-*ú-tu* to a slave of his and one or more others,[24] who will carry out the work together: *a-ḫa-ta-šu-nu dul-lu ma-la-ma-li-iš ip-pu-uš*(sic): "they are companions and will carry out the work in equal proportions". Brewing in Borsippa prebendal circles is well-documented in general.

This, again, is an arrangement coming close to a *ḫarrānu*. Such is the case also elsewhere, an example from the Sippar Bēl-rēmanni file was mentioned above. The involvement of slaves as *ēpišānu*s is certain, at any rate if *ēpišānu* is a general word for someone who carries out the prebendal work. But that is not completely certain for the word may have implications beyond the simple delivery of the goods required for the cult to the owner of the prebend. Jursa qualifies the relevant texts from the Bēl-rēmanni archive as "Dienstverträge". It is possible that some of the constructions mentioned imply that the slave is placed by his owner in a kind of firm for which an entitled person was engaged, nominally or not, to act presumably in the institutional, ritual, context, with the slave representing the business interests of the master and doing the practical manual work. There is the possibility that the entitled person was only involved in the undertaking in order to act especially in cultic respect, which was, possibly, out of bounds for the slave. Whether this construction is correct rests, however, largely on the interpretation given to the Uruk text An Or 8, 44, on which below.

However, exceptionally a *qallu*, "slave", could be directly involved in cultic activities,[25] or was this someone acting the *qallu*?

Both in the Ur III and in the Hellenistic period there are indications that there existed milling establishments explicitly providing for the cult. An indication that grinding of flour for cultic purposes could be organised centrally in the Neo-Babylonian period is provided by some texts from Borsippa. VS 6, 174 (29 VII Šamaš-erība 0) is headed by the words "*iškaru* of flour" plus date. It is followed by groups of posts listing 0.2.0 (of flour or barley) plus PN *ša* PN2, meaning presumably, that (male) PN worked for PN2 and daily had either to deliver two *sūtu*s of a known type of flour or had to grind two *sūtu*s of barley, which of the two is the case must remain undecided. Both PN and PN2 can probably return in different lines of the same text. The PNs are grouped in lists of eight names each and are totalled as "eight *iškaru*s" of respectively the main and the secondary meal of the morning and the evening, which are in some cases called the *naptanu* (BUR) of another person, with still someone else acting as the *pārisu* for the morning meals or as a "receiver" (?, IGI) for the evening meals. The *pārisu* was conceivably the person who handed out the cereals to the actual millers and acted as a kind of supervisor. Directly comparable are VS 6, 159 (14 XI Dar 33) and VS 6, 164 (24 II Dar 35), which are incomplete and skip the organisational details. No doubt these are the meagre remains of a file

---

24 This is problematic: it would be possible to reason that the *ēpišānūtu* is at the disposal of the slave Balāṭu, whose name is repeated and who will do the work with a Nabû-ittannu, assuming that at the end of line 4 <A-*šú šá*> is to be supplied, or less likely <*ù*>, in which case we would be dealing with three men. But in line 9 we have an additional clause "his clothing (written ^{LU_2}TUG$_2$.BABBAR) as much as is his share Balāṭu will give to Nabû-ittannu", which suggests that only two persons are involved. The *šutummu* is mentioned here as one of the localities where the beer was being brewed. BRM 1, 92, dated 3+ VIII, so presumably from the same day as BRM 1, 82, mentions brewery tools handed by Balāṭu to Nabû-ittannu, which could suggest that after all the actual work was done by him.

25 Çagirğan and Lambert, 1991-'93, line 19 ff. It is evident that the *qallu* appears before Bēl with a bull. The exact status of a *qallu* is perhaps not always that clear, however. Strictly spoken he need not have been unfree, as the term can indicate any servant or "junior".

of possibly daily texts, dealing with providing for the cult. Whether there is enough material for a successful prosopgraphical investigation can be doubted for the moment.[26]

VS 6, 173 (23 VII Šamaš-erība 0) is a directly related contract concerning the grinding of monthly eight *iškarus* of flour for the *šapattu* of a named person for which someone is engaged. He will carry the barley from the store. The passage, lines 16-7, mentioning 0.3.2 of barley is damaged, but 120 $SILA_3$ for eight days of work can hardly represent the remuneration. 15 $SILA_3$ per day is probably what the person engaged had to grind, far less than what is mentioned by VS 6, 174. This is to all probability a private contract for auxiliary work. VS 6, 114 (25 II Camb 7),[27] from Borsippa, is also a contract concerning the grinding of -notably- one *iškaru* of *ḫirigallu*-flour during the year Cambyses 7 for the major and the minor repasts of an unspecified god. Strictly spoken, nothing can be said concerning the person who undertook the task, as his status remains unspecified. The document is, however, to all likelihood also a private one and it again does not use the term *ēpišānūtu*, or something comparable, which once more suggests that the grinding of flour was regarded as only a lower, auxiliary, element of the task. Even if there were grinding establishments, it is yet to be expected that the grinding of flour was an activity which was put out by the owners of, particularly, baker's prebends, for the fact remains that the Neo-Babylonian bakers received as an element of the *maššartu* barley and not flour. VS 6, 115 (Borsippa, 15 II Camb 8) and 144 (Borsippa, 1 III Dar 26) are good examples of comparable texts regarding the delivery of beer, of which there are more.[28]

We might suppose that the weaving of the garments used for the *lubuštu* ceremony, which were, it would seem, presented by the prebendal weaver, could be regarded similarly as an auxiliary task. It is notable, however, that Waerzeggers 2001 M.r. 174 explicitly uses the term *ēpišānūtu* for the weaving.[29]

The Uruk one-day roster of mainly personnel providing food, An Or 8, 44, must be discussed again below, in the context of comparable texts, but the fact that slaves figure prominently as those actually involved on the day concerned, must be mentioned already here. That institutions and private persons used non-prebendal personnel for preparatory tasks is evident, not so clear is how far this usage could be stretched regarding actual participation in cult related tasks.

3. Lease or execution: *ēpišānu* and *rāsinu*[30]

In the Old Babylonian period the transfer of tasks by a holder of a prebend is much more difficult to establish than in the late period, though it must have been almost inevitable as

---

[26] Ungnad 1959-60, p. 75 suggested a connection with the Lakuppuru texts from Borsippa.

[27] TuM 2/3, 209, which seems to be a contract concerning the hiring of a baker, has been mentioned already.

[28] In VAT 18499, L. Jakob-Rost Or NS 54, 1985, (Borsippa 16 I Nbk x) the beer for the meal of Nabû is delivered by a *qallu* (line 3, read *qal-la*). Also in the Babylon Nappāḫu text VS 6, 85 (4 XIIb Nbn 12), cf. VS 6, 96, (19 II Cyr 2), a *qallu* is to deliver beer made from barley delivered at the *maššartu*.

[29] The damaged text VS 6, 168 (14 I Dar x) from the Nappāḫu archive deals with the execution of prebendal weaving obligations.

[30] Cf. CAD E "confectioner" (no longer relevant) and *ēpišānūtu* "performance" and CAD R *rā/ēsinu* and *rā/ēsinūtu*, "person performing the service connected with a prebend", and "duties or service connected with a prebend", which passes by the question as formulated following Kessler 1991, p. 79-82, whose contribution to the understanding of *rāsinu* might at least have been mentioned. That *rasānu* means in Uruk "carrying out /taking over prebendal tasks" seems established, AUWE 8 p. 60, BaM 5, 228: 17 IV 20-8. For Sippar Jursa 1999 p. 43ff gives an overview of the formulae of the contracts, which is particularly useful.

functions were fragmented.[31] It was probably also inevitable in this period if a strictly male prebendal function was in female hands. But the situation may have differed somewhat from that in the late period. The Kingsbury text refers to female millers, probably, of a goddess, and in Pre-Sargonic Lagaš we find an occasional female GALA. The exclusion of females from "male professions" may have been less absolute, or rather, such professions had in the wider context of the cult not yet become male.

In the late period transfer of tasks had to take place if a prebendal function was in the hands of a woman, and, if Kessler's theory is correct[32], if the holder of the prebend did not belong to the limited group of those allowed to practice. Such a situation also occurred, according to Kessler, if he was the owner of more than one type of prebend.[33] Whether these reasons really were imperative must be awaited. There are also a number of other, practical, reasons with would have had a comparable effect. Transfer would have been practically inevitable if prebendal rights were owned by people residing in other towns,[34] were young minors[35] or were or became impaired.[36] In practice execution contracts are known for the purveying prebends, only rarely for crafts prebends and for the lower fringe of the prebendal system, where we locate the boatmen or the measurers,[37] while in the ritualistic sphere they are hard to find, but occur. But this may be deceptive and the result of our documentation, in which bakers and brewers abound.

Temporary transfer can take place in a simple form. TuM 2/3, 208 (Borsippa, 12 X Nbn 0) transfers the or a *tardennu*-meal by simply stating that that belonging to PN is *ina* IGI PN2,

---

[31] Charpin 1986 p. 261, BIN 7, 193, Isin; cf. also p. 320 *ad* UET 5, 556 and 586.

[32] Kessler 1991, p.79-82.

[33] In this respect we must, however, refer to Gehlken's remarks, AUWE 11, 1996, p. 16 *ad* no. 174. Of some interest is that the Borger text (1973 p. 165, 27-8) seems to imply that a certain pre-knowledge was not a hindrance to the initiation, if the person concerned occupied already a position in the cult of another god. Multiple initiation, for different gods, was possible. That had little sense if actual service was forbidden, though there is always the aspect of a promotion to a more important or lucrative employment. A further step is whether once initiated a fresh initiation was required on accepting a new function of the same nature. This is of some interest for the question of what made an *ērib bīti* an *ērib bīti*. We must not forget in relation to this discussion that in the early Neo-Babylonian *kudurrus* kings assigned more than one function to a person or functions to persons who already held others. That would have had little sense if they would not be allowed to exercise them.

[34] Best example Beaulieu 1991. It also seems to be the case in some texts from the Borsippa Rē'i-alpi family file. BE 8/1, 108 (28 XII Dar 6), which is obviously a part of the same prebend, or at any rate related to the same prebend as mentioned in VS 6, 113 (21 VIII Camb 6), deals with (shares in) sheep before Nanāia (and Sutiti), according to BE 8/1, 108 line 9 explicitly in Babylon. The text rescinds an inheritance arrangement made by the grandmother, which would have favoured a daughter's son. With the available prosopgraphical evidence it will rarely be possible to recognise such arrangements always, and the importance of inheritance in the female line is probably greatly underrated. Practical tasks attached to prebends owned by females will have been generally exercised by related males, especially if they had a share of their own, which also will have masked the real property relations.

[35] This seems to be evident in texts dealing with Nidinti-Marduk and his mother Inbā in Jursa 1999, whether prebendal functions are handed over *ana ebūri* or obligations *ana ēpišānūti*.

[36] In case of old age, where we must probably add: combined with the lack of a son. For execution by a son seems to have been possible without any problem, adoption of someone who could take over the obligations, in a care context, seems to have been largely a private affair. Automatic, undocumented, execution by a suitable family member can probably always be assumed, also in the case of female owners.

[37] Otherwise the *ēpišānu* could never have become a "confectioner". *ēpišānu* and *ēpišānūtu* are, of course, not words which were used only in connection with prebends.

who is made responsible in an often occurring formulaic manner, usually stressing the punctuality and the quality of what is to be delivered. He obviously carries out the complete task. Whether the owner receives some income is not made explicit here, but we can refer on this point to Ashm A 109, OECT 12 Pl. 12 (12 X Cyr 3), which belongs to the same context, where the executor pays the owner a specified *pappasu*. VS 5, 124 (Borsippa 29 x [Dar] 13) is an accounting document over *idū*, wages, relating to the *maššartu* of two months for meals of Nanāia during $2^{2}/_{3}$ days paid to the person who is made responsible for interruptions, presumably, by the owner. Here the actual tasks seem to have been transferred in a transaction between members of the same wider family. A comparable transaction is VS 5, 97 (2 VII Dar 25).

Though this may in some respects be a question of words, lease and antichretic use of prebendal income must on principle be separated from transfer of obligations and income through an execution contract, in which, to complicate matters, not all tasks and all income pertaining to the prebend need have been involved. Lease is directly indicated by the terms *ana sūti*[38] or *ana ebūri*.[39] This type of transaction should involve a fixed payment in silver to the owner and contain no arrangements for the fulfilling of the functions, which on principle should remain the responsibility of the owner, if we follow the proposed theory.[40] Whether this is true or not is for the future to decide.

A good example of antichretic use of prebendal rights is BaM 5, 228: 17 I 21-8. For a debt of 12 *š* of silver $1^{1}/_{4}$ day of a baker's prebend before Kanisurra is *maškanu,* security. The fact that this is an antichretic transaction is made clear by the statement that no interest on the silver is paid and that there is no *pappasu*, which means that the debtor leaves the *pappasu* to the creditor, and does, probably, the work himself. Even more interesting is IV 20-28, the passage used by Kessler (1991 p. 79 cf. 60) to establish the meaning "to execute the prebendal tasks" for the verb *rasānu*: $6^{1}/_{2}$ days of a baker's prebend are *maškanu* for 58 *š* of silver. "he

---

38 Jursa mentions VS 5, 107 (x x Dar 34) from Dilbat, a lease of a fraction of a measurer's prebend expressed somewhat obscurely as 2 SILA3 ŠE.BAR 6-*šú* ḪA.LA 2) LU2*man-di-di-ú-tu* in the temple of Uraš, held by the owner together with the lessee, for which the owner will receive annually fixed amounts of barley, dates, sesame and emmer at the *maššartus*. Furthermore the lessee will give one *sūtu* per kor *ul-tu* 11) [x-]x-*ni-e* for the EN.NAM(?), the *šatammu*, the *ṭupšarru*, the measurer and the *rab tarbaṣi*(?), obviously a somewhat expanded list of the officials mentioned in the Edict of Belsazzar. The tasks of the function are obviously transferred to the lessee in this case.

39 It is notable that the prebends involved, when specified, seem to be those of ritualists. Waerzeggers 2001 M.r. texts 80 and 157, concerning *ērib bīti*, BM 42408, Jursa 1999 p. 177, mentioned under *āšipūtu* in Chapter IV are real leases. In the case of BM 42408 I cannot but assume that the mother and her young son will not execute the actual tasks involved, the lease is intended to obviate the fact that the owner was too young for the task.

On the other hand *ebūru* payments can be in natura. Berens 106 (Borsippa 20 XI Dar 16) is an *ebūru* payment for an unspecified prebend in barley. Other transactions are perhaps no more than the pre-arranged sale of secure income. CT 55, 70, (7 X Dar II) mentions meat portions "given for a year" against a payment in silver and Peek 7, (15 VII Dar 22), where a similar transaction is recorded, also mentioned by Jursa, only income in the form of elements of offerings is being "given" for silver. Here the possibility that the owner only turns the income into silver, while retaining the obligations should be left open. Perhaps we should see this type of transaction primarily as an attempt to turn income in the form of naturalia into a liquid asset, so why not a simple sale by two people entitled to a fixed income of the goods concerned? Cf. also BM 64182, quoted Waerzeggers 2001 p. 205, ostensibly income in bread and beer from several prebends serving as a *bīt maškanu ana ebūri ina pān* PN "given" to PN2 for 90 *š* annually. A later lease is also mentioned. This suggests that the holder of the security could not provide the service himself and had to find an executor. The complete publication of the texts must be awaited.

40 Jursa 1999 p. 44.

will execute the prebendal tasks of the days instead of interest, there is no interest for the silver and there is no extra for the days(?)[41]; ... on the $1^1/_2$ day PN2 and PN3 (the two debtors) will execute the prebendal tasks." This somewhat cumbrous expression probably means that the creditor enjoys all the prebendal rights, and executes the obligations on five of the $6^1/_2$ days. The five days are practically transferred to the creditor, the debtors retain $1^1/_2$ day. We can only conclude that similar formulas used in documents can express differing situations. There are more examples.[42]

ana ēpišānūti, a phrase used especially in Sippar, should indicate a "Werkvertrag", which comprises the duty to prepare what is required for the cult (for instance) in food, but also, and here we land possibly in difficulties, in textiles. The owner receives a fixed amount (in naturalia) from the executor, the *pappasu*, or more. The executor was responsible for delays and the quality of the products, but perhaps that does not automatically imply that he has taken over the function in its complete extent. The *ēpišānu* must be regarded in these cases as a kind of entrepreneur. In the case of the weaver who provided Marduk-rēmanni, as his *ēpišānu*, with textiles for the *lubuštu*, we would expect that the executor is remunerated by the owner, the executor, as already suggested, being little more than an auxiliary. In the Borsippa text BE 8/1, 117 (22 IX Dar 32) the sons of a presumably diseased owner of an ox-herd prebend settle accounts in silver with a man who had been the *ēpišānu* since Darius 18, that is for 14 years. He was paid for his services by the owner. In the Babylon Nappāḫu *ēpišānūtu* text VS 6, 104 (7 VIII Cyr 8) three days of a baker's and brewer's prebend was to all likelihood the complete responsibility of the executor, as described in lines 7-13. The contract was to last for three years and the owner was to hand the executor an amount of *makkasu*-dates and firewood.[43] BM 77929 (17 IX Dar 19, Bertin 77929) deals with the *ēpišānūtu* of a number of days of a slaughterer's prebend,[44] which are entrusted for 2 *š* per month to two persons. As the owner had to pay a fine of 30 *š* if he transferred the days to someone else, the transaction virtually represents a lease, for which time limits were indicated.[45] At most we can propose that some of the *ēpišānu*s fulfilled the complete tasks of the owners. In itself that increases the possibility that such an arrangement was not exceptional.

In "Dienstverträge" the executor sometimes literally "stands" at the disposal of the owner. Such documents are rare in Sippar.[46] This is Kessler's Pfründendienstvertrag, which can be expressed in Uruk by the executor being *ana rāsinūtu* at the disposal (*ina pāni*) of the

---

[41] U_4.MEŠ *ur-ri-ši-na* 27)*ia-a-nu*. Meaning? This will perhaps indicate that the debtors have no practical interest until payment of the debt. Cf. also H. Hunger, BaM 5, 1970, nos. 21 and 22, a comparable transaction.

[42] The antichretic use of a *mubannû* prebend was discussed under *mubannû* in Chapter IV. In the text BM 79116, Jursa 1999 p. 250, the prebend is stated to be the *maškanu*. The income, flour and dates, is summed up and said to represent the *ebūru*, once more not silver, which is left to the creditor in lieu of the interest on the silver.

[43] Unique seems to be the stipulation 13) ... *ina mas-sar-tu₄ šá* x x 14) 2 $SILA_3$ (ŠE.BAR ras.) *mi-ṭi-is-su i-man-dad*, "at the *maššartu* of x he (the executor) will measure out 2 litres as his "deduction". Meaning? Does this refer to compensation for losses during the production process? Or, rather, does he receive only part of the (net) income?

[44] Jursa 1999 p. 50 note 178.

[45] In Cyr 304 (Sippar, x II Cyr 8) the owners of a boatman's prebend arrange with another person *a-na e-peš*.MEŠ (line 6) for the rest of the year. The executor is responsible. Remunerations: 8) *a-na man-zal-tu*$_4$ 1/2 GIN_2 KB *la-pa-an* [x?] 14) ^{LU_2}EN *man-za-al-tu*$_4$ *e-lat* E_2.SIG_3 [x x] 15) *ki-is-ki-ri* x, remainder of the passage lost. This is difficult to understand, but it seems to suggest that the *ēpišānu* is paid by the owners.

[46] Jursa 1999 p. 50.

owner,[47] though he had to belong to the "inner-circle" of the prebendaries of the profession involved. Regrettably enough the question of the remuneration of the executor in Kessler's texts in which the term *rāsinūtu* is preserved is not unequivocally clear.[48] Kessler suggests that this type of document was automatically valid for one year. The assumption must be that the executor received the *pappasu*, and occasionally, as we noted already in Chapter II, evidently more.

Though as to the form of the contracts this summation of document types may be more or less correct, "socially" it leaves open many practical alternative interpretations, only partially determined by the question whether only one or both parties could perform the task in all its aspects. Jursa, 1999 p. 45-6 also points out that the "Zusatsvereinbarungen" determine the real contents of a document.

Dar 543[49] (24 IV Dar 22) from Uruk is an *ēpišānūtu* (line 6) contract concerning a brewer's prebend. Though damaged, the text is important because it contains both the terms *ēpišānūtu* and *rāsinu* -or possibly *rāsinūtu*?-. The executor is a well-known brewer who almost inevitably belonged to the inner circle of the Uruk prebendal brewers.[50] The crux of the matter is to be found in the damaged lines on the lower edge. After the responsibilities of the lessee have been established we find a rather damaged clause, which I cannot reconstruct with confidence: 12) *lìb-bu-ú ra-si-in-*x [gap = "of function, i.e. brewer"?] 13) *šá* E$_2$.AN.NA *pap-a-su* x [gap, name of lessee?] 44) *a-na* PN (=lessor) *i-[nam-din]*, "the lessee will give the *pappasu* of the *rāsinūtu (?)* (of function x) of Eanna to the lessor". In this -far from securely based-interpretation the *ēpišānu* and the *rāsinu* (of the function) are the same person, he hands on -speculatively- the *pappasu* to the owner. The occurrence of the two terms in one text could be taken as suggesting that *ēpīšānu* equals *rāsinu*. Though Dar 543 is difficult to understand the text obviously has a bearing on the question of remuneration. The supposition must be that anyhow in the purveying trades dealing with food the executor has to hand over to the owner the *pappasu* and even more. I expect that this is also the case in the Bēl-supê-muḫur texts. As remarked, texts dealing with the transfer of prebendal obligations are generally uncommunicative on remuneration.[51]

Special circumstances seem to obtain in YOS 6, 170 (23 X Nbn 11) from Uruk. The text is of interest in that it contains, without mentioning the circumstances, a specification of the number, weight and material of the *makūtu*-cakes and the quantities of dates for the *mirsu*-baskets to be provided by a *rāsinu*.[52] As the *šatammu* and the *qêpu* are in attendance and as no

---

[47] Kessler 1991 p. 79, according to p. 73 the executor had to belong to the "inner-circle" of the prebendaries of the occupation concerned, a conclusion mainly based, it would seem, on prosopgraphical comparison of the SWU and the Bēl-supê-muḫur texts.

[48] In no. 68 Bēl-supê-muḫur is the executor, and he pays the owner an annual amount of 1.2.[0], to which we must return. In no. 60 1 kor of barley seems to go from the executor to the owner, but the text is perhaps too damaged for certainty.

[49] The text is mentioned Kessler 1991 p. 80 and p. 82, as relating to "Pfründendienstleistung" and not -therefore- a "Werkvertrag". Perhaps we must avoid such fine tuning.

[50] Cf. Kümmel 1979 p. 151, Šamaš-mukīn-apli.

[51] But note: AUWE 8 no. 29, concerning the *epēšu* of *takkasû* mentions a *qištu*, gift, of the owner to the executor. The text can be understood only partially. No. 58 deals with flour and mentions payment of wages, but milling is also in Uruk an auxiliary occupation in prebendal respect.

[52] Using, line 3) *šuzzuzu*, "imposed upon (PN)". In YOS 6, 239 1) *nab-ru-ú* SAG.DU *nap-ta-nu*, line 6 mentions *ma-la-a-ta*. Potentially *nabru* and *malītu*, an offering attested as an element of the *šalām bīti* act, could represent elements of the cult which could be split of "vertically" into separate prebends. The *malītu* is connected with the functions of *ērib bīti* and also *zabarūtu*/*āšipūtu* in Camb 236: 1-4 (25 III Camb 4) and Dar 162: 5 (22 II Dar 5).

owner of the prebend seems to be mentioned as far as can be seen from what remains of the text, it might be assumed that some specific administrative problem looms in the background to the document. The text is uniquely focused on the obligations and there is nothing on remuneration. The possibility that a *rāsinu* operated (occasionally?) directly on the orders of the heads of the administration must be kept open. A situation comparable to that found in the case of the milk-herdsmen may have arisen: a prebend had become vacant or had reverted to the king, and some practical solution for the delivery of the products required had to be found. Perhaps the situation is comparable to that found in YOS 6, 239 (20 x Nbn 12), also a detailed specification clearly imposed by the *šatammu*. The obligations connected to prebends in royal hands also had to be fulfilled somehow, we might expect appointment of executors through the intervention of his representatives.

4. Information from rosters: a sign of a degree of vocational autonomy?

The month, with its recurring special days, was in all periods the basic means of subdividing the Mesopotamian cultic year in which all prebendaries operated. Though the monthly lunar cycle was of prime importance for the regular succession of special days, for prebendal purposes, especially in the purveying trades, it was divided otherwise. In Old Babylonian Ur a division into ten-day periods is attested,[53] but other subdivisions also occur.[54] In the Neo-Babylonian period we have clear indications from the SWU texts that in Eanna the purveyor's month was split into three periods, called, as in Old Babylonian Ur, early, middle and late, each of ten days. In Ebabbar in Sippar there was an earlier and a later half, there and in Borsippa such halves were indicated by the term *šapattu*. The cultic and the practical sometimes coincide and sometimes not. That may be the fact with other arrangements too.

Especially in Sippar the more fragmented, but lucrative, prebendal occupations of baker and brewer, but also perhaps sometimes those of butcher and oil presser, were headed on a collegial basis by a *šāpiru*, or, which is perhaps typical of the situation, occasionally by two persons, who obviously shared the obligations and advantages, but not the title.[55] The existence of such *šāpirus* in Uruk is less pronounced[56] and much depends on the interpretation of the few rosters available. The existence of a *šāpiru* was probably an aspect of the non-*ērib-bīti* prebendal professions, some of which showed a high degree of fragmentation, while they were only indirectly linked to the execution of cult. Some practical form of organisation was inevitable in such circumstances.

Though the subdivision of the month into "blocks of time" makes an eminently practical impression, it is not easily reconciled with other *ad hoc* arrangements, which occasionally suggest room for regulation by mutual consent. The blocks of this type play a practical role in the *maššartu* system, but that does not mean that they were universally applied in the locality concerned, and they are perhaps primarily an accounting device in the handing out of the material required. In the case of the fishermen of Uruk periods of five and ten days appear to have fulfilled a practical purpose, but even these short bands of time tended to disintegrate. Other texts suggest no more than *ad hoc* daily arrangements.

---

[53] UET 5, 875, Charpin 1986 p. 263.

[54] A simple Old-Babylonian roster, presumably for a specific month in a small sanctuary of Sakkud is UET 5, 867, Charpin 1986, p. 266-7. The function concerned remains unspecified. The month was divided into one period of twelve days and three of six. Another, badly preserved, Old Babylonian possible roster-like text was published by A. Cavigneau, AUWE 23, 1996, no. 57.

[55] The facts are conveniently collected in Bongenaar 1997 p. 200 for the brewers.

[56] Cf. the discussion on *šāpirus* in Kümmel 1979, p. 151f.

a. Babylon

When dealing with VS 6, 273+ from the Babylon Nappāḫu archive it is evident that in Babylon, as elsewhere, the smaller sanctuaries were to a degree managed by an organisation headed by Esagil. Its *šatammu* ordered assignments of food to prominent members of the personnel of the "small sanctuary" of Išḫara according to a fixed monthly roster consisting of two blocks of five and two of ten days.

b. Uruk

From Uruk[57] there is a small file on "prebendal" fishermen,[58] which suggests, as has been accepted widely, that within an occupation similar to the purveying trades, there was a certain freedom to organise the service to suit those involved, provided, of course, that obligations were fulfilled. That is at any rate what VS 20, 87, lines 1-3, suggests, with one person bearing the final responsibility for the fish of the *naptanu* and the quality of the *šussulum*, probably the basket (or bin for live fish?) of Bēlet of Uruk. The texts discussed by Freydank reflect a number of practical re-arrangements required by changing circumstances, as will have been the case in other comparable trades. These people seem to have been hereditary fishermen of Bēlet of Uruk. YOS 7, 12 and VS 20, 87 speak explicitly of the *manzaltu*/*manzalātu* of the *bā'irūtu*. As in other texts dealing with prebendal rostering family names occur sparingly, which in itself is not particularly significant. But *manzaltu* does not automatically indicate a prebendal position in the sense of our definition. At any rate in this case appearance in the fisherman's rosters does not mean prebendal status, but obligations resulting from an unfree status. In this context the fishermen granted by Nebuchadnezzar to Marduk should be recalled.

TCL 13, 221[59], undated, purports to be a comparable document dealing with the bakers. They work in the *bīt kanni*s of each of the four major goddesses of Uruk, which possibly stand for the central organisation dealing with the bakery products in Uruk. In line 14 we find a total of 19 ^{LU_2}MUḪALDIM.MEŠ ^{LU_2}*e-pe-e ù* ^{LU_2}*ṭe-ḫe-ia šá nap-ta-nu i-na* E_2 *ka-an-na-nu šá* (the four goddesses) 16) *i-pu-ú,* interpreted[60] "19 bakers, (being) ordinary bakers and *ṭēḫû*-"servers", who have to prepare the meal (for the god), are responsible for baking the meal" and who are responsible for the *naptanu* , "meal" and the quality of the *takkasû*, the bakery products. In case of interruptions and bad-quality meals they would have to pay the fines which the *qêpu* regarded as appropriate. These cooks, bakers and "servers"[61] are stated to have deposited the witnessed,

---

[57] Comparable for the limited evidence from Sippar A.C.V.M. Bongenaar and M. Jursa, WZKM 83, 1993, 36-7.

[58] Discussed Freydank 1978 and Kessler 1991 p. 89f., and previously San Nicolò 1934. The word "prebendal" must be used cautiously here, there are only a few Uruk texts putting fishermen in an environment we could regard as prebendal: AnOr 8, 44 and TuM 2/3, 206. They were, however, subjected to specific, inheritable, service obligations and were responsible for deliveries according to a roster, the word *manzaltu* being used. For the amount of the actual obligation *iškaru* could be used, and that could function as the *mandattu* of the (unfree) person concerned. The Sippar "Mäusefänger" is a good example, A.C.V.M. Bongenaar and M. Jursa, WZKM 83, 1993, p. 31. We are dealing with time related tasks and with products destined for the gods, yet over-all these functions cannot properly be included in the prebendal purveying trades. We can probably assume that those involved mainly subsisted from what they caught -or produced?-over and above their *iškaru*, and from sustenance fields.

[59] Edited Kessler 1991, p. 95-6.

[60] CAD E p. 248L.

[61] CAD E p. 248 translates "bread-servers" or *ṭēḫû*-"servers", AHw p. 1385, which gives only this quotation for the occupation, has "Brotteigaufstreicher", *ṭēḫû* II being some action related to the baking of bread. The CAD translation suggests that it consists of actually serving the bread, which would seem to fit

but undated, tablet of their own free accord in Eanna. Notably enough they do not use family names.[62] Only the first person of the first group of six, almost certainly those of Bēlet of Uruk, is certainly qualified as a *ṭēḫu*. All the others are either unqualified, or the qualification is lost, as is the case with the first persons of the groups belonging to the other three goddesses, but who should also be regarded as likely *ṭeḫus*. If the *ṭēḫû* was the principal of the group and if he was the actual server, it would seem to be likely that he actually appeared before the gods and so, possibly, had to be an *ērib bīti*, -among the bakers.[63]

AnOr 8, 44 (9 XI Cyr 4) is a list of the ^{LU_2}EN.MEŠ *man-za-la-a-*tu_4 ^{LU_2}$KU_4.E_2$.[MEŠ] 2) ^{LU_2}ŠEMxNINDA.MEŠ ^{LU_2}$GIR_2.LA_2$.MEŠ ^{LU_2}[MUḪALDIM].MEŠ [EN.U_4].MEŠ of 9 XI Cyr 4 before Bēlet of Uruk and Nanāia. The text has received the attention its importance deserves.[64] Kessler has discussed the difference between *bēl manzalti* and *bēl ūmi*, the first being the "owner", the second in his interpretation the person who had an inherited right to act as the official responsible for a specific "trade" during the period of service concerned. The problem is, that, if *bēl ūmi* does not refer to the status of the two *qallu*s mentioned, it must refer to their masters, who were both brewers: we would have two representatives of the same trade.[65] It makes better sense, as the text seems to do, to note in three cases that the person on the list was merely a *bēl ūmi* (lines 9-10, 10-11 and 19), someone who acted on the day concerned. This is the "traditional" opinion, which implies that unfree persons could fulfil the tasks of a purveying prebendary.[66] The term notably refers to two *qallu*s who served for the brewers of respectively Bēlet of Uruk and Nanāia, the third being a *rab banî*, who presumably stands in for a colleague who is not even mentioned. There is presumably one *ērib bīti*, one brewer and one baker, with

---

the basic meaning of *ṭēḫû*, which is used in line 14 for the *naptanu*, the meal, and not for the bread. For von Soden *ṭēḫû* seems to be the act of putting the dough on a hot stone or on the wall of the oven. The "Brotteigaufstreicher" must represent the person who bakes bread in this manner. That might indicate someone especially "qualified". Whatever the case, prebendal functions tend to specialise, whether "serving" or "baking" is involved.

[62] These persons are not included by Kümmel 1979, nor are the witnesses other than the scribe. The treatment of the bakers and brewers is rather limited, the reasons for which are stated on p. 150R.

[63] On the status of the text cf. Kessler 1991, p. 95-6, stressing not only the unusual solemnity of the words used, but also the absence of a date.

[64] Edited Kümmel 1979 p. 149, Kessler 1991, p. 92-4; cf. for collation of the heading see Freydank 1971, I p. 31 note 3. The text presumably has a simple structure in which first three pairs of functionaries follow one another: *ērib bīti*s (the second, line 7 without title), brewers, and bakers, who are accompanied by a *mubarrû* (*ša našappi*) each. Of these pairs the first person serves Bēlet-*ša*-Uruk, the second Nanāia. The presumption must be that in line 12 Nanāia is a mistake caused by a repetition of the end of line 11. On line 9 cf. next note. Thereafter follows one each of other trades, who will have had to serve both goddesses: slaughterer, fisherman, *rab banî* and ^{LU_2}ŠITIM followed by a person without an indication of an occupation. Separated by a ruling from those mentioned previously three persons are added to the list, two of them being *qallu*s. There must be a special reason for the ruling, but it escapes me. Are these additional servants who had to be at hand?

[65] The problem would loose some of its acuteness if we could follow the copy against Kümmel's, and Kessler's, transcription of line 9, and retain the *pān* Bēlet-*ša*-Uruk of the copy, which has been changed into Nanāia by Kümmel, who only refers to following Freydank's actual readings for lines 1-5. If the change rests on collation my interpretation looses one of its main supports, but on the other hand I find it difficult to accept that all personnel above the ruling would have to be assigned to Nanāia, the junior of Bēlet-*ša*-Uruk, who would only retain the three persons under the ruling after line 14, of whom two are slaves.

[66] Jursa 1999 p. 44.

an attending *mubarrû*[67], per goddess. Other "trades" are represented by only one person, and the list ends with four persons, amongst whom two slaves, without a function.[68] It can be assumed that the list of serving personnel is adapted to the cultic needs of the day, which required, in addition to the daily functionaries, like the *aḫu rabû* and other ritualists[69], nine different functionaries, eight of whom belonged to the purveying trades,[70] plus some unidentified others. Even if Kessler's observations on *bēl manzalti* and *bēl ūmi* are correct, it is clear that a considerable share of the tasks was actually carried out by those entitled to the relevant prebends for the day concerned.

That rostering regularly took place on an *ad hoc* basis is suggested by YOS 6 241, 25 XI Nbn 12,[71] dealing with the first five days of a coming intercalary month.

c. Borsippa

A small file of texts without dates from Borsippa suggests that the *šapattu*[72], "half-month-period", system was difficult to reconcile with realities. No function is indicated but a specific person is made responsible. VS 6, 284 is the clearest, it lists (heading, lines 1-2) the days of the *šapattu* of Kuṣurāia s Mukīn-apli, and registers a number of days plus a personal name. The total reaches $12^1/_3$ day, but without assigning days to Kuṣurāia himself. VS 6, 283 is even less enlightening.

d. Sippar

The question has been discussed by Bongenaar. His conclusion was that the system of half-monthly periods was still more or less intact during Nebuchadnezzar II as far as the bakers were concerned (p. 172). In the case of the bakers, service periods of 7.5 or 15 days were arranged independently of actual ownership, assisted by the fact that the bakers' prebends were in the hands of a limited number of families (p. 200). C. Waerzeggers has, however, revised Bongenaar's reconstruction convincingly, though that does not change the picture fundamentally, as the number of families concerned remains limited.[73] Members of the Rabā-ša-Ninurta family take over the role Bongenaar assigned to the Ṣāḫit-ginê family, which early in the reign of Darius obtained two *šapattu*s and the Šangû-Inanna-Bābili family, especially the

---

67 Twice the *mubarrû* follows a *nuḫatimmu,* and it may be assumed that each pair serves one of the two goddesses. CAD M/2 p. 158 notes the connection with the *našappu* and suggests a link with the presentation of the product, possibly by "announcing" it. This would imply entry into the sanctuary. The *našappu* was used as a serving vessel, CAD N/2 p. 56, where our text is quoted, cf. notably RAcc 90, 24f. This would mean to all likelihood that the *mubarrû* could enter the sanctuary.

68 For an attempt to identify their masters cf. Kümmel 1979, p. 150.

69 Or was on this day just one *ērib bīti* per goddess sufficient?

70 Plus the *ērib bīti*. Another possible exception could be the ^{LU_2}ŠITIM. Possibly at least one member of the "technical trades" had to be at hand, though H. Bongenaar reminds me of the fact that "*itinnus* receive flour remarkably often", with reference to Bongenaar 1997 p. 123. His note 137 connects an *itinnu* specifically with *miḫru* offerings. The *itinnu* certainly had a separate ritual role, but whether that role had a place in the ordinary daily cult is something else. Cf. also Bongenaar 1997 p. 374 on Iddin-Bēl. As noted above we need no longer consider the possible equation of *mubannū* and *itinnu.*

71 YOS 6, 241 (25 XI Nbn 12) deals with the responsibilities as to the days of the brewers and the bakers on the first five days of the (coming) intercalary month. For the brewers the *manzaltu* is that of their *šāpiru*, for the bakers it is shared by three persons: does this really mean that the persons mentioned are the owners, or only that they "stand" the *manzaltu*, "assume responsibility" for the execution? SWU 108 line 9, also represents a kind of assignment of bakers and brewers to tasks.

72 I do not understand VS 6, 318, 9-11.

73 Waerzeggers 2001 p. 141-5.

šangû of the moment, retains the role they acquired in the first decade of Darius' reign. The roster reconstructed by Bongenaar on p. 286-7 must be adapted in the sense proposed by Ms Waerzeggers, but a reasonably regular picture remains. For the brewers there were more problems. Only CT 57, 309 (I-IV Nbn 6) indicates the irregular division of days between the various brewers entitled, though the fragmentation is more serious for some months than for others. (Bongenaar 1997 p. 201ff.)[74]

For the Sippar *ērib bītis* we have the tantalising text BM 77834 ,which is a copy of a text dating to 20 III Nbp 7(?).[75] It gives for thirteen months, including the intercalary one, one named *ērib bīti* per month each. If we could assume, as Bongenaar proposes, that this is close to Nabopolassar's reinstitution or reform of the cult of Šamaš, we might have an excellent indication that the *ērib bīti* function was indeed a kind of "Wechselamt", which in turn might support the idea that there were *ērib bītis* who were not specialists in some (other) function indispensable for the execution of the cult. Yet such a conclusion would be premature as the cult would require -on occasion- a whole range of specialists, all with the status of an *ērib bīti*. The specific reason for the list is not given, just as the task of the *ērib bītis* in AnOr 8, 44 is not specified.

The use of the term *ērib bīti* in the two texts must be explained, however, if we want to accept that the function of *ērib bīti* has in itself occasionally no proper specialist content. There must be a specific ritual obligation, though, perhaps, it would be possible to add: "which could be fulfilled by anyone having the status". The interpretation which makes the *ērib bīti* prebend a Wechselamt would have to assume that a special person was appointed for the intercalary month, though that is not absolutely unthinkable in itself. The matter remains problematic.

e. Elsewhere

Beaulieu[76] has published the best evidence on prebendaries from one town possessing days in sanctuaries in other towns. YBC 3991 consists of two lists of respectively the brewers and the bakers from Uruk having rights before Šamaš in Larsa. The same author[77] also published lists of temple brewers from Nippur, stressing that there again, also in the Neo-Babylonian period, smaller sanctuaries were incorporated into a bigger organisation. Belonging to different organisational structures would have implications for the rostering of tasks.

A roster for a small organisation in Ur is preserved in the administrative text UET 4, 161, date lost, the *gi-ir-ri*, "roster", of *ērib bītis* of Marduk, Palil, Bēl-ālia, Mār-bīti and Bēl-ālia of (Al) It-x, presumably all as minor gods in Ur, from 1 XI Camb 2 onwards. The text is divided into sections, mentioning days held by named persons. Notable is that day 30 is in the joint possession of those mentioned, which makes sense, as not every month would have had 30 days.

We have only two texts dealing with the rostering of *ērib bītis* and one with links them with purveyors. Otherwise only the order in which members of the "purveying trades" served

---

[74] VS 6, 280, listing days of an unspecified month III is stated by Bongenaar p. 192 to mention members of an unspecified prebendal occupation. (The text would involve brewers, but Nabû-apla-iddina is known as a baker.) VS 6, 281 is claimed for the brewers on p. 216 (sub Guzānu s Nabû-nipsari Balīḫu) and would thus well illustrate the individual rostering of the brewers' prebend, with which also 282 dealt. Such small monthly lists will have been routine documents, possibly collected into larger lists encompassing a number of trades or used for compiling SWU-type texts. Perhaps the pieces can be collected and added to somewhere in future: CT 56, 468; 57, 61; 336; 512?; 636; 663; 665; 992. MacGinnis 1991-2 no. 4 is a list -with a complication- of a person's days in one year.

[75] Bongenaar 1998 p. 153ff.

[76] Beaulieu 1993 p. 140-2.

[77] Beaulieu 1995.

can be figured out more or less. Their daily involvement with commodities caused much more "paperwork" and thus provided an improved chance that information would be preserved. In reality there will have been schedules for all those involved in the cultic activities, at the simplest level of the one day type of AnOr 8, 44 from Uruk. Not only because the cult was too important a matter to leave things to the hazard of the moment, but also because leaving matters unorganised would result in an unending stream of litigation, as service meant remuneration. Though the wooden boards with the detailed information can be regarded as irretrievably lost, there are perhaps some copies on clay.[78]

5. Conclusion

The nature of the contracts discussed depends, as always, more on the "small print" and the background than on the standard formulae. The wider interest is perhaps that though the prebendal system could largely operate independently on the basis of goods and products received, we must note that, discounting sales, only leasing and, occasionally, execution arrangements involved the introduction of silver in the system. Perhaps also taxation made silver a part of the prebendal equation in the late period, leading to an increase of the importance of silver in the running of the system in the Hellenistic period. But in itself the prebendal system did not require silver to function and this is perhaps one of the sources of its resilience.

Another observation that should be made, is that notwithstanding the subdivisions, the combination of more than one function, in different sanctuaries, in one hand and a number of obvious personal impediments, the prebendal system seems to have been flexible enough to ensure services without too much trouble in cultic and legal respect. There was, if we may reformulate what we could observe in that way, a working market for the execution of functions, but it operated largely without silver.

[78] Such a possible exception might be the tablet BM 77960, quoted Bongenaar 1998 p. 155 note 177, as possibly from the Šamaš temple in Babylon.

CHAPTER VI
BALANCE

We have attempted to treat our prebends as elements of a structure with a task which entailed remuneration. How the structure developed into what we can actually observe from the later Old Babylonian period onwards, is only partially understood. We assume that it arose because society, consciously or not, felt a specific need, roughly at the same time, in localities belonging to various similarly structured political entities, for which it made available the means. In a sense the personnel was seconded from more ordinary occupations to the special tasks created or, perhaps, rather upgraded. We need more information on this process, or have to understand the material available better. The process presumably originated in the Third Millennium or even somewhat earlier, perhaps as an element contributing to the development of a hierarchical settlement system. Little is known about the higher ranks, with which the process will have started, but by the Ur III period also some of the more modest functions had become involved. Whether the elimination of female functions was a logical consequence of the momentum of a process which gathered speed in later Old Babylonian times, can for the moment only be a question of speculation.

The development induced specialisation, primarily through splitting up of the tasks "vertically", with "horizontal" division[1] limiting the individual periods of service of the lower functions. The practical result was the involvement of far more people than strictly necessary, thus broadening the basis of a phenomenon which created an elite, which was ensured of regular income. The group of people involved became in the course of time an important element of the urban population, for the prebendaries had their families, which spread the economic interests even wider. Tentatively the adoption of family names in the second half of the Second Millennium is proposed to have been an element of the process that created the prebendal elite.

On the negative side of the prebendal balance stands for us that many basic questions remain poorly understood. Especially in the later period the central figure of *ērib bīti* remains problematical. The title of *ērib bīti* certainly imparted status and it is relatively certain that he at least sometimes plied a specific trade, but whether he was always primarily someone who brought a specific skill with him on becoming an *ērib bīti* is not so clear. The situation is more or less comparable with that of those who bore the titles of *ramku* or *pašīšu* (and thus their Sumerian equivalents of ŠITA or $GUDU_4$) in the earlier period. Important though they were, it is difficult to fathom their tasks. The relevant assumption here, which may initiate fresh research, is that the practical task of the system could be seen as the duty to execute a number of ritually determined acts, for which purpose first raw materials and ultimately finished products were required. Providing the special products made from the raw material and executing the rites required specific functionaries, who were remunerated with the material and products involved. Matching the functionaries, the products and the rites must elucidate who they were and what they did.

Prebendaries can be divided into two main groups, those "who had access everywhere in the temple" and those who had not, and who were remunerated in different,

[1] For the observation of this process the later "small sanctuary prebends" are especially valuable.

often obscure ways. Those who had access were classified according to standardised amounts of bread and beer and specific cuts of meat, deriving from the offerings, plus, of course, pro rata additional perks, including probably pieces of textile. Presumably their status was determined primarily according to their basic allowance of bread and beer, always provided in equal volumes. Those who were not allowed to enter acted as purveyors and were remunerated on principle with the material they had to make suitable for consumption or use. On top of that they received certain meat portions from the sacrifices, or if they were butchers, bread and beer, a source of confusion with the *ērib bītis*, for us.

Having a share in the offerings and sacrifices did not automatically imply prebendal status, and persons belonging to the prebendal fringe, notably doorkeepers and measurers, but also others, derived their income, or part of it, from special accounts, which were fed from specially assigned sources of income. There were probably professions where only very few members were prebendaries, perhaps only in the sense that they could act alongside *ērib bīti*s or purveyors on specific occasions. Perhaps the boatmen and the fishermen must be mentioned here. Fishermen were to all probability unfree, and had to deliver an *iškaru*, an obligation sometimes indicated by the term *manzaltu*, thus causing confusion. The possibility that certain (individual) purveyors were -so to say *à titre personnel*- *ērib bīti*s can as yet not be excluded completely. That direct contact with the godhead was of central importance for the place in the system occupied, is an assumption. In many respects only the barest outlines of the system are discernible. We can expect an extremely varied and numerous personnel for Marduk in Babylon and the prebendal system will also have had its ramifications in the palace chapels and the mortuary cults.

This contribution is also based on the still further assumption that if the prebendal functions were not on principle inheritable, they at any rate circulated within the family. This is especially important in connection with the higher functions. Proof is inevitably patchy, but the matter is crucial, if we want to form an opinion on the social status of the clergy as a whole. Ancient Mesopotamia had no organised mechanism of succession other than succession through inheritance or appointment by the ruler. Under normal circumstances for the higher functions, at most tempered by possible manipulation of presages, the king selected the person he regarded as suitable from those entitled. But there was no recognisable general selection process for the ordinary functions, neither by insiders nor by outsiders.[2] What was practically required was registration, giving access to income, and consecration.

What is clear, is that prebendal income was always, early and late, controlled by local organisations centring on the main sanctuary, where royal representatives wielded much practical power. This agrees in every respect with what we otherwise know about the operation of Mesopotamian temples. Under normal circumstances the king dominated the sanctuaries, especially from an economic point of view. They carried out the royal policy regarding agriculture, in name the king provided them with the means to maintain the cult. Major building operations took place in his name, in theory he provided the funding for the offerings, and from the material resulting from the offerings the cultic personnel was paid. We might add: the king also played a prominent role in crucial ritual events, thus creating access to his person for those involved. But we cannot regard the king as the unrestricted owner of the temple. In the late period the temple of Marduk in Babylon constituted a kind of paradigm for the other sanctuaries.

---

[2] This constitutes also an assumption, but I cannot regard resort to some form of selection by omen as an independent, properly independent method of selection, the only answers possible being yes or no to a very specific question.

Al this does not mean that the prebendal class was not in itself socially important, especially in the towns. The sanctuaries played a vital role in maintaining and restoring the position of the old towns. They maintained an important layer of urban settlements between the two purely agrarian layers of smaller settlements on the one hand and the highest level in the settlement hierarchy, the royal residence towns, which regularly doubled as the main religious centres. Kings were careful to have their own men in the top functions, where we find the most overtly political appointments, and also probably had their special supporters among the clergy. Otherwise the prebendaries formed an urban group which clearly distinguished itself carefully from the non-prebendal urban families, even though this conclusion can only be based on comparison of the available family archives: some families, even economically important ones, never possessed prebendal interests. The economic activities of the temple, especially with the system of leasing temple property from the later Chaldean period onwards, created new possibilities for enrichment, even though the expansion of the system of leases may have been intended to loosen the grip of a restricted number of families, which was regarded, perhaps, as becoming stifling by the royal administration.

The prebendal system created a tough, resilient, numerically important elite which sometimes managed to maintain its interests until deep into the Hellenistic period, if not to its very end, after the beginning of what we now call the Christian era, a point in time not marked as special by the contemporaries. The prebendal class probably constituted one of the few recognisable elements of the socio-political structure which could through its own weight up to a degree withstand the monarchy.

The social importance of Babylonia's main sanctuaries and their personnel in retaining and restoring the country's status as an urbanised society can hardly be underrated. Political unification seriously weakened the small regionally based four-tiered hierarchical settlement system that had come to development in the Third Millennium. The status in the religious system of the main local sanctuaries saved a modified hierarchical urbanised system at least partially during the periods of political unification, and it played an important role in periods of restoration, as we may suppose the later Kassite period to have been up to a degree and as the Neo-Babylonian period certainly was, when it resurrected the four-tiered system in a very different form under one large centre.

The fact that the prebendal system was based nearly completely on what was produced locally, in Mesopotamia itself, should provide food for thought. The prebendal system largely eluded, at least until the Hellenistic period, our elusive silver, though we cannot fail to note its increasing impact in the Neo-Babylonian period. This does not mean, however, that the prebendal families had no economic interests other than their prebends.

PREBENDS LITERATURE

Beaulieu 1991 — P.A. Beaulieu, Neo-Babylonian Larsa: a Preliminary Study, Or NS 60, 1991, p. 58-81.

Beaulieu 1992 — P.A. Beaulieu, New Light on Secret Knowledge in the Late Babylonian Culture, ZA 82, 1992, p. 98-111.

Beaulieu 1993 — P.A. Beaulieu, Prébendiers d'Uruk à Larsa, RA 87, 1993, p. 137-151.

Beaulieu 1995 — P.A. Beaulieu, The Brewers of Nippur, JCS 47, 1995, p. 35-96.

Boiy 2000 — T. Boiy, Laatachaemenidisch en Hellenistisch Babylon, Portret van een Mesopotamische stad in een cultureel spanningsveld, Diss. Leuven, 2000.

Bongenaar 1997 — A.C.V.M. Bongenaar, The Neo-Babylonian Ebabbar Temple at Sippar, its Administration and its Prosopography, Istanbul, 1997.

Bongenaar 1999 — A.C.V.M. Bongenaar, Money in the Neo-Babylonian Institutions, in ed. J.G. Dercksen, Trade and Finance in Ancient Mesopotamia, MOS Studies 1, Istanbul 1999, p.160-174.

Bongenaar 2000 — A.C.V.M. Bongenaar, Private Archives in Neo-Babylonian Sippar and their Institutional Connections, in ed. A.C.V.M. Bongenaar, Interdependency of Institutions and Private Entrepreneurs, MOS Studies 2, Istanbul 2000, p. 73-94.

Borger 1973 — R. Borger, Die Weihe eines Enlil-Priesters, BiOr 30, 1973, p. 163-176.

Çağirgan-Lambert 1991-3 — G. Çağirgan and W.G. Lambert, The Late Babylonian Kislīmu Ritual for Esagil, JCS 43-45, 1991-1993, p. 89-106.

Charpin 1986 — D. Charpin, Le clergé d'Ur au siècle d'Hammurabi, Genève-Paris, 1986.

Civil 1989 — M. Civil, The Statue of Šulgi-ki-ur$_5$-sag$_9$-kalam-ma, Part One: The Inscription, in eds. H. Behrens, D. Loding, M.T. Roth, DUMU-É-DUB-BA-A, Studies in Honor of Å.W. Sjöberg, Philadelphia, 1989, p. 49-63.

Cocquerillat 1973/4 — D. Coquerillat, Recherches sur le verger du temple campagnard de l'Akītu, WdO 7, 1973-74, p. 96-134.

Dossin 1938 — G. Dossin, Un rituel du culte d'Ištar provenant de Mari, RA 35, 1938, p. 1-13. (= Durand-Guichard 1997, text no. 2).

Doty 1977 — L.T. Doty, Cuneiform Archives from Hellenistic Uruk, Diss. Yale, 1977.

Doty 1993 — L.T. Doty, Akkadian *bīt pirišti*, in ed. M.E. Cohen, D.C. Snell and D.B. Weisberg, The Tablet and the Scroll, Near Eastern Studies in Honour of W.W. Hallo, Bethesda, 1993, p. 87-89.

van Driel 1992 — G. van Driel, Neo-Babylonian Texts from Borsippa, BiOr 49, 1992, cols. 16-28.

Durand-Guichard 1997 — J.-M. Durand et M. Guichard, Les rituels de Mari, Florilegium Marianum 3, 1997, p. 19-71.

Ebeling 1954 — E. Ebeling, Stiftungen und Vorschriften für assyrische Tempel, Berlin 1954.

Edzard 1957 — D. O. Edzard, Die "Zweite Zwischenzeit" Babyloniens, Wiesbaden, 1957.

Falkenstein 1959 — A. Falkenstein, Zwei Rituale aus seleukidischer Zeit, UVB 15, 1959, p. 36-44.

Freydank 1971 — H. Freydank, Spätbabylonische Wirtschaftstexte aus Uruk, I, II, Berlin, 1971.

Freydank 1978 — H. Freydank, Zu den Einkommensrechten und Dienstleistungen in Eanna, in eds. B.Hruška, G. Komoróczy, Festschrift Lubor Matouš I, Budapest 1978, p. 91-103.

Funck 1984 — B. Funck, Uruk zur Seleukidenzeit, Berlin, 1984.

George 2000	A.R. George, Four Temple Rituals from Babylon, ed. A.R. George and I.L. Finkel, Wisdom, Gods and Literature, Studies in Assyriology in Honour of W.G. Lambert, Winona Lake, 2000, p. 259-299.
Harris 1975	R. Harris, Ancient Sippar, a Demographic Study of an Old Babylonian City, 1894-1595 B.C., Istanbul, 1975.
Hunger 1968	H. Hunger, Babylonische und assyrische Kolophone, AOAT 2, Kevelaer and Neukirchen-Vluyn, 1968.
Hunger 1970	H. Hunger, Das Archiv des Nabû-ušallim, BaM 5, 1970, p. 193ff.
Joannès 1980	F. Joannès, Textes néo-babyloniens de Strasbourg, RA 74, 1980, p. 145-157.
Joannès 1989	F. Joannès, Archives de Borsippa, la famille Ea-ilûta-bâni, Genève, 1989.
Jursa 1999	M. Jursa, Das Archiv des Bēl-rēmanni, Istanbul, 1999.
Kessler 1991	K. Kessler, Uruk, Urkunden aus Privathäusern, Die Wohnhäuser westlich des Eanna-Tempelbereichs, Teil I, Die Archive der Söhne des Bēl-ušallim, des Nabû-ušallim und des Bēl-supê-muḫur, AUWE 8, Mainz am Rhein, 1991.
Kingsbury 1934	E.C. Kingsbury, A seven day ritual in the Old Babylonian Cult at Larsa, HUCA 34, 1934, p. 1-34.
Lackenbacher 1977	S. Lackenbacher, Un nouveau fragment de la "fête d'Ištar", RA 72, 1977, p. 39-50.
Lambert 1957	W.G. Lambert, Ancestors, Authors and Canonicity, JCS 11, 1957, p. 1-14.
Lambert 1998	W.G. Lambert, The Qualifications of Babylonian Diviners, in ed. S.M. Maul, Festschrift für Rykle Borger zu seinem 65. Geburtstag am 24. Mai 1994, p.141-158.
MacGinnis 1991-2	J. MacGinnis, Neo-Babylonian Prebend Texts from the British Museum, AfO 38/39, 1991-92, p. 74-100.
MacGinnis 1999	J. MacGinnis, Additional Prebend Texts from the British Museum, AoF 26/1, 1999, p. 3-12.
Maekawa 1999	K. Maekawa, The “Temples” and the “Temple Personnel” of Ur III Girsu-Lagash, in ed. K.Watanabe, Priests and Officials in the Ancient Near East, Heidelberg, 1999, p. 62-102.
McEwan 1981	G.J.P. McEwan, Priest and Temple in Hellenistic Babylonia, FAOS 4, 1981.
McEwan 1983	G.J.P. McEwan, Distribution of Meat in Eanna, Iraq 45, 1983, p. 187-198.
Nolet-Boeren 1951	W. Nolet, P.C. Boeren, Kerkelijke Instellingen in de Middeleeuwen, Amsterdam, 1951.
Renger 1967/1969	J. Renger, Untersuchungen zum Priestertum in der altbabylonischen Zeit, I: ZA 58, 1967, p. 110-188; II: ZA 59, 1969, p. 104-230.
Renger 1967	J. Renger, Götternamen in der altbabylonischen Zeit, in ed. D.O. Edzard, Heidelberger Studien zum alten Orient, Adam Falkenstein zum 17. September 1966, Wiesbaden, 1967, p. 137-171.
Renger 1971	J. Renger, Notes on the Goldsmiths, Jewelers and Carpenters of Neobabylonian Eanna, JAOS 91/4, 1971, p. 494-503.
Renger 1975	J. Renger, Örtliche und zeitliche Differenzen in der Struktur der Priesterschaft babylonischer Tempel, CCRAI 20, 1975, p. 108-115.
Da Riva-Frahm 2000	R. Da Riva und E. Frahm, Šamaš-šum-ukīn, die Herrin von Ninive und das babylonische Königssiegel, AfO 46/7, 1999-2000, p. 156-181.
Rochberg 2000	F. Rochberg, The ṭupšar Enūma Anu Enlil, in ed. J. Marzahn and H. Neumann, Assyriologica et Semitica, Fs. J. Oelsner, AOAT 252, Münster 2000, p.359-375.
Roth 1989	M.T. Roth, Babylonian Marriage Agreements, 7th - 3rd Centuries B.C., AOAT 222, Kevelaer and Neukirchen-Vluyn, 1989.
Roth 1991	M. Roth, The dowries of the Women of the Itti-Marduk-balāṭu Family, JAOS 111, 1991, p. 19-37.
Sallaberger 1993	W. Sallaberger, Der kultische Kalender der Ur III-Zeit, UAVA 7/1-2, Berlin, 1993.

San Nicolò 1934 — M. San Nicolò, Einiges über Tempelpfründen (*isqu*) und hemerai leithourgikai in Eanna, Parerga Babylonica XII, Ar Or 6, 1934, p. 179-202.

San Nicolò 1935 — M.San Nicolò, Nochmals zum *gullubu* von Pfründeninhabern in den neubabylonischen Tempeln, Parerga Babylonica XVI, Ar Or 7, 1935, p. 16-25.

Sassmannshausen 2001 — L. Sassmannshausen, Beiträge zur Verwaltung und Gesellschaft Babyloniens in der Kassitenzeit, Mainz, 2001.

Seux 1967 — M.J. Seux, Épithètes royales accadiennes et sumériennes, Paris, 1967.

Sigrist 1977 — R.M. Sigrist, EŠ.TA.GUR.RA, RA 71, 1977, p. 117-124.

Sigrist 1984 — M. Sigrist, Les *sattukku* dans l'Ešumeša, BiMes 11, Malibu, 1984.

van der Spek 1985 — R.J. van der Spek, The Babylonian Temple during the Macedonian and Parthian Domination, BiOr 42, 1985, cols. 541-562.

Steinkeller 1999 — P. Steinkeller, Land-Tenure Conditions in Southern Mesopotamia under the Sargonic Dynasty, in eds. B. Böck, E. Cancik-Kirschbaum, Th. Richter, Fs. J. Renger, Münster 1999, p. 552-559.

Tanret and van Lerberghe 1993 — M. Tanret and K. van Lerberghe, Rituals and Profits in the Ur-Utu Archive, in ed. J. Quaegebeur, Ritual and Sacrifice in the Ancient Near East, Leuven, 1993, p. 435-449.

Thureau-Dangin 1921 — F.Thureau-Dangin, Rituels accadiens, Paris, 1921. (Texts quoted as RAcc. + p.)

Ungnad 1959/60 — A. Ungnad, Neubabylonische Privaturkunden aus der Sammlung Amherst, AfO 19, 1959-60, p. 74-82.

Waerzeggers 2001 — C. Waerzeggers, Het archief van Marduk-rēmanni, I Studie van de familie Ṣāgit-ginê in Nieuwbabylonisch Sippar (548-484 v. Chr.), II De tabletten, Dissertatie, Gent, 2001. (Texts: M.r. + no.)

Zettler 1992 — R.L. Zettler, The Ur III Temple of Inanna at Nippur, the Operation and Organization of Urban Religious Institutions in Mesopotamia in the Late Third Millennium B.C., Berlin, 1992.

PART III

MESOPOTAMIAN TAXATION AND LAND USE IN THE NEO-BABYLONIAN PERIOD

THE KING, THE LAND AND THE SUBJECT

CHAPTER I
INTRODUCTION

1. Purpose[1]

a. Preliminary remarks

Defining taxation in an Ancient Mesopotamian context poses a number of problems. Usually taxation is what the subjects pay or otherwise contribute to a government, which uses the income to finance itself and all those other tasks which it deems worthy of financing for one reason or another. Manpower, which is widely used for civil purposes and is militarily a blood tax, plays its own problematic role, as does the incompletely free status of much of the population. But there is also a link with land use in general.

The era studied is the Neo-Babylonian period in its widest sense, particularly that which is covered sparingly by the early First Millennium *kudurrus* to the end of the Achaemenid period.

The government is for practical purposes in our period the king, without his person no government worthy of the name could function at the time.[2] He was the most important land holder[3] and he had, for us largely undefined, rights to water without which no agriculture was possible. He played an important role in religion, the material aspects of which are of especial significance here. Equally undefined for us are the rights the king had over the person of his subjects. Though subjects were regularly called out for civil or military purposes, in this period, they were mobilised mainly, it would seem, as holders of property which had been granted, or was held, specifically against the fulfilling of certain obligations towards the monarch. Through the system of land holding not only the men,

---

[1] It is, of course, a coincidence that the writing of this study took place at the same time as the introduction of a tax reform in the Netherlands. But to the author it is not a coincidence that taxation "systems" are always difficult to fathom: one of the elementary secrets of successful government is to leave the subject in the dark as to the real bill he has to foot, if only by inventing reasons why levying taxes, duties and rights should be left in reality to a whole range of interests and monopolies, while stressing *ad absurdum* that the system is becoming more comprehensible.

[2] The reader will note that the term "state" is used reluctantly or, rather, avoided, especially for this reason. Practically all Ancient Mesopotamian states (of the period) which left written documentation were monarchies, and in none there existed an effective separation between "crown" and "king". In a remarkable number of cases in the Neo-Babylonian period measures and initiatives can be associated with a specific monarch, acting in person. This is not just valid for that monarch's own inscriptions, which will contain a form of propaganda which stresses the king's role, but also for practical documents, however repugnant it may be for a twenty-first century citizen to have to attribute effective government to a single person, and however convinced he or she may be at heart that the monarch merely acts as an exponent of a badly defined "collective". The word "monarchy" represents the facts perfectly, much better than "state".

The term citizen is not used either, a monarch has subjects, especially in Mesopotamia where all were, at least at a rhetorical level, his "slaves". The king could exempt someone from the prevailing formal or customary law, an act which could turn subjects into citizens, in a true sense, of a certain town -or rather, in our case, of a certain god, -but the ensuing *kidinnu* status is, as far as I can see, never being claimed by any individual in a practical text. *mār banî* was the term for a(ny) non-slave, and not a term for a specific, restricted urban class of people. Freedmen are difficult to identify in Mesopotamia.

[3] This is more an assumption than that it can be made hard.

but also the women were incorporated in the system of taxation. Though the nature and the extent of the obligations may be badly known, they were real. What is in practice virtually unknown in this period is the nature of the obligations of the subject as a subject towards the sovereign.

In the Persian period it appears likely that the various obligations were systematised and expanded into a more coherent system. Yet we must start by regarding all individual obligations as the separate elements of a system of taxation and land holding which need to be analysed. Also meriting attention is taxation in the form of duties levied for services provided by the government, always a type of burden which is apt to be stretched further and further, by stealth, we would say nowadays. There are of course also a number of identifiable taxes on commodities and levies in a religious context. A separate question is what the levies amounted to in total, both in theory and in practice, but that is the principal secret of all systems of taxation, especially as all levies also involve costs.

The king is a patriarch and the apparatus with which he governs is relatively spoken small. That means that he transfers rights to income to his entourage, members of his family and officials, to hold at his, the king's, pleasure[4] and he has other rights to income leased to certain persons against a fixed sum. Though he will on occasion receive additional "rations", it is normal that an official draws income from his charge. All officials will use their private dependants for "official" tasks. The patriarchal structure extended downwards in society. As a matter of fact agricultural business enterprises of the type run by Iddina-Marduk Nūr-Sin and his Egibi relations and also the much less transparent structure of the Murašû firm had strongly patriarchal traits: sons and brothers, trusted slaves and clients play a central role, daughters and sisters constitute vital links, mother provides capital. But rivalry within the family also plays a role.

Government is linked intimately to land use,[5] even without proposing the theory that in Mesopotamia all land was basically government property. Such a theory is not needed actually. The government was in a position where it could regulate and stimulate exploitation of much under-used land after the collapse in the second half of the Second Millennium and the ensuing extreme tribalisation. All types of transfer of land by the government, or the institutions it controlled, contained elements of taxation and elements of ordinary tenancy arrangements. Gift-giving is often associated specifically with trade, but like tribute, it has above all a taxation dimension. We must keep in mind that in Mesopotamia itself that will often involve agricultural produce. Officials often derive at least part of their income directly from their charge: such "costs", paid by the underlings, are properly a form of taxation. The "Edict of Belsazzar" is a good example. The transfer of rights over subjects can have serious consequences for the persons concerned, they constantly run the risk of loosing some of their personal freedom: any monopoly in private hands entails risks for those subjected to its workings.

---

[4] The discussion between Maekawa and Heimpel on the status of the possessions reclaimed or expropriated on the death or disgrace of officials attested especially in Ur III Lagaš and in Old Babylonian Mari illustrates the phenomenon best, but it is not restricted to this time and period and not typical for the Ancient Near East only: the appropriations of officials are for the duration of the king's pleasure, must possibly be renewed annually, and certainly on the accession of a new king. Much of the taxation paid by the king's entourage took the form of "gifts", but these were for all practical purposes obligatory. On the status of the "property" of high officials cf. K. Maekawa, ASJ 18, 1996, p.103-168, and 19, 1997, p. 273-286 versus W. Heimpel, ASJ 19, 1997, p. 63-82. A study on aspects of the question in Mari by F. van Koppen will appear in a future Florilegium Marianum.

[5] This should include animal husbandry, but, as we will have to stress, the evidence on this point is limited.

The Neo-Babylonian period in its widest sense saw the re-establishment of an effective centralised government in Babylonia after the collapse and tribalisation of the early First Millennium BC. In addition the Neo-Babylonian kings undertook huge public works. They had to maintain a considerable military apparatus: they will have used all means known to increase their revenue. Though the documentation on taxation is much better for the Persian than for the Chaldean period, that probably does not mean more than that the Achaemenids, notably, we may assume, Darius, increased the effectiveness of what they found on arrival. The evidence available does not suggest that the Persians used their conquest to introduce, for instance, a completely new system of land holding, which is the central factor determining the economic relation between government and subject in an agrarian society.

The period we are dealing with saw a fundamental change in the political map: it stood at the beginning of Mesopotamia as an economically valuable asset in a much bigger political construction. The question of the Mesopotamian "tribute" to the Persian king cannot be completely avoided here. It is clear that much of the taxation levied, the wealth created, in Mesopotamia actually left the country in the Persian period. The fact is suggested by Herodotus and supported, though differently, by the textual material found in the private archives of the period. This is valid not only regarding commodities, including silver, but especially concerning manpower. It betrays the increasing grip of the government on its subjects, but without the implied exploitation stretching the possibilities to the limit. The assumption could be that the actual weight of the tax burden was mitigated by an economic growth which is undeniably visible archaeologically in the considerable long term increase in inhabited space. This, again, was not initiated by the new Persian masters, but economic growth makes the creaming off of income by the government less burdensome, even if it is or becomes a foreign one.[6]

The ultimate sense of a study of taxation, however limited its scope, should not only be to investigate how it worked and what it yielded, but it has to establish what the effects were. In this respect real insights are for the future. No more than cursory impressions are possible and they are strongly coloured by the archaeological message of sustained long term growth. But that message is supported by policies which can be reconstructed on the basis of an interpretation of the material linking taxation and leasehold policies: whatever happened, in the long term the economy grew in this period.

b. A note on procedures

This is not the place to repeat the familiar and list the various archives from which the material used derives. Virtually all administrative and private archives contain information on land use and land holding, this is not for nothing an agrarian society. The exploitation of the land is a central concern. With the passage of time private archives from this period contain an increasing number of tax receipts. References to fiscal practices can be distilled in many cases from tenancy agreements, of both administrative and private nature. But the information on the taxation of animal husbandry and trade is disappointing and even utterly misleading if regarded as a sign of the relative unimportance of these sources of income.

---

[6] We will note the presence of widespread military landholding, but these "military" were also subjects, they are not visibly the tool of an occupier. We notice the presence of Persian officials, but not that of a Persian army of occupation, as far as we can see. Herodotus only tells us that Cilicia had to pay separately for a strategic Persian cavalry force. In general such stationary forces will after one or two generation acquire strong local roots. Where relevant this will also have been the case in Murašû Babylonia.

The importance of the role of the dictionaries, both the CAD and the AHw will be apparent throughout. In general the reader will find an introductory section to each subject, followed by a section on the relevant taxation terminology, consisting of a discussion followed by a selective list of passages, references or summaries taken from texts which constitute the basis for the discussion in the introduction to the section. These references are mainly selected from private archives which are exploited to a varying degree. This introduces an inevitable element of arbitrariness, which is the unavoidable result of conscious selection combined with ignorance. The Murašû archive, for instance, has been studied in the past intensively regarding the terminology discussed, it is therefore not quoted extensively compared to its general importance. Other important material will certainly have been missed, certainly much of what occurs in quotations by others from unpublished texts in secondary literature. The discussion of the taxation terminology is followed by one concerning the basis of the taxation (sub-)system and, very tentatively, by speculation on the level of taxation and its consequences, where such is feasible.

The text summaries included are only intended to provide the reader with information which gives an idea about the relative importance of the text for the subject in hand. They are not intended to replace the editions available, to which the reader is explicitly referred. Occasionally a text provides information on more than one of the terms relevant for our subject, it may therefore be quoted twice, but in general the reader will be referred back or forward to one occurrence. Damage to the text concerned will only be indicated sparingly, on principle only if the author is of the opinion that it seriously affects his way of using the material. On principle the reader should consult a complete edition of the text.

In many cases names have been shortened. Often PN stands for PN son of PN2 family PN3, especially where the author is of the subjective opinion that the additional information does not add to the argument. In other cases a shorthand version of a recurrent PN is used, for instance MNA stands for Marduk-nāṣir-apli s Itti-Marduk-balāṭu Egibi, which saves space. Such abbreviations are listed at the end of this contribution. In summaries of texts, contrary to common usage, PNs, names of places and occupations are not put in italics, as ordinary Akkadian text is.

2. Aspects of the documentation used[7]

a. Terminology and limitations

We can assume that the written material from which our knowledge derives is not of necessity explicit or precise in its formulations. Those involved knew the backgrounds, we do not. An unspecified receipt can deal with payment of tax, even though the fact is not stated with so many words. Only prosopography could provide a clue regarding the backgrounds of the payment, but we do not always know the persons involved and there are also other reasons imaginable for a transfer between known people.

The technical terminology of taxation consists of terms which could be used in a non-tax-related context. Words like *dullu* or even *urāšu* can have a very general sense and are only tax related in a specific situation. Sometimes they even have another technical meaning in a different context, like *dullu* and even *ilku* in the cult. *rikis qabli* is strictly spoken not a fiscal term, but it has socially spoken considerable taxation related implications

[7] An interesting overview of types of Ancient Near Eastern taxation has been provided by J. Nougayrol in PRU III, 1955, p. 225, dealing with Ugarit in the second half of the Second Millennium. Not all forms of taxation found there can as yet be documented for the Neo-Babylonian period, but it is unlikely that they were unknown. A poll tax is a simple form of taxation after all and it certainly existed in Mesopotamia in Parthian times. Being a member of an *eširtu* possibly had a comparable effect.

in specific circumstances. Other words like *irbu* and *tēlītu* are basically not tax related either, but can easily be used regarding taxation-based income or expenditure respectively. The context is all-important.

Understanding the terminology does not imply understanding the workings of the form of taxation concerned, the burden it constituted or the extent to which it was levied and from whom. All practical information is, however, limited and must result in subjective interpretation of limited scope. There is no basis for quantification proper, as yet. Herodotus' annual Persian tribute paid by Mesopotamia of 1000 talents of silver cannot be verified or rejected and his additional delivery of 500 boys remains for the moment unsubstantiated by the material from Mesopotamia itself. But he certainly misses Babylonia's most evident subservience to the economy of the Achaemenid heartland: its yearly contribution of a labour force to what is indicated in the texts as Elam or Susa. Is that the prosaic translation of what Herodotus really meant by the 500 boys, and is not its importance in that case probably grossly underestimated? Again it is impossible to put a figure on the total costs involved, but there are texts which suggest that these were not negligible, certainly not at the level of, minimally, some individual tax payers.

b. Administrative practice: manipulation of weights and measures

As always weights and measurements and the related question of the purity of the silver used for payments and in calculations constitute a problem. But so does the chalk mixed with the flour or the water in the milk. We will not worry about the question of purity of the silver. But we must take notice of the fact that the purity of the silver used as currency by the subject in the Achaemenid period increased, impurities accepted declining from 1/8 to 1/10.[8] There are signs that silver was in reasonable supply, but the manner in which it was earned remains badly understood.[9] We must also accept the fact that one type of Neo-Babylonian surface kor is 4000 square cubits larger than the other, 54000 instead of 50000, and that the older surface kor of 60.000 square cubits cannot be excluded from our considerations completely.[10]

---

[8] P. Vargyas, Silver and money in Achaemenid and Hellenistic Babylonia, Fs. Oelsner, AOAT 252, 2000, p. 513-521, esp. p. 515, cf. P. Vargyas, *Kaspu ginnu* and the Monetary Reform of Darius I, ZA 89, 1999, esp. p. 247-268 and F. Joannès, Métaux et moyens de paiement en Babylonie achéménide et hellénistique, Transeuphratène 8, 1994, p. 137-144.

[9] Best indication: 1 kor, in this period 180 SILA3, of dates has a kind of standard price in the period of the Murašû texts of 1 shekel of silver, a kor of dates in the Neo-Babylonian period in general is equal to a kor of barley in the payment of rations or prebendal income. The early standard price of a kor of barley of 300 SILA3 was 1 shekel. I would hesitate calling this inflation but prefer regarding it as a sign that the supply of silver had increased, silver being still primarily one commodity amongst others. This type of an "accounting price" is of course not the same as a "market price". These were in the late period always higher, if we may follow the calculations of A.L. Slotsky, The Bourse of Babylon, Bethesda, 1997, p. 50, which first of all points out that in reality an equal amount of dates was less valuable than one of barley and also, for instance, that the median value of barley is to be put at over 2 *š* per kor (of 180 SILA3), which only underlines the changed position of silver even more convincingly: 1 *š* for 300 SILA3 had become 2 *š* for 180 SILA3 in roughly 1500 years. But we must note perhaps that most of the usable evidence from the diaries dates to the later Seleucid period and after. We may not apply these facts automatically to our period, though the 2 š per kor price occurs earlier.

[10] A surface kor declined from 1.5 ha. to 1.35 ha. in private archives and 1.25 ha. in institutional context, if a standard cubit of 50 cm. is accepted.

But especially solid volume measures have a real, practical meaning for our subject.[11] In agrarian Mesopotamia they are used to express the volume of taxation in the most literal sense of the word. That different measures were used at the different stages of agricultural manipulation from seed through harvest and thereafter from delivery to expenditure and processing is more than a suspicion. For dates and barley the *mašīḫu* (0.1.0), basically of 36 SILA_3, will have been the main measure for solid volumes, the half *mašīḫu* or *ṣimdu* (0.0.3) also played a role and that is in taxation also the case with the *sūtu* (0.0.1). There are five *mašīḫu*s in a Neo-Babylonian kor and I take it for granted that if a text states "he will give *itti* 1 kor 0.1.0 or 0.0.3 or 0.0.1",[12] that means that either a *mašīḫu*,[13] a *ṣimdu* or a *sūtu* was to be delivered additionally. Such additionals are not indicated as implied when the "*mašīḫu* of Mr. X", "of god Y"[14] or the palace is being used. Especially not when that is the special *mašīḫu* belonging to a specific stage of manipulation, for there are various *mašīḫu*s of more SILA_3s than the 36 of the standard one. A quick look in the CAD is sufficient. In general in private documents an attempt is made to keep the relation between the seed used and the harvest delivered constant by prescribing the use of one particular *mašīḫu*. But manipulation of *mašīḫu* sizes is always likely, perhaps that is one of the reasons for the importance of the role of "measurers". The effects immediately run into percentage points, with a range of $3^1/_3$ to at least 20.

In a text like CT 56, 225, 6 XI Cyr 7, from Sippar, of which lines 17 and 18 will appear to be of importance for our subject, the delivered amount given in line 16, resulting from the amounts listed, can, barring gross mistakes in the copy, never be correct, unless the amount, 148.4.1 3 SILA_3 or $744^1/_4$ *mašīḫu* is the result of playing with the number of SILA_3s in various *mašīḫu*s used, presumably. I cannot figure out what is done, one of the reasons being that *adi* (line 4), *ina libbi* (line 9) and *elat* (line 11) pose an intractable problem concerning what must be included and what not.

It must be evident that many aspects of the problems posed by the measurements used will escape us.

---

[11] We will not discuss again the question of the size of the SILA_3. The reader can either accept or reject the one litre equivalent, 0.84 litre, or any other alternative, important though the question is.

[12] These readings in themselves are already problematical: *itti* 1 GUR 0.1.0 *inamdin* can also be understood, if an amount precedes the phrase, as "with it he will deliver 1 GUR 1.0, i.e. 6 *mašīḫus*, that is not 20% extra but only 1.1.0 in toto. I am convinced that this is not the intention, however.

[13] In the Murašû text TuM 2/3, 147 this seems to be called, lines 9 and 16: *ina* ^{GIŠ}*ma-ši-ḫu tar-ṣu-ú it-ti* 1 GUR 1 PI. It is said of the fixed yield to be paid annually to the rent farmer of the Nār-Sin for an irrigation system. To complicate things PBS 2/1, 163 (date lost) has 4) ... *ina* ^{GIŠ}*ma-ši-ḫu tar-ṣu ù* KI 1 GUR 0.0.3.AM_3 ... *inamdin*. AHw p. 1331R translates "richtig, angemessen". See also Cardascia 1951, p. 141. This type of additionals is also of importance in taxation matters. There are cases, we will see, in which these seem to be intended to pay for specific forms of taxation.

[14] For a case in which calculation is possible cf. P.-A. Beaulieu, NABU 1989/65, NCBT 620, (16 VI Nbk 43) where in Eanna in Uruk a *mašīḫu* of 45 SILA_3 is used in administering various forms of allocation of barley. x *mašīḫu* are provided for every purpose listed and the total is given in kors. No motive is provided. Rations and fodder for horses would be shared out normally in the form of an amount representing a fixed number of SILA_3 per day. A closer inspection of the two persons who put the remainder into storage in Udannu may have been advisable: which *mašīḫu* did they use when handing out what was transferred to them? Or is this the manner in which the inevitable storage losses were compensated administratively: incoming 45 SILA_3 equals 36 SILA_3 in spending? The administrative problem of storage losses remains generally intractable. The 45 SILA_3 *mašīḫus* are also otherwise identifiable as we will see. Beaulieu's text provides a welcome occasion to ponder the reasons for their use.

3. Some problematic aspects of taxation

a. The limits of government

Our Mesopotamian monarch does not govern a modern state which extends to known borders and has a more or less uniform grip on all its subjects. His rule is effective near the centres of power, and questionable in border areas, in general there where communications are difficult. This type of complication is particularly relevant in Southern Mesopotamia, where strong tribal units persisted at least in the Chaldean period. In such circumstances the subject often has to accept a regime of contributions to local, traditional, potentates of various kinds, combined with additional tribute payments to the centre through these local rulers. "Centre and periphery" has a very real meaning for the subject under these circumstances. This represents an unstable mixture, in which the person of the ruler plays an important role.

The existence of an asymmetric system of mutual gifts which must be observed by superiors and inferiors plays an important role in keeping this type of society functioning. There are aspects of such a system which can be regarded as a type of "trade", especially at an "international" level, but it is as much a system of taxation and tribute through which on balance goods flow from the lower to the higher echelon. As this system functions in practice at a higher level than that of the private and institutional archives of local, urban nature we possess for the Neo-Babylonian period, it must remain largely undiscussed here,[15] though there are clear signs of promises and favours in order to obtain opportunities in the documentation available.[16] If we want to know how "taxation" works in an economic respect, obligatory "gifts" must be regarded as an essential element in the total equation. The fact that this aspect is badly documented does not indicate its lack of importance, but it illustrates the limited means available for assessing taxation in its totality as a phenomenon.

One aspect related to taxation and the relative weakness of government structure, and perhaps not only in peripheral regions, is, as far as I can see, only directly documented in the Old Babylonian period. The sale of functions belongs to the realm of taxation as the official concerned buys his function to recoup his costs from the subjects placed under his jurisdiction, and with interest. It occurred notably in Mari: it is the payment by the *sugāgu*, commonly regarded as a local official acting in a tribal environment, to the king for the right to exercise his function. It is unlikely that *rabiānu*s, *bēl āli*s, *ḫazannu*s and their likes in general were not often in a similar position in later periods. The Nuzi *ḫazannu* Kušši-Ḫarbe is a good example of the financial possibilities open to a functionary of this type in dealing with the subjects, even in one of the centres of a kingdom. The borderline between "tribute", "taxation" and "extortion" will often have been hazy, especially at this level. Petty corruption in local government is notoriously difficult to eradicate, but it weighs heavily on the subject.

On the evidence from the texts and from archaeological survey this period sees a notable internal colonisation. We can assume a parallel increase in the strength of the grip which the government exercised on the subject in general. This is demonstrated already by the fact that subjects retain tax receipts. From their virtual absence from texts dating to the Achaemenid period, the tribes of Southern Mesopotamia seem to have lost their separate

15 The importance of direct contact with the sources of power transpires, however, even in the private archives at our disposal. Not just in the importance of the Egibi contacts with Neriglissar already before he became king, but also in Itti-Marduk-balāṭu's visits to Susa, and in the hiring of a house in Babylon by the head of the Murašû firm, explicitly, "until the king leaves". Visiting the king is expensive, but essential for the upwardly mobile.

16 Such additional "gifts" can be found openly in rent farm documents, TCL 12, 57, 13 VIII Nbk 41, is a good and early example.

identity, a phenomenon probably assisted by the steady infiltration of their Arabian successors. Internal colonisation will inevitably have reduced tribal lands. As we will see, kings occasionally granted members of the tribes to the temples or their personnel. We also have a rare instance in which the buying of tribal land is being alluded to.[17]

There is another area where the subject comes into financial contact with his rulers which is difficult to treat. It is that of jurisdiction, which leads to costs, official, semi-official[18] and no doubt through outright bribery,[19] but which also entails fines and payments in lieu of other punishments. Whether the often high fines payable to the "government" in case of breach of ordinary contracts between private individuals had a basis in reality can be doubted, but they belong in this ambience. Though there is ample information on litigation, its costs are seldomly documented. The question must certainly be included in the considerations, if only in a theoretical manner. The role of supreme royal jurisdiction in expanding the area under effective monarchical control is also never to be underestimated. This is an important subject which cannot be treated effectively. It compelled the subject to visit the royal court, it caused local judges to be present there. In the Persian period it explains many of the visits to Susa or Ecbatana.

b) The role of the institutions

Much production, not only in the field of agriculture, took place in an institutional context. This masks certain aspects of taxation, for what was produced contributed to the financing of "government and what it deemed worthy". Little is known about the productive capacity of the various palaces in this period, but the statement is certainly valid for the temples. Though ideology might perhaps prescribe a *kidinnūtu* or *šubarūtu* status, with exemption from taxation and service obligations, it is beyond doubt that temples definitely had to contribute to the system of taxation we can identify. The same is valid for the upper layer of their personnel, who would have been the best placed group for claiming a privileged position. The temple functioned economically as an extension of the monarchy.

Direct production for own use was probably, at least in the Third Millennium, a very important source of disposable income for Mesopotamian governments. Much of what could be actively spent was the result of the production by government-related institutions themselves. The most direct and complete form of "taxation" was, in the prevailing circumstances, that in which the people who acted as producers were the property of an institution, worked for that institution and received (a meagre) sustenance: this is in fact, if not a form of slavery, at least one of servitude in relation to the government.

The "incorporation of labour" found in Mesopotamian institutions will not be classified under the term "slavery" or even "(absolute) taxation" by many, because the persons concerned are assumed to have led an "embedded" existence, which is supposed to have cared as much for them, as it exploited them. Yet, involuntarily, in this context people are, with a creeping universality, being increasingly regarded as having been a means of

---

[17] AnOr 9, 19, quoted Chapter III under *nakkandu*.

[18] Such costs can perhaps be found in unofficial notes concerning expenditure, which will not be preserved generally. An example is perhaps VS 6, 309, undated and belonging to a group of similar documents from the Ilšu-abušu family files. Lines 1-2 register a payment consisting of 8,5 *š* of silver and a *gandu* of wine to a named judge, rev. 5-6 four sheep, four *dannu*, presumably of beer, and 1.3.2 of both flour and barley for "the judges".

[19] Typical are the MA *šulmānu*-payments to someone of status by someone who wanted to go to court. Is it a fee required on starting a case, a payment for interesting an official in one's cause, or an outright bribe to determine the outcome?

production which could be made, and was made, productive at will. There are some signs that this situation had already come into being in the Late Uruk/Jemdet Nasr period.[20] Institutional servitude is not usually included under the heading "taxation", but in reality it constitutes the ultimate example of the manner in which labour and toil can be appropriated for purposes deemed "public". Whether wage labour, or rather, at which rate of remuneration the use of such labour can be regarded as a form of exploitation is an old and insoluble question, but it is difficult to regard the early Mesopotamian institutions as examples of what should be seen as a social ideal.

The important question in this respect in the context of overall taxation is that of the size of the share in the total population of this embedded institutional work force, compared to, for instance, personnel on other estates, the military land holders and the subsistence farmers providing their own sustenance outside the various institutional or estate systems. These are matters of quantification which can only be approached in a subjective manner. My own guess is that even the Third Millennium institutions covered only a restricted share of the land, but with an even more limited share in the population, which makes it likely that the institutional subjects were burdened with a heavier work load than their contemporaries in general.[21] At any rate in the First Millennium there are signs that becoming a *širku*, an institutional dependant, was not being regarded favourably: it was probably considered less disadvantageous to become a client of a private person, presumably because it was easier to escape from that condition.[22] The institutions can legitimately be seen as a part of the apparatus which burdened the population, and particularly, possibly even excessively so, their own subjects.[23]

This confronts us with a problem. It is clear that in the Neo-Babylonian period the institutions had considerable trouble in finding the labour required for a proper exploitation of the land they held. The government can be seen to encroach on this land, giving out shares in it and favouring outside leases. A logical outcome of this situation would be that the grip of the institutions on their subject population would have become difficult to maintain, which in turn would encourage the development of more contractual relationships between the institution and its subject personnel. This question will have to be considered further.

---

[20] As suggested, probably too speculatively, by the present author BiOr 57, 2000 col. 499.

[21] Cf. the contributions to ed. A.C.V.M. Bongenaar, Interdependency of Institutions and Private Entrepreneurs, MOS Studies 2, Istanbul 2000, p. 11-13 in general and AfO 46-47, 1999/2000, p. 80-91, for especially, Umma. Both these attempts should be seen primarily as intended to stimulate discussion, but I find it increasingly difficult to imagine (Third Millennium) Ancient Mesopotamia as one huge collection of temples and palaces managing the complete agriculture and assume that especially the tribal and "military" aspect of the economy is grossly underrated.

[22] G. van Driel, The Neo-Babylonian period, in ed. M. Stol, S.P. Vleeming, The care of the elderly in the Ancient Near East, Leiden, 1998, p. 176.

[23] We can perhaps admire Mesopotamian institutional agriculture for the manner in which it used the available ample supply of land for an effective system in which relatively spoken limited labour, extensively used traction with a sparing application of seed provided a favourable yield. We cannot, or can hardly, compare the results obtained with those of agriculture outside the institutions. The only case I know of, where direct comparison is possible consists of three texts from Mari, in the Old Babylonian period, which can be used to put a question mark behind the proposed institutional effectiveness: the *muškēnu*s, who operated outside the institution, in Mari the palace, in a wide sense, produced more in relation to the amount of land available, than those working in an institutional context. It should be noted, however, that doubts have been expressed concerning the validity of the results attributed to the *muškenu*s: F. van Koppen, JESHO 44, 2001, p. 483.

Whether in the Neo-Babylonian period the institutions were still as important as producers as they were in the Third Millennium can be doubted: the share of the institutional sector in the overall production had, at least relatively spoken, shrunk. To all probability the private sector had become much stronger than before and especially less subsistence oriented, even if such a statement is mainly based on impressions. All attempts at quantification remain ineffective.

An increased role of the private sector presupposes the existence of a market for agricultural produce. That means that by the First Millennium B.C. the relative importance of private producers for taxation by the government will have increased. Measuring this increase is again not possible, but the easiest way to obtain more will have been to use the methods available in a more intensive manner. Privatisation of the exploitation of the institutional assets is a fact in this period. But perhaps it was attempted earlier and belonged to the known arsenal of means of increasing production.[24] For a government, especially for a monarch, it was essential to have access to the proceeds of the most productive sections of society, loosing that access would always sooner or later be fatal. That was certainly so if the government was for all practical possibilities an alien power, as was the case in Mesopotamia in the Achaemenid period.

It must be kept in mind that, though the relative importance and perhaps even the absolute size of the institutions did not reach that of the earlier periods, the institutions remained important producers of essential goods, which were at least partially at the easy disposal of the government, the king.

The increased distance, especially in Persian times, between the king and the Babylonian subjects probably added to the importance of liquidity, that is of silver, when

---

24 This can possibly be illustrated by speculating in the grand style on an Ur III-Old Babylonian example, with its antecedents. Ur III institutional agriculture in Lagaš on the main local waterway to the South, the "Canal running to Nina", is known from texts from the archive of the local ENSI, indicating exploitation organised in a number of divine estates managed in the end by the ENSI in an institutional structure. When we turn to the Old Babylonian period we find in the Birot-Ellis group of texts (TÉBA 1-11 and JCS 29, 1977, p. 127ff.) something very different: land in the same general area is being managed by leaseholders, presumably for the government of the day, but there is certainly no direct exploitation. Was this the result of a complete restructuring of the exploitation, or was at least some of the land in this area always exploited indirectly, and is there merely a shift in the nature of the documentation? A systematic search of all documentation available on evidence for the relation between direct and indirect exploitation is required. A cycle suggests itself. The kings of Akkad concentrated in the Lagaš area much of the exploitation of agricultural land in their own estates and in those of their followers (OIP, 104, 1991, Ancient Kudurru no. 24 and P. Steinkeller, Fs. Renger, Münster 1999 p. 558ff.). The Ur III kings in turn, especially Ur-Nammu, probably "returned the land to the gods", an assertion based on the material published by F.R. Kraus, ZA 51, 1955, p. 45ff., which, though referring to a different area, yet suggests a political principle, the application of which can be related directly to what can be observed in practice in the Lagaš area. This should remind us of the earlier Uruinimgina "Reforms", also "restoring" divine property. "Reforms" of this type were well within the means of the rulers of the day. The practical effects of the Uruinimgina example could indicate that the real difference was marginal. Perhaps it could be characterised as determined by the status occupied by the person who fulfilled the tasks of the NUBANDA.GU_4 or the DUB.SAR GU_4, more or less the level of the Old Babylonian managers. An example of the cyclical "change" we also experience and could call that of "nationalisation and privatisation". What is really interesting is the question of who are the movers and who foots the bill in this permanent experiment. In the Neo-Babylonian period we could perhaps suggest that (in the later Chaldean period) the temples had got far more land than they could manage, probably as a result of attributions in the ninth and eighth centuries. As soon as a demand for land, especially near the towns would arise, "insufficient management" would become an argument for taking it away.

dealing with taxation. The consequences remain largely obscure, but must have been significant. Also the institutions were forced into a more market oriented economy: they had to exchange their produce for silver even more than was the case earlier on. Mesopotamia would have required more silver, which had to come from the outside and had to be earned.

CHAPTER II
SERVICES PROVIDED BY THE AUTHORITIES AND RELATED COSTS

1. Introduction

The first aspect of the Neo-Babylonian taxation that must be studied is that of the costs charged by the government. These were claimed for what were initially specific services provided, but there were also costs related to administration in general. It is, however, not certain whether some of these administrative costs were not often rather estate-related than a government matter. The estates, especially those of the gods, can be seen, however, as an extension of government. There are clear indications that especially in the Persian period government intervention in property matters gave rise to the levy of duties. Such interventions nearly always begin as a "service", but they inevitably acquire fund raising aspects, which makes the government dependent on them. In this chapter we deal only with administrative matters, not with, for instance, payments for the use of roads or canals, without forgetting that boundaries are vague, also in this respect.

2. The Evidence

a. The "Edict of Belsazzar"[1]

General (production) costs like payments for water and energy and taxation are not easily separated. Governments at all levels are clever in this respect.[2] Access to water is essential for agricultural production, and especially in an irrigation-based society it must be manipulated. That providing water for irrigation entails costs stands to reason. We will deal separately, and rather ineffectively, with the matter, for especially here "taxation" and "rent" are closely related and difficult to separate.

In the "Edict of Belsazzar", YOS 6, 103, "costs" are listed in the form of rights to income for certain officials, but the practical work, the form of the services involved, is nowhere specified. This possibly implies that these "costs" were primarily duties levied, with additionally means being provided, intended to compensate for the expenditure caused. The fact that these compensatory measures were not yet incorporated in the main stipulations of the transaction could suggest that we are dealing with a recent adaptation of what were to all likelihood customary payments of long standing. These are certainly not the costs involved in the upkeep of irrigation systems or in the delivery of water. The payment, partially or in full, of officials through the granting of perks payable by those under the say of the person concerned, has a proper Ancien Regime flavour.

---

[1] Though not an edict in the proper sense of the word, we will continue to call the text "the Edict". The following repeats in the main van Driel 1987-'88 pp. 61-64.

[2] A prime modern example is the stealth tax introduced through the privatised water companies in the Netherlands called "contribution" -mark the possibilities for expansion- to costs in water caused by the operation of the fire brigade, payable as a fixed amount by those paying for a water meter, which is a fictitious, but obligatory, apparatus for people living in apartments, who are prevented in this manner to monitor their own water use and compelled to pay a collective bill, thus reducing the costs for the company. The fire brigade is paid anyhow by the taxpayer, but it asks increasingly for payment for the services it provides. This is only an example. The practical implication is that even now it is virtually impossible to calculate the total tax burden in an objective manner.

To all likelihood the text containing what we call the Edict was found in Uruk. It should be classified as a "note", which makes its status strictly spoken questionable, and it is not particularly well-phrased. It refers to rent farm arrangements on the estates of Marduk, therefore deals primarily with what was or was to be the rule in the Babylon area. The text does not belong to a "private archive", but the "rights" mentioned are probably a reflection of what could be applied generally to institutional land and, in some respects, also regarding land belonging to private persons. In fact it states a norm for what was expected from a standard plough team on arable and from a standard area of date orchard. The object of these leases was, as is known, to expand the area under the plough by offering incentives to the lease holder to engage tenants of his own in addition to the institutional personnel put at his disposal by the grantors of the lease.

The rights listed in the Edict are in themselves probably not typical for lease arrangements in general, they belong to agricultural management by the government, payments to gate keepers (of storehouses?) are perhaps primarily applicable in an institutional context. But there is no reason to suppose that only institutional land should have been obliged to contribute to the upkeep of a provincial governor, if that is indeed intended by the title of ^{LU_2}EN.NAM used for one of those entitled to payments.[3] As the following sections of this chapter will demonstrate, payments analogous to those in the Edict can be shown to have existed and there is much more, but almost exclusively in texts with an institutional background only. The few exceptions from private archives are therefore important in suggesting that measures regarding institutional property were also applicable to private owners. We could ask ourselves, however, whether the land concerned might have been held by the institutions at some stage in it its recent history. Whether it was also subject to *ešrû* might be relevant in the context. The institutions would have retained certain vestigial rights in such circumstances. Regarding the stipulations in the Edict, it could be argued that it made sense to specify the obligation to pay official costs in an institutional context, but less so in private documents, where, in theory, payments to the government or other authorities would be self-evident and an unavoidable element of lease contracts, where they did not require being spelled out. All lease contracts are always based on "traditional" elements, which are well known to the parties and need not be mentioned. "Good practice" is always implied.

The "Edict of Belsazzar" is an unusual text in that it alludes to general principles, which could apply anywhere. Few Mesopotamian texts mention general principles, and in this case these can even be compared with actual practice. Jursa has shown convincingly regarding the *ešrû,* as will be underlined below, that this tax was levied over what was kept by the tenant after the share of the temple as holder of the land had been deducted. This may have been the case with other forms of taxation too, but we must consider the possibility that they must, on principle, be added to what was to be paid on other accounts. All the accumulating deductions had in the end to be met by the tenant.

Especially in an institutional context we must regard the leasing of land as having some fundamental relation to taxation, if only because the lessor and the tax man, who normally compete for a share in that part of the harvest that can be taken from the tenant, are in this case close associates. The tenant is reduced as much as possible to a scantily paid unfree employee. The institutional rent farm arrangements betray aspects which involved the rent farmer in tax farming, even though that is not made explicit in the Edict of Belsazzar: lines 1-3, which deal with "Land of Bēl which in Nisan of year 7 of Nabonidus, king of Babylon, Belsazzar, the crown prince, assigned on the orders of the king to the

---

3 We will see that there is a likely alternative within the institutions for this assumption, below note 31.

head-farmers". They are to make lump sum payments to the institutions and must try to recoup their costs, also those involving the authorities, from the two types of "tenant" who were subject to the effects of the contracts. The Edict has a special position in that it grapples with the manner in which the costs to the tenant could be met, that is theoretically, for on this point practical traces of the execution of the measures are wanting elsewhere and the amount of land assigned to a plough team was for practical purposes definitely too much.

We start with a translation of the date palm section (lines 4-14). "For 1 kor of land planted (as a date orchard) they will give 40 kor of dates, including 5 kor for the remuneration of the gardener, who digs the ditches and performs the digging, who constructs the wall of the garden and carries away the hard lumps of earth, which the crown prince allows them. As payment for the services and for the rations of the governor, [the scribes], the measurers and the gatekeepers 11½ $SILA_3$ per kor as payment for their services [and rations] is retained at the store. Per kor they will give 3½ $SILA_3$ as rations for the governor, scribes, measurers and gatekeepers, which they keep."

The lessee(s), the rent farmer(s), (^{LU}2GAL(.MEŠ) ^{GIŠ}BAN$_2$) has/have to deliver per kor of land 40 kor of dates, of which 5 kor constitute the *sissinnu* for the actual gardener for digging, walling and clod breaking.[4] For *kiṣru* and *kurummatu*, payment for services and sustenance of the ^{LU}2EN.NAM, the "governor", the UMBISAGs, "scribes", who are the keepers of the accounts, the *mādidu*s, "measurers", i.e. the surveyors, estimators of the yield and measurers of the rent, and the gate keepers (*atû*), presumably those who took ultimate delivery,[5] per kor 0.0.1 5½ $SILA_3$ is retained, and (additionally?) *kurummatu*, "sustenance", of these officials takes per kor 3½ $SILA_3$, that is a total of 15 $SILA_3$ per kor or 1/12th, 8.33%. Let us regard this total as "costs", in the sense of the Edict, of which possibly only 3½ $SILA_3$ reached those for whom the deductions were made. The remainder is pocketed by the institution, Esagil, which probably had a special right, as we will see. This interpretation is confirmed by the arable section.

This sounds reasonably straightforward, but the contents of the text are in reality problematical: though the yield depends on a number of factors, the number and the age of the trees are of elementary significance. The relation between surface and number of trees remains unspecified, but must have been subsumed, in a manner unknown to us, in the

---

4 Theoretically the size of the *sissinnu* depended on the amount of work done, derived from the surface tended. It was not visibly related to the number of trees or the yield. The text of the "Edict" expresses this well. Much material is quoted CAD S p. 326f. The question is whether under normal circumstances the *sissinnu* was the complete remuneration of the tenant, or only a minimum, which cannot be recognised as such, because the share of the tenant in the main product, dates, is not specified or mentioned in a normal *imittu* document, since this only registers what the tenant had to deliver to the owner, not whåat he could retain. This leaves open the theoretical possibility that on principle the complete (date) harvest went to the owner. Probably the *sissinnu* was something additional and a remuneration for additional labour. Cf. Ries 1976, p. 63 and 104ff. Especially the texts quoted in Ries' notes 720 and 721 suggest that *imittu* and *sissinnu* were completely separate matters. The question is in reality even more complicated on account of the lesser cultures practiced under the trees. If these additional cultures were indeed intended to be (normally) for the sole benefit of the tenant, it is possible that he indeed did not receive a share in the main harvest. In those cases in which the *imittu* document results in round amounts it is, however, likely that the tenant kept the surplus -or had to make good the shortfall- and there are rare instances in which documents stipulate delivery of products of the lesser cultures. In all these matters local circumstances will have determined actual practice. We will see that there are clear cases in which the tenant had to make payments over and above the *imittu*, which, at least in those cases thus cannot represent the whole yield.

5 This implies transport by the tenant, which also has taxation aspects, as we will see.

specified dimensions of the land assigned. Not unlike other rent farm documents the text imposes a fixed rent, while known practical arrangements always suggest that the specific amount to be delivered was to be estimated and established through an *imittu* procedure just before the harvest, dependent as it was on the size of the year's harvest. Exactly that, we could assume, provided a reason for payments to surveyors and scribes. Perhaps in these general farm arrangements very global averages were used, which we find difficult to compare with reality, especially as practical evidence from institutional Babylon itself is not available. It might be expected that such averages would be on the lower side of what was actually regarded as an average yield. We can assume, however, that the net-yield to cost relation in the Edict had roots in reality, possibly the amounts mentioned were applied to the real yields of the *imittu* procedure, which had to be adapted somehow to the fixed yields required of the rent farmer. It would be possibly to attune actual yield and the surface used. That costs comparable to those mentioned by the Edict were indeed payable together with *imittu* yields in institutional contexts in Uruk and Sippar will become clear from what will be discussed below.

If the 15 SILA$_3$ due were paid over each of the 40 kor of the yield destined for the owner, that would have included taxation paid over the *sissinnu*, which was paid out of the 40 kor, if we take the text literally. In turn that would imply that the taxes would have to be paid over a possible yield over and above the net rent, which is (in this case) only that, that was to be delivered to the owner of the orchard. That yield would have been payable, at least nominally, by the rent farmer, whose gains would consist of what was produced over the 40 kor mentioned, unless the actual gardener also had a share and had to foot the tax bill. He or they probably had to pay the 15 SILA$_3$ costs over this extra amount. The consequence would be that representatives of the authorities levying these charges would have to be present at an *imittu* procedure, hence, again, the payments. Taxation brings in income but it entails costs which are made payable by those liable for the tax. There is also always the case in which payment for a service rendered becomes a duty to be paid at the moment the service has lost its purpose, or, as is the case here, the payment is much higher than the service provided warrants. Collection of the right can be left to a tax farmer. Any form of taxation creates further new rights in this manner.

That in an institutional context payments for the governor, the scribes, the measurers and the doorkeepers after the amount of the *imittu* had been established, were customary long before the Edict, is clear from a number of Sippar texts dating back to at least the early reign of Nebuchadnezzar. The texts can be found easily in Jursa's overview of the typology of the Sippar *imittu* lists.[6] The amount of the costs remains unspecified, but they are stated to have been deducted from the *imittu*-amount in CT 56, 185+ rev 2'-4', which should indicate that at that moment the landowner regarded these costs as being subtractable from his share in the production. The state of preservation of texts like CT 56, 185+ and CT 57, 365+, where a comparable statement is found is, however, not good enough to provide a definite solution on this point. Especially CT 57, 365+ suggests that we are dealing with these costs in the context of an accounting model which we cannot reconstruct and which also involves the *sissinnu* paid to the gardener.[7] That such rights had to be paid before the "Edict" was written down, is certain, however.

After the date palm section we must discuss that on arable: lines 15-30 of the Edict. "[Per plough] they will give 25 kor of arable. (The farmer) will give 12 kor of barley per kor (of land) as a net rent, but 5 kor of land is granted for costs (*gimir*) and for rations

---

6 Jursa 1995 p. 150ff. A relevant date, 25 x Nbk 3, is preserved in the text Nbk 36.

7 As in the Edict it must have been based on a fixed amount of land.

(*kurummatu*) of the governor, scribes, measurers and gatekeepers. For one plough four oxen, two cows (and) four ploughmen are provided. The oxen do not die, they are of iron. Per kor they add $11^1/_2$ $SILA_3$ of barley (or) dates for rations to the rent and give it to Esagil. They must give the barley and the dates net in Esagil. Per kor they will also give $3^1/_2$ $SILA_3$ for rations to the governor, the scribes, the measurers and the gatekeepers over and above their rent. In the first year (of the lease) they will give per plough 25 kor of barley for seed and 20 kor for rations of the ploughmen. In toto they will give 45 kor of barley".

The lessee received per plough team (of a given standard composition) 25 kor of land, and paid a 12-fold rent in relation to the 25 kor of seed required, that is 300 kor. He might till an additional 5 kor of (institutional) land for his costs and the *kurummatu*, sustenance, pertaining to the same officials as mentioned in the date section. Per kor, presumably of the yield, if we accept that arable and date plantations are treated in an analogous manner, he adds $0.0.1.5^1/_2$ to the rent as *kurummatu* for Esagil, and he gives on top of his rent per kor $3^1/_2$ $SILA_3$ as *kurummatu* to the officials. i.e. per kor of land he pays additionally 12 times 15 $SILA_3$, i.e. one kor over each of the 25 kor of land, again 8.33 % of what must be paid to the institutional owner, -that is, as said, additionally. "They" -the institution- provide (per team) 25 kor of seed and 20 kor for food/fodder, which means that the lease holder had to find the seed for the additional 5 kor of land made available to him and had to recoup these costs himself.

Again we have a fixed rent, but still in a rent farm context where it is not uncommon for arable, contrary to what is stipulated in ordinary leases. Securing a fixed income for the institution is clearly a purpose of this type of leasing. A twelve fold yield is not impossible, but on much not too good institutional land it might be problematic in certain years, to put the point cautiously. If the payment of the costs was yield related, we must consider the possibility that it had to be made also over what was produced over and above the fixed rent. Though the evidence for this type of taxation on arable is much less strong than for that on date plantations, the Edict suggests that on principle both were treated in a similar manner.

There is in this manner nothing in the Edict about the *gugallu* or payments for water, also a form of costs. This could be, however, an element of the actual lease, while what we have is a note dealing with a limited number of matters, notably payments to institutional authorities, or, less likely, authorities at a provincial level. It is striking that the other texts to be referred to also make no direct link between Edict-type costs and payments to the *gugallu*, even though both occur in the same texts. This suggests that, whereas the Edict-type costs were due to the central institutional administration, the *gugallu* related payments were local, though also estate related. That the *gugallu* generally was more of an estate manager than an official of the central government needs not be argued.

One effect of the "costs" is, however, visible: the lease holder is expected to finance them from an increase in the land under the plough, with the subtlety that no additional seed and fodder is made available for the five kor of land extra, 20% more, that had to be sown. A twelve fold yield would bring in 60 kor of barley, which would amply make good the "costs", but ploughing a total of 30 kor of land with a normal plough team is something of a task and the additional 60 kor of barley would not be produced easily, if not to say that the solution for the problem of the costs provided is unrealistic.

It is not easy to determine what is the case: certain is a payment for some real services provided by officials, plus the collection of a right, in the first case possibly over the whole yield, in the second over the share of the owner only, with a premium for the entrepreneur. Of the 15 $SILA_3$ of dates or barley paid $11^1/_2$ went to the institution and $3^1/_2$ to the officials for whom the payment was nominally intended. "Costs" contain additional taxation. What is clear is that anyhow the situation required clarification, and that is usually a suitable occasion to increase the burden. That is what the Edict implies.

b. *gimru*[8]

"Costs" (*gimru*, often written *gi-mir*) is not a specific taxation term, it is often regarded in particular as a payment for transport costs,[9] but the term is applied to a specific form of obligatory payment -by rent farmers- in the Edict of Belsazzar. It can be found in certain documents from private archives. First comes a group of texts from the Egibi archive with a rent farm background. In Bertin 2587 and (with less confidence also in) 2576 the (additional) payment amounts to the round sum of 10% of the total mentioned.[10] This is already somewhat more than what we found in the Edict. The texts suggest by their wording a tax on barley and dates, but perhaps this can be expanded to agricultural products in general, according to Bertin 2587 levied (by the *šākin ṭēmi,* a high-ranking government official in the main towns) specifically from rent farm arrangements. This will have been true for all the Egibi texts listed, they acted as rent farmers of the badly documented land belonging to the palace, and managed ultimately under the responsibility of the *šākin ṭēmi* through a hierarchy of officials.[11] We can find confirmation both for the general nature of the payment and for the higher amount payable.

The Borsippa and Dilbat entries indicate clearly that we are dealing with a customary right: payment will take place by the tenant according to the custom of Borsippa or Dilbat.[12] VS 3, 165 even mentions in this context a specific (private?) estate. The amount of the Borsippa *gimru* can be calculated on the basis of VS 3, 105, though the text is perhaps not completely unequivocal.[13] In line 9 we find *ù* 1.0.3 *gi-mir ... i-nam-din*. We could arrive at either just over 7% if we understand 1.0.3 over the (relevant) yield of 15.2.3, or at 10%, one *ṣimdu* per kor, if we take the passage to intend the same as what is specified unequivocally in later texts, in which 0.0.3 is to be delivered on top of one kor. This second interpretation is to be preferred, though it is hardly allowed by the formulation used. It agrees with what the Egibis pay and what is unambiguously recorded in other texts. We can conclude that the payment of *gimru* is intended by the use of formulaic passages of the type "with one kor he gives a *ṣimdu*", even if there is no explicit reference to the term. Unequivocally this represents an additional payment. We will find other examples where use of a larger *mašīḫu* signifies the payment of a tax.

---

8 Literature: CAD G p. (77R-)78L.

9 As a general word for costs it occurs, for instance, in the Uruk texts TCL 12, 29: 7 and Sack, CD 64: 2.

10 This cannot be regarded as the norm, however, and in texts "costs" may include the obligatory taxation costs and other expenditure, for instance on transport. In Nbn 786, Sippar, 15 VI Nbn 14, an accounting document, *gimir* amounts to only 5 kor out of 270.0.3, but there are other "costs" adding up to 55 kor. Whether an institution had to pay "taxation *gimru*" is in itself questionable, the text may be irrelevant for the subject in hand.

11 On the role of the later Egibis and their relation to the palace cf. Wunsch 2000a, p. 105ff. The payments are receipted by various Aramaic scribes, *sepīru*s, of the *šākin ṭēmi*.

12 In the relevant passages I prefer reading *a-ki(-i)* over *adi*, as Ungnad does in NRVU, though he translates, for instance NRVU 421, "nach den Vorschriften von Barsipa". The possibility should be considered, however, whether the levy in these cases could be identical with, or include, the *kāru* (of the king) discussed later on.

13 The best solution would be to read *ki* instead of *ù*.

Nearly all texts belong to the later part of the reign of Darius I, but that this type of expenditure also occurred in earlier periods needs no discussion since it is sufficiently attested by the Edict.

Babylon, Egibi and related files

Bertin 2567 7 IV Dar 25, barley, *gi-mir* of ?, at the disposal of Bēl-x is received by x-la-a, *ša rēš šarri*, the *sepīru*, from Širku s Iddina on the orders of Guzānu.

Bertin 2587 17 V Dar 25, 20 kor *gi-mir* of 200 kor of barley from the rent farm (*sūtu*) of Iddina-Bēl on the orders of Guzānu, *šākin ṭēmi* of Babylon, received by Mamusu s x-ga-ia, *sepīru* of the flour, from Š s I.

Bertin 2576 28 VII Dar 25, 10 kor(?) *gi-mi-ir* of 100 kor barley Ṣillaia *sepīru* of the gardeners and irrigators of the Great Palace and the New Palace has received on orders of Guzānu, *šākin ṭēmi*, from Š s I. Mentions an earlier amount received by Bēl-upaḫḫir and Ḫašdā.

Bertin 2574 x x Dar 25, 50.3.3 kor of barley *gi-*[*mir*] of the rent farm of Bēl-ittannu is received by Bēl-mušallim, *ša rēš šarri*, on the orders of Guzānu, *šākin ṭēmi*, from Š s I.

Bertin 2613 18 II Dar 26, 15 kor of dates with a tablet of 40 *š* of silver at the disposal of Iqūpu s Nādinu Arad-Marduk is received on orders of Guzānu, the *šākin ṭēmi*, by Bēl-ušallim, *ša rēš šarri*, from Š s I. (Same context as the other texts?)

BRM 1 81 4 VIII Dar 26, Apla, *ša rēš šarri*, *sepīru* of the *ša rēš* of the New Palace, has received the *gi-mir* due on account of 316 kor of dates from Š s I. Identical Bertin 2623 (4 VIII Dar 26).

BM 30591[14] 27 VII Dar 35, 24.3.2 of barley to be paid by Š s I as *gi-mir* to PN the *ša rēš* in V.

Borsippa

VS 3 74 26 VI Camb 3, archive unassigned, *imittu*, dates, 7) *gi-mir šá a-ki* Barsip^{KI} *i-nam-din*, follows passage on dates due to Nabû.

Ilia file

VS 3 105 13 VI Dar 9, at Āl-Eššu, *imittu* share of PN in dates (amounting to 15.2.3 kor) 9) *ù* 1 GUR.0.3 (read KI 1 GUR 0.0.3?) *gi-mir ina* UGU Nār-Eššu *i-nam-din*.[15]. The reverse mentions a list of additional payments not included in the sum mentioned previously.

Dilbat

VS 3 153 25 V Dar 33, (Amat-Bau), date *imittu*, *gi-mir šá a-ki-i* Dilbat^{KI} *i-nam-din*.

VS 3 165 13 VI Dar 36 (Amat-Bau), date *imittu, gi-mir šá a-ki-i* É Nabû-aḫa-ittanu *i-nam-din-nu-'u*.

Murašû

BE 9 10 3 III Art 28, lease of bow land for three years, lessee pre-pays 5 *š* of silver as *gi-mir* A.ŠA$_3$-*šú-nu*(!) for the three years.

c. Uruk and Sippar: the institutional *imittu* documents with *kurummatu, kiṣir esitti* (and) *balāṭu* (*ana*) *Bēl* and *suluppu ša gugalli*[16]

The *imittu* documents dealing with the date plantations of Eanna which became part of rent farm arrangements constitute one of the most interesting files from institutional

---

[14] K. Abraham, OLA 65 (Fs. Lipinski), 1995 p.1-9, suggests for *gimir* in the late Egibi texts "transportation costs". In view of the frequency in which ships occur in this group of texts this is not *a priori* impossible, though occasionally a connection of the term with the rent farm complex seems to be suggested explicitly: Bertin 2587 and 2574. We must await a full publication of the material, but for the moment I prefer a connection with Edict-type costs.

[15] The writing allows possibly two interpretations. If 33 *sūtu* are paid on 463 that amounts to 7%, in the other case we would have 3 *sūtu* on 30 or 10%. This should be preferred as argued in the text.

[16] Literature: D. Cocquerillat, 1968, Chapter 3, p. 55ff., cf. CAD K p. 439 *kiṣru* 3) rent (payment), payment (in kind) for services or taxes.

archives from the Neo Babylonian period available. The yield first went directly to Eanna, later on it became part of what was turned over to rent farmers and enabled them to pay their fixed dues to the temple. The texts demonstrate that the change over to rent farming did not fundamentally alter traditional practices, the *imittu* remained a normal procedure. This group of texts also illustrates the problems involved in studying taxation in this period well: the phrasing, its occurrence in time and the amounts all pose their own problems. Mrs. Cocquerillat has studied especially the background of the contents and the geographical reality at the basis of the texts, there is no need to repeat this discussion or list the texts, as they can be found easily in ADFU 8.

Before the reign of Cambyses these texts do not contain a phrase that could be related to taxation. That does, of course, not mean that no taxes were levied, nor does it signal that the reign of Cambyses meant a change, for the only relevant text from that of Cyrus I know of, BIN 1, 111, is damaged in the crucial place.

When the documents become available, in the accession year of Cambyses, a short statement concerning the $SUKU_6$.ḪA_2, *kurummatu*, to be delivered by the tenant appears, which, like the other phrases to be discussed here, can be absent if the amount of the *imittu* established is small.[17] For whom this sustenance, which is never specified, was intended, is not spelled out, but it is unlikely that the owner or the rent farmer was meant, for the statement would have lacked sense in that case. That a third party is intended is confirmed by the sequel in later years. In the available texts from Cambyses yrs. 2 and 3 the *kurummatu* phrase is not found, but instead we do find: "*itti* 1 GUR 0.0.1 $4^1/_2$ $SILA_3$ *kiṣir esittu u balāṭu ana* ^{d}*Bēl*[18] (plus the secondary date palm products) he (the tenant) will deliver", a phrase occurring only in these texts from Uruk, and obviously indicating an amount due: $10^1/_2$ $SILA_3$ had to be added to every 180.

The phrase also occurs in texts from the same file for the years Cambyses 4 to 7, but in these documents we regularly find that additionally either 1 or 2 kor of dates are marked as *ša* $^{LU_2}GU_2$.GAL, "for the *gugallu*", but always at the end of the text, immediately in front of the witnesses, not as an immediate sequel to the phrase quoted earlier. These are separate payments. The destination of this second post is clear, but there is in this case no visible, direct, relation between the amount mentioned for the *gugallu* and the total imposed. This suggests that the amount is in this case an arrangement between the rent farmer and the tenant, or an imposition by the first, not a standard amount calculated on the basis of the yield to be delivered.

The last known texts belonging to this set files are those of the *imittu* of what is called the first year of Nebuchadnezzar IV.[19] The *kiṣir esitti balāṭu ana Bēl* phrase is gone and replaced by *itti* 1 GUR 0.0.2.3 $SILA_3$ $SUKU_6$.ḪA_2 "pro kor 15 $SILA_3$ of sustenance" (plus secondary date palm products, but that is not relevant here) he will pay". This is the 8.33% of the Edict. Again at the end of the texts we find: *elat* 1 or 2 (and once 4)[20] GUR *suluppu šá* $^{LU_2}GU_2$.GAL, over and above what is listed before (he will pay), which, again, in view of the separate position in the text is a different matter, that of the remuneration of the *gugallu*.

---

17 For instance in YOS 7, 98, the *kiṣir esitti* phrase is not found in BIN 1, 129; there are no dates for the *gugallu* in YOS 17, 290.

18 CAD E p. 337; CAD B p. 51.

19 Texts collected by D. Cocquerillat, RA 77, 1983 p. 163-5.

20 YOS 17, 298.

That *kiṣir esitti*[21] with *balāṭu ana Bēl* replaced *kurummatu* for a number of years seems likely, and that the short period of independence under Nebuchadnezzar IV when *kurummatu* returns, definitely shows an increase in what was due, is also certain. The different terms indicate the same basic purpose, a payment to central authorities. The elimination of the reference to Bēl may have significance, it could suggest interruption or fragility of the link with Babylon owing to the political circumstances. It may also have no practical meaning at all. But the question is of some importance for the ultimate destination of the payments: Bēl, Marduk, may have had a share, as we noticed already in Babylon, and the level of taxation is certainly influenced by political events.

What the *gugallu* was to receive begins to be listed in Uruk from the middle of the reign of Cambyses onwards, it comes over and above the "costs" which are the real subject of this paragraph. The level of payment is agreed by parties on an individual basis, which is not directly related to the total yield in the particular case. But we must not regard this as a new tax, as *gugallūtu* occurs separately elsewhere and earlier. New is only that it is written down in the *imittu* document. With the Edict type payments, which are also additional, the explicit mention of this payment makes clear that the *imittu* does not represent the complete yield, but no more than what pertains to the owner of the land. That is understandable, even if this amount now went towards what the rent farmer had to pay, but possibly the actual farmer had a share.

The date *imittu* files from Uruk are relatively well-preserved, but comparable material on the barley harvest is much more limited in scope, and not very informative regarding our subject. Only during the reign of Cambyses do a few texts contain a short phrase concerning *kurummatu* payable to the *gugallu*, but solely as a matter of principle. $SUKU_6$.$ḪA_2$ *ša* $^{LU_2}GU_2$.GAL is mentioned as something payable, but not the amount.[22] Compared to what we found in the date documents this is rather striking: there the *gugallu* got "that of the *gugallu*" and the *kurummatu* was obviously a payment for various other officials of the type intended in the Edict of Belsazzar. In support the Edict itself can be quoted: *kiṣru* and *kurumattu* for the governor,[the scribes], the measurers and the gate keepers. There is no point in speculating since the amount is not specified. Non-occurrence of phrases dealing with standard procedures is not significant and the assumption must be that, as in the Edict, dates and barley, and presumably other arable products, were treated in a comparable manner.

Comparison of the payments to the officials in the Edict, where it amounts to 15 $SILA_3$ per kor or 8,33% (additionally) under Nabonidus in Babylon, to the *kiṣir esitti balāṭu ana Bēl* of 10.5 $SILA_3$ per kor or 5.8% under Cambyses in Uruk and the 15 $SILA_3$ per kor as *kurumattu* or 8.33% under Nebuchadnezzar IV in the same place, suggests that the marked local rise in Uruk in reality only constituted a partial adaptation to what was habitual elsewhere, notably in the Babylon area. This form of taxation was virtually stable from Nabonidus to the coming of Darius, that is, if we assume that the purpose of the various payments was identical. During his reign, according to non-institutional texts from Babylon, Borsippa and Dilbat it had become 10% under the name of *gimru*. By that time the institutional archive from Uruk is no longer available to us.

---

[21] Note that the Edict itself uses *kiṣru* (sec) with *kurummatu* for the payment in the date palm section retained by the institution. Possibly this *kurummatu* is the equivalent of *balāṭu ana Bēl*. Cf. below, the texts from Sippar.

[22] The texts are YOS 7, 167 (x I Camb 4) and YOS 7, 180, (7 II Camb 5), where the passage is damaged, but restoration is reasonably certain.

Two occurrences of *balāṭu ana Bēl* from Sippar can be quoted, one of these combines the expression with the term *kiṣir*. BM 75829[23] a list of expenditure in dates, headed by ZU$_2$.LUM.MA *te-lit-tu*$_4$ *ša ina qāt* ^{pd}Bēl-it-tan-nu ^{LU_2}GU$_2$.GAL, after the subscript, giving the total and the remark *te-lit*-<<UT>>*tu*$_4$ EDIN, "expenditure outside the town", has some additional information on the left edge: (a) [*ina muḫ-*]*ḫi* 1 GUR 2.3.0 *ba*(!)*-la-ṭu* ^{d}*Bēl* (b) [x x x] *u-ma-su*, "on each kor 90 SILA$_3$, 50% [are to be paid as?] *balāṭu ana Bēl*". I do not have a solution for the second line. Though this is much more than the *kurummatu* amount we noted in Uruk under Nebuchadnezzar IV, and thus cannot not be regarded as directly comparable, the text yet helps us to link the various formulations found in Uruk, and it also seems to confirm the general nature of these payments, which were also levied in Sippar. The text itself is probably a list of expenditure and previous payments deducted by the *gugallu* on the delivery of his quota at the central store. The sense of the phrase at the end is that it serves as a reminder that the tax also had to be paid over payments deducted already[24] from the (taxable) harvest by the *gugallu* concerned, who acts here as an official and is not the receiver of the sustenance. Probably his own remuneration consisted of additional further *gugallūtu* payments, which are not mentioned, unless he was a leaseholder himself, in which case the official remuneration may have merged with the expected gains.[25] The reference to Bēl is of some importance when we consider the final destination of the payments.

CT 56, 225, 6 XI Cyr 7, is damaged at the crucial place, the beginning of lines 17 and 18, and on top of that, as mentioned in Chapter I, the calculation of the amount of dates provided cannot be made to fit. The names occurring, crucial for better understanding, are also extremely common, which means that prosopography does not help. A clue as to the meaning of the text is provided by lines 13-15 according to which two persons, Šamaš-kāṣir and Iddina-Nabû received dates as a *sissinnu*, with some silver. To all probability they were the orchard men whose account was being made up in this -ostensibly?- sloppy way. One could toy with the idea that the amount mentioned in line 1 is the *imittu* imposed,[26] and that the slightly higher amount in line 16 represents what was actually delivered. This should have been specified in line 17, but of one word of two signs only traces of the first remain, or perhaps one long sign could fill the space. This is followed by *ki-ṣir ù* TIN *a-na* ^{d}EN. These terms were subsumed by the lost first word of line 19.[27] The missing word is possibly ZAG, *imittu*, or ^{GIŠ}BAN2, *sūtu*, "rent". In this way the gardeners will have had to pay not only their *imittu*, but also, like their counterparts in

---

[23] The text is known to me in the form of a transliteration by H. Bongenaar, who dates it in a general manner to "end Darius".

[24] This is the meaning of the word *tēlītu*, discussed below, Ch. VI. The *gugallu* will have made, if he abided with the rules, only payments authorised by the central administration of the institution, probably in the form of letter orders, which he would have had to present at the accounting regarding his quota, or, perhaps, his lease. Other payments were specifically forbidden, but were probably not exceptional.

[25] In theory such payments can, however, only be expected from tenants, and not from institutional farmers, who are supposed to receive wages and to deliver the entire yield to the institution. The institution would have to remunerate the *gugallu* in this case with "rations" or with land. If the *gugallu*, or the person who fulfilled his tasks had a lease, remunerations had to come from the net yield of the lease, though tenants may have continued to pay *gugallūtu* duties. We are not dealing with a situation which was uniform for all tenants. The rent farm complicates these matters, but there are also circumstances suggesting that the head of an institutional plough team was, at least occasionally, more than a mere wage earner.

[26] Is this word missing at the end of line 1 on the edge of the tablet?

[27] The singular of [*it-*]*ta-din* in line 19 is an obvious mistake.

Uruk, *kiṣir <esitti>*, "collection costs" and *balāṭu ana Bēl.* As in Uruk this may actually have constituted one overall sum.

kiṣru for scribes, for the measurers and for the gate keepers is each mentioned separately in texts from Sippar, this is possibly short for the Uruk *kiṣir esitti.* There were obviously deductions called *kiṣru* destined for these "officials", possibly within the institution, but these payments can for the moment only hypothetically be related to the fees mentioned in the Edict or in other taxation clauses.[28] Similar payments in an arable context have been collected by Jursa.[29] The lease BM 75542, 25 x Cyr 5,[30] explicitly states, without using the term *kiṣir* (*esitti*), that the tenant will also pay additionally 9) SUKU$_6$.ḪA$_2$ ^{LU_2}EN.NAM ^{LU_2}TIL.LA.GID$_2$.DA ^{LU_2}UMBISAG 10) ^{LU_2}I$_3$.DU$_8$ ù ^{LU_2}*man-di-di*, in which list the *qêpu* figures together with the officials already known in Edict context. This could suggest that this type of payment was primarily intended for the temple officials, as could be concluded from the actual *kiṣru* and related payments known. The "governor" would also be an institutional functionary.[31] As yet we know little about the special accounts in institutional context used to finance certain occupations and supervised, in the Hellenistic period by a special *bēl mindi.*

d. *kuṣurrānu* and *balāṭu ana Bēl* in Murašû texts[32]

A standard phrase in a small group of contracts which deal with the stocking of land with plough teams and a wide variety of types of seed by the Murašû servant Ribat refers after the phrase stipulating payment of the rent agreed, first to an additional payment of

---

28 Cf. Dar 116, 23 IV(?) Dar 4, dates, rest *imittu* on PN s PN2 4) *ina kiṣir šá* ^{LU_2}UMBISAG.MEŠ PN5 s PN6 /Šangû-Innanna-Bābili (one of the scribes), received from Bulṭā s ?, rest lost; Nbn 898, 21 VIII Nbn 15, 7) 5 minas of wool *ina ki-iṣ-ru* 8) ^{LU_2}*ma-di-di-ú-tu;* Camb 264, 28 XI Camb 4, dates 2) *ina ki-iṣ-ru* ^{LU_2}I$_3$.DU$_8$-*ú-tú* of yr 4.

29 Jursa 1995, p. 138ff. He stresses the general nature of the payments in institutional contexts and accepts the plough team as a possible basis for the calculation of the amount, with, of course, as in the Edict, the team representing a fixed amount of land to be tilled. That does possibly imply again a recalculation related to the realities of the harvest concerned. There is perhaps one standard payment known: 10 kor of barley per plough team for the *qêpu* in CT 56, 490, dating to the reign of Nebuchadnezzar II, quoted by Jursa.

30 Edited by Jursa 1995, p.139-40.

31 That this EN.NAM possibly could be an institutional functionary is supported by a number of texts. Significant in this context are the ^{LU_2}EN.NAM E$_2$.SAG.IL$_2$ in Dar 215, see Chapter VI under *šibšu* and the comparable ^{LU_2}EN.NAM-u? in the passage in SWU 117 (line 12') dealing with rights belonging to the clergy of Šamaš in Uruk discussed in Prebends Chapter III. For Dilbat we have VS 5, 107 (x x Dar 34) concerning a measurer's prebend, where we find that the co-owner/lessee will give one *sūtu* per kor *ul-tu* 11) [x-]x-*ni-e* for the EN.NAM(?), the *šatammu*, the *ṭupšarru*, the measurer and the *rab tarbaṣi* (?), obviously a somewhat expanded list of the officials mentioned in the Edict of Belsazzar. It should be noted that EAH 214, quoted in Chapter VII under *nisḫu ša māti*, Nippur, mentions a ^{LU_2}NAM I$_7$.ḪA$_2$ who has *ikkarus* of the king at his disposal. On ^{LU_2}NAM of canals see also Stolper 1985 p. 39 nos. IV and V. Cf. also Chapter III note 43. M.W. Stolper, JESHO 41, 1998 goes further and regards these "governors" as elements of the rent farming system. I am not completely convinced, for the other "officials" benefiting from Edict-type payments belong to the institutional personnel and the SWU occurrence certainly does not fit a rent farm context. Also the date of SWU 117 is rather "early". EN.NAM is probably one of the many Mesopotamian titles of which the status and importance depends on the context in which it occurs. For good measure we can refer to BBSt 36 II 5, dealing with income deriving from offerings taken from what was assigned to the *šaknu* of Esagil. Babylon is normative, but there are local variations.

32 CAD K p. 597: comparable to what in Uruk is called *kiṣir esitti* (*u balāṭu ana Bēl*).

10%,[33] and then to a reservation regarding payments called *kuṣurrānu, balāṭu ana Bēl* and *akal ša mandattu,* or *ana uš-ta-ma-nu.*[34] This last word clearly belongs to the Persian administrative jargon and will indicate a specification of the rather general term *mandattu*[35] used by PBS 2/1, 44, which makes clear that a payment -in bread(?)- for some official service is intended. The string of standard clauses in these contracts ends with the specification of the amount of barley seed made available by the lessor to the tenant, but before making this last point it deals with obligations of the tenant. The contracts mostly date from a few specific days in month V in Dar II yr. 2 and they were written by the same scribe. The only text from Dar II yr. 3, also by the same scribe, refers only to the unspecified 10% payment.[36]

As the CAD has stated there is a clear parallel between *kuṣurrānu* and the Uruk *kiṣir esitti*, strengthened by the shared use of *balāṭu ana Bēl* in both the Murašû and the Uruk texts. These payments are restricted in the first group of texts to the Ribat documents, their general non-occurrence in other similar material from the same period does therefore not say much. These are obviously obligatory payments which ultimately had to be met by the cultivator, either directly or through the holder of the land.

We again find a reference to Bēl. Though there is a chance that this is a mere phrase, or otherwise possibly refers to the local Bēl of the Nippur area, Enlil, the possibility that this still indicates a payment to be made to the head of the (royal Mesopotamian) pantheon cannot be excluded. We can assume that these payments will not have been less than the amount we found under Darius I in texts from Babylon and neighbourhood: 10 % is reasonable.

The importance of the Ribat contracts is that they provide firm proof that these payments were due over arable products in general. PBS 2/1, 44 and its parallels list a whole range of arable products for which seed is asked to be provided to the prospective tenants by the lessor. The ten percent is paid over every kor of yield, whatever the nature of the product.

On top of this payment of at least 10% for Edict-type dues, the Ribat texts refer to an additional payment of 10% on rents contractually payable. The purpose of this payment is not specified, it may be intended for the receiver of the rent, but there is also the possibility that this had to be passed on to the ultimate owner, the king and that it was in fact a tax.

---

33 Or 0.0.3, two cases mention 0.2.0, which is, perhaps rashly, regarded here as a mistake.

34 The Persian term in PBS 2/1 154 could be *uš-ta-ma/ba-nu*, 155 seems to give UŠ or DU followed by ta ab ba or ta um ma, in 157 we seem to have *uš-ta*-KA(read um?)-*ba/ma*. Collation is obviously required, there is little sense in a whole range of exclamation marks with every sign. Possibly there is some connection with the plural of *uštiamu*, a function discussed by Stolper, 1985 p. 22, who considers the possibility that the term indicates the equivalent of a *sepīru*, a(n Aramaic) scribe, as discussed by Cardascia, 1951, p. 15, also from a prosopographical angle. In the texts collected here we must expect a payment to some official, if the proposition made is correct the one fulfilling the role of the *gugallu*. If, however, the main lease, held by the Murašû "firm", included the water rights of the canals concerned, Nār-Simmagir and Nār-Sîn, the *gugallu* payments would probably be part of their income from the lease. One thing is certain: the tenant would have to pay.

35 Cf. CAD M/1 p. 15-6, *maddattu* as additional fee besides the rent, but in the instances referred to, the fee is for the land owner, here the term is used for an official payment, in combination with *aklu*.

36 The first verb describing the transfer of the seed by Ribat to the tenant is difficult to read in all texts, one expects perhaps *i-maš-šaḫ*, but in PBS 2/1, 154 there is a PA, in 155 the remains of the sign look like $AŠ_2$, 157 makes no sense to me; in 44 we seem to have again *i-maš*-$AŠ_2$.

PBS 2/1, 79 from the next year is of the same type as the texts from Dar II yr 2 mentioned, but it contains only a short phrase referring to the unspecified extra payment of 10%.[37] The same terse phrase returns twice in PBS 2/1, 104, a receipt for the payment of water rights on the same Nār-Simmagir. The text not only demonstrates the hierarchy of leases and sub-leases, it also makes clear that, as is to be expected, the obligation to pay for taxes was passed on down the line. The ten percent was possibly a tax to be paid on top of rent paid for water.[38]

It is perhaps possible to provide some proof for this contention. TuM 2/3, 147 (see p. 194) is a lease of water rights and land by Rēmūt-Ninurta Murašû from the lease holder of the Nār-Sîn. Of special interest are lines 9-10: *it-ti* 1 GUR 1 PI *ana muḫ-ḫi* Nār-Sîn *lud-dak-ka*, "I will give you per kor a *mašīḫu*, 20%, additionally for/on the Nār-Sîn", repeated in lines 16-17. This could simply indicate delivery of the rent on the Nār-Sîn, the lessor is after all holder of the lease of that canal. But the possibility should be kept open that this is meant as a payment of 20% instead of 10% as an additional payment for (water from) the canal. That is a much more realistic interpretation. We must see this promised increase as belonging to the haggling over terms between participants in the lease system. The man at the top will have to pay to the administration, the man under him "helps" with a higher contribution in mixed tax and rent payments, which he in turn will pass on to his own tenants.

The payment for the Edict-type services of the officials in this way now amounted to minimally 10%. The additional payments for the use of water rights -for the water itself?- is making the step from 10% to 20%. The local payment for the services of the *gugallu*, possibly a fixed amount per tenant came on top of that. A total almost certainly exceeding 30% of the harvest had now to be paid, probably, at least over what was due from the tenant to the owner, but possibly over the whole harvest. Whatever the case, this group of taxes had certainly increased in terms of percentage points during the Persian period. But we can also note a certain keenness to retain the leases, at least on the part of the principal tenants.

Murašû

PBS 2/1 154 15 V Dar II [2], 20) KI 1 GUR 0.0.3 *i-nam-din-'u šá la ku-ṣur-ra-nu* TIN *ana* ^{d}EN 21) *u a-kal ana uš-ta-ma-nu* 20 GUR ŠE.NUMUN Ribat 22) *i-maš*-PA *i-nam-di-sú.*

PBS 2/1 49 16 V Dar II 2, 22-23) virtually lost, but contained a comparable phrase.

PBS 2/1 155 16 V Dar II 2, 19) ...... *šá* KI! 1 GUR 0.0.2 (sic) *šá la* x[....] 20) *a-ka-la šá uš-ta-um-ma* SE$_3$-*in* [....] 21) 40 GUR ŠE.NUMUN Ribat *i-maš*-AŠ$_2$ [....].

---

37 In the context of these payments of 10%, presumably for water rights, reference must be made to two texts from Babylon. Bertin 1790, 84-2-11, 90, 5 VI Camb 4, is a date *imittu* text belonging to the Babylon Eppeš-ili file. After the clause dealing with the delivery of the secondary date products the lower edge has: *it-ti* 1 GUR 0.0.1 *i-nam-din*, which represents an additional payment of 1/30, 8.33%. The same is found in Dar 563, from the Rabā-ša-Ninurta file, a receipt for *šibšu* paid by the tenant to the owner: 3) KI 1 GUR 0.0.1 ŠE.BAR *gam-mir-tum ina* x x etc PN has received. Here it is a payment on top of the barley which is the harvest share of the owner. Neither of the two texts specifies the reason for the payment, which suggest for these payments a generally known background.

38 It is perhaps useful to point out already here that in a hierarchy of leases rents are paid at the higher level for the lease of a canal, that is for water and lower down for the land on the canal, implying the use of water taken from it. How this worked in cases where land had been distributed by the government or was the property of smaller owners, is generally far from clear. Perhaps the water had gone with the land, but in that case those entitled can be expected to be responsible for the upkeep of the installation. This could explain why water plays a limited role in private archives.

PBS 2/1 157 20 V Dar II [2], 19) KI! 1 GUR 0.0.2 (sic, on/for the Nār-Simmagir and the Nār-Sîn) *i-nam-din-'u ša la-'a ku-ṣur-ra-nu* TIN *ana* ^{d}EN *a-kal* 21) *šá uš-ta*-KA-*ma* 20 GUR ŠE.NUMUN Ribat *i*-x-*maš i-nam-di-in.*
PBS 2/1 44 22 V Dar II 2, 22) KI 1 GUR 0.0.3 *šá la-'a ku-ṣur-ra-nu* TIN *ana* ^{d}EN 22) *u a-kal šá man-da-tu*$_4$! 20 GUR ŠE.NUMUN Ribat *i-maš*-AŠ 23) *i-nam-din-šú.*
Cf.:
PBS 2/1 79 x VI Dar II 3, 10) ....<<*ina*>> KI 1 GUR 0.0.3 *ina muḫ-hi* Nār-Simmagir *i-na* GN 11) *ina-an-din.*
and:
PBS 2/1 59 (Dar II yr 2), fragment of a receipt for payment of rent for several canals by Rēmūt-Ninurta) 2') .... *ina* ^{GIŠ}*ma-ši–ḫu šá it-ti* 1 GUR 0.0.3 (received).[39] The rent amounts to 2000 kor *zitti šarri* for the canals, and is to be registered with Napsanu the ^{LU_2}NAM *šá* CL *šá* Nār-Sîn, "the (royal) procurator for the left bank of the N.-S.".
PBS 2/1 104 22 V Dar II 5, 1) 1800 kor of barley KI 1 GUR 0.0.3 ^{GIŠ}BAN$_2$ *šá* Nār-Simmagir 2) for yr 5 which is in the hands of PN s PN2 3) *šá muḫ-ḫi sūti* Nār-Bēl-ab-uṣur which is due from Rēmūt-Ninurta s Murašû. 1800 kor KI 1 GUR 0.0.3 rent of the Nār-Simmagir (is received).

e. *gugallūtu*[40]

That *gugallu/ūtu* is a payment for the services of the *gugallu* would seem to be obvious, occasionally it is explicitly stated to be intended for his *kurummatu*, "sustenance". That this was related to water rights can be proposed but not really be made hard. As a *mušannītu* or *appu* are occasionally mentioned in direct context with the *gugallu*, his involvement in water works is beyond doubt.[41] But that does not in itself mean that *gugallūtu* is a payment for water. In BM 42374+ there is a fixed annual payment for (the upkeep of) one particular structure, but not even that is a payment for water. These are only water-related payments, not payments for actual water. A special connection of the *gugallu* with areas with date plantations makes sense in view of the additional water requirements of these trees, a consideration which would also be valid for areas with summer products.

Many texts, especially date *imittu* documents, only state whether the *gugallūtu* or the *kurummatu* have been paid or not,[42] though such statements are not to be regarded as obligatory and occur usually in a string of stereotype phrases, they attest the common nature of this type of payment. In contrast relatively few texts mention dues paid for water. The explanation is that payments for water are in general included in the rent paid for the land, we leave this question until the next chapter. That the provision of water is a common reason for corvée work goes without saying, but that is not the point here either.

A text like VS 3, 14 indicates that payment of *gugallūtu* was due, as is to be expected, when the harvest became available. It was levied not only on dates and barley, but also on onions, and thus, no doubt, on other products. The *gugallu* was involved in many aspects of local administration, not just in water. BE 8, 80,[43] from the neighbourhood of Nippur combines the functions of *ša muḫḫi āli* and *gugallu* in one

---

[39] Such a *mašīḫu* is difficult to envisage as it would contain a broken number of SILA$_3$s, again suggesting that the use of a specific *mašīhu* sometimes indicates no more than that a specific "right" is included in the payment. The use of the word *mašīḫu* in this text, and not in others, does not mean that a different procedure was being followed. The superfluous *ina* in PBS 2/1, 79, where the scribe abruptly stopped, but possibly intended to write the same phrase, probably indicates a mistake.

[40] Literature CAD G p. 122 and cf. *gugallu* p. 121-2. D. Cocquerillat, RA 78, 167; Jursa 1995 p. 49ff., discussed M.W. Stolper JESHO 41, 1998, p. 500ff.

[41] Especially BM 74538, Jursa 1995 no. 65 is clear, copy M.W. Stolper AfO 46/7, 1999/2000, p. 49.

[42] Such texts are not listed here.

[43] Quoted, but not fully understood, under Cost of water, below.

person, the first of six, the elders of the village concerned, who were required to make a statement concerning local water use, which cannot be reconstructed completely. In an institutional context the *gugallu* represented the authorities at village level, which does not, however, mean that he always had to belong to the village concerned.[44] He could also act for a private estate and even, it would seem, for an individual owner: in Nbk 244 the fact that barley is due from the *gugallu* should be noted, he could be a kind of estate manager. It is clear that a *gugallu* should not be seen as a government official but as an estate functionary, as such he represented the landlord's interest in the village.

The most informative document illustrating the role of the *gugallu* in the managing of the inhabitants of institutional villages is the Uruk text YOS 7, 186, which will be discussed when the evidence regarding the hold of the institutions on their personnel is considered.

In institutional Sippar, according to BM 76034 the *gugallūtu* seems to have been leased occasionally by the authorities of Ebabbar.[45] BM 42374+ and BM 42541, with the same amount paid for *gugallu* for a number of successive years under Darius, could indicate that payments had become standardised, but this need not have been universally so.[46] Cyr 225 not only uniquely deals with barley, it also indicates the area concerned as *bīt* ("district"? of) PN *gugalli*, but there may be a link with the fact that he is attested as a local *errēšu,* therefore factually was a "(small) lease holder".

The two texts from the Tattanu archive indicate again, but this time in the later Achaemenid period, that the function of *gugallu* was leased regularly. By the reigns of Artaxerxes I and Darius II the leasing of such functions can no longer be regarded as something exceptional. What is of some importance is, however, that the text suggests that we are dealing with a complicated layered system in which dependants ultimately act for superiors who are not practically involved, to all likelihood. This is, however, a common feature of rent farm arrangements.

VS 3, 17, from the Babylon Sîn-ili archive is thus a remarkable text with its late Nebuchadnezzar II date. Ṭabia, as owner, will not only receive the *imittu,* but also the *ešrû* and the *gugallūtu*. Did he have the lease of these rights or did he have to act as his own *gugallu*? Not necessarily so: the tenant had the task to provide the owner with the means to pay for the dues. The fact that he had to pay *ešru* suggests that the land had been institutional property in the past.

TCL 12, 85, from a Borsippa archive, possibly provides some further insight in the volume of these payments, if not into the whole structure of tenancy payments. In this

---

44 For a "*gugallu* of Borsippa" operating as receiver in a taxation context cf. below sub *zebēli ša upiyati*.

45 Or was this amount included in the lease of land in this case? The question of the lease of *gugallūtu* has been dealt with extensively by M. Jursa, 1995 p. 49ff. That means of course that the function was "sold" for a certain period. This is a rare, but practical, example of the sale of offices in the Neo Babylonian period, and it implies a routine practice. Jursa has pointed out the fact that members of prebendal families in Sippar were active as *gugallu*s at a certain stage in their carrier. It was probably not only a lucrative occupation, but possibly also an essential step in an administrative career.

46 The two sums in silver followed by the huge amount of 23 minas of silver for 1,5 minas of gold in Sack CD 5, from Uruk, *ana ša-ka-an* PN the *gugallu* of Bīt-Simmagir finds no real explanation. It can hardly be an appointment fee, as there would be no logical reason for the exchange into gold. The translation provided by the editor does not help.

imittu document 13 kor of dates[47] is due to the owner, with delivery in Borsippa.[48] On top of that the *sissinnu* due to the tenant equals 5 kor, and the *kāru*, to be discussed below, amounts to 1.2.0 or 7 *mašīḫu*, to which the *gugallūtu* adds 0.3.0 or 3 *mašīḫu*. The total estimated yield for delivery by the tenant is thus 20 kor, which can be translated into 100 *mašīḫu*. The dues are therefore, if we include the special payment by the owner to the tenant in the basic amount, 10%, otherwise, using the owner's net share as the base, 15.4%. The round numbers involved make it somewhat doubtful whether we are dealing with a real *imittu* document or with a kind of arrangement on principle.[49] It is difficult to find effective support for these findings and to use them for generalisations, even if we could assume that various local levies amount to at least 10% and possibly to 20% if not of the harvest, at least of the share of the landowner.[50] But we must keep in mind that date plantations are not in every respect comparable to ordinary arable.

We have seen that there are clear cases in which the *gugallūtu* is leased. But it is not clear what the exact content of the lease is: some obligations are listed, not the normal duties or the remuneration. *gugallūtu* seems to imply on the one hand a kind of right to an official income, but it is primarily an estate function with responsibility for deliveries by subjects, who had to be kept in their places. We will return to this point.

Babylon, Egibi

W, IM, 175 27 I Nbn 10, *gugallūtu* on onions belonging to the treasury of Nabû at the disposal of IM is paid by IM to Padā s Ezida-x *širku* of Nabû.[51]

Uncertain connection with Egibi:

Nbk 244 14 V Nbk 31, 50 kor of barley of Nabû-nāṣir s Aplā is due from Amurru-lū-dārī the *gugallu* of Itti-Nabû-balāṭu in II in the town of Ma-x to Bēl-aḫḫē-iqīša.

Non-Egibi Babylon

---

47 There is also "0.0.3 of sesame as *šibšu* for one kor of land", but that is something additional, dealing with the minor summer cultures.

48 That means that the tenant had to arrange for transport and its costs. These costs may have included payments for *kāru* or similar expenditure. Transport clauses may hide more than the simple burden of delivery.

49 Note that Joannès 1989 p. 308 reads 4 and not 5 kor for the *sissinnu,* which makes calculations less neat. The round sum strongly suggests that the tenant may have retained all that was produced above that amount, or, had to pay for a shortfall. *kāru* and *gugallūtu* are dues payable to "authorities", if their size is dependent on an *imittu* procedure, that *imittu* procedure, even if it relates to a private tenancy arrangement, can hardly constitute a completely private procedure, as we have already proposed. This has consequences for our ideas about the "size" of government: it was directly involved in basic agricultural procedures.

50 TuM 2/3, 157, Ea-ilūta-bāni-file, Borsippa, 21 VI Nbn 1, is less clear. The *imittu* amounts to minimally 60 kor (number damaged) plus the customary additional minor products. The *sissinnu* amounted to 7 kor (per kor of land, this was not the actual amount?) and a sheep was to be given on 20 XII. The *gugallu* received 1 kor, which is less than 1/60 of the yield. In TuM 2/3 158 the *gugallūtu* is explicitly 0.3.0 per kor of land, 3/5 of what it is in TuM 2/3, 157. It is difficult to generalise from this type of evidence, as has been observed in the case of institutional Uruk.

51 This would constitute a clear case in which divine property was subjected to ordinary taxation. Perhaps we must understand the text in such a way that the onions belonged to the Nabû temple, but were at the disposal of Iddina-Marduk who was obliged to pay the *gugallūtu* to a *širku* of the temple, who served in the capacity of *gugallu*. This is perhaps comparable to the sharecropping tenant of a temple paying *ešrû* to the temple over his share in the harvest. There is a private interest and that is taxed. If the *gugallu* was primarily an estate official it would be intrinsically unlikely that the estate itself paid the relevant dues.

VS 3 17 1 VI Nbk 37, at Kiš, see Chapter VI under *ešrû*.

VS 3 170 19 VI Dar x, *gugallūtu* for 0.3.2 of land in Nabutum, the share of Ina-Esagil-ramat dr Balāṭu Egibi is received by Aplā s Rēmūt-Bēl Eppeš-ili from IN s NBZ. IN retains his right to a promissory note of 19 kor of dates(?).

Borsippa

VS 3 24 26 I Nbk 29, PN, PN2 and PN3, brothers, 6)^{LU}2GU$_2$.GAL.MEŠ *šá* PN4.

TCL 12 85 20 VI Nbn 5, Ili-bani-file, 13 kor *imittu*, 5 kor dates for *sissinnu,* 1.2.0 in *kāru* and 0.3.0 for *gugallūtu* are paid additionally.

TuM 2/3 157 21 VI Nbn1, Ea-ilūta-bāni file, 1 GUR šá ^{LU}2GU$_2$.GAL *e-lat e-ṭer*.

Sippar

Cyr 225 8 II Cyr 6, *meš-ḫat* ŠE.NUMUN ŠE.BAR ZAG *šá* GARIM-Gi-lu-šu NIG2.GA ^{d}UTU *šá* E$_2$[52] Šāpik-zēri ^{LU}2GU$_2$.GAL.

Dar 43 1 VII<Dar> 2, quoted in Chapter III on the status of villagers.

BM 76034[53] Dar [yrs 25-8], fragmentary, following the interpretation given by MacGinnis a lease of land of Šamaš in an irrigation area (GARIM) by the authorities of Ebabbar to more than one person, 10) ^{LU}2GU$_2$.GAL*-ut-su šá* ŠE.NUMUN *šú-a-tim*<<šû>> *ip-p*[*u-šu-ma*] 11) *a-na* MU.AN.NA.MEŠ ZU$_2$.LUM.MA [amount] *u* ŠE.BAR [amount] 12) [*a*]*-na* NIG$_2$.GA ^{d}UTU *i-nam-din-nu-ú*, other standard stipulations concerning date products and digging.

Private, Šangû-Šamaš:

BM 42301 1 XI Dar 13, lease of a date plantation for eight years against a fixed sum of 45 kor of dates per annum and pro rato secondary products, (*sis-sin-nu* PN, the lease holder, will pay), *dul-lu mu-šá-ni-tum ap-pu ša* GN, dates ^{LU}2GU$_2$.GAL*-lu-ú-tu*, dates *eš-ru-ú* and dates *ma-la* ^{LU}2*šangû* Sip-par^{KI} *u* [^{LU}2UMBISAG] [*i-na-áš-š*]*u-ú* are payable by the lessor.[54]

BM 42374+ Dar yrs. 14-19, *taḫsistu*, list of expenditure in dates from yield accruing to Nidinti-Marduk (Ile'i-Marduk), mentions: *šangû* of Sippar (not every year), the *ap-pu* (of Zanzana), 6 kor per annum, the *gugallu*, 1.1.0 per annum, once 2.2.0 and the *ešrû* 4.2.3 per annum.

BM 42541 Dar yrs. 15-21, similar text, only expenditure on the *appu*, *gugallu* and *ešrû,* same amounts.

Uruk

Sack CD 5 6 IX Nbk 1, a total of 43 minas of silver as price for [?] *a-na šá-ka-an* PN s [PN2] ^{LU}2GU$_2$.GAL *šá* E$_2$ ^{LU}2UD.SAR-SE.GA.[55]

YOS 7 38 3 VIII Cyr 4, date orchards of Bēlet of Uruk belonging to the *bīt ritti* of Innin-zēr-ibni s Rēmūt are entrusted (*i-na muḫ-ḫi ip-qí-du)* by the administration of Eanna to PN *a-na* ^{LU}2*gú-gal-ú-tu*. PN is obliged to deliver to Eanna the *imittu* imposed and he must use *uḫinnu* dates belonging to Eanna received from the gardeners as fodder. He will give half the expenditure of/for the king (*a-ḫi ina te-lit-ti šá šarri*) imposed on a certain Nidintu, and he will do all work required (*dullu*) in the fields. (There is an additional note on the responsibilities for other *bīt rittis*, which involves still another person.)[56]

YOS 7 186 23 I Camb 6, see Chapter III under *aššābu* and *naiiālu*.

---

52 Jursa 1995 p. 50L.

53 J. MacGinnis, Iraq 60, 1998, p. 213-4 no. 7.

54 Cf. Jursa 1999 p.17.

55 Sadly not very clear, but certainly a *gugallu* of a specific estate, that of the Simmagir. No speculation on the meaning of the text is warranted.

56 The text, cf. F. Joannès 1982 p. 13, is not an ordinary contract between representatives of Eaṇna and the person concerned, Nanāia-ēreš s Gimillu. It is rather an arrangement which solves a number of problems between him and his colleagues. The role of the Nidintu of lines 12-13 remains unexplained, but was certainly known to the parties. Joannès regards him as a tenant, and the arrangement concerning the responsibility regarding the other *bīt rittis* and the *limu* of Lasūtu is also not directly related to the main subject. This is rather an attempt to solve a number of administrative complications than a contract.

Tattanu

VS 3 188 25 III Art I(?) <20/1>, dates *sūtu* ^{LU_2}*gú-gal-ú-tu* GARIM-Bir-[tu$_4$(?) ...] for Art yr 20 [due from] PN1 *šá* PN2[.....], those dates and the ?, according to his written document, the lease of the GU$_2$.GAL-*ú.tu* of GARIM-Birtu-šá-Šušinnu PN3 has received from PN2 *šá*(?)-*pir* of PN5.[57]

VS 5 122 21 x Dar II 2, ^{LU_2}GU$_2$.GAL-*ú-tu šá* ZU$_2$.LUM.MA, leased by son of Tattanu.

f. *kādu* in combination with *gugallūtu*[58]

Only the close association of payments for *gugallūtu* and for *kādu*, "guarding" in unspecified phrases stating that these are either paid or not,[59] which are not excerpted here, could suggest that this could represent a separate official levy. It, however, cannot be totally excluded that the payment was a result of private arrangements or specific for certain estates only, or, probably the best interpretation, that it was normally included in the *gugallu* payments.

Borsippa

Ea-ilūta-bāni file

A 86 27 VI Nbn 12, 2.5 *š* silver PN1 *šá ka-a-da ina* ŠU^{II} PN2 *ma-ḫir*.

g. Registration by government agencies: an Achaemenid innovation?

We have become accustomed to the idea that on being born or having died, and on many other occasions some sub-section of government wants to register the fact and accompanies that action by the claim to a certain fee. The same is valid for spiritual authorities. Any new form of registration entails a fresh fee. We can assume that at any rate the institutions kept registers of those pertaining to them, if only to avoid unnecessary payments of rations. Hence the existence of Ur III texts of the at first sight somewhat unusual type "from 26 VIII yr. x PN is dead", which, however, administratively makes good sense, or, for us more immediately comprehensible, “from such and such a date PN is assigned to this or that occupation”. Whether PN had to pay for this type of note is, on balance, not likely, yet that does not change the fact that government involvement generally means the paying of taxes. Stolper, the first to write systematically about this matter, regards forms of registration of this type under the Achaemenids a fact and payments of dues virtually certain. In general we can be sure that especially in military affairs a register was kept, listing in which unit a subject had to serve. We do not know at what age someone was registered as a member of an *eširtu*, but we know for certain that as soon as male persons received the (age or wage?) classification "three"[60] they started to be listed by their given name in institutional documents in which also able bodied men, *itbāru*, and *šību,* old men appeared. This type of registration made a subject liable for service and taxation. The fact itself was probably not taxed directly, though some doubt is possible as soon as in the Hellenistic period the services for which registration took place (occasionally) assumed a prebendal aspect, involved payment of certain emoluments.

If property was involved the idea that some payment might be the consequence of registration is not to be excluded. Though for the Neo-Babylonian period signs for a

---

57 This follows Ungnad NRVU no. 388; the text contains many difficulties.

58 Literature: CAD K p. 33-5.

59 VS 3, 66, 67, 69.

60 This is valid for people classified as *itbāru*, for the possible meanings of this "three" see Chapter III under *itbāru*.

general taxation of slaves are lacking, there are traces of a form of taxation of slave sales, which, as is well known, in the Hellenistic period caused the disappearance of relevant contracts in Akkadian, when the use of Greek in such cases was prescribed for taxation purposes.[61] The scant signs of Neo-Babylonian taxation of slave sales[62] consist of two contracts mentioning the fact that the seller of the slave in question was obliged to have the slave sold pass the *bīt miksi*. Registration, expressed by the term "causing to pass the *b. m.*", and thus the payment of some fee, is the likely reason. As will be seen below under *miksu*, the expression is also used for registering payments on other occasions. The action is probably supposed to be seen by the buyer as a strengthening of his position, which probably meant that the government regarded an unregistered sale as void. The government may have sold the measure to the public as beneficial on account of the additional security implied in registration, that is, if it felt a need to provide a reason.

There are also -scant- traces of (general) registers of real estate, almost inevitably also requiring a fee on the occasion of a mutation. The best known, and for us of special importance as it is explicitly stated to have been in existence during the reign of Darius I, is Stolper's *karammaru* in EE 106.[63] If Murašû had been obliged to pay a duty, the investment proved worthwhile on this occasion. Registers of real estate, if only for the purpose of collecting rent, certainly existed in the institutional administrations, that comparable lists existed of property belonging to land for service systems is more than likely. A considerable number of texts insists on the proper registration of payments relating to services attached to such property in the relevant accounting documents. Which those properties were, was known evidently. It was only a small step to a general register of real estate and even slaves, at least for the area under effective government administration.

Uruk

BM 30126[64] 1 I Dar II 7, Bertin 2106 sale of slave, after the warranty clauses 14) .... *ina* E$_2$ *mi-ik-su šá* [LUGAL] x x PN1 15) $^{\mathrm{LU}_2}$IR$_3$ MU-*ti tu-še-ti-*[*iq* (subject the female seller) *ana* P]N2 (buyer) *ta-na-din*;

Where?

BM 62588[65] 21 XI Art 35, at Gummanu 12) .....$^{\mathrm{LU}_2}$*a-me-lu*[*-tu*$_4$[...] 13) [xx *šu*]*-a-tim i-na* E$_2$ *mi-ik-su šá* LUGAL PN1 s PN2 (seller) 14) [*ú-še-ti*]*-iq-ma a-na* PN3 s PN4 (buyer) *i*[*-nam-din*]

ROMCT 2 35 1 IX Art II(?) 10, (after warranty clauses) 14) ... *ina* E$_2$ *mi-ik-su šá* LUGAL LU$_2$*-ut-tim š*[*uati uštētiq* (seller) *ana* PN (buyer)] 15) *it-ta-din*.[66]

Babylon

Dar 551 17 IX Dar 22, 9) .... LU$_2$*-tú* 10) *šá* Bēl-iddina AD *šá* 11) Bēl-uballiṭ *u* ŠEŠ.MEŠ-*šú i-na* MU 19 KAM$_2$ Da-a-ri-ia-muš 11) LUGAL *ina kar-ri-am-ma-ru šá* LUGAL *a-na* UGU Bēl-ēṭer ŠEŠ.AD-*šú-nu* Bēl-uballiṭ 12) *ù* ŠEŠ.MEŠ-*šú-ú-še-ti-iq mim-ma* ḪA.LA-*šá* Bēl-eṭer ŠEŠ.AD-*šu-nu i-na* LU$_2$*-tú šu-a-ti ia-a-nu* LU$_2$ *šu-a-ti šá* Bēl-uballiṭ *ù* ŠEŠ.MEŠ-*šu ši-i*.

BM 115716[67] small fragment, lines 4'-6' possibly similar clause.

Murašû

---

61 Doty, 1977, p. II.

62 M.W. Stolper, 1977, p. 259-266 and 1989, p. 80-101. Nothing can be added to what was available to Stolper. Cf. also Stolper 1985 p. 29-31.

63 The text mentions a registration in Darius I yr 20: Stolper 1985 p. 31 with note 116, cf. earlier Stolper, 1976 p. 195-6.

64 Stolper, 1989 p. 93.

65 Stolper, 1989 p. 95.

66 Cf. McEwan, 1982 p. 46-7.

67 Stolper, 1989 p. 99.

EE 106 6 IV Art 20, court case concerning a house 8) .... *ár-ki* Murašû s Ḫatin *ra-ga-[mu] ina muḫ-ḫi* E_2 MU.MEŠ *ú-šib-šu-ú iq-bu-u* 10) *um-ma* E_2 MU.MEŠ *at-tu-ú-a šu-ú* [x (x)] *ina ka-al-am-ma-ri šá šarri ina* MU 22 KAM_2 *šá* Da-ri-ia-a-muš *ina muḫ-ḫi-ia šá-ṭer.* (In Art 20 the question was probably resolved in the sense that Murašû paid for work executed on the house by the other party.)

3. Conclusions

Attention must be drawn to three points, which require further consideration.

We have seen that there are grounds for the assumption that in later Achaemenid times, under lease conditions, the payments to the administration in general may have risen to over 30% of the yield, but this was in a context where a lease holder obviously wanted to obtain or retain the lease. The context is that of haggling about the price. This may not have affected those who held land belonging to (former) land division schemes. The borderline between tax and rent is fluid in the case of these payments.

In his study of the Neo-Babylonian *ešrû* Jursa has argued that *ešrû* was paid by tenants of temple land over their own share in the harvest, on top of what they delivered as rent to the god as owner of the land. Payments ostensibly for the benefit of Bēl, evidently Marduk, by holders of leases of his land on top of the sum of the lease therefore stand to reason. We have also found payments called *balāṭu ana Bēl* in Uruk and Sippar in documents dealing with the estates of the local gods, though we also noted similar 10% payments to the treasury of Nabû. We could consider whether payments from the estates of at least some of the gods may have been due ultimately to Marduk, possibly as a kind of tax paid to the principal god of the pantheon. The term is also found in a small group of texts from the Murašû archive. Land belonging to Enlil, or people from Nippur, is not completely absent from the Murašû archive. There is perhaps, after all, some ground for reconsidering the non-existence of a kind of "Kirchensteuer". The relation of some of the payments mentioned to the term *ešrû* needs better documentation. The payment may have been included in the over 30 % already suggested for the later Achaemenid period, and some form of absorption of the payments involved into those due to the government would then be likely. Costs of at least 20% payable to the government -on top of other payments- can be regarded as considerable.

The registration of property transactions by the government in the Achaemenid period may have had a precursor in the activities of a group of scribes as notaries, which in turn may have been related to the activities of the royal courts.[68] Though the texts are generally silent on the costs involved in the production of legally valid documents, we can assume that certain payments were due. After all the Edict mentions scribes as involved in activities for which payments were due from rent farmers, and thus at a lower level perhaps also from ordinary tenants. Official scribes would also have to be paid. It is known that scribes sometimes derived income from the keeping of certain accounts.

---

68 Cf. the preliminary publication by H.D. Baker and C. Wunsch on scribes as notaries in eds. W.W. Hallo and I.J. Winter, CRRAI 45, 2001, p.197-213.

CHAPTER III
THE STATUS OF WATER, LAND AND PEOPLE AND GOVERNMENT POLICIES

A. Means

Taxation must tap the most important sources of wealth. Mesopotamian society was agrarian. Wealth was primarily created through arable agriculture and animal husbandry. People, water and land were the most important basic means of production in agrarian Ancient Mesopotamia. If, in future, we want to understand the social and economic structure of the country better, we will have to know more about the manner in which land, water and population related to one another in the past. A real insight into this fundamental question cannot be obtained from texts alone, it requires integration of the archaeological and the archival evidence, and also a greater availability of narrative sources. Here we must discuss the manner in which the relation between man and land were structured according to the written evidence available. The following will not contain fundamental new insights or material. The next chapter will deal with what could be called the "land for service system", which is of prime importance for the question of the relation between subject and government in the countryside and we will separately discuss the urban aspect of this question. Here we must try to assess what is known about land held by "the government", in practice that means the king, and in relation to that, the status of the people living on it.[1]

The archaeological map suggests insight into the development of settlement and thereby land use, the texts suggest the existence of policies and provide some limited insight into the changing profitability of the exploitation of land. We accept that the major archaeological survey in the alluvium suggests overall expansion of exploitation in the relevant period.[2]

No text which explicitly states that "land without an owner"[3] belonged to the king seems to exist for this period.[4] In practice such land will have abounded, though perhaps less so close

---

[1] Sources are silent on general rules. Only the letter BIN 1, 70 suggests a "rule of behaviour" but it must be quoted in a context, and that is not made explicit, beyond the fact that there is some sort of difference of opinion between officials: rev. 1) [x x GIŠ.]ŠUB.BA.MEŠ 2) *u* KIRI$_6$.MEŠ *šá* TIN.TIR^{KI} 3) x x (= *ina* ŠU^{II}?) *šá* LUGAL *ta-at-taš-kan*, after which the "rule" follows later on: 16) *man-nu ina* ŠA$_3$ GIŠ.ŠUB.BA-*šú* 17) *u* ^{GIŠ}KIRI$_6$-*šú ú-šu!-uz-zu* 18) *ni-di-it-tu$_4$ a-na* LUGAL 19) *i-nam-din u ú-tur ik-kal*, "You have put the allotments (prebends?) and gardens of Babylon in the hands of the king", and: "whoever has the use of a prebend and a garden must give a present to the king and is allowed to enjoy the remainder". Cf. CAD N 207L, which does not differ fundamentally from other interpretations. The exact meaning of GIŠ.ŠUB.BA, *isqu*, is not clear, it could refer to prebendal rights or, in view of the context, possibly, to a share in a land division, where the order in which a share was taken may have been determined by lot. Though *isqu* is hardly used in the context, a direct link with the garden mentioned could be intended, which suggests that the letter deals with a *rab banî* prebend and its date plantation. It is difficult to grasp the right tone in these cases. Jursa 1995 p. 59f has established that VS 6, 255 (Nbk II 0) registers garden plots which *rab banîs* "took" under supervision of the *šangû* of Sippar. In general the link between this prebend and its garden is nor very strong, and this not only in Sippar.

[2] For rapid orientation Adams 1981, Chapter 5.

[3] This is, of course, a dubious concept in a country where sedentary and non-sedentary merge gradually and where extensive grazing is common. "Land without an owner" will in practice mean "land not used for arable agriculture". But that does not constitute a proper definition, for at least under-used land in the hands of the institutions is attested in the documents and there will always be some form of rough grazing

to the main towns than further away.[5] I imagine that the situation did not differ very much from a situation as found during the Turkish attempts at regulating land holding in the 19th century, at any rate not at the beginning of our period. Everywhere there would be people who had, and were acquiring, a right to the land they occupied by tilling it. The administration would attempt to get as much as possible of this land subjected to some administrative system of land holding and taxation. For the Neo-Babylonian period the practical modalities of much of these efforts are next to invisible for us. Royal land division schemes, of which the *ḫanšû* land near the towns is the best known, are, however, more or less recognisable.

We regard the Neo-Babylonian state as a monarchy, starting from a very restricted basis at the beginning of the period. The practical power of the king was not unlimited, it operated from centres, its hold on the periphery was limited and it had to cope with the fact that even in the vicinity of the main centres there was a tribal presence. In such a situation the practical relation of the monarch to land and people could not be uniform. Though we do not have statements claiming that all the land was on principle the property of the king, all his subjects were on principle his "slaves". But that means in practice that only those who recognised themselves as the king's slaves were his subjects, which is something different: royal power had to grow, especially in the tribal areas. Concerning land the situation will have been comparable, there too the direct say of the king had to grow from the depth reached in the early First Millennium. The fact applies to rights to both water and land, which are, of course, intimately connected, particularly in the alluvium. The land of the subjects could be taxed and they could be regarded as willing to enter into the various schemes implementing royal policy. There existed a poorly specified but concrete link between the population and the land it lived on, especially in the countryside.

We must first deal with the terminology, for its existence is the best indicator of the presence of means with which to carry through a policy. Policies can best be understood through the manner in which the means available were used, for we cannot generally expect them to be formulated explicitly.[6]

---

to which there will have existed a system of entitlements, which the government no doubt will have attempted to tax, if it could.

[4] In the text published by E. Weidner in AfO 17,1954/6 p. 1ff., land belonging to a person who had been executed for high treason and which was therefore ownerless, is sold on behalf of Nabû and not by the king. This is certainly too flimsy a basis for a theoretical divine ownership of unoccupied land, especially not as the land may always have been intended for the god. In various periods houses or house plots in towns without known owners were occasionally sold as if the property of the gods.

[5] Unused and unusable land will have been visible everywhere. Lease contracts based on water rights accept restrictions in the use of land by the limiting clause "as far as the water reaches". Who was protected by this stipulation is not immediately clear, expansion was possible, but practically the clause may refer to annual fluctuations in the water supply. The area which could be tilled would have to be adapted to the supply. This marginal land was practically without owner, but theoretically it belonged to the lease. Real land without owner is extremely rare in texts. The Marduk-zākir-šumi donation, Thureau Dangin, RA 16 p. 117ff., has after a description of land 8) NAM *la man-ma-an*, which, perhaps significantly, is not even being claimed by the king who grants the property concerned. Yet he could possibly dispose of "land without an owner".

[6] I can find only one, rare, indication for payments for the right to graze animals on otherwise unused land in the Neo-Babylonian period, but that does not mean that there were no such rights. They are mentioned already by Nougayrol in his list of taxes in PRU III p. 255.

1. Water rights: rent or taxation?[7]

The importance of the involvement of the Mesopotamian kings in the provision of water in the alluvium cannot be underrated. If Samsuiluna can be held responsible for, if not causing, at least accelerating the decline of much of the South by his cutting off of the eastern branches of the Euphrates system, the fact that the main artery which re-supplied water to the middle of the southern alluvium in the Neo-Babylonian period was called the Nār-Šarri, "King's Canal", in that period, is significant. Only the king had the resources to undertake the construction of a major canal of this scale. Only he could make use of corvée labour on an appropriate scale. The canals were exploitable as a source of revenue and they were at the basis of a policy of agricultural expansion. As such they appear in an elaborate system of leases and sub-leases, principally in the Murašû texts in the later Achaemenid period. Not for nothing is most evidence concerning the exploitation of water rights found in the area of artificial canals in the neighbourhood of Nippur, where to all likelihood a northern and a western source of water came together and from where there ran the previously mentioned major canal to the South. But that does not imply that all water everywhere belonged, on principle, to the king, nor does it mean that a system of canals did not exist already in the earlier part of the period. Its reconstruction is fundamental to the phenomenon of growth in the Neo-Babylonian period. The importance of the Murašû material is that it derives from the specific social-economic level where transactions of a size involving complete irrigation systems took place.[8]

The supply of water for irrigation purposes implies costs and their payment in the form of silver or produce and (corvée-)labour. In the whole of Mesopotamia water was a prime concern, but the question cannot be treated in terms of taxation only. Strictly spoken the 10% or 20% levy discussed in the previous chapter probably contained payments for the services of officials, but in view of the *balāṭu ana Bēl* formula, there was probably a religious dimension to the payments as well. Only marginally this included direct payments for water itself. Payment for *gugallūtu* may imply only that the supervision of the sharing out of the water was being paid for. Two of the Sippar texts quoted above under *gugallūtu* indicate that certain tracts of land were obliged to pay for, or had to contribute to the upkeep of certain specific constructions which ensured security against flooding or regulated the provision of water. That stands to reason, such constructions might ensure or improve the exploitation of a particular area. But again that is not equal to the provision of water in general, which lies at the basis of at least some of the Murašû leases, explicitly mentioning a canal, with the land on it as something secondary. A sub-lease only mentioning land on the canal covered the water needed from the canal for that land, which was paid for by an unspecified share in the total rent to be paid. We have noted that there were additional payments, which may be regarded as more explicitly taxation related and probably resulted from the haggling over lease conditions. Leasing of government rights and taxation cannot be properly separated in irrigation matters.[9]

At the lowest level actual use of water and the manner in which it was obtained influenced what had to be paid as rent, normally a share in the yield. Direct payments for water

---

[7] In this context Stolper's discussion of water rights in EE p. 36-51 should be referred to explicitly.

[8] Use of the term "the Murašû firm" does not imply that the structure of the "company" is not a problem. The relation of the Murašûs and the people who are their main "employees" is far from clear, but it must be noted that even the relations with their simplest gardeners regularly are formal and contractual.

[9] Speculation along these same lines suggests that land in private hands, often resulting from a land division, had to include rights to water from the canal on which it was situated. That would explain why there are so few documents on water rights in private archives. The owners of such land would have to maintain the canal. Some payments for *dullu* or *urāšu* may actually be the result of this situation, and a strong government, able to assert that the land was shared out by it, may in the course of time have claimed full rights to the complete *ilku*.

are rare, PSBA 17, 278 can be mentioned. A tenant retained more of his harvest when he had to draw water with a bucket than when he irrigated his land by gravity irrigation. This seems to have been a generally accepted principle. BE 9, 7 is a particularly good example, as it indicates that the principle even applied to the size of the *ešrû,* "tithe", payable. Even at the lowest level of the hierarchy of leases the tenant could profit, if the circumstances were right, from increasing the amount of land under exploitation, but at the price of an increase in the work load. The owner, and the lessee of the water rights, when he gave a sub-lease, in this way could be seen to encourage a maximisation of the use of water for irrigation. Whether the manner in which irrigation water was applied influenced contracts with a fixed rent is not visible for us, but we can assume that the question plays a role when low fixed rents in speculative situations were agreed between parties. Increasing the yield not only increased the volume of the rent paid when a new contract was made, it also increased the income from rights as discussed in Chapter II. It remains, however, difficult to assess practical results.

We have already seen that it was common practice in the Neo-Babylonian period to lease agricultural assets of every nature. But direct exploitation often seems to precede leasing. It is therefore reasonable to assume that the owners of water resources, rivers and canals, also exploited these resources directly at first, before they made them the object of a lease. Statements in contracts referring to inclusion of access to water in the sale or lease contracts of land are rare, however. What is clear, is that the parcellation always was arranged in such a manner that access to water was generally guaranteed by locating one of the short sides of a field on some water course, thus implying access. This is not the same as ownership of the water concerned, though if the watercourse carried the same name as the owner or holder of the land that possibility should be left open.[10] Certain land holders do seem to have been able to improve their access to water.

The only explicit case mentioning water rights known to me is late: TÉBR 31 from Šaṭir.[11] VS 6, 66 is not so much a sign that owners of land had a right to exploit water, as an arrangement between two parties that they will not cut off access to water from main canals to one another: the water itself could possibly be owned by a third party. TuM 2/3, 7 from Nippur expresses the same thing differently: PN must not fill the construction at the inlet with sand.[12] Such stipulations are extremely rare, they possibly refer to specific problems in the past. In general granting a lease of land automatically implied inclusion of access to the water that makes the land cultivable. We might expect that the owner's rights to water are covered by the total rent paid, but that is not of necessity always the case. BE 8, 80, which I do not understand completely, no doubt belongs to an investigation into a case where access to water was, intentionally or not, made difficult. In this case the right to water was the result of a governmental grant.

It is in the nature of things that rights to complete canals can only have pertained to major estates. What constitutes a "complete canal" is a matter of definition. Some canals play a central role, for instance the Nār-Sin in the world of the Murašû contracts. The lease of such a canal provided the holder with a dominant role, at a higher level than that at which the Murašûs usually operated. If a leased canal stretches "from its intake (KA_2) to its tail end (*šiliḫtu*)" it obviously represented a branch canal deriving water from a main artery. But it does not only

---

[10] But such names also occur on land of important landowners, even the king, where such names are those of their agents. Bīt-Ḫaḫḫuru is the best example.

[11] Leasing land automatically includes normally the practical rights and obligations of the owner, but this is not expressed explicitly. A rare case is the Murašû text EE 27 (25 VII Art 40). The warranty clause, lines 14-16 not only mentions the land but also the ḪA.LA *me-e*, "share in the water", which is not mentioned at all, as is done normally, in the core of the text.

[12] Comparable is EAH 214, 7, Stolper JCS 40 p. 144, quoted below under *uzbāru*.

contain the water, as the land on the right and left banks, or at least only on one bank, is included in the lease. Such complete irrigation systems occur only in the leases of the Murašû archive. It constitutes the maximum level at which they operated. We must not overrate the size of such a system. At the Murašû level we have probably a system consisting of an artificial ditch with an intake which probably could be closed, if necessary by simple infilling, and which served to irrigate the land on both sides, up to what is called the *šiliḫtu*, an area where water did not reach every year. The land was used as arable and cultivation could therefore not take place every year, over not counting the normal fallow of half the land. The lessee was allowed to use as much land as he deemed suitable. A stretch of the bank of the main cannel from which our system takes off could be included in the system leased, which was limited by the two, sometimes three, similar systems to its left and right, drawing water from the same main canal. Some idea about the size of the individual system can be obtained by comparing the amount of seed provided by the owner or the yield promised to the lessor. There is, of course, the possibility that water had to be bought incidentally, in a bad year.

Most texts derive from archives of which the owners operate at a much lower agricultural level or in systems based on a division of land to private persons by the king. But even the Murašûs did not operate at the highest level, they were the sub-lessees of other lessees. The dealings of that type of lessee with the real owner, or rather with those acting for the owner, are not documented by the material available: only at that level we would be able to establish whether payment was due for water taken from the main natural arteries, Euphrates or Tigris. It is notable that the Nār-Sîn, the main artery of the artificial canals in the Nippur area, had a panel of administrative judges. The question of whether there was a general tax on irrigation water or whether dues were levied only on water deriving from specially constructed canals cannot be answered effectively. The impression is that water was paid for through the leases of the land in the Murašû texts, but that does not tell us much that is relevant in cases in which people were the outright owners of their fields or in cases in which the land had been granted in the land division schemes. That people occasionally had to buy water for their date plantation seems to be implied by BE 9, 16. In BE 9, 7 a payment for water for a bow fief is mentioned. Narrative sources providing insight in these matters are not available.

It is unlikely that all the land on a major canal was included in a Murašû-type lease, as there were others who had rights. The question is whether the amount payable by those others to the ultimate owner was included in the rent. Only one text explains what can be expected: the right to draw water from a canal was limited as to time, transgressing that period involved a fine: BE 9, 7.[13] Time during which it was permitted to draw water had a value which could be expressed in silver. It is somewhat disturbing that documents illustrating such payments are extremely rare. Perhaps these questions were the responsibility of the *gugallu*. The contract implies supervision and thus additional costs, possibly the payments to the *gugallu* discussed in the previous chapter. We do not know how access to water in royal land division schemes was arranged. We can only note that all such land, as far as we can see, was on a canal. The names, for instance the "New Canal", suggest that these were at least sometimes dug on purpose.

The question of what was included in a lease always remains unclear, sometimes land held by others was excluded explicitly, but in general there will have been no need to list an area to which neither party had an interest. Especially with the larger canals this would be valid. Another question is whether a lease did include responsibility for the collection of dues from others in the whole area concerned, or not.

Perhaps the two payments for water from Sippar from the reign of Nabonidus are signs of direct exploitation of water rights by the government. Leasing is far less difficult to prove.

[13] Note that the rent payable, 25% of the yield, is identical with the amount asked normally from land irrigated by hand.

This is directly related to the fact that the evidence mainly derives from late Achaemenid texts, a period in which leasing was a wide-spread mode of exploitation, if the documentation available is to be believed. But the leasing of complete canals is definitely older and there is no reason why it should have been invented in the reign of Cambyses: Nippur, BE 8, 85. It is a basic element of the system of rent farming as it began to develop before the end of Chaldean rule, when the intentions of the system were already clear. In Uruk we can note that while the upkeep of the existing system was the task of the lease holder, major digging operations remained the responsibility of the institutional owner.[14]

It is of some importance that the one explicit text available, BE 8, 85, mentions one of the canals which figure prominently in the Murašû archive: the (Nār-)Purat-Nippur. What was common practice in their time in the area can be projected back, just as the system of land for service, which gave the Murašûs many of their other opportunities, can be projected back. As is to be expected, assignation of land, for whatever purpose, and royal canal building went together. BE 8, 80 deals with a Nār-ša-Gubāri, a name suggesting a recent development, although politically correct renaming does always remain a possibility.

That there was a standard set of stipulations applicable under standard circumstances is likely. This is supported in the sub-lease BE 8, 85 by a clause like "additionally a sheep for 10 kor of land", in a lease dealing with 15 kor of land. The fixed low rent of four kor of barley per kor of land in that text, called "the king's share", instead of an assessed share in the crop also suggests standardised practices.[15] This applies to un(der)-used land for which a low rent was asked. The rent paid was a kind of recognition, it thus comes close to a land tax, but it differs from that in that the amount would be increased if the venture was successful. What was recognised is that the government could give out land, while the tenant obtained a degree of security of tenure in this way. A theory that unused land belonged to the king is not formulated in any text available, but it operates in practice where it has a practical purpose. We find un- or under-used land connected in some way or another to the king in the margin of a range of contracts dealing with land.

The late Achaemenid texts with a Murašû background suggest that ultimately the king was the virtually exclusive owner of water rights. This is partially due to the fact that the texts share a similar background, but it will also reflect the reality that only the king had the power and the means to handle major land and water resources, quite unrelated to theoretical considerations of ultimate ownership.

In this context the Sippar text Cyr 175, with the more difficult to read Camb 240, 4 VI Camb 4, stands out through the curious manner in which it is formulated. Fishermen of Šamaš engage themselves to pay a "price for water", if this is correctly read, at two specified localities. To all likelihood this price was payable to the administration of the temple. The silver is called "silver of Šamaš", but who the contractual partner of the fishermen was, is left open. This could be regarded as a lease of fishing rights, but to fishermen who were to all likelihood obliged to provide the temple with fish. The texts are rather exceptional.[16]

The lease of a canal presumably implied a right to use or sub-lease the land on it, that is the unused land and this may even have been the intended purpose of the grantor of the lease.

---

[14] TCL 13 182: 31, (13 IV Dar 2).

[15] I do not understand the line on the lower edge of the tablet referring to the Nār-Sin. That canal obviously plays a central role in the canal system in the neighbourhood of Nippur in the period of the Murašû texts. Especially the presence of the judges of the Nār-Sin as witnesses is a sign of the permanent importance of that canal. The central role of the Nār-Sin goes back to at least the early Achaemenid period if we accept what BE 8, 85 seems to suggest.

[16] Also the two Murašû contracts PBS 2/1, 111 and 112, 18 XI Dar II 5, signify that holders of rights to water wanted to have their rights to the fish in it safeguarded.

Other users of the source of water concerned would probably have to pay according to custom or according to their existing contract with the owner or the previous holder of the rights. That such payments could take a considerable share of the yield is indicated by BE 9, 16, where Murašû passes on water in the Nār-Bēl taken from the Nār-Sin against a share in the yield of 25% of the dates. Such information is rare and not easy to extrapolate, but, possibly, this indicates no more than a lease of manually irrigated land, compare BE 9, 7 with its rent of 25% from manually irrigated land and $33^{1}/_{2}$% from gravity irrigated land, 25% for water alone can be regarded as a hefty imposition on a land holder if he also otherwise had to pay a rent for the land.

Not unexpectedly the use of the major sources of water is ultimately in the king's gift. The term *ṣibitti šarri* is probably specifically used to express this right, rather than a word for some reservoir or pond as the dictionaries suggest. That *ṣibittu* is nearly always clarified by the addition "royal" is of some importance: even if the right was temporarily transferred, it explicitly remained royal property. BE 10, 43 is an exception, but we can assume that there too a right ultimately belonging to the king is implied. Especially TuM 2/3, 147 connects the source of the water and the *ṣibitti šarri* directly. The other texts use the same phrasing, though sometimes in a more convoluted manner.[17] BE 9, 7 is of special importance for the question of the status of bow fiefs in this connection, as will be discussed below. If *ṣibittu* primarily refers to the right to draw water, *mûṣānē*, always in this form of a plural, probably represents a term for a point where water could actually be drawn from a main canal. In BE 9, 65 this is what was leased with a stretch of river bank.[18]

The policy of exploiting rights to water through leases may potentially have reduced direct income for the owner, but it created an atmosphere where all sub-lessees could gain by increasing their exploitations, which in turn will have increased the income from taxation rights. The question remains whether these taxation rights were included in the leases or had to be paid for additionally. From the point of view of the government additional payment would make most sense, and this is possibly implied by the "with one kor he will pay a *ṣimdu/mašīḫu*" passages as discussed in Chapter II. Otherwise water was included in the rent paid. Many leases were short term, three years is normal and the lessor could at the end try to obtain improved rents. He held the land and the water, and leaving aside the managers, the main problem would be labour and stock. That made finding tenants such an important job.

Direct exploitation by or on behalf of owner:

Babylon

Sin-ili

VS 6 66 9 XII Nbn 2, document concerning sale 2) *šá ta-lu-ku me-e šá ul-tu* Nār-Banitu 3) *i-na-áš-šu-ú* ... 21) *me-e* Sin-ili *u* ŠEŠ.MEŠ-*šú a-na* ŠE.NUMUN 22) šá PN1 *ul i-kal-lu-ú ul-tu* 23) Ḫar-ri-ša-GARIM-Banitāia *šá* PN1 s 24) PN2 Eppeš-ili *a-na* ŠE.NUMUN *šá* Sin-ili 25) *u* ŠEŠ.MEŠ *me-e ul-tu ḫar-ri-šú* 26) *i-nam-din*.

Nippur

BE 8 80 15 VIII Camb 1, Širikti-Ninurta file, PN1 the *ša muḫḫi āli* and *gugallu* s PN2 and 6 others, *mār banî*s and *šibūtu* of Āl-ša-Ḫandidi swear in the presence of two servants of Širikti-Ninurta the *guennakku* 12) ... *ki-i* A TA I_7.MEŠ 13) *ku-um* Nār-ša-Gubāri *i-*⌈*ke*?⌉*-me-šu-nu-tú* 14) PN3 *rab bīti* of Gubāru 15)x x x Gú-bar-ri I7 *a-na* 16) ^{LU_2}Gi-mir-ra-a-a *u* ^{LU_2}Su-bar-a-a/ 17) [*id-di*]*n-nu*; place and date.

---

[17] Literature: AHw p. 1097R, "Einfassung, Bassin"; CAD Ṣ p. 155 3) "pond, reservoir", but cf. especially Cardascia 1951, p. 160 note 5.

[18] *āṣītu* possibly has a similar meaning, possibly at a lower level.

TuM 2/3 7 25 VI Art 30, 17) *mu-ša-an-ni-tu₄ a-na muḫ-ḫi* 8) PN *ul ip-pir-'u*, cf. 15) *mu-šá-an-ni-tu la e-pi-ri*.

Šaṭir

TÉBR 31 1 IX Art I 41, arable belonging to a number of persons, all in Šaṭir in Bīt-Ḫarbate is sold (16-17) *a-di* I₇.MEŠ-*šú*.

Sippar

PSBA 17 278 1 XI Nbn 0, silver, included in a larger sum, as the ŠAM₂ *me-e šá* Āl-Šamaš.

Nbn 245 27 XIIb Nbn 6, silver, price of ? (*me-e*!? x?) *šá la-pan* PN1 *bēl piqitti* of PN3 ^{LU_2}GAL A.MEŠ *šá šarri*, brought by PN4 s PN5, follows expenditure against this amount. Dubious whether relevant.

Cyr 175 3? VII Cyr 4, 1) x MA.NA silver NIG₂.GA ^{d}UTU ŠAM₂ *me-e*! at two localities from VII yr 4 to VI yr 5 is due from three named persons, all said to be members of the family Fisher[19] 7) *ù* ^{LU_2}ŠU.KU₆.MEŠ *šá* ^{d}UTU *gab-bi* and the other fishermen of Šamaš in two instances per annum. Cf. the parallel Camb 240, 4 VI Camb 4, where the amount payable is 1 mina.

Leasing:

Pre-Murašû

BE 8 85, 2 I Camb 3, from the Nippur Enlil-šākin-šulum file, PN1 s PN2 addresses PN3 s PN4 the *bēl piqitti* of PN5 the *šá muḫ-ḫi sūti šá* Nār-Purat-Nippur concerning the lease of 15 kor of land. This is granted at a rate of 1 EN 4, explained duly as a rent amounting to 60 kor (lines 8-9), *zitti šarri ga-mir-šú i-gam-mar-ma a-na ka-a-ri šá šarri i-nam-din* (with additionally one sheep per ten kor of land).

Murašû cf. also the final section of this chapter

BE 9 16 25 XII Art 28, lease of water from Nār-Bēl, which draws water from the Nār-Sin for land in (Āl) Bīt-^{LU_2}DUMU.NUN.NA by two persons from Enlil-šum-iddina for a 25% share in dates.

Explicit statements concerning rights to water: *ṣibittu ša šarri*

Murašû

EE 2 5 V Art [24], 14) ... A.MEŠ 15) [*ina ṣi-*]*bit-tú-a₄ ina* Āl-Bīt-[x] 16) Enlil-šum-iddina *i-šad-dad*. (Additional statement with lease).

BE 9 7 12 XI Art 26, six persons address Enlil-šum-iddina and two others with the request for 6) A.MEŠ *ina ṣi-bit-*[*ti*] *šá šarri arḫussu ištu* U₄ 12 KAM₂ *adi* U₄ 15 KAM₂, for irrigating (explicitly) their bow land (ŠE.NUMUN E₂ ^{LU_2}BAN-*ni*) in Bīt-Sin-erība; the request is granted against $33^{1}/_{2}$% of the yield from gravity irrigated land and 25% from manually irrigated land, plus for *ešrû* respectively per kor 1 or 2/3 of a šekel in silver. If they irrigate additional land it is charged in the same manner and taking water outside the period mentioned is fined with 5 mina of silver per day.

EE 1 25 x Art 34, see below under *uzbāra*.

BE 10 43 15 VI Dar II 1, lease by Rēmūt-Ninurta of oxen for land of the master of the lessee in Naqidini on the Nār-Aḫu-le'u, land in (Āl) Paršušu on Nār-Miṣirāia, land in (Āl) Bīt-Bēltum, land in (Āl) Arazūa, in Āl-A.QAR-qabušú, in (Āl)Bu-šu-'u, in (Āl) Bīt-Rab-kāṣir, in (Āl) Bāb-Dirat, in (Āl) Kuzabatu, land *ina mi-ṣa-ri-ši-na it-ti ṣi-bit-tú* A.MEŠ-*ši-na*, "within their boundaries with their rights to water", plus acceptance by Rēmūt-Ninurta of *pūt pišku* of the lessee, his brother and their *kinattu*.[20]

TuM 2/3 147 17 VII Dar II 4, request of lease by Rēmūt-Ninurta s Murašû from Libluṭ s Iddina-Nabû the *ana-muḫḫi-sūti* Nār-Sin of the Nār-Badi'atu *ša ina šupal* Nār-Ruḫē which carries water to Bīt-Bulliṭ and Āl-Arbā right and left, wherever water reaches, with arable *uz-bar-ra šarri* on it and 5)A.MEŠ *ṣi-bit-ti šá ina lìb-bi* and land *uz-bar-ra ša šarri* from Bāb-Nār-Piḫāti *adi tu-ru-un* (=?) *a-di miṣir* of Nār-ša-Nergal-dānu (above (Āl) Ḫarubatu), for a total rent of 250 kor in products, and with a *mašīḫu* per kor additionally and one ox and ten sheep as *mandattu*.

---

19 It is slightly disturbing the all fishermen should belong to a family of that name, or rather, that family names are common and general at this social level.

20 On this clause cf. this chapter, below.

The acceptance refers to all elements including the Nār-Badiatu, the royal *uzbāra* land on it and (12) the *ṣibitti šarri ša ina lìb-bi-šú*.[21]

PBS 2/1 158 20 VII Dar II x, lease by Rēmūt-Ninurta of land on the Nār-Šarri which branches from the left bank of the Nār-Sin with land (type or status lost) with water *ṣi-bit-ti šarri* "which is in it", with oxen, ploughs, tools and seed; the delivery of the rent, in total 400 kor, has to take place on the Nār-Sin in the *mašīḫu ša ú-si-iš-tu*$_4$. The acceptance phrase is damaged on this point but contained a further specification.

EE 25 date lost, cf. below under *uzbāru*.

Ownership of points where water could be drawn:

mûṣānē[22]

Uruk

Florenz 155 [x x] Nbn 13, dispute between PN s PN2, the *ša muḫḫi sūti* of Bēlet of Uruk, and PN3 s PN4 *ša ina muḫḫi mu-ṣa-ni-e* of Bēlet of Uruk, fragmentary. 12) *um-ma* PN2 ..... 14) *i-na* ŠE.NUMUN *šá* ^{d}Bēlet-šá-Uruk^{KI} *šá mu-ṣa-ni-e šá* ^{d}Bē[let-ša-Uruk^{KI}] 15)^{GIŠ}APIN *šá*(?) *a-na lìb-bi ul a-bu-ku-šú* ...?

Murašû

BE 9 65 28 x Art 38, contains two leases, the first is a request for a lease from Enlil-šum-iddina Murašû of the right bank of Nār-Bēl-aba-uṣur from (Al) Galutu to (Al) Bīt-Bagadāti, *mu-ṣa-né-e šá šarri u* ŠE.NUMUN ^{LU_2}*pa-'a-ṣi-e-ti šá ina muḫ-ḫi u* ŠE.NUMUN *šá* ^{LU_2}NIBRU^{KI} plus oxen, tools and seed. Considerable yield, see below under "Policies".

PBS 2/1 83 20 IV [Dar II] 4, small fragment, request for internal lease by Ribat to Rēmūt-Ninurta of Nār-Simmagir *it-ti mu-ṣa-ni-e* [.....] *šá ik-kaš-ši-da-áš-šú*, Nār-x. x from Nār-Kuta.

2. The terminology concerning royal land

makkūr šarri used for land does occur, but sparingly. The word *makkūru* is perhaps the most explicit indicator of ownership. Barring oversight, the term is not used for land held by private individuals, it is reserved for gods and kings. The estates of the gods are their NIG$_2$.GA, *makkūru,* they are managed by the higher officials of the temples, who are under close supervision of royal appointees, but that does not mean that there is not also a persistent direct intervention by the royal central administration, even in minutiae. The introduction of the system of rent farming on temple estates was pushed through by the king in person, at any rate by Nabonidus, and the accounting at the level of the ploughmen and herdsmen, who certainly were more than mere herders, was closely supervised by the vice-regal administration in Babylon in the Persian period.[23] It would be useful to collect the references to *makkūr šarri* applied to land, regarding divine property the remark that the term is commonly used is sufficient.[24]

The ordinary terminology used to indicate "royal" land is complex[25] and incompletely understood, but it is of considerable importance for the reconstruction of the tax basis in Neo-

21 On the possible importance of lines 9-10 cf. above, Chapter II, *kuṣurrānu* section.

22 Literature CAD M/2 p. 249R 4.

23 Some will object, and with reason, against calling a governor of Babylonia and *ebir nāri* a vice-roy, but the person in question was certainly not a simple provincial governor. The precise status of a satrap in a Babylonian context is not clear to me. The upper levels of the Persian administration in Babylonia are still opaque, at any rate seen from Babylonia. Cf. M. Dandamaev, Nippur at the Centennial, 1982, p. 29-32.

24 Estates of members of the royal family, including the crown prince are called their *bītus*. The word *makkūru* is not used either in the context of aristocratic estates. *bīt šarri* does not seem to be used for land, as far as I can see, though it occurs in the context of the payment of rights which pertain to it.

25 In slave sales a guarantee is (seldomly) given against that slave belonging to a *bīt kussi*, which is possibly a word for land in the royal domain, but the term is hardly ever used in Neo-Babylonian texts in

Babylonian Mesopotamia. For that reason the following compilation may be of some use. Simple "land of the king" is rare[26] and, what is of equal importance, "land without an owner" is even rarer[27]. That could suggest that "land without an owner" was automatically attributed to the king, though there is no support for the formulation of a general principle, as is often the case in Mesopotamia in similar circumstances. But I find it difficult not to assume that squatter's rights on unused land could not evolve into property rights, for the simple reason that sedentary and non-sedentary are shifting categories in Mesopotamia and "squatting" will have been common. The degree of practical occupation, which would influence "ownership", would vary. We can assume that normally contracts delineate properties by listing the factual holders of neighbouring land without bothering about the degree of "ownership".

Though there is a rich terminology relating to "royal land", there is, for all practical purposes, little sign of the land being directly exploited by the estate of the king or even "the palace", unlikely though that may sound. For, as can be best illustrated for Old Babylonian Mari, the system of government implies that the king had a *fundus* of land, with human and animal stock from which he could grant elements to his queens, the other members of his family and also to high ranking servants for their sustenance for the duration of his pleasure. The Neo-Babylonian term *niditti šarri* probably expresses this situation. There can be little doubt that the king had cultivated land at his disposal. In studying the terminology we are confronted by the fact that the land the king disposed of, regularly proves to be badly located and under-used.

a. *gizzatu*[28]

The existing literature is unanimous in accepting that the term refers to land which came into royal possession through confiscation. This interpretation is based on occurrences in earlier *kudurrus* where the term clearly indicates some form of reduction of what has been granted, which -in itself- was formally forbidden. As far as I can see a comparable interpretation does not find a firm basis in the occurrences which can be quoted from Neo-Babylonian practical texts. Though *gizzatu* of the king occurs, the term is also associated with gods, where "confiscation" makes little sense, unless a reference to an earlier juridical status remained stuck to certain property, even though it had been regranted. A recollection of a former juridical status in a geographical name, a phenomenon known not only in Babylonia, might also be a possibility. Where private persons or groups of persons are mentioned the land may actually have been confiscated recently. The term occurs already in practical texts from the Chaldean period.

YOS 6, 40, difficult though it is, suggests that land was involved which was granted in the Uruk area in the system of grants practiced in the early Neo-Babylonian period, to which

---

a "practical" context. CAD K p. 593 a knows only of a neighbouring E_2.GIŠ.GU.ZA in 8th Congress 31 (Manaḫtu, 17 IX Art 40).

26 CTMMA 3, 109 11 X Camb 2, mentions, line 7, the king as a neighbour, with another person, just as the *kamru* of the king, line 4, is said to be next to the field, but that seems to be explained as someone's estate (E_2). The date plantation concerned measured 0.1.0, or 1/4 of a ha. The role of the Egibis in the exploitation of palace land has been mentioned.

27 See above note 1.

28 Literature: AHw p. 496R: *kizzatu*, "Vorbehaltsland". What that means is difficult to understand. Is the meaning of the word to be related to "Vorbehaltsgut", i.e. that part of an inheritance which is assigned without restriction to the surviving spouse? Most unlikely. "Land reserved for the king"? CAD G p. 115f. "encroachment on land by royal authority" and "the land thus acquired"; D. Cocquerillat 1968, p. 35: "terres provenant d'empiètement du pouvoir royal", assigned as "fiefs" to meritorious subjects; detailed discussion Van der Spek 1986, p. 95-98: confiscated land (in Uruk, Nippur and Kuta). The term occurs as an element of geographical names already before the coming of the Persians: Dūr-Gizzati, YOS 6 82 (8 x Nbn 7) and cf. also Tamirtu-Gizzati, TÉBR 39 (25 V Camb 2).

also the *ḫanšû*s belonged and in which sanctuaries received shares called (one) *līmu*. The lease includes low quality land. In TÉBR 39 *gizzetu* seems to occur in a geographical name, the possibility of which seems to be confirmed by CT 57, 5 from Sippar and by other names. The grantor will have been the king.

According to TCL 13, 190, the king possibly retained some of this land at Dūr-ša-karābi near Babylon after a *ḫanšû*-type of land division, of which Dar 335, quoted sub *ḫanšû* in Chapter VII preserves the traces. This *gizzatu* constituted clearly the lower, down slope land, away from the source of water, which, in this case, had not been shared out. Whether BE 9, 107 similarly represents the same type of retention could be doubted,[29] *gizzatu* indicates in this text a juridical status differing from that of a bow fief, though it could be leased by the *šaknu* of a *ḫadru*. A certain juridical status will also be intended in BRM 1, 188. A translation "confiscated from PN" could perhaps be considered in these cases, but without much conviction.

I am inclined to consider the possibility that the term *gizzatu*-land refers to some general measure, taken for instance in the period of the (piecemeal) introduction of the "*līmu-ḫanšû* system" near the old towns, which probably required some measure of rescinding of older rights. The following land division would have compensated the owners for lost claims. But such an explanation is not likely for all the occurrences found, certainly not for the persistence of the use of the term into the Hellenistic period.

Uruk

YOS 6 40 23 VI Nbn 3, lease, 3) ... ŠE.NUMUN *šá* ^{d}Bēlet-ša-Uruk *šá* UGU Nār-Šarri E$_2$ *dul-lu ka-sa-al ka-lu-ú* 5) *u ga-bi-bu* give me ... 11) (that land) *šá ul-tu* UGU 1 *lim šá gi-iz-ze-e-tu*$_4$ *šá* ^{LU_2}La-'e-et-u-ú-a 13) *a-di* GARIM-Ḫamar-šá-Ialliqa (excepting ...), etc.

YOS 6 67 14 XI Nbn 4, lease for planting date palms, 3) ...... ŠE.NUMUN *ina gi-iz-ze-tú* 4) *šá* Nār-^{d}Innin *a-ḫi ul-la-'a šá* Nār-Gabadē 5) *qaq-qar šá* ^{d}Bēlet-šá-Uruk.

TÉBR 39 26 V Camb 2, dates, *imittu* on land on 2) Nār-eššu, GARIM-*gi-iz-ze-t*[*i*], 3) next to PN, *makkūr* Inanna of Uruk and Nanāia.

Babylon, Egibi

TCL 13 190 6 II Dar 12, date plantation on the Nār-eššu at Dūr-ša-karābi on the eastern side, furtherest from the canal, next to 8) *gi-iz-za-a-ti šarri*. Identical Dar 321, W, E I 202.

Murašû

BE 9 107 6 VIII Art 41, lease of land belonging to seven bow fiefs and 8) ŠE.NUMUN *gi-iz-ze-e-tú* (identical with line 2: ŠE.NUMUN *gi-iz-ze-e-ti šá* PN) *šá ina* (Āl-)Bīt-rab-uratē, subsumed as PAP 7 ^{GIŠ}BAN *gi-ze-ti* are leased for five years by PN, *šaknu* of the *šūšānu šá* ^{LU_2}*ma-šá-a-ka* to Enlil-šum-iddina.

Hellenistic period

BRM I 188 11 IV SE 125, land *ni-din-tu*$_4$ *šarri šá ina kišad* Nār-Puratti *šá ina gi-iz-za-tu*$_4$ *šá* Bēl-apal-uṣur ^{LU_2}*āšipu* s Bēl-balassu-iqbi.

Sippar, in a geographical name

CT 57 5 19 VI Dar 5, *imittu* dates at Gi-iz-a-ta-šá-^{LU_2}SIPAD.MEŠ *ša* Āl-Šamaš.

b. *makkūr šarri* said of land[30]

As will be noted below under "land of the king", it is notable that royal ownership is explicitly noted down in the direct manner implied by this term in a context which refers to "land held against service obligations". This underlines the fact that the holders were well aware of the fact that they were not the real owners of the land they held. Notable is also the use of the

[29] I find it difficult to accept that BE 9, 107 intends to state that all bow fiefs were "of *gizzatu* type" as CAD G proposes, for in the list of the land included in the lease *gizzatu* only refers to specific plots, not to the fiefs in general. It is not used in apposition to the bow fiefs mentioned in general.

[30] Cf. CAD M/1 p. 136R.

term *bīt ritti* in the same context. We could proceed one step further and consider the possibility that the need to stress the real owner was a result of the fact that service land also could be held on land of other "owners", primarily, of course, the temples.

It is of some importance that in the reign of Darius it was still considered necessary to note down in a routine document that the land used by the *rab banîs* for the production of dates for the table of the gods belonged in reality to the king and the crown prince.

makkūr šarri occurs at least once as an indication of a neighbour in a field plan.[31] and BE 9, 32a, a Murašû text, indicates that it could be leased. For NIG_2.GA LUGAL in connection with *bīt ritti* see Chapter VII. Also Nbn 350, 13 V Nbn 9, quoted under *niditti šarri* in Sippar can be mentioned.

Sippar, private archives

VS 5 55 13 V Camb 7, see under horse fiefs, sub *bīt aspatu*, in next chapter.

Murašû

BE 9 32a 5 V Art 31+, at Bīt-Zēr-līšir, receipt rent land NIG_2.GA LUGAL, mentions Lābâši 2-*ú* ^{LU_2}*mašenni*.

c. *nakkandu/nakkamtu*[32]

nakkandu, or one of the several other variant writings in which the word occurs, indicates land belonging to large estates, those of the king and of the temples in Uruk and Sippar. We assume that texts use the term *nakkandu* intentionally and not as a synonym for, for instance, *makkūru*. In some cases the sum paid as a rent for this land can be regarded as nominal. In YOS 6, 150 the land involved was not intensively cultivated, though the avowed intention of the text was to increase the amount of land under the plough. Even if it was not the most intensively used land belonging to large estates, it could still contain date palms: CT 55, 136, Sippar.[33]

The Monserrat text published by C. Wunsch is perhaps the most informative on the term. The text deals with the registration of measured fields, for a number of which the circumstances surrounding the acquisition by the temple are specified. The third plot is situated next to the, or a, *nakkandu*, presumably that of Bēlet of Uruk, to which land planted with date palms is to be assigned from the plot acquired, after deduction of a specified area already in use with the *rab banîs*, the prebendal date orchard keepers responsible for the provisioning of the divine table. YOS 6, 150 and Monserrat 1 thus suggest for *nakkandu* a meaning "land (belonging to an estate) available for assignation", of which the manner of exploitation, direct or not, could be decided depending on the circumstances. According to An Or 9, 19 a stretch of land in the middle of a/the *nakkandu* in Uruk could have a separate status, which, incidentally supports the idea that the word represents a kind of reserve, from which the area with the best soil quality would be used first.

A meaning "land held in reserve" thus suggests itself: land which the owner decidedly wanted to be exploited or to be exploited more intensively. It is at any rate not a term for "land without an owner which is attributed to the king". In Marduk-rēmanni 88 land from the royal *nakkandu* is incorporated in a complete hierarchy of leases.

---

31 K.R. Nemet-Nejat, Late Babylonian Field Plans in the British Museum, Rome, 1982, no. 1, "Achaemenid period".

32 CAD N/1 p 184, Cocquerillat 1968 p. 20-1 note 38; Stolper 1985 p 90. Possibly *nak* LUGAL in ROMCT II 9, 18 IX Camb 2 is short for *nak(kandu) šarri*. So already Jursa 1995 p. 144, note 291.

33 In Sippar we always must reckon with the possibility that a term with geographical connotations indicates a specific locality, compare the pertinent remark under Nidinit-Šarri.

Nippur

BE 8 13 15 I Nbk 28, 1) *i-mit-ti ša* ŠE.BAR *šá nak-kan-du šarri.*

Uruk

YOS 6 150 20 x Nbn 11, 11) ... ŠE.NUMUN E_2 *me-ri-šú nak-kan-du ša* ^{d}Bēlet-ša-Uruk 12) *šá ina pa-ni-šú* ŠE.NUMUN *ma-la ib-bal-lak-ki-tu ina* ^{GIŠ}APIN.ME *šá ina pa-ni-šú ina lìb-bi er-ri-šú* 13) ŠE.NUMUN *ma-la* ŠE.NUMUN *ul-tu* ŠE.NUMUN *šá ina pa-ni-šú a-na nak-kan-du šá* ^{d}Bēlet-ša-Uruk 14) [*ú-maš-*]*šar ù* ŠE.NUMUN.$AM_3$2 lim 81 GUR *nak-kan-du pi-i šul-pu* 15) [*ša ana*] ^{GIŠ}BAN_2-*šú at-ru* (will be tilled by *errēšus*).

Monserrat 1[34] (after Nbn 13), list of measured orchards and fields which had become temple property for various reasons, of these the third (on two sides, 10'-11'), is next to (the/a) *nak-kan-du*; 13') *napḫar* 167.3.4 3 $SILA_3$ of land *ina libbi* 24.1.0 ŠE.NUMUN *zaq-pi* ŠE.NUMUN *šá* ^{LU_2}GAL.DU_3.ME 14') *ina libbi ṣab-tu a-na a-ma-ri re-ḫe-et* ŠE.NUMUN *zaq-pi a-na nak-kan-du ana ša-ṭa-ri,* "in total 167.3.4.3 land, of which 24.1 planted with date palms, of which the *rab banî* have the use, for review, the remainder of the land planted with trees to be added to the *nakkandu*, for registration".

AnOr 9 19 no date, includes various stretches of land bordering on *nak-kan-du*; the first is in the *līmu šá* GARIM-Ḫarratu on the Nār-Ḫarratu and the (Nār)-Takkiru next to the/a *nak-kan-du* and Bāb-ḫiltu and the *maḫīṣu*, on which the next parcel borders; there follow passages on date plantations, mentioning both their size and the number of trees; 34) deals with land indicated as 35) *ši-i-ḫi šá* $ŠU^{II}$-*nu* GAL-i; 39) *li-i-mu šà* Ḫulḫulli, (identical with?) 45) ŠE.NUMUN *šá* E_2 ^{d}Nabû, on the two long sides, lines 39-40 next to *nak-kan-du* and with a short side of notably 1100 cubits[35] on the Euphrates and next to the *maḫīṣu*; line 46 deals with a parcel which has at any rate two sides on a *nak-kan-du*, and lines 47-51 seem to mention a parcel completely enclosed by *nak-kan-du*, but perhaps the text is not fully understandable here; in 47 we find the remark : *ši-i-mu šá* KI.LAM *ina* E_2-A-muk-a-nu, which is partially planted with date trees; follows another parcel 57) *qaq-qar šá ina ši-i-ḫu šà* GARIM-šá-Killatu also bordering on *nak-kan-du*, cf. also line 62.

Sippar

Administrative

CT 55 136 x+2 XI Nbn 14, PN ^{LU_2}GU_2.GAL *iq-bu-ú* 4) *um-ma* ŠE.NUMUN x ^{GIŠ}GIŠIMMAR *na-kan-du šarri ša* PN *a-na* (context vitually lost);

CT 55 83 (late Darius), request to authorities of Ebabbar for lease of arable 4) .... E_2 *na-an-kan-du ina* E_2-Miṣirāia, follows description of situation. (The rent proposed is difficult to assess, but as to the amount of barley decidedly nominal, possibly the land was leased especially for the (summer) cultivation of sesame.)[36]

Marduk-rēmanni[37]

M.r. 9 25 I Camb 7, two parcels of 15 kor of land respectively *ina ḫu-ú-pu* and *ina ḫa-am-ma-šá-*tu_4, total 30 kor 3)... *ina* ŠE.NUMUN *nak-ka-du* LUGAL at the disposal of two persons, representatives of the *šanû* of the *mašennu*, leased by Bēl-muballiṭ s Iqīša Ṣāḫit-sattukki, is leased on by him for joint exploitation. The two partners will pay9) ... *a-ḫi* ḪA.LA *gi-mir* 10) *u na-sa-ḫi* to the representatives, plus another damaged clause. (BM 74487)

M.r. 88 26 V Dar 14, lease given by Marduk-rēmanni as *errēšu* to two persons of 30 kor land *šá nak-ka-du* LUGAL *šá* (Al)Bar-tibni/Barinnu(?), belonging to the rentfarm of PN, the rent farmer of the *ḫa-za-*tu_4, the *bīt rittis* of several persons separately and jointly; various stipulations, *zitti šarri* payable by M.r. (BM 74622)

Murašû

Ist 9 15 XII Art 35, see below under policies.

---

34 C. Wunsch, Aula Orientalis 15, 1997, p. 141ff.

35 This 1100 could represent the "1000" of a temple, compared to the one of the palace, which actually measured 1000 cubits.

36 Edited Jursa 1995 p. 144.

37 Texts published Waerzeggers 2001.

BE 10 43 15 VI Dar II 1, see below under *perku*.

PBS 2/1 31 29 x Dar II 1, promised delivery of dates by a member of the Ḫadru-ša-maqtūte in Āl-ša-Maqtūte, bow land on Ḫarri-Piqudu in Āl-ša-Maqtūte next to ŠE.NUMUN *nak-kan-du šarri* pledge.

PBS 2/1 123 22 VIII Dar II 6, PN servant of Ribat and [PN] address Ribat and another servant of Rēmūt-Ninurta for the lease of 4) ŠE.NUMUN.MEŠ *šá nak-am-du šá a-na sūti la-pa-ni* Rēmūt-Ninurta 5) *[ku]l-la-tu-nu*, with trained oxen, tools and seed, fragmentary.

Later, Nippur:

TCL 13 203 10+ VI Art II 2, division of bow fief for 14 yrs, 15) ... *a-di* ŠE.NUMUN *nak-kan₂-du šarri.*

d. *niditti šarri*[38]

BE 9, 99 and its parallel Ist 31 are clear catch-all attempts to list the various types of juridical status pertaining to land, as the real situation of the orchards involved is of little importance in an internal lease contract of the Murašûs. This suggests that the place of *niditti šarri* in a scala of possibilities is somewhere between bow land, which is land held against service, and bought land, which is probably intended to represent unencumbered property, *bīt maškanu* being, of course, land held only as a pledge.

Also because in several cases, e.g. OECT 10, 192 and BE 9, 102, the holder is clearly an official of some sort, *nidittu šarri* will be the appropriation put at the disposal of the beneficiary for the length of his tenure at the king's pleasure.[39] In Sippar Nidinti-Šarri is (almost?) a geographical name, but that would represent a gift to a god, which could not be reclaimed so easily.[40] The term is used for a dilapidated house in Babylon in BM 54205[41] and Kelsey 89490.[42]

Uruk, private

TCL 12 38 25 III Nbk 22, 3 *me qaq-qar šá ina lìb-bi ina ni-din-tú šarri* PN1 s PN2 *a-na muḫ-ḫi* PN3 *na-šu-u₂*.

Kiš, Mušallim-Bēl s Nidintu file

OECT 10 192 15 II Art 14, date *imittu* land *ni-din-tu₄ šarri ša* PN ^{LU_2}*se-pi-ri.*

Murašû

BE 9 99 4 VII Art 41, internal lease of E₂ ^{GIŠ}*ga-pan* E₂ ^{GIŠ}GIŠIMMAR E₂ ^{GIŠ}BAN *ni-din-tú šarri ma-ḫi-ri kaspi* E₂ *maš-ka-nu* from the border of Šalame to the border of Bīt-Galalānu leased to slave (IR₃) by Enlil-šum-iddina for three years *ana nukarribūtu*; he will enjoy the yield of the secondary cultures and deliver *imittu* on the dates. He will receive *sissinnu* even if there is

---

38 CAD N/2 p. 207: royal property, (an income due to the crown), regularly written *nidintu šarri*. Only clear cases referring to land are listed. Stolper, 1985 p. 129 *ad* BE 9, 102 “royal grant”; much late Achaemenid material is collected by Stolper Iraq 54 p. 126, "crown grant", *ad* OECT 12, AB 243, at Dilbat, with the remark (note 11) that the holders often are Persian officials. The mechanism through which the land is exploited fits the concept "appropriation" well. M. Jursa, 1995, p. 121 note 235 on the (geographical) ambiguity of the expression.

39 This is a situation comparable to that of Old Babylonian Mari office holders described by F. van Koppen in his unpublished master’s thesis.

40 Jursa's solution 1995 p. 252 "Geschenk des Königs" in the index of place names, see especially p. 174L and p. 223L. In Nbn 350 the ENGARs will not be a gift of the king, the term is used to indicate a locality. In Sippar the administrative texts are sparing with the use of the determinative URU before localities in the country side. That is probably the reason why such localities in the Sippar area are underrepresented in RGTC 8. The gap is filled more or less by Jursa 1995 p. 251-2.

41 8 VII Art 12 (according to M.W. Stolper, Iraq 54, 1985, p.126.) W. Eilers, Iranische Beamtennamen in der keilschriftlichen Überlieferung, Leipzig, 1940, Plate 3, where line 2 still has *ni-din-t[u4 šarri]*.

42 M.W. Stolper, Iraq 54, 1985 p.136-9, line 2, (8 II "Art" 37), a building plot.

no *imittu*. Clauses on work to be done, and a 30 mina fine on not doing work. Cf. Ist 31, same day and scribe.

BE 9 102 16 VII Art 41, see below under "Policies".

Hellenistic period

BRM I 188 11 IV SE 125, quoted above under *gizzatu*.

Nidinit/Nidintu-Šarri in Sippar: a locality

Nbn 350 13 V Nbn 9, 20) 250 kor (of barley) *šá* ^{LU}2ENGAR.MEŠ 21) Ni-din-it-Šarri at the disposal of [PN1 and/s? 22) PN2 *ina* E_2.NIG_2.GA.LUGAL

BM 74439 26 XII Nbn 16, (Jursa 1995 p. 133) land NIG_2.GA ^{d}UTU Ni-din-it-tu_4-šarri on the Nār-Ḫabūru, a vineyard of 0.2.2 is leased for 13 yrs.

e. *piḫat šarri*[43]

The particular meaning of this term for land in connection with ownership by the king escapes me. It occurs with certainty in an Egibi document dealing with land on both sides of the Nār-Eššu, Northwest of Babylon.[44] The term does not seem to return in a recognisable manner in other documents from the Egibi archive dealing with the same general area, though TCL 13, 190, quoted under *gizzatu*, concerning a different date plantation in the same area, mentions *gizzeti šarri*, on its eastern side, also away from the canal. In 5 R 67 the field sold extends on both sides of the Nār-Eššu, a *makallû* is probably in general a lower, down levee, demarcation of a field, in this case occurring on both sides of the Nār-Eššu. As C. Wunsch suggests the *piḫat šarri* can be situated beyond, on one of them. This implies that the term *piḫat šarri* possibly refers here to the juridical status of (unattractive) land not used in the land division scheme.[45]

Babylon Egibi

5 R 67, 1 8 XI Ner 0, date plantation, arable and freshly broken land on both sides of the Nār-Eššu outside the Enlil-Gate at Babylon, with the short upper northern side next to 11) .... $A.ŠA_3$ *pi-ḫa-at šarri*, and the southern, lower, side on 12) ... *ma-kal-lu-ú ša* 50.MEŠ-*e*, bought by Nabû-aḫḫē-iddina s Šulā Egibi from members of the Eṭeru family. (=W, E I no. 6)

f. *uzbāra* (of king and queen)[46]

I know of no occurrences earlier than the Murašû archive, where virtually all references can be found, though this is hardly significant since the word is obviously Persian in origin, with

---

43 For the use of NAM, *pīḫātu*, as a characterisation of the status of land cf. the remark above on ownerless land. The king disposed of it. EN.NAM can possibly be used in an estate context, cf. below under "land *ša šarri*", possibly Nbk 115. Cf. also the remarks on the EN.NAM in the discussion here, in Chapter II note 31.

44 Discussed Wunsch, 2000, I, p. 71. All relevant documents can be found Wunsch 2000 II nos. 5ff. It is restored in no. 5 [6'] ff. She translates *pīḫāt šarri* by "königliche Domäne", with which one can agree broadly, but does not discuss the matter.

45 I do not regard a term like *raqqatu ša šarri* as indicating a similar primarily juridical status: Bertin 3043, BM 41511 line 17, small plot bordering on *raq-qa-tu_4 šá šarri*, cf. Nbn 193, 25 VI Nbn 5, line 4, Nbn 178, 6 XII Nbn 5 *raq-qa-tu_4 šá kišad* Puratti, with Nbn 203, 6 X Nbn 5 :16-7 all in the same area. (See Wunsch E I nos. 48-51. There are several *raqqatu*'s of Šamaš. If *raqqatu* is a general term for marshy land on the bank of a river, so the flood plain in a narrow sense, it should be noted that much labour is spent on (the) *raqqatu*(s) of Šamaš, whereas it might be expected that regularly flooded land was preferably left alone.

46 Literature: Stolper 1985 p. 42; p. 127 translates "crown land". Many of the texts are badly preserved, but reconstruction is often possible by comparing the request and the grant passages in contracts of the Zweigespräch-type. What derives from which section is not indicated in detail here, the reader is referred to the reconstructions of the original edition in, especially, Stolper 1985.

a plausible Persian etymology. The question is thus whether there is a native Babylonian term that was (partially?) replaced by this designation, or whether this represents something really new introduced by the later Achaemenids. That would be the case if this were land with a specific status, for instance being subject to special duties.

The word *uzbāru* is generally reserved for land of the king, but BE 9, 28 (and possibly EE 1?) refer to a consort, in which case the term to all likelihood indicates land that was transferred by the king. In EE 11 the *uzbāru* land is held by Aršam, who also belonged to the immediate royal entourage. Where *uzbāru* land on its own is an element of a lease, a source of water is indicated, for which there may have been a special reason. Receipts and texts mentioning *uzbāru* as a neighbouring parcel do not contribute much to our understanding. An occasional very low rent paid by the Murašûs could be suggestive, especially as comparable low rents occur on all forms of royal land: tenants were sought for all these types of land in the hands of the king, though in BE 9, 67 it is explicitly excepted from the sub-lease. It can also be leased separately: EE 1, where it is located in the tail end section of a canal, but draws water from another.

"Crown land" is hardly a Persian invention, *uzbāru* land is certainly not land incorporated in the "land for service" system, though that too was subjected to payments to the king. It probably incorporates, but has not entirely superseded, land indicated by the other terms already studied here. Use of the term can possibly be seen as an attempt at simplification of the terminology. It is perhaps another catch-all expression, possibly, as a Persian term, that used by the administration. The ^{LU_2}*uz-ba-ri* of EE 1 is notable and possibly problematic.

Murašû

EE 2 5 V [Art 24], lease of Nār-Bēl (identical with the Nār-Sakiri) and Nār-ša-Mušezib-Bēl by Enlil-šum-iddina from Iadiama s Banaiama with(out?) x and its *uzbāra*, for 200 kor and additionals, delivery of rent in (Āl) Bīt-x.

BE 9 28 18 VII Art 31, (// TuM 2/3 179) receipt of rent 1) .... *uz-ba-ra ša* E_2 MI_2-*ša*-E_2.GAL at Baṣṣanu and (Āl-)Parakku, *usalla* on Ḫarri-Piqudu, at (Āl) Bannišú, at (Āl) Ḫidu'a, excepting the bow fiefs. (The same land in Ist 2, date lost.)

EE 1 25 x Art [34], Enlil-šum-iddina s Murašû requests the lease of land 3) ... ŠE.NUMUN ^{LU_2}*uz-ba-ri šá* [*šarri u ṣi-bit-tu*$_4$ *šá šarri*] 4) *ša ina ši-li-iḫ-tu*$_4$ *ša* Nār-Badiāti *ša* [Amisiri], mentions water of the king and Amisiri drawn from Ḫarri-Piqudu. The rent is nominal: half a kor of barley for a kor of land.

BE 9 67 28 VII Art 39, (// EE 29) request by two persons for the lease of Nār-Dirat, the right and left banks from its intake to its tail, as far as the water reaches 3) .... E_2 *rit-ti-ka u* E_2 *maš-ka-na-ti-ki šá ina lib*$_3$*-bi e-lat uz-ba-ri šá šarri* for a mixed rent of 800 kor.

EE 11 10 III Art 40, request by a group of (5+) persons addressed to Enlil-šum-iddina for the lease of land of Aršam, 4) ..... ŠE.NUMUN KA *šul-pu uz-ba-ri* 5) *šá* Nār-Simmagir, land of Itti-Šamaš-balāṭu, land of Malaḫānu, land KU UD DA AM ḪU(?) in the Tamirtu-ša-Ḫumāia *u* Ḫuṣṣētu-ša-Zaruttu from ? to *kālû* Bīt-Kīki plus the *bīt ritti* of DUMU.MEŠ Ḫ-š-Z, within a circumscribed area, ending with land E_2 [*rit*]-*ti šá* DUMU.[MEŠ] *šá* Ḫ-šá-Z, plus oxen, tools and seed; lease granted without repetition of the area concerned; delivery of rent on the Nār-Sin, at least 1418+ kor.

EE 14 25 VII Art 40, cf. below under "Policies".

BE 9 73 16 XIIb Art 40, sesame *zitti šarri ša ina uz-ba-ri šarri ša ina muḫ-ḫi* Nār-Šarri, receipt.

EE 118 16 x [Art] 41, [lease?] date orchards on Nār-Sin at Til-Ḫurdu, land belonging to at least two other persons and 4) *uz-ba-ri šá šarri*, remainder lost.

BE 10 32 24 IV Dar II 1, promise to deliver dates, Ḫadru-ša-Ustaribarra in Bīt-Arza, bow land on Nār-Purat-Nippur next to 10) ŠE.NUMUN *šá* ^{LU_2}*ga-ar-du* and to 10) *uz-bar-ra šá* [*šarri*] pledged.

BE 10 31 26 IV Dar II 1, promise to deliver dates by members of Ḫadru-Bīt-mār-šarri in Ḫuṣṣēti-ša-Babu-ēreš, bow land on Nār-Šum-ukīn in Ḫarri-ša-Babu-ereš pledged next to ŠE.NUMUN *uz-bar-ra šarri.*

TuM 2/3 147 17 VII Dar II 4, see above, under rights to water with *ṣibitti ša šarri.*

EE 2 [x x Dar II] 5, lease given by Ribat, mentions 6) 6 ... *uz-bar-ra šarri*, context lost.

PBS 2/1 150 19 III Dar II 6, lease, fragmentary, includes land in Bīt-Dibin *uz-bar-ra ša šarri* on Nār-ša-Addu-aba-uṣur with oxen, tools and seed.

PBS 2/1 124 2 X Dar II 6, lease arable on Nār-Ṭupsar-Ekalli, 2) *uz-bar-ra šá šarri* in Āl-ša-Ab-ba-a-a (=Ar-ba-a-a?) at the disposal of Ribat given *ana errēšūtu* to PN for 1/3 of the yield.

EE 25 (date lost), request 2') ... A.MEŠ *ṣi-bit-tu*$_4$ *š[á šarri ša ina* ?] 8') *u* ŠE.NUMUN *uz-bar-ra ša muḫ-ḫi* ... granted by Enlil-šum-iddina; rent 800 kor excepting that resulting from another lease.

Ist 27 (date lost), fragment, lease *uz-bar-ra šá ina mi-ṣ[ir*] below Til-Gurdia; includes rights to water.

Nippur, Late Achaemenid

EAH 214, 5 VII Dar II 3, land , arable 1) ... *uz-ba-ra šá kišad* Nār-Sin *u* Nār-Balāṭu PN1 s PN2 2) and PN3 s PN4 DUMU.MEŠ ^{LU_2}ENGAR.MEŠ *šá šarri* at the disposal of PN5 4) ^{LU_2}NAM I$_7$.ḪA$_2$ *ki-i* KA *šá* PN6(?) *a-na* ^{LU_2}ENGAR-*ú-tu a-na* PN7 5) s PN8 *id-din-'u pu-ut* G U$_4$ ŠE.NUMUN *u ru-ub-bu-ú* 6) PN7 *na-ši pu-ut la pa-qa-ri šá* A.ŠA$_3$ MU.MEŠ 7) [*la se*]-*ke-ri šá* I$_7$ PN1 *ù* PN3 *na-šu-u*; (11) *lib*$_3$-*bu-u* KUR 12) 3 GUR ŠE.BAR *ana nis*(!)-*ḫu i-nam-diš-šú-nu-tú*); (Stolper suggests the reconstruction *libbû nisḫi ša māti,* see below, Chapter VI)). (JCS 40, 1988,144f.)

g. Land "of the king", *ša šarri*

Land belonging to the king without further specification, with or without ordinary *ša*, occasionally actually held in some quality by an ordinary subject, is rare in Neo-Babylonian texts, though a few cases from Babylon, Sippar and Ur and the Murašû archive can be quoted.[47] The exchange of land published in RA 83 mentions simply "land of Nebuchadnezzar, king of Babylon", obviously in an area where there had been a land division, at Burbissu, in which of those recognisable also the Simmagir had participated.[48] We must assume that for some reason or another directly exploited royal estates, perhaps land *ša ekalli*, is severely underrepresented in the documentation. The interest of the Ur text is perhaps that it again recognises land for service holdings explicitly as belonging ultimately to the king. Also Nbk 115 is notable because it concerns the granting of a perpetual lease for the planting of a date orchard on royal land.[49] The copy of the text is rather difficult to use.

ŠE.NUMUN *ša šarri*, "land of the king" is strikingly rare, but it existed. The Uruk text YOS 7, 156 (4 XI Camb 3) in which people are engaged to guard against wild donkeys mentions land of Bēlet of Uruk, Šamaš, *ša šarri*, "of the king" and *šá* ^{LU_2}BAN, "of the bowmen", Such land occurs also in CBS 5316 together with land belonging to the ^{LU_2}*gardu* on the Nār-Kasal.

Babylon, Egibi related?

Nbk 115 29 VI Nbk 18, at Ḫuṣṣētu-ša-Ḫaḫḫuru. Arrangement between Šulā s Nabû-gāmil Egibi and Ḫaḫḫuru s Nadnā servant of Zēria, ^{LU_2}EN.NAM of Bīt-x-gal (or E$_2$.GAL!?)

---

[47] On the Sippar text see the note in the section on the status of the large estates in the next chapter. Cf. also note 45, above, on *raqqat šarri.*

[48] F. Bruschweiler, RA 83, 1989, p.153ff., cf. also under *ḫanšû.*

[49] This "Reedhut-of-Ḫaḫḫuru" developed into Bīt-Ḫaḫḫuru and Āl-Bīt-Ḫaḫḫuru, the geographical name thus suggesting some success of the royal development policy.

concerning 0.1.0 ŠE.NUMUN *ša šarri* on ^I7^Ḫarri-ša-Lāḫišu on which a date plantation is to be planted. No time limit. Proceeds to be shared with the king?

Sippar

Šangû-Šamaš

BM 42371 27 VI Dar 23, ^GIŠ^GIŠIMMAR *ze-qé-pi ša* A.ŠA$_3$.MEŠ LUGAL [*u*] A.ŠA$_3$.MEŠ *ša* ^LU2^DUMU.LUGAL *šá i-na li-mi-tu$_4$* UD.KIB.NUN^KI *ša ina* MU.AN.NA ^LU2^GAL.DU$_3$.MEŠ *ša* ^d^UTU *a-na nap-ta-nu ša* ^d^UTU *i-zaq-qa-pi-'u* (context lost).

Administrative

BM 50505[50] (Nbk?), measurements of three parcels in the hands of Šulā s Šāpik-zēri and brothers fam. Rab-banî; respectively next to A.ŠA$_3$ *ša* LUGAL (lines 5 and 19) and to the Euphrates.

BM 75502[51] Nbn 12, uncollected *ešrû* 4) *šá bīt ritti* PN 5) *šá ina* ŠU^II^ PN2, parcels 1 and 2 amount of barley *šá* PN *šá* E$_2$ *re-du-tu* E$_2$ (^LU2^)BAN (*ina muḫḫi* PN), amount of barley *ešrû ul iddin*, or variant; parcels 3 to 9: amount of barley *ša* PN *šá ina lìb-bi šá* LUGAL *i-re-eš*, "who cultivates (land) in that of the king", amount of barley *ešrûšu ul iddin*.

Ur

UET 4 194 5 X Art I 39, statement by Nidintu-Sin, son of ^f^Taštibi, an *atkuppu*, to descendants of the Gallābu family 9) *mim-ma* ḪA.LA-*šú ina* ŠE.NUMUN 10) *zaq-<pu> pi-i šul-pu šá šarri ù* 11) *mim-ma-ku-nu šá e-lat šá šarri ana ma-la* 12) ḪA.LA-*ku-nu šá it-ti* ŠEŠ.MEŠ-*ku-nu* 14) *ù* ^LU2^EN.MEŠ.BAN-*ku-nu a-di u$_4$-mu* 15) *ṣa-a-ta it-ti-ku-nu ia-a-nu:* "Forever I hold no share whatsoever with you in orchards or arable belonging to the king or whatever else you hold over and above what belongs to the king, which you share with your partners and co-owners of bow fiefs. (Follows the waiving of all future claims and court procedures by the other party.)[52]

Murašû

CBS 5316[53] 30 III Art 31, lease from Enlil-šum-iddina by a slave of land on Nār-Kasal, including ŠE.NUMUN *šá* LUGAL *u šá* ^LU2^*ga-ar-du*, excepting that irrigated by hand on Nār-Kasal and Nār-Sa'idu, with plough and seed for three years for an *ebur,* (lit. "harvest") of 400 kor, no additionals.

3. Land and the subject

Not only land and water but also personnel constitutes an essential means of production, all the more so because there are signs that there was a shortage in this respect in the Neo-Babylonian period, at any rate in the institutions.

There is no need to discuss a word like *širku*, it applies to many inhabitants of the estates of the gods. The term indicates a juridical status which obviously was hereditary and tied the person concerned to the sanctuary to which he, she or their ancestors had been given. People with this status certainly belonged to a labour force which could be employed wherever required. They worked the land, were herdsmen, could be put at the disposal of the king for military or civil service, could be craftsmen and sometimes played important administrative and commercial roles. The problem for the institutions was, however, that this commodity was in short supply. Individually, certain of these people could exercise a considerable influence, especially the rent farm system created fresh opportunities for them, but they were and remained unfree. The rent farm system also put groups of these people at the disposal of the rent farmers, one of whose prime tasks was to find additional labour. Here the important point is that the

---

50 Jursa 1995 no. 12, p. 60.

51 Jursa 1998 no. 2, p. 102f., cf. p. 11.

52 The backgrounds of the case remain unexplained. In view of the fact that the (former) claimant is called explicitly the son of a named woman, it may be surmised that at issue is the status of the relation between the father of the Gallābu brothers involved and the mother of the person who relinquishes the claims.

53 Stolper JCS 53 no. 6

divine estates had a subject rural labour force, obviously living in the villages where the administrative texts locate the plough teams.

We can assume, but only provide limited proof, that if rights to other estates, including those of the king, were leased, the subject population of these estates, whatever their juridical status, was also included in the lease. These people remain practically invisible. They will have belonged at least in part to the *arad šarrūti* who could not be sold or bought by private persons. Sellers of slaves had to guarantee that the person sold did not belong to this category of people.[54] But such persons do not actually appear in the texts available. Xenophon relates that there were villages on the estates of Parysatis; they were, no doubt, part of the royal grant to her, but they could not be disposed of arbitrarily.[55] All the bigger royal grants will have included rights over the people living on the land included in it.

We can equally assume that such a fact applies at least down to the level of the chariot fief. This must have had a more complicated structure than that required for the provision of a simple chariot with its equipment and immediate crew. We must probably accept that the ordinary bowman worked his own land. But even that is no absolute certainty, nor does it of necessity apply in all instances. If the members of *ḫadru*s were, on principle, obliged to serve as bowmen, and were made land holders especially for that purpose, some of them had to fulfil other regular occupations, with the land no doubt also serving for (a part) of their regular remuneration for that function. Some of these lower fief holders cannot have combined regular agriculture with the occupation which lay at the basis of their holding the land and these persons may have been granted workers. We can not expect that all holders of a bow fief received a holding of equal size, at least occasionally it will have been sufficiently large to accommodate the agricultural labour required. This will certainly have been the case with people like scribes and "merchants".[56]

The Murašû archive[57] contains many texts about the stocking of specific parcels of land, some contracts even restrict themselves to making available stock, draught animals and seed, notable in its variety. Such contracts were thus part of a "policy" intended to diversify what was produced. But there are only a few marginal remarks on the essential people who worked this land. It is too simple to conclude that granting the lease of a team of oxen automatically implied that of a crew to go with it. The Murašû text EE 27 stands apart in that it explicitly states that the lease is given "without oxen or plough men": was that the normal situation, or the other way round? Inclusion of people may have been common, but doubts will linger.

One of the more intriguing aspects of the Murašû texts is therefore that of their hold on people. The other (private) archives of substance are socially not at a level which can provide relevant information. The rare information on people contained in the Murašû texts is therefore not generally valid for the late Achaemenid period. The earlier tenants of the Egibis were different people, often using family names. It can be assumed that they had an urban background.[58] There is the possibility that, (like, for instance those coming from the Ur III Umma administration,) the documents are generally so concerned with the land and its products that the villages with the workers and plough teams, which constitute an essential element of the production apparatus, disappear from view. If that were true the estates and the *ḫadru*s from which the Murašûs leased their land must have leased their labour force together with the land. This is not in itself impossible, but it hardly goes without saying. The Uruk rent farm documents

---

[54] For full examples of these clauses cf. F. Joannès 1982 p. 26.

[55] Anabasis II 4: 27.

[56] Cf. the list of *ḫadru*s provided by Stolper 1985, p. 75-79.

[57] We must not discuss again the restricted background of the available Murašū texts.

[58] These tenants are listed conveniently in Wunsch 2000b, Band I, p. 54-8.

indicate that labour itself was a problem, but though it was scarce, as far as available, it went with the lease.

It is their hold on people which provided the Murašûs, and those underlings who acted for them, with the labour required for the undertaking of the leases we find in the archive. We can assume, on account of the information available, that there is not just one reason for this grip on people, there is a complex of circumstances which applies to individuals in a varying manner. We can simply note that in a lease, EE 14, the sub-lessee, the frequently occurring servant (IR_3) Ribat is promised that two villages will only do plough work for him and not for others, but that is to all likelihood only valid as far as the head of the firm is concerned, it need not be true in an absolute manner.[59] We could assume that this isolated piece of information refers to standard practice, but that in this case the sub-lessee wanted to take no risks, for the size of this contract is considerable.

There are a few documents in the Murašû archive registering the selling and buying of slaves, but this is purely incidental, it does not explain the availability of an agricultural labour force.[60] The term IR_3 probably implies absence of freedom, in the sense that the person in question could be sold, that is probably a lower status than that of the institutional *širku*, but some IR_3s, as has been noted before, were practically entrepreneurs in their own right, though others were ploughmen or gardeners. But is that the ordinary labour force? The Murašû *nukarribūtu* contracts are perhaps of some importance here and the fact that contracts were made out at this humble level is in itself notable.

The question is thus: what do we know about the rural population in general? The subject has already been touched upon when the tasks of the *gugallu* were discussed, and it was suggested that he was primarily a kind of estate manager or bailiff, who could be an inhabitant of the village where he exercised his function. Alternatively he could belong to the prebendal families, in which case we must regard him as belonging potentially to the entrepreneurs to which also the rent farmers can be reckoned, with whose tasks those of the *gugallu* will have blended up to a degree.

A number of terms requires discussion. We must not expect that their use was restricted to the countryside, but they do also occur in a rural context. The texts illustrating the role of the *gugallu* mention the *aššābu*, here probably "the ordinary villager", who belongs to the estate, i.e. is on temple estates comparable to a *širku*, who was subjected to its authority. Relevant is perhaps also *itbāru* as it is a status or situation in which the most essential element of the village population, the adult members of the plough teams, found themselves. The word seems to be used only in an agrarian context where it indicates an adult worker, the meaning in literary texts is much less circumscribed. Another relevant, but problematic, term is *šūšānu*, which is in slave sales a status which makes the acquisition of the person concerned undesirable, but which, on the other hand, occurs in the names of various *ḫadru*s in the Murašû countryside and is also a kind of worker who can be made available. In the name of one *ḫadru* we find the "occupation" *ēpiš ṭīṭi*, this is, as Stolper has seen, in the Hellenistic period clearly an indication for one of the lower, unfree social categories. In a similar context we must probably place the *gardu*, who, as a

[59] There are some other snippets of information. First the Istanbul fragment 67, published by F. Joannès in Anatolica 14, where not only the habitual oxen and tools are made available but also two ploughmen: 3) 4 GU_4.MEŠ 2 ^{LU_2}ENGAR *u ú-nu-tú*. Cf. also BE 9, 80, 4 IX Art 40, 1) ŠE.UD.E.NE *ḫar-pu u up-pu-lu* ...... 4) ... *šá* I_7.MEŠ-*šú 5) šá* ^{GIŠ}APIN.MEŠ-*šú u er-re-šú*.MEŠ *šá ina* ^{I_7}Ḫarri-Piqudu which have been registered, are receipted by the *ša muḫḫi sūti* of the Ḫarri-Piqudu and Nār-Sūru.

[60] These people are probably primarily house personnel, as is the cook in PBS 2/1, 65; Ist 104 can be classified not as an investment, but as being of a consumptive nature: female singers, though one never knows, "singer" is after all an euphemism and a brothel an investment.

document from Egypt indicates, could be branded with the name of the owner, as slaves or *širku*'s were.

There also are the indications that a certain layer of society, to which the principal Murašûs belonged, had a personal following, which was perhaps seen with a certain apprehension by outsiders: ^{LU_2}DUMU.MEŠ E_2.MEŠ-*ka* ^{LU_2}*a-lik na-áš-par-ti-ka u* ^{LU_2}IR_3.MEŠ-ka,[61] which has in this context a distinctly unfavourable catch-all collective meaning which is difficult to translate: "your *familia*,[62] your men of all jobs and your slaves", in short "your henchmen".[63] Strong-armed tactics are clearly the background of a number of preserved court documents. In several Murašû texts the request by one individual to another "to assume his *perku*" also indicates that for a group of persons protection from a socially stronger person was desirable.[64] The patron was not necessarily the master himself, his subordinates could also fulfil the role, but it is significant that the relevant documents were sometimes kept in the archive of the head of the firm. Accepting patronage, as one text formulates it, being someone's *ṣāb qatē*, was a feature of this society, and it provided a hold on people. I do not expect that this in our eyes "unhealthy" aspect of patronage was typical for the later Achaemenid period, only when information about a comparable social level in the earlier phases of the period becomes available we will know for certain. The role of the entourage of Neriglissar in the early phases of the Babylon Egibi archive is comparable and there too we find the accompanying signs of high-handedness.[65]

There can be little doubt that indebtedness played a considerable role in the relation of, for instance, the Murašûs and those who were dependent on them. They will in no way have been unique, the phenomenon is general in the Ancient Near East. It can be traced back on a considerable scale at least to the Ur III period, but it will not have been an invention of this period: rural credit is a problem and people fail to fulfil their rent and taxation obligations. The Murašûs were certainly not the only ones to distrain such people, about which we are only

---

61 Stolper 1985 p. 20ff.

62 A translation "side kicks" is too familiar, but these are the unspecified people around when one visits a person of status. We will not discuss the status of royal and palatial *mār bītis* in general, they were, or are supposed to have been, (some of?) the male members of the royal family.

63 Sometimes the order of the terms changes, but not the innuendo. In BE 9, 69 (4 XII Art 39) 2-3 they are the supporters of an unfriendly brother of the plaintiff. Their action is rectified by Enlil-šum-iddina, whose degree of involvement is unclear, everybody accepting the suggestion or fiction that he was not really involved. Possibly more serious is the very damaged Ist 105, with EE 109, as it will relate to the uncertain situation surrounding the succession after the death of Artaxerxes I, where the same list of hangers-on is given in different order, complemented by "the Nippurians". Stolper suggests that the claim was bought off by Enlil-šum-iddina. A third case is BE 10, 9, 16 I Dar II 1, a date which in itself suggests an aftermath of a situation of comparative lawlessness, where the same followers are again expanded with "the Nippurians" and accused, with Enlil-šum-iddina at their head, of having illegally taken silver from a "town" and of having broken (*ta-aḫ-ti-pi*) into another and having removed all sorts of assets from still another and its neighbourhood. Though the action is denied, pursuit of the matter is bought off by a hefty payment. Having this type of following makes the use of force possible. We find these people also in PBS 2/1, 140, x X Dar II 7, where the Murašûs are bound over to halt a certain type of behaviour, cf. below *pirku*. The Murašûs will have kept these documents for some timebecause the arrangements imposed guaranteed future indemnity from prosecution. The Murašû-type of agricultural entrepreneur had a following which enabled him to act high-handedly. Less negative is probably *kinattū*, "associates, dependants", probably including family, and perhaps the phrasing in BE 9, 25 where a favour is requested and the Murašû entourage is indicated by *atta* ŠEŠ.MEŠ-*ka* ^{LU_2}IR_3.MEŠ-*ka*, which no doubt encompasses the same group of people, but the context is not intentionally negative here.

64 The result of such a request was, it seems, that one became a *ṣāb qātē* of the person who accepted it.

65 Cf. perhaps Nbk 266.

informed when others formally stood bail[66] or, more usefully, they accepted to provide labour instead of the backlog.[67] Pledged property constituted a special category of the land held by people like the Murašûs. This question requires a new and separate study, indebtedness may have been a considerable source of labour for those to whom people were in debt.

Another method of exploring the presence, if not the actual status, of the underlings of those involved in the hierarchy of leases, is to examine the secondary elements of the lease contracts. That agricultural products are the main element of the rent to be paid stands to reason. But secondary products are also listed and they additionally involve work: delivery of flour, beer and textiles, and we can also mention animals, which in turn need fodder, but possibly provide the wool for the textiles. The obligation to deliver common but labour intensive products can be regarded as a sign not only of subordination, the confirmation of which was the intention of such payments, but of the practical presence of a labour force connected to the execution of the prime purpose of the lease, the production of agricultural staple products. The owner was used to the receipt of the token products mentioned, he saw no reason to leave them to his new tenant, or more realistically, he was himself obliged to pay these products as taxes, especially in a system in which he too was only a link in a hierarchy of leases. These payments are the marks of the grip of the ultimate owner and possibly his tax man, as we will see below, on the subjects in general.[68]

a. *aššabu*[69] and *naiiālu*[70]

There must be a subtle difference between those who "sit" and those who "lie" on the estates of others, as represented by the *aššābu* and the *naiiālu* respectively. Both words had a long previous history, but they were, it would seem, used in the Neo-Babylonian period to indicate (also) the status of inhabitants of estate villages, *aššābu* more so than the rare *naiiālu*.[71] That *aššābu* is often simply someone who lives in a house, is not relevant here, but the word also has a special, more restricted "social" meaning.

As is the case with the Nuzi *aššābu*, the translation "tenant", "resident" is much to bland for the Neo-Babylonian representative of this type of person, though in Nuzi the usage is much more specific than is the case later on, to all probability. In the Middle-Babylonian period the term can indicate the status of being a *metoik*.[72] The Neo-Babylonian *aššābu* as found in a text like YOS 7, 186 is a villager, probably living in a house belonging to the estate to which he or she pertains as a dependent, on temple estates almost invariably as a *širku*, as is the case in YOS 7, 174. The word seems to be used in this meaning in a generalising manner.

---

66 EE 104, Ist 103, there are more texts of this type, but they do not refer explicitly to agricultural debts. Debts in general are mentioned in PBS 2/1, 21, but criminal cases, that is seen from the view point of the Murašûs, also occur: PBS 2/1, 85.

67 EE 113, quoted here under *šušānu*.

68 We could consider the possibility that there was an important difference between town and country regarding the status of the king's subjects: in the town they were "free", in the country they were "serves". That is too absolute, but the mixture will have contained more of the one than of the other in the two environments, and we refer to the king's subjects only.

69 Literature: CAD A/2 467.

70 CAD N/1 p. 152-3 "tenant with special status".

71 There is a possible complication in the form of *āšib/pu* in Bertin 2235 from the Egibi archive, where *āšib/pus* are holders of a bow. The text is quoted in the next chapter under *qaštu*. *āšibu*, as far as can be seen ,without extensive search, from CAD A/2 p. 429ff, occurs in Neo-Babylonian in expressions like *āšib āli* in "learned texts", otherwise it seems to have been replaced by *aššābu*, which pleads against reading *āšibu* in Bertin 2235 and compels us to a reluctant acceptance of *āšipu,* "exorcist".

72 CAD A/2 p. 462, discussion.

This is one of the complications, and not only in the Neo-Babylonian period. In the institutional archives the core of the agricultural labour force consists of the plough teams. Additional seasonal labour could be drafted in, if the institution employed workers for other purposes, e.g. textile production and milling, or it might be hired if the means and the people were available. There were local reserves of labour in the country side. But villages hardly figure in the texts. YOS 7, 186 from the administration of Eanna in Uruk is an exception in that it shows that institutional estates, and therefore also the estates of other landowners, exercised a general grip on the inhabitants of their land. That is what is indicated by the use of the term *aššābu* in these cases. Grinding flour is obviously a general obligation, one might expect that also the weaving of simple textiles falls in this category of obligations.[73] YOS 7, 186 makes supervision the task of the *gugallu*, with, probably, the consequence that he had to fulfil a quota for a village under his responsibility. The subordination of the village population will have been something that went without saying for the contemporaries, therefore in practice written evidence is limited.

Unmistakable is the promise by the head of the Murašû firm, referred to above, to one of his underlings on his undertaking a sub-lease:[74] two villages will not have to do plough work for other contractors.

There is only one relevant Neo-Babylonian passage possibly using the term *naiiālu* known to me. It is slightly dubious, on the left edge of Dar 43, quoted below under "other relevant material", where it probably serves to summarise the people who have been registered above: x *na-a-la-a šá* ^{d}*Šamaš*. I assume that there is not much difference in status between the *aššābu* of YOS 7, 186 and the *naiiālu*, if the identification of this term in this document is correct.

Babylon

Bertin 2235 25 VII Dar 12, see sub *qaštu*. (Barley and wheat NIG$_2$.GA LUGAL *šá* ^{GIŠ}BAN ^{LU_2}*a-ši-b/pu*.MEŠ . Not relevant here.)

Uruk

YOS 7 174 1 IX Camb 4, Āl-Naṣibate, *ad* Uruk, empty tuns in the hands of *aššābus* of two localities and other people, amongst whom ENGARs.

YOS 7 186 23 I Camb 6, at Šingu, a *šīḫu* (in the text: *qaq-qar*) of Bēlet of Uruk, five named persons and the ^{LU_2}*áš-šá-bi-e* in general are told by the *šatammu* and the *bēl piqitti* of Eanna to grind flour of the proper quality *a-ki-i* ^{LU_2}*áš-šá-bi-e šá i-na* URU.MEŠ *šá* ^{d}Bēlet-ša-Uruk *a-šab-bu*/ ZID$_2$.DA *it-ti* PN s PN2[75] ^{LU_2}GU$_2$.GAL *šá* ^{d}Bēlet-šá-Uruk^{KI} *ṭe-e-na-'a*; this is confirmed by four of those named.[76]

---

[73] For weaving as a task imposed on widows cf. from Sippar Dar 43, 1 VII <Dar> 2; on textiles included in the rent of institutional houses Cyr 163, 8 III Cyr 4. The virtually totally undocumented, but essential, task of spinning probably also belongs in this context. It is to be connected with the obligation to deliver skeins of linen thread in a number of Murašû texts. Examples: EE 14: 26; Ist 16: 18; Ist 18: 24; PBS 2/1, 150: 20'; BE 9, 65: 21.

[74] EE 14, quoted here under "Material on the status of villagers" and "Policies".

[75] This same man is the subject of an injunction in TCL 13, 150, 14 III Camb 2, quoted below under *urāšu*, dated at Āl-Maškan-ili, also a *šīḫu* of Bēlet-ša-Uruk, to deliver 10 *urāšus* for canal work on pain of the displeasure of Gubaru, who more or less occupied the position of a viceroy. It is probably a sign of the friction caused between the managers of the estate and the lessees by the imposition of the rent farm system, that the person to whom the *urāšus* are assigned is the *ša muḫḫi sūti* of the canal concerned, the Nār-Ḫarri-Kippi.

[76] There must be a reason why the name of the first person named at the beginning is erased, possibly he refused to comply or for some reason he was personally exempted, which is interesting in itself.

b. *itbāru*[77]

Jursa's conclusion that *itbāru* are adult workers, is supported by other Sippar texts. The word was used there for agricultural personnel in groups. BM 60158[78], and 60280 are lists of male personnel of all ages including small children, arranged, as far as can be seen according to family relationship with individual age qualifications, running from ^{LU_2}AB.BA, "aged (and infirm)" to *pirsu,* "weaned infant", and *ša šizib*, "baby at the breast", who, it would seem, do not yet have a recorded given name. Adults are indicated by ^{LU_2}*it-bar.*[79] This and other variant writings of *itbāru*, indicates the male adult members of the group in the probably vocation based summaries in BM 60280, which gives numbers of *itbār,* "adult", *marē* "(male) children" and AB.BA "(too) old" after a grand total. BM 60453 is probably an inspection of personnel *ēpiš dullu* of the *qēpu*, "labourers of the *qêpu*", who eat *kurummat šarri*, in this case probably "sustenance (officially) provided by the king". This text has an appendix concerning females, similarly categorised according to age. The term *itbāru* in these texts is no more than "man capable of performing a full task", the word has no direct status implications, beyond the fact that they, but not they alone, for the list also includes boys with qualifications ranging from 5 to 3,[80] are obliged to do "the work of the *qêpu*", that is perform the corvée work imposed on the temple estate and supervised by this official.[81] Only the AB.BAs escape from this obligation, it seems.

itbāru can probably be excluded from our investigations, it does not mean something like "member of a labour or corvée unit", it is basically an age related term. It is, however, notable that in Sippar the term *širku* seems not to be used for plough men. Yet Āl-Itbārāte occurs as the name of a small settlement in the Babylon countryside, and it also turns up as an element in a geographical indication in Dar 520,[82] a text from the file of the Babylon Ea-eppeš-ili family. Dar 43, quoted below under "further relevant material", could suggest, notwithstanding its damaged state, that *itbāru* is a word which could be used to indicate the persons with whom institutional widows in a village, supervised by a *gugallu*, were allowed to remarry. In a village the word therefore indicates in practice a status with limited freedom, in a sense it may have replaced *širku*. Perhaps the word had after all if not "rustic", at least subject-related overtones.

Sippar

Dar 43 1 VII <Dar> 2 see below, this chapter, "other material".

---

[77] Literature: CAD I/J p. 294; Jursa 1995 p. 8ff; F. Joannès, KTEMA 22, 1997, p. 121 "laboureur", "équipier"; certainly unfree, MacGinnis in press.

[78] BM 60158, 60280 and 60453 were made available in transcriptions by H. Bongenaar.

[79] Possibly the same as the also attested ^{LU_2}*it-bar-tu*$_4$ or *i*-LU-*bar-tu*$_4$, with perhaps once *i*-DI-*bar-tu*$_4$.

[80] "Years" is Joannès' preferred choice, "cubits" or "palms" being hardly convincing if the cubit is put at the "conventional" 50 cm. A six year old can perhaps guide an ox, but he can hardly be classified as an adult worker. The remnant CT 56, 805 was much more detailed as to the age of those involved. Is a ration based classificatory system impossible? The difficulty is that a full-grown man receives a standard kor per month, and if we might suppose *mašīḫus* being intended by the numbers, five would equal a kor. We might speculate that a boy on the verge of being classified with the men could be indicated in this manner, but this remains questionable. The rating of people according to their basic wage has a long history in Mesopotamia.

[81] The runaways are all *itbārus*. Working with the *qêpu* was, it seems, a favoured occasion for absconding, Cf. Cyr 292, 8 I Cyr 8, a text listing, on the occasion of an inspection, seven runaways and four deaths. That this type of administration still served to control the amount of rations spent is explained by CT 56, 761. This is comparable to the procedures in the Ur III period.

[82] Read, perhaps, following CAD I/J 294 AN!.TA-*nu ša* ^{LU_2}*it-ba-ra-a-tu*$_4$.

c. *šūšānu*[83]

This is obviously a term with juridical implications which make sale to a private person impossible or undesirable, because the status indicated invalidates the contract. This suggests a link with the government, or with estates ultimately deriving from the government. That the term also in later Babylonia has a connection with the care for horses is beyond doubt.[84] But the term occurs most notably as an element in a range of names of *ḫadru*s listed by Stolper.[85] These can be divided into several distinct types. In the first the *šūšānu*s are indicated as belonging to an estate which is held by a specific person. In Stolper's nos. 40, 42, the dependence is expressed by *ša*, "belonging to". So also no. 9, the *šūšānus ša bīt rab uratē* will be dependants of the estate of the *rab uratē*, which will be comparable to no. 41, whatever the *bīt* ^{LU_2}*šaknūte* may represent. The variant *šūšānu māru* ^{LU_2}*šaknūte* is important for Stolper's interpretation: the *šūšānu*s are the "sons (i.e. members of the class) of foremen", probably on the assumption that the *šaknu*s intended are the "managers" of the *ḫadru*s we encounter as the business partners of the Murašus. In some of the other *ḫadru*s *šūšānu* is either linked to the occupation mentioned, or not: 44, 47, in others in all occurrences *ša* is found: 48, or it is always absent: 43, 45, 46 and 49. Inclusion or omission of the *ša* may be a whim of the scribe, or it may have some real meaning. If it has real meaning and indicates a dependence on the occupation mentioned, these *šūšānu*s are at the service of those who exercise the occupation. If the lack of a linking *ša* is significant, if we are dealing with a real apposition, which would be the case with the *ēpišānu ša ṭīṭi,* the DUMU.MEŠ *ḫisannu*, the DUMU.MEŠ *ikkarāte*, and the *šadidi ša sisî,* these *šūšānu* could themselves execute the occupation indicated. At least three of these four are not high ranking occupations, and what the *māre ḫisanni* are, is unknown to me. That *šūšānu* represents a lowly status is generally assumed and it would be confirmed in this manner. The *šūsānu*s would either belong to the estate of an official, be subordinated to persons fulfilling a specific job or themselves fulfil some not very elevated task. Yet they could hold land in their own right, if we accept CBS 7961:2, where a named *šūšānu* is the neighbour of a holder of a horse fief on the Nār-Šapputtu.[86]

But this is probably all wrong, or at least not the whole truth. Slave sales specify a number of situations making the acquisition of a person of a specified status undesirable and impossible. The status of belonging to a horse or chariot fief is explicitly mentioned, but that of possessing or belonging to a bow fief is not. We might expect that such persons deserved equal protection as they were intrinsically all the more vulnerable than the underlings of horse and chariot fiefs, who were under the protection of their direct chiefs, if only because the king would not have liked to loose his investment. *šūšānu* is an element of many names of *ḫadru*s. Members of *ḫadru*s are in general holders of bow fiefs, also if they belonged to, for instance, a chariot fief. I would not be surprised if *šūšānu* was, or had become, the, or at least a, term used to indicate the holder of a subordinate(?) bow fief, even if that would differ fundamentally from the earlier and persisting link with horses. An institutional *širku* could also be a bowman, but he was unfree and did not possess a "fief" which enabled and obliged him to serve. There evidently was some service to be executed by people specifically called *šūšānu*, as EE 113 indicates. A limited number of persons of that status had to be provided. Actual military service seems to be

---

83 Literature: CAD Š/3 p. 378-80. On the Neo-Assyrian *sūsānu* cf. recently K. Radner, StAt I, 1999, p. 114, *ad* rev. 18f., where the connection with chariots and horses is evident. A long discussion can be found in M. Dandamayev, Slavery p. 626-642. Stolper 1985 p. 79-80 observes: "belongs to an estate or to some skill or employment".

84 Cf. the Eanna text published by P.-A. Beaulieu, NABU 1989/65 where a *šušānu* handles fodder for horses. The connection is also evident etymologically through Hebrew sūs, as Stol points out.

85 Stolper 1985 p. 76-78 nos. 40-49.

86 Stolper 2001 no. 8.

possible. PBS 2/1, 186 could link a specific person both with the status of being a *šūšānu* and with holding a bow fief. The text is unusual in mentioning this explicit combination, no doubt on account of the fact that the holder was a woman. Again a case in which doubt lingers: normal or not? Probably not, unless the holder of a bow fief was always a free man, who therefore could not be sold. That again is questionable. The fact that there is no explicit place for the personnel of the ordinary bow fief in the list of status's precluding sale as a slave remains suspicious.

Babylon

TÉBR 120 mentions Art (which?) yr. 29, fragment of a lease of land belonging to Esagil 6) [*šá*?] ^{GIŠ}BAN$_2$ *ša* P[N s PN2?] 7) *šá ina muḫ-ḫi* ^{LU_2}*šu-šá-an-na* [.....]. Here?

Murašû

EE 113 [x x Art 33], four persons address Enlil-šum-iddina of their own accord: 6) .... *ku-um* 7) NIG$_2$.KAS$_7$-*ka ra-šu-tu šá ina muḫ-ḫi-i-ni* 8) ITI 40 ^{LU_2}ERIN$_2$.MEŠ [*ni*-]*dak-kam*$_2$-*ma dul-lu* 9) *ina muḫ-ḫi* E$_2$-*ka li-pu-uš-ú* 10) *ù i-di mu-un-na-šú-nu-tu ù* 10 ^{LU_2}ERIN$_2$.MEŠ 11) *a-na* ^{LU_2}*šu-šá-ni-e ni-dak-ka e-lat* 2 *ù mi-šil* 1) ^{LU_2}ERIN$_2$.MEŠ *šá at-ta tu-maš-šir*.[87] "On account of the sum which is due to you from us we will provide you for a month with 40 men to work on your estate, assign them a wage (<and regard that as payment>) and we will provide you with ten men as š., on top of that you will concede us $2^1/_2$ men." Accepted. Damaged clause concerning failing to appear for work.

PBS 2/1 186 3 VII Dar II 1, dates of Enlil-šum-iddina s M. PN1 s PN2 3) *šá* ^{GIŠ}BAN *ša* ^{f}GEME-ia$_2$ *šá* ^{LU_2}*šu-šá-ni-e* 4) will deliver in VII, bow fief security.

d. *ēpiš ṭīṭi*

In the Murašû texts occurs a *ḫadru* of the *šūšānu ēpišānu šá* IM,[88] which Stolper has connected with a number of Hellenistic dedications of slaves to sanctuaries.[89] The term used is obviously intended to suggest menial work, possibly of a simple nature, in the building trade. Though not occurring in practical texts, this seems to represent a specific class of people.

The only exception could be Ist 2. In that text *ēpiš ṭīṭi u mašaka* is taken to represent *šūšāne ēpiš ṭīṭi u šūšāne ša mašaka* by Stolper. The text is badly preserved and difficult to reconstruct. It would mean that the person who grants the lease, a manager acting for the queen, was in the position to grant outright leases concerning bow fiefs "which belonged to the estate of the queen". The context is dubious and all conclusions based on it are subject to the same qualification.

Murašû

Ist 2 (before Art 31?) see Chapter IV under Terminology, status of large estates.

e. *gardu*[90]

The role of the *gardu* has been discussed recently by P. Briant, who has pointed out the fact that they were/could be branded with the mark of an owner, which indicates that they were unfree. In Babylonia they worked on the land of the king and the aristocracy. In this way they would be, it would seem, comparable to the *širku*s on the temple estates, but only as to status. The Murašû texts confirm that they could hold land and could be organised in a *ḫadru,* as the

87 Cf. Stolper 1985 p. 81.

88 Stol points out that it would be correct to read *ṭiddu*.

89 Stolper 1985 p. 77, no. 43 with note 32.

90 CAD G p. 50 (a military class or profession): AHw p. 282L "Arbeitsverpflichtete", P. Briant, Histoire de l'Empire perse I, Paris, 1996, p, 471, "travailleur" (translation given in the register), also for equation with (Persepolitan) *kurtaš*.

*šūšānu*s were. This again suggests that *ḫadru*s could consist of people not entirely free in status, who could yet hold land and be obliged to perform military service. They seem to fulfil some specific purpose, as CT 22, 74 seems to stress, ordering their release from, we may assume, active service. Specific comparison of especially them with the later *laoi basilikoi* is therefore not immediately obvious. A special connection with the king seems warranted on the grounds of the contents of BE 10, 127 and there is -in the Babylonian- texts no link with specific other individuals. Perhaps the *gardu* could be included in royal appropriations to consorts or officials, which would be understood to be limited in time.

Sippar

VS 3 138/9 — 7 V Dar 36, (sustenance) 2) *ša* ^{LU_2}*ga-ar-du* ^{LU_2}*ma-gu-še-e*.MEŠ *ù* ^{LU_2}DUMU.MEŠ E$_2$.GAL *šá* E$_2$-Ḫa-re-e *ša* ŠU^{II} PN ^{LU_2}*se-pir-ri*.

Murašû

CBS 5316 — 30 III Art 31, cf. above under "Land of the king".

BE 9 101 — 16 VII Art 41, land 2) ... US$_2$.SA.DU ŠE.NUMUN *šá ga-ar-du*.

PBS 2/1, 2 — 11 x Dar II 0, dates A.ŠA$_3$.MEŠ *šá* ^{LU_2}*ga-ar-du* [x].

BE 10 32 — 24+ IV Dar II 1, promise of delivery of dates from pledged land next 10) ^{LU_2}*ga-ar-du* next 11) *uz-ba-ra ša* [*šarri*].

BE 10 92 — 13 IX Dar II 4, arable *šá* ^{LU_2}*ga-ar-du*, situation, of PNs1-5 and colleagues *gab-bi šá* ^{LU_2}*ḫa-ad-ri šá* ^{LU_2}*ga-ar-du ša ina* GN.

PBS 2/1 91 — 27 IX Dar II 4, receipt rent land of PN ^{LU_2}*ga-ar-du-pa-ta*, sealed by PN2 *šá* ^{LU_2}*ga-ar-du šá* MU 4-*i* ^{P}Da-ri-'-muš LUGAL.

PBS 2/1 204 — 12 XII Dar II 4, rent *šá* A.ŠA$_3$.MEŠ *šá* ^{LU_2}*ga-ar-di* in Āl-Banišāia.

BE 10 127 — 4 IX Dar II 7, receipt *ilku* land in (Āl-)Bīt-Murašû 4) *u ina* Bīt-Ḫanana'-ḫarbatu *šá* ^{LU_2}*ga-ar-du ša* LUGAL at the disposal of PN.

Ist 32 — x V Dar II x, lease of land *ana* ^{LU_2}NU.KIRI$_6$-*ú-tu* next to 4) ... PN *šá* ^{LU_2}*ga-ar-du*.

Where?

CT 22 74 — (letter), 26) *ṣābe ša ga-ar-du ša ṭēme aškunuka puṭṭeršunutu*.

f. *perku* or rather *pišku*[91]

The word has been discussed before and the meaning remains uncertain, the same is the case with the expression *pūt piški našū*, which is relevant for us. PBS 2/1, 140 clearly suggests that high handed behaviour involving the yield of land constitutes the background of the text. A comparable link is also suggested by BE 10, 43 with its unique clause on the non-entry of what are generally the estimators of the yield, here on both date plantations and arable. The strange fact is that this text also states that the land involved belongs to the "master" of the person who solicits both the use of stock and the "*našū* of his *pišku*" from Rēmūt-Ninurta. The *ēmidu*s will normally be the estimators acting on behalf of the "master". In this case the transaction is possibly of limited duration, at least initially.

Specific circumstances are also indicated in PBS 2/1, 28. The person who addresses the Murašû *mār bīti* Tirikama gives as a reason for his request that "they" already "for the second time must [not] carry off all his .... (word lost)", the crucial line in the acceptance section of the document is also damaged, but "he will not undertake his (own) *pišku*" against a payment of 20 kor of barley per annum to Tirikama. No time limit is indicated. Without time limit is also PBS

---

[91] This passage had been written when Stolper 2000a arrived in Leiden. Acknowledging Stolper's prior findings I leave the text as it is, because it is has the greater explicitness required here. Literature: A.L. Oppenheim, JQR 36,1945-46, p. 171-6, "forced labour, corvée", Cardascia 1951 p. 165 ff. Stolper, 1985 p. 280 note 1 proposed a much more general meaning, "harm, injustice". The link with patronage is found in Stolper 2000a. Cf. AHw *perqu*.

2/1, 107, where the request is made collectively and notably involves a payment which derives from bow fiefs and land held as a pledge. These people did not act because they were primarily in financial difficulties, there must be another motive. Noteworthy is that the payment is also, in view of the fact that it is made by six people and their following, not very high, not exceeding four kor of dates per person per annum.

What occurs in these texts is explained best by EE 112: a person declares himself for the rest of his life a *ṣāb qātē*[92] of Rēmūt-Ninurta against a payment of 10 kor of barley (per annum) on condition that he, Rēmūt-Ninurta, will "carry the responsibility for his *pišku*": the request regards patronage and protection. In BE 10, 43 this was sought (on a limited basis?) against the "master" of the person concerned, in PBS 2/1, 107 it collectively involved holders of bow land.[93] Incidentally we have learned another term for someone requiring patronage and protection: *ṣāb qātē* (PN).

Whatever the exact meaning, the situation in the countryside was not favourable even for collective groups of small landholders. The possibility that tax claims are pursued in a high handed manner always exists, while redress is difficult for the individual subject. This could be one of the practical backgrounds.

Murašû

EE 112 x VI Art 41, PN s PN2 addresses [of his own accord] Rēmūt-Ninurta: 3) *lu-u* ^{LU_2}ERIN$_2$ ŠU^{II}-*ka ana-ku pu-ut p*[*iš-ki-a*] 4) *lu-ú na-šá-a-tú u$_4$-mu ma-la bal-ṭa-ku* [(x)] 5) [10] GUR ŠE.BAR *ana* E$_2$-*ka lu-ud-din*. Request granted.

BE 10 43 15 VI Dar II 1, PN1 s PN2 requests from Rēmūt-Ninurta the lease of oxen for use on land belonging to PN3, his master (EN-*ía*), in (Āl)-Naqidini on the Nār-Aḫu-le'i, land in (Āl) Par-šu-šu (on) the Nār-Miṣirāia, land in (Āl-)Bīt-Bēltum, land in (Āl) Arazua, in Āl-A.QAR-qabušu, in (Āl)Bušu'u, in (Āl) Bīt-Rab-kaṣir, in (Āl) Bāb-Dirat, in (Āl) Kuzabatu, *it-ti* 9)*ṣi-bit-tú* A.MEŠ-*ši-na šá iq-bi-ši-na*, for three years for 50 kor per annum; follows a damaged clause regarding the lease, possibly on its beginning in month VII, after that: *pu-ut* 11)*pi-iš-ki-iá pi-iš-ki šá* PN4 Š[EŠ-*iá u* ^{LU_2}]*ki-na-at-ti-iá* 12) *lu na-ša-a-tú u e-mi-du a-na* ŠE.NUMUN-*iá zaq-pu u pi šul-pu* 13) *la ur-rad*.[94] Request granted.

---

[92] This is also the term used in the letter YOS 3, 38 for the person with whom the letter deals, but it continues 15) ... *man-ma* 16) *pir-ki ina pani-ku-nu* 17) *it-ti-šú*, addressing the addressees and not referring directly to the person mentioned. Kessler, AUWE 8 no. 45 is too damaged to be useful, the term refers here to persons who can be hired. Kessler suggests a translation "Hilfskräfte". "Client", in a social sense, fits most (NA and NB) passages quoted CAD Ṣ p. 1, but the term will have a more occupation related sense in the case of the institutional *nāqidu*s and *ikkaru*s, who can be regarded as a kind of foremen of shepherds and plough teams.

[93] There is the possibility that the protection was especially related to the payment of dues. The "township" of Ḫasbāia was obviously a centre of Murašû interests. Amongst other affairs they were associated with the exploitation of bow fiefs of members of the *ḫadru* of the *šūšānu ēpišānu ša ṭīṭi* in this and neighbouring localities in the Nār-Simmagir area. The curious fact is that in PBS 2/1, 193, 25 VII Dar II 2, their *šaknu* Nabu-nādin receives the *ilku* payment from Rēmūt-Ninurta. But PBS 2/1, 120, 23 V Dar II 6, that is after the *pišku* contract PBS 2/1, 120 records that Rēmūt-Ninurta is the person who has received the *ilku* payment for bow fiefs belonging to the same *ḫadru* under (*ina qātē*), no doubt, the same *šaknu*. (This man is also found in PBS 2/1, 117, 4 II Dar II 6, another *ilku* receipt, together with Rēmūt-Ninurta, lines rev. 2-3, but the text is too damaged to reconstruct the sequence of events. It involves another *ḫadru*). These sums will not have been kept by either the *šaknu* or Rēmūt-Ninurta, but they will have had to be passed on. It is possible that the Murašû undertook, against the payment of a fee, the responsibility for the proper registration of payments. Another burden on the tax payer. In BE 10, 43 they possibly undertook to protect the protégé against high impositions, in PBS 2/1, 28 against double claims.

[94] Cf. Ries 1976 p. 95 on the exceptional nature of this clause, but without discussion of the relation to the *pišku* clause.

PBS 2/1 28 6 x Dar II 1, PN s PN2 addresses of his own accord Tirikama *mār bīti* of Enlil-šum-iddina): *pu-ut* 4) [*pi-iš-k*]*i-ia i-ši šá-niš-ma mim-ma-ú-a* 5) [x x] x x *i-na-aš-šu-ú u ana-ku* 6) [*ina* MU.A]N.NA 20 GUR ŠE.BAR TA E_2-*ia a-nam-dak-ka*, request accepted. (8) [x x x] x-*bi pi-rik-šú la ip-pu-uš*).

PBS 2/1 107 20 VII Dar II 5, six named persons and their associates (*kinattu*) in the township of Ḫašbaia adress of their own accord Rēmūt-Ninurta: 5) *pu-ut piš-ki-ni i-ši* and from VII yr 5 we will give you yearly 20 kor of dates on our bow fiefs and pledged holdings. Request accepted with the remark "one stands in for the other".

Cf.

PBS 2/1 140 x I Dar 7, 30) *ki-i ul-tu* ^{ITI}BARA$_2$ MU 17 KAM$_2$ Rēmūt-Ninurta 31) *piš-ku a-na* ^{LU_2}ra-ku-se-e šá gi-iš-ri *šá ina* ŠU^{II} 33) Aḫu-ú-a *i-te-puš* (he will pay a fine).

Tattanu

VS 6 183 12 IV Art 38, at Tabalu, PN asks Šamšāia s Tattanu 3) [*ma-am*]-*ma-am piš-ki-ka-a la ip-pu-šú* 4) x [x] x *ina* ITI II 25 GUR ŠE.BAR *ina* ITI VIII 5) 25 GUR ZU$_2$.LUM.MA *a-na muḫ-ḫi* ŠE.NU[MUN] 6) *ù* E_2-*ia* (for three years) I will give you. Text not in order.[95]

g. Other material on the status of villagers

The Uruk text YOS 7, 186 centred on a conflict between the administration of Eanna, or its representative, and a group of villagers, whose duty to grind flour, like other villagers in a similar position, as the text specifies, was confirmed. Here we encounter what can be regarded as a rule. The Sippar text Dar 43 is very fragmentary and only a guess can be made about its purpose. This text is probably not written down as the result of a conflict, it rather sets out the duties of the villagers of a specific settlement under a specific *gugallu*, in this case a *širku*. Possibly all the inhabitants were listed, male and female in a document setting out the particular responsibilities of this *gugallu*. The nineteen *itbārus* were the adult men and there is special attention for the widows of the village, presumably because they had (male) children, destined to take over the tasks of their deceased fathers. The widows are forbidden to take up residence with free men or to allow their sons to be adopted by free men: that, at least, seems to be the best interpretation of the damaged passage. From amongst the women three are registered with the obligation that they must deliver each year a piece of textile produced at their own expense. This is clearly a form of imposition which is not unknown in other periods, it is comparable to the TUG$_2$.GU$_2$.NA of the Ur III period. Traces at the end of what remains of the text seem to deny the persons involved a right to reside elsewhere. The edge classifies those concerned as *naiiālus*, if the interpretation already proposed above is correct.

From the Murašû archive EE 14, already quoted above, is of importance in that it suggests that villages implicitly went with leases of agricultural land. If this indicates that "villages" somehow constituted a recognisable economic entity, it is still striking that they only rarely appear as such. Ist 13 is a rare case in which a village as such seems to be leased. Villagers acting together as tenants are another indication of a certain basic form of organisation at low level. This was not completely unknown.

The Murašû archive contains several types of texts illustrating indirectly the situation of the ordinary rural labourer. If he does not do his work properly he will be beaten and shaved in an ignominious manner, but this type of punishment is also the acknowledgement of a relative powerlessness on the part of the landowner: if the labourer does not want to work the investment is lost.

Of much more interest is Ist 22 where a person addresses Tirikama, one of the Murašû henchmen, and obviously an agricultural entrepreneur in his own right, with a request for land,

---

95 Stolper 2000a p. 471 reads *piš-<<ki>>ka-a la* etc., "my *p*.". The statement is made by the person concerned

oxen and seed, against which he will serve as one of his "ploughmen who are in your townships". This looks like a very simple transaction, but in reality someone without possessions is joining the labour force of an entrepreneur. The attempts to hold on to possessions which have been lost already for all practical purposes are illustrated by requests not to be driven from one's land, but to be allowed to continue farming it, sometimes with loaned stock. This belongs to the question of agricultural indebtedness in general and will not be examined here.[96] The phenomenon is in itself timeless.

Of some interest is that there are also a number of cases in which groups of villagers managed to retain or gain a certain amount of independence, though the price is difficult to assess. In BE 9, 25, 17 I Art 31, a certain Iadiḫiama asks to be allowed to keep his *bīt ritti*, his *eqel našparti* and his *bīt maškanāti*, with a canal called Nār-ša-Uratē, for a rent of 200 kor per annum. In BE 9, 45 we find the same man with two sons and six named other men undertaking a new lease in the same area, against, altogether, a rent of 700 kor. This suggests some stability, perhaps even the modest success of a joint venture by villagers.[97]

Sippar

Dar 43 1 VII <Dar> 2, fragmentary, remains begin with PN, *širku* of Šamaš, *gugallu*, follow the names of a number of women, who are generally qualified as *almattus*, "widows", after a long break follows a date, and the remark *e-lat* 19 ^{LU_2}*it-bar-re a-na* PN2 x 9) *a-ša-tu*$_4$ *ina lib*$_3$*-bi*, after which follow a number of injunctions: *it-ti* ^{LU_2}DUMU.DU$_3$ *ul tu-šu-bu* 10) x x x *a-na* DUMU-*ú-tú a-na* DUMU ^{LU_2}DU$_3$ *ul ta-nam-din* 11) *ina lib-bi* FPN1 FPN2 *u* FPN3 12) *ina* MU.AN.NA 3 ^{TUG_2}*gu-li-en iš-ka-ri a-na* ^{d}UTU 13) TA *ra-man-ši-na i-nam-din-na-'a ina* URU *šá-n*[*a-ma*] 14) *ul ú-šu-ba-'a ki-i man-ma ina lib*$_3$*-bi a-*[*na* x x 15) x x x]*it-tal-ku* PN2(?) rest lost, but for on L.E. x] x *na-a-la-a šá* ^{d}UTU [*šu-nu*](?) plus date.

Uruk

YOS 7 186 23 I Camb 6, see above under *aššābu*.

Murašû

BE 9 25 17 I Art 31, request for the lease of Nār-ša-Uratē *bīt rittia eqel našpartia* and *bīt maškanāti;* you, Enlil-šum-iddina will not take away from (former owner?) Ia-di-iḫ-ia-a-ma s Ba-na-a'-ilāni, but lease for 200 kor per annum for three years; delivery of rent in (Āl) Gira'a. (Cf. below BE 9, 45, 20 V Art 34.)

EE 14 25 VII [Art] 40, important lease, see below under "policies", granted by Enlil-šum-iddina to his servant Ribat 28) Āl-Sin-bēlšunu *u* (Āl-)Uš?-x-ta?-ra-'a *ana dul-lu* ^{LU_2}ENGAR-*ú-tú ina* IGI ^{P}Ri-bat 29) *dul-lu šá-nam-ma šá* Enlil-šum-iddina *ul ip-pu-uš*.

BE 9 45 20 V Art 36, lease by Ia-di-iḫ-ia-ma s Ba-na-a'-ilani and two sons and six named others with more unnamed persons from Bit-Gira'a from Enlil-šum-iddina at (Āl) Bit-Gira'a of Nār-ša-Uratē from its intake to its tail, the (or: which is a) *bīt* 10-*ú*, the *bīt ritti* of Ia-di-iḫ-ia-a-ma on the canal, and land left of the Nār-Milidu excepting land which draws water from Nār-Enlil and three DIM$_3$.ME.MEŠ[98] to the right of the Nār-Milidu for three years for 700 kor per annum and additionals. (Cf. above BE 9, 25. Also quoted sub water rights.)

Ist 13 28 V Art 38, lease of (Āl-)Galia, land *ina ḫu-ú-pu ša ina* Dūr-Ṣenu(?) (plus or equals?) *bīt ritti* of Enlil-šum-iddina, with oxen, tools and seed to PN IR$_3$ PN2 for an *ebur* of 300.1.4 in mixed products. (No additionals.)

---

[96] BE 9, 34, 7 IV Art 34; EE 12, 13 VIII Art 37, Ist 17, 22 XII Art 40, where the tenants will do ^{LU_2}ENGAR-*ú-tú-ka*, against the usual *imittu* on (your) plough men, but with a heavy fine for leaving work, BE 9, 88, 10 III Art 41.

[97] There are a number of texts in which groups of persons together act as tenants, they are probably real farmers and not "entrepreneurs": BE 9, 3 (26 II Art 13); BE 9, 7 (12 XI Art 26); BE 9, 35, ([7] IV Art 34); EE 19 (1 III Art 38) and EE 11 (10 III Art 40).

[98] LUGAL.KAM.ME.MEŠ, studied by M.W. Stolper, JCS 53, 2001, p. 123. The passage clearly refers to land irrigated by hand, and suggests a standard size for the DIM$_3$.ME.MEŠ.

Ist 22 14 XI Dar II 0, Iddina-Enlil s Iddina-Bēl addresses Tirikamu *mār bīti* of Enlil-šum-iddina concerning land in Ḫuṣṣētu-ša-Zaruttu, oxen and seed, he will serve *libbu* ^{GIŠ}APIN.MEŠ-*ka ša ina* URU.MEŠ-*ka ebūr ludakka.*

Leases of own land, *bīt ritti*, cf. BE 9, 25, above.

BE 9 34 7 IV Art 34, lease of own *bīt ritti* with two oxen and seed by PN from Enlil-šum-iddina on Nār-Namgar-Dūr-Enlil for three years for 100 kor of mixed produce. No additional deliveries.

EE 12 13 VIII Art 37, lease of 4 oxen and tools by Enlil-šum-iddina, for use on PN's *bīt ritti* on Ḫarri-Piqudu. at (Āl)Ḫa-ni-'i-ki-ni for 150 kor, payment in (Āl) Ḫa-a-a-x-x on Ḫ-P.

Ist 15 x VIII Art 38, request by Marduk-bēlšunu s Bēl-erība to Enlil-šum-iddina for land of his bow fief, his *bīt ritti* in Ḫuṣṣētu-ša-x with oxen, tools and seed, for a rent of 150 kor; no additional deliveries.

Ist 17 22 XII Art 40, lease of oxen, tools and seed by sons of Iltammes-barakki for their(?) *bīt ritti* in Āl-Išqallunu, for ^{LU_2}ENGAR-*ú-tú-ka*, against the usual *imittu* for (your) plough men; a 60 mina fine on leaving work.

BE 9 88 10 III Art 41, lease to sons of Dide of 20 kor of land *šá* ^{LU_2}*se-pi-re*.MEŠ in GARIM-Bīt-Dide in Ḫuṣṣētu-ša-Magušu with oxen and seed for three years, delivery of 150 kor in rent, with minor products, on Nār-Sin.

Leases by groups of villagers, Murašû

BE 9 3 26 II Art 13, five named persons ask Enlil-ḫatin for arable 6) ... *bīt re-e-ti* of named persons on Nār-ša-Iqīšā s Šamaš-zēr-ibni for *dalūtu*, leased with oxen and seed? Fragmentary, dated at Bīt-Murānu.

BE 9 7 12 XI Art 26, see above under "direct exploitation".

BE 9 35 [7] IV Art 34, lease by six named persons from Enlil-šum-iddina of Nār-Enlil in Til-Ḫurdu and land of your *bīt ritti* on it, with oxen, tools and seed. for three years for an *ebūr* of 255 kor per annum.

BE 9 45 20 V Art 36, see under material on the status of villagers. (Cf. BE 9, 25, 17 I Art 31)

EE 19 1 III Art 38, lease from Enlil-šum-iddina by six named persons of land belonging to three persons, without *bīt aspastum* and E_2.SUM.SAR, with oxen, tools and seed for over 760 kor per annum and additionals, note concerning water from Nār-Kittumannu and Nār-SAL.ŠA_2.NA.A.

EE 11 10 III Art 40, quoted sub *uzbāru*.

EE 23 x x [Dar II] 5, lease by Ribat to four named persons, fragmentary, mentions *uz-ba-ra šarri* land, dated at Til-Gabbara.

h. A note on the Murašû *nukaribbus*[99]

The Murašû *nukaribbūtu* contracts are of interest in that a written document was used to set out the obligations and rights of the individual gardeners, who must be regarded as being of a lowly status. The reason was probably that their action or inaction determined the yield of what was regarded as a valuable investment, whether it was Murašû property or not. The documents ended up in their archive anyhow. The texts document the convoluted manner of leasing and sub-leasing both within and outside the firm. BE 9, 99 and Ist 31 were written by the same scribe on the same day, but only in the first case it is certain that the lessee was a direct subject of the lessor. In both instances the status of the orchard concerned is described in a general catch-all manner and the remuneration consists of the under cultures plus a payment for *sissinnu*.

BE 9, 10 is obviously a mixed lease granted by outsiders, including arable, of which they received a share in the harvest of 25%, which suggests a case of manual irrigation. PBS 2/1, 159 is likewise a lease granted by outsiders in which the under cultures plus *sissinnu*

---

[99] Especially discussed Cardascia 1951, p. 136ff.

constituted the remuneration of the lessees. PBS 2/1, 81 and 115 again granted the proceeds of the under cultures to the tenants, who were submitted to *imittu*, at any rate in the first case.

BE 9, 101 is properly spoken an injunction placed on two Murašû servants to do their work in the correct manner, there is nothing on remuneration. The same could be said of EE 91, were neglect results in beating and defamatory shaving of head and beard. Other texts are damaged, whereas BE 8, 124 is rather curious in that it suggests the planting of an orchard on land held as a pledge. The situation was obviously regarded as sufficiently permanent for such an investment.

The group of texts indicates that the Murašûs could dispose of a number of persons, often unfree servants, who could undertake leases of orchards, generally against the yield of the under cultures, but sometimes even without specification of a remuneration. Yet the obligations were registered.

Murašû

BE 8 124 8 V Art 23, sub-lease of E_2 ŠE.NUMUN on the Nār-Sin, share of PN, pledge held by Enlil-ḫatin at the disposal of PN to another person *ana ebūr* MU.AN.NA at 20%. He will plant fruit trees. No time limit stated. Cf. Cardascia 1951 p. 197 and Ries 1976, p. 47-8.

BE 9 10 3 III Art 28, lease of bow land of two pairs of brothers *ana nukarribūtu* and *errēšūtu* to a *qallu* of Enlil-šum-iddina who will give 25% over the arable and *imittu* on the date palms; 3 kor as *sessinnu*; he has paid 5 *š* in *gimir* to the holders.

BE 9 99 4 VII Art 41, see Chapter III under *nidintu šarri.*

Ist 31 [4 VII] Art 41, 1) internal lease granted by Enlil-šum-iddina of orchard and date plantation, *bīt qašti, nidintu šarri, maḫīri kaspi* 2) *bīt maškanu* on the right bank of the Ḫarri-Piqudu and x on the left bank of the Ḫ-P at Bīt-x; *nukarribūtu*. Cf. BE 9, 99, same day and scribe.

BE 9 101 16 VII Art 41, lease *ana nukarribūtu* of land on bank of Namgar-Dūr-Enlil, next to *umaspitru*, next to land belonging to *gardu*, next to land of the smith of Al-Bannešš̌āia, bow land of Murašû, to two IR_3.MEŠ of Enlil-šum-iddina, clauses on work to be done, nothing about rent.

PBS 2/1 159 x VII Dar II 1+, lease by holder to two *mār bītis* of Enlil-šum-iddina of his bow land on the Nār-Ninurta at Bīt-Abdia (cf. Ḫarri-Piqudu), *imittu*, *sessinnu* as the neighbours, the yield of the under cultures is for the tenants.

PBS 2/1 81 20 II Dar II 4, internal lease of bow land of three persons, among them Ribat, on the N-Š *ana nukarribūtu* for 2 years to two brothers, they keep the under cultures and pay *imittu*. Note on sesame.

PBS 2/1 115 28 x Dar II 5, *nukarribūtu* lease of bow land on Nār-Simmagir in (Al) Gammale of Ribat to his own IR_3, who received all the under cultures; fine for not doing the work. Dated in Til-Gabari.

EE 91 x x [Dar II] 5, lease of date plantation, bow land of Rēmūt-Ninurta in Til-Gabbari and (other?) *bīt ritti* of PN, will be worked (*rapāqu*) by PN2; beating if work not is done properly. Damaged.

PBS 2/1 215 23 VI Dar II 6, lease of date plantation, *qu-ta-nu šá* ^{LU_2}*paḫḫāru*, bow land on the Nār-Kuta in Gadibatum belonging to the bow land of two brothers, leased by another person to IR_3 of Rēmūt-Ninurta, against *imittu*. Other clauses damaged.

Ist 32 x V Dar II x, land of various persons *ana nukarribūtu* for 3 years to two IR_3.MEŠ of Ribat, against *imittu*, fragment.

EE 20 date lost, fragment *nukarribūtu* lease.

i . The marks of subordination

YOS 7, 186 and Dar 43 provide meagre information on the ordinary duties of villagers towards the owners of the land on which their villages stood: the grinding of flour and the production of textiles. These are no innovations of the Neo-Babylonian period and the tasks are not restricted to the temple estates from which these texts derive. At any rate for the flour that is certain, textiles are much better attested in previous periods but there is in our period an otherwise not attested type of obligation which belongs to this category of impositions.

We must regard the grinding of flour, often not in excessive amounts, and thus more or less a token act, as a sign of subordination, not so much of the land as of the people who tilled it. We find such clauses regularly as secondary obligations in Murašû leases. Those subjected to the obligation clearly went with the lease. Delivery of flour and beer are regular requirements from bow fiefs. These clauses regarding additional commodities to be delivered are therefore one of the best indications of what is silently passed over by the texts: the close ties between the estate labour force and the land it tilled.

Textiles are rarely mentioned in connection with this labour force in Neo-Babylonian texts. This is not completely explicable for me, spinning is just as time consuming as grinding flour, though it is done whenever other tasks or rest permit it. The Murašû texts, however, add one new element to the equation: the contracts stipulate the delivery of specified numbers of skeins of linen thread. Examples have been given above. The curious fact is that the agricultural texts, which mention a considerable diversity of products, omit the production of flax. It is possible that the villagers had to cultivate the flax and produce the linen thread completely at their own costs. Flax is a labour intensive product.

The importance of these "secondary products" is that they offer the one clear indication that landed holdings and population coincided, also, and this is important, especially at the level of the bow fief. It suggests that the actual holders of the fiefs at least in a number of cases were not the people who worked the land, that was done by the villagers who went with that land. But we must not expect a completely uniform system.

Uruk

YOS 7 186	23 I Camb 6 see above under *aššābu*.

Sippar

Dar 43	I VII <Dar> 2, see above, Other material on status of villages.

B. Policies

As has been touched upon above, it is certain that at any rate the temple estates did not possess sufficient labour for an adequate exploitation of their land, and there are sufficient signs, notably in the shape of low nominal rents stipulated in leases at various levels of the system, that the same situation obtained on land which can be linked to the king. For the temple estates the best information comes from Uruk: YOS 6, 150 (20 x Nbn 11), quoted already above under *nakkandu* and TCL 13, 182, the well known text dealing with the Uruk lease given up by Gimillu, of tarnished repute, which clearly identifies the shortage of *ikkaru*s owned by the temple as the reason why an insider like Gimillu refused to continue a major contract.

This did not change anything in the determination of the royal administration to bring as much land as possible under the plough. The Murašû archive suggests that one of the means used was the offering of low rents, of the type one kor of land for one kor of barley, with somewhat higher variants, to entrepreneurs, at any rate in the initial stage of a lease. Whether such a policy also applied to the same degree in the Uruk contracts, can be doubted, as land already under cultivation played an important role in contracts there.

There are some signs that the lessees undertook, at least occasionally, improvement work on the land, particularly regarding the access to water, but that only makes the question of how these people managed to obtain the labour required, which the administration did not have, more intriguing. Access to a reservoir of labour could be obtained in several ways, but none of them is very apposite under the circumstances. There are no signs of an influx of immigrants whose labour could be engaged by entrepreneurs either from the same or from a different background, though it is a fact that kings occasionally granted members of tribes to institutions

background, though it is a fact that kings occasionally granted members of tribes to institutions or even to individuals, even if this evidence is limited to the earlier part of our period.[100] There are indications that the entrepreneurs were in a position to exploit the fact that people were in debt and such debts were occasionally tax related. There are, especially in the Murašû archive, listed above, leases in which a person in obvious difficulties asks not to be thrown from his (pledged) land, but to be allowed to continue to cultivate it as a tenant. Such arrangements are rarely successful, for they do not fundamentally change the situation of those concerned. Whether this type of arrangement is really a means of getting more workers can be doubted, for though this may tie people to the land, it does not attract new workers, which clearly was the intention in the relevant Uruk texts. In the documentation from Sippar there are possibly signs that at least some of the institutional plough men profited from a stronger position caused by the personnel shortage. Their relation to the institution was becoming a contractual one, and that is also the interest of the Murašû *nukarribu* contracts. Overall the evidence from the texts which helps to explain the phenomenon of the increasing number of larger settlements the archaeological surveys show us, remains, however, limited. The texts suggest labour shortage rather than expansion of the population. But that makes the phenomenon no less real.

In general we can note that the temple estates had to deal with a labour shortage, that royal estates in Mesopotamia in direct exploitation are practically undocumented, and that entrepreneurs undertook both leases with low rents, and leases which were more demanding. The conclusion must be that they at any rate could solve the labour problem, either by driving those at their disposition harder, by attracting outsiders, or by a combination of both. Technological innovations are unlikely, though the Murašû archive seems to suggest an intentional change from a two to a four ox plough team, as had been employed since long by the institutions. This implies the employment of at least one extra worker per team. A fact is also that entrepreneurs of the Murašû type had a surplus of stock which they made productive by leasing it to others, instead of using it themselves. In itself this suggests that there was a certain amount of free labour, or labour of small farmers, available. Small groups of tenants act together in Murašû texts. We can also notice, especially in the file on the work on the *mušannītu* at Gilušu, that the temple in Sippar could hire local labour. There were villagers who availed themselves of the opportunity to earn extra income. Though the origin of both this additional labour and the surplus Murašû stock may remain a problem, its presence is evident.

We can safely assume that the lease of a canal implied the right to use or sub-lease the land on it, that is, probably, the unused land.[101] Other users of the source of water concerned would probably have had to pay according to custom or according to their existing contract with the owner or with the previous holder of the rights. The unused land often seems to have been given out at low rates. Though it may, on principle, have been beneficial to bring more land into exploitation, irrigation inevitably had negative effects in the long run. It is difficult for us to assess the result at this distance in time. The efforts to increase productivity should be acknowledged, however. Taxation and the leasing of sources of government income play some

---

[100] According to BIN 2, 132 members of the Puqudu tribe had been given to Eanna by Sargon II and Sennacherib, which was confirmed by Esarhaddon, obviously a problematic affair. An Amukannu family occurs in F. Thureau-Dangin, RA 16, 1919, p. 117ff., 14-18, as an element of a donation of Marduk-zākir-šumi. We must assume that this was witnessed by a (prominent) member of the tribe: IV 20.

[101] The question of profitability has exercised many people. Notably M.W. Stolper, 1985 pp. 134ff, and this author, JESHO 32, 1989, but it remains difficult to understand the size of an enterprise like that of the Murašûs. We do not have even the faintest indication either regarding the size of one of the large princely estates of the Achaemenid period, nor, for good measure, of what an "average" bow fief amounted to.

part in this, as the phenomena are closely associated, although the full implications are not easily understood.

Some of the sub-leases involved will have implied a certain amount of speculation, probably on the part of both parties, as is indicated by the nominal character of the rent stipulated. The entrepreneur could sub-lease land he had leased himself for a nominal sum. A good example is the Murašû text Ist 9, a low-level sub-lease. We may assume that the tenant had at least one plough team with which he would attempt to exploit at least 10 kor of land -much less than the standard amount for a plough suggested by the Edict-, for which he paid a rent of one kor of barley per kor of land. He would probably be able to manage more land, and he is in fact promised unlimited access to water. This is only possible if land and water are in good supply. The lessor expects that he will be able to increase the rent if the speculation succeeded. There are two examples of a rent of one kor of barley per kor of land, and also an example where there is what could be called a moderate fixed rent, but that already amounts to eight kor of barley for a kor of land.[102] In general and on principle all fixed rents must be regarded as fixed on the low side: the tenant simply would not be able to survive otherwise - or, indebtedness was (already) a way of life. As we have seen not fixed rents amounted to 25% of the yield on land irrigated by hand and to $33^{1}/_{3}$% on other land.[103] We have also noted that on principle this differentiation according to effort can be regarded as an incentive.

As has already been stated only the archival material of the Murašûs derives from a level in the economic system at which irrigation systems as complete entities play a role. The smallest type is that of a branch canal which does not supply water to other canals. A full description, containing a number of standard elements, has been given above. Such "systems", basically a small canal and the land depending on it, need not have been very large. BE 9, 65, 28 x Art 38, and BE 9, 67, 28 VII Art 39, deal with three neighbouring canals of this type, deriving from the left bank of the all important Nār-Sin (BE 9, 65 line 7 and BE 9, 67 line 6) There are three systems next to one another: the Nār-Tattanu, the Nār-ša-Natunu and the Nār-Diratu. The fact that two contain a personal name is immediately indicative of the modest size of the system concerned: it was constructed or managed by the person mentioned. Two of the three canals were being leased. The middle one, the Nār-Natunu required 40 oxen and for seed a mixed quantity of cereals of 250 kor. It was assessed at a rent of 3005 kor, inclusive of products for which no seed was provided by the lessor. Some of these were summer crops, which opens the possibility of a limited double cropping on favourable land. The lessee was a "servant" of the lessor, but he seems to have provided some categories of seed himself, so possibly also additionally some of that of the categories listed as provided by the lessor. For the other, the Nār-Deratu, the lessor did not provide extra oxen or seed and the yield (for the lessor!) amounted to 800 kor, but not all land on the canal was included, the *uz-ba-ri ša šarri* was excepted.

Direct comparison of the two leases is not without problems, just as the two leases of BE 9, 65, to two different underlings of the firm, but with a clause which made the two lessees jointly responsible for both leases, an unique configuration, are difficult to compare. All rents were fixed and the leases ran for three years, which makes it inevitable that there must have been provisions for fallow. Even if the number of oxen is given, the number of ploughs is not known, for, as was mentioned, in the Murašû archive a change over from a plough with two oxen to one with four was on its way. The amount of seed does not tell all either, as the tenant, even the one who was a servant, himself also contributed. In BE 9, 65 2900 kor of cereals were the yield of 250 kor seed used, a ratio of seed to yield of 1:11.6, which includes payment for

[102] In several of the texts quoted here some of the essential numbers are difficult to read and choices are sometimes unavoidable.

[103] In BE 9, 7, 12 XI Art 26, this is to pay for water alone on bow land.

oxen and seed and the compensation for the fact that the tenant was a "servant".[104] In the other case the rent paid could represent the ordinary 1/3 share of the owner, which would result in a total of 2400 kor as the yield. The "fixed" cereal yield of a basic, small irrigation system (on the Nār Sin) could be around 2400 to 2900 kor. We assume that one kor of land produced at least 10 kor of any cereal and that a kor contained 54000 square cubits of 50x50 cm each, i.e. that a kor equals 1.35 ha. We could propose, for all it is worth, that such a system measured, with provision for fallow, some 800 ha. For a full team of four oxen 30 kor of land is something of an absolute upper limit for what it can cope with. There would be ample opportunity for sub-leasing. But the conclusion must also be that the tenant could never have produced the rent required on his own. He inevitably would have required personnel.

The other case, on BE 9, 65, is that of a different type of irrigation system in which part of a bank of a major or secondary canal is included, that is of the canal supplying water to a number of minor irrigation systems of the type just discussed, which was leased with the right to draw water directly from that canal. Here speculation on the size of the system is not warranted.

EE 14, with its parallel EE 15 is perhaps a good example of a sub-lease in a system which had become fully productive. The head of the Murašûs can be regarded as the real lessee, and it must also be assumed that some of his, named, previous tenants did not continue their lease. Why, we are not told, either of the parties involved may have been dissatisfied, or the old tenants were out-bidden by the new one. But that is perhaps not really the case. The sub-tenant undertaking the lease is a well known Murašû servant, but the importance of the text lies in that he is careful to stipulate an additional clause, which gives him the exclusive right to the plough services of two villages. But only as far as his master is involved, third parties are not excluded. As already remarked, the clause is unique for the Murašû archive, but probably indicates that in this type of lease labour was usually included and constituted a source of friction.[105] The lease proper concerns a canal with the land on its two banks, "from the intake to the tail end, as far as the water goes". This can be regarded as a catch all phrase, which required practical specification, understandable only for those who knew the situation: the horse fief, the royal *uzbāra* land, and land leased to four other persons in three separate leases. But that is still with unused land.

A rough idea about the practical size of the area involved could, with some risk, be derived from the amount of seed involved and the fifteen teams of four oxen requested, assuming that the tenant did not himself have to contribute. The seed included some 260 kor of cereals, which indicates roughly an equal amount of land planted if the tenant did not provide additional seed and not including the fallow implied in a three year lease. Some more land would have been required for the "lesser crops", of which, however, some are summer products, suggesting that also here some double cropping can be assumed on good land close to the source of water. 275 kor would be about the maximum, which results in 18 kor of land per team, some 24.5 ha each, which is, certainly compared to known earlier Ur III standards, extremely reasonable, and better than what the Edict prescribed. The total arable involved could be some 675 ha. The 260 kor of land planted with cereals will have had to deliver 3750 kor of cereals to the lessor, which gives a seed to yield rate of 16.15, which is not impossible, but means that the lessee would have no income excepting that from his own farming, beyond that from the water leased. This is unlikely in view of the phrasing of the contract which places the canal, and not the land in first position. The contract tells us that land involved in the earlier leases was

[104] This is marginally lower than what is stipulated in the arable section of the Edict.

[105] It is notable that this lease does not mention the normal additional contribution in flour, the grinding of which would be the task of the villagers: this could suggest an additional perk for the lessee, unless such payments are automatic.

situated at two different localities. These villages are not the same as those where the ploughmen lived, thus there must have been other farmers who depended on the canal.

But the dubious character of these reasonings are made clear by EE 17 and its near duplicate of about a year later, BE 9, 30: the 74 kor of cereal seed in that text cannot reasonably result in a (partial) yield of 1500 kor, the seed provided by the lessor to his "servant" is only a form of additional stocking. But this perhaps is exactly the fact which should claim interest: both parties are expanding requirements. And expansion is the purpose of the leases.

Uruk

YOS 6 150 20 x Nbn 11, see above under *nakkandu*.

TCL 13 182 13 IV Dar 2, Bēl-gimlanni s Mandanu-ereš, *ša muḫḫi quppi* Eanna accepts a lease to the value of 10000 kor of barley and 12000 kor of dates given up by the *širku* Gimillu of 1000 kor of land with 200 oxen and some iron for tools. Gimillu had asked for 400 plough men and 600 oxen with 1000 kor of seed. The new lessee is promised 200 additional oxen and 50 additional plough men at the beginning of the next agricultural season. He will give additionally 10 fattened oxen. Major canals will be dug by Eanna. Additionally the lessee will give *kurummatu* for the EN.NAM of Esaggil, the scribes, the gate keepers and the measurers. The arable and waterlogged land will serve as grazing for the herds of Inanna.

Murašû:[106] Low rents

Ist 9 15 XII Art 35, land *nak-kan-du šarri* delimited roughly by two (smaller) canals and by land exploited by two other persons, belonging to the lease of PN *ša ana muḫ-ḫi sūti* of a stretch of the Nār-Sin at the disposal of Enlil-šum-iddina is (sub)leased to PN for a (nominal fixed) rent of 10 kor of barley 8) *ma-la* ŠE.NUMUN *šá ina lìb-bi ip-pu-uš* A.MEŠ Enlil-šum-iddina *ana* PN *i-nam-din*.

BE 9 102 16 VII Art 41, lease of 21.2.x kor of land by Enlil-šum-iddina on the Nār-Sin on both sides of N-x, [x kor] in Ḫuṣṣētu-ša-Nāṣir, 60 kor [at ?] on the Nār-Šapputtu, in (Āl) Šapputtu, 4.1.4 kor [in ?] and on Nār-Dūr-pānia in (Āl) Mamšam, [x kor] in x Āl-Ḫūpu-ša-Bariki-Iltammeš, in GARIM-ša-(Al)Makmanu, in total 107.1.4 kor land NIG$_2$.SUM$_3$.MU LUGAL of the *šaknu ša* ^{LU_2}ba-na-i-ka-nu, leased by him for five years to Enlil-šum-iddina, at 1 kor of barley per kor of land (?) (1:1).

PBS 2/1 182 11 V Dar II 1, lease by Rēmūt-Ninurta of 30 kor land on N-Š and Nār-Zame for five years for 30 kor barley per annum. (1:1)

PBS 2/1 20 8 VIII Dar II 1, lease 8 kor land of a *mār-bīti* in Abastanu on Nār-ša-Salā by his *paqdu* to Rēmūt-Ninurta, rent 64 kor per annum(?) for three years. (1:8)

Murašû: irrigation systems

EE 17 30 III Art 31, internal lease from Enlil-šum-iddina of (your) bow and (your) *bīt ritti* land at Bit-Murānu and in the *zi-im-ma-nu* Nār-ša-Reš which draws water from the Ḫarri-Piqudu and "as far as it reaches" and (my) *bīt ritti* land in Āl Bīt-Nadini with oxen and seed. Damaged. Subject to *imittu* by Enlil-šum-iddina.

BE 9 30 12 V Art 32, next to identical with EE 17, gives with 12 ploughs of 2 oxen and 74 kor of cereal seed, a fixed combined rent of 1700 kor of which 1495 kor in cereals.

BE 9 65 28 x Art 38, a) internal lease on the right bank of the Nār-Bēl-aba-uṣur from (Āl) Galutu to (Āl) Bīt-Bagayadāti, *muṣṣane* of king and land of inhabitants of Nippur, plus oxen, tools and seed for an *ebūr*, "harvest", of 2005 kor.

b) internal lease of Nār-ša-Natunu on the left bank of the Nār-Sin from *miṣir* of Nār-Dirat to *miṣir* of Nār-Tattanu in its totality with oxen, tools and seed for an *ebūr* of 3005 kor and additionals. Note lines 22-23 Nār-Bēl-ab-uṣur Bēl-apal-iddina (lessor 1) *it-ta-nab-ba-ku*, <<Nār ša>> Nār-ša-Natunu Nabū-ušēzib (lessor 2) *it-ta-nab-ba-ku*.

BE 9 67 28 VII Art 39, Lease Nār-Dirat, see above under *uzbāra*.

EE 14 25 VII Art 40, Ribat s Bēl-erība addresses his master Enlil-šum-iddina with a request for the lease of Nār-Ugari-Dūr-Nippur which draws its water from the Ḫarri-Piqudu 3)

106 The examples are very selective.

right and left *ištu* KA$_2$-*šú a-di ši-li-iḫ-ti-šú a-šar* A.MEŠ *il-la-ku-'u* 4) [A.ŠA$_3$].MEŠ KA *šul-pu šá* E$_2$ ^{GIŠ}GIGIR ŠE.NUMUN.MEŠ *uz-ba-ri šá* LUGAL *šá ina muḫ-ḫi* ŠE.NUMUN.MEŠ E$_2$.^{GIŠ}BAN.MEŠ 5) *ša* PN *ù* PN2 in GN and two other stretches of land leased in GN2 to two other people, with stock (60 oxen, with ca 275 kor of various types of seed (of which 259 kor of cereals), for a rent of in total 4019.3.0 3 sila$_3$, (of which in cereals 3750 kor) plus 20 kor of GAZI and as extras 500 skeins of linen thread, 2 oxen and 20 sheep).

PBS 2/1 32 7 x Dar II 1, receipt barley ḪA.LA LUGAL, ^{GIŠ}BAN$_2$ *šá* Nār-šá-Add[u-ab-uṣur].

PBS 2/1 59 (Dar II 2), fragment cf. sub *kuṣurrānu.*

PBS 2/1 50 12 IX Dar II 3, barley, *imittu* ḪA.LA ŠE.NUMUN.MEŠ K[A *šul-pu ša* GU$_2$ Nār-ša-Addu-ab-uṣur.

PBS 2/1 104 22 V Dar II 5, receipt payment of ^{GIŠ}BAN$_2$ *šá* Nār-^{LU_2}Simmagir given by the *ša muḫḫi sūti ša* Nār-Bēl-ab-uṣur for yr 5; lines 1) and 4) note payment of KI 1 GUR 0.0.3, i.e. per kor 10% additionally.

C. Practical results

The two important Uruk leases, YOS 6, 150 and TCL 13, 182, indicate that one of the considerations which made leasing more attractive for the institutional owner than direct exploitation, was the need to attract more labour, which was expected to be within the means of the lessee, who had to have access to labour in order to be able to undertake the lease. In the case of the Murašûs there are reasons for the supposition that up to a degree they had their own following which could be employed, but what could be expected from a *širku* like Gimillu in this respect is less clear.[107] We must assume that initially the "owner" had to make circumstances attractive for the taker of the lease. But leases where short term, three years being normal, which made a steady improvement in the share of the owner possible. Reclaiming contracts ask a lower rent from the tenant than ordinary contracts. In the previous chapter we have seen that there are reasons for the assumption that the administration received anyhow a *ṣimdu,* 10%, but that with a tendency to expand into a *mašīḫu,* 20%, per kor of the complete yield on top of the rent stipulated from the tenant or lease holder. Under such circumstances expanding production even in an indirect fashion would have been extremely attractive for the administration. It would have limited the costs of supervision and provided all possibilities to adapt conditions at regular intervals, whereas the lease holder would try to retain the land he had reclaimed and thus was ready to pay more. And that, to repeat the fact again, in an economic atmosphere of persistent growth.[108] Taxation and leasing, even outright privatisation, by the government are related matters, again, then as now. However, over-exploitation and dependency on the high yields of lease contracts are, then as now, problematic.

Though our documentation is of a limited nature, particularly compared to the importance of the subject for contemporary society, the conclusion that the government had a

---

107 In this respect we must reconsider Joannès' idea that somehow the use of persons like Gimillu represents an attempt by the leading circles of Eanna to regain the control of the institutional economy, which had been weakened by introduction of the outside rent farmers by the royal administration: TÉBR p. 150. On the other hand Gimillu is not easily seen as the man of the inner circle, an argument which could be met with the remark that he was forced out of business.

108 Even though I do not regard it likely that the end of the Murašû texts as we have them represents the abrupt end of the firm, I am still convinced that the society in which the Murašûs operated knew a considerable amount of arbitrariness and organised violence. Setting one's feet in the wrong place in a political sense will have had grave consequences for the Murašûs and their colleagues. Not for nothing do they rent a house in Babylon "until the king leaves" in the crucial months of the stabilisation of the rule of Darius II. That is what I meant with "tyranny" in the Murašû environment, which seems to have been problematic to some: being economically active entails political risks, both for the holders of fiefs and for those who exploited on a large scale the opportunities created by the system.

grip on both water and land is hardly unexpected. In the documentation available labour is not well-represented beyond the fact that the existence of a subject population in the countryside is sufficiently attested. That there were villages containing a population partially tied to the land is certain for the temple estates and likely for such land which can be linked in one way or another to the king. Through land for service arrangements and leases this labour was partially transferred to certain sections of the private sector. On the one hand there was the aristocracy, including the military, the subject of the next chapter, on the other the entrepreneurs who were supposed to be able to increase the yield by enlarging the agricultural labour force through sub-leases. That certain entrepreneurs, notably the Murašûs, had their slaves, servants, debtors and "clients" is evident. Some of these clients could be other people's men, certain persons were more successful than others in retaining followers. These clients were, at least in part, "smallholders", who for one reason or an other sought their protection. In this indebtedness, including that to the taxman, played a role. Incidentally, the documented loss of independence by a certain group of people is potentially one of the best indicators available for the existence of a layer of independent subsistence farmers. The role of tribal organisations, another source of labour in the Chaldean-Achaemenid period is poorly documented.[109] We assume a decline in importance of the Chaldean and Aramaic tribes, but must regard Arab penetration as likely.

Not unexpectedly taxation policies had both a positive and a negative aspect. They stimulated expansion by making available land and water against a sliding scale of payments, but they also had negative effects on certain farmers by contributing to their indebtedness. For a cynical politician that was perhaps a purpose: it compelled people to make themselves available on the labour market. Taxation and indebtedness are clear elements of the land for service system of land holding we will discuss next.

Excursus: The situation of a Sippar head of an institutional plough team.

We have learned to accept that the Neo-Babylonian institutions had to deal with personnel shortages. A consequence would be that that personnel was in a relatively strong position. Since the publication of Jursa's dissertation on the agriculture of the Šamaš temple in Sippar the number of indications that the institutional personnel had an interest in the exploitation of institutional land has considerably increased. Jursa has remarked that the agricultural personnel in Sippar is not indicated formally by the term *širku* in the texts available. Though that will not mean much in itself as we see herdsmen, ploughmen and gardeners being called up for military service for the temple as a result of their unfree status, it is still notable that the relationship between the institution and its *ikkarus* can in Sippar at least occasionally be regarded as a contractual one. Though less pronounced in Uruk, the same situation may have obtained there. This does not, of course, automatically apply of necessity to all those potentially involved, the documentation is rather haphazard, but what was branded "total taxation" of the institutional agricultural labour force at the beginning of this study is perhaps no longer completely applicable, at least not for a number of individuals. We must pursue this matter somewhat further.

We have regarded the Edict of Belsazzar as a basic set of rules applying to the institutional rent farm, in reality it could equally apply to the individual institutional ENGAR, *ikkaru*, the head of a plough team. Regarding him in the Neo-Babylonian period primarily as a wage earner, possibly with a sustenance plot, is possibly not the whole picture, almost certainly not only in Sippar, but also in Uruk. His relationship to the institution is contractual, as indicated by the fact that he has to pay *sūtu*, a fixed rent, together with probably the other dues,

---

[109] We therefore cannot automatically justify the supposition, that, as often in similar circumstances, for the central government tribal holdings present themselves as the holdings of their leader, therefore "function" as another large estate.

as mentioned by the Edict.[110] Jursa has published a number of documents which indicates that the ENGAR/*ikkaru* has on his land his *errēšu*. This is a sharecropper, who as such pays *šibšu*, "rent" to the institution, with *ešrû*, "tithe". He exploits that share of his land which the *ikkaru* did not manage to till himself and made the rent burden, directly related to the surface of the land leased by the *ikkaru* easier to bear. The *errēšu* was not solely an employee engaged by one of the big rent farmers of the period from Nabonidus onward, but he also fulfilled a role in earlier institutional agriculture, where he was engaged if not by, at least alongside the simple *ikkaru*. The texts published by Jursa have made possible a better interpretation of already available comparable material. Usually the *errēšu* is mentioned by name, only occasionally he is not.

A direct lease to a Sippar *ikkaru* is Jursa 1995 no. 51 (22 XII Nbn 6), which was to run for 5 years and bring in 25 kor of barley for the temple. The amount of land is unspecified, but the stipulations of the Edict clearly do not obtain, for notwithstanding the use of the expression *ana errēšūti*, "for exploitation as arable under the plough" the five years term and the 25 kor possibly suggest a reclamation contract. Otherwise the contract would involve only a small piece of land of perhaps some two kor, which is Jursa's preferred solution. The fixed rent is a fact, but it is possibly not very high. Jursa 1995 no. 1 (20 I Nbn 11) is even more revealing: two brothers, otherwise known as *ikkarus*, receive an unspecified amount of land as a *bīt sūti* and they will pay in barley "like the *ikkarus* of Bēl, Nabû and Nergal". This suggest that contracts with *ikkarus* were not uncommon, all the more so as a reference to the by now known exemplary position of the estates of Marduk is included.[111]

The combination of (institutional) *ikkarus* with (additional) *errēšus* is also found in Nbk 131 (18 I Nbk 22). The *ikkarus* of Āl-Šamaš were subject to *imittu*. The amounts they had to deliver are mentioned first in the first four posts listed, followed by a much smaller amount "in the *mašīḫu* of one PI", *zittu* of PN *errēšu*. The text is only partially preserved, there were separate subtotals for *ikkarus* and *errēšus*, but also for the "*errēšus* with the *ikkarus*" (rev. 17). In Nbn 398 (Nbn yr. 9) we find in line 7 a Lâbâši *errēš ša* Nabû-eda-uṣur, whose own contribution was listed in the previous line and who is also found in the next. Clear is especially Jursa 1995 no. 2 (date lost, probably Nbn), where we follow Jursa for lines 3-5: "in toto x barley is the *sūtu* of the *ikkarus* [at the disposal of PN], barley, *šibšu* and *ešrû* of the *errēše* who are [on the *sūtu* land] of the *ikkarus* at the disposal of PN", for which we can compare the situation found in CT 56, 505+526, also edited by Jursa.[112]

From Uruk there is no useful comparable information. All smaller lease contracts deal with date plantations, usually involving new planting, while the larger ones belong to the rent farm sphere. But the conclusion that the institutional *ikkaru* was a proper tenant seems to be warranted not only in Sippar, but occasionally also in exemplary Babylon. The rent farmer of institutional land in this manner had a modest, and probably older, "little brother", who belonged to an early phase of the system he operated.

---

110 On the position of the *ikkaru* in Sippar cf. Jursa 1995 p. 24. The lack of information on rations for *ikkarus* can possibly be explained by the supposition that they were no longer mere employees, but often tended to have a more tenant-like position. Unlike the *errēšus*, who were sharecroppers, it would seem that they did not pay *ešrû*.

111 As Jursa 1995 p. 14 points out, fixed rent and *imittu* procedures which link actual yield and actual *imittu* are difficult to square. In view of the date Jursa proposes to regard the text as an *ad hoc* document stipulating complete delivery. But that does not explain the reference to what had to be done on a regular basis in Babylon, Borsippa or Kuta in comparable circumstances.

112 Cf. Jursa 1995, p. 15 and 16.

CHAPTER IV
THE LAND FOR SERVICE SYSTEM: MILITARY AND CIVIL OBLIGATIONS IN THE NEO-BABYLONIAN PERIOD[1]

1. Introductory remarks

The assignation of land with the obligation to fulfil specified tasks and to pay specified contributions is far older than the Neo-Babylonian period, but in that period we can speak with confidence of a system which is reasonably documented and encompasses in its ramifications a considerable section of society in the countryside, with extensions into the towns.[2] Strictly spoken this does not represent taxation, as it is formally no more than complying with obligations which are a result of the tenure of land on which the obligations rest. Though the holder will not have been completely free in engaging in the contract, compulsion as the overriding motive for entering into the transaction is also unlikely. As the obligations answer public needs, they can not be dissociated from the impositions of a government on its subjects in general, especially not if the impositions are variable as to their height and linked to the governmental requirements of the moment. The fact that land was available made the policies followed an easy option.

This is the best documented type of "taxation" in the Neo-Babylonian period, but only in the sense that there are many texts dealing in some form or another with the subject, not that the texts illustrate the whole complex matter. What is striking, is that it is present, in varying guises, in archives with different local backgrounds. This does not mean primarily that basic obligations differed, but that the phrasing of the documents varied somewhat from one place to the other and that there was an observable development in time. Another reason for variations is that, socially spoken, obligations, and therefore holdings on which the obligations rested, were not only unequal, but are also unequally documented. Particularly clear is that the qualitatively and socially more important military obligations, those associated with serving with a chariot or a horse, which merge with impositions on “aristocratic” estates, are less easily paralleled with their immediate civil obligations than those resting on the simple bowman.

In translating phrases like *bīt narkabti*, *bīt sisê* or *bīt qašti* we will use the terms chariot, horse or bow fief. This is a land for services system in which holdings and obligations were hereditary and probably had been intended to be that from the outset. But it is a far from fully fledged "feudal system" as developed in mediaeval Europe or as was created in a purer form in its extension in the Holy Land. Like earlier structures of this type which have left documentation, Old Babylonian, Nuzi, and perhaps Neo-Assyrian, the different elements of the system remained subjected to the monarchy, which had, if not created it, at least regularised it, in order to obtain a grip on the personnel it required for military and other purposes through providing land -with water, but not even that was automatically the case, as BE 9, 7 demonstrates. The system was never entrusted with general tasks in the sphere of civil

---

[1] Literature in general: primarily Joannès, 1982, p. 16ff., Stolper, 1993-7, p. 205-207, with literature. For the Old Babylonian period the introduction by F. Thureau Dangin 1924, p. 3-6, is still the excellent concise introduction to essential aspects of the phenomenon.

[2] Texts in the Murašû archive occasionally mention not only land held by Nippurites, which may have had a different background (BE 9, 65), but also fief land in Nippur: BE 9, 8, BE 9, 44 or near Nippur PBS 2/1, 128. Stolper 1985, p. 79 no. 66.

administration, even though officials with civil tasks participated in it. In Mesopotamia the combination of regional military and civil power did not develop, as far as we can see, into a serious menace for the monarchy,[3] though every participant in a land for service scheme inevitably will have been involved in succession problems and revolts. There inevitably existed a political dimension, as befits all elite structures. But this did not constitute a menace to the basic structure of the political system. A particular benefit of the structure was that it provided a means for regulating and canalising the integration of fresh elements into the population. Such elements could be of nomadic, deportee or mercenary[4] stock.

We may expect that a specific administrative act constituted the basis for every local land for service scheme, instituting and regulating the local system of land holding, in which local circumstances, especially the people participating, influenced details. There is no text which can be compared with those which can be related to the implementation of the *bīt ḫanšû*-schemes of the earlier Neo-Babylonian period, which are, perhaps in size, if not in purpose, of a similar nature. The likelihood of a link will be considered in Chapter VII. Inevitably there will have been an administration dealing with the land for service systems.

The particular schemes we can identify in a limited fashion in the textual material always had already gone through a certain development by the time documentation becomes available. We do not know their beginnings, but can only note -partially- how existing obligations were fulfilled under particular circumstances. Equally we do not know their final phase, though we can imagine that a system which was not used actively and where obligations became increasingly of a financial nature, would become difficult to mobilise when real need arose. Perhaps especially in the South the dissolution of any local system can be regarded as inevitable if it is accepted that the possibilities of permanently exploiting any piece of land were limited. Though this may seem to be highly theoretical, for both social and environmental reasons land for service systems were finite in the South. In social respects the various schemes will have gone through a parallel process of fragmentation and concentration, which will have changed the social structure of the individual schemes fundamentally, while ecologically land will have deteriorated, as irrigation subjected it to salinisation.

Terminology defines three standard types of service obligation: with a chariot (*bīt narkabti*), with a horse (*bīt sisê*) or as a bow man (*bīt qašti*), but this cannot have constituted the complete system. At any rate a man with a chariot will certainly not have served alone, probably not even a horseman will have done so. Any obligation implied provision of one's own basic equipment, including a certain amount of selective foodstuffs and probably some silver for occasional expenditure on the road. This will have been a "traditional" obligation, dating back from long before the Persian period, for this was not something new in the Neo-Babylonian period. Yet basic conditions like the length of the annual(?) period of service are unknown, nor do we know whether the men had to appear under arms every year, whether there was a difference between having to appear for civil duties, with hod and shovel, and armed only when a real mobilisation took place, which may have meant a difference as to expenditure on equipment. We do not know whether a bowman had to practice his skills on a regular basis. The obligation to serve was not strictly military, that much is absolutely certain at least for the holders of chariot- and bowland, but it will also have been true for the horse fiefs, which anyhow, like the bowmen, paid *ilku* in silver in lieu of service, when the case arose. We may also expect that there were people who primarily had to provide transport, by boat, with carts or with oxen, horses or, more practically, with donkeys or mules. Providing for these tasks simply belongs to the system of services which had to be organised in order to obtain a working

[3] With a possible exception towards the end of the Ur III dynasty?

[4] In this respect we must mention especially the Bannešāia, Carians, who came form outside the Chaldean sphere of influence, and who can also be found in Egypt.

apparatus. This is virtually unknown as yet, but see below under *kanšu*. The little that is known in this respect hardly stands in a realistic relation to the importance of the matter.[5]

The lowest tier in the land for service system in the Neo-Babylonian period seems to have been the bow-service, but the question is whether "bow-service" was something uniform. There were certainly unfree bowmen amongst the institutional personnel and on other large estates, in *ḫadrus* or not. Some of the bow fief holders may have been primarily bowmen, but others, with an occupation, will have been assigned land, for which they could be mobilised. In institutional context bow-service was imposed at any rate on selected *širkus*, who were not free. The same could be true of the *šūšānu* or the *gardu* in the context of an aristocratic estate or on that of a high official. If members of a *ḫadru* held on principle a bow fief, that perhaps did not strictly mean that they served with a bow. This is immediately suggested by Stolper's list of *ḫadrus*[6] where at any rate the *taššalīšānu*[7] and probably the *aštebarriānu*, "lance bearers", but perhaps not the *māḫiṣū*[8] served otherwise in a military fashion. Service in connection with a bow-fief seems to have covered a varied range of occupations, definitely including some of a low social status. But it could be questioned whether scribes or merchants were expected to serve personally, which in turn would put a question mark behind *ḫadru* as a basically military form of organisation. We must not expect a rigid, uniform system but something which had grown piecemeal, and kept growing in that manner. At any rate some *ḫadrus* were linked to estates, and there were *ḫadrus* which were probably unfree. We must not assume a monolithic organisation.

The duration of the period of obligatory service is a problem. To a considerable degree this determined the weight of the burden. The term *ilku* covered on principle all obligations of a person involved in a land for service system. For the Old Babylonian period Landsberger[9] proposed that the complete *ilku* of a fief-holder covered all days of the year, but that the obligations were shared equally between the official holder, the *qaqqad redîm* in the case of the Ubārum texts studied by him, and his *taḫḫu*, "substitute", perhaps with the additional complication that in Landsberger's interpretation the official holder, Ubārum, and his brother served in alternate years, implying that they also performed one another's agricultural work every other year.[10] The interest of the Ubārum texts is that the relation between the holder and

---

[5] The workings of the Ur III "*zikum*" have been studied by W. Heimpel, Toward an understanding of the term *sikkum*, RA 88, 1994, p. 5-31. It seems to include the use in an institutional context of oxen "normally" used for other purposes, i.e. ploughing, when available. This could imply that men were also required. Being required to provide transport, food and shelter for the army was/is the common lot of subjects and conquered alike. In the Ur III period there was a proper organisation for post and transport services, if such an organisation did not exist in later periods, as Heimpel suggests, we must reckon with *ad hoc* requisitions. At least in Assyria some comparable system existed and the Persians could not do without.

[6] Stolper 1985, p. 72-79.

[7] Stolper: "shield bearer", but possibly essentially as a member of a chariot crew?

[8] Stolper: "scout", CAD M/1 p. 102, "hunter, scout", yet primarily: "bowman"?

[9] 1955 p. 128. There may be some doubt whether there is proof for the assertion, but it considers the maximum possible. Reduction of the length of service periods by Old Babylonian kings is a well known propaganda devise, so is later *kidinnu* or *šubarû*, but these terms do probably not refer to land for service arrangements, which may in part have been intended to replace the old subject related obligations, which had lost much of their contents. Perhaps that is one of the reasons why the subject serving as a subject is difficult to detect in our period.

[10] 1955 p. 126. In the small Old Babylonian "Larsa" group of texts published by P. Mander and F. Pomponio in JCS 53, 2001, p. 35f. a person assigned to a service regularly has a DAḪ and sometimes additionally a TUR or a DIRI, who are members of the same family, and a *puḫḫu,* occasionally also with a

the *taḫḫu* changed in so far as that the holder at first kept two-thirds of the obligations and the land, and later only half of each. If the original obligation to serve covered the whole year, both men would serve now half a year each. Though such arrangements look reasonable, they do not really inform us about a solution for the most pressing problem. These people are supposed to have been farmers, and that meant that they, that is all of them, had to be present on the land in certain periods of the year, unless holding a fief implied a family business, with more than one adult male for each person obliged to serve. That seems to have been the case with Ubārum, but it obviously led to friction between him and his brother. There is also the possibility that a land division scheme made additional agricultural personnel available.[11] Inevitably service must otherwise have been limited to a certain number of days or months per annum. But perhaps an Old Babylonian *redûm* like Ubārum with his police duties is not a good example for comparison with the Neo-Babylonian bow man in general.

The best evidence for a time limit for the duration of service in the Neo-Babylonian period is PSBA 7, 148, quoted below under *eširtu*: the actual service required perhaps one month out of every six, but again: in this particular case.[12] The interest of the text is that it makes the existence of time limits for actual service a distinct possibility. Under *rikis qabli* a small file from Sippar will be quoted, which could suggest another type of time limit as the persons concerned seem to have been destined for a three year stint. Such an arrangement was of course possible only in an institutional context where certain individuals could be selected for service from a much larger group of people with the same occupation.

Though we have PSBA 7, 148, we do not have, for example, notes certifying the fact that a soldier had entered service or had been granted leave on a certain date, types of documents not unknown in Mesopotamia in other periods.[13] BM 42432 from the Bēl-rēmanni archive, confirmed by the seal of the person responsible, quoted below under *ešírtu*, comes close, however. We will note below that people were engaged for special civil duties for periods of three months. We must again not expect uniform obligations anyhow, certainly not in cases where services were replaced by payments. As soon as actual service was replaced by payments, authorities entitled to services will have been inclined to replace aspects of length of service by higher payments in the name of efficiency, for instance in order to reduce overall travelling time by engaging a limited number of persons for longer.

Perhaps we must assume on principle that all persons obliged to serve belonged to a unit, a *kiṣru* or a *ḫadru* and at a lower level, as far as service was concerned, to an *ešírtu*. Perhaps we can speculate about the practical course of action followed. Those in authority assessed the amount of service required, depending on the situation, either in manpower or in silver and divided thereafter the assessed requirements over the various groups, which had to arrange the fulfilment of the assigned quota internally. Relating to taxation the question is whether there was a fixed or customary limit to what could be asked for or not. That applies to both the duration of the service and to the payments. The nature of the documentation is such

DAḪ, who replaces him. The service involved, either by being incorporated into it, or by leaving it, is that of AGA.UŠ. It was probably the intention that the "soldier" could dispose of an adult who could do the (agricultural) work. Under such circumstances he, or someone else, would always be available for service.

[11] Possibly the rare Third Millennium ENGAR.ERIN$_2$.NA? On the other hand the military campaigning season was not for nothing adapted to the constraints of the agricultural year.

[12] Stol has studied aspects of the duration of Old Babylonian service obligations, eds. P.J. van den Hout and J. de Roos, Studies Houwink ten Cate, Istanbul 1995, p.293-307. He mentions one or two months, but the evidence derives, in general, from payments to people engaged for specified periods, which is, strictly spoken, inconclusive.

[13] For Old Babylonian documents on entering service cf. JCS 7, p. 83 no. 2.

that no firm conclusion will be possible, but we must pose the question and be prepared to collect the evidence.

2. Terminology

a) The status of the large estates

Scarce though the information on cultivated land held by the king may be, as we noted in the previous chapter, kings granted estates to members of their family and to officials. For the Neo-Babylonian period the phenomenon is not well documented,[14] but it is probably to be linked with a kind of terminology which hardly appears in the texts otherwise than in status related phrases which indicate that the person concerned was not completely free or could not be sold. To belong to a *bīt kussi*[15] figures here, besides pertaining to a *bīt narkabti* or a *bīt sisê*, but, as already noted in the previous chapter, being a *šušānu* also had a link with certain estates, besides possibly having a more general meaning.

A daughter of Nebuchadnezzar could give a considerable amount of land to Eanna in Uruk.[16] Some of the large estates had a more or less institutional status. The rise of the Babylon Egibis is linked to their being an agent for the estate of Neriglissar, who held the position of Simmagir[17] during Nebuchadnezzar II, before taking the throne. In the Murašû texts we find a certain Tattanu, who is called the Simmagir and a Bīt Simmagir, his estate, which had a *ḫadru* and therefore contained military fiefs.[18] Though it is difficult to prove with the evidence available, we can assume with virtual certainty that such large estates were obliged to contribute to the civil and military undertakings of the kings already in the Chaldean period. The Simmagir of the moment, Neriglissar, figures in the list of officials who were obliged to perform menial labour of a ceremonial nature amongst other worthies:[19] more practically they will have contributed to the labour force required for the royal projects.

There are prosopographical arguments for considering the estate of Neriglissar as the precursor of what was during Nabonidus the estate of the crown prince, possibly with other property elements of different origin, for, as we noticed, the Simmagir estate seems to have continued to exist separately. Such estates had their own household staff and were no doubt subject to various obligations, which inevitably included those linked to the military status of the holder. An estate like that of the crown prince will have consisted of elements scattered over the whole kingdom and it will have shared characteristics with the land held by the king himself, including under-exploitation, as is attested in a text published by F. Joannès,[20] where

---

[14] For the later Achaemenid period Stolper 1985, Chapter 3; a detail: M.A. Dandamayev, The Domain-Lands of Achaemenes in Babylonia, AoF 1, 1974, p. 123-129.

[15] Mentioned in the previous chapter in connection with royal land.

[16] R. Labat, RA 54, 1960, p. 85f., cf. J.A. Peat and W.G.E. Watson, NABU 1999/29 p.27-9, also edited by P.-A. Beaulieu, Or NS 67, 1998, p. 194-5.

[17] On this functionary W. von Soden, Or NS 35, 1966, p.19ff, cf. ZA 62, 84ff. and CAD S p. 272-3.

[18] Stolper 1985 p. 73 no. 10.

[19] E. Unger, Babylon, die heilige Stadt, Berlin-Leipzig 1931, p. 290 IV 21.

[20] Joannès-Lemaire 1996, p. 41-60, the estate of the crown prince is called the *bit redūti* in the date *imittu* documents nos. 2, 3 and 4. That the land in text no. 6 belonged to the estate of the crown prince seems to be a reasonable assumption. The lease holder was at any rate his *rab bīti*. Cf. the comments RA 90 p. 53f. Joannès interestingly suggests that the bow fief was additional to the 45 kor of land mentioned, and that the rent of 60 kor barley can be taken as suggesting that the size of the bow fief amounted to 15 kor of land. This would result in a nominal rent of 1 kor of barley per kor of land. Even if the rent amounted to 60 kor over 45 kor of land it would remain a "nominal" amount. The suggested size for this/a bow fief cannot be compared with other evidence, we must regard it as a valuable piece of information in need of confirmation. As always practical problems abound. Fallow is probably included, which could double the practical rent over the actually planted area, which, however, still remains modest. More important would

land, including a bow fief, is leased against a low nominal rent.[21] The GAL ^{GIŠ}BAN$_2$ *šá* E$_2$ DUMU.[LUGAL] mentioned in OECT 10 345: 4, from the Mušallim-Bēl file, will hardly have been responsible for the exploitation of the complete estate of the crown prince. With varying intensity all large estates will have had their local administrators.

Status and tax obligations merge imperceptibly. All dignitaries were givers and receivers of (obligatory) gifts. In the temples such gifts are booked not only under the neutral term *irbu*, "incoming goods", but also as *ešrû*, tithe.[22] They used for the exploitation of their land not only their own staff, but also leased elements of their estates to local entrepreneurs, directly or indirectly through their staff. An example is the *ganzabaru*, who had a long-running contract with the Babylon Egibis during the reign of Darius I.[23] The large estates mentioned in the texts of the Murašû archive were subject to obligations which were linked to the prominent political role of their owners, who had military units linked to them on a permanent basis. That was not something new, as it was a direct result of the monarchical-patriarchal structure of society in which a king bound his followers to himself by granting them estates.

As Stolper has explained[24] the large estates of the later Achaemenid era were not monolithic structures, but they contain land assigned to (military) personnel and local elements of these estates were leased with or without 'rights' regarding this already assigned land.[25] The estates of the members of the royal family and the dignitaries were incorporated in the land for service system.[26] This occurred at least at two levels. Land belonging to the estate was given out as fiefs of a lower order and the directly exploited segment was subject to a levy of its own. Both were probably linked to the obligations imposed on the holder. This is comparable to what can be found on temple estates. This type of arrangement can be regarded as universal in similar circumstances.

---

be that the bow fief could easily be tilled with one plough team. But the official concerned was certainly not expected to till the land himself and he obviously did not possess the wherewithal.

[21] BM 75502, Jursa 1998, no. 2, p. 102-3 and p. 6, quoted under land of the king in the previous chapter, illustrates problems related to the large estates well. The text deals with *ešrû* barley which had not been collected from a number of holdings in a specified geographical area (obv. 2). These are stated to belong to or to constitute the *bīt ritti* of Aplā s Mušēzib-Bēl, which were at the disposal of Šamaš-apal-uṣur s Niqudu Rē'u-sisê. (For collection? Or for actual exploitation?) The first two parcels are said to be *šá* E$_2$ *ri-du-tu*/ E$_2$ (LU$_2$).BAN (lines 7-9 and 10-11). In both cases persons are mentioned as responsible for delivery, in one case the responsibility has been transferred to another. Seven other parcels are said to be <on land> *šá ina libbi ša šarri*, "on that belonging to the king", which is probably an intentionally vague expression, avoiding reference to any specific other obligations of those responsible for the payments. At least one of the persons concerned was to all likelihood a foreigner. The text is for Jursa the basis for a "military" interpretation of *bīt ritti*, about which, as will transpire, I feel some doubt. The text dates from Nbn yr. 12. I would prefer to regard the holder of the *bīt ritti* in this case as someone who has undertaken the exploitation of the holdings mentioned through the people who are listed in connection with the individual parcels which are subject to *ešrû*. It would mean that already during the reign of Nabonidus there were bow fiefs which were "unoccupied" in a technical sense. That is in no way remarkable, for soldiers holding land were a persistent feature since, at least, the Third Millennium.

[22] I would like to interpret in this way the fact mentioned by Jursa, 1998 (esp.) p. 8: costly presents at a, as Jursa remarks, politically sensitive moment. I assume that the word *ešrû* in such a context does not indicate a fixed recurrent obligation, but represents a label used by the administration in booking the sum.

[23] Dandamayev 1968, p. 235-239; Wunsch, 2000a, p. 107.

[24] Stolper 1985, Chapter 3, p. 54ff. deals especially with this matter.

[25] The estate of Aršam also encompassed herds, and with herds belong rights to pasture. This cannot have been unique, but we know next to nothing about the arrangements required.

[26] There is nothing new is this. A *kiṣru* of the queen was known in Neo-Assyrian times, but this would not have made the queen the honorary colonel of some regiment. It would indicate a unit (mainly) provided with land on the estates of the queen and personnel drawn from such estates.

Three texts dealing with a Murašû lease of land belonging to the estate of the queen, the E_2 MI_2-*ša*-E_2.GAL, in a number of places, presumably on or near the Ḫarri-Piqudu illustrate these phenomena.[27] Intended initially to last for three years the arrangement was obviously continued. It specifies that the bow fiefs associated with the estate[28] were not included in the lease. The document states that the tenant would pay a basic amount of 100 kor of barley and 400 kor of dates, but over and above that, that he would provide 25 *ṣāb šarri ana dullu*, "king's men for (corvée) work", and a *kurummatu* consisting of 15 kor of barley in flour, 10 *dannus* of beer and an assorted number of 25 sheep and goats. The earlier receipt is not informative as it merely records the payment of unspecified commodities, but the second confirms the difference between the basic rent and the extras delivered by the tenant. The directly exploited part of the estate was thus subjected to a levy of 25 *ṣāb šarri*, as the word suggests ultimately to the king. The population of the estate was also subject to the ordinary obligation to grind flour, primarily a female task. We could suppose that this was not strictly an imposition which had to leave the estate, but the possibility should be considered that it was intended as a delivery due to the ultimate provider, the king. As we will see the delivery of flour was a not uncommon standard obligation.

The most important contribution of these three texts is that they explain how this estate of the queen contributed directly to the land for service system, not alone through apportioning land to fief holders, but also by providing men from its core personnel for direct service and female labour for onerous routine tasks. This is not surprising, but for once some of the aspects of the system are specified.

Bīt mar-šarri at Bīt-Abī-rām

RA 90, no. 6 18 VIII Dar 26, at Babylon, lease by a Persian official of 45 kor of land (and? or equalling?) his E_2 ^{GIŠ}BAN for four years for 60 kor of barley per annum.

Nippur, Murašû

Ist 2 date lost, lease of land of E_2 MI_2-*ša*-E_2.GAL *ša ina* (Āl) Baṣṣanu, [x Āl Parakku, (Āl)Bannēšu, Ā]l Ḫiduia and *usallu* Nār-Piqudu [without bow land] *šá ina lìb-bi e-piš* IM *u ma-šá-ka* for three years for 100 kor of barley and 400 kor of dates and 25 *ṣāb šarri a-na dul-lu ù* $SUKU_6$.$ḪA_2$ [and additionals, cf. BE 9, 50] (only specification of animals preserved), leased by PN to [M.]. (Same land as in BE 9, 28).

BE 9 28 18 VII Art 31, receipt of rent *uz-bar-ra ša* E_2 MI_2-*ša*-E_2.GAL at (Āl) Baṣṣanu. and (Āl)Parakku, *usalla* on Ḫarri-Piqudu, at (Āl) Bannešú, at (Āl) Ḫidu'a (// TuM 2/3, 179).

BE 9 50 20 VIII Art 36, receipt of rent as in Ist 2 with additionals specified as 15.0.0 ŠE.BAR *ù qé-me* 10 ^{DUG}*dan-nu* KAŠ.SAG *ma-lu-ú* and in total 25 UDU.SIZKUR and 25 $^{LU_2}ERIN_2$.LUGAL for the same land as in BE 9, 28, but with a different manager.

b) *bīt narkabti* and *bīt sisê*, service with chariot or horse[29]

The two superior forms of military service obligation, *bīt narkabti* and *bīt sisê*, chariot or horse fief, are rare in the early Neo-Babylonian private archives, even though in the Murašû archive, the horse fiefs occur in close association with the ordinary bow fiefs, and were

---

27 The lease is Donbaz-Stolper Ist 2, to be dated before Art 31. There are two receipts for rent, BE 9, 28, 18 VII Art 31 and BE 9, 50, 20 VIII Art 36. The three documents each mention a different steward, but that is not important here, the estate is the same.

28 These are qualified *e-piš* IM *u ma-ša?-ka*?, on which Donbaz-Stolper, 1997 p. 79, with a link with *šūšānu*, discussed in Chapter III. Though no exact definition of *šūšānu* is possible, their status was not completely "free", cf. the discussion in the previous chapter. Perhaps the limitation of their status consisted exactly in the fact that they were obliged to serve not in their own "right", but through holding land from an estate. Ist 2, refers explicitly to bow fiefs.

29 Literature: CAD N/I p. 359-360; CAD S p. 334-5; Cardascia, 1983 p. 62, note 3.

therefore not particularly elevated socially. Furthermore they were often subdivided. Babylonian town dwellers probably were no horsemen, or rather a horse was outside the military sphere a useless luxury for which they had no employ. Here again we are dealing with a type of obligation which had a long history, but which did not belong to the strata of the "commoners" from which the private archives derive in general. Involvement with these higher fiefs is mainly indirect. The possibility seems to exist that the holders of chariot fiefs provided the "military" cadre for the bowmen, with whose *ḫadru*s the horsemen may have been associated. There are signs that people like the Murašûs became more directly involved with the higher fiefs through adoption, a phenomenon which has earlier precedents, especially in Nuzi.

The pre-Persian text from a Nippur environment BE 8/1, 52 is difficult to understand, but it refers to a property related obligation and is best regarded as dealing with a chariot, thus automatically including horses, as well as other horses. It is striking that the persons concerned bear non-Babylonian names and in fact seem to belong to a specific, Aramaic, ethnic group. CBS 7961, for the later Achaemenid date of which see Stolper 2001, 102 *ad* line 3, deals only with a part of a horse fief, not all of it will have been leased as a date plantation.

The Borsippa text VS 6, 155 provides the written evidence that a *bīt narkabti* involved more than a chariot and its equipment. It had a *rab qašti*, "commander of the bowmen" and therefore involved more people than those manning the chariot.[30] It also entailed high costs, in this case for corvée work done for the king in Susa. Though the text is a private debt note, the chariot and the service connected with it will probably have belonged to the obligations imposed on the Nabû temple, as its *qēpu* was in charge. The Egibi text quoted could indicate that the high ranking officials who had to field chariots, in this case the *šākin ṭēmi*, "governor", of Babylon had rights over (possessions of?) inhabitants of the town, in this case Marduk-nāṣir-apli Egibi, for which he could require men. The wage paid covers the period from the middle of month I to end VII, which could suggest travelling plus labour obligations. The text refers anyhow to a voyage to Elam. Such trips occur more often in the "land for service" texts, illustrating the manner in which Babylonia had to contribute to public works in Elam. The (institutional) Sippar text Dar 9, on canal work, indicates that holders of chariot fiefs could be required to act collectively, parallel to the institutions and were made responsible for the digging of stretches of an irrigation canal. That the owners of chariot fiefs belonged to the higher strata of society is evident. In BE 10, 91 (11+ IX Dar II 4) a *bīt narkabti* has its own *ḫadru* of bow-fief holders. In this case *bīt narkabti* probably is short for *bīt narkabti* of someone. A clear link between a horse fief and bows is made by PBS 2/1, 63 and 99.

A *bīt narkabti* or a *bīt sisê* involved not just the personnel required directly, but also included other support personnel.[31] An owner willing to sell slaves had to guarantee against the possibility that the slave concerned belonged to a *bīt narkabti* or a *bīt sisê*, a clear indication that this type of fief was granted together with its unfree, probably agricultural, personnel. That these could be made to serve militarily stands to reason. What we do not know is whether chariot, horse and bow fiefs were always linked in a fixed (command?) structure, through which the other fiefs were grouped around the chariot fief. The Murašû archive contains a number of texts in which combined payments for chariot or horse fiefs and bow men, identified as belonging to specific *hadru*s, are mentioned.[32]

---

30 The holder was possibly callcd ^{LU}2GAL ^{GIŠ}GIGIR, Sippar, Dar 9, or was he only a manager of such a fief?

31 For a small file of Sippar texts suggesting service with horses cf. here *rikis qabli*, but this service with horses may have concerned a horse depot, either for the remounts or for breeding purposes, which makes it less relevant here.

32 The lease PBS 2/1, 30 (18 x Dar II 1) contains a share (?) in a horse fief and much bowland, but the text is too damaged.

As in the Neo-Babylonian South there existed in Nuzi after the middle of the second millennium a graded system whereby service either with a chariot, i.e. as a *rākib narkabti*, as a *nakkuššu*, as an *ālik ilki* or as an *aššābu* had to be provided. We can safely assume that this represents a scale of obligations in which at any rate that with a chariot and as an *ālik ilki* are recognisable as implying military obligations, the *ālik ilki* being the common infantry man armed with a bow.[33] What the *nakkuššu* had to do is not so clear, but the word is occasionally connected with messengers.[34] The position in which the obligation is listed, between the charioteer and the bowman, suggests some mounted form of service. The Nuzi archives abound with texts in which people with *ālik ilki* status alienated rights to land they were holding, but remained burdened with the *ilku* obligations resting on that land. Similar Nuzi texts without statements about *ilku* arrangements tend to come from specific localities: it could be assumed that we are dealing with no more than local scribal habits which in reality refer to the same situation, with the same *ilku* arrangements as mentioned explicitly elsewhere. The interpretation of what occurred is hotly debated, but the likeliest solution remains that these people were alienating rights to land which was formally not their own.[35]

The Neo-Babylonian texts pledging land belonging to our types of fief are unspecific. The pledge, as the *tidennūtu* in Nuzi a means of circumventing the rules forbidding sale of land held against service obligations, probably does not imply in the Murašû archive, where bow land was regularly pledged as a security for the delivery of produce, automatically that the land was actually being alienated. Access to the produce was probably the main aim for the Murašû. On the other hand pledged land regularly figures in enumerations of the possible status of land

---

[33] The specific type of service imposed on the Nuzi *aššābu* is not clear to me, they rank under the *ālik ilki*. The matter has been studied Dosch 1993, p. 85ff. There are clearly foreigners amongst them.

[34] N. van Brock, RHA 65, 1959, p.130. It is clear that the *n.* could be released from service and therefore actually served during a certain period. A survey of the Nuzi material on *nakkuššu* is provided by Dosch, 1993, pp. 77f., who gives a useful list of the disparate facts. The *n.* was socially spoken of a middle rank. Dosch concludes on p. 79 that in Nuzi the *n.* held land for which they were not obliged to do service, and that they could be compared to the *eḫele/šūzubu* in Alalaḫ, who should be some form of "freedmen". This would negate the proposed parallel of Neo-Babylonian serving with a chariot, a horse or the bow with *rākib narkabti, nakkuššu* and *ālik ilki*, which is in itself not completely unlikely as serving on horseback in Nuzi could be regarded as already possible. The evidence for the ranking of the *nakkuššu* under the *rakib narkabti* but above the *ālik ilki* and the *aššābu* is conveniently collected in Dosch 1993 p. 75. On p. 83 the author denies a link between *ilku* and military obligations in Nuzi, though there too the *ilku* obligation results from the holding of land. To her conviction *ilku* obligations in Nuzi were irregular as to incidence and contents, but that is not of necessity exceptional: requirements would vary from year to year everywhere. Though there is fighting in Nuzi towards the end of the archival material available, much of the property related text material dates from considerably before that point in time. I find it difficult to dissociate social status from military obligations in a land for service system, as (also) existed in Nuzi, if only because on principle no difference should be made between military and civil obligations. There was an *ilku* of the *aššābu*, but they were not numerous.

[35] The other now, perhaps, principal interpretation, that of G. Dosch, in 1993, p. 144f., explains the Nuzi-type adoptions as a means by which the adopter obtained the patronage of the adoptee, certainly deserves serious consideration. In the Neo-Babylonian period a person acquired a patron by asking someone else to assume certain responsibilities for him and by handing over regular token payments, cf. the previous chapter. I find it significant that in the Neo-Babylonian period adoption manifestly leads to transfer of property in the land for service sphere in the one case documented, where again the stronger party has been adopted by the weaker and assured itself of the practical services of that party in order to comply with the obligations. This one parallel is for me essential for the overall interpretation of the phenomenon, also in Nuzi.

in leases.[36] But retaining access to the labour of the former holder is both in Nuzi and in the Neo-Babylonian period a purpose on the part of the adoptee or holder of the pledge.

Only one instance of partial transfer of a fief through adoption is known in the Neo-Babylonian period, the UCP 9 text originally published by Lutz.[37] In this case the Murašû family had acquired through adoption a part of a horse fief. A kinsman of the adopter, of whom it is not certain that he had remained the main person responsible for the service, now arranges with the adopted co-owner concerning the practical execution of the service: he is willing to undertake the obligation, but needs support regarding his equipment. It is obvious that the person who undertook the service was, in this case, in a somewhat diminished situation. It is also clear that the man prepared himself for actual military service. When we discussed the terminology of royal land in the previous chapter we encountered several cases in which holders of fiefs were well aware of the fact that they were not the real owners. Also in this respect the Neo-Babylonian period did not invent new solutions. What occurred in our period can help to understand what took place earlier.

The term *bīt aspatu* has been seen as a rare alternative expression for *bīt sisê*.[38] The land was leased *ana errēšūtu*, "to be exploited as arable" and the alternatively proposed emendation into (*bīt*) *aspastu*, "lucerne field", is no solution, as in other instances that type of field is carefully excluded from leases.[39] The irony of the case is probably that lucerne fields can be regarded as an innovation, especially intended for the keeping of horses.[40] The land was royal property, and was as a *bīt aspatu* the *bīt ritti* of someone else.[41] The text does not refer to special obligations involved in holding such land, which is, as we will see, usually the case with land called *bīt ritti*.

Whether the owners of chariot or horse fiefs were obliged to fulfil corvée duties in person is unlikely, such duties meant mobilisation of the personnel belonging to these fiefs, which took part in canal building and which had to go to Susa, possibly with the charioteer as leader, just as the *qēpu* of Borsippa, like other *qēpu*s, was in charge of working parties provided by the temples, in which his "chariot" played a role. "Chariot" in such instances indicates a unit of a certain composition.

Babylon Egibi and related

Dar 154 — 15 I Dar 5, Š s I hires Kuṣuraia s Ibnia Ban-x for 40 š to the end of month VII to go for him to Elam *it-ti* ^{LU_2}ERIN$_2$.MEŠ *šá* ^{GIŠ}GIGIR *šá* Bēl-aplā-iddina, the *šākin ṭēmi* of Babylon. Guarantor is Napsanu s Nergal-uballiṭ.

Borsippa

VS 6 155 — 6 VIII Dar 39, at Susa, 36,5 mina silver due to Iddina-Bēl s Nurea Ilija from Ša-Nabû-idušu s Lāqīpu, *rāb qašti šá* E$_2$ ^{GIŠ}GIGIR *šá* Nergal-nāṣir, *qêpu šá* Ezida, silver spent *a-na dul-lu šá šarri* and ? on account of the *bīt narkabti* of the *qêpu*.

---

36 The status of the pledged land in BE 8, 124 is not specified and, as is known, the Murašû texts are uninformative concerning their property rights. EE 87 is too damaged to serve as an acceptable example of a bow fief actually held as a pledge.

37 H.F. Lutz, UCP 9, 1928, p. 269ff. and E. Ebeling, ZA NF 16, 1952, p. 203ff.

38 Obscure according to CAD A/2 339L; the connection with a "horse fief" (Sanskrit aspa, "horse") was suggested by Cardascia 1983, p. 63, where there is also an extensive discussion of the Lutz text. CAD R p. 388L returns to the emendation *as-pa-<as->tu*$_4$ rejected A/2 p. 339.

39 Cf. EE 19; it is possible that in VS 5, 55 the end of line 1 also contained an exemption (*e-lat*), in which case the emendation could be accepted without problems and the text can be eliminated from the discussion.

40 The exclusion of this type of field from *errēšūtu* contracts practically excludes the idea that lucerne was knowingly applied as a green manure.

41 On *bīt ritti* see the discussion in Chapter VII.

Nippur environment

BE 8/1 52 (+)2 x Nbn 13, at (Āl-)Guzānu, (unassigned to an archive) 3 mina of silver repayable to Ninurta-ana-bītišu s Baba-iddina from five persons on orders of Nabû-uballiṭ ⌈*na-ad*⌉*-na-šú-nu-tu*, KB *šá a-na* x [x x (x)] 11) ^{GIŠ}GIGIR *u* ANŠE.KUR.RA.MEŠ *šá* E$_2$ ^{P}Ú-x-x-AN-ia 12) SE$_3$*-nu a-di-i* 1/2 MA.NA KB *šá* $^{\text{URU(?)}}$ E$_2$ x-nu-e-x x 13) *na-ad-*[*n*]*a-šu-nu-tu*.

CBS 7961[42] x V x, lease of arable on the left bank of the Nār-Šapputtu 2) E$_2$ ANŠE.KUR.RA next to PN *šu-šá-an-nu* and next to the šandabakku and PN2 *šá* E$_2$ *qa-bu-ut-tum*, "of the animal pen" is leased as a date plantation.

Nippur/Murašû

BE 9 8 12 VIII Art 27, receipt for the rent of land of complete, partial and *pa'iṣu* bows in Bīt-Šulaia and in (Āl) Ḫambari and a E$_2$ ANŠE.KUR.RA in Nippur in the hands of Enlil-šum-iddina given by *šaknu* of $^{\text{LU}_2}$*šu-šá-ni-e*.

BE 9 66a 19 VII Art 39, receipt for rent 2) *šá mi-šil* A.ŠA$_3$ *šá* 3) E$_2$ ANŠE.KUR.RA at Bīt-Balassu. Cf. PBS 2/1, 48 (13 V Dar II 2) with a link to the 3) *ḫadru šá* $^{\text{LU}_2}$*šu-ša-ni*.MEŠ *šá ki-ri-ki*.MEŠ.

BE 10 7 2 I Dar II 1!, receipt for 1) the yield of and of E$_2$.ANŠE.KUR.RA E$_2$ ^{GIŠ}BAN.MEŠ *ina li-mi-tu$_4$* 2)NIBRU^{KI} *šá* GU$_2$ Nār-Sin *šá* GU$_2$ Nār-Ḫarri-Piqud *šá* GU$_2$ Nār-Purat-Nippur šá GU$_2$ Nār-Namgari-Dūr-^{d}En-líl and elsewhere *ša ḫa-da-ri ú-qu šá* $^{\text{LU}_2}$*se-pir-ri*.MEŠ in the hands of the *šaknu* at the disposal of Enlil-šum-iddina; paid. (= TuM 2/3, 181).

PBS 2/1 3 5 I Dar II 1, receipt of complete *ilku*, (formulated as in BE 10, 91), amount lost, for horse fief and bow fiefs on the Ḫarri-Piqudu, horse fief of Bēl-bulissu and [bow fiefs] on the Nār-Sin at Āl Galia, [? and] bow fiefs *ḫa-da-ri šá* $^{\text{LU}_2}$*se-pir-re-e* at the disposal of Enlil-šum-iddina paid over yr 41/Dar II 0. Damaged.

PBS 2/1 228 x III Dar II [1], promise to deliver dates by a member of *ḫadru ša ḫuṭari* in Bīt-Bania, horse land on the Nār-Purat-Nippur in B-B pledge.

BE 10 35 1 V Dar II 1, promise of delivery of dates by holder of bow fief and his associates in Bīt-Balassu, horse land in B-B pledge.

PBS 2/1 48 13 V Dar II 2, receipt of *ebūru* of half a horse land of PN in Bīt-Balassu, *ḫadru ša* $^{\text{LU}_2}$*šu-šá-ni*.MEŠ *ša ki-ri-ke*.MEŠ, and land $^{\text{LU}_2}$Ar-ba-a-a in Bīt-Murašû, in (Āl) Ḫambari (on the Nār-Šarri), in Āl-Puṣāia and on the Nār-Purat-Nippur (which is bow land? in the hands of the *šaknu* of the Arbāia, given by him. Cf. BE 9, 66a, 19 VII Art 39.

Lutz UCP 9 18 X Dar II 2, arrangement between PN and PN2 concerning the equipment of PN as the horseman due from the E$_2$ ANŠE.KUR.RA of the father of PN which had become the partial property of PN2 through adoption by PN3.[43]

PBS 2/1 63 x V Dar II 3, receipt of 5 mina of silver, two *dannu* of KAŠ.SAG, two sheep and one kor of flour and [barley] <*ilku*> (formulated like BE 10, 91) over months I to XII yr 3 for land belonging to a quarter of a quarter E$_2$ ANŠE.KUR.RA and land of two bows in Kār-Ninurta on Ḫarri-Piqudu, 3 *'u-du* in a bow in Bīt-Marudu, 3 *'u-du* and four (complete) bows in Bīt-Murānu, a bow in (Āl)Ḫambari, a bow in Bīt-Šulā, and a bow in (Āl)Ḫadala', summarised as 13) 10 bows 1*-en*(!) *u'-du* (=1/5) and 1/4 of an 1/4 horse fief, received by *šaknu ša šūšāni* DUMU.MEŠ *ḫisannu*. (PBS 2/1, 87 (1 VII Dar II 4) comparable for yr 4, PBS 2/1, 99, Dar II 4, for yr 3 related small fragment also mentioning a payment of 5 mina.)

PBS 2/1 66 x VI Dar II [3], receipt of 4 mina of silver, *ilku* on a E$_2$ANŠE.KUR.RA, over months I-[XII] yr 3 as much as the share of PN and PN2, brothers, at Ḫuṣṣētu-ša-Kalbā (so Zadok), which is at the disposal of the second in command of the *šaknu ša* A.BAL *ša ú-qu*.

PBS 2/1 76 8 x Dar II 3, receipt of 16 mina of silver, *ilku* of land of eight occupied and unoccupied bows in Āl-Bēl, Āl-Sin-bēlšunu, (Āl) Bīt-Ukkamā, (Āl) Bīt-Reḫēti, on the Ḫarri-

---

[42] Stolper 2001 no. 8.

[43] There is no sense in summarising this text extensively here, though it provides a good insight in some of the obligations involved. It is for instance clear that this horseman would not have been able to carry all the equipment listed, he would have needed one or more attendants, and probably a donkey.

Piqudu, and a horse fief belonging to at least five named persons and others at Bīt-Kinā (DU.A) for the year Dar II 3, received by the *šaknu* of the *ḫadru* of the *šūšānu* of Bīt-Zuza.

BE 10 91 11+ IX Dar II 4, receipt of 5 mina of silver *il-ki* TIL.MEŠ [LU]$_2$ERIN$_2$.LUGAL *qé-me šá šarri bar-ra u mim-ma na-da-na-a-tú šá* E$_2$ LUGAL from I yr 4 to XII yr 4 for one bow in Bīt-Sin-līšir on the Nār-Sin, and one in Ḫuṣṣētu-ša-Addia belonging to the *ḫadru ša* E$_2$ [GIŠ]GIGIR in the hands of PN, *šaknu* of the E$_2$ [GIŠ]GIGIR, paid to his *mār bīti* by Rēmūt-Ninurta.

BE 10 102 21 VIII Dar II 5, 1 MA.NA KB *il-ki* TIL.MEŠ [LU]$_2$ERIN$_2$.LUGAL *qé-me šá šarri bar-ra* 2) *ù mìm-ma na-da-na-a-tú šá* E$_2$ LUGAL of yr 5 3) ... *ina* UGU ŠE.NUMUN *zaq-pu ù* KA *šul-pu* E$_2$ ANŠE.KUR.RA *šá* PN and PN2 in Larak and the towns *ša limēti* L., *ḫadru* of [LU]$_2$A.BAL.MEŠ *ša ú-qu* received by *šaknu* [LU]$_2$*sepīri*.MEŠ *ša uqu*.

PBS 2/1 209 4 X Dar II 5, receipt imittu dates E$_2$ [GIŠ]GIGIR on the Nār-Namgar-Dūr-Enlil given by Murašû servants.

Sippar

Dar 9 17 x [Dar] o, [x], Nār-Su-ma-an-[da-]ár *šá ina* A.ŠA$_3$.MEŠ 2') *šá* Bēl, Nergal, Šamaš [LU]$_2$GAL.MEŠ E$_2$[GIŠ]GIGIR *šá i-ḫe-ru-ú*, follows number of stretches (*mišḫu*) of which the first is to be dug by Šamaš, with whose share the text is primarily concerned. Fragmentary.

Related: *bīt aspatu*

Sippar

VS 5 55 13 V Camb 7, 1) A.ŠA$_3$ NIG$_2$.GA LUGAL *šá ina* BIR ḪU KA x x 2) E$_2$ *as-pa-tu*$_4$ E$_2$ KIŠIB *šá* PN s PN2 leased *ana errēšūtu* for six years by PN against 1/5 of the yield on newly reclaimed land and 1/3 on land already under the plough.

c) *bīt qašti*, bow land[44] and *bīt azanni*

Though the terminology is explicitly military, and refers to the land and obligations of the ordinary Babylonian foot soldier, it is also certain that these people had to accomplish other services. CAD Q p. 153, "bow fief", explains that "land (was) granted by the king to which originally was attached the obligation to outfit an archer". This is to all likelihood correct. The terminology used is not always explicit, especially not in the Chaldean period, where much is, or can be, masked by *ilku* and the related set of terms, and from which we do not have so many ephemeral documents of receipt-type as we have for *qaštu* payments from the reign of, for instance, Darius I. The term *bīt qašti* is extremely common in Murašû texts, but though it occurs only sparingly earlier, the ordinary bowman was no Persian or even Chaldean invention. Serving with a bow was not only the consequence of holding a bow fief, BM 79128 from Sippar explicitly links bow and *ḫanšû*, a connection we reserve for Chapter VII. The bow was the ordinary weapon of the Babylonian. Though the term *bīt qašti* is pre-Persian, the Persian administration possibly named the obligation to serve systematically for its military aspect. In reality nothing fundamentally changed under the Persians, as the same people continued to be mobilised, also for civil projects. We can not identify with certainty the Babylon Egibis as holders of bow fiefs, although in Dar 307 someone held bow land on arable of Marduk-nāṣir-apli.

With other texts Bertin 2619 indicates explicitly that the duties connected to the possession of a bow-fief could be called *ilku*. This makes it evident that at least *rikis qabli*, *ṣāb šarri*, *ilku* and *bīt qašti* represent one complex, to which some more specific terms referring to special aspects of the service can be connected. Having a *bīt qašti* does not imply strictly spoken military duties only, but, like *ṣāb šarri*, accomplishment of all duties that were imposed, also in a civil context. The *nidintu*, "gift", of the bow paid by the head of the Egibi family in Bertin 2093 for the person who was formally summoned to come to an arrangement was possibly the sum paid for his *ilku*. The automatic fine imposed on non-appearance was (in this case) one mina, which though probably not the absolutely fixed sum which is sometimes

[44] Literature CAD Q p. 154R-155L, M. Dandamayev, 1983, p. 57.

proposed as a standard payment in lieu of bow fief service obligations, would seem to be suitable to be regarded as a kind of notional average. Additionally we find at the end of sequences summing up the obligations of fief holders the expression *u mimma nadinăt bīt šarri*, "and all that is to be handed over to the house of the king", which could probably indicate the "extras", on which below, which were probably not handed over in silver but as commodities. It is anyhow a catch-all phrase.

CT 44, 82, later Achaemenid, and from the neighbourhood of Babylon, explains that two brothers held a bow fief for which they paid *ilku* and which they probably leased to a tenant. Nothing remarkable, but for the fact that the text provides us with the notable information that the bow fief was somehow connected to the status of *mār banī*, a "free man", of the holders. But serving with a bow is not specifically the sign of being a free man. It is difficult to fathom the implications of this information. Making a slave a *mār banī*, which any owner of a slave could do, certainly did not imply that the owner was in the position of granting the slave concerned a bow fief.[45] Otherwise we can only refer to Dar 351, where there is an *ušurtu* of *mār banī*s. This text will be discussed under proto-*ḫadru* in Chapter VII. That having a bow fief was not just a burden, but also a source of income, perhaps also of status is indicated by the Šaṭir text TÉBR 31 where a share in one is sold, but within the group of persons entitled.[46]

Though only of the later Achaemenid period, UET 4, 39 is remarkable, as it mentions a (dilapidated) house as an element belonging to a bow-fief. In this respect it is joined by the recently published UCLM 9-2919 and the freshly identified text BM 136872, both from a Babylon environment and quoted below, of the same general period. In UET 4, 53 a house belonging to the temple is mentioned, which may have been assigned to an individual with the obligation to serve as a bowman. This again suggests that not just land, but also houses could be an element which could be subjected to this kind of obligation. We will have to collect this type of evidence. For the conditions of tenure BE 9, 7 is of some importance, as it confronts us with the unexpected fact that not all land granted as a bow fief had an automatic right of access to water.[47] This can, however, hardly be a general phenomenon.

A number of texts from Borsippa uses the term *pānāt qašti*. Two of these also include *urāšu ša šadādi ša kāri* and *ẓebēli ša upiyāte,* but as VS 6, 160 indicates, these phrases can individually indicate separate obligations, see the separate discussion of these terms. In my view *pānāt qašti*[48] in Borsippa does not represent a separate duty, but it constitutes a general, comprehensive, term for the total of the obligations, as indicated by expressions like *ù mimma pānāt qašti gabbi* "and all obligations of the bow-fief in their totality", which is evidently a catch-all term. As such it stands at the end of a list of specified obligations. In some texts it occurs after one specific obligation, directly preceded by *ù*, "and". In these cases it indicates all obligations, other than the specific one on which the text concentrates, which have not been mentioned separately. Nothing is forgotten in this way.[49] All these separate obligations could also simply be subsumed under the term *ilku*.[50]

---

[45] Does the text possibly refer to a specific earlier land division scheme in which slaves were granted their freedom on condition that they would undertake bow service?

[46] Cf. the comments by Joannès 1982. p. 99ff. This does not mean that fiefs can be sold freely.

[47] Text quoted in the previous chapter under *ṣibittu šarri*.

[48] CAD Q p. 153R translates with a question mark "preferential share".

[49] Only in one case, L 4720, it is followed in such a situation by *ù ḫi-šá-ru-ú*, "and *ḫ*.", as indicated, a hapax. But see below for Jursa's solution, which fits our context well.

[50] Marduk-rēmanni no. 41 is damaged, and it would be unwise to suggest that the total amount was a payment for *ilku*, for that would mean that Marduk-rēmanni had to pay for three separate amounts, a share in a *qaštu*, for an *urāšu*, as in no. 47, and for something else, constituting this *ilku*. That *qaštu* and *urāšu*

The importance of the Borsippa texts is that they derive from the archives of urban families, which where obviously subjected to obligations similar to those on bow fiefs. The same is true for people from Nippur and Dilbat and, no doubt, from other towns.[51]

Sack CD 98 from Uruk is a definitely Chaldean occurrence of a bow fief[52] and in this context the well-known Camb 85 underlines that the phenomenon of the bow "fief" already existed in the year of the co-regency of Cyrus and Cambyses, the first full year of Persian rule. But the feature will have been much older as the text suggests the existence of a full-grown *ḫadru*-type organisation of these fiefs.[53] Both the splitting up and the dissolution, presumably due to not having a (male) successor, meant that financial arrangements inevitably became much more important in the course of the existence of a particular arrangement. Mutation of actual service into payments ultimately leads to freezing the amounts of silver paid. This cannot be strictly proven in Mesopotamia, but in this respect we can perhaps point out the small amounts of silver paid in Nippur, listed under *ilku* and *urāšu,* which might indicate a final stage of a land for service scheme.

That an important element of the Murašû business consisted of taking the lease of under-manned bow-land is well-known. The collective groups of bow-fief owners, *ḫadru*, concerned, had, it would seem, to guarantee payment of a certain sum, either fixed permanently or for the occasion only. This had to be divided over the number for which they were assessed and they were only too glad to find a lessee willing to accept the use of the land at cost level. Whether the fact that the lessee undertook the financial obligations also meant that he, in cases where this was required, became involved in the putting into the field of a man, or whether it indicates that by this time the incidence of actual service was rare and had been replaced by payments, is not clear.[54] In the Murašû archive we find mainly texts dealing with the countryside, but owners of bow land were present also in the towns.

At least in the Persian period the ownership of many of the bow fiefs had become divided. BRM 1, 83 is one out of many examples. The problem whether an agriculture based bow fief could be kept functioning properly by a single person operating alone has already been addressed. That involvement of more than one person could lead to friction was demonstrated by the Old Babylonian case of Ubārum. That will have increased the inclination to split up the fiefs. In the Neo-Babylonian period there existed a special terminology for fractions of fiefs, discussed below under *kutallūtu*, but these fractions may sometimes have been structural elements of the system and not a result of splitting originally large fiefs amongst several entitled

---

occur parallel in one text is anyhow remarkable. It suggests that these payments could accumulate, and that paying for armed service did not exclude additional payments for labour. This is what one would expect in the Persian period, additional *ad hoc* payments becoming more and more the rule.

[51] Cf. Joannès, 1989 p. 275; Stolper 1992, p. 134, and, 1988 esp. p. 138 note 25.

[52] The matter has been discussed recently by Jursa, 1998 p. 17f. and NABU 1998/124.

[53] Postgate 1974, p. 224, note 2 concluded from the similarity of the Assyrian and the Neo-Babylonian terminology that the Chaldean kings had taken over the land for service system from their former Assyrian masters. Though a certain amount of continuity of Assyrian arrangements in Babylonia is more than likely, land for service is a much older institution, even a permanent feature in Ancient Mesopotamia, as it answers basic needs and problems of society. It existed at least from the Third Millennium onwards.

[54] The workings of the system are discussed by Stolper, 1985, Chapter 5, with much attention for the (exceptional) situation surrounding the disputed succession by Darius II.

persons. As many texts in the Murašû archive indicate, other fiefs had become "dissolved" or "unoccupied" (*pa'īṣu*).[55]

The idea that the system of holding property as a bow fief was to all likelihood expanded by the Persian kings is not new, but it makes sense to collect as much evidence as possible.[56] What is important, however, is that this was not a new phenomenon. Extension of obligations is possibly a general feature of Persian taxation, if it is not an aspect of taxation in general. In the later Achaemenid period BM 50021 speaks of bow land "held by the inhabitants of Dilbat", which might suggest that townspeople as a group had been granted such land, or possibly, that what they held earlier, possibly *ḫanšû*-land, was classified as such. The Seleucid texts from Uruk possibly illustrate the process of the blurring of separations between systems best: *qaštu* seems to have been in Seleucid Uruk not only an obligation, but it had become also an *isqu*, "prebend", not in a clerical sense, we may assume, but in the sense that it may have developed into a specific task resulting in a saleable right to income.

For want of better *bīt azanni/u*,[57] "quiver fief" is probably a rare variant of *bīt qašti*. The only occurrence is found in a Nippur environment. The holder is of foreign descent and the land, of unknown size, has to be reclaimed. That *bīt azannu* belongs in a land for service context is suggested especially by a Neo-Assyrian text, ND 5550,[58] where a possible contestant of a contract is someone's *bēl a-za-ni(-šú)*, who has a claim on the person concerned. The fact that the term is used in Nippur may be significant in view of the fact that the town was one of the Assyrian bases in the South.

qaštu-related payments
Babylon Egibi and related

Bertin 2093 12 VII Dar 6, on 20 VII Guzānu s Nabû-zēr-līšir Gaḫul will come and speak with MNA about the silver *ni-din-tu₄ šá* ^{LU}2BAN which MNA gave to Guzānu. If he does not turn up he must pay one mina of silver.

Dar 307 19 VIb Dar 11, land ploughed with the *maiiaru* in the *bīt qašti* of Nergal-nāṣir which has been given to Iddina s Arad-Bēl in the plough land of MNA. Fragment. (Not in W, E I.)

---

55 The acceptation of the interpretation that this type of "fief" no longer had a holder is based on the assumed opposition implied by the expression GIŠ.BAN.MEŠ *uzzuzēti u pa'iṣēti*, in which the first represent the occupied bows and thus the second the unoccupied. The phrase is not used for a sub-type of fiefs, it mainly occurs in contexts where the intention is to provide a comprehensive enumeration of existing situations, though *pa'iṣētu* fiefs of known persons occur. Note that CAD Q p. 153 translates *ušuzzēti* and *pa'eṣēti* as "whether released or not", thus understanding it, it would seem, in the sense of whether the service due had been performed or not. But this is of no relevance in lease contracts which deal with exploitation of the land for which the service was to be performed and whether actual service happened to be due or not was a secondary matter. The question is extensively rediscussed in M.W. Stolper's comment on his text no. 7 in Stolper 2001. As these fiefs had had known holders, "unoccupied" remains the best interpretation.

56 Stolper 1988, p. 139, esp. note 27.

57 Cf. CAD A/2 p. 526, *azannu* B, "quiver", without discussion.

58 Iraq 19, 1957, Pl. XXXIII line 18, parallel, amongst others, with his *bēl ilki*.

59 The text is also otherwise problematic. In the first place in the manner in which it indicates the amounts of cereals, in that it puts KI.LA$_2$ between the amount and the cereal indicated. The second problem are the *di-pa-ni-šú/di-*<<pi->>*pa-ni-šú* of, presumably, the holder of the fief, who/which seem to belong to Bīt-šangû-parakki. The first sign is almost certainly a DI and not a KI. A reading *qí-pa-a-ni* does nor make

Bertin 2235 25 VII Dar 12[59], barley and wheat NIG$_2$.GA LUGAL *šá* ^{GIŠ}BAN $^{\text{LU}_2}$*a-ši-b/pu*.MEŠ[60] at the disposal of Nabû-šum-ukin, *šākin ṭēmi* of Babylon, NIG$_2$.GA ^{GIŠ}BAN Ba-zu-zu *ù* 9 $^{\text{LU}_2}$*di-pa-ni-šú šá* E$_2$ $^{\text{LU}_2}$SANGA.BARA$_2$. Liblut̩ s Murašû Sin-tabni will pay for Bazuzu $^{\text{LU}_2}$*di*-<<pi->>*pa-ni-šú* to MNA. Liblut̩ and another person are responsible for the payment of barley and wheat.

Bertin 2619 20 III Dar 26, 40 *š* of silver, *ilku* for yr 25, due from the bow of Bēl-erība s Nādin Lūṣi-ana-nūr-Marduk and his $^{\text{LU}_2}$*di-pa!-ni(-šu)* is received by Š s I from Iqūpu, brother of Bēl-erîba.

Bertin 2621 20 XII Dar 26, [x] GIN$_2$ *di-pi ša* BAN! *u ú-na-at* $^{\text{LU}_2}$BAN of Dummuqu s Balāṭu Gaḫul from month IX yr 25 to end I yr 27 is received by Š s I from Nabû-iddina s Eṭel-pî for Dummuqu.

Babylon: Nappāḫu and related

VS 4 77 4 V Camb 5, silver, amount lost, NIG$_2$.GA *ṣābe qašti* from V yr 5 to end X received by Nabû-nādin-šumi s Iddina-Marduk Gaḫal (husband Širā dr NBZ N) from Bēl-iddina s Kunā Aḫu-bani.

VS 4 96 6 III Dar 3, silver of *di-pi ša qašti* from III Dar 3 to end III yr 6 received by Rēmūt s Marduk-šakin-šumi Atkuppu from Ina-Esagil-zēri s Nergal-uballiṭ Sagdidi on behalf of Nabû-mukīn-zēr s Marduk-erîba Marduku. Nabû-mukīn-zēr will show earlier tablets to Rēmūt. IN s NBZ N witness.

Dar 199 x I Dar 6, Marduk-šum-ibni s Šulā has paid 8 *š* belonging to the bow of Bēl-kīšir s Šūzubu Adad-šammê, on behalf of Iqūpu s Murānu. (To whom?)

VS 4 125 12 VII Dar 9, 20 *š* silver, one third of a [*qaštu*] up to end X of Šūzubu s Nabû-šum-uṣur Babûtu is due from IN s NBZ N. Follows damaged passage mentioning x s Bēl-usippe and Šūzubu. Cf. VS 4, 127.

VS 4 127 26 x Dar 9, for half of one bow of x s Nabû-šum-uṣur Babûtu and IN s NBZ N for 6 months of yr 10 Šūzubu will serve for Iddina; Iddina has paid the silver to Šūzubu.

Babylon(?)

AfO 44-5 29 [Nbn yr 9-12], Fragment. Sale(?) of land with judges as witnesses. Mentions 2'-3' neighbouring bow-land in such a manner that it could belong to the land of which the measurements are given.

Camb 85 22 IX Camb kB (= Cyr yr 1), land, bow-land of the *kiṣru* of the Miṣirāia at the disposal of Nabû-nāṣir, the head of the boat men, about which in the council of the elders of the Miṣirāia Mašdesu s Šarrua, Ki-Šamaš s Sin-ittia, Ḫapidišballa s Pišamiš have cast lots: one bow

much sense, *ṭepū* is probably to be preferred, whether *ṭepani* or *ṭepini* is correct or possible is another question. The identity of the ten persons in Bertin 2235 can only be an object of speculation. The same word occurs in Bertin 2836 (13 IV Dar 2[5]), as *di-pi-ni-šu*, quoted under *ilku*. A connection with VS 4, 96 *di-pi ša qašti* is strongly suggested by Bertin 2621 which contains the same phrase and extends it with *u unāt* $^{\text{LU}_2}$BAN, "and equipment of the bowmen". Ungnad NRVU 1 no. 551 note 1 emended into *di-ki*! In Bertin 2235, 2619 and 2836 an interpretation which turns *dipāni(šu)* into another word for *bēl qašti(šu)*, "his co-owners", might make sense but can be no more than a suggestion. F. Joannès, 1982 p. 22 read *ṭi-pi* in VS 4, 96 and translates "supplement sur les (*bīt*) *qašti*", cf. AHw p. 1392, "Belag, Auflage, Umschlag (med.)" and "Eintragung, Addition", (but referring also to AHw p. 167, *dēpu*, a weapon). In the three texts the "*dipānu*" are inevitably humans, however. In Bertin 2621 and VS 4, 96 a payment which is equipment related is possible. In both cases a third party is involved, so this might be *rikis qabli* related. Bertin 2235, earlier than the other Egibi texts, mentions barley and wheat as *makkūr*(?) *šarri* due from the bow of *āšipu*s. The other texts mention payments in silver. Bertin 2619 and 2621 belong to the file on collection of *ilku* duties by Širku alias Marduk-nāṣir-apli Egibi, quoted under *ilku*. A possible connection with AfO Beih. 6, Tell Halaf no. 6 3) *emūqika* 4) *ša ḫarran šarri* 5) *ana mala di-i'-pa* could be considered. Weidner's comments on p. 15 make little sense, the text refers to mobilisation, not to actual fighting.

60 For the reluctant acceptance of *āšipu* cf. the section on *aššābu* in the previous chapter.

in (Āl-)Iškillu, one bow of (the) *akullātu* (land/type?)[61] of Bīt-x-ṣir and 1 bow in Āl-Bīt-da-x. Damaged.

CTMMA 3 124 5 VIII Dar x, sworn deposition, fragmentary, concerns receipt of silver and 6) ^{LU_2}BAN, period of service?

Babylon environment?

CT 44 82 27 V Art 36, at Bīt-Aḫḫē-šullim, *imittu* of dates 1) ... A.ŠA$_3$ *šá* E$_2$ BAN 2) *šá* E$_2$ DUMU.DU$_3$-*ú-tu šá* Bēl-uballissu ù Zitti-Nabû ss Arad-Tašmētu[62] due from etc. (7) KI 1 GUR 0.0.3 *e-piš-tu*$_4$ and (other) date palm products he will give.[63]

UCLM 9-2919[64] 11 IV "Art" 19, [at Babylon?] contract combining reconstruction by and lease for 10 yrs. to a neighbour of a reed-house, next to other houses 4) E$_2$ ^{GIŠ}BAN *šá* PN. No clause on responsibility for the service.

BM 136872 x x Dar II 12,[65] where? contract combining reconstruction and lease for 14 yrs as in the previous text; line 3: E$_2$ ^{GIŠ}BAN.

Borsippa

Ash A 107 26 VII Nbn 16, (Ea-ilūta-banî file) 5 kor of dates *i-na* ^{GIŠ}B[AN] *šá* PN1 *i-na na-aš-par-tim šá* PN2 ^{LU_2}GAL ^{GIŠ}BAN *šá* PN *ina* ŠU^{II} PN3 PN4 *ma-ḫir.*

TuM 2/3 169 16 VI Dar 17, (Nanāḫu-file) see *qēmu* in *ilku* texts.

Borsippa

(examples for) *pānāt* ^{GIŠ}BAN

L 4720	24 IV Dar 25, quoted under *ilku*.
NBC 8371	26 VII Dar 29, see sub *urāšu*.
VS 6 160	21 XI Dar 33, see *zebēlu ša upiyāti*.
L 4740	22 IX Dar 21, // TuM 2/3 220, see sub *urāšu*.
TuM 2/3 221	14 IV Dar 32, see sub *urāšu*.

Dilbat

BM 50021[66] 17 VI Art 40, land leased for three years 3) next to ŠE.NUMUN E$_2$.^{GIŠ}BAN šá ^{LU_2}Dilbat[^{KI}-a-a (x x)].

Nippur

BRM 1 83 25 XII Dar 31, at Nippur (archive unassigned), lease of arable É ^{LU_2}BAN of Iddina-Enlil and ^{d}Nin-x-x-x, x *šá*(?) Arad-Ninurta and ^{LU_2}EN ^{GIŠ}BAN.MEŠ-*šú-nu*, (follows the situation of the land) for tilling to Aḫḫē-bulliṭ s Balāṭu for four yrs. including fallow; owners receive a one third share in the yield.

Nippur/Murašû, no texts quoted here

cf. especially the material listed under chariot and horse fiefs and under *ilku*.

Šaṭir (Barbora group , TÉBR)

TÉBR 1 no date, see below sub costs holders of fiefs.

---

[61] CAD A/1 p. 276L where *akkullātu* land is obviously of a less desirable quality, and *akkullātu* is not a known type of bow. Is some small locality meant? Not very likely.

[62] Possibly related: Michigan 24 (I-XII Art 26), a fragmentary receipt for the payment of *ilku* silver.

[63] *e-piš-tu*$_4$ indicates in this context some manipulation of the dates carried out by the gardener, cf. B. Landsberger, AfO Beih 17, p. 43 and 44, esp. TCL 13, 208, 8 where the formula is more complete. This additional(?) payment would be quality and not taxation related.

[64] Stolper 2000b p. 668-672. The lack of an obvious clause on who bears responsibility for the service connected to the house is disturbing. The tenant is a neighbour and pays the owner for the construction materials, and also each year 1 *š* of silver plus trice per annum *nuptu*. We might expect that a builder-tenant could use, especially if he paid for the materials, the construction free of costs. Is the payment of 1 *š* per GI of land by the tenant to the owner a payment for service obligations?

[65] C.B.F. Walker, JCS 30 p. 237-240. For the date and identification as a bow-fief, see Stolper 2000b p. 670.

[66] Stolper 1992 p.132-4, cf. comments on line 3.

TÉBR 31 1 IX Art 41, at Šaṭir. Arable of numerous persons *u* ^{LU_2}EN ^{GIŠ}BAN-*šú-nu gab-bi šá* Šá-ṭir^{KI} *ina* E$_2$ *ḫar-ba-a-ta*, situation, *a-di* I$_7$.MEŠ-*šú*, a 1/3 share of a number of persons and ^{LU_2}EN ^{GIŠ}BAN-*šú-nu gab-bi* sold to two persons.

Sippar

Camb 13 x X Camb 0, silver taken by two brothers when(? *e-ma*) going to Laḫiru, 6) *te-lit a-na muḫḫi* ^{GIŠ}BAN-*šu-nu* 7) *ú-še-li-'u ù* ^{LU_2}ERIN$_2$ LUGAL-*šú-nu* 8) *ú-zi-zu-ma*: "They will charge the costs to their *bīt qašti* and shared out (the costs of) their *ṣāb šarri* from IX onwards, PN, their *ṣāb šarri*, has received from them 33 *š* of silver *ṣi-i-ti-su*.[67]

Šangû-Šamaš/Ile'i-Marduk (and related)[68]

BM 79128 2 IV Dar 19, dates (resulting from *imittu*) due from PN s PN2 fam. Ile'i-Marduk and mother, the value of silver *ša a-na* ^{GIŠ}BAN *ša* Marduk-šum-iddina s Marduk-nāṣir 9) *ša a-na* PN1 *ša it-ti* EN 50-*ú an-né-e* 10) *a-na ma-la* ḪA.LA *ša* PN! 11) (*u* KU$_3$.BABBAR *ša ta-bal a-na ma-la* ḪA.LA 12) *šá* PN1 *u* KAŠ.SAG *u* 13) UDU.NITA$_2$ *ša a-na qí-na-a-ta* SE$_3$-*na*.) Mentions backlog in dates *šá* ^{GIŠ}BAN! since year 17. (Not all these payments are related to our subject.)

BM 42352+ 15 x Dar 20, 30 *š* silver *ma-la* ḪA.LA ^{GIŠ}BAN of PN (fam. Balīḫu) and PN2 (fam. Šangû-Šamaš) *ša dul-lu ša* I$_7$ *ša* Āl-(^{KUR})Elam^{KI} *ša* MU 17.KAM$_2$ *ša* ^{LU_2}ERIN$_2$ *ša* Ubar (s Bēl-iqīša Isināia) *ina* ŠU^{II} ^{LU_2}*šākin ṭemi* TIN.TIR^{KI} *ip-pu-šu*, received by Ubar. (Share of another person mentioned.)

BM 42548 3 VI Dar 20+, silver for ^{GIŠ}BAN for half a year received by Kāṣir s Kinā Isināia from Nabû-aḫḫē-šullim s Mušēzib-Marduk Šangû-Ištar-Babili.

BM 42577 19 I Dar x, silver *ilku* PN1 received by PN2 for Nidinti-Marduk s Suqaia Ṣāḫit-ginē.

Ṣāḫit-ginê, Marduk-rēmanni

M.r. 41 x x Dar 4, sum, split up into several amounts of silver, first unidentified 2) ... 20 *š šá* ^{GIŠ}BAN *šá* UGU–*šú ma-na-tú* 4) x *š* KB *šá* ^{LU_2}*si-i?-di šá na-aš-par?-tu$_2$?*[69] 4) x *š* KB *šá a-na* Kalbā < s Ṣillā Nabāia> 6)[*a-na*] ^{LU_2}*ú-ra-šú a-na muḫ-ḫi* Marduk-Rēmanni *na-ad-din*, received by PN from M-r. (Cf. no. 47 under *urāšu*)

Other related material:

BM 42444 (no date, but cf. 42633), seven persons, presumably all members of the Ṣāḫit-ginê family under Kiribtu s Iqīša are from VII yr 9 *ina* IGI Kiribtu, 1 MA.NA 50 GIN$_2$ KB *qa-lu-ú šá* ^{GIŠ}BAN-*šú ina* IGI Ki-rib-t[u$_4$ ^{LU_2}*s*]*e-pi-ir*, 1 MA.NA KB *šá ina* 1 GIN$_2$ *bit-qa šá gi-na i-di* 1-*en* ^{LU_2}A.GAR *šá* 6 ITI *ina* IGI Ki-rib-tu$_4$.

BM 42633 x IX Dar 9, as BM 42444, with statement that Bēl-rēmanni has received the last amount for Kiribtu.

BM 43300+ 6 II Dar 17, 10 (rather 11) named men [PAB x] ^{LU_2}ERIN$_2$.MEŠ *a-na* ^{GIŠ}BAN *i*[*na pān* N]idinti-Marduk (s Suqaia).

BM 42432 9 XII Dar 18, PN s PN2 ^{GIŠ}BAN *šá* Nidinti-Marduk s Suqaia Ṣāḫit-ginê, 1-*it* ^{GIŠ}BAN *ina* IGI PN, who seals.

BM 43429 date lost, fragment of list of payments by ERIN$_2$.MEŠ(?) LU$_2$ ^{GIŠ}BAN *ša* Nidinti-Marduk?

Ur

UET 4 39 10 XII Art x 37, (archive unassigned) house plot [E$_2$] *kám-mar* next to other houses, 8) E$_2$.BAN *ša* Šamaš-iqīša s Iddina-Nabû at the disposal of Nidintu-Sin s Sin-aḫa-utir Nidintu-Sin, who transfers it for the building of a brick house to Bēl-iddina s Sin-aḫa-iddina for 20 yrs. Incomplete.

Gallābu archive

---

[67] Text studied Dandamayev 1983, p. 57-59; *ṣi-i-ti-su*: here"his (travel) provisions".

[68] All Šangû-Šamaš family texts quoted by BM numbers are from the edition of the Bēl-rēmanni archive in Jursa 1999, where they are edited in numerical order.

[69] C. Waerzeggers suggests "zilver voor steuntroepen", "silver for support personnel". Not understood by me.

UET 4 194 5 X Art 39, Nidintu-Sin, the *atkuppu*, son of ^{f}Taštibi, declares to Sin-aḫḫē-bulliṭ and Sin-mušallim ss Balāṭu Gallābu that he has no rights to date 10) plantations, arable *šá* LUGAL *ù* 11) *mimma-ku-nu šá e-lat šá* LUGAL *a-na ma-la* ḪA.LA*-ku-nu šá it-ti* ŠEŠ.MEŠ*-ku-nu ù* ^{LU_2}EN.MEŠ BAN*-ku-nu*, on which the brothers on their part relinquish all claims against Nidintu-Sin.

UET 4 60 25 II Art II 1, division of a date plantation and arable E$_2$ ^{LU_2}BAN of Iqīša s Sin-iddina Gallābu *ù* ^{LU_2}*ku-tal-la-a-tú* and prebends between two sets of two brothers. Mentions 9-10) *mimma il-ki* LUGAL *ù na-da-na-a-tu il-ki* LUGAL in damaged context.

UET 4 42 6 IV Art II 35, at Ur, date plantation at 2) A.QAR ^{URU}Madumme, province of Ur, on both sides next to land NIG$_2$.GA ^{d}XXX E$_2$ ^{LU_2}BAN PN1 and PN2 which is at the disposal of seven persons, of whom three, 11) ... ^{LU_2}EN.MEŠ BAN.MEŠ*-šú!-nu* x-x *a-tar ina-a'-na a-ḫi ma-la* ḪA.LA*-šú-nu* 12) *šá ina* A.ŠA$_3$ *u* ŠE.NUMUN MU.MEŠ *šá ki* Aḫušunu s Šamaš-iddina *a-na ma-dat-tú* A.ŠA$_3$ [*ana*?] 13) 4*-ta* MU.AN.NA.MEŠ *a-na* MU.AN.NA 10 *š* KB *qa-lu-ú* 14) *a-na* Sin-iddina s Sin-aḫḫē-šullim *id-din-nu-u'*. The other half of the field is *ana mandattu* at the disposal of Sin-iddina. Incomplete.

UET 4 106 12 I Art II 42, at Ur, barley, *šibšu* arable E$_2$.BARA$_2$*-a-nu* ... GARIM-Makke, province of Ur, 4) E$_2$ ^{LU_2}BAN *šá* PN1, PN2 and PN3 *u* ^{LU_2}EN.MEŠ BAN*-šú-nu* Ea-ēriš s Šamaš-rēu'a will pay for Niḫištu in Ur. Mentions other debt.

UET 4 3 x x Art II 45, at Ur, damaged, statements in court case, mentions number of persons called ^{LU_2}EN.BAN*-ia* but deals with prebends (line 11) and household goods (line 17).

UET 4 53 x x Dar II 7, Ur, damaged, division mentions (rev. 3) E$_2$ NIG$_2$.GA ^{d}XXX E$_2$ ^{GIŠ}BAN PN as a neighbouring house plot of that involved in the transaction.[70]

Uruk

Sack CD 98[71] 3 XI Nbk 35, debt in barley due from PN1 to PN 2, 15) land E$_2$ ^{GIŠ}BAN *ša* PN3 which PN1 *a-na er-ru-šu-tú i-ir-ši maš-ka-a-nu šá* PN2.

YOS 7, 156, 4 XI Camb 3, arrangement dealing with the guarding of land against wild donkeys 9) ŠE.NUMUN *šá* ^{d}GAŠAN *šá* UNUG^{KI} *šá* ^{d}UTU *šá* LUGAL *ù* ^{LU_2}BAN.

YBC 5600[72] 25 VI Art (I/II) 33, dates due from PN and PN2, brothers, to PN3, 9) E$_2$ LU$_2$.^{GIŠ}BAN*-šú-nu šá* [(Al) K]ār-Nanāia 10) *šá šal-šú ina a-ḫi* ḪA.LA *ša ki* PN5 [u?] PN 6 *maš-ka-nu ina pa-ni* PN3.

Seleucid Uruk

BRM 2 29 1 VII? SE 96?, 5) ... *ana* 1*-et qa-áš-tu*$_4$ *ina* U$_4$ 13.KAM *ša arḫussu*.

TCL 13 242 13 ? SE 99, two brothers 2) GIŠ.ŠUB.BA*-šú-nu* 3) *gab-bi* (follows list) 5) *gab-bi* 6) *šá ik-kas-šá-du a-na* 1*-it-tu*$_4$ *qa-al-tu*$_4$ *šá ši-iš-šú* 7) LA$_2$*-ú šá* KI ^{LU_2}UNUG^{KI}-a-a EN.MEŠ *qa-šá-a-tú šá* KA$_2$.GAL ^{d}Adad 8) *šá* ITI*-us-su kal* MU.AN.NA, sold.

Where?

VS 6 302 Date lost. 18*-ta* GIŠ.BAN *ú-šu-uz-za-a-a-i-tu*$_4$ [*ša*?] *ḫa-ad-ri ša* ^{LU_2}*Ki-ir-ka-a-a ana di-ke-e šá* [x?] *ka-a-ri šá* ŠU^{II} PN1 ^{LU_2}GAL *ka-*[*a-ri*] PN1 *a-na ša-da-da šá* 2*-ta* ^{GIŠ}[MA$_2$(?), remnants].

bīt azanni

Nippur

ROMCT II 9 18 IX Camb 2, at Al-ša-Rē'i, lease, 1) A.ŠA$_3$ E$_2$ *a-za-nu*, arable and land to be reclaimed, land of Dakiki s Ammekubabbu to Bēl-āb-uṣur s Barik-iltammeš, from the bank of Nār-Sin to the border of (the land of) the *rab ṣibti* and from the border of $^{(P)}$Galu to the *nak*(*kandu*) of the king, *bīt ritti šá a-na*(sic) Iqīša,[73] leased for six years for 20 kor for the land

[70] Though the passage is damaged, enough remains to suggest that this *bīt qašti* could belong to the treasury of Sin.

[71] M. Jursa, NABU 1998/124, the text holds the present earliest explicit *bīt qašti* record.

[72] M.W. Stolper, BaM 21, 1990, p.567f. no. 4.

[73] The function of the *a-na* is not clear. Iqišā probably reappears in line 25 where we are told that the witness of line 24 will reclaim one kor of land on the boundary with Iqišā.

under the plough and at the rate of one kor of barley per kor for land to be reclaimed during the first three years, after which all the land must have been brought under the plough. Other clauses.

d) *ṣāb šarri*[74]

The ordinary foot soldier, the person with the lowest grade in the hierarchy, who was not of necessity the holder of his own bow fief, but who was made available by others and who was often employed specifically for civil projects, was the *ṣāb šarri*. He was the actual person fulfilling the obligation, not only if it rested on him alone, but also if he served from amongst or in the name of those who were involved together. That such a specific term was required, other than the expected *ṣāb qašti*, or perhaps *bēl qašti*,[75] is the result of the fact that obligations were often shared by several people. Someone hired to fulfil the obligations as an outsider also became the *ṣāb šarri* who was put into the field. Actively serving *ṣāb šarri*s were also due from certain estates. *kutallūtu*-payments allude to the fact that the holders of fiefs (originally) had a fixed substitute, but this will have become something different from the hiring of a *ṣāb šarri,* an *ad hoc* arrangement, the *kutallūtu* being originally a fixed element of the system.

The *ṣāb šarri* and related *rikis qabli* documents from the Egibis and their relations illustrate the manner in which this type of expenditure contributed to the indebtedness of the rural personnel who had come into the grips of people like the Egibis. Another instance in which some of the workings of the taxation system become visible.

Of some interest is TCL 12, 76, where Iddina-Marduk acts as a witness. Three brothers divide obligations, two will work on the onion field, the third one will be maintained by his brothers, while he performs their share in a *ṣāb šarri*. *ṣāb šarri* is clearly the person who fulfils the actual duty, but the way the arrangement is phrased could indicate that he had to be available for service all the time. There is no explicit indication that *ṣāb šarri* indicates involvement in strictly military obligations, but he will have had to serve as a bow man, if required to do so. For the later Achaemenid period we can refer to Stolper's discussion (2001, p. 123ff.).

Babylon Egibi and related

Lab 3 4 II LbM 0, for (the interest on) a promissory note of 30 *š* of silver of IM due from Nādin, ᶠBau-ilat and Marduk-erība s Nādin Nergal-ibni, the *ṣāb šarri,* has been given by Mandanu-šum-iddina s Zēria and Rēmūt to Marduk-erība and ?[76] W, IM no. 85.

TCL 12 76 24 IV Nbn 2, x and Nabû-nāṣir ss Nabû-aḫḫē-iddina will do the work related to onions and barley. Their brother Ṣillā, the *ṣāb šarri,* will enjoy a third share. He will receive sustenance from the paternal home. IM witness.

Cf. also under *rikis qabli.*

---

[74] Literature: CAD Ṣ p.1f., where actual service and payments in lieu of service are separated. There is a wide ranging discussion by Stolper, 2001, no. 13, A 34117, p. 123ff.

[75] It should be noted that in the texts we are dealing with *bēl qašti*, cf. CAD Q p. 154, is not the "master of a bow-fief" or its superior, but a co-owner, unspecified, of a person specifically mentioned earlier.

[76] Understanding depends on the meaning of *ina* in line 1. The best interpretation probably still is that in lieu of a debt, or rather the interest due, a *ṣāb šarri* is provided. The problem is the role of the Marduk-erība mentioned twice, as both sharing in the debt and receiving the "payment". Is this the same person?

Nippur

A 34117[77] 10 I Xer 13 PN the *qalla* of PN2, the x of Nippur, has received 1)LU$_2$.ERIN$_2$ LUGAL for two months, II and III, from PN3 and PN4, brothers, sons of PN5. PN is responsible for proper execution of the service.[78]

Murašû

Cf. texts discussed above under large estates and *ilku* payment formulas.

e) *allāku ša uqu*[79]

The expression is found in a text from the Ur archive of the Gallābu family, thus late in our sequence. It is, in my opinion, to be linked to *ilku* and *rikis qabli*. The costs are clearly customary: "provisions and (taking the word in its widest sense) all sorts of equipment required for those doing obligatory duty as required from inhabitants of Ur". (^{LU_2})*uqu* is possibly a kind of approximate "translation" of *ṣāb šarri,* thus indicating a general, both military and civil, category of persons obliged to fulfil certain tasks "in the muster of the king".[80] The text is a substitute arrangement in the form of a dialogue document, in reality Kuṣurea will have taken the initiative and engaged Nidintu-Sin.

UET 4 109 25 IV Art II 8, at Ur (Gallābu archive). Nidintu-Sin s Sin-aḫḫē-iddina asks Kuṣurea s Sin-aḫḫē-bulliṭ for 2) ... *kaspu ṣi-di-tum ù si-im-me-nu-ú gam-ri lìb-bu-ú* ^{LU_2}*al-lak*.MEŠ *šà* ^{LU_2}*u-qu šá* ^{LU_2}ŠEŠ.UNUG^{KI} ... 4) *lul-lik ina an-de-e-su šá* LUGAL of yr 8 in your place.

f. *pasa'du*[81]

That we are dealing with an obligation to provide labour for projects in Elam put on institutions and fief holders alike, is made clear by the two Sippar texts which happen to deal, it would seem, with the same imposition for Dar yr. 9. Dar 293 indicates that we are dealing with a mobilisation with the purpose to provide labour, the text is an account registering the days spent by personnel of various departments in the town, indicated as É.ŠU^{II}. In this context, this will not have been the total account. The text indicates that the personnel the Šamaš temple had to provide included craftsmen like smiths, besides less specialised workers like those in the cowsheds and the sheepfolds. The text is rather damaged and it is not clear whether each "department" had to provide more than one man,[82] but at least one smith was absent for 8 months and 23 days, a cattle man was away for 10 months and 13 days and an attendant of the sheepfold for 9 months and 27 days. Such long periods suggest possibly that one man undertook the obligations imposed on his group. The period encompassed by the account suggests that the

---

77 Stolper 2001 no. 13.

78 This is therefore a receipt for payments in lieu of service. which still had to be performed. Perhaps the *qallu*, free or unfree, of the unidentified official organises the proper amount of manpower required. The text dates to month I and the service is due in II and III.

79 Discussed by M. Jursa, NABU 1995/61, p. 54-55.

80 CAD A/1, p. 353 sub 3. "agent" (LB) does not accept a military context for the passage and translates "agents of the people of Uruk (for: Ur)". The passage suggests the possibility of a military context, which is not excluded with *uqu,* cf. AHw p. 1427. There was a *ḫadru* of the *sepīru ša uqu*, Stolper EE no. 35, which in itself militates against a strict equation of *ṣāb šarri* and *uqu*, as *ṣab šarri* is not a permanent "employment" and belonging to a *ḫadru* was a permanent "status"; the members of this *ḫadru* were, however, primarily *sepīrus*, Aramaic scribes.

81 M. Jursa, NABU 1995/61, p. 54, with previous literature. Dar 293, mentioned by Jursa, is quoted after collations by H. Bongenaar.

82 Some lines, obv. 6' and 7', give PN and the name of a department, this can hardly mean that all the personnel had to go.

obligations extended for longer than a normal military campaigning season lasted. Dar 293 registers days, not costs made on account of equipment.

How to relate this to the 20 *š* paid by the individual in VS 4, 126 is unclear, but the amount is anyhow probably a share in a joint obligation of the unit of which the *rab qašti* who received the silver was the head. *pasa'du* is not a straightforward Persian equivalent of *rikis qabli*, but it is perhaps too early to assume a mangling of *padašūtu*, which after all was used in the same context of civil work in Elam, see below under *dullu*. C. Waerzeggers has published Bertin 2249, where we find silver paid for the *pa-se-ed*, payable ultimately by *rab banîs*, who as she emphasises, held land on the estates of the king and the crown prince.[83]

Sippar, Šangû-Šamaš

VS 4 126 6 XII Dar 9, 20 *š* silver, 2) *pu-ut* ḪA.LA *šá* PN 3) .... *šá* 4) *pa-sa-'a-du šá* MU 9 KAM$_2$ *ša* ^{KUR}E-lam-mat^{KI} 5) received by PN 2 ^{LU}$_2$GAL ^{GIŠ}BAN *šá* PN from FPN, his (PN's) mother.

Ṣāḫit-ginê, Marduk-rēmanni

M-r no. 83 20 XII Dar 12, PN and PN2 promise to deliver 380 kor of dates to Marduk-rēmanni 13) KB BABBAR-*ú šá pa-se-ed šá a-na muḫ-ḫi* [x x] 14) *u* ^{LU}$_2$GAN$_2$.DU$_3$.MEŠ *a-na* PN3 SE$_3$-*na* (Bertin 2249).

Sippar, administrative

Dar 293 (II Dar 9-x .x.yr 10), rev. 1) *e-pe*[*š*] NIG$_2$.KAS$_7$ *šá pa-sa-a'-du šá* ^{LU}$_2$ERIN$_2$.MEŠ *e-peš* 2) [*du*]*l-lu šá* ^{KUR}Elam-mat^{KI} *šá* E$_2$.ŠU^{II}.MEŠ *šá ina* ŠU^{II} 3) Bunene-šimanni ^{LU}$_2$x.x *šá* ŠU^{II} Ina-ṣilli-šarri (the *qēpu*), from II yr 9 to ? yr 10.[84]

g) *kutallu*[85] and fractions of fiefs

Strictly spoken it is not certain whether *kutallu* and the fractions discussed here belong together, but as the most important text TÉBR 1 somehow connects the two in dealing with sums due, we can treat them together. There is a difference between fractions arising from the splitting up of fiefs and properly instituted fractional fiefs, for the moment only existing theoretically, instituted from the beginnings of a system, for instance, in order to provide for servants. The *kutallu* on principle belongs to the system, either with a specially assigned minor fief or as established on the fief of a fief holder. We will not discuss here the fractionating of horse fiefs, the evidence can be found in the texts quoted above under the heading concerned. It will be an accident of the documentation that complete horse fiefs are scarce.

The term *kutallūtu* is connected by Dar 430 with a bow-fief, thus indicating an obligation to pay for a fixed substitute, but such substitutes could obtain an independent status.[86] The text could suggest that the payment amounted to half a mina payable over the complete fief, but this idea is undermined by Bertin 2318 from the previous year, which probably deals with a similar payment, assuming that the otherwise unknown Zargāia are the

---

83 Waerzeggers 2001 text 83.

84 Collated Bongenaar, 1997, p. 38 note 65.

85 Plural *kutallātu*. Literature CAD K p. 607L and CAD K p. 606.

86 This is comparable to what we noted as taking place in the Old Babylonian Ubārum text group. In all land for service systems there will have been changes as a result of the particular set up of arrangements between those involved. The position of the substitute may, for instance, be strong, as in the case of Ubārum or weak, as suggested by the low share in the payments due from the *kutallu* in TÉBR no 1. The workings of inheritance arrangements are always subject to the circumstances of the moment. Though basic structures are similar and comparable, we must not expect that developments result in the same outcome in different periods or even in the same period in different schemes of land holding. The dissolution of the scheme is also influenced by other economic possibilities open to the participants and the degree to which actual service is replaced by (fixed) payments.

kutallu meant.[87] Camb 292 strengthens the idea that *ṣāb šarri*, *rikis qabli*, and *kutallūtu* constitute one and the same complex with *ilku*, though *ṣāb šarri* is no more than a reasonable restoration. Consequently the bow-fief, *ṣāb šarri* and *kutallūtu* seem to constitute here the (financial) obligation of one and the same person. Either the holder of the bow fief was responsible for his *kutallu* or, in this case, he happens to have held both the fief and the *kutallu* "holding". It should be noted that the Murašû *ilku* receipts, which specify the obligations for which the payment concerned was valid, never mention *kutallu(tu)*.

There seem to have been "official" terms for fractions of bow fiefs, probably with specific obligations attached to them. These fractions seem, however, to have been something different from what resulted from the division of complete bows. The important text edited by Joannès, TÉBR 1, which is undated, is probably the most explicit text regarding payments by owners of fractions, but it is not without its problems. Compare also EE 3a (20 I Art [22]) as it also deals with its *judu'*[88] and *rabia* in their own right. The fact that the lease granted in this text was to cover ten years and only yielded 50 *š* per annum suggests that the fractional rights leased were not very substantial. That a *rabia* represents a quarter fief seems etymologically certain. The relative size of a *judu'* can be calculated from PBS 2/1 63 and 87, *ilku* receipts quoted under chariot and horse fiefs, above. In both texts we find nine complete bow fiefs and twice 3 *'u-du* (PBS 2/1, 63) or *'u-ú-du* (PBS 2/1, 87), summarised as 10-*ta* GIŠ.BAN.MEŠ 1-*en 'u-ú-du* (PBS 2/1, 87: 12), which assures the meaning "1/5". A small Murašû file deals with *ilku* payments for the *ud-du*/(^{LU_2})*'u-ú-du* of the Murašû servant Ribat s Bēl-erība.

In TÉBR 1 (full) bows are followed by *kutallu*s, who precede the ^{LU_2}*rabia ša* ^{LU_2}*ḫadar*, presumably "persons with a fourth share belonging to the *ḫadru*". Not only are the shares of the members of each sub-group as unequal as the amounts they contribute are dissimilar, but they are also disproportionate: a ^{LU_2}*rabia* pays much less than a quarter of any of the unequal amounts listed as paid by holders of complete fiefs, and the *kutallu*s pay the higher amount mentioned for the various *rabia*, 7.5 *š*. This text will play an important role in the discussion of the payments in silver by holders of fiefs at the end of this chapter.

The term *kutallu*, when used for personnel, does not always belong to the land for service sphere.[89] A clear case is the Murašû text BE 10, 4 (15 XII Art 41 = Dar II 0), a contract for the brewing of date "beer", where Enlil-nādin-šumi is asked to provide brewers, "our associates" (^{LU_2}*ki-na-at-i-ni*) and ^{LU_2}*ku-tal-la-a-tú*, "substitutes"[90] in addition to the ingredients required.[91]

Babylon Egibi and related

Camb 292 7 XI Camb 5, at Saḫrinu 88.3.0 of dates, 11.0.2 4 SILA$_3$ of barley and 4½ *š* of silver of IMB due from Mušēzib-Bēl s Zēr-iddina. Arrangements concerning payment and security. Line 16 mentions *ni-*]*din-tu šá* LUGAL *u ṣi-di-it-tu*$_4$ which might refer to dates and barley. Silver was spent on 18) [*ṣāb šarri, ri*]-*kis qab-lu u ku-tal-lu-u-tu* of year 5. Incomplete.

---

87 The writing of the name of the *šanû* in both texts differs, but is probably intended to represent the same person.

88 For previous literature see R. Zadok, BiOr 41 cols. 34-5.

89 TuM 2/3 128, (18 X Nbk 37) a receipt given by Nabû-šum-iškun s Ṣillā Balāṭu to Lūṣi-ana-nūr-Marduk s Nabû-mukīn-zēr Ili-banī, 5) ... *e-lat e-pu-uš* NIG$_2$.KAS$_7$ 6) *maḫ-ru-tu šá ku-tal-la*, is probably prebend related, cf. much later texts like Ash A 159, 1 X Dar 30+ and VS 6, 180, 13 XII Xer 1, from the Mannu-gērûšu files.

90 It may be doubted whether replacements are intended, "support personnel, helpers" might be considered, this could change the meaning in a military context, but that would probably be against the parallel with earlier *taḫḫu*, who is supposed to have been the regular replacement.

91 The term does not recur in the regular repeat confirming the request in this type of documents.

Bertin 2318 3 V Dar 15, 20 *š* of silver for the rations of the LU2*za-ar-ga-a-a* of yr. 15 *šá* GIŠBAN of Bēl-iddina s Nabû-zēr-ušabši Nabû-uṣur s Rēmūt messenger of Amurru-šarussu-ukīn (sic) LU2*2-ú* has received from Mandanu-bēl-uṣur slave of MNA and Iddina s Ardia for Bēl-iddina. Cf. Dar. 430.

Dar 430 30 VI Dar 16, 30 *š* silver *ku-mu ku!-tal-la-ú-tu* of yr 16 *a-na muḫ-ḫi* GIŠBAN of Bēl-iddina s Nabû-zēr-ušabši at the disposal of Palil-aḫa-iddina s Nabû-aḫḫē-bulliṭ Nabû-nipšari s Iqīšaia messenger of [Amurr]u-šar-kini (sic) LU2*2-ú* from Mandanu-bēl-uṣur slave of MNA and Iddina s Ardia. Continues with a damaged statement concerning their share in the payment. Cf. Bertin 2318.

Borsippa

VS 6 131 11 x Dar 13, SUKU6.ḪA2 *gab-bi šá* FPN fam. DU3.ḪAL[92] *šá ku-tal*[-x?] *a-di qi-it šá* VI yr 13 PN fam. DU3.ḪAL brother of FPN *ma-ḫi-ir*.

Ur

UET 4 60 25 II Art II 1, see above sub *qaštu* related payments.

Nippur/Murašû

EE 3a 20 I Art [22], lease of bow land of named persons, with or without the LU2*ia-di-du-'u* and the LU2*ra-bi-ia* at Bīt-Murānu on the Ḫarri-Piqudu is requested by Enlil-ḫatin from the *šaknu* of the *šušāne māre* LU2*ḫi-sa-nu* for ten years at 50 *š* per annum.

Šaṭir

TÉBR 1 no date, see below sub costs holders of fiefs.

h) *rikis qabli*[93]

"Equipment costs", is, obviously, a very general term. In a technical sense it is a type of costs incurred in connection with obligations resulting from holding a fief, which clearly existed already under the Chaldean kings.[94] Later in the reign of Darius *ṣidītu*, "provisions", was added explicitly to *rikis qabli,* but that will not of necessity have meant an actual increase in the obligations, as the Sippar text Camb 13 from Cambyses' *rēš šarrūti* attests. On principle these will have been costs born by the holder of the fief, or by the institution responsible for providing the man. Such costs could be paid to others if these were not the holders but only the performers of the duty concerned. In such cases payments were sometimes made by third parties with a hold on those who should perform the service, but who were unable to pay, thus increasing the already existing indebtedness.

Of special importance is Bertin 3065-66. Though the text is formally not concerned with taxation or related questions, it mentions an earlier debt, involving silver paid for *rikis qabli* and corvée work on a *mušannītu*. We can speculate whether this refers to one or to two obligations, *rikis qabli* either has to be paid in the case of "civil" work, which is in itself immediately understandable, or, the same person pays both for *dullu*, civil "corvée" and military obligations. That *rikis qabli* was not only paid for military obligations, but also in other contexts, is clear in VS 4, 139 from Borsippa, where it is required for boatmen. We must, however, reckon with the possibility that terms can be used in a specific "service" context and in a more general sense. Dar 156 could possibly not even refer to a service obligation at all, but, for instance, to a business trip. No time limits are indicated.

Though the intricacies of the Egibi relations with others will be avoided, their texts dealing with *rikis qabli* indicate the importance of the members of the family as creditors, providing silver required by people subject to service obligations. These remain unspecified as

---

92 Reading?

93 Literature: A.L. Oppenheim, OrNS 4 p. 239-241; CAD R p. 345.

94 Oppenheim thinks of an annual payment. The term is also attested in institutional documents. A text like Dar 141 makes it clear that silver for *rikis qabli* is meant for the persons who actually serve.

to their origin, but are of the same type as can be associated with holding a *bīt qašti*, a term which is, however, not used regularly before the early reign of Darius. The texts go back at least to the beginning of the reign of Nabonidus. It can be assumed that as soon as the Egibis became land holders during the short reign of Neriglissar, they became the creditors of those who worked the land for them or were their neighbours. The Egibis held land in areas where earlier *ḫanšu*-type land divisions had taken place, and their debtors were possibly those who had themselves received shares in these divisions. We find here a situation comparable to that of the Murašûs, but at a much more modest, urban based level.

Bertin 3065-66 and Dar 164 and 167 belong to a small file dealing with transactions between Marduk-nāṣir-apli Egibi and the brothers Rēmūt-Bēl and Nabû-makû-uṣur ss Nabû-šum-ukīn, who held land of an unspecified nature on the Nār-Barsip for which they were obliged to go to Elam. The equipment costs were financed by Marduk-nāṣir-apli, with their land serving as a pledge and one of the brothers performing the service in Elam. Comparison of the dates of the documents and of the delivery of the commodities suggests that the nature of the relationship between the parties was not one caused by indebtedness due to service obligations, but that we are dealing with a more normal business relationship, though Marduk-nāṣir-apli seems to have been in a strong position as he was able to provide the necessary silver. The relationship with Rēmūt-Bēl continued at least until Dar yr. 11 when Dar 310 shows Marduk-nāṣir-apli financing 8 mina of silver out of an obligation of 15 mina incurred by Rēmūt-Bēl and a partner, Kīnā s Dannu-aḫḫēšu-ibni.

The term *rikis qabli* is explicitly related to *ṣāb šarri* in three other Egibi/Nūr-Sin texts, Nbn 103, Bir 47 and Dar 481. Payments in silver were due from third parties on account of silver paid by a member of the Egibi family for *rikis qabli* on their behalf to those entitled. Such payments need not strictly have been in silver, and other commodities occur. Nbn 103 connects *rikis qabli* with the term *ṣāb šarri Bābili*. As we saw Camb 292 lists [*ṣāb šarri*], *rikis qabli* and *kutallūtu* in one go, indicating that a full payment at least comprised elements for these items.

That silver for *rikis qabli* could be paid to officials transpires from Camb 322, where a payment in dates is to be provided in lieu of equipment costs for a *ša muḫḫi ṣindata*.[95] In Camb 276, mentioned already, the *šākin ṭēmi* of Babylon was the intermediary for payment to someone qualified as a *rab a-šu*(?)-*mu*(?). In Dar 206 the *šākin ṭēmi* of Babylon ordered the remainder of the silver for someone's *rikis qabli* to be taken from the house of Marduk-nāṣir-apli Egibi. That higher authorities intervened in questions regarding payment of *rikis qabli* or *ṣidītu* stands to reason: the person who provided the actual service could not do so effectively without being properly equipped, so also in this case the sum involved was intended for the person actually serving. It is of course theoretically possible that elements of these types of expenditure were, or could become, the perks of intermediaries, especially of those in authority. Historically, military units or a ship could represent a source of income for their commanders. Tribal and mercenary units for which occasionally payments may have been due from central authorities, will have been known in our period, but the phenomenon is not documented, providing such units with land was the natural solution.

In Lab 3 we find a payment by one of Iddina-Marduk's factotums, no doubt on his orders, probably on behalf of the son (and the wife?) of the person from whom payment was due, possibly for a replacement for the missing father. This is a usual type of indebtedness in cases where an advance had been given. Though W, IM 110 does not state the reason why a mother and son contracted a debt, the link with Nbn 103, two months later, suggests that equipment costs of the father, who possibly had already disappeared or for whom a third party had to be engaged, constituted the background of both tablets. Other texts from the Egibi files

[95] CAD Ṣ p. 199R translates "custodian of the teams", connecting the term with plough teams. Whether this makes sense will have to be awaited.

indicate that debts on account of *rikis qabli* payments were one of the obvious reasons for the accumulating debts of some Egibi clients, cf. especially Camb 17 and 104. The fact that the silver was not paid to the head of the family but to the wife and others suggests that *rikis qabli* under circumstances could entail payments for a replacement.

Bir 47 mentions *ilku* paid in silver to a woman and her son(?) whose husband and father(?) is/was a *ṣāb šarri-* for his *rikis qabli,* thus indicating that *ilku* could be a general term also including payments for *rikis qabli*. *ilku* was, however, paid to the authorities and not to individuals performing service, so on principle, would not be spent on equipment. The term *ilku* may have been used in this case because as an element of their total obligations those responsible for the fief concerned had engaged a *ṣāb šarri* and therefore also had to pay for his equipment. In this case not too much meaning should be attached to the fact that such payments were made to the wife of the man who actually fulfilled the obligation. If *ṣāb šarri* was the term for the person actually responsible for the fulfilling of the obligation, the *ilku* payable in silver may also have been collected by the "active partner" from those who were his co-responsibles.

Some other cases of involvement of a woman with a son possibly indicate that the son was a minor who could not acquit his obligations after the disappearance of his father. W, IM 110, with Nbn 103 (no. 112), indicates that widows(?) and minors could come into difficulties, presumably especially when they had to find replacements: in these circumstances their land had to serve as a pledge. The text is, however, not specific enough to clarify whether the land pledged was the same as the land for which service was due. If that were the case, the passage could suggest that this land was, under the specific circumstances, transferable, contrary to what is suggested by material from other periods. The persons concerned were already in debt. Dar 323 indicates the final result: sale of a house. Cf. also Dar 156, if military, and Bertin 2041: *rikis qabli* expenditure is a burden because it demands an unusual concentration of expenditure at a specific moment and thus leads to problems resulting in indebtedness. Especially in the Egibi archive advances for *rikis qabli* are common transactions involving people with whom ordinary business relations existed, Bertin 3065-6 is a good example. In Dar 308 the silver was provided by Mandanu-bēl-uṣur, the slave-manager of Marduk-nāṣir-apli Egibi. Not only the obligation to serve, but also financing the person serving was a problem. Much of the actual burden which this form of taxation caused will not be visible in the documents.

Bertin 2614, and other texts, indicate that the Egibi themselves also had to pay *rikis qabli*, probably collectively as a family. It is only a small step to suggest that this type of payment was due for a specific property.[96] Such a relationship is strongly suggested by Camb 276 where silver *of a house* is mentioned. That house will have constituted, alone or with land, the object for which the obligation was due. The use of *bītu* in the context of service obligations is too rare to regard it simply as generally indicating someone's "estate". There is a possible link with obligations via the *babtu* and the *eširtu.*

If institutions such as temples are regarded from an economic perspective as elements of the government apparatus, it stands to reason that their resources would be used by that government. Whether that is regarded as a form of taxation is a matter of choice. BM 64707 and Dar 253 belong to a small file of texts dealing with semi-military personnel made available by the Šamaš temple in Sippar. Dar 253 is of particular interest in that it stipulates a service period of three years. All foodstuffs assigned, and the fodder for the donkey, could be made to cover a 36 month's period. The equipment in both texts is of a defensive nature: *širiam* (otherwise TUG_2.KUR.RA), a "buff coat", *karballu,* a (reinforced?) cap, *nūṭu*, a "leather water container",

[96] References to property stated to be encumbered with military obligations are rare in the texts dealing with Egibi land edited by Wunsch, 2000b: only no. 48 line 11 mentions the inclusion of tiny *bīt qaštis* of uncertain nature. We return to this matter in Chapter VII. Anyhow Egibi and Nūr-Sin involvement with property burdened with "military" obligations is certain, cf. for instance Wunsch, 2000a p. 111.

(*me*)*šēnu,* "sandals", being listed in BM 64707, amounts of salt, oil and cress being other standard elements of what was provided. It is possible that this group of eleven or twelve people worked in a local depot, but the fact that a donkey was made available to them, no doubt for the transport of equipment, indicates a certain amount of mobility. The importance of these texts is that they again suggest a preference for longer service periods in an institutional context. Such long stints would be practically impossible for individuals having to tend a farm.

Often payments would be made or expenditure was incurred for equipment costs without the fact being stated explicitly. An example could be Bertin 2537, an Egibi payment on the orders of an official to people in charge of a transport. Often we will not recognise this.

Babylon Egibi and related

W, IM 110 16 XII Nbn 2, 5 *š* of silver of IM due from Nabû-apal-iddina s Šum-iddina and his mother Bau-ēṭirat dr Šamaš-ibni with interest payable in XII. Land serves as security. The silver was given for the [*rikis qabli* of] Šuma-iddin? (= BOR 5, 52, cf. Nbn 103.)

Nbn 103 28 II Nbn 3, 1 mina of silver of IM due from Nabû-apal-iddina s Šum-iddina and mother [f]Bau-ēṭirat dr Šamaš-ibni, with interest, in VII. Land security. The silver has been given for *rikis qabli* of *ṣāb šarri Bābili.* The interest must be met by the *imittu* on the date palms on the land. (W, IM 112)

Cyr 331 Cyr 8, memo to "my master", accounting, dates, onions, silver. 12) 40 *š* has been paid for *rikis qabli* of Cyr yr. 8.

Camb 17 1 XII Camb 0, 100 kor of dates and 20 *š* of silver of IMB due from Nergal-nāṣir s Nādinu in VII and XII yr 1. Mentions earlier debt. 11) The silver is the price of dates and onions given for *rikis qabli* of yr 1. Cf. Camb 104 (30 II Camb 2).

Camb 104 30 II Camb 2, 106 kor of dates, 21 *š* of silver and onions of IMB due from Nergal-nāṣir s Nādinu in VII and XII. Mentions earlier promissory notes for which land is security and on left edge: *rikis qabli*(!) of yr 2. Cf. Camb 17 (1 XII Camb 0).

Camb 276 12 III Camb 5, 1 mina of silver of the house of Ḫašdā s Arad-Gula Dīkî, *rikis qabli* of Itti-Nabû-balāṭu for Camb yr 3 and 4 Marduk-zākir-šumi *šākin ṭēmi* of Babylon will hand over to Esagil-šarra-uṣur the *rab a-šu?-mu.* (Reading? Function?) IMB scribe.

Camb 292 7 XI Camb 5, see under *kutallūtu.*

Camb 322 13 VII Camb 6, (?) 75 kor of dates of IMB due from Nabû-ēṭer-napšāti s Ibnā and Šum-iddina s Nabû-aḫa-iddina in VII yr 6. 12. The silver has been given for *rikis qabli* of yr 6 to Aḫa-iddina s Aplā, the *ša muḫḫi ṣindāta.* Mentions earlier dues. Cf. Camb 261 (24 XI Camb 4) mentioning deliveries for debtors to palace.

Dar 156 25 I Dar 5, Bēl-iddina s Itti-Marduk-balāṭu Aḫu-bani receives 25 *š* (after an earlier payment of 3 mina) from MNA at the orders of Murašû s Marduk-šum-iddina Baliḫu (for) 8) equipment *a-na a-la-ku a-na pa-ni šarri.*

Bertin 2041 19 IV Dar 5, 10 kor of dates of MNA due from Mušēzib-Bēl s Šum-iddina in VII. Land on Harri-ša-Nergal is security, as is land on the Nār-Tupašu for an earlier debt. Both the earlier and the later silver has been given for *rikis qabli.*

Bertin 3065-6 x x [Dar] 5, 3 mina $57^1/_2$ *š* of silver and onions of MNA due from Rēmūt-Bēl s Šum-ukīn, arrangements concerning date of payment. All land between Nār-Borsippa and the *ḫarran šarri* serves as security for MNA. Mentions earlier tablet of 297.3.0 kor of dates and 11.2.3 of barley, silver for 18) *dul-lu ša mu-ša-an-ni-tu*$_4$ 19) *ri-ki-is qab-lu.* Is to be paid from the *šibšu* of the onion field of Mandanu-bēl-uṣur. Defines on edge share with (brother) Nabû-makû-uṣur. Cf. Dar 144, 25 XI Dar 4, where the same amounts of dates and barley are mentioned.

Dar 164 1 V Dar 5, 30 *š* KB and 30 bundles of onions of MNA are due from Nabû-makû-uṣur s Nabû-šum-ukīn in I yr 6, mentions earlier debt of 245.3.0 of dates, 8.1.2 of barley, 50 *š* of silver and 44 bundles of onions for which his land is security and of which the silver has been paid 12) ... *a-na ri-ki-is qab-lu šá* MU 5.KAM$_2$ 13) *šá a-na a-la-ku* [*a-na* [KUR]]E-la-am! 14) to Nabû-makû-uṣur.

Dar 167 x V Dar [5], 50 *š* of silver and 50 bundles of onions of MNA are due from Rēmūt-Bēl s Šum-ukīn in I from the *šibšu*, "yield", of the field; mentions a number of earlier promissory notes. Land security for 12) KB *šá a-na ri-ki-is* $MURUB_4$! *šá* MU 5.KAM_2 x? 13) URU.[KUR]E-l[a-am?] given to Nabû-makû-uṣur. Cf. Dar 144, 164 and 310.

Dar 206 2 VII Dar 6, x silver remainder of 6 mana equipment costs for the complete yrs. 2 and 3 for Arad-Marduk s Kittia Šangû-Ea "given" from the house of MNA on the orders of Bēl-aplā-iddina *šākin ṭēmi* of Babylon, is received by Marduk-x [son] of Arad-Marduk from MNA.

Dar 220 6 II Dar 7(?), Nabû-šum-uṣur s Marduk-šum-ibni Ile'i-Marduk receives 10 *š* of silver in the equipment costs of yr. 8 from Nabû-ittannu (s Bēl-iddina Irani). Cf. Dar 481.

Dar 308 26 VII Dar 11, 30 kor of dates, 30 *š* of silver of Mandanu-bēl-uṣur, slave of MNA, due from Iddina-Bēl s Nabû-zēr-ušabši in VII yr 12. Land in Šaḫrinu security. 12) The silver has been given for *rikis qabli* for going to Elam.

Dar 481 29 I Dar 19, silver *ri-ik-su qab-lu* of Nabû-šum-uṣur s Marduk-šum-ibni s Ile'i-Marduk the *ṣāb šarri* of Nabû-ittannu s Mušēzib-Marduk Egibi for yr 18 and 19 has been paid.

Bertin 2614 26 V Dar 26, BM 31528 1 mina silver for *rikis qabli* from yr 24 Nabû-aḫḫē-bulliṭ s IMB has received from Nabû-zēr-ibni s Itti-Nabû-balāṭu Egibi, no other sum is due. Mentions earlier document of 1 mina for *rikis qabli* in yr. 23.

Bertin 2554 28 II Dar 36!, 1 MA.NA KB ... 2) *ku-um ri-ki-is* $MURU_4$ *ù ṣi-de-e-ti* up to end month XII yr 36, as much as is the share of MNA, is paid by Nidintu-Bēl to Nabû-aḫḫē-bulliṭ s IMB Egibi. Identical with Bertin 2740 (dated x II? yr 35?).

Babylon

Bir. 47 8 VI Nbn 4, $3^{1}/_{2}$ *š* of silver, of *ilku* of Nabû-mušallim received by Nabû-taklak and Paliti, wife of Bēl-mušallim. The silver is for *rikis qabli* of Bēl-mušallim *ṣāb šarri*. Additional is the promissory note of $1^{1}/_{5}$ *š* of last year, received by Nabû-taklak and Paliti.

Borsippa

VS 4 139 27 XI Dar 14, Atkuppu-file: silver of the *rikis qabli ša* $^{LU_2}MA_2.LAH_4$ *mala zitti ša* PN1 until end of VII(?) yr 14 received by Iqīša s Aplā Gabbi-ša-ilia (?) from PN1.

Comparable? (from Babylon Egibi)

Bertin 2537 2 VII Dar 24, 3 kor of barley given on the orders of Ina-Esagil-lībur *šākin ṭēmi* of Babylon by Š s I to Nidintu-Bēl as sustenance for the boatmen of a beer ship (going to URU.KUR.URU).

Sippar

Ṣāḫit-ginê, Marduk-remanni

M.r. 132 (ca Dar 26), 3 mina of silver .... 2) ... *ri*]-*ki-is qabli šá* $^{LU_2}ERIN_2$.LUGAL.[MEŠ] 3) *šá* Šu-sá-an Dar yr 26 4) at the disposal of PN *qêpu* of Ebabbar, received by PN2, his second in command, from PN3, scribe of Ebabbar, not to mention 307 mina of wool, 0.1.0 of salt, cress and oil each and 10 (pairs?) of sandals received from Marduk-rēmanni.

Comparative institutional material: equipment provided

Sippar Ebabbar

BM 64707[97] x V Camb 7, 6 plough men and 5 shepherds are equipped with [one line lost] 11-*et šir-a-*[*am*] 11 *me-e-š*[*e-nu*] 0.0.5 3 $SILA_3$ *šam-ni* 0.1.5 MUN.HA_2 11 ^{KUŠ}*nu-ú-ṭu* [11] ^{TUG_2}*kar-bal-la-ta ina ri-kis* $MURUB_4$ [*šá*] MU 8 KAM_2 (note difference in date!).

Dar 253 10 V Dar 9 silver, *rikis qabli ša* $^{LU_2}ERIN_2$ *ša* ANŠE.KUR.RA *šá na-ak-x-tu*$_4$[98] *šarri* [*ša*] 3-*ta* MU.AN.NA.MEŠ, follows expenditure on a donkey and its fodder and on items of equipment, 12 of each and on food, explicitly for three years, from I yr 9 onwards.

---

97 J. MacGinnis 1998, p. 177.

98 *na-a-*x-*tum* is tentatively combined with *nakkamtu* CAD N/1 p. 184L and equally tentatively read *na-ak-rám-tu*$_4$ Joannès, 1982 p. 18, with translation "de la réserve". That we are dealing with a royal horse depot is supported by BM 60756, probably a fragment of a related list of personnel belonging to the bowmen of the herdsmen and 2) the *šu-šá-nu*.MEŠ *šá* ANŠE.KUR.RA 3) [*šá* L]UGAL *na-ak-ka-du ša* LUGAL.

Excursus: arrangements for practical service

Bongenaar (1997 p. 37-38) has collected much material on the obligations Ebabbar incurred in connection with corvée labour it had to supply for work in Elam. Some of the more explicit texts have been quoted here. The institutional working party was ordinarily led by the *qêpu*. We can assume that the other institutions were equally obliged to contribute in a similar manner. Bongenaar stresses that Ebabbar obviously had problems in finding the personnel.

Four texts from the Murašû archive illustrate the practical arrangements which were made by individuals under the obligation to provide men for actual services as a consequence of their holding land against service. That such is the case is clear from the well-known Lutz text, quoted above in the section on chariot and horse fiefs: the Murašûs had acquired through adoption a share in a horse fief and were therefore themselves co-responsible for the service, in this case consisting of going to Uruk under arms. It is perhaps not remarkable that there is one perhaps directly comparable text involving infantry men in the same year, PBS 2/1, 54, where three men were engaged for doing service. There is one associated text, Ist 83, where silver and barley are advanced for equipment costs, for which bow land was pledged. After the events surrounding the disputed succession of Darius II the mobilisation system probably needed an overhaul, which meant that it was tested practically. Three years later, PBS 2/1, 114, paying and equipping three *ṣāb šarri* for the next year required 100 *š* and 120 $SILA_3$ of barley per head, which could perhaps suggest a four months' tour of duty.

In PBS 2/1, 114 Rēmūt-Ninurta paid as the lease holder of bow land belonging to the *ḫadru* of the *šūšānus* of the estate of the *rab uratē*. In all three texts from Darius II year 2 a certain Aplā, brother of Bēl-šar-uṣur, *šaknu* of the *šūšānu mar ḫisannu*, was present. The year 2 texts can possibly be combined with the long term Murašû interests concentrating at Ḫambari on the Nār-šarri. In BE 10, 61 and PBS 2/1, 63, from the same year Darius II 2, bowland of the same *ḫadru* was pledged and the *šaknu* of the same group received *ilku* payments for land belonging to horse and bow fiefs, thus further suggesting a link between the various types of tenure. The structure is not clear, but an infantry *ḫadru* might be linked to a chariot fief and some horse fiefs or rather the other way round, the chariot fief constituting the military core of the mobilisation system, as had already been the case in Assyria.[99]

Murašû archive

Lutz UCP 9, 3 18 V Dar II 2, arrangement of Rēmūt-Ninurta with Gadaliama s Raḫim-ilāni quoted already under horse fiefs, sealed by Aplā, brother of Bēl-šar-uṣur *šaknu* of the *šūsānus māre ḫi-sa-a-nu,* son of Marduk-bēlšunu.

PBS 2/1 54 20 X Dar II 2, contract of Rēmūt-Ninurta with three men regarding *i-di ṣi-di-it lu-bu-uš u ú-nu-tu(-ka)*; sealed by the same Aplā, fragment.

Ist 83 x x Dar II 2, contract with more than one person in which bow land is pledged, price silver *lu-bu-uš u ú-nu-tú* x (gap) paid for going to Uruk; Aplā witness, fragment.

PBS 2/1 114 20 XIIb Dar II 5, 1 MA.NA KB, 2 GUR ŠE.BAR *i-di u ṣi-di-tu₄ gam-ri/ šá* 3 ^{LU_2}ERIN₂.LUGAL *šá a-na a-la-ku a-na ma-dak-tú šá* MU 6 KAM₂ (of Darius II) *šá* ŠE.NUMUN *zaq-pu* [*u*] KA *šul-pu šá* ^{GIŠ}BAN.MEŠ *ú-šu-uz-za-'a-e-ti* [*u*] *pa-'a-ṣe-e-ti šá* ^{LU_2}*ḫa-ad-ri šá* ^{LU_2}*šu-ša-ni*.MEŠ [*šá*] E₂ ^{LU_2}GAL *ú-ra-a-tú* is at the disposal of Rēmūt-Ninurta, received by the *šaknu* of that *ḫadru*, who seals.

i) *ilku*[100]

The general word for "service for land" was *ilku*, which combined with the verb *alāku* indicates in an unspecified manner "performing service". The expression had acquired, at least from Old Babylonian times onwards, a specific meaning: doing something as the result of an

[99] As best illustrated by the Tell Halaf text AfO Beih. 6, no. 48.

[100] Basic literature: CAD I/J p.76 h); p. 78f), g), 80 b); Joannès, 1982 p. 16-46.

obligation undertaken in consequence of the acceptance of some piece of real estate from a higher authority.

Occasionally, however, what is intended by the term *ilku* is further specified. Bertin 2619 (20 III Dar 26) directly links, as would be normal, the payment of *ilku* and someone's *qaštu*. The linkage of *qaštu*, and less often, but none the less regularly, *bīt sisê*, and *ilku* is, of course, also usual in the Murašû texts. The texts from Babylon are usually not very informative, but that is compensated by those from Borsippa. There *ilku* payment involved as a total something called *pānāt qašti*, but it is specified as *urāšu* and the related *zebēli ša upiāte*. The text L 4720 (24 IV Dar 25), published by F. Joannès, unmistakably connects both civil and military obligations with the same, unspecified, tax basis, thus again indicating that we are dealing with one and the same complex, which is not so explicit in Babylon texts. YBC 11599 (11 VIII Art II) unequivocally states that the owner of the house remains responsible for the *ilku*, the *urāšu* and an "obligation" called ^{LU_2}KU.GAR.MEŠ, though the tenant possibly has to contribute with a fixed sum. Military and civil obligations are here linked to a house.[101]

In Neo-Babylonian times TuM 2/3, 132 expresses the relation between the obligation and the land held concisely: "give me a share in the land shared out by the king and I will execute the (ensuing) duties (*ilku*) with you". This is confirmed by Bertin 2033, which mentions land on which rest general *ilku* obligations. In Bertin 2619 *ilku* is due "from the bow of PN". The acceptance of the obligations was a formal affair. VS 6, 70 is explicit on this: someone refuses to undertake a certain duty (*ilku ul allak*) but wants to be inscribed (in the roster of the) bowmen, in such a manner that he can perform his duty for the crown prince: *ilki ša mar šarri lūllik*. This is comparable to TuM 2/3, 172, where two persons, one a slave, will perform their *ilku* amongst (*libbu*) the gardeners.

The Murašû archive *ilku* receipts, in their intention to give a complete summing up of all elements for which payment has been received, provide a fairly precise insight into what was understood by *ilku* in the later Achaemenid period. For instance Donbaz-Stolper Ist 52 (25 XIIb Art I 29) enumerates: "(silver), the complete *ilku*, *ṣāb šarri*, *qēme* <*ša šarri*>, *bāra* and all gifts pertaining to the house of the king". The word *ilku* can be omitted occasionally in this sequence, indicating that the other elements listed together represent it adequately, e.g. PBS 2/1, 203. That *ilku* and the specifications listed are meant to be identical is stressed by the beginning of PBS 2/1, 66 which is damaged, but probably formulates [4 MA.NA KB *il-k*]*i gam-ri ku-um* ^{LU_2}ERIN$_2$.LUGAL *ba*[*r-ra* etc., as Ist 52 indicating even clearer, that the *ilku* payment subsumes the other obligations. This manner of phrasing is also found in the repeat clauses as in PBS 2/1, 76: 17-18. The same is the fact in cases where *ilku* follows the same list of specified obligations, as for instance in BE 9, 83, (Art 40, Larak file). By this time the term had probably become especially associated with payments in silver. We will look at the *ilku* elements mentioned in the Murašû receipts individually, only rarely some other minor element is added.

In general the term used (*ilku* of PN) remains unspecified as to its contents, with the Nidinti-Marduk text BM 42302 as an exception. There the *ilku* is "for Elam", which will mean that here payment for corvée is intended. *ilku* is on the one hand clearly connected with the military terminology already studied, on the other with "civil" concepts like *dullu* and *urāšu*, especially through the persons who collected these dues. In civil cases the obligations were

101 Stolper 2000b, p 673-675. Stolper suggests that the high *šugarrû* payment of twice 40 *š* should be regarded as the contribution of the tenants toward the service obligations of the owner. We can only note that this represents a fixed sum, and that it should make us aware that unspecified extras equally could represent similar contributions. What ^{LU_2}KU.GAR might represent is discussed by Stolper in his remarks to line 16. mentioning VS 6, 99 and 192. Th. Krispijn suggests a reading DUR$_2$.GAR, *āšibu*, which might fit VS 6, 99, but not VS 6, 192. The meaning might be, that the tenant is responsible for who lives in the house, but we will not link that for the time being to what was discussed under *aššābu* in Chapter III.

regularly transmuted into payments. In the Egibi archive in the later years of Nabonidus especially Nurea s Bēl-iqīša Šangû-Nanna acted as a collector. Texts like Nbn 757 and CTMMA 3, 81, record payments which, though no reasons are given, obviously belong here on prosopographical grounds. Whether the collector was a tax farmer having acquired the right to collect, could be considered. The fifteen texts listed here registering the receipt of *ilku*-silver by Širku s Iddina Egibi, thus Marduk-apal-iddina, the head of this branch of the family in Darius I years 25-27, are best understood as indicating that he was involved in such collecting of *ilku*-money. In what capacity is not completely clear for the moment, but we could compare his position with that of the Nurea mentioned above.

The way in which *ilku* payments were officially collected is possibly also indicated in some texts from Nippur. The note (*taḫsistu*) BE 8/1, 66 (2 IX Cyr 5) mentions a *dēkû,* the person who calls up people for service, and his messenger. TÉBR 18 (18 V Art 37), from the Louvre Acquisition Barbora, establishes the link between the *dēkû*'s (plural here) and the *ḫadru* of those due to pay. This is of course important, though not unexpected: these vocational or ethnic organisations, relatively well known from the Murašû archive, are obviously responsible for the fulfilment of obligations by their members. The role of the *dēkû* in collecting the *ilku* silver suggests a context for the Borsippa text NBC 8337, with its monthly collecting *dekû*. The presence of the *dēkû* constitutes a link with the types of taxation to be discussed in Chapter VII. Presumably he was an official rather than a tax farmer.

The texts from Nippur from Nabonidus to Smerdis are notable for the low amounts paid in silver and for the fact that these are said to cover a full year. Perhaps, as suggested above, we could be dealing with an arrangement at the end of its practical viability. BE 8/1, 92 mentions a significant combined payment of silver and flour. Cf. also the administrative document BE 8/1, 37, Ner yr 2, quoted under *urāšu*.

ilku payments through the heads (*šaknu*s) of the *ḫadru*s, (a group of people with the same background and sharing the same obligations,) to higher authorities are one of the central elements in the Murašû archive. Such payments often contained also an element due from the higher types of fiefs, thus suggesting again that the various types of fiefs were structurally linked. Amounts of silver paid in connection with *ilku* were always, in the end, intended for the authorities, even though collection might go through several different stages, from private collection among co-holders, through the (collegial) head of the group to the official in charge or perhaps even the person who had leased the right to collect. Cases of *ilku* payments to others than the authorities always require a special explanation, of which the fact that the object for which the payments were due had a divided ownership, one of whom collected what was due from the others, is only the commonest.

For the moment it can not be confirmed or denied whether *ilku* obligations which originally probably ensued from certain specifically allotted types of land, were in due course extended to cover other land and finally even other sources of income. These developments will have taken place especially in the Achaemenid period. Bertin 2569 could be especially relevant, the text must be connected to the Egibi activities regarding the floating bridge in Babylon, to which we will have to return. VS 4, 121, from the Babylon Nappāḫu archive records an *ilku* payment by a person and his *mubannû*s, which might suggests a prebendal context.

Babylon Egibi and related

Nbn 741 14 VII Nbn 13, x mina of silver out of the *ilku* of IM is received from Ina-Esagil-ramat by Nūrea s Bēl-iqīša s Šangû-Nanāia; mentions earlier payments. (W, IM 218)

Nbn 757 24 I Nbn 14, 15 *š* of silver is received by Nabû-ēreš s Ṣillā Mandidi on orders of Nurea s Bēl-iqīša from Esagil-ramat, wife of IM. (W, IM 224)

CTMMA 3 81 18 III Nbn 14, 10 š of silver is on the orders of Nūrea s Bēl-iqīša Šangû-Nanāia received by Nabû-ereš s Ṣillā Mandidi and Bēl-šunu s Bēl-iqīša Šangû-Nanāia from Esagil-ramat, exclusive of 25 *š* in earlier payments. (Mold I 30; W, IM 225)

Dar 323 24 II Dar 12, Marduk-ēṭer s Nabû-mukīn-apli Dābibī buys a house in Saḫrinu from Nabû-bēl-kalama and Nabû-mukin-zēri ss Nabû-mušēzib-napšāti Lakuppuru and their mother Inbā dr Nabû-mukīn-apli Šigua for five mina of silver. The silver had been given for the *ilku* of the king (line 42). Cf. Dar 325 (15 IV Dar 12) in which MNA acquires the house, and Bertin 2244.

Bertin 2331 17 VII Dar 15, 2 mina of silver *šá* ŠE.NUMUN *il-ki* [x x] of Nabû-ittannu and Bēl-zēri ss Nidintu-Bēl and Balāṭu s ? is received by Š s I from Mukkê(?)-Bēl s x Bēl-ēṭeru.

Bertin 2548 8 VII Dar 24, [x?] *ilku* to the end XII yr 24 (!) as much as represents the share of Rēmūt-Bēl s x-Bēl Nabûnnaia is received [by] Š s I.

Bertin 2542 6 VIII Dar 24, *ilku* of Nabû-ittannu s Suḫaia for I-XII yr 24 is received by Š s I from Nabû-ittannu, the total *ilki?-šú* for yr 25 is also received.

Bertin 2836 13 IV Dar 25, *ilku* of Rēmūt-Bēl s Bania Itinnu and *di-pi-ni-šu* up to end yr 25 is received by Š s I from Nabû-ittannu.[102]

Bertin 2583 16 IV Dar 25, whole *ilku* for I to XII yr 25 as much as the share of Nabû-bullissu s Nabû-ittannu amounts to, is received by Š s I from Nabû-ittannu.

Bertin 2581 4 VI Dar 25, *ilku* for four months and 6 days from 25 II up to end VI Dar 25 has been paid by Bēl-iddina s Zēria Rab-bani to Š s I.

Bertin 2573 1 XII Dar 25, *ilku* of Aplā and Iddina-Nabû ss Bazuzu Kāṣir x s Itti-Marduk-balāṭu s ? and Šum-ukīn s Bēl-ēṭer up to end XII yr 25 is paid by Aplā to Š s I.

Bertin 2575 5 XII Dar 25, *ilku* of Barsia s Marduk-šum-uṣur Babûtu for the whole yr 25 is received by Š s I.

CTMMA 3 68 12 XII Dar 35, (at Laḫiru) *il-ki* of Amurru-aḫa-ušur s Šum-iddina until end XII is received by Š s I

Bertin 2569 4 x Dar 25, *ilku* of Bēl-asua s Nabû-iddina Babûtu to the end XII yr 25 *šá i-da-šú* 5) *šá gi-ši-ri* TIN.TIR^{KI} *šá ina* ŠU^{II} PN, "of his hire of the bridge of Babylon at the disposal of Bēl-ēṭer" is received by Š s I.

Bertin 2557 25 x Dar 25, *ilku* of Muranu s Marduk-ibni Aḫu-bani and half the *ilku* of x[103] s Nuḫsia for the whole yr 25 is received by Š(?) s I. from Murānu.

Bertin 2572 7 VIII Dar 25, 21 *š* of silver *ilku* of Bēl-mušallim and Bēl-ēṭer ss Bēl-iqīšā Šangû-Ea for the whole yr 25 is paid to Š s I by Rēmūtu s Kalbā for them.

Bertin 2620 5 I Dar 26, *ilku* of Tattannu s Nabû-balassu-iqbi Babûtu for the whole yr 25 is received by Š s I from Iddina-Nabû s Aḫḫē-iddina-Marduk for Tattannu.

Bertin 2619 20 III Dar 26 cf. sub *qaštu*.

TCL 13 197 27 VIII Dar 26, *ilku* of I yr 25 to XII yr 26 of Murānu s Marduk-ibni Aḫu-bani is received by Š s I from Rē'ušunu-Marduk s Bēl-apal-uṣur x-āia for Murānu.

TCL 13 198 11 I Dar 27, *ilku* of Guzānu s Ḫambaqu Mandidi for the period I 26 to XII 27 is received by Šamaš-iddina s Arad-Marduk Dēkî from Š s I for Guzānu. So text, but is this correct?

Babylon, Nappāḫu

VS 6 70 24 VII Nbn 6, at Āl-ša-errēši-ša-Ellipāia. PN declares to PN2, the messenger of the *mār šarri* and PN2 the *dēkû* of the ^{LU}2BAN *ša eššēti ša bīt ridūtu*: *il-ku ul al-lak* [*itti*] ^{LU}2BAN *šu-ṭur-a-in-ni-ma* [*il*]-*ki ša* ^{LU}2DUMU.LUGAL *lul-lik*: I will not perform the *ilku* (you order me to do?), but register me with the bowmen and I will perform service with the crown prince.

VS 4 109 4 I Dar 6, $7^1/_4$ *š* of silver *ilku* of IN s NBZ N is received by Bēl-iqišā s Nabû-uṣuršu Tunā. (PV 53)

---

102 On Bertin 2836 cf. remarks in note to Bertin 2235 sub *qaštu*.

103 Line missing in text.

VS 4 121 21 XII2 Dar 8, 30 *š* of silver part of a promissory note of x mina 4 *š* of the *ilku* of IN s NBZ Nappāḫu and his *mubannûs* is received by Mušēzib-Bēl s Rēmūt Egibi. Joins VS 4, 122.

VS 4 123 20 I Dar 9, 28 *š* of silver, *ilku* up to end II of Guzānu and Šulum-ana-Bābili ss Bēl-ušappi Babûtu is received by IN s NBZ Nappāḫu from Arad-Bēl s Guzānu Tunā.

VS 4 132 11 XI Dar 10, 12 *š* of silver of IN s NBZ Nappāḫu is due from Tabluṭu dr Iqīša on the 15th. Guarantor is Ḫammaqa s Ina-Bēl-ultaraḫ. The silver is that of the *ilku* of Libluṭ, brother of Tabluṭu up to IV yr 11. (PV 60)

Nbn 962 2 IV Nbn 16, (Dullupu-file) 5 *š ilku* of half a GUR.ZAG,[104] of Arad-Gula s Kiribtu, from 1 I onwards, Ša-pî-kalbi s Šellibi, the messenger of Iddina-Nabû the servant of the *šākin ṭēmi* of Babylon, has received.

Bir 47 8 VI Nbn 4, see under *rikis qabli.*

Borsippa (cf. Joannès 1998)

Nanāḫu file:

L 1643 23 III Dar 9, 3 *š* of silver *i-na su-ú-ti ba-ab-tu₄ il-ki* of V Dar 9 is received by Aḫušunu from Nabû-aḫa-iddina s Nabû-zēr-iddina Rēmūt-ili (a clear case of a lease of the collection of *ilku* payments according to Joannès).

Ash A 118 10+ XI Dar 14, *ilku* receipt, from ? to end II yr ? given by Aḫunu s Nabû-uṣuršu Ta[b-x-x] after payment by Nabû-tabni-uṣur s Nabû-nādin-x Arkat-ilani for Aḫušunu N.

L 4720 24 IV Dar 25, see under *zebēli ša upiyāti.*

Rē'u-alpi file

Mich 26 21 X Dar 10, see under *urāšu.*

BM 82666 Bors 21 IX Dar 16, see *zebēlu ša upiyāti.*

BM 82716 Bors 20 VI Dar 17, see *zebēlu ša upiyāti.*

Other

NBC 8337 II-IV Dar 10, see sub *dēkû ša babti* in Chapter VII.

Berens 105 Bab 19 VI Dar 16, (Borsippa, Ilia related?) 1) *il-ki qé-me ḫi-li-ru-ú* AB SU U_2[105] ^{GIŠ}BAN 2) *gab-bi* from VIII yr 15 to X yr 19 is received by the *šāpiru* of the brewers.

TuM 2/3 172 1 VII Dar 34, at Rimme, (Borsippa, Edu/a-ēṭer[106]-file) *imittu* imposition on a slave of the owner as (principal) tenant, who involves a third party, *il-ki lìb-bu-ú* ^{LU_2}NU.KIRI$_6$ *il-lak-ku*, "they will perform *ilku*-service amongst the gardeners".

VS 4 180 17 VII Dar 36, (file unidentified) 6 *š* of silver *il-ki šá ul-tu* (month) I *šá* yr 36 *a-di qi₂-it* XII *gab-bi šá* yr 36 Nādin s Zērūtu Kidin-Sin has received from Arad-Gula s Mušēzib-Marduk Sikkua on behalf of Itti-Nabû-I(?) A Balāṭu.

Nippur

BE 8/1 45 17 II Nbn 3, at Āl-x-^{d}BE, (Zēr-ukīn s Pir'u file) promissory note for 2 *š* of silver due from two persons to Zēr-ukīn; KB *šá il-ki šá pu-ut* Zēria *na-šu-ú.*

---

[104] A reading *qurbūtu*, with CAD I p. 78 L, must be regarded as highly dubious, as this term does not occur otherwise in a Neo-Babylonian context and is anyhow out of place if the Assyrian meaning is taken into consideration, as that places these people in the royal entourage. No effective interpretation can be suggested.

[105] The reading of the line after *qe-me* is dubious. *ḫi-li-ru-ú* can be compared with some difficulty with *ḫillūru*, "chick peas", which could be turned into flour. For *ab-su-ú* there could be a link with *ab/pšu* B (CAD A/1 p. 66, "(a grass seed)" AHw p. 7R "eine Art Erbse", cf. J.N. Postgate, BSA 3, 1987, p. 94, which is never attested in Babylonia but might perhaps appear as *absu*. Postgate proposes, however, identification of (Assyrian) *abšu* with Babylonian *kakkû*. That the delivery should represent the "total bow" is equally suspicious. The involvement of the *šāpiru* of the brewers could suggest a prebendal context.

[106] The reading of this name remains uncertain as to the subject of the sentence, if SUR is interpreted as *eṭēru*. Aš-šur persists as a faint possibility as Aššurāia occurs as a family name. The question is discussed anew by Zadok NABU 1997/11 *ad* line 22.

SCAC Sc 134 18 XII Cyr 2, (Bēl-ēṭri s Aplā file) B. pays $1^{3}/_{4}$ *š* KB to Rēmūt s Bēl-uballiṭ *ina ilku* of yr 2; mentions responsibility of B for *kutallātu* and *ṣāb šarri* in damaged context.

BE 8/1 66 2 IX Cyr 5, (unassigned) $3^{1}/_{4}$ *š* KB, *il-ki šá* yr 2 received by PN *dēkû* and PN2 messenger from Bunene-ibni s Širikti; *taḫsistu*.

BE 8/1 92 26 XI Camb 5, (Lābāši s Zēr-ukīn file) x *š* KB 0.1.4 *qé-me il-ki* of Lābāši s Zēr-ukīn(sic) is received by Nergal-iddina s Šamaš-aḫa-iddina from Ninurta-re'ussunu s Ninurta-mušētiq-udda.

BE 8/1 99 15 XI Camb x, (Arad-Gula s Šamaš-iqīš file). A. pays 5 *š* KB *ilku* of Nabû-it-[x] s Rape[x] for 15 months to 15 IV to Ḫašdaja s Talim.

BE 8/1 100 13 VI Barz 1, (same file) A. pays 3 *š* KB *ilku* from VI yr 1 to VI yr 2 of x-ia s Mušēzib to Šamaš-erība s Ninurta-aḫa-iddina.

Anatolica 14 38 (Nippur unassigned) Small fragment, seems to mention dates *šá il-ki*.

Nippur/Murašû, examples only, cf. also under chariot and horse fiefs

Ist 52 25 XIIb Art I 29, 6 MA.NA KB *il-ki gam-ru-tu* ^{LU_2}ERIN$_2$.LUGAL *qé-me ba-a-ri* [*ù mim-ma na-da-nu-tu*$_4$ *šá* E$_2$.LUGAL].

PBS 2/1 203 24 VII Dar II 4, 1 MA.NA KB ^{LU_2}ERIN$_2$ LUGAL *qé-me ba-ra u mim-ma na-da-nu-tu šá* E$_2$.LUGAL *gab-bi*, from I to XII yr 4.

PBS 2/1 217 10 VIII Dar II 6, 2 MA.NA KB *1-en* ^{DUG}*dan-nu* KAŠ.SAG 0.2.3 *qé-me u* ŠE.BAR 1 UDU.NITA$_2$ *il-ki* TIL.MEŠ ^{LU_2}ERIN$_2$.MEŠ LUGAL *qé-me ša* LUGAL *ba-ra ù mim-ma na-da-na-a-tú ša* E$_2$.LUGAL for I-XII yr 6.

Šaṭir

TÉBR 2 18 V Art 37, see sub *dēkû*, Chapter VII.

Sippar

BM 62561[107] 15 III Dar 14, at Akkad, deals with 1 mina of silver, *il-ki šá* MU.9.KAM due from PN, presumably to PN2 ^{LU_2}GAL 10-*ti-šú*, refers to royal *dātu*, "decree".

Ile'i-Marduk, Nidinti-Marduk

BM 42312[108] x x Dar 19, 66 *š* KB of PN due from Nidinti-Marduk and mother, prebend(al income) antichretic security, Bēl-rēmanni guarantor 11) silver which Nidinti-Marduk and his mother gave 12) *a-na il-ki šá* ^{KUR}ELAM.MA^{KI}

Uruk

"Claremont"[109] 20+ XI? "Art" 8?, 1)[x x] x-*nu e-piš* KU$_3$.BABBAR(?) *šá ina* ^{URU}UNUG^{KI} 2) [*ù ina*] *li-mi-tu*$_4$ ^{URU}UNUG^{KI} 3) [*šá*] *ina* ŠU^{II} PN ^{LU_2}GAL *um-ma?-nu* 4) ... PN ^{LU_2}*um-ma-nu* 5) *a-na il-ki* from 1 VIII 6) until end XII yr 8 7) *a-na* 1 MA.NA KB, half in each of two types of silver, to PN2 and PN3 *id-din*. Half the amount is paid.

Other

YBC 11599 11 VIII Art II 20, at (Al) Bīt-Nabû-dūr-edu, slave of owner leases a house at his disposal for 3 yrs. to two brothers, rent 3.5 š, mentions dates of payment. 10) *šu-gar-ru-ú šá* month IV and IX 11) 40 *š* KB *i-nam-din*(!) repair clause, date of beginning of lease; 16) *pu-ut il-ki ú-ra-šú ù* ^{LU_2}KU.GAR[MEŠ] PN (owner) na-ši.

---

107 M. Jursa, WZKM 87, 1997 p. 101, seriously damaged, and as to the reconstruction of the first line dubious.

108 Jursa, 1999 p. 133f.

109 M.W. Stolper, BaM 21, 1990, p. 582-3. That the text involves an *ilku* payment for the period of a year is certain, but the manner in which lines 1-2 indicate an area is unusual for fiefs. It is, however, unlikely that it refers to people, as what is intended is handed over for the payment of *ilku* amounting to 1 mina per annum. Not much can be lost at the beginning of line 1 according to the copy. See Stolper's interpretation.

j. *dullu*

dullu, "work", is, again, not a taxation specific expression,[110] but in many instances it unmistakably indicates "corvée"[111]: civil tasks or their costs, generally payments for labour which were imposed upon certain members of society because they were of a suitable age, possessed the specific means required, or had property burdened with the obligations concerned. That these obligations generally were property related seems to be certain, whether that was always the case is, however, not so clear.

A number of texts from Babylon (Egibi conglomerate) suggests that payments for *dullu* were regular features in connection with work on canals and defensive installations. The payments were collected by the same person collecting for, for instance, *urāšu*. Cyr 10, a payment for work on the walls of Babylon immediately after the taking of the town by Cyrus strongly suggests that payments for *dullu* could be required on an *ad hoc* basis for a specific purpose. The consequence would be that those liable also could be called up when the need arose, perhaps even in an unlimited manner. Some of these payments were to all probability recurring impositions on an annual basis. If *dullu* was intended for a specific purpose it could possibly be an additional payment, for a specific purpose. The king can build palaces or dig canals in Elam on a permanent basis, but if the local town wall collapses that might require specific measures at short notice. The texts from the Babylon Egibi archive indicate that such payments occurred already in Chaldean times. The term is, however, used less regularly, especially, in the later reign of Darius.[112] It is too early to suggest that a more *ad hoc* type of taxation was increasingly being replaced by regular fixed payments. After a steady rise in obligations that might have been perceived if not as a relief, at least as a stabilisation. For the question of the total burden of taxation in general this is a matter of considerable uncertainty. Corvée work outside one's own town was already known in the Chaldean period, as the material from Borsippa indicates.

On the length of the obligation the Dilbat text BM 49718 provides some information: the person concerned will work for three months in Elam. This could be understood as including the time needed for travelling, if we take the etymological interpretation of *pa-da-šu-tu*[113] proposed by Jursa literally. The text is dated to month XII yr. 10 and the obligation is to reach its term in VI (yr. 11). But we cannot be too certain about that, as we are dealing with the hiring of a worker from his father for a three month's period: an obligation to perform work is changed into a financial transaction for which personnel is engaged. Such a person may be a professional "worker in Elam", for whom there seems to have been a going rate as the default clause suggests. Also the Egibi text Dar 572 mentions hiring for a period of three months for work in Elam of, in this case, four persons, who have to be engaged and provided with sustenance. In neither case it is certain that the obligation imposed on the tax payer also

---

110 A whole range of Borsippa *imittu* documents includes the standard phrase *dullu u gú-gal* (*ul*) *eṭer*, in this form or in slightly different combinations. I assume that *dullu* in these cases represents the work that is remunerated by the *sissinnu* mentioned in other texts, the agreed payment to the tenant for doing the digging, etc., required. As the *gugallu* is to my conviction primarily an estate official, the payments alluded to in these texts do not refer to taxation by the government. Example from Babylon: VS 6, 130. Cf. TCL 12, 97 line 26. Generally such passages are not considered here.

111 There is no adequate English word for this. The (military) "fatigues" is too narrow, CAD D p. 173 accepts "corvée work".

112 Only VS 6, 150, Borsippa (25 XII Dar 27), which mentions *urāšu ša dullu ša ikkarāte*, "corvée workers doing the work imposed on the ploughmen", an anyhow exceptional passage, attests use of *dullu* in a corvée context in the later reign of Darius. The probable intention was to all likelihood that the *urāšu*s concerned were selected from the plough men.

113 Discussed by M. Jursa, NABU 1995/3 p. 54-5.

involved a period of three months, we are possibly dealing with a kind of rationalisation of obligations in which certain persons were engaged for a period which made sense.

Two texts are perhaps not sufficient for a firm conclusion that the period for obligatory *dullu* (or *urāšu*) in Elam amounted to three months. It would mean that 25% of the working year of certain categories of persons would be available for obligatory work in foreign parts, but of this group certain persons may have been made available for much longer as institutional material from Sippar suggests. It is almost unimaginable that all Babylonians liable for *ilku*, that is all involved in a land for service system would have been obliged to work for three months per annum in Elam. The burden would have been staggering. The person who hired the labour possibly organised the individual liabilities resulting from some collective imposition into something more effective. In a positive sense this obligation created opportunities for paid labour,-and possibly for those who acted as organisers-, in a negative sense it withdrew labour from Mesopotamia itself for the benefit of the Susa area. As labour was to my conviction a scarce commodity, at least in some periods of the year, these arrangements could develop into a serious burden. Dar 572 is dated to the last day of month IX, the three month's period mentioned would include some of the harvest period. The text published in NABU dates from month XII, thus to the period when the harvest would be about to begin. Removing labour at this point would disfavour Babylonia, a matter of some importance in considering the effects of a tax related withdrawal of labour from Babylonia benefiting Susiana.

A payment of 1.5 mina of silver in Dar 411 for work on a canal in Elam can be considered as considerable if it really represents an imposition on one taxable person, even if he was a senior Egibi. We must, however keep in mind that the Egibis were financially involved with government business at an official level, which makes it uncertain whether we are really dealing with taxation imposed on them personally. But, whatever may have been the case, and however impossible to quantify it is, Babylonia had to shoulder a considerable workload in Susiana: this is an element of the "Persian tribute" that is not considered by Herodotus.

VS 6, 84 is possibly not a question of taxation, but a private contract, even though the intervention of the *šākin ṭēmi* suggests an official context, perhaps one in which a contractor supplied the personnel and the *šākin ṭēmi* the materials. What, possibly, was imposed on the brothers could be the *mišḫu* mentioned, a specified stretch of, for instance of a wall or a quay, known to the parties, but not mentioned in detail in the text, for which labour with the required skills and materials had to be provided for work according to specification. But there is perhaps also the possibility that such work had been put to tender, and thus had to be implemented by those who had accepted it.[114] Imposition of certain specific tasks on a tax payer and a kind of tender are not, however, strictly mutually exclusive. The tax payer could be obliged to engage specialists just as he could hire unskilled labour to perform his tasks. Cf. the Borsippa text L 1632 concerning the preparation of baked bricks for work on the quay of Babylon. We know little about the organisation of public works, beyond the fact that institutions and holders of chariot fiefs could be made responsible for a stretch of a canal. Some special skill will have been needed occasionally. In general it would not be unlikely that a certain task would be split up in a number of obligations, of which providing a specific type of material could be one, which were finally imposed on an individual tax payer. The tax payer concerned would have to contract a "specialist". VS 6, 66 is a receipt for baked bricks given by a *rab eširti* for an imposed *iškaru*. This is almost certainly tax related. That is perhaps more likely than a local governor contracting with an entrepreneur to have a certain piece of work done for a lump sum

[114] CAD M/II p. 121, *mišḫu*, mentions the word in several contexts where the completion of building work is required, especially in an institutional context. This should not be regarded automatically as a question of "taxation", but primarily be regarded as an assignation of a certain amount of work to a labour unit. But institutions certainly had to contribute to public works.

in silver. Having work in Elam done certainly meant contracting labour by tax payers. Several of the *dullu* related terms explicitly connect the tasks performed with Elam.

Babylon Egibi and related

Nbn 657 19 X Nbn 12, 4 *š* of silver due from Ina-Esagil-ramat dr Zēria wife of IM for *dul-lu* on the Nār-Ninlil, received by Nurea s Šāpik-zēri.[115]

Nbn 727 6 IX Nbn 13, 10 *š* of silver due to Nūrea s Bēl-iqīša *ina dul-lu šá* IM received from Ina-Esagil-ramat, mentions earlier documents.

Cyr 10 x x Cyr 0, 19 *š a-na dul-lu šá* BAD_3 at the Enlil Gate from 14 X to 6 XII received by Nūrea s Bēl-iqīša Šangû-Nanāia from Marduk-rēmanni s IM.

W, IM 387 x VII x x, Nur-ea s Bēl-iqišā Šangû-Nanāia has received from Ina-Esagil-ramat, wife of IM, [silver for work?], not including the silver received from Iddina and the hirelings who performed the work.

Camb 73 14 VIII Camb 1 KB, $20^1/4$ *š* received by Nabû-ban-zēri s Daiian-Marduk Sin-šadūni for work (*dullu*) (due from) Marduk-ban-zēri s Eṭellu Bēl-ēṭeru from Aḫḫē-iddina-Marduk s Šākin-šumi Eṭēru for Marduk-ban-zēri.

Bertin 3065-6 x x [Dar] 5, see sub *rikis qabli.*

Dar 411 22 VIII Dar 15, 2 mina of silver of Tattannu s Rēmūt due from Š s I will be paid in XII, encompasses(?) an earlier document of $1^1/_2$ mina for work on the Nār-Šarri of Elam.

Dar 572 30 IX Dar 23, Marduk-iddina and Zitti-Nabû ss ?, Suqaia s Kalbā and x-ēṭer s Kalbā Šumu-libši have received from Š s I hire and sustenance (*i-di ù* $SUKU_6$.$ḪA_2$) for going to Elam for three months.

Babylon: Sin-ili and Nappāḫu files

VS 6 84 8 VI Nbn 12, the *dullu ša kāri mišhu* of Marduk-šum-ibni and brothers ss Ṭabia Sin-ili will be performed by Nabû-balassu-iqbi s Ša-Nabû-šu Raksu, who will receive the materials needed according to the decision of the *šākin ṭēmi* of Babylon. He can dispose of three slaves, and he will receive $2^1/_2$ *š* of silver per month. He will not leave the slaves unsupervised in charge of materials and tools.

VS 6 130 10 V Dar 13, 2.1.0 of dates and other products, rest of the harvest of yr. 11 of IN s NBZ Nappāḫu is due from Balāṭu s Nabû-bašti-ilāni Atkuppu in VII. The dates of the *dullu* and the *gugallu* are paid. Incomplete statement by Balāṭu.[116]

Borsippa

Ash A 99 VI Nbk 35, (Zēr-Babili Ea-ilūta-bani file) 5 *š* K.B *ina dul-lu šá* Zēr-Babili Ina-teše-ēṭer *ina* UGU ZB *ina* $ŠU^{II}$ Nabû-aḫa-iddina *ma-ḫir.*

L 1632 22 VIII Nbk 40, (same file) *dul-lu šá ka-a-ri šá* $TIN.TIR^{KI}$ *šá* Dadia ^{LU_2}*qal-la šá* Nabû-ēṭer-napšāti *a-na* UGU Zēr-Babili *ip-pu-uš a-ki-i* 3 *lim a-gur-ru* TIL-*tim ina ka-a-ri a-na* 1 MA.NA KB *a-na* UḪU Zēr-Bābili *i-nam-din.* Arrangements concerning payment.

(TuM 2/3 215 10 V Cyr 5, involves members Ilūta-bani family, lines 6 and 7 mention *ilku*(?) and *dullu*, probably in Babylon, but all context is lost).

NBC 8340 4 II Cyr 6, (Širiktu Ili-bani-file) *dullu ša* A.MEŠ *šá* PN *šá* MU 5 KAM_2 *šá a-di qi-it šá* ^{ITI}II PN2 *ina* $ŠU^{II}$ PN_3 *ma-ḫi-ir*; possibly a completely private affair.

VS 6 150 25 XII Dar 27, (Rē'u-alpi file) see sub *urāšu.*

"Building material file", taxation related?

VS 6 166 9 V Dar 36, 410 *a-gur-ru a-na dul-lu šá mu-še-ḫi-ne-e*.MEŠ *šá* E_2 ^{d}Mār-bīti *ina* $EŠ_3$.QAR *šá* Itti-Nabû-guzu Ša-Nabû-šu GAL 10 $ERIN_2$(!) *ina* $ŠU^{II}$ Ša-Nabû-šu *maḫir*, cf. VS 6, 177 (11 V Xer 0) and VS 6, 178 (9 XI Xer 0).

---

115 Eliminating with C. Wunsch the *šá* in line 1.

116 In passages like this *dullu* refers to the digging performed by the gardener, not to taxation. Also in the Borsippa text NBC 8340 a link with taxation is dubious.

dullu and *padašūtu*
Dilbat

BM 19718[117] 27 XII Dar 10, (unassigned) PN1 (will go) 2) ... *ana pa-da-šu-tu*$_4$ *šá* PN2 3) ... *ana* ^{KUR}Elam^{KI} *il-lak* 4) 3 ITI.MEŠ *dul-lu ina* ^{KUR}Elam^{KI} *ar*$_2$*-ki* 5) PN2 <<*dul-lu*>>> PN1 6) *ip-pu-uš*. If he does not work until month VI in Elam his father will pay hire according to the rate for hirelings working in Elam for three months.

k. *zebēli ša upiyāti*[118]

zebēli ša upiyāti (=ukpiyataš), is best regarded as a specific type of *dullu*, or, more generally, according to BM 82666 and 82716, of *ilku*, specifically related to Elam. It is also closely associated with *urāšu ša kāri*, and therefore inevitably indicates a form of corvée work. To all likelihood it constituted some form of transport obligation. Strictly spoken this brings us no nearer to what *upiyāti* was. In Dar 244 there is a special store for the delivery of what was due as *u.*, which leaves open the possibility that *zebēlu* was only the corvée related to the transport of what was due as *u*.

The importance of the Borsippa texts in creating a firm link between the military and civil obligations implied by the term *ilku* has been discussed under *ilku*. The involvement in the collection of what is due by someone called the "*gugallu* of Borsippa" should be noted. We can not regard a town as an estate, but if his tasks were the practical ones of supervising the distribution of water, that task would also have to be accomplished in areas were land had been distributed to townspeople. We will see that Borsippa provides especially good information on the local *ḫanšus*. Could we locate this functionary there? In L 4720 the terms following *ilku* specify that term, therefore it could be skipped in VS 6, 160.

Borsippa

BM 82666 21 IX Dar 16, (Rē'u-alpi file) *il-ka šá za-ba-lu šá ú-pa-a-tú šá* ^{KUR}Elam^{KI} from month X yr 16 to end month III Dar 17, as much as was the share of Rēmūt-Nabû s Nabû-mukīn-zēr Rē'u-alpi and his father, is received from Rēmūt-Nabû [s x] by Nabû-bulissu *gugallu* of [Barsip], son of Taqiš-Gula.

BM 82716 20 VI Dar 17, (Rē'u-alpi) *il-ki ša* [cf. 82666] *šá* ^{KUR}Elam^{KI},[share of R.] s Nabû-mukīn-zēr from month X yr 17 to month III yr 18 Bēl-ittannu s Taqiš-Gula family x has received on orders of Nabû-balassu-iqbi the *gugallu* of Borsippa, his brother, from Rēmūt-Nabû.

L 4720 24 IV Dar 25, (Nanāḫu-file) Mušallim-Nabû s Nabû-mukīn-zēr receives from Nabû-aḫḫē-iddina s Kalbā Nanāḫu *il-ki ma-la* ḪA.LA-*šú šá ze-bé-e-li šá ú-pi-a-ta šá* ^{LU}*2ú-ra-a-šú šá kar-ri ù pa-na-at* BAN *ù ḫi-šá-ru-ú*[119] from yr 21 to end II yr 25.

VS 6 160 21 XI Dar 33, ^{LU}*2ú-raš šá šá-da-du šá ka-a-ri šá ze-be-lu ša ú-pi-a-tu*$_4$ *šá* ^{URU}Šu-un-ša-an from 1 III yr 32 to II yr 33 *ma-la* 5-*šú* ḪA.LA *ša* Nabû-kāṣir s Nabû-balassu-iqbi s ? *ù pa-na-at*! ^{GIŠ}BAN yr 32 PN is received on orders of Iddina-Nabû ^{LU}2GU$_2$.GAL Barsip^{KI}.

Babylon, here?

Dar 244[120] 26 XII Dar 8, before 10 IV [Nabû-rēmua] slave of Širiktu will measure out 240 kor of barley *makkūr šarri* of Marduk-šum-iddina the ? 4) *i-na ka-a-ri šá šarri ša up-pa-ia-a-ta*. Nabû-remua stated "I have handed it to Arad-Bēl-ṣarbe s Nurea". He will register the 240 kor

---

117 Published R. Zadok NABU 1995/4, re-edited M. Jursa, NABU 1995/61. I would consider the possibility that PN2 organises a working party for *dullu* in Elam led by him. If PN replaced PN2, he would have acted as his *kutallu*.

118 Literature: M.W. Stolper, 1977, p. 254f. and R. Zadok, BiOr 41, 1984 p. 36b; Joannès 1989, p. 153-4.

119 On this hapax cf. Jursa 1999 p. 104 note 440: *ḫišārū* is attractively proposed to indicate "die Zehnerverplichtung". Are we to suppose that *pānāt qašti u ḫišārū* indicate in this case together the whole complex of obligations?

120 Edited Stolper 1977 p. 255, see his remark with collations by E. Leichty on the title of Marduk-šum-iddina.

barley with Arad-Bēl-ṣarbe and hand proof to Iqūpu s Bēl-x the *bēl piqittu* of the *mašennu*. (See Stolper 1977, p. 255)

l. *kanšu*[121]

The texts are all from an institutional context, including BM 42347, which need not be non-institutional, but possibly is not related to an imposed transport duty. TCL 13, 165 is perhaps the most explicit in suggesting transport obligations.

Nbn 237 and BM 74964 suggest that manning could be organised in a manner similar to that of the recruitment of the bowmen the temple estates had to provide: they were selected from the *širku*'s on a semi-permanent basis. There could be some connection with the Sippar texts quoted under *rikis qabli* dealing with institutional obligations towards the horses of the *nakkandu* of the king, but the occurrence of (nominal) groups of ten in both sets of texts is no proof in itself as the group of ten constitutes the basic structure for all civil, military and labour units. There is, however, a difference between serving in groups of ten and being drafted from a similar group which constitutes the mobilisation and taxation structure. In Sippar herdsmen were generally amongst those used for this type of semi-military obligations.

Transport duties were a general "old-regime" imposition on the population, their existence in Mesopotamia stands to reason, and they will have applied to both land and water transport. *rikis qabli* is once found for boatmen, but, as stated, it is a term which need not be restricted to civil or military service obligations, the term might be used for any undertaking.

Sippar Šangû-Šamaš/Sippar

BM 42347 13 XI Camb 5, dates received by Eṭellu s Itti-Bēl-lummir Šangû-Šamaš for the donkeys *šá ka-an-šú šá it-ti* ^{LU_2}KU$_4$.E$_2$ ^{d}UTU.

Sippar Ebabbar

Nbn 237 22 VI yr 6, (dates for in) total 10 ERIN$_2$.MEŠ *šá itti ka-an-šú il-lik.*

BM 74964 no date, barley *a-na* ^{LU_2}SIPA.MEŠ *šá it-ti ka-an-šú il-li-ku.*

Uruk

TCL 13 165 15 VI Camb 4, 1 ANŠE *bab-ba-nu-ú ana ze-bi-lu ša ka-an-šu ša šarri.*

Mich 89 no date, silver for fodder for 10 donkeys and 10 birds[122] *ša* 10 ^{LU_2}ERIN$_2$.MEŠ *ša itti* ANŠE.MEŠ *ša ka-an-šu.*

m. *urāšu*[123]

The *urāšu* was a corvée worker, who was to be made available or for whose hire had to be provided. There is not much difference with *dullu*, which often also implies the provision of labour. The term is not specific to private taxation obligations, it occurs in institutional context and notably also in Assyrian royal inscriptions in passages referring to the imposition of tribute, which could imply the regular provision of a specified labour force. In a Babylonian taxation context the tax basis must have been real estate. TuM 2/3, 218, from Borsippa, explicitly mentions the fact that the *urāšu* concerned was due on account of a *house.* This is confirmed by YBC 11599. The texts constitute two more pieces of evidence not completely unexpectedly suggesting that houses could be an element of the tax basis. An obligation of this type could be shared by several persons, as VS 6, 119 indicates.

---

121 Literature: CAD K 158 (donkey caravan); W. von Soden OrNS 35 p. 12 no. 63 (Arbeitskommando) and especially Jursa, 1999, p. 100, a general discussion. We will not discuss Hittite transport arrangements.

122 A confident interpretation cannot be given, but the reading seems to be assured.

123 Literature: basic S. Weingort, Das Haus Egibi, Diss. Berlin, 1938, p. 27-30; Joannès 1989, p. 151-9; Jursa 1995 p. 121, note 234.

The tasks imposed will have been specific to the occasion: earth work, the making of bricks and transport related tasks are being mentioned.

The direct connection between *ilku*, *dullu* and *urāšu* exists in both private and institutional texts and is underlined by the fact that in the Nūr-Sin section of the Egibi archive in Nbn yrs. 12 and 13 sons of Bēl-iqīša collect what is due under all these headings, as does (Nabû-)Ban-zēri in the early years of Cyrus. One of the surprises of the Marduk-rēmanni archive from Sippar is that Kalbā s Ṣillā Nabāia, the father-in-law of Marduk-nāṣir-apli Egibi also served as collector of these dues, with the possibility that these persons acted as a tax farmers,[124] though strict proof is not available for the moment.

Mich 26 explicitly refers to *ilku* of the *urāšu*. The *urāšu* was, however, not used for military purposes in the documentation available, but he was due for the same (property related) reason for which military personnel could be levied, in which the explicit texts from Borsippa are important. Several texts combine the town of Susa and transport work for the quay, here again Babylonia contributes to the "Persian tribute". In Mich 26 the *ilku* of the *urāšu* of Elam seems to have evolved into a special payment, it thus could represent a separate form of annual taxation. In this way L 4740 and TuM 2/3 222 cover half a year, but other texts deal with even longer periods.

L 1651, from Borsippa could suggest that gods had rights to *urāšu* workers, and these were indeed occasionally employed in projects figuring in the Ebabbar administration from Sippar, but there is of course always the possibility that such workers were made available for the occasion by the royal administration. The clearest examples occur in the file on the work on the *mušannītu* at Gilušu between (minimally) 30 X Nbn 13 and 11 X Nbn 14, but in this group also the limited importance of *urāšus* for the project becomes clear,[125] certainly compared to, for instance, local hirelings. In the headings of the texts they predominate, *urāšus* occur in only three of the texts[126], DU$_3$.E$_2$s[127] and *ummanus*[128] are, however, even rarer. Many hirelings were engaged locally, but there are also many members from the various vocational groups of institutional personnel. Such personnel was employed by the institution on a regular basis, why they appear in documents headed by the word "hirelings" is not self-evident, the best interpretation is probably that all labour costs related to the project figured on these daily lists.

The Nippur text BE 8/1, 12 indicates a payment in commodities for the *urāšu*. The amount paid agrees well with the sums spent according to BE 8/1, 37, which are in turn in line with the payments in Nippur listed under *ilku*. The undated text TuM 2/3, 217 cannot be located with absolute certainty in Nippur, but is of some interest for understanding the procedures followed. A group of 22 people[129] is, for reasons which are not stated, assessed for providing collectively seven *urāšu* workers. As so often, the texts from Borsippa specify the period for which payments were made. These statements do, however, not indicate the period of actual service. At most the text implies that it deals with a given period and a given, known, obligation, which is not to be exceeded by further unexpected demands. But: only for the specific purpose mentioned and not for fresh tasks?

VS 6, 150 with its "*urāšu* of the plough men" is remarkable. Payment is due from an ostensibly private landowner, who is known to possess land subject to *ilku*, but the dues are

---

124 As C. Waerzeggers remarked.

125 *urāšus* are also found in CT 56, 596, 4 *urāšus* at the disposal of Guzānu, and CT 57, 288, a damaged passage concerning a named *urāšu* at the disposal of PN (name lost).

126 CT 56, 572 (30 X Nbn 13), BM 68211 (28 x Nbn 14) and CT 56, 792 (Nbn 14).

127 CT 56, 572, restoration based on line 6.

128 In the headings in BM 68211, but more frequently in the text itself.

129 Some of those listed are obviously more prominent than others, whose names are indented, the reasons are not clear.

collected on behalf of a rent farmer.[130] A possible interpretation is that the ploughmen concerned constituted a unit, possibly an *ešertu*, one member of which had to serve as an *urāšu*, or otherwise the members had to pay together for an *urāšu*. The Eanna archive text Birmingham 7 is of some importance in this context, as it explicitly indicates that the obligation to provide an *urāšu* was linked to the *ešertu*-structure. We will have to return to this question.

Babylon Egibi related

Nbn 632 9 VIII Nbn 12, two *urāšus* for earth work (2 ^{LU_2}*ú-ra-šú šá dul-lu e-pi-ri*) due from IM from VIII to end I yr 13 received by x-mušallim s Apkallu Mušēzib from IMB s NAI Egibi. (W, IM 202)

Nbn 713 16 V Nbn 13, 11 mina of silver *ina ú-ra-šú* due from IM paid by him to Bēl-šunu s Bēl-iqīša Šangû-Nanā and Nabû-LIL[131] s Bēl-uballiṭ Ea-ibni on orders from Nūrea s Bēl-iqīša Šangû-Nanā. (W, IM 213)

Cyr 8 21 XII Cyr 0, Marduk-rēmanni s IM pays 6 *š* for *urāšu* of IM to Nergal-aḫḫē-iddina s Erība-Marduk Šigua; mentions earlier payment of 9 *š* by Marduk-rēmanni to Lābāši. (W, IM 261)

Camb 88 14 I Camb 1 kB, 30 *š šá ú-ra-ši-šú a-na ṣa-ra-pu šá a-gur-ru* of IM from IV yr 1 to *ṭup-pi a-na ṭup-pi*,[132] received by Ban-zēri. Identical Camb 419. (W, IM 265)

Nbn 1091 18 VI Cyr 1, 3 *š* of silver *ina ú-ra-šú* of IM received by Ban-zēri s Daiian-Marduk Sin-šadûnu from IMB s NAI, mentions earlier payments. (W, IM 266)

Cyr 48 13 V Cyr 2, 1 mina $46^1/_2$ *š* of silver from 13 VIII yr 1 to 13 V yr 2 is received from Ina-Esagil-ramat, wife of IM, by Nabû-ban-zēri s Daiian-Marduk Sin-šadūnu and Šamaš-šum-ukīn *ina ú-ra-ši-šú*. (W, IM 275)

Cyr 86 8 XII Cyr 2, 5 *š ina ú-ra-šú* of IM is received by Ban-zēri s Daiian-Marduk Sin-šadūnu from Marduk-rēmanni s IM. (W, IM 282)

Cyr 102 27 I Cyr 3, silver *ina ú-ra-ši-šú* is received by Šamaš-iddina s Ban-zēri Sin-šadûnu from Bēl-rēmanni s Iqīša Nūr-Sin. Mentions earlier documents. (W, IM 283)

Bir 46 22 x Cyr 4, *e-puš* NIG$_2$.KAS$_7$ *šá ú-ra-šú* of IM from 1 V yr 3 to III yr 4 with Ban-zēri s Daiian-Marduk is completed, but that from XII yr. 2 to III yr. 4 is not.

W, IM 296 9 V Cyr 5, *ú-ra-šú* of IM to 1 VII is paid to Bulṭā s Šamaš-aḫḫē-iddina by IM.

Cyr 212 22 X Cyr 5, 1 *š* of silver received by Šapik-zēri from Marduk-rēmanni *a-na ú-raš šá par-di-su*. (W, IM 297)

Cyr 224 3+ II Cyr 6, Nummuru s Zēria has received from Nergal-reṣua slave of IMB s NAI the *ú-ra-šú* up to 1 III yr 6. (W, IM 302)

W, IM 346 x III Camb 7, Arad-Nabû s Ki-Bēl Aškappu has been paid the *ú-ra-šú* up to VIII yr 7 due from IM by IMB.

Dar 56 21 XII Dar 2, Šamaš-iddina s Šāpik-zēri Sin-šadûnu has received 5 *š* of silver of the *urāšu* of IM from Marduk-rēmanni s IM on the orders of his father Ban-zēri s Daiian-Marduk. Mentions earlier documents. (W, IM 349)

Bertin 2534 15 x Dar 24, [*ú-*]*ra-šú šá-da-du šá ka-a-ri* of Ina-Esagil-ŠEŠ s Zēr-Babili of 3? months and 12 days yr 24(?) received by Š s I from Bēl-uballiṭ s Iddina-Nabû Ba'iru for Nabû-x s Zēria Mu-x.

Bertin 2566 23 III Dar 25, x x E$_2$/ú(?) ^{LU_2}*šá-di-du* for a month and 6 days to end VIII yr 25 of Marduka s Nabû-uṣuršu Šumu-libši Š s I has received from x s Lāqīpu on behalf of Marduka. Cf. Bertin 2534.

Non-Egibi Babylon

Camb 260 8 XI Camb 4, Marduk-šum-ibni and Nabû-iddina ss Šulā Eppeš-ili pay silver for an *urāšu* up to XI yr 4 to Bēl-ban-zēri s Nurea Šangû-Nanna.

---

[130] His title or exact occupation is an old problem.

[131] I regard the reading of the name as Nabû-lillu, as proposed by Tallquist, "impossible", but have no solution.

[132] Probable meaning here "as long as it takes to finish the job".

Dar 84 24 VII Dar 3, 2 *š* of silver with the *urāšu* Samaš-iddina s Šāpik-zēri Sin-šadûnu has received from Šum-ukīn and his brothers, sons of Aplā Gaḫul.

Borsippa

Texts from file on Ahušunu Nanāḫu

L 1651 22 IX Dar 27, receipt of silver *šá* ^{LU}$_{2}$*ú-ra-šú šá ka-a-ri* ^{d}Na-na-a *šá ḫi-ri-tú* I$_{7}$ ḪA.LA *šá* Aḫušunu N. given by Nabû-zēr-līšir s Arad-Bēl Zērūtu, mentions additionally silver [*ana dullu ša*] *mušennītu*.

NBC 8371 26 VII Dar 29, receipt of *ú-ra-šú šá šá-da-du kār ša* ^{KUR}E[lam^{KI}?] *qe-me šá ḫi-ru-gal-lu-ú ù mim-ma pa-na-at* ^{GIŠ}BAN *gab-bi ma-la* ḪA.LA PN *šá* Aḫušunu N., up to end VIII given by Šamaš-iddina s Nabû-nādin-aḫi Ili-bani.

L 4740 22 IX Dar 21, receipt *ú-ra-šú šá šá-da-du šá ka-a-ri šá* ^{URU}Šu-šá-an *ù pa-na-at* ^{GIŠ}BAN *gab-bi a-na ma-la* ḪA.LA Aḫušunu N from 1 IX to end II yr 32 given by Šamaš-iddina. Identical TuM 2/3, 220.

TuM 2/3 221 14 IV Dar 32, receipt ^{LU}$_{2}$*ú-ra-šú šá šá-da-da šá ka-a-ri* from III yr 30 to VIII yr 32, *ma-la* ḪA.LA *šá* Aḫušunu N; 9) *ù mim+ma pa-na-at* BAN *gab-bi* x), given by Šamaš-iddina Ili-bani.

TuM 2/3 222 4 I Dar 33, receipt ^{LU}$_{2}$*ú-ra-šú šá-da-da* 2) *šá* ^{URU}Šu-šá-an *šá qa*-a[t PN?] 3) ^{LU}$_{2}$*gú-gal* Barsip^{KI} x [x] 4) [*šá*] MU 32 KAM *ana ma-la* ḪA.LA *šá* A s N from IX yr 33 to II yr 34 (*sic*!) given by Šamaš-iddina Ili-bani.

Other Borsippa

TuM 2/3 218 14 X Nbk 15, (Ili-bani file) 1 *š* of silver PN *ina* ŠU^{II} PN2 *ša urāšu ša* E$_{2}$ PNx *ša* ^{GIŠ}MESMAGANNA [x x (x)] *ana* UGU PN2 *u* PN3 *ma-ḫi-ir*.

TuM 2/3 219 XI Cyr 7, (Ili-bani, unidentified file) ^{LU}$_{2}$*ú-ra-šú šá dul-lu a-di qí-it* ITI XI yr 7 ... *ma-ḫir* on orders of Arad-Nabû s Nabû-ēṭer-napšāti Itinnu.

VS 6 119 12 x Dar 1, (Ilia-file) *re-bu-ú šá* ^{LU}$_{2}$*ú-ra-šú a-n*[*a* x] 1-*en* A NI PA[133] ^{LU}$_{2}$*ú-ra-šú*, period, paid to Rēmūt-Bēl s Silim-x Raksu.

NBC 8337 IV Dar 10, see Chapter VII sub *dekû ša babti*.

Mich 26 21 X Dar 10, (Rē'u-alpi file) *il-ki šá ú-ra-šú šá* ^{KUR}ELAM.MA^{KI} from X Dar 9 to end X Dar 10, of Rēmūt-Nabû s Nabû-mukīn-zēr Rē'u-alpi due from Nabû-mukīn-zēr his father, Nabû-balassu-iqbi Taqiš-Gula Nagar x of Rēmūt-Nabû has been paid by [? = Rēmūt-Nabû], both took a receipt.

VS 6 150 Bors 25 XII Dar 27, (Rē'u-alpi file) ^{LU}$_{2}$*ú-ra-šu šá dul-lu šá* ^{LU}$_{2}$ENGAR.MEŠ from I yr 26 to end XII Dar 27 *šá* Rēmūt s Murašû Re'u-alpi, three persons, messengers of PN[134] have received from Rēmūt.

VS 6 160 21 XI Dar 33, see *zebēlu ša upiyāti*.

Kiš

OECT 10 133 x.x Dar x, (ḪSK Eppeš-ili), badly preserved, ^{LU}$_{2}$*ú-ra-áš-šú šá* x *šá* LUGAL, receipt

Nippur

BE 8/1 12 29 I Nbk 26, at Al-ša-Lûṣianuru. (Nippur unassigned) Barley *imittu* of 6 kor of Lābāši on Lûṣianuru, of which (5) 5 kor barley *a-ki-i ú-ra-áš* Lûṣianuru has paid.

BE 8/1 37 Ner yr 2, administrative?, 1) [*ina*?] date 2) [*a-na*?] *ú-ra-šú u ni-is-ḫu e-šír* immediately followed by amounts of silver of maximally 6 *š* (twice/) or 5 *š* (once), otherwise between 4 and 2 *š* + PN.[135]

---

133 Obscure.

134 (lines 8-9) x-Na-na-a the *ša muḫḫi* GIŠ.BAN$_{2}$ *šá* UGU ŠE.BAR *šá up-pi-qu-du*, obscure, but probably a rent farmer, possibly *šá* $^{\text{KUR!}}$Pi-qu-du? That would be a rare late reference to a tribal area, deep into the reign of Darius I, and thus highly dubious.

135 Some twenty payments are more or less preserved, but note that the first line of the reverse, and even the first of the lower edge may mean a shift to payments of house rent, which would leave only some eight payments for *urāšu*. What *nisḫu* means in this context is not clear to me, for *nisḫu ša māti* see below, this must be something different, however.

TuM 2/3 217 no date, list of PNs followed by a fractional number, ending with PAP 7 ^{LU_2}*ú-ra-šú* [more than half of line lost].

Sippar

Ṣāḫit-ginê, Marduk-rēmanni

M-r 41 x x Dar 4, see sub *qaštu*. (The text mentions Kalbā < s Ṣillā Nabāia>).

M-r 47 24 III Dar 6, 1) x+1 ^{LU_2}*ú-ra–šú gi-ši-ir* 2) from I yr 3 to XI yr 5 Kalbā s Ṣillā Nabāia has received from Marduk-rēmanni.

CT 56 572 30 X Nbn 13, 1) [^{LU_2}DU$_3$.]E$_2$ ^{LU_2}*ú-ra-šú ù* ^{LU_2}ḪUN.GA$_2$ *šá ina* UGU *mu-šá-*[*ni-tu*$_4$] *šá* ^{URU}Gi-lu-šú *dul-lu ip-pu-šu.*

CT 56 569 x x Nbn 13, 21) 4 ^{LU_2}*ú-ra-šú ina* IGI ^{P}Gu-za-nu, at the end of a list of various other groups of workers.

CT 57 288 [PN] [^{LU_2}]*ú-ra-sú šá ina* ŠU^{II} [PN], no context.

Uruk, Eanna Archive

Bir 7 30 IV Nbk 38, PN1 stands security for PN2 and sons with the *qêpu*, 1-*en ú-raš a-na* ^{LU_2}GAL 10-*ti-šú i-nam-din u* PN2 *dul-la ina* Eanna *ip-pu-uš.*

TCL 13 150 14 III Camb 2, at Maškan-ili PN (known as a *gugallu*) receives an injunction that he is obliged when asked in writing to deliver 10 *urāšus*[136] for canal work to the lease holder of the Nār-Ḫarri-Kippi; if he does not comply, he will have to bear the displeasure of Gubāru, governor of Babylon and Transeuphratia.

Other

YBC 11599[137] 11 VIII Art II 20, see under *ilku*.

n) *qēmu* (*ša šarri*)[138]

This type of taxation occurs especially in the Murašû texts, where it is included in the string of obligations mentioned in the *ilku* receipts. Frequently without *ša šarri*, it is a very general, though not widely attested, obligation imposed on holders of *ilku* land. That more or less symbolic amounts of flour were actually delivered is certain, a number of texts, e.g. PBS 2/1, 217, add a pot of beer, and a sheep or other small numbers of animals. Sometimes an equal amount of barley accompanies the flour. This is not just a purely financial transaction, but it had probably also a symbolic meaning, underlining the acceptance of a subordinate position in general. As we have seen, similar obligations were imposed on institutional underlings.

The texts from Borsippa are again the most explicit among the earlier Achaemenid material. The obligation is generally an element of a list which sums up all responsibilities, the texts concerned are quoted under *ilku* or *urāšu.* TuM 2/3, 169 could refer to a special milling obligation, as the material seems to be provided.

VS 6, 114 does not provide an explicit link with the *ilku*-complex, but it mentions the in the Neo-Babylonian period rare *ḫirigallu*-flour, also occurring in NBC 8371, and specifying that there is a "big" and a "small" type, presumably a coarse and a fine variety.[139] The member of the Rē'u-alpi family concerned is, however, both a prebendary and a holder of service land.

---

136 The *urāšus* are qualified as *šá* ^{LU_2}URU.MEŠ ^{LU_2}ERIN2 ŠU^{II}-*šú šu-ul-su-du-ú-tu.* ^{LU_2}URU.MEŠ could perhaps be *ālāiu* (or even *aššābu*? cf. perhaps YOS 7, 186 quoted under *gugallūtu* and involving the same *gugallu*) or require emendation into ENGAR.MEŠ. *šu-ul-su-du-ú-tu* might be, with CAD D 127R *šušdušu*, "divided into groups of six" which would complicate the usual division in groups of ten, and is thus not assured. Rather *šuršudūtu*, "equipped", which would clarify the injunction? On *ṣab qatê* cf. the section on *pišku* in Chapter III.

137 Stolper 2000b, p. 673-675. Stolper proposes to regard the high *šugarrû* payment of twice 40 *š* as the contribution of the tenants toward the service obligations of the owner. We can only note that this represents a fixed sum, and that it should make us aware that unspecified extras mentioned elsewhere could equally represent similar contributions.

138 Literature: CAD Q p. 208-209.

139 Cf. CAD Ḫ p. 297 L.

Though the text to all likelihood deals with the milling aspect of an obligation, it is more likely that the milling is related in this case to prebendal obligations than to the holding of service land. Flour combined with *ilku* definitely occurs in a Nippur text.

qēmu (in *ilku* texts)

Borsippa

VS 6 114 25 II Camb 7, (Rē'u-alpi archive) *qé-me ḫi-ri-ga-lu qal-la ù* GAL-*ú šá* MU 7 KAM$_2$ Camb due from PN1 [x-x-]*su-u*K(?) PN2 *pu-ut ṭe$_4$-ni-šú a-na* UGU PN1 *na-ši*.

TuM 2/3 169 16 VI Dar 17, (Nanāḫu-file) *qēme* (and) barley due from Aḫušunu s Nabû-mušētiq-udda Nanāḫu received by EN.DUMU-*ka* s ? Iddin-Papsukkal from Nabû-aḫḫē-iddin s Kalbā Nanāḫu. ŠE.BAR *ma-la* ḪA.LA *ša* Aḫušunu *a-ki* ^{GIŠ}BAN.MEŠ *ša* Barsip^{KI}.MEŠ EN.DUMU-*ka a-na* Nabû-aḫḫē-iddina *i-nam-din*.

NBC 8371 26 VII Dar 29, see under *urāšu*.

Nippur

BE 8/1 92 26 XI Camb 5, at Nippur. (Labaši s Zēr-ukīn group) x *š* of silver and 0.1.4 of flour *il-ki* Lābāši s Zēr-ukīn(sic) has received from PN.

Nippur/Murašû (cf. CAD Q p. 208-9), some selected quotations only

BE 9 13 24 IX Art 28, *qe-me ša* LUGAL *ba-a-ri šu-ga-ar-ru ša* ZU$_2$.L[UM.MA].[140]

Ist 52 25 XIIb Art I 29, 6 MA.NA KB *il-ki gam-ru-tu* ^{LU_2}ERIN$_2$.LUGAL *qé-me ba-a-ri* [*ù mim-ma na-da-nu-tu$_4$*] *šá* E$_2$.LUGAL.

PBS 2/1 203 24 VII Dar II 4, 1 MA.NA KB ^{LU_2}ERIN$_2$.LUGAL *qé-me ba-ra u mim-ma na-da-nu-tu šá* E$_2$.LUGAL *gab-bi*, from I to XII yr 4.

PBS 2/1 217 10 VIII Dar II 6, 2 MA.NA KB 1-*en* ^{DUG}*dan-nu* KAŠ.SAG 0.2.3 *qé-me u* ŠE.BAR 1 UDU.NITA$_2$ il-ki TIL.MEŠ ^{LU_2}ERIN$_2$.MEŠ *qé-me ša* LUGAL *ba-ra ù mim-ma na-da-na-a-tú ša* E$_2$.LUGAL for I-XII yr 6.

Kiš?

OECT 10 241 date lost, (Kiš? unassigned) (Statement concerning half share of king?: PN will?) with(?) PN1 and PN2 ss PN3, with PN4 and PN5 <ḪA>.LA(?) LUGAL *ú-ša-az-zi-iz* (sic?) and if PNx does not deliver (*ú-šu-z i-iz*) that 1 kor of flour with PN4: punishment of the king. Damaged.

o) *bāru*[141]

This term occurs regularly in the Murašû archive in formulaic lists which enumerate the obligations of holders of bow fiefs. It therefore belongs to the *ilku*-complex. In PBS 2/1, 62 it seems to be the only obligation required from a certain piece of land, while bow fiefs in general are stated there to be excluded from the lease. The two texts from Ur, on the other hand, seem to refer to a payment related to *bāru* at the *irbi šarri ša* IG.GUR^{KI}, "transport" related to the "entry of the king in Susa".[142] The importance of the texts lies in the fact that here the *širku*'s, temple oblates, who do not normally belong to a land for service system, are obliged to contribute.

This is also a clear case in which the fact that taxing people involves costs is specifically mentioned. In UET 4, 49 wages and provender for those who collect what is due, are listed. The extension of the obligation to include subjects of the temple could be an indication of a general tendency to extend obligations pertaining to one sphere of taxation to another.

We are dealing with a Persian word with the meaning "to carry", either in a specific or very general sense, cf. perhaps the *zebēlu ša upiyāti* discussed above. BE 10, 13, quoted under *qēmu*, mentions *bāru* between *qēmu* and *šugarru ša suluppe*, which according to CAD Š/III p.

---

140 CAD Š/III p. 198.

141 Literature: CAD B, 120R.

142 This is a rather colourless translation, but the passage refers at any rate to Susa. Whether in reality the coming of the king to Susa is intended, is something else.

198, are separate obligations.[143] CT 57, 23 (lines 7, 19 and 20) and CT 56, 222 could, though unspecific, suggest transport duties.

Ur

UET 4 48 4 x Art II 6, (Gallābu archive) damaged, receipt, 6) *i-di u ṣi-di-tu*$_4$ *gam-ri lìb-bu* ^{LU}2*al-la*[*k*.MEŠ] 7) *šá ba-a-ri šá* ^{LU}2*ši-rak*.MEŠ PN 8) *ina* ŠU^{II} PN2 9) *ma-ḫir e-ṭer pu-ut šá* PN 10) *il-lak-ku-ma ba-a-ri šá* K[U$_4$.LUGAL] *a-na* IG-[GUR^{KI}] 11) yr 6 12) *a-na muḫ-ḫi* PN *i-za-ab-bil* 13) FPN AMA-*šú* 14) *ki-i* PN *la it-tal-ku-ma ba-a-ri* 15) *šá* KU$_4$ LUGAL *a-na* IG.GUR^{KI}[144] *ina* yr 6 16) ... *ana muḫ-ḫi* PN2 *la iz-zi-bil* 20 *š* 17) KB *qa-lu-ú* PN *ù* FPN AMA-*šú a-na* PN2 *ina-an-din-nu-ú.*

UET 4 49 12 x Art II 6, (Gallābu) PN 2) *a-na za-bi-lu šá ba-a-ri šá* KU$_4$.LUGAL *a-na* IG.GUR^{KI} 3) *i-na* MU 6.KAM$_2$ ... KI ^{LU}2*al-lak* 4) *šá ba-a-ri šá* ^{LU}2*ši-rak*.MEŠ *il-lak-ma* 5) *ba-a-ri a-na muḫ-ḫi* PN2 6) *i-zab-bil i-di u ṣi-di-tu*$_4$ *gam-ri* 7) *lìb-bu* ^{LU}2*al-lak*.MEŠ *šá ba-a-ri šá* ^{LU}2*ši-rak*.MEŠ PN 9) *ina* ŠU^{II} PN2 *ma-ḫir e-ṭer*, continues like UET 4, 48.

Murašû

PBS 2/1 62 8 IV Dar II 3, lease of land in ? and Ḫuṣṣētu-ša-Babu-ereš *ina* IGI PN s PN2(?), *ḫu-ú-pu* of Bīt-Murānu (on Ḫarri-Piqudu), ŠE.NUMUN *ba-ri šarri*, *bīt ritti-ka u* E$_2$ [*maš-k*]*a-na-ti-ka šá ina lìb-bi e-lat* É.^{GIŠ}BAN.MEŠ-*ka* plus stock and seed, fragmentary. Meaning?

3. The burden on the holders of the fiefs

Two aspects require attention, that of the length of the service and that of the costs in silver and other commodities. The question of the length of the service has been broached in the discussion of the various terms which have passed the review. We have not been able to determine whether actual periods of service were subject to time limits, but concluded that the lack of a time limit in an agrarian society is virtually impossible, unless there were specific manpower arrangements in order to compensate for it. In the Old Babylonian case of Ubārum these seem to have existed originally, but they were replaced by a division of obligations and rights, which indicates that such arrangements in practice led to nothing but litigation. This was at the level of a fief exploited by a simple soldier and his replacement. As we have seen, newly published Old Babylonian texts suggest, however, that land for service arrangements involved, on principle, extended families. Occasionally such arrangements are also found in our period. For the Neo-Babylonian period we have hardly any useful evidence, though many payments explicitly state that they cover (more than) a full year- or occasionally a shorter period. In the previous chapter some evidence was collected for the supposition that at least sometimes labour went with the land shared out, especially in the case of the more important fiefs, though it also may have been the case with those held by people like scribes and merchants. This does not solve the question of the length of the periods of service.

There can be little doubt that the obligatory work for the king in Elam constituted a considerable, if unquantifiable burden. It is not realistic to assume that all Babylonians subject to *ilku* had to work every year for three months in Susiana. People were specially engaged for this task, there was possibly a special annual levy in silver for this special purpose. Michigan 26 could imply working there for the whole year by specially engaged personnel. That opens the possibility that there were special middlemen, to whom our Babylon Egibis may have belonged. They will have taken their cut. Taxation opens possibilities for entrepreneurs, as always. Construction of defensive and water works in Babylonia itself may have created similar opportunities, as such constructions will sometimes have required special skills. Special payments for specific purposes do occur and corvée labour was used widely.

143 The "basket of dates" seems to have been a choice present, it occurs as a -compulsory?- gift from a prebendary to a superior in BM 42424, Jursa 1999, p. 180f.

144 On the reading of IG-GUR as ŠUŠIN, Susa, cf. F. Joannès, NABU 1988/1.

Here we are especially concerned with the costs in silver. In this respect the matter of equipment has been discussed under *rikis qabli*. The sums mentioned in e.g. Camb 276, one mina of silver as (only) a brother's share for two years, both passed, suggests that this could constitute a real burden. When a fief had just one holder this type of cost will normally have remained hidden: the holder had to provide the equipment for himself and it would not appear in the books. This was not introduced by the Persians, it already existed in Chaldean times. No amount can be mentioned confidently, but it is evident that especially if there was no adult male available for the job, this was expensive and contributed to indebtedness, probably especially if the holder of the fief had disappeared and a new set of equipment had to be provided.

The other important question concerning taxation is that of the *ilku*-related payments. Are we dealing with fixed amounts or was the height of the payments related to circumstances? Perhaps we must not expect fixed sums, these would only come into being when a particular system of service against land approached its final stage. It could perhaps be proposed that in the later Achaemenid period the administration was still generally in a position in which it could relate the sum asked to overall requirements. Customary rights, as for instance mentioned by the texts from Borsippa and Dilbat would in that case mean no more than that the person in question would have to contribute no more than other inhabitants of these localities in the same position. Yet there are several occasions in which a receipt states that the payment is for a whole year or for a very specific period and for the complete *ilku* or other type of payment. I am afraid that this means little more than "the specific *ilku* or task for which the receipt is given by a specific collector".

VS 4, 25 could indicate that the fixed amount payable for a certain type of bow-fief was ("already") one mina (per annum?), and the Murašû archive occasionally mentions payments in silver for "the entire *ilku*", which was thus stated to amount to a fixed sum, again one mina in BE 10, 102. We must regard this as not generally valid, but as dependent on the occasion and not really indicating a fixed amount that could be required in a year.[145] Caution is certainly due.

The in more than one respect important text edited by F. Joannès, TÉBR no. 1, mentions a standard sum of $1^5/_6$ mina for each of a distinct group of fiefs, with variable amounts for others, and nothing for still another group. Only 7.5 š is mentioned for the *kutallus*, and that same amount or less is taken from the holders of fractions.[146] The term *kutallūtu* is connected by Dar 430 with a bow-fief, it will be, on first sight, (an obligation to pay for) a fixed replacement, but such replacements could, as suggested above, obtain a (minor) fief of their own. The text could suggest that the payment amounted to half a mina payable over the complete fief. On the other hand Bertin 2619 registers a payment of only 40 *š* for a full year. Even more uncertainty is added by VS 4, 125: if one third of a bow requires 20 s for four months, a complete bow would thus require 3 mina for a year. These amounts differ considerably from the assumed norm of one mina, which therefore can not be regarded as a standard amount proper.

Though of minimal size, the one fifth of a bow (*ud-du*/(^{LU}2)*'u-ú-du*) for which Ribat s Bēl-erība paid *ilku* in the years 1 to 4 of Darius II is of some interest. In PBS 2/1 24 we find a *nidintu maḫrītu u arkītu*, which is said to represent the complete *ilku*, of 90 *š* on 4 XIIb Dar II 1. In PBS 2/1, 46 (26 IV Dar II 2) it amounts to 10 *š* for the earlier *nidintu* of the year, the same occurs for the later *nidintu*, said to represent the complete *ilku* of year 3 in BE 10, 78 (1 XII Dar 3), but in PBS 2/1, 92 it is 24 *š* for the complete year Dar II 4. We seem to be dealing with

---

[145] However dubious the procedure may be, we can perhaps tentatively continue to use the "one mana per annum" formula as a kind of standard payment expected from holders of bow fiefs.

[146] Joannès has suggested several possible explanations for the differences in treatment, the problem being that we do not know the exact backgrounds of the text. An additional complication is that the amount mentioned at the end of the text cannot be related properly to what is listed or left open.

annual payments in two instalments of amounts which vary from year to year. These texts indicate better than others that payments fluctuated from year to year.

On top of that we cannot be always certain whether the amounts mentioned in the texts quoted represent a payment in lieu of service or a fixed payment in silver due in any case, whatever practical service might have been required additionally, as seems to be certain in a number of cases. In VS 4, 125 we obviously have a payment for someone serving. Some of the texts, like Mich 26, quoted under *urāšu*, suggest that payments for labour in Elam were recurrent annual levies, but that does not imply that no other *-ad hoc- urāšu* or *dullu* payments could be asked. Under such circumstances a fief was no more than an element in a system over which any requirement could be shared out when the need was felt.

We will not re-discuss the regular additional contributions in flour or animals asked.

Šaṭir

TÉBR 1 no date, list of GIŠ.BAN plus PN, but for the first group of ten, preceded by amounts of silver; the second group pays 1 mina 50 *š* (2) 1,5 mina (2) or 1 mina (1); in a third group 1 mina (1), 1 mina 10 *š* (1) and 50 *š* (5) occur; after a gap follow amounts of 7,5 š for persons *ina kutalla*, after that follow *ra-bi-ia šá* ^{LU}2*ḫa-dar* with smaller payments. General total *ki-i* 15 ^{GIŠ}BAN *a-na* ^{GIŠ}BAN 1 5/6 MA.NA KB *u re-eḫ-tum* ^{GIŠ}BAN.MEŠ *lìb-bu-ú* [Ša-]ṭir(?) *šá* x x x(x), follows a total amount of 33 mana 13 *š* of silver, which is not reached by adding up the sums mentioned.

4. Conclusion

Land for service was a very common phenomenon in a world where payment in money, or rather, in some commodity that was generally accepted, silver, was not the absolute rule. There is a certain irony in the fact that this obligation to serve could, universally, be bought off by a payment, generally in silver, which required conversion of the commodities produced on the land by the holder of the fief into the accepted means of payment. This involved outsiders and it became inevitably one of the ways in which indebtedness arose. Already in the Neo-Babylonian period payment of a certain amount of silver, possibly at least partially depending on the needs felt by authorities as they presented themselves, seems to have been a general obligation imposed on holders of fief land and, rarely attested, houses. That again would automatically involve those who dealt in the commodities produced on the land. By Murašû times, but probably already in the period of the later Egibis, if not earlier, the holders of the fiefs, and perhaps even (other) tenants, will have had to produce for the market in order to obtain the necessary silver. The notable widening of the range of products found in the Murašû archive is possibly one of the signs betraying an increasing market orientation, even though the archive contains no information whatsoever on the actual marketing. Such evidence is, however, in a latent fashion already present in the background of the Egibi complex, but there the link with the holders of fief land is less easy to make.

If we do not like the inference of a market, another strategy could be suggested. The Murašûs and before them the Egibis had to cope with huge amounts of staple commodities, and, especially the Murašûs, also with a smaller stock of special products. The Egibis in particular had their onions. They received receipts in silver for payment of feudal duties from the holders of fiefs and their superiors to whom they advanced silver. For this they were paid by the same fief holders in products, which they also obtained through other channels, such as rents. These products were delivered to the government and used for public works, for which the Murašûs received credit in silver on a government account, which they, in view of the fact that no silver actually changed hands, used to grant credit to the fief holders, who made their land available and who, using the credit, paid the government in their turn. All these transactions would only nominally be in silver. This is not documented, but it is not wholly impossible. It would require considerable transports of commodities to, for instance, Susa, where these commodities had to be used on the public works.

Nevertheless this is a not a convincing scenario, even though it should be taken for granted that the institutions constituted an important market for a whole range of goods, already in the Third Millennium. This is especially valid for food stuffs in processed form. Brewing, as we saw, is probably the first of the purveying prebends. In the First Millennium not only many prebendaries, but also people like the Egibis and the Murašûs are involved in the processing of food stuffs, especially the brewing of beer.

The fact remains that those who were hired in Babylonia to do the job in Elam were certainly paid in silver and not primarily in the agricultural products, which they took along. We have little idea about the amount of silver in actual circulation, and this remains a crucial question, though silver played undoubtedly an essential role and it undoubtedly had to be earned.

There are two other subjects which require investigation: what is the evidence for taxation on the trade in commodities and what are the other conditions of land holding, which are possibly related to land for service systems? The first question will occupy us in the next chapter, the second will be part of a discussion of the question of the wider tax basis in (Neo-Babylonian) Mesopotamia in Chapter VII.

It is the cumulative character of the various tax burdens on the holders of land for service which makes the real burden and therefore the workings of taxation in this period difficult to assess. Even if we accept that we are dealing with an expanding economy, the several forms of taxation were probably only sustainable through the relatively spoken high yield of agriculture. The land for service system had evolved into a system of taxation in which all sorts of obligations had to be fulfilled by payments in silver. The system could only exist because in the end there was a market for agricultural commodities. Ultimately part of that market had to be found outside Babylonia in order to continue to earn the essential silver, which, if Herodotus was correct, was drained away and hoarded by the royal administration.

CHAPTER V
TAXATION RELATED TO THE TRANSPORT OF COMMODITIES: THE *kāru* CLUSTER

1. Introduction[1]

There existed an organisation in charge of the collection of taxation. It was indicated by the term *kāru* (*ša šarri*), of which the local office was called *bīt kāri* with a local representative, the *rab kāri*, occasionally with underlings in even smaller places and with guards in rural centres and on the various canals (VS 3, 159), but the evidence in our possession is unrepresentative.[2] Those who staffed the organisation locally will not have belonged to the upper layers of society.

Though the *bīt kāri* as a border or inland customs office is in a sense better attested in Assyria[3] than in Babylonia, there can be little doubt that its presence was a normal phenomenon in the Babylonian towns and villages. There are some indications that this tax office system also coped with other, "land for service", forms of taxation, and it was also as *kāri ša šarri* the office at which the rent for land leased from the king might be paid.[4] VS 3, 159 suggests that payments were carefully checked and had to be registered in order to be valid. Significantly the text dates to the reign of Darius. Leasing the rights connected to a local office will have been relatively easy, but concrete evidence is not available. The use of private personnel is in itself no proof, as all ancient Mesopotamian officials will have used their private servants for official duties in this manner. That rights were maintained occasionally by those in charge of an office in a highhanded manner, seems to be clear from a letter like YOS 3, 74, where we hear that textiles and weapons were taken.

For practical purposes we are only informed on the taxation of agricultural products in the Neo-Babylonian texts. The local officials will have had the power to take a share in the commodities transported, but they probably will have been obliged to pay their superiors, the royal administration, in silver. So, as the texts indicate, they were paid in silver and they sold the products they received, and possibly also produced themselves, to the same shippers they charged for the amount of taxation due from their loads. We can expect a system of price reductions along Old Babylonian lines benefiting those who

---

[1] In general: Dandamayev 2000.

[2] In the Iddina-Marduk texts we find a small group of associated localities in the countryside, not too far from Borsippa, we can assume, probably near the Borsippa-canal. The *rab kāri*, as far as can be established successively, Gimillu, Šum-ukīn, Nabû-aḫa-rēmanni and Nabû-rēmu-šukun, probably had his seat in Til-Gula. We find a *bêl piqitti* (*ša kāri*), a certain Itti-makû-Bēl in Bît-Ṭab-Bēl in the years Nbn 7 and 8. This will have been a very subaltern post as the earlier *rab kāri* Gimillu employed a slave there (W, IM 54), whereas another slave, of another person, possibly another *rab kāri*, appears there in Nbn 106. Gimillu also operated as a *rab kāri* in Āl-ša-Ṣilli-Ea in Nbn 30. We may probably envisage a system in which smaller rural localities were grouped together under a *rab kāri* who used his personal servants to control the neighbourhood. This underlines once again the importance of the role of slaves in the managing of firms and offices.

[3] ADD 952 rev. 5, with 50 ^{LU}2GAL.KAR, "50 heads of customs and excise offices", this must have been a very common, low ranking, official.

[4] BE 8, 85, quoted Chapter III under water rights.

disposed of the commodities, but this remains a conjecture. The supposition must be, again, that the commodities involved found a market.

2. Terminology: *kāru* and related

We have three main terms: *kāru*,[5] *miksu*, *mūṣû* and a number of other words, applied more informally, such as *nēbiru*, which were used in the ostensibly similar context of shipments of agricultural commodities. There is, however, no reason to assume that only agricultural products were subject to this type of levy, but there is no relevant information of substance for other than these products being treated in this manner. That onions ostensibly play such an important role in the documentation, results from the fact that the relevant texts mostly come from the Nūr-Sin component of the Egibi archive. The recently published text CTMMA 3, 74, from the same context, mentions fish. Iddina-Marduk and his associates dealt prominently in onions and for the moment the texts from his files are the best information on agricultural products being shipped from the countryside to the towns in the Neo-Babylonian period.[6] Neo-Babylonian trade in general is badly documented, especially in relation to marketing, where we might expect further taxation.

The central term for this type of taxation is probably *kāru (ša šarri)*, *miksu* referring primarily to the cut taken and the infrequent *mūṣû* and the virtually unattested *nēbiru* primarily to the occasion of the levy. This is, however, no more than a theory, mainly based on the frequency of the words in the material available. That we are dealing with one and the same complex is also suggested by (earlier) standard phrases like *ina miksi kāri nēbiri zakû*, "he is free from 'deductions', 'harbour duties' and 'ferry duties'".[7] The impression can only be that agricultural products were preferably taxed (additionally?) when they were being transported, though there is at least one link with *gugallūtu* and that could suggest that *kāru* was a tax levied, or levied also, where production took place. Some link with *gimru* can be expected here. This was discussed under "costs" in Chapter II, and it had an unmistakable taxation aspect. Excepting the *ešrû* due to gods, there is no useful information on additional taxation of agricultural products on the field or at harvest. That would have been relatively easy in view of the next to universal *imittu* procedures, which would already have entailed involvement of officials, if yield related "costs" were indeed levied in the manner the material collected in Chapter II suggests. The possibility that there existed a tax called *kāru* on agricultural products for local consumption must be left open, compare the remarks below on TCL 12, 85.

We will regard *kāru* as the general term for this complex of taxation of commodities, but there is a possibility that it was slowly being replaced by *miksu* in the Achaemenid period. We have already seen that slaves were registered in the later part of our period in the *bīt miksi*. By that time *miksu* may have been due on importing or acquiring a slave, but whether registration also had to take place regarding home produced slaves is unknown.

mūṣû[8] was paid, as etymology suggests, when the products left an area. A right called *kāru* was possibly levied on transit, on a canal or when loading a boat, but there is no reason to assume that this payment was limited to transport by water. *kāru* (*ša šarri*) was paid especially for (ships with) onions in the Egibi related Iddina-Marduk group of texts, a ship occasionally being mentioned explicitly in combination with a specific month: this type of transport was organised on a regular basis by the dealers in agricultural produce. Duties

---

[5] Literature: CAD K p. 236R.

[6] For the complete corpus of texts see Wunsch 1993, it can be supplemented marginally with some later material from the Babylon Egibi archive proper.

[7] ADD 646 rev. 3 and related texts, but from Assyria.

[8] CAD M/2 p. 249, b) "exit dues".

for such ships could possibly be prepaid, we must assume that a kind of laissez-passer valid for the occasion was issued in those cases, as Camb 272 seems to suggest. The letter YOS 3, 71 refers to a covering letter sufficient for getting a vessel past the toll bar. Promissory notes given for later payment seem to have been a general rule, though the delay in payment granted amounts often to no more than a few days. Whether this type of arrangement for the payment of these taxes by one payment guaranteeing free transit, stood open to everyone, is another question, however. There must have been a way in which payments to central offices were reconciled with possible local leases of the collection of the taxes.

A ship of the *kāre šarri* occurring in PSBA 7, 148 and the active involvement in that text of a *rab ḫanšû*, "head of fifty" seem to be isolated phenomena in the texts available. As the contributions can be called *kāri ša šarri* some transport obligation may be involved, but this would be a form of taxation differing from that discussed here, it would belong to the obligations to provide labour and not constitute a form of taxation of goods transported. VS 6, 302 is too damaged to contribute.

We assume that *kāru, miksu*, etc., were related payments. TCL 12, 85, from Borsippa, has already been discussed sub *gugallūtu*. The text is, however, also important for *kāru*, as it confirms that *kāru*, with *gugallūtu,* could be a levy on goods produced, together amounting to a total of 10% of the rather artificial amount of 20 kor payable by the tenant this text refers to. The fact that these rights are mentioned together could mean that occasionally *kāru* is linked with *gugallūtu,* which, as we could notice in chapter II, is probably a levy of which the amount was fixed according to individual circumstances between owner and tenant. If *gugallūtu* was primarily an estate affair, the final payment of the *kāru* was possibly formally the duty of the owner, who would, however, try to shift the obligation on the tenants of the estate.[9] Or otherwise, the buyer of the commodities was in a position in which he could compel the producer to answer for transport to the town and its attending costs. If this is true, we may conclude that whether the ultimate buyer was an institution or not, the producer worked for the market. At any rate transport costs could include also those of passing the toll bar. This would be very much a question of the relative strength of the parties involved.

C. Wunsch has referred to a specific amount for *miksu*, $3^1/_3$ percent, for the Babylonian "a *sūtu* per kor", calculable from one specific text.[10] But as a rule we must not expect precise formulations in these texts, especially not if *kāru* is the general term for a complex of payments. If passing every toll bar took $3^1/_3$ %, costs would increase rapidly.

Notable is also that in the Borsippa texts A 173 and TuM 2/3, 169 the same person, Bēl-maruka[11] received both the silver of the *kāru ša šarri* and the land for service imposition of flour due from the bow fiefs. The various types of taxation were locally collected by the same persons.

a. *kāru* "harbour(-duty)"[12]

Babylon, Egibi related (mostly Iddina-Marduk Nūr-Sin)

Nbk 357 2 x Nbk 39, at Bīt-Ṭāb-Bēl, 6.5 *š* of silver *ka-a-ri šá šūm*[*i*] (on garlic) 2) *šá* Gimillu s Šamaš-zēr-ibni 3) Sin-šadûnu ^LU^2GAL *ka-a-ri* 4) [*ša šarri*] will be paid by Širikti s Nūrea Dannea in III. (W, IM 34)

---

[9] The possibility that the *nisḫu ša māti* (see below, Chapter VI) is a similar form of taxation on the exploitation of land should be considered. Could this represent the direct tax on the produce of the land, which, though unidentified, may be suspected to have existed?

[10] Wunsch 2000a p. 106 note 29, mentioning BM 31347.

[11] Both instances give EN.DUMU-*ka*, which looks unfamiliar and is thus suspicious.

[12] Cf. CAD K p. 236 dues, p. 238R sub 2 b) and p. 239 under *rabi kāri*.

CTMMA 3 74 15 I Nbk 40, at Bīt-Ṭāb-Bēl, 7 *š* of silver *ka-a-ri šá* KU_6.ḪA_2 *šá* Gimillu s Šamaš-zēr-ibni Sin-šadûnu LU₂GAL *ka-a-ri šá* LUGAL will be paid by Nabû-šum-iddina s Bēl-uballiṭ Sagdidi and IM at the end of I.

Nbk 358 10 III Nbk 40, at Til-Gula, 9 *š* KB *ša ka-a-ri ša šarri šá* Gimillu s Šamaš-zēr-ibni LU₂GAL *ka-a-ri ša šarri* due from Bēl-aḫḫê-erība s Nabû-nāṣir Paḫāru and Marduk-nāṣir s Bēl-aḫḫê-iddina Rē'u-sisê on 20 III. (W, IM 35)

Liv 21 15 VI Nbk 41, at ?, 6000 *gidlu* of onions due to Gimillu s Šamaš-zēr-ibni Sin-šadûnu *rab kāri ša šarri* from Lūṣi-ana-nūri s Marduk-zēr-ibni Nappāḫu and Nabû-aḫḫe-iddina s Kabtia Adad-šum-[x] in Babylon. (W. IM 38)

Nbk 384 16 VIII Nbk 41, at Bît-Ṭāb-Bēl, 23 *š* of silver, *ka-a-ri* of the onion ship due to Ḫašdā and Lūṣî-ana-nūri from IM in IX. (W, IM 41)

Nbk 389 5 x Nbk 41, at Til-Gula, 28 *š* of silver of Gimillu s Šamaš-zēr-ibni Sin-šadûnu *rab kāri ša šarri* due from Nabû-mušallim s Inia in XII. Mentions partial payment. (W, IM 43)

Nbk 397 25 III Nbk 42, at Bît-Ṭāb-Bēl, 5500 bundles of onions, *kāri ša šarri*, of Gimillu s Šamaš-zēr-ibni Sin-šadûnu *rab kāri ša šarri* due from Nabû-mušētiq-udda s Tabniea in IV in Babylon. (W, IM 45)

Nbk 400 19 V Nbk 42, at Til-Gula, 1500+ bundles of onions *kāri ša šarri* of Gimillu s Šamaš-zēr-ibni Sin-šadūnu *rab kāri ša šarri* due from Nergal-mušallim s Zērūtu Dābibī, damaged. (W, IM 46)

Speleers 277 26 XII AM 0, at Til-Gula, 50 *š* of silver *šá kāri šá šarri* of Gimillu s Šamaš-zēr-ibni Sin-šadūnu *rab kāri ša šarri*, due from Nabû-mušallim s Inia on 20 I, with onions of the ship of Bunene-ibni. (W, IM 52)

AM 8 28 XII AM 0, at Til-Gula, 17 *š kāri šá šarri* of Gimillu s Šamaš-zēr-ibni Sin-šadūnu *rab kāri šá šarri* due from Kurbanni-Marduk s Bēl-zēri Adad-šum-uṣur on 5 I. (W, IM 53)

W, IM 54 6 x AM 1, at Al-Ṭāb-Bēl 80 kor of barley, 25000 bundles of onions, 30 *š* of silver of Nabû-mušallim s Inia and Mandanu-šum-iddina s Zēria Nabaia due from Lâbašî, slave of Gimillu the *rab kāri* in IV.

TCL 12 63 28 III Ner 1, at Bît-Ṭa[b-Bēl]. 23 *š* of silver *kāru* of the king of Gimillu s [Šamaš-zēr-ibni] Sin-šadûnu due from Šûzubu s Nabû-ēṭer Aḫu-bani on 30 III. Oath sworn by Šûzubu.

Nbn 30 19 III Nbn 1, at Til-Gula, 32 *š* of silver of[13] Gimillu s Šamaš-zēr-ibni Sin-šadûnu *rab kāri* of the king of Al-Ṣilli-Ea is due from Mandanu-šum-iddina s Zēria and Nabû-mušallim s Inia end III. (W, IM 95)

W, IM 381 date lost, silver *ša kāri ša šarri* of Gimillu s Šamaš-zēr-ibni Sin-šadûnu *rab kāri ša šarri* due from Bēl-aḫḫê-iddina s x in II.

W, IM 377 date lost, ? of Mandanu-šum-iddina s Zēria and Nabû-mušallim s Inia due to (?) Šum-ukîn s Aplā Itinnu *rab kāri* of Til-Gula. Mentions Iddina-Marduk?

Nbn 106 18 III Nbn 3, at Til-Gula, 1 mina 2 *š* of silver of IM due from Nabû-aḫâ-rēmanni *rab kāri* of Til-Gula slave of Bēl-x on 10 IV. (W, IM 113)

W, IM 219 13 x [Nbn 5] at Saḫrīnu, mentions 1000 *gidlu* of dates 9) *šá* Nabû-rēma-šukun in connection with *ḫarrānu,* involves Nergal-rēṣua, slave of IM, Ea-nāṣir and Rēmut-Bēl.

Nbn 268 27 VIII Nbn 7, 254 kor of dates of IM due from Itti-makû-ili *bēl piqitti ša kāri* of Bît-Ṭāb-Bēl in IX(!). (W, IM 146)

CTMMA 3 55 2 XI Nbn 11, 30 *š* of silver of Nabû-rēmu-šukun *rab kāri ša šarri* due from NAI the judge in XII, remainder of $2^1/_2$ mina *ina ḫu-šá-e ša sarri*(?). Here?

Cyr 12 7 I Cyr 1, [x+?]3000 bundles of onions of Nergal-rēṣua, slave of IM due from Nabû-šum-ukîn s Nabû-bēlšunu Lakuppuru in II. The *kāru* is the responsibility of Nabû-šum-ukîn, expressed by the phrase (lines 7-8) *ka-a-ri* N. *ú-še-ti-iq-šú*. (W, IM 263).

---

[13] C. Wunsch: *šá* + Rasur.

Peek 19 x VII Dar 26, Iqūpu s Bēl-iddina Egibi and Nādinu s Bēl-iddina Rē'u-sisê[14] are guarantors for one another *a-di muḫ-ḫi* 5) *ka-ra-am šá* Nār-Sin Aplā 6) s Šum-uṣur ^{LU_2}<MA$_2$.>LAḪ$_4$ *šá* LUGAL *šá* x(-x) 7) Rēmanni-ili ^{LU_2}*ka-a*[*-ri*] 8) *šá* LUGAL *ina* ŠU^{II} Š s I 10) *ma-ḫi-ir*.

Unassigned archive, possibly Nappāḫu?

CTMMA 3 123 x I Dar [32?], damaged 1) *ka-a-ri šá* (Al)Ka[-a-ri-^{d}Taš-me-tu$_4$?], mentions 15 XII Dar 31.

Borsippa (file on Aḫušunu s Mušētiq-udda alias Bazuzu Nanāḫu)

Ashm A 173 (IV Dar 18), receipt of silver *šá ka-a-ri šá šarri* until end IV yr 18 given by EN.DUMU-ka to Aḫušunu (N) after payment by Nabû-aḫḫē-iddina s Kalbā Nanāḫu.

TCL 12 85 20 VI Nbn 5, at GARIM-Surmarrati, Ili-bani-file, 13 kor of dates *imittu*, 5 kor for *sissinnu*; 1.2.0 in *kāru* and 0.3.0 for *gugallūtu* are paid additionally. (Total amounts to exactly 20 kor.[15])

NBC 8364 20 III Nbn 7, (Ea-ilûta-bâni-file) partnership(11) *i-di ka-a-ri ina ka-re-e-š*[*u-nu*]; (Probably not relevant, but referring to a store room?).

b. *miksu*[16]

miksu, "cut", "levy", does not occur often in published Neo-Babylonian texts, but it is related to *kāru*. Basically it is also an unspecific term, used in the specific taxation context of "levy". *kāru* and *miksu* may actually have referred to the same payment, as both were paid to the *rab kāri*. But in the Borsippa text VS 4, 194 we find a special *rab miksi*, though we must note that this is in connection with a payment in Susa. Whether these various payments were cumulative or not, remains a question, if they were, this would have taxed the trade in foodstuffs between the various towns and the countryside in a rapidly increasing manner.

If not the same thing, *miksu* was levied (as *kāru* was) by or on behalf of the *rab kāri* in Wunsch IM 251, and in the *bīt kāre* in VS 3, 159, there on behalf of what is called the *bīt šarri*. Dar 268 shows that *miksu*[17] was a term indicating the same type of levy on products passing through a canal and possibly also on material being unloaded, as *kāru* did. It was not necessarily a certain amount taken from the material taxed, but it could (also) be paid in silver: W IM 339. That the amount of the *miksu* was fixed by royal decree is made explicit in VS 3, 159.

The preponderance of texts dealing with onions is, again, misleading, Dar 268 concerns barley.

Babylon Egibi and related

W, IM 251 20+III Nbn 17, *mi-ik-su* for the onion ship of month III yr 17 of *kar-ri šá* (Al-)Til-Gula is received by Rēmūt s Nabû-iddina Isināia [^{LU_2}*b*]*ēl pi-qit šá* Nabû-rēmū-šukun *rab kāri ša šarri* from ?

W, IM 339 Camb 4, at Tillu-Gula, Rēmūt has received from Nabû-aialu, slave of IM, the *ka-sap mi-ik-su*(*-šú*) due from Aḫû-ilia s Kiribtu for the onion ship of Marduk-bēl-uṣur slave of IM, which he caused to pass (*ú-še-ti-iq*)[18] the barrier; Marduk-bēl-uṣur has received nothing from what was due from Aḫû-ilia.

---

[14] Both qualified as GAL ^{LU_2}KAŠ.

[15] But, as remarked already, note that Joannès 1998 p. 308 reads 4 and not 5 kor for the *sissinnu*.

[16] CAD M/2 p.65 and *rab miksi* p. 65-6.

[17] CAD M p. 65R, "customs duties".

[18] The texts use *šūtuqu*, in this case *ú-še-ti-iq*. We assume that Marduk-bēl-uṣur slave of IM, the boatman, is the subject and not Aḫu-ilia, who was probably the owner of the load in W, IM 339. The *miksu* is paid by another slave of IM to Rēmūt who probably belonged to the tax office. We assume that

Camb 272 19 I Camb 5, the(?) *miksu* for one onion ship in III has (already) been paid by IM to Bēl-rēmanni s Ṭabia Šangû-Ninurta. (W, IM 347)

Dar 268 18 IV Dar 10, *miksu* for 70 kor of barley paid by Š s I to Kulbibi s Bēl-kāṣir Eppeš-ili *rab kāri* of Sippar, received by Irani.[19]

Borsippa

VS 4 194 3 XII Xer 1, (at Šušan, belongs with Inṣabtu Naggāru group) 4 mina 5 *š*. KB PN *ina na-aš-pa-<ar->tu₄ šá* Bēl-iddina (the?) Miṣirāia LU₂GAL *mi-ik-su ina* ŠU^II PN2 *ma-ḫi-ir*.

VS 6 307 no date, list of various expenditure, Ilšu-abušu group, including payments from/to(?) *qēpu*: 6) x GIN₂ *a-na mi-ik-s*[*u*?].

Where?

VS 3 159 24 III Dar 35, at Damar, *mi-ik-su* on amounts of barley, wheat and cress of Nabû-ittannu PN2 and PN3 ("Persians") have allowed to pass through (*ú-še-ti-qu*) the *bīt ka-a-re* of the x-canal, *mi-ik-su a-na bīt šarri it-tan-nu, ...* they will register (the payment) before the judges for PN4, if not *mi-ik-su ana bīt šarri a-ki-i da-a-ti šarri i-nam-din* (sic).[20]

CT 22 44 letter

c. *mūṣû*

mūṣû, "exit(-duty)" is extremely rare in the Neo-Babylonian period.[21] In Nbn 280 it is clearly the person who delivered the barley in Babylon who paid the levy. I assume that *gimru* refers here to the transport costs in general and not specifically to the form of taxation discussed in Chapter II. It could be assumed that this duty might be identical with *kāru* and *miksu* but the term would specifically refer to rights levied in the place of production. *mūṣû* is linked to *kāru* in Nbn 280 by the person of the *bēl piqitti* of the *rab kāri* in Nbn 268. The *mūṣû* went therefore through the same hands as the *kāru* payments.

Nbn 280 1 I Nbn 8, 80 kor of barley is due from Itti-makû-ili, *bēl piqitti* of Bît-Ṭab-Bēl to Nergal-reṣua slave of IM in II. 5) ... *gi-mir* 6) to Babylon he will give, 7) *mu-ṣu-ú šá* Barsip^KI *iṭ-ṭir*. (W, IM 149)

d. *nēbiru*[22], *gišru*[23], *maṣiru*[24] and comparable terms

In the context of taxation *nēbi/eru* may have belonged to the same complex as *miksu* and *kāru* as is indicated by Esarhaddon's claim[25] to have freed certain elements of the population from this complex of levies, which, however, hardly can have meant that all ferries became free, even for the inhabitants of Aššur. *nēbiru* in texts can therefore indicate

---

the load was destined for IM or one of his dependants. But in Camb 272 we must assume that Bēl-rēmanni has received the *miksu* from Iddina-Marduk, that he will cause the ship to pass the tax barrier and hand over to IM. This will also refer primarily to the load. Bēl-rēmanni will probably pay the *miksu* on passing the toll bar. In Cyr 12, sub *kāru*, transport and duties payable are the responsibility of the supplier, this is also expressed by the use of *šūtuqu*.

19 Text edited by K. Abraham, NABU 1997 p. 50.

20 The text is a receipt of a well known type for Nabû-ittannu, who has paid PN2 and PN3. If the matter is not settled administratively PN2 and PN3 are made responsible and must pay. The singular of *i-nam-din* is therefore a mistake. Though the text is obviously difficult to read, the type of transaction is not uncommon.

21 CAD M/2 p. 250L knows only of Old Assyrian texts. Of dubious relevancy are the Sippar texts Nbn 893, 12 VII Nbn 15 and CT 55, 392, 15 X Nbn 10.

22 Cf. CAD N/2 p. 145 which accepts "crossing fees" for OB *nēbertu*.

23 CAD G p. 107-8.

24 CAD M/1 p. 332.

25 Borger, Esarhaddon, Ass A III 9, referring to the inhabitants of Aššur.

both a payment for the services of the ferryman and an "(official) right levied at crossing". Either of these could be intended in the only text quoted here. As a type of taxation the term is not really attested in the Neo-Babylonian period, as a phenomenon it comes close to the "payments for services" discussed earlier.

For *nēbiru*[26] as a possible tax in an early Neo-Babylonian context there is only one rather dubious and not very informative occurrence in a list mentioning various forms of expenditure: 0.0.3 *ša ne-bi-ri*.[27] The passage needs not refer to more than a payment to a ferryman. The word in itself occurs more generally as a geographical reference point in land sales. The pontoon bridge in Babylon in which the Egibis were involved, would have been an ideal point for levying these duties, both on traffic over land and by water. That such levies existed is clear from TCL 13, 196, discussed in the next section and by the occurrence of payments for *gišru* in notes dealing with expenditure.

But as soon as this type of material is drawn into the discussion more payments crop up, whether these were "official" or not. It is difficult to treat this material in a systematic fashion, and it cannot be separated from the payments discussed in Chapter II. We have seen there that the Edict of Belsazzar prescribed certain payments to "governors", scribes, measurers and gatekeepers. Marduk-zākir-šumi assigned a scribe of Eanna rights to incoming and outgoing goods. Keeping an account also entailed income for a scribe. Payments to officials executing their tasks were normal, they were an official element of their remuneration. Various types of payment in this sphere can be covered by *irbu ša bābi,* as found in Dar 533, mentioned in the next chapter in relation to *ešrû*. There are also *gišru* and *maṣīru* which occur together in UET 4, 133, YOS 6, 171 and TCL 13, 216.

In this last note, possibly from Uruk, we can identify, next to normal expenditure in dates, also a payment to a GAL.DIR.RA (0.0.3), an unidentified official, a post for *giš-ri*, "bridge", *ma-ṣi-ru*, an "unidentified right", and *šá* KA_2.GAL, "(payment) for the gate", each of 0.0.2, which suggests a certain standardisation. The context in which these costs were incurred is not obvious. UET 4, 133, from Ur, is a much more formal accounting document, but it is damaged. It deals in an uncertain context with recurring shipping costs, which involve the hire of two boatmen (rev. 8) and five towers, which indicates that the recurring undertaking concerned was of a modest size. It entailed payments of 0.0.4 to the ^{LU_2}GAL *gi-ši-ir šá* $BARA_2$.ŠAP^{KI}, the keeper of the bridge at Borsippa (obv. 6 and rev. 3) and, obv. 5, which is more completely formulated, 0.0.3 (rev. 2 has 0.0.4) *a-na* $^{GIŠ}BAN_2$.MEŠ *šá ma-ṣi-ir-nu,* which, literally, means "three *sūtu* measures (of barley?) for the *sūtu*-measures of the *maṣirnu*", suggesting that the term *maṣirnu* could imply a payment for the use of the (local) measuring vessels. YOS 6, 171:20 links, however, *gišru* and *maṣira*[*nu*] in one payment. In this case we can figure out the importance of that sum. The complete transport, from Uruk(?) to Sippar amounted to 226.1.2 kor of barley, of which 5 towers received 1.1.5, the boatmen 0.3.2 and *gišru* and *maṣiranu* amounted to 1 kor, which thus remains well under 0.5%. These were obviously relatively small additional costs.

This evidence from "notes" is yet of a certain interest because it gives some idea of the variety in which these types of payment could occur, but it is even more difficult than the other evidence to use as a basis for generalisations.

---

26 CAD N/2 p. 146.

27 AfO 2 p. 59, Itti-Marduk-balāṭu yr. 1, rev. 3.

e. Related: *isirtu* "collection of payments"[28]

The term occurs once in a tax- and lease-related Neo-Babylonian context: collection of rights on bridges and quays from traffic moving up or down stream.[29] This will probably refer to the collection of duties of the type discussed in this chapter, but the term may imply more than just the taxation rights mentioned. For the text refers to costs involved for those who manned the bridge. *našpartu*, in line 20, means in this context "anything that has to be done -and involves expenditure", which might have to be deducted from the takings, but only after those concerned had been asked. The explicit mentioning of bridge and quays indicates that traffic both on land and on the river was involved, but the fact that only three mina of silver per annum was required, suggests either that this pontoon bridge in Babylon was not a really important link in the transport system, or -perhaps- that transit payments were generally settled elsewhere.[30] Another possibility is that we must take *isirtu* literally as meaning only the right to collect, excluding the yield of what was collected, in which case the sum represents only the yield for the lease holder of the task to collect the rights due at the bridge. Perhaps that is the best interpretation, for these people also will have had to live and for that purpose there would be a surcharge on the leased governmental rights: that constituted another right which could be leased. The right to levy a form of taxation results in a right to make costs, and this can be exploited in turn.

Babylon, Egibi

TCL 13 196 1 VII Dar 26, 1) *i-si-ir-tu*$_4$ *šá ina muḫ-ḫi gi-iš-ri ù ka-a-ri* 2) *e-re-du ù e-lu* E$_2$ *qip-tu*$_4$ *šá* PN 3) ^{LU_2}*šākin ṭēmi* Bābili *šá i-na pa-an* Š s I 4) Š s I *a-na a-ḫi* ḪA.LA *šá i-na ir-bi* 5) *šá gi-iš-ri šá* PN *šākin ṭēmi šá it-ti* PN2, PN3 *u* PN4, PN5 8) ^{LU_2}EN.NUN.MEŠ *gi-iš-ri* Š s I 9) ... *u* PN2 10) ... *a-na su-ú-tu a-na* ITI 15 *š* KB ... 11) *a-na* PN6 ... 12) *ù* PN7 *id-di-nu-u'* ^{GIŠ}MA$_2$.MEŠ *šá ina muḫ-ḫi gi-iš-ri* 15) *i-ki-il-la-a'* PN6 *u* PN7 16) *is-si-ru-u'* KB *ir-bi šá gi-iš-ri* 17) *šá* ITI-*us-su šá* Š (s I) *u* PN2 18) ^{LU_2}EN.MEŠ ḪA.LA-*šú* PN7 *ù* PN7 19) *šá la* Š (s I) *ul i-na-an-di-nu-u'* 20) *na-aš-par-tu*$_4$ *ma-la a-na muḫ-hi giš-ri tal-la-ku* 21) PN6 *u* PN7 *a-na* Š (s I) 22) *u* ^{LU_2}EN.NUN.MEŠ *giš-ri ú-kal-la-mu-u'*. (Identical: Peek 18)

3. The context of these payments

That agricultural -and other- products were subject to taxation during transport to town, that is to market, is certain. A reason would be that waterways and roads required upkeep, but straightforward raising of revenue is just as likely, even inevitable as any government always becomes dependent on sources of income it creates initially for the upkeep of specific public utilities. In fact some of the costs discussed earlier, notably those paid to gate keepers on arrival, mentioned by the Edict of Belsazzar, imply transport. Such duties were levied from what was intended for the institutions themselves. That rights were levied on the use of canals or roads in general is therefore less of a problem, even if the transports were intended for an institution.

---

28 CAD I/J p. 197-8.

29 Cf. possibly UET 4, 133 6) 0.0.4 *a-na* ^{LU_2}GAL *gi-ši-ir šá* Barsip^{KI}, cf. rev. 2'. CAD G p. 108L. These are possibly regular, recurrent payments.

30 As I understand it, the contract is between Š s I alias Marduk-nāṣir-apli Egibi and PN8 and PN9. It involves his interest in the half share he has leased from (or has been "entrusted with", the situation depends on the interpretation given to E$_2$ *qip-tu*$_4$, by) the *šākin ṭēmi* together with four persons called "watchmen of the bridge". Whether the *it-ti* refers to the same half share or to the other half is not completely clear, but MNA and the first of the keepers lease whatever they hold of the right leased for 15 *š* per month to PN 6 and 7. The further phrasing indicates that MNA is the principal party, if not in the complete affair at least in the contract.

Our problem is more what the payers of the duties, people like Iddina-Marduk Nūr-Sin and the Egibis, but also the Murašûs about whose payments of these rights we are not informed, but who also collected huge amounts of agricultural products, did with the commodities they had transported to the main towns or caused their suppliers to transport. During the lifetime of Iddina-Marduk the shippers seem to have preferred the commodities, otherwise they would not have disembarrassed the tax officials of their takings in the form of products.[31] The institutions had their own system of supply. If the Ur III situation provides a valid parallel, much of the practical transport will have been left to the receivers of rations, who themselves had to transport what was assigned to them from the silos in the countryside to their homes. Almost certainly that type of arrangement was still the background of the Neo-Babylonian institutional letter orders and parallel to the injunctions to rent farmers and other keepers of supplies not to hand out staples without a specific authorisation from the administration. This type of private transport was probably taxed and the fact that it was taxed presumably was next to the other costs yet another incentive for the stronger parties in contracts to shift as much as possible of transport costs unto their weaker partners.

Two texts quoted under *kāru*, especially W, IM 54 and to a lesser degree Nbn 268 provide some information on the manner in which the commodities received by the tax collectors were disposed of. We must assume that on principle a fixed amount of the goods transported was taken *in natura*. In both texts mentioned Iddina-Marduk Nūr-Sin or his close associates were due to receive barley and onions[32] from persons associated with the tax office of the *kāru*. This can be best understood by the assumption that these commodities would be dealt with in the same manner as those Iddina-Marduk and company normally disposed off, after having them transported to the town, for which they paid tax. Nbn 280, quoted under *mūṣû* is a similar text. As a rule Iddina-Marduk and company themselves paid in silver and retained the commodities for disposal, presumably by selling the goods in Babylon. Here we inevitably introduce a market for these goods in the town. Whatever is the case, we must stress that people like Iddina-Marduk and his Egibi relations preferred keeping the products and paying taxes in silver on the canals to Babylon: they had a destination for the goods involved.

[31] The material from the Iddina-Marduk archive is extensively studied by C. Wunsch, 1993 I p. 35ff.

[32] But we must not forget: in one case also silver, which may betray other business links.

CHAPTER VI
OTHER TAXATION RELATED MATTERS

1. Introduction

This chapter deals with a number of terms which are related in various degrees to taxation. Several of those discussed must be regarded as dubious in the context. Others have been accepted in the past as typical for taxation terminology, but they must be eliminated, as they represent very general terms, which only occasionally cover expenditure or income relating to taxation. As said earlier, taxation terminology in general consists of words with a broad general sense used in a limited, technical context.

2. Terminology: certainly taxation related

a. *ešrû*[1]

This levy, "tithe", possibly not only on agricultural produce,[2] but best known there, has recently been treated in a monograph by M. Jursa, so there is no need for much additional discussion here. Only some selected texts from private archives will be listed. Unusual and therefore important, because it corroborates information regarding other forms of taxation, is Bertin 2809 (25 XI Dar x), where a house is subject to payment of *ešrû*, if the interpretation given is correct. The right to levy tithes is probably best seen, if Jursa's conclusions are correct, as an "encumbrance"[3] resting in a far from general manner on specific property. If Jursa's collection of material is representative, *ešrû* was levied especially from property that had been in the hands of the temples, but of which the tenure had been taken away in a legal manner, or of which the exploitation had been ceded to others, for instance to a tenant. He had to pay *ešrû* over his share in the harvest on top of what the temple received in rent as owner of the land.

If the interpretation as a kind of encumbrance is correct the difference between *ešrû* and, for instance, *mandattu* payable by certain (unfree) individuals becomes relative and *ešrû* cannot be seen anymore as a form of taxation. The idea that *ešrû* is not something universal is supported by the Murašû text BE 9, 45, which classifies some land as *bīt ešrû*, land subject to the payment of *ešrû*, that is thus land with a special, separate status. It is perhaps a tithe levied from a limited group of people, it is thus certainly no universally levied "Kirchensteur".[4] The tax base needs not be land, but it also can exist of other real estate.

---

[1] Literature: Jursa 1998, mentioning previous studies.

[2] In Old Babylonian Ur *ešrû* was after all paid by certain merchants, presumably on the gains they made in trading with Dilmun. Having the Lord, not the Church, as a kind of shareholder in one's business is not unattested in Western European history.

[3] Perhaps a "(special) right *in rem*" is the proper English term. "Encumbrance" is meant to indicate an obligation which is attached in perpetuity to the holding of a specific property. Such obligations can vary from payment of substantial sums to being no more than a mere token imposition.

[4] This agrees with Jursa p. 84. I am, as yet, somewhat more reluctant where he, p. 86, denies the value of tithes on private land. We know little about *gugallūtu*, but can assume that it was a next to universal payment. If *ešrû* was levied at a similar early stage, immediately after the harvest, transport being the obligation of the person/institution entitled, it will have been just as invisible for us.

I would regard Nbk 430 and Nbn 270 as consistent with the not universal nature of *ešrû* payments. The estate, first presumably held by Neriglissar and later that of the crown prince under Nabonidus, which probably were largely identical, was under the obligation to pay *ešrû* to certain gods for certain possessions, the office knew the exact details but required the liquid assets to be able to pay. Ultimately responsible for providing the (liquid) means was Nabû-apal-iddina Egibi, his accounts would probably be settled later on. That persons belonging to institutions, as is the case in Nbn 270, used silver belonging to the institution for the financing of their private affairs had a long history behind it in Mesopotamia, especially in the case of the temples. On principle, a levy on products or income would be expected, but there would have to be some geographical division between the various spiritual authorities entitled to these dues, with all sorts of additional arrangements. Jursa has made it abundantly clear that the tithe was not automatically 10% of the yield, net or otherwise. Especially the conditions of the lease influenced the amount of the *ešrû*, it would seem.

Whether the term *ešrû* was always used in the sense of a recurring payment due from known property can be doubted. We noted already that there is the possibility that gifts, which would be normally registered as *irbu*, "income" (in the widest sense of "all incoming goods") were occasionally called *ešrû*. Especially a text like Dar 533 should warn us. Presumably it belongs to the Egibi archive, it deals with the same area from where the *kāru* documents we collected came: Āl-Ṭāb-Bēl (obv. 9) and the neighbourhood of the Nār-Barsip (obv. 10) where Mandanu-bēl-uṣur, the factotum of Iddina-Marduk and after him of Marduk-nāṣir-apli Egibi had his stamping ground. Ostensibly the text deals according to the heading with *ešrû* of Nergal, but in reality we also find payments for *sūtu*, GIŠ.BAN$_2$, ordinary tenancy payments (lines 11 and 12), for *irbu ša bābi* (line 16) and on the reverse a whole range of *šibšu* payments, payments for the share in the harvest of the land owner, which possibly include *ešrû*. The exact nature of each payment was known and did not require specification, and effectively one person was being made responsible for the total amount payable.

Babylon, Egibi related

Nbk 430 17 V Nbk x, at Sippar. 4 mina of silver *ešrû* of Bēl, Nabû, Nergal and [Bēlet of Uruk] of Neriglissar(?) payable by Naid-Marduk s x Eppeš-ili and Kalbā s [PN] in XI. All possessions security. NAI guarantor. Cf. Nbn 270.

Nbn 270 9 XI Nbn 7, 45 *š* of silver *ešrû* of Bēl, Nabû, Nergal and Bēlet of Uruk due to Nabû-ṣābit-qāte *rab bīti* of Bēl-šar-uṣur from Nabû-mukīn-aḫi, *sepīru* and slave of Bēl-šar-uṣur, *mār šarri,* which had been paid for Nabû-ṣullê-šimê his slave, is paid by NAI in the presence of Dikītum, wife of Nabû-mukīn-aḫi.

Camb 54 21 V Camb 1, 12 kor of dates, *imittu* on land of Nergal-nāṣir s Nādin, which is the security of Nergal-rēṣūa, is due from Bēl-iddina s Nabû-balassu-iqbi Egibi in VIII. The *ešrû* of Nergal is paid.

W IM 357 no date, list of bundles of onions, *šibšu eqli* of named persons belonging to PN ^{LU_2}*aš-pa-ga-a* of Šaḫrinu, the *ešrû* of Nergal is not paid.

Dar 359 29 X Dar 13, 51 kor of dates of MNA at the disposal of Šamaš-ina-tēšê-ēṭer s Šamaš-iddina Šamaš-abāri for *ḫarranu*. The dates are *ešrû* of Bēl.

Bertin 2809 25 XI Dar ?, at Kār-Parakki, 50 mina $4^2/_3$ *š* of silver part of the promissory note of 64 mina 15 *š* price of a building plot in Šuanna which MNA transferred to Anu-mukīn-apli s Anu-aḫa-iddina Ea-ME.ŠE.GA, 8) E$_2$-*šú a-na* 10 *a-na* NIG$_2$.GA E$_2$.SAG.IL$_2$ *in-dag-lu*, "his house which is subject to the payment of *ešrû* to Esagil", is received by Anu-mukīn-apli from MNA. The silver is paid in the shape of 2 kor of date plantation, 4.3.2 of arable and 10 slaves, handed by MNA to Anu-mukīn-apli.

W, IM 371 29 x x x, fragment, promissory notes amounting to in total 82.1.0 of dates inclusive of (? *a-di*) *ešrû* of Nergal and Bēlet-šame, *imittu* on land held by Nergal-nāṣir s Nādin which Šum-ukīn s Ša-Nabû-šu, the *bēl biti* of Nergal-nāṣir, imposed, sum due to IM, ... Šum-ukīn will deliver? Mentions earlier debt of Šum-ukīn.

Dar 533 Dar 21, list of barley purportedly *ešrû makkūr* Nergal. Mentions localities (canals and places) plus *ina pān* PN, but deals not only with *ešrû*.

Non-Egibi Babylon

Sin-ili

VS 3 14 15 VI Nbk 36, at Marad, 100 kor of dates of Ṭabia s NAI Sin-ili, as much as constitutes the share of Nabû-šum-uṣur from Marad, is due from Nergal-šum-ibni slave of Nabû-šum-uṣur and Balāṭu s Erîba Nappāḫu. Ends: *ses-sin-na eš-ru-ú* ^{LU_2}GU$_2$.GAL.LA *e-ṭe-ru mim-ma ma-la ina muḫ-ḫi ip-pu-šu a-ḫa-ta šú-nu.*

VS 3 17 1 VI Nbk 37, at Kiš. x+13 kor dates, *imittu* on Ḫarru-ša-qêpi *a-di eš-ru-ú u gú-ú-gal* of Ṭabia s NAI Sin-ili is due from Babia s Apla x in VIII, *ešrû* and *gugallūtu* of yr 36 paid.

Nappāḫu?

VS 3 212 no date, 35 kor of dates, *ešrû* of Nabû-ēṭer, the *suk-kal-lum* Bēl-rēmanni s Nabû-bēlšunu Rab-bani has received from Iddina-Nabû s Šûzubu Kānik-bābi, at the disposal of Iddina *ērib bīti* of Išḫara.

Kiš

OECT 10 73 10 x [Nbk] 34, date *imittu*, possibly *ešrû* (line 2) and *gu-gal-la šá* ^{d}[x?] *šá* FPN, due in VII.

OECT 10 278 no date, dates, *ešrû* of Zababa, list, damaged.

Nippur

BE 8/1 76 15 XI Cyr x, damaged *elat* clause in lines 11-12.

BE 8/1 94 6 IV Camb 7, at Tilli-zibari, dates *a-di*(?)*-i eš-ru-ú* of Enlil, *imittu* imposed by the *guennakku*.

BE 8/1 136 no date, administrative, *taḫsistu*, barley received from Mûrânu ^{LU_2}GAL *eš-ru-ú šá* Enlíl.

Nippur, Murašû

BE 9 45 20 V Art 36, see Chapter III, sub material on status villagers.

Sippar

CTMMA 3 92 30 I Dar 21, lease by Nabû-uballiṭ s Ṭabia from Šamaš temple in Sippar against the payment of a 50% share of the yield plus *ešrû*.[5]

BM 101334[6] (end Camb. -beg. Dar) PN requests from administration of Ebabbar 6) *eš-ru-ú* NIG$_2$.GA ^{d}UTU E$_2$ *ri-it-ti-ia* 7) [*i*] *bi-in-nim-ma ina* MU.AN.NA *a-na* Ebabbar x+60 kor of dates and 2.3.2 of barley *a-nam-din.*

Ur

UET 4 107 29 V Dar 18, at (Al-)Bīt-Kušê (Iṣṣur group) date *imittu*, *e-lat eš-ru-ú* of Sin.

UET 4 108 15 VI Dar 12, identical.

b. Taxation on prebends/prebendal income?

This question was already raised in the discussion of *ilku* in relation to the payment in VS 4, 121, where the presence of *mubannûs* suggests a prebendary context, but there is some additional information.

Payment for *kurummat šarri* is not to be regarded as a type of taxation, but a payment in lieu of prebendal income which was due to the king for prebends which were his property or for remnants of offerings which belonged to him. In the case of the Nappāḫu Išḫara butcher's prebend the king, or his *bēl piqitti*, probably left the meat due to

---

[5] Quoted from Jursa 1998 p. 256-7.

[6] Also Jursa 1998 p. 19.

him, perhaps but for a token amount which was actually sent to the king, to the (other) prebendaries, who paid him in silver. We can assume that such meat was sold in order to obtain silver. Again we are forced to assume the existence of a market. The likelier it becomes that a market for commodities existed, the likelier the conclusion must be that it was taxed. Pieces of meat were indeed available, but amounts and frequency are imponderables.

VS 5, 72, reign of Darius, is the most intriguing of the prebend related texts. It deals with a levy imposed by the palace for which no reasons are given. The idea that we are dealing with a specific measure for a specific purpose is, however, not supported by the fact that a time limit with a beginning and an end is specified. That suggests a recurrent obligation or imposition. VS 6, 169 is sadly damaged.

The texts are not very explicit, but taxation of prebendal income seems at least to belong to the possibilities.

A possible integration of "priestly" personnel in the land for service system might be suggested by the Murašû text BE 9, 72, where date plantations and arable belonging to bow fiefs of $^{LU_2}E_2$BAR.MEŠ, thus *šangûs*, of Larak, which is at the disposal of a ^{LU_2}GAL *um-ma*[7] is leased for three years.

Babylon, Nappāḫu archive

VS 4 121 21 XII2 Dar 8, see sub *ilku*.

VS 5 72 21 III Dar 9, barley, to the value (ŠAM$_2$.ḪA$_2$) of the bread, beer, meat and *makkasu* dates, sustenance of the prebend of IN s NBZ, 4) .... *šá* TA E$_2$.GAL *ina muh-ḫi-šú šá-kan-nu* from III yr 4 to end x yr 6 Ina-ṣilli-Esagil s x, the *sepīru* (has received from) IN(?). Fragmentary, earlier tablets mentioned. (PV 57)

VS 6 143 28 II Dar 25, the *kurummat šarri* of the sheep and lamb offerings in the temple of Išḫara of months III, IX and X of yr. 25 have been paid by Šellibu to Nidinti s Bēl-eṭēri-Nabû, *širku* of Marduk, the *ša kurummat šarri*. (PV 140)

VS 6 153 26 III Dar 28, meat shares until end III yr 28 Zumbu s Iddina and Bēl-iddina s Damqia have been paid by Šellibu. (*kurummat šarri*?) Identical VS 6, 152.

Bertin 3055 12 x Dar 30, (BM 77563) (payment for meat portions?) belonging to an Išḫara prebend from IV yr 29 to III yr 30 Itti-Nabû-balāṭu s Lūṣi-ana-nūr the *bel piqittu ša muḫḫi quppi* has received from Šellibu.

VS 6 179 x III Xerxes 1, (payment) belonging to the *kurummat šarri* of the Išḫara temple for yr 1 Bēl-ittannu s Marduk-zēr-ibni Šumu-lībši has received from Šellibu.

VS 5 136 (date lost), receipt(?) for meat portions (?). Fragmentary.

Other

VS 6 169 (reign of Darius) badly damaged *ēpišānūtu* contract for a slaughterer's prebend in the Eulmaš temple of Bēlet-Akkade in Sippar; 11) ... *ebūr* GIŠ.[ŠUB.BA]-*šú* LU MU *il-ki šá* ^{LU_2}ERIN$_2$.MEŠ LUGAL x x (= *il-lak*?).[8]

Murašû

BE 9 72 5 VI Art 40, date plantations and arable at [x x] E$_2$ GIŠ.BAN.MEŠ 2)*šá* $^{LU_2}E_2$BAR.MEŠ *šá* Larak$_2^{KI}$ *šá* ŠU^{II} ^{LU_2}GAL *um-ma* PN has leased for three yrs to PN2.

c. *ṣibtu*: taxation of animal husbandry

The term *ṣibtu* occurs in relation to animals, but it should be kept in mind, contrary to the interpretation given by the CAD, that *ṣibtu*, when dealing with animals, primarily

[7] On this functionary Stolper 2001 no. 9 *ad* line 3.

[8] I cannot reconstruct the passage with confidence. Whether the phrases are connected directly or not, the fragment suggests that prebendaries had already been drawn into the structures through which military and civil projects were financed. We can safely expect earlier indications.

refers to culling in general, and that *ṣibtu* as a (likely) form of taxation only represents a narrowing of that general meaning. In this narrower sense it will occur in the title of the (royal) *rab ṣibti*, "chief of the tax (on animals"), whom we find acting in the Murašû text PBS 2/1, 224 and who also occurs in Sippar documents mentioning the presence of herds of sheep in Raṣapa. In the sense of a "tax on herded animals" *ṣibtu* occurs in Sargon II's Annals, Lie 331, where it is payable to "Bēl and his son". The letter CT 22, 80, from the correspondence between Iddina-Marduk and his slave-manager Mandanu-bēl-uṣur, which mentions a *rab ṣibti* (line 17) and taxation (*šá ṣibti šá bir-ri* I_7.MEŠ, line 19) does not help, though CT 22, 82 from the same correspondence informs us about animal husbandry in the area.[9]

In institutional texts, however, *ṣibtu* often clearly indicates animals taken from the institutional herds and transferred to the institutional fattening pens. The term does not refer to taxation in such cases.

That herds, and probably grazing areas, were taxed if the opportunity presented itself, is extremely likely, but the documentation is wanting for this period.[10] The private archives available are, however, not concerned in a meaningful manner with animal husbandry. In the Nippur text quoted, in which the partners anyhow share the costs, the in itself superfluous statement concerning *ṣibtu* suggests that this form of payment was common.

Wool could certainly be expected to be taxed. Transport would pose identical opportunities as were available regarding onions and barley, but there is simply no information.

Small deliveries of animals, ten sheep and one ox, for instance, often belong to the additional payments in larger arable lease contracts. Delivery of such animals to owners, who include the king and the institutions, cannot be regarded in a direct sense as a form of taxation as the payments belong to the conditions of the leases. The habit forms, however, part of the system of gifts which was definitely taxation related, certainly so in land for service contexts. What is of importance, is that these additionals suggest that such animal husbandry was a regular component of ordinary arable agriculture. Yet its taxation aspects remain obscure.

In arable agriculture taxation and leasing of land by the government are elements within a single continuum. That the same is the case with animal husbandry is suggested by the Uruk text YOS 6, 26, in which a person entitled "herdsman of Bēlet of Uruk" requests the lease of land belonging to the temple against a rent payable in barley in order to obtain space to station herds of sheep and cattle belonging to the temple itself. We need not discuss the backgrounds of the text,[11] but can note that people working for the temple were not free to use land belonging to the temple without payment of a duty. This suggests that in general, where possible, authorities would indeed claim such payments, also in this period.

---

[9] Literature CAD Ṣ p. 166, *ṣibtu* C. Cf. also M. Dandamayev, The Neo-Babylonian *rab ṣibti*, in ed. J. Marzahn and H. Neumann, Assyriologica and Semitica, Fs. J. Oelsner, AOAT 252, Münster 2000, p. 29-31, which deals with *ṣibtu* and temple herds, and animals used for "royal offerings". The Author concludes that something like 1.5% (Uruk) or 2,5 % (Sippar) was taken. What should be considered is what could be culled from the herds of the temple. A few percent of the male animals were required for breeding purposes, and cattle were also needed in the form of oxen, but only 2.5% percent available for offerings would suggest a terrible waste of male animals, and female animals had to be culled when they had become useless for breeding, before they died of illness or old age. This is unpractical.

[10] For the grazing tax in second millennium Ugarit cf. I. Márquez Rowe, More Evidence of the Grazing Tax in Ugarit, UF 27, 1995, p. 317-331.

[11] Cf. M. San Nicolò. OrNS 17, 1948, p. 279-284. The lease holder *in spe* is (later on) a *rab būli*.

The date suggests that the arrangement belongs to a kind of reorganisation of the management of temple property which took place in Eanna on the succession of Nabonidus. The text indicates that this type of "herdsman" had in fact become already an entrepreneur in the rent farm system.

Still another form of taxation involving animals is suggested by TCL 13, 153, where the impression must be that the king had a right to sheep, possibly on a daily basis, which had to be delivered by local authorities, but were payable, possibly according to a roster, by people of certain means. The text is an isolated phenomenon, but the phrasing suggests a routine matter. Too little is known about the backgrounds, but we know that also the temples were accustomed to charge those who rented a house from the institution with fattening a sheep.

Nippur

BE 8/1 63 6 x Cyr 4, at Āl-ša-Addidāia. Herding contract. (Ninurta-mutīr-gimilli s Zēr-kitti-lišīr group) *ṣib-tu*$_4$ *it-ti a-ḫa-meš i-nam-din* (sic).

Uruk

YOS 6 26 12 III Nbn 1, Iqīša s Nanāia-eriš, *nāqidu* of Bēlet-ša-Uruk, asks the royal representatives in Eanna for a *maškattu* in the form of land of Bēlet-ša-Uruk for the 2000 sheep and 500 cattle of the goddess for which he was responsible, *in concreto* land in the *šiḫu šá* (Āl)Til-Ḫurāṣi for a rent of 400 kor of barley. The land was the remainder of land given to (*nadānu*, means: exploited by) *širkus* of Bēlet of Uruk (as lease holders?,) at the disposal (*ina* IGI) of the *šākin ṭēmi*.[12] Additionally: one head of cattle and 10 sheep. *qêpu* and *ṭupšar* Eanna present.

Murašû

PBS 2/1 224 13+ VI Dar II [7]?, receipt of 40 *š* of silver paid by Šum-iddina and Aḫušunu the ? of Rēmūt-Ninurta as *ṣi-ib-ti* for yr 7 Dar II to Iddina-Bēl *rab ṣibti* (written, as usual, MAŠ$_2$), son of Tattannu, who is one of those sealing.[13]

Other evidence for taxation of herds, possibly related

TCL 13 153 x X Camb 3, Borsippa, 1-*en* UDU.NITA$_2$ *šá* LUGAL *šá* ^{LU_2}*ḫa-za-nu* of day 10 of Zēr-Bābili Iddina-Papsukkal, *šá ina muḫḫi šá* Arad-Gula s Nabû-aḫḫē-iddina Ili-mudammiq *is-su-ku*, Bēl-šarra-bulliṭ the *rab ekalli* of Borsippa has received from Arad-Gula.

d. *nisḫu ša māti*[14]

nisḫu is a not very specific word either. It can presumably be used for any form of "deduction", but *nisḫu ša māti* will to all likelihood indicate some form of taxation as

---

[12] This is probably the reason why the matter is decided by a *ša rēš* and the *bēl piqnēti* and not by the *qêpu* and other temple authorities: this land was not really controlled by the temple any longer.

[13] The first five lines of the text are damaged, but it seems to begin with the sum due for which period by whom (Murašû, his brothers, his agents, *mār bītis*, and his servants, IR$_3$.MEŠ) , then possibly it specified the actual animals due, mentioning goats before sheep. Thereafter the actual receipt is formulated. The importance of the text might be that this could represent an arrangement covering the complete holdings of the firm in its widest sense, though 40 *š* is not an important sum, possibly suggesting a limited geographical range for the document. A completely different interpretation of the text has been provided by Cardascia, 1951 p. 121.

[14] Literature: CAD N p. 267, Cardascia 1951 p. 57, notes 5 and 6, Augapfel 1917, p. 23; AHw 795 L, "landesübliche Zahlung"; Stolper 1988, p. 144, translates this text, EAH 214 lines 11-12, which were somewhat garbled by the scribe: "he will pay them (silver equivalent to) three kor of barley, according to the current posted rate (?) of the country", with the comment ".... the expressed volume of barley appears to be a measure of value for a payment that is to be made in another commodity, presumably silver". I cannot see any indication of a change in commodity, and I see no reason for such a change in the modest amount that would be involved, certainly by Murašû standards.

already Augapfel suggested, without finding much acclaim, for the texts concerned are far from explicit. The proposition that we are dealing with a form of taxation definitely finds some support in cases where *urāšu* and *nisḫu* are found next to one another. But not even there matters are clear cut.[15]

CAD N/2 p. 267 quotes RA 25, p.78, no. 7, one of the texts from Neirab, dealing with the payment of silver and containing the phrase *aki ni-is-ḫu ša māti*(!), "according to the current tariff of the land", *nisḫu* being interpreted as a kind of record, in the same way as is done with PBS 2/1, 110:6, 204:6, 108:4, 219:5 and BE 10, 121: 4. In my opinion a passage like ROMCT 2, 16 indicates that *nisḫu ša māti* probably was a customary levy, in this instance on bow fiefs. The phrasing with *libbu* in some of the Murašû texts makes an interpretation "according to the tariff" less likely, though, in case a form of taxation was involved, there would have been rules.

Especially PBS 2/1, 201 suggests a levy on (leased?) land burdened with "military" obligations. In the Murašû texts we find that the amount of (always!) barley due, belongs to (NIG_2.GA), generally, the main partner, only once to the factotum, almost a junior partner, Ribat, who, like his superior acts in practice through agents. Those obliged to pay were also personally linked to the firm. In PBS 2/1, 204 the payment due is part of the rent. Why the rent should be paid explicitly "according to the tariff of the land" is not clear as the term *nisḫu ša māti* is not used ordinarily in leases, and leases always anyhow contain a good deal of customary law. A likely interpretation of the Murašû texts is probably that the head of the firm is obliged to pay an overall *nisḫu ša māti*, hence the occasional *libbu*, which indicates, in the interpretation given here, that only a share in the total obligation (of the senior partner) is covered by the amount mentioned. It is each time only a part of the means to pay which he is to receive through his (local) agents from his tenants, who will be sub-tenants in the complicated system of leases of land encumbered with service obligations. But it must be conceded that PBS 2/1, 110 clearly has *a-ki-i*, "according to". The amounts mentioned by the Murašû texts concerned are relatively minor compared to what is usual in this text group in general.

The possibility should be considered that *nisḫu ša māti* represents a levy on the agricultural products harvested, possibly levied from the landowners, but shifted by them on to their tenants.

As to the date, the involvement of silver and the fact that there are no reasons not to assume that the text refers to a private transaction, the Neirab text is an exception, the other texts are all later Achaemenid and belong to a land for service environment.[16] Whether we are dealing with a new tax or with a new manner of indicating something old, cannot be decided for the moment. EAH 214, quoted under *uzbāru*, and dating to Darius II yr 3 probably mentions the same levy.

---

[15] BE 8/1, 37, see sub *urāšu*.

[16] PBS 2/1, 126 (6 XI Dar II 6) is a court case, which mentions incidentally land in Al-Banešš̌āia, like PBS 2/1, 204, in which the looser is condemned to pay *lìb-bu-ú ni-is-ḫu ša* IG.GUR[KI] (= Susa), if he failed to make his point. The case is possibly being referred to a higher court. Here clearly local circumstances are alluded to and the matter is completely different from the *nisḫu ša māti* which interests us. Here *nisḫu* certainly refers to an obtaining rate. *nisḫu* is a general word, like many of the terms we are concerned with and the meaning depends on context and circumstances. In CTMMA 3, 128, 26 I Dar II 5,: 9-10 two kor of barley IGI-tu_4 *šá ni-is-ḫu* are still due from the debtor. This may or may not refer to outstanding tax obligations.

Neirab

RA 25, 7 7 x N[bn?] 4, silver [of] PN1 s PN2 due from PN3 s PN4; at the end of the month he will pay the silver 5) *a-ki-i* 6) *ni-is-ḫu šá* KUR! (The copy gives GAR NU, the emendation was proposed by Cardascia.) At Bît-Daiian-Addu.

Murašû archive

PBS 2/1 204 12 XII Dar II 4, 11 kor of barley NIG_2.GA of Rēmūt-Ninurta/Murašû at the disposal of PN 1 and PN2 due from PN3 s PN4 and PN5 s PN6; they will pay II yr 5 *lìb-bu-ú ni-is-ḫi šá* KUR (according to the *kuruppu*-measure) *ina* GIŠ.BAN_2 A.$ŠA_3$-*šú-nu šá* A.$ŠA_3$.MEŠ *šá* ^{LU_2}*ga-ar-di šá* ^{URU}Ba-na-UR.MAḪ(!).

PBS 2/1 108 11 X Dar II 5, 10 kor of barley NIG_2.GA of Ribat s Bēl-erība servant of Rēmūt-[Ninurta] due from PN3 s PN4, he will pay x yr 6 [*lìb-bu*]-*ú ni-is-ḫu ša* KUR.

PBS 2/1 110 10 XII Dar II 5, 9,5 kor of barley, NIG_2.GA of Rēmūt-Ninurta/Murašû at the disposal of (his servant) PN s PN2 due from PN3 s PN4, he will pay in II yr 6 6) *a-ki-i ni-is-ḫu šá* KUR.

PBS 2/1 219 2 X Dar II 6, 2 kor of barley NIG2.GA of Rēmūt-Ninurta/Murašû at the disposal of PN1, PN2 and PN3 due from PN4 s PN5, he will pay in II yr 7 *lìb-bu ni-is-ḫi šá* KUR; cf. PBS 2/1 127, 7 XI Dar II, where the payment of 5 kor is due from a servant of Rēmūt-Ninurta.

BE 10 121 20 I Dar II 7, identical, 3.5 kor (?) *lìb-bu-ú nis-ḫu šá* KUR.[17]

Nippur

EAH 214[18] 26 VII Dar II 3, 12) 3 GUR ŠE.BAR *ana nis-ḫu* (with interpolated *lìb-bu-u* KUR) *i-nam-diš-šú-nu-ti* (i.e. the lessee to the lessors, ENGAR.MEŠ *šá* LUGAL *šá* $ŠU^{II}$ PN ^{LU_2}NAM I_7.$ḪA_2$) [Already quoted under *uzbāru*.]

Where?

ROMCT 2 16 24 XI Art 33, *a-ḫi ni-is-ḫi šá* KUR *ina* GIŠ.BAN x x *ša* PN.

BE 8/ 37 no date, *urāšu u ni-is-ḫu* in a list of payments.

3. Dubious or rejected taxation terms

a. *palāḫu ša šarri*

The phrase, a general obligation of all subjects, is used in a particular manner in the Murašû archive. As explained by M. Stolper,[19] it indicates the leasing of land belonging to *ḫadru* land-holders as a collective through their *šaknu* to a person or persons who was/were willing to take the lease of land which would otherwise remain untilled, but for which the *ḫadru* probably had to pay to the king duties of the types discussed earlier. The tenant paid only the amount of these duties to the *šaknu* of the *ḫadru*, who had to forward this sum in the end to the authorities. The expression is best seen as a catch-all phrase, what was actually due remained unspecified.

Ur

UET 4 43 22 IX Phil.-Ar. 7, Gallābu archive; 1) 12 *š* KB .... 2) *man-dat-tú* TIL-*ru* (date) 3) *šá* 5-*šú ina* A.$ŠA_3$ (land and situation) 7) .... A.$ŠA_3$ *u* ŠE.NUMUN MU.MEŠ 8) *šá* E_2 PN *šá a-na pa-làḫ ša*[*rri*] KI E_2 PN2 .... 9) *šá a-na man-*[*dat-tú*] 10) *ina* IGI PN3 (is paid).

---

[17] PBS 2/1, 93, dealing with 11 kor of barley possibly belongs here too, and involves Ribat, again also possibly, BE 10, 104. In the same general context PBS 2/1, 129 (13 XIIb Dar II 5) can be mentioned, with 1,5 kor, but the "owner" is in this case Libluṭ s Lābāši, who occurs in other texts. The person obliged to pay is a servant of Ribat, the amount is 10 kor. All these documents date roughly to the same period towards the end of this text group.

[18] Stolper 1988, p.144.

[19] Stolper 1985 p. 61.

b. *šibšu*

In Neo-Babylonian texts, in so far as they are comprehensible, *šibšu* is not a term for some form of taxation. This had already been seen by F.R. Kraus in the study of the expression in his Edikt.[20] *šibšu* seems to be used often in connection with secondary crops like sesame, particularly in Borsippa. In Dar 315 two Egibi brothers concede their mother's brother's son a one third share in the proceeds of a huge transaction involving the share in the onion harvest belonging to Bēl, if that is meant by "the governor of Esagil"[21] which they had bought from the lease holder concerned.

In a text like VS 5, 33 *šibšu* denotes the (in this case, one third) share of the land owner, as in YOS 17, 8 from Borsippa. In Dar 314 the share of the *šibšu,* charged as rent, amounts to a quarter. We find in this way, but the fact may be accidental, the ordinary percentages for respectively gravity and manually irrigated land. In leases a tenant who leaves land unused can be compelled to deliver a *šibšu* equal to that of his neighbours: BM 97354. In institutional texts *šibšu* is due to the institutions as landowners, occasionally together with the *ešrû* levied from the share of the tenant: e.g. YOS 17, 46, from Uruk. Misleadingly the combination of the two could suggest a form of taxation for both terms.

A form of taxation amounting to 25 or 30% would perhaps be bearable, but 50% of the harvest on top of the share of the landowner, combined with *ešrû* and "costs", plus the necessity to reserve seed and fodder, would leave extremely little for the tenant. The fact underlines the necessity to regard taxation, rent and agricultural costs in general as one complex: there comes a moment at which the tenant can no longer survive. Also for this reason *šibšu* can not be a tax in the Neo-Babylonian period.

BM 97354 is also of some interest on account of the extra payment of 0.3.2 of barley as a *šulmānu eqli*, presumably to the owner. Only a few examples of the use of *šibsu* have been selected.

Babylon

Egibi

Dar 315 — 21 XII Dar 11, 1) *šib-šu šá* ŠUM.SAR NIG$_2$.GA ^{d}*Bēl šá* ^{URU}Šaḫrinu (period) 3) .... *šá ina* IGI ^{LU_2}*er-re-še-e šá* 4) MNA and Nabû-aḫḫē-bulliṭ ss IMB Egibi *šá ina* ŠU^{II} 6) PN 7) *šá* GIŠ.BAN$_2$ *šá* PN2 ^{LU_2}EN.NAM E$_2$.SAG.IL$_2$ 8) *a-na* 42 1/2 MA.NA KB .... 7) *šal-šú* ḪA.LA *i-na ú-ṭùr* PN4 [will enjoy with the two Egibis].

Dar 533 — Dar 21, mentioned above under *ešrû*.[22]

Borsippa

Ea-ilûta-bâni file

BM 97354[23] — 25 III Nbk 37, at Nuḫšanitu, land in GARIM-Qutanu *ina* Bāb-Ni-gi-iš(?) is leased by Zēr-Bābili to a slave of Nabû-zēr-ušabši Ardia, 6) ŠE.NUMUN E$_2$ *dul-lu ma-la ú-šad-du-ú* 7) *a-ki* US$_2$.SA.DU *šib-šú ú-šal-lam* 8) MU.AN.NA 0.3.2. ŠE.BAR *šu-ul-ma-nu* A.ŠA$_3$ 9) *i-nam-din* ŠE.NUMUN *ma-la* 10) *ip-pu-uš šal-šu šib-šu* SE$_3$-*in*; additionally: *ina si-ip-ḫu u ši-ri-in-du a-ḫa-meš* A.ŠA$_3$ *ik-kal*.[24]

---

[20] Kraus 1958 p. 128-9. CAD Š/2 p. 385 sees *šibšu*, as in other periods, also in the Neo-Babylonian period as a form of taxation on yields. Ries 1976, p. 78 deems "Worfelertrag", which must mean the complete, cleaned yield, the right interpretation. The complete yield as the amount of the levy would be stifling, even though it would typify the tax man's paradise.

[21] He is probably the unspecified "governor" meant alongside the scribes, measurers and gatekeepers in the Edict of Belsazzar, see above, in the study on prebends.

[22] Line 18 mentions *šibšu* and ḪA.LA *šá kap-pa-ri-in-ni ina* IGI PN, of whom/which *šibšu* is also mentioned in line 30. Nothing can be added to CAD K p. 185L.

[23] Quoted from a transcription by H. Bongenaar.

[24] Cf. CAD S p. 300, *sippiḫu*, for TuM 2/3, 140: 4-8.

Ili-bani file
TCL 12 85 20 VI Nbn 5, at GARIM-Surmarrati, contrasts the dates of the *imittu* and 3) ŠE.GIŠ.I$_3$ *šib-šú ebūr* 1 GUR ŠE.NUMUN which pertain to the husband of the woman owning the *nudunnu* land. (See also above under *kāru*.)
Ash A 114 12 VII Camb 5, at Surmarrati, 1) 0.1.2 ŠE.GIŠ.I$_3$ *šib-šú* A.ŠA$_3$ *šá* PN (owner) 3) *ina muḫ-ḫi* PN2 and PN3 *ina* VIII ...5) *i-nam-di-nu*.
Nanāḫu
TuM 2/3 168 13 I Dar 14, at GARIM-Ḫallat, 1) 3 kor barley *šibšu* A.ŠA$_3$ *šá* GARIM-Ḫallat *šá* ^{GIŠ}KIRI$_6$ ^{GIŠ}GIŠIMMAR 2) *a-di muḫ-ḫi ú-šal-lam ina* Al-šá-Šaddinu, belonging to PN and PN2, undivided with their father's brother.
Other:
TuM 2/3 166 2 II Dar 7, at GARIM-Ḫallat, 1) 2 kor barley *i-mit-tum* 2) *šib-šu* A.ŠA$_3$ *šá* GARIM-Ḫallat *šá ku-pa*-[x(-x)] *šá* PN due from PN2 in Borsippa in III.
Lakuppuru
VS III 157 16 I Dar 35, receipt dates *imittu* yr 34, 7) ... *ù*(?) x(?) ŠE.GIŠ.I$_3$ *šib-šú šá* UGU *ḫa-re-e* (plus secondary products of the date palm).
VS III 161 5 VIII Dar 35, 1) 0.1.4 ŠE.GIŠ.I$_3$ *gam-ru-tu šib-šú* A.ŠA$_3$ *šá* GARIM-Tamtim-šá-Bīt-ḫarê NIG$_2$.GA ^{d}Nabû (paid); will be registered in the register of Nabû with proof for the receiver of the receipt.

c. *tēlītu*

tēlītu is often regarded as a form of taxation, but in a clear majority of cases "costs" seems a more appropriate translation. Cf. for Borsippa the "notes" Ash A 111, 15 IV Xer 1, A 182, 22 II Xer 2, and VS 6, 307 all belonging to the Ilšu-abušu group. This text group contains many notes regarding all sorts of payments, in which not only a *qêpu* and a person with the Persian name Uštanu figure, but also all types of household expenditure are listed. For Nippur: Durand EHE 27: *tēlît ša* PN1 *ina muḫḫi* PN2 *ušēlû*: small amounts for food, "costs which PN charged to PN2". Cf. also TÉBR no. 6, X Art 23 etc. Especially no. 14 *te-lit ṣe-en*, and no. 16 *te-lit ṣe-en* TA *mi-il-du*, "from the increase". Intriguing, but hopeless(?) Kiš, unassigned, OECT 10, 94, mentions AM yr. 2. Ur: UET 4 122, 128, 135 and 119, 121, 118, 117 from the Sin-uballiṭ file. It is of course possible that among the posts listed there are taxation payments, which are, naturally enough, referred to as costs in private administrative notes.

Uruk
YOS 7 38 3 VIII Cyr 4, see below Chapter VII under *bīt ritti*.

d. *tillūtu*

The phrase occurs in the curses of the text Binning 1, from the time of Bēl-ibni[25] line 26', which concerns those who mobilise the people of the reinstated town mentioned by the text *ana il-ki ù til*(=BE)*-lu-ti*. The parallel indicates that both *ilku* and *tillūtu* are obligations. *tillūtu* does not occur unequivocally in this sense in other texts.[26] Perhaps the term had become obsolete in later Neo-Babylonian. A dubious instance from Borsippa possibly mentions the word in relation to flour, which is one of the taxation "additionals".

---

[25] Published by C.B.F. Walker, Iraq 44, 1982, p. 71ff.

[26] E. Leichty's translation of Izbu VII 3 makes "good sense", but what is the basis for the translation "work-gang"? AHw 1359 L registers a parallelism between *itbarūtu* and *tillūtu*, *itbarūtu* can possibly represent a collective term for "workmen".

Borsippa

Ash F 2 20 IX - 14 X, *qēme ša ana* [NINDA.]ḪA$_2$ from 20 IX *i-na* TIN.TIR^{KI} *i-lu-ú*, list of amounts, mentions total x *qēme til*(=BE)-*lit-tum šá* X, also in last line. Possibly prebendal.

e. *zitti šarri*

What the "king's share" means in BE 8/1, 85 is not clear. It is better to regard the king in this case as a landowner or rather as the owner of the water concerned, which is here in the hands of a rent farmer. This is not a special form of taxation but literally "the share belonging to the king", the rent payable to him as owner of the land.

BE 8/1 85 12 I Camb 3, Enlil-šākin-šulum s Līšir leases land *ana sūti* from Anum-šar-uṣur s Šamaš-zēr-ibni the *bēl piqitti* of Šamaš-x-uṣur the *ša muḫḫi sūti* of the Nār-Purat-Nibru; additional clause ḪA.LA(?) LUGAL *gam-mir-šú i-gam-mar-ma a-na ka-a-ri šá šarri i-nam-din.*

5. Conclusion

The list of dubious or insufficiently identified taxation related words could probably be extended further. Passages containing the term *kudurru*, especially in Neo-Babylonian texts, I have not considered as referring especially to taxation-related activities,[27] though carrying the hod can indicate being subject to corvée obligations. *nāmurtu*, CAD N/1 p. 255 is also in NB a not frequent word for a(n official) gift. *nuptu*, CAD N/2 p 343, "additional payment" belongs to the more or less regular "gifts" which, if traditional, would be taxable themselves in present day Holland. *kinâtu* represents a comparable term. There are many more words of this type. CAD N/2 *nidintu*[28] (p. 207 1b) quotes PBS 2/1, 24 and other Murašû texts, suggesting that "an earlier and a later gift due to the king" were de rigueur when paying *ilku*, but the term indicates that what was due was paid in the form of an earlier and a later instalment. The relevant texts have been discussed at the end of Chapter IV.

---

[27] This is of course the case in Binning 1, 13', where freedom from *ilku* and *ṭupšikku* is established.

[28] Not to be confused with *niditti šarri* said of land and discussed in chapter III.

CHAPTER VII
LAND AS A BASIS FOR TAXATION: THE LAND DIVISION SCHEMES

1. Introductory

Of the three grounds for taxation identified, the first, payment for services provided by the government, and the last, taxation on commodities, require little additional comment, even though they cannot be completely separated. But concerning the second, "land for service", combined with leasing, some further observations must be made. We must accept that the impositions by the government on the population at large, on the subject as a person, can not properly be identified and that impositions on townspeople use a terminology which can not be separated adequately from obligations deriving from specific grants with the intention to obtain services from the grantee. The townspeople also bear the *qaštu* and are subject to the related civil dues. We surmised already that there is a link with the *ḫanšu*-system found in a number of old towns. The Sippar text BM 79128 clearly implies a connection between *qaštu* and *ḫanšū*. The result is a not very transparent system. But taxation systems in general are not intended to be transparent. The system of holding land inevitably evolved through time and we can assume that it was in the interest of the (Persian) government to play down differences between urban and rural land holders, who anyhow over time would tend to merge. We are dealing with a patchwork of rights and duties, in which it was often hardly relevant to spell out the details.

Land holding is the most obvious tax basis in Neo-Babylonian texts. Though not many in number, there are still some texts indicating that houses, that is houses in the towns, not in the countryside, where they might be regarded as belonging to the adjacent fields or even an estate, held against the obligation to serve, were the reason for the fact that taxes were being levied: cf. here sub *ilku* (and *urāšu*) YBC 11599 (in a village, but, it would seem, with named streets), sub *qaštu* UCLM 9-2919, BM 136872 (JCS 30, 239), UET 4, 39 and 53, sub *rikis qabli* Camb 276, sub *urāšu* W, IM 346, TuM 2/3, 218 and sub *ešrû* Bertin 2809.[1] The texts mentioning *dekû ša bābti* constitute perhaps the best general reference to the taxing of houses, or rather of people, families, because they lived in a house in a certain urban quarter. These texts belong to a specifically urban context. The question is whether such houses were granted with the intention that their owners should serve or whether a real estate based system of impositions was extended to cover (also) already existing urban property. The bases of property holding and taxation are, as always, linked, but one might

---

[1] We can add the two *nidittu šarri* houses mentioned under that term in Chapter III, but they are not of the same importance for the subject in hand here. All this must be seen in addition to the small plots, outside the built up area, which seem to occur in relation with bow service in the recently published text from the Egibi archive W E I no. 48: 11) in total 0.2.3 3 $SILA_3$ of land *a-di* 14 GAR.$ḪA_2$ ŠE.NUMUN E_2.BAN.MEŠ. As the Author remarks (2000b I p. 94-5) a mere 105 m^2 cannot be regarded as a bow fief in the usual sense. It is difficult to assess the meaning of this passage, but the possibility could be considered whether on the land originally assigned to persons of more elevated rank, the *rab ḫanšūs*, for instance, there was after all room for "common soldiers" of a very modest social level. Bow land on Egibi fields is also found in Dar 307, 19 VI^{II} Dar 11, quoted under *qaštu* related payments in Chapter IV. Though many of the texts are late Achaemenid, houses subject to service obligations clearly occur earlier.

expect to find here the connection with the general service obligations of the subject. The relation between general and specifically property based obligations constitutes a problem, but probably primarily for us. In a tribal context, outside the towns of the first half of the millennium, everybody would act as the members of his tribe did, if such a tribe could be regarded as something stable. Notwithstanding manifest party allegiances, town dwellers could be expected to act in a similar manner: they acted as their group did. All submitted to what was accepted collectively.

2. The structure of the service: the urban aspect, *dekû* and related matters, *eširtu*[2]

As we have seen there are indications that taxation was, at least partially, based on a property for service system. But there was also the *eširtu* system, which, as Jursa has recently stressed,[3] had a structure directly connected to the social realities of society, members of prebendal families being grouped with their likes and plough men with plough men. Primarily we can expect the *eširtu*, as far as was possible, to have been based on family relationships, automatically so as there existed a degree of correlation between family and occupation that was much stronger than is the case nowadays. In this way the *eširtu* also had an inbuilt property link, in which general obligations of the subject were linked to, or could evolve into a primarily property based taxation system. It should not be assumed that a property linked system, such as we are dealing with, had in itself anything to do with ideas of social justice or equality. Group interests are even more likely to influence behaviour if family and property operate in tandem. A rich *eširtu* would have had less difficulties in hiring a substitute than a poor one, but the possibility that a rich person was taxed for more than one property also complicated the situation, for he could only serve for one property at a time.

For the relation between the various relevant terms a small group of texts from Borsippa is important, not in the least because these texts clearly link obligations to urban property. As elsewhere the subject was obliged to fulfil certain tasks. Mobilisation took place through a "summoner" working via the "heads of ten". I understand VS 4, 150 in such a manner: the *dēkû* gives his orders through the *rab ešerti*.[4] A link with "holding a house" can be made in any case, at least at a certain level, for it can be assumed that the organisation of a "mobilisation" took place at several levels, of which the *babtu*, -with its *eširtus*?-, was perhaps the lowest.[5] YOS 3, 44 indicates that *eširtu*s were under the supervision of *rab ḫanšû*s when actually serving, but we must consider -again- the possibility that the *eširtu*s to which the male population belonged were not identical with actual serving units of ten, grouping men from different "local" *eširtu*s.

In both Borsippa Atkuppu file tablets the owner of the leased house remained responsible for the tax-related payments involved. The third case is too damaged for a definite conclusion on this point. This does not signify, however, a real deviation from what seems to have been a general tendency, signifying that owners of property subject to obligations managed to transfer the practical implications of those obligations on to their tenants. VS 4, 150 is, however, an antichretic loan, in which the owner of the house presumably was the weaker party, but that is not so clear in VS 5, 77.

---

[2] Literature: *dekû* CAD D p. 123, meanings 2 and 3; *dēkû* CAD D p. 128-9; *dēkû ša babti* CAD B p. 11; *eširtu* CAD E p. 365L and *rab eširti* p. 365.

[3] Jursa 1999, p. 104.

[4] Perhaps the *dēkû* was responsible for having all males assigned to an *eširtu* on reaching the appropriate age.

[5] A. Ungnad NRVU I *ad* no. 126 note 5 regarded a mobilisation context too uncertain, CAD B p. 11L speaks of "tax due (in lieu of corvée work)".

A link between *babtu*, quarter of the town, place of residence, and *eširtu*, the (family based) unit through which mobilisation took place, seems certain. This is, of course, not a uniquely Babylonian phenomenon, it is a typical aspect of a certain type of urban structure and it confronts us with our factual ignorance about the manner in which Mesopotamian towns were governed. But that should not bother us here.

The *dēkû* and *dekû ša babti*[6]

Borsippa

VS 6 70 24 III Nbn 6, see Chapter IV sub *ilku*.

VS 5 77 12 XI Dar 13, (Atkuppu-file) lease of a house by PN to PN2 23) *pu-ut de-ek-ki šá ba-ab-tu*$_4$ PN (owner) *na-ši*.

VS 4 150 4 V Dar 18, (Atkuppu-file) antichretic lease of house to FPN by PN2. 10) *pu-ut de-ki šá ba-ab-tu*$_4$ *šá* ^{LU_2}GAL 10-*tim*.MEŠ PN2 *na-ši*, he will recompense FPN for costs incurred.

VS 4 154 2 XI Dar 20, (Rē'u-alpi-file) payment of rent for a house by Rēmūt-Nabû s Nabû-mukīn-zēr Rē'u-alpi to Nabû-ittannu s Nabû-mi-iš-ḫi-da(?) Širik-Nabû 6) ... *a-ḫi de-ki šá ba-ab-tu*$_4$ to end X Rēmūt-Nabû *it-ti* x (= erasure?) Nabû-ittannu *ú-ta-ṣi*-x(?).axation: the land divisions 294*i* ^{ITI}II, III and 2) IV *šá* MU 10 KAM Darius 4) 3 GIN$_2$ 2-*ta* ŠU^{II}.MEŠ KB 5) Iddina *ina* ŠU^{II} Mušēzib-Bēl 6) *ma-ḫir e-lat* 1 *š* KB 7) Nabû-bulliṭ *ma-ḫir*! 8) Iddina *ina* ŠU^{II} Mušēzib-Bēl 9) *ina us-ḫa-ri(?) e-lat* 0.0.4 ŠE.BAR 10) *šá ul-tu* 10-*šu iš-šu-u* 11) *e-lat šá-pat-ti šá ul-tu* 12) *ú-ra-šú né-e-si-iḫ*.[7]

rab ešerti

Sippar Ebabbar archive, institutional

BM 74659 19 XI Cyr 7, PN1, *rab širkāti*, and PN2-5 individually qualified as GAL.10-*tu*$_4$ and 8 others, probably *kizûs*, make a no longer identifiable request relating to their *dullu*, involving the *qêpu*.

Borsippa

VS 6 166 9 V Dar 36, 410 see Chapter IV under *dullu*.

Uruk, Eanna Archive, institutional

Bir 7 30 IV Nbk 38, see Chapter IV under *urāšu*.

eširtu

Borsippa

BRM I 71 11 III Dar 7, 1) KU$_3$.BABBAR UDU.NITA$_2$ *qé-me* MUN.ḪA$_2$ *saḫ-le-e* 2) I$_3$.GIŠ KAŠ.DUG$_3$.GA *ḫu-un-zu*[8] SUG.ḪA$_2$ *gab-bi* 3) *ša* (months) I, II, III yr 7 5) *šá* 10-*tim šá* Bēl-kāṣir s Rēmūt-Nabû 6) Arkat-ilāni *ù* ERIN$_2$.MEŠ *šá* 10-*tim-šú* 7) Lukšu ^{LU_2}*kar-dak-a ma-ḫi-ir* 8) *e-ṭe-er* (amongst witnesses two other ^{LU_2}*kar-dak-a*-"officials").

Sippar Bēl-rēmanni archive

BM 42384 no date, Bēl-rēmanni, followed by incomplete list of names, rev. 2) PAB 10 ^{LU_2}ERIN$_2$ *a-na* 1-*en* 3) ^{LU_2}BAN *šá* Bēl-rēmanni.

BM 43300+ 6 II Dar 17, Nidinti-Marduk s Suqaia, Bēl-rēmanni s Mušebši-Marduk, more names ... 14) ... [PAB 10?] ^{LU_2}ERIN$_2$.MEŠ *a-na* 15) ^{GIŠ}BAN *i*[*na* IGI N]idinti-Marduk, date.

BM 42432 9 XII Dar 18, Šamaš-nāṣir s Mušebši-Marduk ^{GIŠ}BAN *šá* Nidinti-Marduk s Suqaja, 6) [1]-*it* ^{GIŠ}BAN *ina* IGI 7) Šamaš-nāṣir, date, sealed by Nidinti-Marduk.

---

6 For the role of the *dēkû* in the countryside cf. VS 6, 70 (24 VII Nbn 6) quoted sub *ilku*.

7 Line 9 is problematic, the two other *elat* clauses are remarkable. I assume that Iddina is the subject in line 10, which probably means that he was assigned "the fortnight out of the *urāšu*": an alleviation or an extra duty? Whether Iddina was an official or a substitute is unclear.

8 A hapax according to CAD Ḫ 238L.

(Payments to) *rab ḫanšū*

Babylon

Nbn 480 13 XII Nbn 10, 32 *š* of silver of Tukulti-Bēl s Šamaš-iddina s Rabā-ša-Ninurta due from Erîba-Marduk s Šamaš-iddina Rabā-ša-Ninurta. Interest clause. Mentions earlier debt of 33 1/2 *š* KB, which silver had been given to the *rab-ḫanšū* on behalf of Erîba-Marduk.[9]

PSBA 7, 148 13 IV Dar 24, PN has performed a month of corvée work since II with PN2, his *rab ḫanšū*, PN 2 will not mobilize him (again) until end VII.

Uruk, institutional

YOS 3, 103 letter, 6) *mi-nam-ma* SUKU$_6$.ḪA$_2$ 7) *ù* SIG$_2$.ḪA$_2$ *šá la* PN1 *ù* PN2 9) ^{LU_2}GAL 50-*ú a-na* 10) ^{LU_2}GAL.10-*ti*.MEŠ 11) *ta-ad-din*?

3. The early "urban" terminology: *zu'uzti šarri* and *ḫanšū*

The system of land for services was not an invention of the Neo-Babylonian kings, it had a long history behind itself. As far as can be seen the land was provided by the government against delivery of services and payments, but it was convenient for both parties that the services could be commuted into payments in silver.

The kings of the first half of the First Millennium had to deal with the effects of the tribalisation of the country caused by the entry of new population elements and the decline of the towns with their autochtonous population. That this was a cause of permanent stress need not be doubted and without a sound basis in agriculture the towns were doomed. Creation, or, minimally, strengthening of a town-based land holding group of people seems to have been one of the purposes of the policies of the kings of the period. An important element of this restructuring of urban land-holding was the *bīt ḫanšū,* "the fifty-estate". The information available does not amount to much over all, but it is perhaps just sufficient to suggest a structure linking institutions, individuals and land into one urban based system. Such a system would be status and wealth linked and changes in wealth would inevitably result in changes in the manner of land holding. It is obvious that this land was being bought and sold without reference to the organiser of the schemes, the king, even though it seems evident, especially in Borsippa, that people tried to retain their family link with this land. The parcels sold are sometimes tiny. The only text from Nippur quoted links a royal land division, having a share in a *ḫanšū* and *ilku* obligations, as observed earlier. This is crucial information. The outlines are thus relatively clear.

The question is how the *eširtu* we discussed already and the *ḫanšū,* "fifty" were connected. There are several possibilities, and it is likely that "fifty" had different meanings, depending on the context in which it was used. That a *rab ḫanšū* was a headman over a group of "50" workers seems to be inescapable from, for instance, the text published in PSBA 7.[10] But though the "military" groups of 50[11], divided into sub-groups of 10, may have been a reality, this reality must be reconciled with the fact that the "fifties" as pieces of land are consistently associated with family names and occur in standard sizes in which "fifty (cubits)" at least occasionally plays a role. These are the "fifties" of, for instance, the Ṭabīḫus or the Esagilmansums, and even if they had owners outside the family they could

---

9 The edge mentions a commodity measured in talents which "he" will give to Tukulti-Bēl (s Šamaš-iddina Rabā-ša-Ninurta) in the *bīt šukutte* on behalf of Bēl-ēṭer. Not understood.

10 Material quoted CAD Ḫ p. 81 *ḫanšū* in *rab-ḫanšū* where Neo-Assyrian occurrences support NB letters like RA 11, 116 and YOS 3, 103.

11 The word of course indicates an ideal type of uniform unit seize, the reality, certainly after an amount of time, will have been that the unit led by PN is only traditionally a "*ḫanšū*". In a sense it can be compared to the old English Hundred as a (there) geographically based element of military and political organisation.

still be called the *ḫanšū* of the *bītu* of the family concerned. VS 5, 140 and Ash AB 140 are good examples. These families, as discussed elsewhere, often occupied prebendal functions and belonged in general to the local elite. Originally such a piece of land would have comprised a fixed stretch, peculiar to the scheme in which it originated, with one short side along the principal source of water and with or without a specified length. That is: it stretched to the point where it met some pre-existing boundary, or possibly a specially constructed drainage ditch (*makallû*) or a dam (*kilâtu*) at the lower short side, phenomena occurring with a certain regularity in connection with the *ḫanšū* land in the texts. The principle is made especially clear by AnOr 9, 1 and directly related texts, where the "owner" of each of these strips of land is called a *rab ḫanšū*.

The narrow shape of the fields virtually precludes the possibility that it was exploited by settling the presumed fifty underlings of the *rab ḫanšū* on it. But it is certain that *ḫanšu*s could participate in more than one scheme near the same town.[12] The possibility that *ḫanšū* in the context of the title *rab ḫanšū* represents a grouping of *eširtu*s, "military" structures which had in turn a basis in the family structure, is at least as likely as that the term *ḫanšū* may represent the basic block of land in a land division scheme. That the land *ḫanšū* is based on division is indicated by the regular size of the plots belonging to a specific scheme. TCL 12, 11 is a prime example and it could even suggest that, on principle, the term *ḫanšū* indicated a basic unit of fifty of the (from scheme to scheme variable?) blocks of land on which land divisions were founded, in this particular case a strip of 250 cubits wide. This idea is reinforced by the fact that an *eširtu*, one fifth of a "fifty", measured 50 cubits in this text. On the other side of the scale in a land division came the *limū*, "thousand", which was assigned, it would seem, to (urban) institutions.[13] Only the publication of more material can solve the problem, but land division and mobilisation structure are related. At least in Borsippa, shares in a land division scheme were also indicated as *zittu*/ḪA.LA, both with and without indication of the size. This suggests again that in a particular scheme there was a basic standard size.

That the land *ḫanšū* and the groups called *ḫanšū* were somehow linked in the person of the *rab ḫanšū* seems to be certain. In Uruk the same *rab ḫanšū* was apportioned land in different land division schemes in the neighbourhood of the town at roughly the same time and in Borsippa land in different *tamirtu*s is linked by belonging to the same family *ḫanšū*.

The concepts *zu'uzti šarri*, *ḫanšū ša* PN or *ša bīt* PN constitute the relevant (early) terminology, which persists sparingly until the reign of Darius I. Land in *ḫanšū* PN is called *zu'uzti šarri*. The texts published by Jursa in his book on the Bēl-rēmanni archive suggest a regular connection between *eširtu*-obligations and belonging to a specific (extended) family. These texts date to the reign of Darius. In the earlier period (Marduk-apal-iddina to Šamaš-šum-ukīn and onwards, but there are earlier indications) we find a link between family and the holding of property belonging to a land division scheme. Where we have information, especially in Borsippa, the families concerned belong to the group of

---

[12] Note also that the Dilbat text OECT 10, 395 indicates that the width of an individual holding could be measured in furrows, in this case four, which might represent no more than 2,5 m. and that in TuM 2/3, 12 a subdivision according into cubits is referred to: "one third of a share consisting of 18 cubits", no more than 6 cubits, 3 meters (for 2,5 *š*). Other plots measured in cubits are larger, 13 or 16 cubits occur. In these cases the length of the plot is not specified. In TuM 2/3, 14 we find 2 $SILA_3$, 60 cubits, 15 m^2, for 4.25 *š*,, which results in a price per kor of 6 mina 22.5 *š*, which is considerable, if not exorbitant.

[13] That a "thousand" plays a role in the system of surveying belonging to these land divisions is probably echoed by the *makallû ša šēpīt* 5 *lim* found outside the Uraš Gate in Babylon in Dar 152 and related texts edited by C. Wunsch recently. This suggest a rather modest scheme at this locality.

prebendal families of the sanctuaries.[14] The later texts mentioning *ešírtus* and shared obligations, the providing of "soldiers", deal in Sippar, as Jursa has pointed out, with members of the same extended family, who were closely related, brothers and their sons for instance. Though these people belonged to prebendal families in Sippar, the *ḫanšû* land seems to have become institutional property there, at least according to the information available.

The members of the prebendal families acquitted their obligations in general by payments in silver, but as the *ešírtu* texts published by Jursa indicate, there was at least a vestige of actual service: a member of an *ešírtu* actually was issued a bow. Nbn 480 is a rare text in which a *rab ḫanšû* actually officiates, some service obligation is certainly involved in the payment recorded, but not even that is completely certain. The PSBA text refers to actual service, but for a specialised category of people.

The *ḫanšû* families were in many cases known owners of prebends. They therefore should have enjoyed, in theory, *kidinnu* status, be free from all sorts of corvée duties. Such prebendal families should, as a rule, not be connected with service land. Yet there are some clear, important exceptions. In Babylon we have the Nappāḫus, in Borsippa the Rē'u-alpi family -perhaps only in the figure of Rēmūt-Nabû s Nabû-mukīn-zēr-, and in Ur the Gallābus. These were prebendal families, but that does not automatically imply that the branch concerned with service obligations also possessed the prebends, or that there existed a *ḫanšû* to which its name was connected[15] and in which various members of the family possessed land. The individual case matters. Nabû-mukīn-zēr was involved with prebends[16] and so was his son[17], but he also paid for *ilku*, *urāšu* and related matters.[18] In this manner we are forced to accept that *kidinnu* status had not much practical effect, at any rate not when the obligations were the result of holdings belonging to land for service schemes. In turn that would make taxation of prebendal income only a minor step. When Nabonidus appointed his daughter in Ur he allowed freedom of *ilku* obligations to the personnel, but by the Persian period *kidinnu* and related concepts had become obsolete, possibly exactly because those who might aspire to it had accepted shares in land for service schemes.

zu'uzti šarri and *ḫanšû* can be regarded as parts of the "early" urban land division terminology, which still persisted in the Achaemenid period in certain old Babylonian towns, but the type of land division which lies behind the terms was not being used as a policy tool anymore, as far as we can see. We can regard the land transactions of the Egibis, especially those near the Ḫarri-Piqudu, but also elsewhere on the right bank near the Nar-Eššu as a kind of dissolution phase of the local *ḫanšû* schemes.[19] The newer terminology using at first predominantly *ilku* and then *qaštu* and the associated terms took over, a process starting already under the Chaldean kings. But that terminology belonged primarily to the settling of military, non-urban, and at least partially ethnic, groups, which constituted a kind of second phase in a policy in which land division played a major role, even though

---

[14] That means that the family archives concerned not only contain texts dealing with their *ḫanšû*-land but also with their prebends. In information from Dilbat individuals dominate.

[15] BE 8/1 44 land *ina* 50-*e ša* Nabû-zēr-ibni s Nabû-apal-iddina Rē'u-alpi.

[16] Text published by J. MacGinnis AoF 26, 1999, no. 3 and AfO 38/9 no. 12. Also BE 8/1 103, 106. This makes the inclusion of the flour text VS 6, 114 among the *ilku* texts, as suggested under (flour and) *ilku* on account of the rare *ḫirigalû* flour somewhat dubious.

[17] TÉBR no. 84, VS 5 102, BE 8/1 117.

[18] Mich 26; BM 82666, 82716, VS 6, 150.

[19] Cf. the discussion by C. Wunsch, 2000 p. 161ff. concerning land outside the Uraš Gate in Babylon near Litamu.

the traditional term of *ilku* could be used without problem in indicating the obligations of holders of *ḫanšū* land.

As remarked, *ḫanšū* in Sippar texts constitutes a problem. In other towns *ḫanšū* can be connected with families, though sometimes especially an individual member of a -known- family is specially connected with the land. In Sippar we do find the individuals connected with the *ḫanšū*s, but not the family link, there is only a Bīt-(p)Ikla'a in CT 56, 538. BM 79746, however, published by Jursa, strongly suggest that *ḫanšū* land in a particular locality had been assigned to a specific group of temple personnel, those prebendaries designated as *ērib bīti*s. Such an assignment to a specific status group must somehow remind us of the (later) *ḫadru*s. It is of importance, because it stresses again that these prebendal families were the important families in the towns in the period that the *ḫanšū* land divisions took place.[20] The main problem is that in the texts from Ebabbar *ḫanšū* land, even though it is indicated as *ḫanšū ša* PN, is exploited in the for the temple estate normal manner by the administration of Ebabbar. Perhaps this Sippar *ḫanšū*-scheme was devised in a period when such schemes were a thing of the past. We can perhaps assume that certain parcels had come into the hands of the administration, but that would not explain the fact that all -known- *ḫanšū* land pertains to the administration in Sippar. The name *ḫanšū ša* PN, and especially "large *ḫanšū*" and "upper" or "middle *ḫanšū*", will thus indicate no more than a locality. Such "geographical" indications for *ḫanšu* land are not prominent elsewhere. The Sippar *ḫanšū* land is found especially, as Jursa has noted, in a locality called Til-Qaqulli, which he connects with the neighbourhood of Āl-Šamaš, a centre of temple held property.

a. *šuzu'uzti šarri*

Babylon

Bertin 1007 22 V Ššk 18, Land, damaged, A.QAR URU?/GARIM?-Li-ta-mu *ina* KI.TA ^{GI}Ḫu-ṣe-tú-šá-Bēl-ēṭer *ina šu-zu-'u-uz-ti šá* LUGAL.DU (= Sargon II), neighbours, short side on the Euphrates, broken.

Nippur

TuM 2/3 132 17 VI Asb 36, Šamaš-erība Šarrāni to Arrabu Šarrāni: 2) ... ḪA.LA-*ka ina zu-'u-uz-ti* LUGAL 3) *ina* 50?-*še-e šá Nabû-zēr-ibni a-ḫu ina lìb-bi* 4) *bi-nam-ma il-ku-šú it-ti-ka* 5) *lul-lik.*

TuM 2/3 280 27 IV Ššk x, Small fragment. Share in plantation of *di-ku-ti* palm trees, *ina* 3) [*zu-'u*]-*uz-ti* LUGAL field etc.

b. *ḫanšū*-land

Babylon

"early Neo-Babylonian texts"

TCL 12 11 20 IX Ššk 14, Bēl-emuq-kullabi Saggilāia *šākin ṭēmi* of Babylon buys 1) 1-*en* 50-*ú i-na* GARIM-B/Maḫe *šá pi-i* GARIM-Litamu 2) 250 $KUŠ_3$ SAG *ul-tu* GU_2 (Nar)Purattu 3) *a-di še-pit* 1 DANNA 1-*en* 50-*ú* 4) *i-na* UGU Nār-Kiš^{KI} 250 $KUŠ_3$ SAG 5) *ù* 1-*it* 10-*ti* 50 $KUŠ_3$ SAG PAP 3 *me* SAG 6) *ul-tu* UGU Nār-Kiš^{KI} *a-di ma-kal-le-e šá* 7) ^{LU_2}TIN.TIR^{KI} PAP 2 50.MEŠ 1-*it* 10-*ti* "of Bēl-epuš Asû" from Bēl-mušallim Irani.

BM 64162[21] 16 I Ššk 19, 1) 100 *ina* 1 $KUŠ_3$ SAG.KI GU_2 I_7-UD.KIB.NUN^{KI} 2) *ina šu-pal* Ḫuṣṣēti-šá-^{d}Bēl-ēṭer *ina* 50-*e šá* Nabû-ēreš Sin-ili.

VS 5 4 28 X Kand 18, Nabû-šum-ibni s Bēl-iddina Eppeš-ili buys 4 kor of a date plantation near the Zababa-Gate from Zēria, Marduk-šum-ibni and Nādin, sons of Bēl-aḫḫê-iddina

[20] The reference to Ḫumāia, Cilicians, as being settled in the neighbourhood is of some interest. Land shared out to townsmen and to a foreign ethnic group, who elsewhere often constituted a *ḫadru*, bordered on one another.

[21] E. Weidner AfO 16, 1952-3, p. 36-7.

Eppeš-ili for 19 mina of silver and 30 *š* as an extra. From the same persons he buys 30 kor of arable in the (15) 50-ú elû in the field at the Bēl-Gate on the Nār-Gubbat for $7^1/_2$ mina(?). Damaged.

VS 5 3 6 X Kand 1, Bēl-aḫḫê-iddina s Bēl-le'u Eppeš-ili buys 30 kor of newly broken land in 1) ... 50-ú kas-lu![22] elû, GARIM-Bāb-ša-Bēl on the bank of the Nār-Gubbat, province of Babylon, from Erišu s Nādin Arad-Nergal for 3 mina 45 *š* of silver. Retro with VS 5, 4.

Egibi

W, E I 116 16 V Nbn 8, land which NAI 2) ... *ina* 50-*e šá* Ša-Nabû-šu, situation, *imḫur*, more land which IMB *imḫur* and another parcel from a *nudunnu* will not be objects of claims by FPN and FPN2, her daughter, and FPN 3 and FPN4, her granddaughters, IMB will not complain regarding a further parcel.

Dar 152 29 XII Dar 4, date plantation at A.QAR (Āl-)Litamu outside the Uraš-Gate in Babylon, the eastern lower side being 8) ... *ma-ak*!*-lu-u šá* 50.MEŠ *šá še-pit* 5-*lim*, (W, E I 181), demarcation *še-pít* 5-*lim* also in Dar 227 (3 VII Dar 7) line 15. (W, E I 184).

Dar 335 28 X Dar 12, (blank) amount of dates, *imittu* 1) ... *šá* 50-*e šá* Itti-makû-Bēl s Nabû-zēr-ukîn Miṣirāia *šá* Dūr-ša-karābi 3) *šá* MNA 4) *ina muḫ-ḫi* PN 5) *i-'i-lu* PN2 paid on orders of PN. (Dūr-ša-Karābi was situated in the Nār-Eššu area). (W, E I 205)

Babylon neighbourhood, (*pi-ḫat* E_2.DURU$_5$.BI$_2$.SA$_6$^{KI})

RA 83 p. 153 x x Nbk 6, exchange of 120 kor of land situated between the Euphrates and 12-13 (= 20-1) *ma-kal-li-e ša* 50.MEŠ *ša* ^{LU_2}TIN.TIR^{KI}.MEŠ.

Borsippa

Bēliau-file

VS 3 104 21 V Dar 9, *imittu* dates undivided land 5) .... *šá* 50-[*e*] *šá* E_2-Sag.íl.man.sum.

VS 3 119 16 V Dar 18, *imittu* field 3) *šá* GARIM-E_2-Ḫabṣirtu *šá* 50-*ú šá* E_2-Ṣillaia.

VS 5 92 15 V Dar 20, *imittu* 1) ... *ina* 50-*ú* 2) *šá* E_2-^{LU_2}GIR$_2$.LA$_2$ *ú-ga-ri* GARIM-E_2-Ḫabṣirtu.

Gallābu-file

BM 85641 [23] 7 I Nbn 15, land in (Āl-)Dunnidē *ina* 50-*e šá* E_2-^{LU_2}NAGAR security for dates, barley and silver.

Ḫuṣābu file

TuM 2/3 106 26 I Nbk 15, land 7) *ina* 50-*e šá* E_2-Ḫuṣab owned by members of that family security.

BE 8/1 43 13 II Nbn 3, land 2) ... *i-na* 50-*e ša* E_2-^{LU_2}[SIPAD.ANŠE].KUR.RA bought by a member of the Ḫuṣābu family.

Iliia-file

RA 10 (Pl 6) 46 8 XI Šmšk 4, 1) 50-*ú šá* Nummuru s ^{LU_2}NAGAR *šá* GARIM-Ḫallat sold by members of the Naggāru family for 5 *š* to a member of the Ilia family.

(Ea-)ilūta-bani-files, early texts

TCL 12 9 3 XII Šmsk 7, 1) 13 KUŠ$_3$ *šá* 50-*e šá* Balassu Ilūta-bâni 2) *ina* 50-*e* [*šá* Iddina-aḫ]a [Ilū]ta-bani 3) *šá ina šu-p*[*al* Āl-B]ēl-iqbi, sold to members of the Iddina-Papsukkal family for 6 *š*.

TuM 2/3 11 19 IX Šmšk 8, 1) 1-*it* ḪA.LA *šá* Nabû-aḫa-ēreš Ilūta-bani] 2) *ina* 50-*e šá* Iddina-aḫa Ilūta-bani 3) *ina šu-pal* Āl-Bēl-iqbi, 16 KUŠ$_3$ *šá* 50-*e*, sold to members Iddin-Papsukkal family for 6 *š*.

TuM 2/3 12 5 III Šmšk 10, 1) *šal-šu šá* ḪA.LA 18 KUŠ$_3$ *šá* 50-*e ina lìb-bi* 2) *šá* Nabû-ereš *ul-tu* UGU 3) Nār-Barsip *a-di ki-la-a-ti* 4) *ina* 50-*e šá* Iddina-aḫa Ilūta-bâni, sold to a member of Nappāḫu family by a member of Iddina-Papsukkal family for $2^1/_2$ *š*.

---

22 Emendation AHw III, Ergänzung p. 1567a, reference M. Stol.

23 R. Zadok, IOS 18, 1998, p.285-6.

Ash A 163 9 x x, [share] PN Gallābu family in 2) ... GARIM-Qut[anu *u*] 3) GARIM-Ḫallatu *ina* 50-*e šá* Iddina-aḫa fam. Ilūta-bâni 4) *ul-tu* UGU Nār-Edu *a-di ki-l*[*a-ti*, bought by a member of the Ilūta-bani family from a member of the Gallābu family.

BRM I 35 x x Šmšk 12, x ḪA.LA.MEŠ of four brothers of the Ea-ilūta-bani family 4) *a-di ḫir-ši-i ina* 50-*e šá* Il-lu-ú-a 5) Ea-ilūta-bani *ina* E_2-Ḫa-'a-la-a 6) *ul-tu* x x ⌈Í7⌉[Pu-rat-ti⌉, rest lost.

Puḫḫūru Ilūta-bani and sons

TuM 2/3 23 7 X Šmšk 12, 3) 2 PI ŠE.NUMUN *ina* 50-*e šá* Il(!)-lu-[ú-a] exchanged by Puḫḫūru (Ilūta-bani) with the *šapīru* of the brewers for 12) 2? ḪA.LA.MEŠ *ina* GARIM-Gura'bi 13) *ina* 50-*e šá* Suppē-Bēl Ilūta-bani.

Ashm A 131 9 x [Šmsk] 12, land 3) *šá ina* Bāb-Bitqa-šá-Azili 4) 50-*e šá* Il(!)-lu-ú-a Ilūta-bani bought by Puḫḫūru from other members of the Ilūta-bani family for $1^3/_4$ *š*.

TCL 12 6 16 III Kand 7, 0.0.2 date plantation 2) *ina* GARIM-Bāb-kirāte *ina* 50-*e* 3) *šá* Suppē-Bēl Ilūta-bani sold to Puḫḫūru by other members of the Ilūta-bani family for 1 mina KB, with two kor of barley as an extra.

TuM 2/3 14 21 VI Kand 13, 2 $SILA_3$ ŠE.NUMUN *ina* <A.?> $ŠA_3$ Nār-Labiri 2) *ina* Bāb-kira *ina* 50-*e šá* Il-lu-ú-a Ilūta-bani, sold to Puḫḫūru by other members of the Ilūta-bani family for $4^1/_4$ *š* of silver.

TuM 2/3 5 16 I Nbp 16, arrangement concerning inheritance of (more) land situated like that in TuM 2/3, 14.

Ash A 98 23 VIII Nbk 8, 1) 2-*ta* $ŠU^{II}$.MEŠ *šá* ḪA.LA GARIM-Qutanu 2) *ina* 50-*e šá* Iddina-aḫa Ea-ilūta-bani 3) *šá* PN2 Ilūta-bani 5) *ù a-ḫi* ḪA.LA *šá* PN3 Ilūta-bani, with identical location, bought from PN4 Ilūta-bani by PN5 Ilūta-bani for 21 *š*., total summarised as (17) 1 ḪA.LA *ù* 6-'*u* ḪA.LA.

TuM 2/3 153 3+ VIbis Nbk 41, at GARIM-Ḫallat, dates *imittu* 2) ... *šá* 50-*e šá* E_2-Ilūta-bâni due to sons of Puḫḫūru Ilūta-bâni in VIII.

Mušezib-Bēl s Zēr-Bābili Ilūta-bani

YOS 17 8 24 VIII Nbk III 0, 1) ŠE.NUMUN *šá ina* 50!-*e šá* E_2.sagíl[-mansum][24] 2) *šá* Mušezib-Bēl A-*šú šá* Zēr-Bābili 3) Attabani, who grants a lease for 2 years.

TuM 2/3 6 7 IX Nbk III 0, dates, land *šá ina* GARIM-Qutanu *ina* 50-*e šá* E_2-Ilūta-bani *ul-tu* Nār-x-E_2.GAL *a-di ki-la-a-ti šá* 50-*e*.MEŠ, transferred to wife.

NBC 8376 18 X Dar 7, dates 2) *šá* GARIM-Ḫa[llat *ina* 50]-*e šá* [x] 3) *pu-ut* ḪA.LA (context lost) to be paid in VII.

TCL 13 189 11 I Dar 12, barley, *šib-šú* $A.ŠA_3$ *šá* GARIM-Ḫallatu 2) *šá ina* 50 E_2-Ilūta-bani *šá* PN1 *ina* UGU PN2, *gugallu* not paid.

Ea-ilūta-bani texts not connected with main files

NBC 8400 11 X Nbp 14, land 3) *ina* GARIM-[x x] *ina* 50-*e šá* 4) Il-lu-ú-a Ilūta-bani leased for planting onions.

TuM 2/3 111 8 XII Nbk 27, 10 *š* of silver, half the silver of PN due from PN2 5) A_2 2-*ta* $ŠU^{II}$.MEŠ ḪA.LA *šá* PN2 6) *šá ina* 50-*e šá* E_2-Ilūta-bani *šá bat-ti*-x[x] 7) *šá* E_2-Bi-be-e *ul-tu* 1 *me* 40 [$KUŠ_3$?] 8) *a-di ki-la-a-tú* at the disposal of PN 1. Antichretic clause, but PN 2 will pay (a fixed share in the harvest) to PN1.

Ili-bani files

Ash A 95 14 VIb Nbk 41, (dates) 2) ... *šá* 50-*e* GAL-*i ša ina* UGU(?) Nār-Eššu, 10) *ka-a-ri* 11) *e-ṭir* $^{LU_2}GU_2$.GAL *ul e-ṭir*.

TuM 2/3 137 4 V Camb 2, 1) ŠE.NUMUN *šá* 50-*e* $ŠA_3$ E_2-Bi-ib-bi-e 2) *šá* PN leased; 8) *dul-lu* $^{LU_2}GU_2$.GAL-*ú-tu* 9) *e-ṭer*, follow various specific obligations relating to the palm trees.

Ili-bani unclear file

TuM 2/3 15 28 II Nbk 18, date plantation 2) ... *šá ina tam-tim ina* 50-*e šá* E_2-Ilūta-bani which PN (Damqa family) sold to a member of the Ilūta-bani family.

---

24 According to Joannès 1989, p. 326.

Nanāḫu unclear file

TCL 12 30 13 I Nbk 11, date plantation, first parcel 2) *ina* 50-*e šá* E$_2$-^{LU_2}AD.KID *ul-tu* UGU 3) I$_7$ *a-di* UGU KASKAL^{II} LUGAL, 4) UŠ AN.TA 50-*e šá* E$_2$-Nik-ka-a-a, second parcel same 50-*e* UŠ KI.TA 5) 50-*e šá* E$_2$ La-ḫa-šú, third parcel next to the same 50-*e*.

Rē'u-alpi file

Mich 54 2 X Nbn 2, date plantation 2) *šá ina* 50-*e ša* E$_2$ ^{LU_2}SIPAD.GU$_4$.MEŠ, additional payment after transfer for debt within the Rēu-alpi family.

BE 8/1 44 7 V Nbn 4, date plantation 2) ... *ina* GARIM-Ḫa-mar *ina* 50-*e ša* Nabû-zēr-ibni s Nabû-apal-iddina Rē'u-alpi sold to member of the Maqartum family.

BM 82607[25] 1 XI Dar 5, 1) ŠE.NUMUN *šá pa-na-at* KA$_2$.GAL-*tam-tim ina* 50-*e šá* ^{LU_2}*mu-ban-nu-ú*.MEŠ, element of *nudunnu*, same plot in BE 8, 108, 28 XII Dar 6.

BE 8/1 108 28 XII Dar 6, first parcel same plot as in BM 82607, second parcel 6) ... *i-na* KA$_2$ Ḫarri-šá-Nabû-šum-ukīn (s Apla Rē'u-alpi) *šá i-na* 50-*e šá* E$_2$-Kidin-Sin.

Other

Ash A 83 24 II Šmsk 4, land, share of three persons, of whom at least two DUMU.MEŠ E$_2$-Aqar-Nabû 3) ... *ina tam-tim ina* 50-*e šá* DUMU.MEŠ Aqar-Nabû, divided.

BE 35275[26] 22 XI Nbk 11, rev. 2) land *ina* 50-*e šá* E$_2$-AD-na-a sold on behalve of treasury of Nabû after confiscation.

VS 3 24 26 I Nbk 39, dates land *šá a-ḫa-la*.MEŠ *šá* Nar-Eššu 3) *šá ina* 50!-*e* (text 40-*e*) *šá* E$_2$-SAG.IL$_2$.A.AN, *imittu* imposed by PN1 and PN2 ^{LU_2}GU$_2$.GAL.MEŠ *šá* PN3, PN4 and PN5(?), received.

VS 5 36 12 VIb Cyr 2, land GARIM-x-x-da-qa 3) *ina* 50-*e šá* Nabû-mutakkil, share of PN. Context not clear.

Ash AB 241 21 XII Cyr 6, date plantation A.QAR GARIM-KA$_2$-Su-ú-ru 2) *pi-ḫa-ti* Barsip^{KI} *i-na* 50-*e šá* E$_2$-Iddina-Papsukkal, sold by a member of the Aqar-Nabû family and his wife from the Ḫuṣābu family to a member of the Aḫḫiutu family.

VS 5 140 date lost, land in Al-Šá-Nabû[šu] [*ina* 50]-*e šá* Nabû-rēmēni family Adnaia, share of member of Šá-ṭabtišu family sold to member of Kidin-Sin family.

BM 82609[27] 19 XI Dar 1, various parcels of land, 5) *šá* E$_2$-^{LU_2}KUR.GAR.RA. MEŠ i-*na* 50-*e šá* ŠE.NUMUN-*šú*; 6) ... *ina* 50-*e šá* DUMU pa-ni-a-su-šu-du; 9) ... *ina* 50-*e šá* A ^{LU_2}SIMUG.

Dilbat

OECT 10 391 26 VI Bēl-ibni 2, date plantation 2) *ina* UGU Ḫarri-šá-Lagamal 3) *i-na* 50-*e šá* Iddina s Zākir.

OECT 10 392 29 XI Bēl-ibni 2, date plantation 2) *ina* UGU Ḫarri-šá-(old break) 3) *ina* 50-*e šá* Iddina Eppeš-ili.

OECT 10 395 17 V Ash 7, 9) PAP 4 [*ši*]-*er-e-ti* ("furrows") *ina* GARIM-Kār-Uraš 10) *ina* 50-*e šá* Balāṭu s Numra(?).

BRM 1 38 15 IV Šmšk 20, 9 = 1) ... ŠE.NUMUN *ina* UGU GARIM(?)-Aṣunu 10) A.QAR Dilbat *ina* 50-*e šá* Iqbi-Uraš 11) A-*šú šá* Kidin (between lines 2 and 3: [A?] ^{LU_2}SIPAD.GU$_4$).

OECT 10 399 29 I Asbp 23, land planted with young date trees 2) *ina* GARIM-Bazia A.QAR Dilbat 3) *ina* 50-*e šá* Uraš-iddina s Saggilu.

Kiš

OECT 10, 3 25 VII Šmšk 10, land *ina* 50-*e* 2) *šá* Nabû-le'u dumu Lú-a(?) *šá i-na* 3) GARIM-Ḫa-a'-ḫu-šá-Marduk-šum-ibni dumu Lú-a-a, lower end on 9) ... *ma-kal-le-e šá* 50.MEŠ sold by Marduk-šum-ibni to a member of Eppeš-ili family.

OECT 10, 7 12 XII Šmšk 19, Babylon, land bordering on western side on 5) *ma-kal-le-e šá* 50.MEŠ, also in line 12.

---

25 M.T. Roth, The Material Composition of the Neo-Babylonian Dowry, AfO 36/37, 1989-99, App C, p. 53 no. 12.

26 E. Weidner, AfO 17, 1954-6, p. 1-5.

27 M.T. Roth, AOAT 222, no. 22. Some of the geographical names in this text are exceptional.

Nippur

TuM 2/3 132 17 VI Asbp 36, see sub *zu'uzti* LUGAL: 50?-*še-e šá* Nabû-zēr-ibni.

Sippar

CT 56 44+[28] (before Nbk 9), parcels of land "to be taken" by named persons: Ki-Šamaš; Nabû-BAD_3.MAḪ; Bēl-Ebbara-ibni; Šamaš-iddina s Ubar; Bēl-reṣūa; Nergal-aḫa-iddina; 50-*ú rabu-ú šá* Aḫušunu Ša-Nabû-šu; Aḫušunu s Arad-Nanna; Nabû[-x] and Bunene-ab-uṣur; mentions 50-*ú rabû* twice in broken context, once possibly indicating a surface of 10 kor.

VS 6 30 4 II Nbk 9, barley, *imittu* on ? Line 2 contained fixed amount of barley payable for 4 kor of land? 17) x land *še-pe-e-ti* 50-*ú*.MEŠ *šá* Šamaš-iddina; 19) total *a-mir-tu*$_4$ 18) *šá* 50-*ú*.MEŠ *pu-*[*u*?-]*tu*, date 22) *ina lìb-bi* ^{LU_2}UMBISAG *u* ^{LU_2}*man-di-di i-ni-ṭer*, followed by total general.

Nbk 131 18 I Nbk 22, delivery of barley: *imittu* of the *ikkarus* of Al-Šamaš, mentions amount together with share of the *errēšu*, who remain unnamed in several instances: Erišu with Nabû-zēr-ukīn *errēšu;* Isinnaja with unnamed; Bēlšunu with Šamaš-šum-ukîn; Bēl-ab-uṣur with unnamed; *šibšu* (+) *ešrû* payable by Šamaš-iddina s Balāṭu 10) for 50-*e šá* Nabû-tabni-uṣur at his disposal; Nabû-tabni-uṣur for *sa-pan ap-pa-ri*; 12) amount *ina* 50-*e* GAL-*i* Arad-x; Bēlšunu s x; rev. total due from *ikkarus* followed by that of the *errēšus*, (small) total of what the *errēšus* who "were with the *ikkarus*" had to pay; total of *errēšus* in Til-Qaqulu; total of the *ḫazannu*; small amounts of Nabû-mukīn-aḫi and Šamaš-mukīn-aḫi ^{LU_2}SAG.

BM 77841[29] x V Nbn 2, date *imittu* 3) amount 50-*ú šá* Arad-aḫḫēšu; 7) amount 50-*ú šá* x *šá muḫ-ḫi ap-pi*; 10) amount 50-*ú šá* Šamaš-aḫa-iddina, treated parallel with known localities: (Al-) Alku, Bīt-Diḫummu; Til-Qaqqul.

CT 57 300 28 x Nbn 3, dates delivered by [gardeners] of Šamas 50-*ú š*[*á* Ba-su-ru] ù Šamaš-mušēzib *id-di-nu.*

Cyr 34+Dar 370[30] 17 I Dar 14, III 25 PAP amount *ina* 50-*e*.[31]

BM 79746[32] 7 X Cyr 8, measurements *ḫarran šarri pu-ut* A.$ŠA_3$ 2) *šá* 50-MEŠ *šá* (A)l Til-Gubbu *šá* 3) $^{LU_2}KU_4.E_2$ ^{d}UTU, which the *šangû* measured; 7) 4400 *ul-tu* UGU 50-*e* 8) UGU-*ú šá* Šamaš-šum-līšir 9) s Nabû-šum-iddina Ile'i-Marduk to the lower border of Šamaš next to the Ḫummāia; 88 *aslu*; (mentions also 26 palm logs of PN in the hands of PN2).

BM 74422[33] 19 VI Camb kB 1, dates delivered to Šamaš 2) *šá* 50-*ú qab-lu-ú kišad* Puratti. (Prosopgraphical link with CT 57, 300)

BM 79128 2 IV Dar 19 see Chapter IV under *qaštu*.

CT 56 498 ?, fragment; mentions Napsari; *errēšus* with him; Nabû-zēr-iddina; *zitti* 50-*e ša* Aḫušunu; Šamaš-iddina s Balāṭu <*rab ikkarāti*>; Šamaš-aḫa-iddina; x s Kuna; x x *šá ḫa-am-ri.*

CT 56 538 ?, amount, factor *šá* PN (+ *e-la-'a:* "the field carries factor x") mentions Ebabbara-ibni; Bulṭā, Bēl-reṣūa, Nergal-aḫa-iddina "in the *ḫanšū* of Bît-Ik-la-'a; Šamaš-x *šangû*? of Inanna?? in the *ḫanšū* of Bīt-Ik-la-'a; Nabû-aialu; Šamaš-iddina s ?.

Uruk

Official

AnOr 9 1 Marduk-apal-iddina yr 4, 1) ^{LU_2}GAL 50.MEŠ *šá ina pa-ni* ^{pd}Marduk-apal-iddina 2) king of Babylon GU_2 ^{I_7}Ḫarri-šá-Marduk-apal-iddina 3) *ul-tu* UGU *mi-ṣir šá* E_2-Zu-gu-na-bu 4) 1 *me* 50.AM_3 *qaq-qa-ru ṣab-tu* 1 *lim* 1 *me* E_2.DINGIR 1 *lim* LUGAL; (colophon:) 96) PAP 91 ^{LU_2}GAL 50.MEŠ *šá ul-tu* ^{I_7}Ḫarri- 97) šá-Marduk-apal-iddina 1 me 50.AM_3 *qaq-qa-ru ṣab-tu-ma* 98) *a-di* UGU *ma-kal-le-e-šá*-50.MEŠ *šá* ^{I_7}Ḫarri-šá-Nabû-šum-līšir 99) *i-šad-da-du*, date.

---

[28] Edited Jursa 1995 p. 12f.

[29] Jursa 1995 no. 58.

[30] Edited Jursa 1995 p. 174ff

[31] I prefer a reading 50-*e* above TIR, especially on account of the connection with Til-Gubbi, see Jursa 1995 p.174.

[32] M. Jursa, ArOr 63, 1995 p. 153ff, see his comments, but the purpose of the note in the text on palm logs is obscure.

[33] From a transliteration by H. Bongenaar.

NBC 4848[34], 4 VIII M-a-i 4, 1) ^{LU_2}GAL 50.MEŠ *šá ul-tu* Ḫarri-šá-E$_2$.DINGIR[x x] (old break) 2) 70.AM$_3$ SAG.KI 5 *lim* [old break]; 35) 91 ^{LU_2}GAL 50.MEŠ *šá* 1-*en* ^{LU_2}GAL 50-*e* 4.4.1 ŠE.[NUMUN .x], situation damaged, date.

Private(?)
TCL 12 8 5 II Šmšk 1(?), land 9) *ki-ma* 50-*ú*.MEŠ *šá* Unug^{KI}-*a-a* 10) *a-na ru-da-a-a ú-ra-du*.
FLP 1533[35] 13 XII Nbk 17, (arable and date plantation on the (Nār-)Guzaru in the Uruk province) 50-*ú šá* PN s PN2 family Sin-leqqê-unini *šá* PN3 s PN4 of the same family *a-ki-i* E$_2$ AD-*bu-tu*(?) *ina tap-qer-tu*$_4$ (as paternal estate? through vindication) *ú-ter-ra* (short side of 250 *ammātu* next to PN1, length *a-ki-i* 50.MEŠ *i-šad-da-ad*) is bought (in Babylon) by Marduk-šākin-šumi s Taqīš-Gula Nūr-Sin from PN3 (only future claims by the family of PN3, and not of the whole Sin-leqqê-unnini family are declared invalid).
Mich 9 1 VI Nbk 18, silver of PN due from PN 2, 3 *me qaq-qa-ru ina muḫ-ḫi* ^{I_7}Ḫarri-^{P}x-[x] 4) *gim-ri šá* 50-*e-šú e-lu-ú ina* IGI PN; antichretic arrangement.
Bir 36 date lost, interest bearing amount of silver due from PN (sing.) 50-*ú-šú-nu šá* ^{LU_2}x(= re??)-x-x(= ma or ku??)-ta *maš-ka-nu*

4. A complication: *bīt ritti*[36]

A complication is caused by the term *bīt ritti*, often discussed and sometimes translated rather vaguely as "hereditary tenure". Its occurrence goes back to before the Persian period.[37] A discussion could be avoided here by stressing that there is nowhere any indication of tax related obligations imposed on holders of this type of land or possession on account of holding land indicated in his manner, or even that obligations could be imposed upon them at all, other than those resulting from a lease. Only arrangements regarding the payment of *ešrû* are occasionally found, but these refer to obligations towards the gods, which could be regarded as something separate from what was directly taxation related and due to the king. The *bīt ritti* is generally seen as a form of property which does not belong in the full sense of the word to the person who was the "holder".[38] The "real/nominal" owner could be a god, generally the main local deity, and the king also occurs occasionally. In Uruk in Hellenistic texts the god Anu is often the nominal owner of *bīt ritti* houses.[39] But normally land is simply a *bīt ritti* PN, without indication of a "real"

---

[34] A. Goetze, JCS 1, 1947, p. 352, who also gives a copy of the remaining part of the colophon of Crozer 201, either the same or still another variant exemplar of the *rab ḫanšû* list, which leaves open the possibility that these *rab ḫanšûs* received a third parcel. In NBC 4848 each *rab ḫanšû* is assigned a plot of 75 x 5000 cubits, equalling 175 BAN$_2$ of land, implying that a kor (still) equalled 60.000 square cubits.

[35] R.B. Dillard, Neo-Babylonian Texts from the John Frederick Lewis Collection of the Free Library of Philadelphia, Diss. Dropsie Univ., 1975, no. 15.

[36] Literature: H. Petschow, Neubabylonisches Pfandrecht, Berlin, 1956, p. 143f. ("geteiltes Eigentum"); Ries 1967 (with the observation that rights of the king or a temple are never stated to be a *b.r.*), p. 39; Joannès, 1982 p. 11ff.; Stolper 1985, p. 25; Van der Spek 1986, esp. p. 32-33; Jursa 1995 p. 120f.; Jursa 1998 Exkurs p. 13-18, CAD Q *bīt qaštu* p. 154-5; CAD R p. 387-8.

[37] Jursa 1995 p. 120, note 229, one text dating from Nabopolassar. Cf. also MacGinnis, Iraq 60, 1998, p. 214 comments on no. 8 for several texts going back to Nebuchadnezzar II.

[38] Sometimes the background is intriguing, as in Dar 328, on which C. Wunsch 2000b I p.80-1. The Egibis are not known as holders of land belonging to temple or king, other than as lease holders. The passage is "unusual" for Babylon private texts.

[39] We will not discuss the question of the houses or storerooms qualified as *bīt ritti*. Houses in the Inanna-gate district of Uruk are *makkūr Anu* and *bīt ritti* (of one of the parties in the document concerned). The store rooms are located in Irigal, where mention of a specific divine owner is omitted. These objects

owner. *bīt ritti* "sec", without some link with a person, significantly, does not occur in the texts, as far as can be seen. Real estate is not a *bīt ritti* but a *bīt ritti* PN.

Temples retained, or had regained, an explicit hold on the exploitation of certain *bīt ritti* land, presumably on that which had been their property, just as they were able to claim *ešrû* from it. In the Sippar text BM 101334 the holder of such a *bīt ritti* asks the authorities for the lease of the *ešrû* from that land, which means that he proposes to pay a fixed sum over land which he actually exploits. YOS 7, 38, already quoted in the previous chapter under *tēlītu*, is probably an arrangement imposed by the administration of Eanna in Uruk. A *gugallu* was appointed over land of Eanna belonging to someone's *bīt ritti* with the obligation to deliver the *imittu* imposed, together with various other stipulations. There is also a decision regarding various other *bīt ritti*s. In this case Eanna seems to have had effective administrative jurisdiction over *bīt ritti*s which presumably were located on land which originally had belonged to it, but it would seem that the holders of the *bīt ritti*s were not even involved in the arrangements. BIN 1, 111 also from Uruk is a case in which a *bīt ritti* belongs to a lease granted by a temple. In Dar 427, in Sippar, the relations are singularly complicated: the owner was Šamaš, but though it was the *bīt ritti* of his *širku* Marduka, it belonged to the rent farm of Bulṭā, who leased it to someone else for three years. The temple had thus been able to include this land in a rent farm arrangement. Jursa refers to a number of texts in which Ebabbar draws income from leasing *bīt ritti* land of certain persons. In these cases the rights of these persons are, it would seem, completely vestigial.

In BE 8/1, 132 a lease of land is given which was the *bīt ritti* of a slave but belonged to the *bīt qašti* of his master. In the Murašû archive a distinction is made between *bīt ritti* and land held as a bow fief, as a *maškanu*, "security", probably in an antichretic arrangement, and, once each, as *uzbāri* or *bāri šarri.* These terms are found together in PBS 2/1, 62, where the bow land was explicitly excluded from the lease. BE 9, 25 is exceptional in that the person who demands a lease asks permission to keep his own *bīt ritti*, his *eqel našparti*[40] and his *bīt maškanāti*. *bīt ritti* can belong to a bow fief (BE 8/1, 132) or it can explicitly not be a bow fief (PBS 2/1 62), in three cases it is contrasted with *maškanu* land (PBS 2/1, 62 and BE 9, 25 and 67), so this had probably a different status, presumably such land still was regarded primarily as the property of the person who had handed it over as an antichretic pledge. On temple estates *ešrû* was due from a *bīt ritti*, but in BE 9, 45 that was regarded explicitly as not being the case. *bāri* and *uzbāri šarri* land are different in BE 9, 67 and PBS 2/1, 62, but they pertain to the king, who is occasionally the ultimate owner of a *bīt ritti*. The overall impression must be that a *bīt ritti* is only that what the persons concerned want to include. That a *bīt ritti* could be exploited by its "holder" is clear from the fragment BM 10334, where this holder agrees with the authorities of Ebabbar concerning a fixed annual payment in dates and barley for the *ešrû* due from him.

The holder of a *bīt ritti* was to all probability someone who held the land, or other property, in order to exploit it, perhaps even to built his house on it, but that was not always the case in a practical sense. It could be land burdened with military obligations, but that was not a direct result of it being or becoming the *bīt ritti* of someone. *bīt ritti* in itself does not automatically imply obligations to others,[41] though the holder is not or needs not be the

can be sold. Land as a *bīt ritti* possibly occurs in an early Seleucid context. Cf. Doty 1977 p.145ff. In a specific context Van der Spek has concluded that there was little difference between owning a house and holding it as a *bīt ritti*.

40 What *eqel našparti* is in this sequence is not completely clear, it is land on which a person has "some business". *našpartu* PN *alāku* is "to do what PN orders", it has no specific military connotations.

41 As already correctly observed by Stolper 1985 p. 25 note 97.

owner, occasionally the rights involved seem to have lapsed in practice. Perhaps this "neutrality" regarding obligations and rights represents the essence of the term *bīt ritti*: the specific purpose of the term is to leave the strict juridical status of the rights the holder has on the property unspecified. The holder has undefined rights and there is even the possibility that the property consisted of holdings of different status. This could be the case especially in the Murašû texts.[42] The particular rights the holder had, could be leased, sold, certainly if the ultimate owner was mentioned, or used otherwise: for the purpose of the document no specification was required, or the specification differed for the various elements involved, which precluded the application of a more specific term. *bīt ritti* is therefore not a type of holding comparable to, for instance, *bīt qašti*. Applying the term was a convenient manner of avoiding difficult specifications which were irrelevant in the context of the transaction concerned. It is once more a kind of catch all phrase, it means no more than "holdings (as far as they are) in the hands of PN", even though practically they could be held by someone else or an institution. As we noticed already a *bīt ritti* has no raison d'être without someone specific being involved.[43]

Babylon[44]

Nbn 7 11 VI Nbn 0, at ?. 5.5 (sic) kor(?) of dates of the *bīt rit!-ti* 2) *šá* Kiddia and Sin-tultabsi-lišīr 3) *u šá* Bakua *šá ina* Gur-ḫu-ba-an-ni (?) 4) *i-mit-tu*$_4$ of Zēr-ukīn at the disposal of Šamaš-iddina s Nabû-nādin-aḫḫê *bēl piqitti* of Bēl-uballiṭ, are due from Zēr-ukīn s Nabû-tabni-uṣur and Aḫimme s Gigia in VIII.

Dar 328 19 V Dar 12+, at Dūr-ša-karābi[45] dates, *imittu* on land, situation, 3)[*a-d*]*i* E$_2$ KIŠIB *šá* MNA due from a member Sin-ili family, guaranteed by a member of Miṣirāia family.

Sippar

Šangû-Šamaš

CTMMA 3 93[46] 27 VI Dar 35, land at GARIM-Bir-ili, lease of land of PN, at the disposition of PN2, the *bīt ritti* of PN3, are transferred on a 20 yrs.(?) lease to PN4.

Ardija Balīḫu

NBC 6170[47] 19 VI Camb 7, dates, imittu on 2) *bīt ritti* PN1 NIG$_2$.GA ^{d}Bēl 3) *šá* ŠU^{II} PN2 and PN3, members of the Balīḫu family, are due from PN4 and PN5, a *širku* of Marduk in VIII.

Other

VS 5 55 Camb 7, A.ŠA$_3$ NIG$_2$.GA LUGAL *ina* (location?) E$_2$ *as-pa-tu*$_4$ E$_2$ KIŠIB PN.[48]

Institutional Sippar, sample only:

CT 55 75[49] 15 II Nbn x, barley x [of the] 2) E$_2$ *rit-ti š*[*á* PN] 3) *e-lat eš-ru-ú šá* ^{LU}$_2$x-[x x] 4) *ina muḫ-ḫi* PN, PN2..., they will pay.

---

42 Cf. also Jursa 1995 p. 120 note 230, BM 75502, text 2 in Jursa 1998, "ein recht komplexes Gebilde".

43 Why such an undefined holding would be called a *bīt ritti* and not, for instance, a *bīt qāti*, in the same manner as someone has a hold on his *ṣāb qātē*, is another question, but perhaps the term *bīt qāti* had too explicit "architectural" overtones.

44 These quotations are extremely selective.

45 This is in the Nār-Eššu area, which was old *ḫanšû* territory, see under *ḫanšû*. This fits in with the fact that *gizzatu* of the king constitutes the lower limit of the land in Dar 321 = TCL 13 190, W E I 202, line 8. See under *gizzatu*.

46 Quoted from Jursa Bēl-rēmanni.

47 Transcription H. Bongenaar.

48 See discussion under *bīt qašti*.

49 Mentioned M.A. Dandamayev, OrNS 55, 1986, p. 466, more *ešrû* documents Jursa 1995 p.120 note 221.

BM 75542[50] 25 x Cyr 5, dialogue contract, PN leases from administration of Ebabbar 5) E$_2$ UZU.KIŠIB PN2 *šá* ^{GIŠ}BAN$_2$-su[51] *la ú-šal-lim* with additional land, oxen and personnel.

BM 101334 (end Camb - beg. Dar) see sub *ešrû*.

Dar 427 27 VI Dar 16, 1) ŠE.NUMUN E$_2$ *li-mi-tu*$_4$ NIG$_2$.GA ^{d}UTU *šá* x x 2) *šá* UTU *ina* Bir-tu$_4$-šá-Ki-na-a E$_2$ *rit-tu*$_4$ *šá* 3) Marduka $^{\text{LU}_2}$*ši-rik* UTU *šá* ^{GIŠ}BAN$_2$ Bulṭā, leased by him *a-na* 5)$^{\text{LU}_2}$NU.KIRI$_6$-*ú-tu* for three years to PN.

Uruk

BIN I 111, 16 V Cyr 2, dates, *imittu* A.ŠA$_3$ 2) x x-*šú* E$_2$ *rit-ti šá* PN, belonging to Bēlet of Uruk and Nanaia pertaining to the rent farm of Ardia due from FPN.

YOS 7 38 3 VIII Cyr 4, see Chapter II under *gugallūtu*.

Nippur

Murašû

BE 9 25 17 I Art 31, lease of *bīt rittia*, *eqel našpartia* and *bīt maškanāti* (not to be taken away) with? Nār-ša-Uratē (from former owner) granted by Enlil-šum-iddina for 200 kor per annum for three years, delivery of the rent in (Al) Gira'a.

EE 17 30 III Art 31, internal lease from Enlil-šum-iddina of (your) bow and (your) *bīt ritti* land at Bīt-Murānu and in *zi-im-ma-nu* Nār-ša-Rēš which draws water from the Ḫarri-Piqudu and "as far as it reaches" and (my) *bīt ritti* land in Al-Bît-Nadini with oxen and seed. Damaged. Rent 1700 kor? Subject to *imittu* by Enlil-šum-iddina.

BE 9 34 7 IV Art 34, lease of own *bīt ritti* with two oxen and seed by PN from Enlil-šum-iddina on Nār-Namgar-Dūr-Enlil for three years for 100 kor of mixed agricultural products. No additionals.

BE 9 45 20 V Art 36, see Chapter III sub material on the status of villagers.

Ist 15 x VIII Art 38, request by Marduk-bēl-šunu s Bēl-erība to Enlil-šum-iddina for land of his bow fief, his *bīt ritti* in Ḫuṣṣētu-ša-x with oxen, tools and seed, for a rent of 150 kor; no additionals.

BE 9 67 28 VII Art 39, (// EE 29) request by two persons for lease of Nār-Dirat, right and left banks from its intake to its tail end, as far as the water reaches 3) .... E$_2$ *rit-ti-ka u* E$_2$ *maš-ka-na-ti-ki šá ina lìb-bi e-lat uz-ba-ri šá šarri* for a mixed rent of 800 kor.

PBS 2/1 62 8 IV Dar II 3, request for a lease of land in Ḫuṣṣētu-ša-Bēl-ēriš *ina* IGI PN, *ḫu-ú-bu*[52] of Bīt-Murānu, land *bāri šarri*, your *bīt ritti*, your *maškanāti* but not your bow land for three years with oxen and seed (on Ḫarri-Piqudu), fragmentary. Granted by Rēmūt-Ninurta.

Where? Nippur?

BE 8/1 132 date? date plantation and arable 5) ... *ina bar-ra-at-ta* ^{GIŠ}BAN *šá* PN 6) ... E$_2$ *rit-ti šá* PN2 $^{\text{LU}_2}$IR$_3$ *šá* PN 7) PN3 gives (the date plantation) *a-na* $^{\text{LU}_2}$NU.KIRI$_6$-*ú-tú* for five years to PN 4.

5. The "countryside" structure of the service: *ḫad/ṭru* and *ḫad/ṭru*-related[53]

In the late Achaemenid texts we regularly find the term *ḫadru* used for groups of people subjected to "military" obligations. Not that we can observe them being created, but they function as (circumscribed) groups of people in the Murašû texts and obviously had already a certain amount of history behind them: fiefs belonging to them are regularly fragmented or have no longer an occupant. The idea that this type of organisation was introduced by the Persians is almost certainly incorrect, there are clear precursors, but the possibility that the system was expanded is a real one, for some *ḫadru*s use Persian terms to indicate their function.

---

50 Jursa, 1995, p. 139f.

51 Note this manner of writing.

52 CAD Ḫ p.216.

53 Literature: principal discussion Stolper 1985 p. 70ff, with the literature mentioned there.

VS 6, 70 does not specify the unit in which the applicant wanted to serve as a *kiṣru* or a *ḫanšū* or the like, but it clearly had a definite structure of it own and it was affiliated to the "house of the crown prince", just as some *ḫadru*s later on were linked to certain estates. The name of the place in which the text was drafted suggests that we are dealing with a community with a foreign origin, possibly already located there in Assyrian times.

Though Camb 85 does not use the word *ḫadru* but *kiṣru* to indicate the unit involved, it demonstrates the activities of an ethnic group, Egyptians, in the first full year of Persian rule, when Cambyses functioned as king of Babylon under his father Cyrus.[54] These Miṣirāia seem to have organised their affairs in a more or less autonomous manner. We are dealing with a proto-*ḫadru* which presumably existed already before the few months elapsed since the arrival of the Persians. The text has *kiṣru* where later texts would use *ḫadru*.[55] Dar 351 is also of some interest. It mentions three ill-assorted *ušrēti*, "groups of ten",[56] of the "herdsman of the regular offerings", of the Ludia[57] and of the *mār banî*, "free men". The mixture of vocational, ethnic and status backgrounds is the same as that found with the later *ḫadrus* and if the Nār-Piqudu is identical with the Harri-Piqudu, or similarly located, we are even in classical *ḫadru* territory. The Cimmerians and Subarians of BE 8/1, 80 also point back to earlier ethnic realities. The occurrence of a group of ten "of the free men" must remind us of the bow land of the *mār banî* we already encountered in CT 44, 82, discussed under *bīt qašti*.

At least the direct precursors of the *hadrus* functioned under the Chaldeans. That is not strange, for the Chaldean kings will have had to recreate the basis for an army of which agriculturists constituted the main body. In so far as they could not be levied from institutional personnel, townspeople or tribal organisations, they will have had to come from the (proto-)*bīt qašti*s, which will have been settled on royal assignments of land and which will have required a mobilisation structure. The possibility that the *ḫadru* had taken in the Persian period the place of something called *kiṣru* in at least Assyrian times could be considered, though that word is often used in the general sense of "the troops". *kiṣru*s could be located in Assyrian times on large estates, for instance on that of the queen or the crown prince, and ethnic overtones are not excluded, as Assyrian kings regularly drafted deported foreign troops into their *kiṣru*s, which will have implied assignment of land.[58]

Though it is difficult to provide strict proof, here again a certain amount of "harmonisation" may have been at work. In the Murašû texts there are *māḫiṣus* of the right and the left, a division which inevitably indicates military employ. The CAD[59] suggests "military scouts", even though the literary texts quoted indicate that manipulating the bow was a notable distinguishing trait of these people. So why not a term for a certain type of bowmen? They occur as neighbours in one of the Uruk land register texts and later on in Nippur in *ḫadru*s "of the left and the right".[60] There is also a canal named after them.[61] I would consider the possibility that we are dealing with military groups provided with land

---

54 This was reluctantly accepted by M. Dandamayev, 1983, p. 57 note 4.

55 J.N. Postgate AnSt 30, 1980, p. 75 already proposed that the Assyrian *kiṣru* was the forerunner of the *ḫadru*, Camb 85 offers distinct support.

56 Singular *ušurtu*, paralleling *eširtu*.

57 Hardly Lydians, who are Sapardāia. Not in RGCT 8 (p. 213).

58 Cf. CAD K *kiṣru* 2, p. 437-8 and also *rab kiṣri*, p. 442-3.

59 M/1 p. 102, AHw p. 584 gives no usable identification, but probably sees no reason not to regard these people simply as weavers.

60 Stolper 1985 p. 75.

61 PBS 2 39: 12 Nar-^{LU_2}Ma-ḫi-iṣ.MEŠ.

in the not too distant neighbourhood of several towns and (later on) incorporated into the *ḫadru* system.

Moore, Mich 43 belongs to the Kasr archive and is to be dated to the reign of Darius II. It shows a curious mixture of obligations. In Babylon under Darius I the *urāšu* is a corvée worker who had to be provided for certain tasks, or for whom silver had to be paid. In the Michigan text a group of *urāšu*s constituted a *ḫadru* and belonged to the estate of the (or a?) *mašennu*. They were therefore landholders for whom was provided on an estate. An *ad hoc* levy had in this way become one with an "occupation", perhaps to be compared with those *mār banî*s whom we encountered as holders of bow land. All these groups of people had their own individual history, they had somehow been incorporated in the land holding and taxation system.

The *ḫadru* constituted the basic structure, based on the assignment of land, in which the ordinary foot soldier in the country side found his peacetime place. There is the likelihood that horse fiefs on principle belonged to the same organisations and it is certain that at least some *ḫadru*s were linked to estates and chariot fiefs. Possibly all *ḫadru*s were somehow linked with commanders in chariots, just as the urban institutions will have known comparable military structures, in which their heads and the royal administrators with their chariots played a leading role.

Proto-*ḫadru/kiṣru*[62]

Babylon

VS 6 70 24 VII Nbn 6, see Chapter IV under *ilku* (Babylon, Nappāḫu)

Camb 85 22 IX Camb kB, see Chapter IV under *qaštu.*

Dar 351 25 V Dar 13, dates and barley due to MNA from Nidintum-Bēl s Nabû-šum-iddina, Baba-ēreš s Nabû-rībi-aḫa and Nabû-zēr-ibni s Giraḫi (?) will be paid in II yr 14 and VII yr 14, yield of their *bīt qašti*s belonging to the three *eširtu* of the *rē'u ginē*, the Ludia and the *mār damqa* on the Nār-Piqudu. Fragment.

Nippur

BE 8/1 80 15 VIII Camb 1, at Āl-ša-Ḫandidi. The *šibûtu* (among whom Šāriḫ *ša muḫḫi āli u* ^{LU_2}GU$_2$.GAL) swear an oath (before the ? of the *guennakku*) concerning rights to water granted by Gubaru to the Gimirāia and the Subarāia.

ḫadru (other than Murašû)

Nippur

TÉBR 2 18 V Art 37, at Nippur (Šaṭir/Barbora group) receipt of $13^{1}/_{8}$ *š* KB *ilku* for Art 37 is received by Enlil-tattannu-uṣur s Ninurta-aba-uṣur and Nusku-iddina s Enlil-šum-iddina ^{LU_2}*di-ki*.MEŠ *šá* ^{LU_2}*ḫa-dar šá* ^{LU_2}SAG.URU-*a* from Ninurta-aḫḫê-bulliṭ s Bēlšunu.

Babylon Kasr?

Mich 43 15 IV Dar II 14, 1) 3 MA.NA KB *a-na taš-lin-du* 2) *šá* 14 MA.NA KB *ina il-ki* 3) *šá* ^{LU_2}GIR$_2$.LA$_2$-*ú-a šá* ^{LU_2}*ḫa-ad-ri* 4) *šá* ^{LU_2}*ú-ra-šú šá* E$_2$-AGRIG 5) *šá ina* ŠU^{II} PN ^{LU_2}*šak-nu šá* ^{LU_2}<*ú*->*ra-šú* 6) *šá* E$_2$ ^{LU_2}AGRIG ŠU^{II} PN2, for Darius yr 14.

Where?

VS 6 302 date lost, 18-*ta* ^{GIŠ}BAN *ú-šu-uz-za-a-a-i-tu*$_4$ [x?] *ḫa-ad-ri ša* ^{LU_2}ki-ir-ka-a-a *ana di-ke-e šá* [x?] *ka-a-ri šá* ŠU^{II} PN1 ^{LU_2}GAL *ka-*[*a-ri*?] PN1 *a-na ša-da-da šá* 2-*ta* ^{GIŠ}[MA$_2$?], remnants. Not understood.

---

62 *kiṣru* was still used in the days of Cambyses. Camb 316 (22 IV Camb [6?]), an isolated text which deals in a stereotype manner with the payment of varying numbers of *arṭabu*s of grain *a-na ki-ṣir ša* Bagapana (lines 2, 6 and 11). Line 2 indicates that it consisted of Egyptians and thus suggests that it can be compared to an ethnic *ḫadru*. The use of the *arṭabu* is uncommon in "native" Babylonia.

6. Land for service: a shifting background and a degree of harmonisation?

We now are in the position that we must construct a theory. Kings like Erība-Marduk and Marduk-apal-iddina II, but not they alone, realised that they had to solve the problems between the old southern towns and the Chaldean and Aramaic tribes in the countryside, and also had to strengthen and restore the main remaining urban institutions, the temples. Land division schemes near the main towns were the result. We can find the traces of *ḫanšu*s near Babylon, Borsippa, Dilbat, Kiš, Nippur, Sippar and Uruk, that is practically near all old towns from which we have information. Among the beneficiaries were the families holding the prebendal functions in the temples and to all probability the temples themselves: the *limū*s, "thousands" granted to the temples parallel the "fifties" granted to the heads of the families. The texts dealing with land tell us little about the obligations attached to the land granted as *ḫanšū* land, and it could be sold without problem, it would seem. At least one text mentions *ilku* and *ḫanšū* together and another refers to *ḫanšū* land of *ērib bīti*s. But we note that the *eširtu*s of the later texts also had members amongst the prebendal families, who were therefore also subject to obligations imposed on this type of organisation. It is probably correct to conclude that families, including those from the prebendal milieu, participating in the early land division schemes, undertook military and civil obligations from the outset.

The main obligation may have been indicated by the title of the principal beneficiary, the *rab ḫanšū*: he was made responsible for a certain "military" unit, which was probably split up in sub-units called *eširtu*, which had a basis in the family structure and thus were also property linked. If we accept this, the temples had to answer for their *limū*s and were also subject to comparable obligations. Possibly *limū*, *ḫanšû* and *eširtu* are not to be taken at face value, but primarily are indicators of a certain share, though an *eširtu*, often, but not always, consisted of ten men. Occasionally, notably in Babylon but also in Uruk and elsewhere, it is clear that those who participated in the various schemes received land in more than one field. This is a common method of spreading the risks if the fact is regarded as having an economic purpose, but it also makes it difficult to estimate the actual amount of land assigned to a *rab ḫanšû*: was it sufficient for providing for his *ḫanšū,* or not? There begins to come some information that people could be located on such land, but it is still difficult to grasp the meaning.

We might expect that somewhere in the *ḫanšū*-system there existed a link with houses, or house plots, in the town, to which obligations could be attached, but this remains elusive. UET 4, 39 is explicit in linking bow service and a house plot, but the text belongs to the "late" group in the sense used here. In general we could assume that in a town any house was located in a *babtu*, "neighbourhood", which was called out for service by a *dēkû*, with the *eširtu* to which the members of a family belonged as a basis for the assessment required by the occasion.[63] There would thus exist a link between being taxed or called up and the place of residence in the town. *urāšu* obligations on houses are known and *urāšu* is a civil aspect of *ilku* obligations. Though there is only a weak direct link between *ilku* and the *ḫanšū* complex, indirectly it is inevitable that they are intimately connected, it would seem. The *ḫanšū*-type of land division, aiming at an urban based segment of the population was no longer practiced in the later Chaldean period.

A different development was taking place in the countryside. It was certainly on its way in the Chaldean period, had possibly started in the period of Assyrian domination, but it no doubt had good earlier Mesopotamian antecedents. This was the provision of land to vocational, ethnic or status groups of limited size, in this period called *ḫadru*s. In an earlier

63 Thus: so many or so much for this or that task, possibly every time a certain task arose.

phase these were possibly dessignated as *kiṣrus*, a word with military overtones in, at least, Assyria. Without the fortuitous find of the Murašû texts the phenomenon of the *ḫadru* would hardly have been known to us. Terminologically we can regard the *ḫadrus* as something particularly late-Achaemenid, but as a general phenomenon this type of organisation was much older. It belongs to a military organisation which had to provide chariots, cavalry, bowmen - with the necessary servants- through a linkage with the most important form of earning a livelihood: agriculture. We can assume that in the early Neo-Babylonian period the granting of this type of fief by the kings meant a second, countryside oriented, stage in regaining a grip on the land. As such land grants belonging to the *bīt qašti* system were elements of a system which remained active for much longer than the *ḫanšū* based system. In its higher grades it had its aristocratic aspects. The commoners, and possibly often even unfree personnel, were holders of bow fiefs, as the lowest grade in militarily organised land holding. Bow fiefs were occasionally also in the hands of urban families, there is therefore in this respect an overlap with the urban *ešīrtus*, which also served with the bow.[64] But overwhelmingly the bow fiefs and their *ḫadrus* are a rural phenomenon.

If the Persian administration consciously tried to harmonise the various types of urban and rural land-holding and obligations, the structures they found offered ample opportunity. That the terminology adopted was mainly that of the still "active" *bīt qašti* organisation is not strange, but there were shared elements, the time-honoured term *ilku* being one. Any impression that the Persians subjected the urban population to a land for service system which burdened the countryside, is misleading: townspeople were already incorporated in a similar system, in which *ḫanšū* and *ešīrtu* were associated with the *ilku*-terminology complex to indicate the obligations. All are variants of "land for service"-type obligations.

One of the aims of the royal settlement policy, involving townspeople, foreigners and tribal elements alike, was to create a better foundation for royal power, since each scheme meant expansion of the area directly administrated by the government, subjecting more people directly to its control. In southern Babylonian circumstances that meant particularly weaning them away from the sway of tribal rulers. The intention was certainly also to make more land productive, with as a direct result a more substantial tax yield. Good but unproductive land was taken from other holders/owners, including the gods, resulting in the complicated land holding system partially masked by the neutral term *bīt ritti*, in which the payment of *ešru* preserves a vestige of the former devine ownership. In a number of cases the temples were able to re-obtain say over such properties.

The *ḫanšūs* and *ḫadrus* together are for us now the lower tier of the land holding system, but with the institutional land they were, however, not the whole pattern of land-holding. The *ḫanšūs* and *ḫadrus* were supplemented by the chariot and horse fiefs, which will have had their complements on institutional land. That the higher urban office holders, *šākin ṭēmi*s, *šatammus*, *šangû*s and *qêpu*s had their chariots is clear at least, but as the first three belonged to all likelihood to the leading local families, their obligations may have been incorporated somehow in the *ḫanšū* system.

It must also be recognised that in the Chaldean period, and probably after it, there were tribal areas, with their own structures, also regarding taxation. Their history is virtually unknown, even though *ḫanšūs* and *ḫadrus* were part of the encroachment policy applied by the royal government. That will not have meant their end, which is unknown to us and

---

64 Already the Mār-Issar letter ABL 340, SAA 10 no. 348, reports a disturbance in Babylon during the reign of Esarhaddon, when silver was being collected for the equipment of, notably, chariots.

which probably cannot be dissociated from the coming of new, Arabian, elements, even though Achaemenid rule will have reduced their importance for the time being.

In this way we have a slowly evolving system which carried in it the possibility of a considerable expansion of the yield to the government, supported as it was by an ample supply of usable land. An increase in the degree of administrative unification, if the will and the power could be found, could contribute. We can look in the direction of the Achaemenids, but the seeds for all developments noted were already present under the Chaldeans.

CHAPTER VIII
NEO-BABYLONIAN TAXATION: AN UNTIMELY ASSESSMENT

1. The imperfect information

We cannot assume that all the taxes levied and all tax-related terms used in the Neo-Babylonian period in its widest sense have been dealt with. Understandably, the terminology of taxation utilises words with very general meanings in a technical sense, which makes it sometimes difficult to decide what belongs to the realm of taxation and what not. Most texts are routine documents and there is no need to be precise since the context was known to those concerned. Catch-all terminology is not only sufficient but also desirable for the purpose of the document. *tēlītu* is a perfect example: payment of a tax is one of many forms in which costs to the individual occur. The use of a term like *bit ritti,* if the interpretation given here is correct, has the intentional purpose to be unspecific. It made the drafting of a document much easier. Time and again the unspecific nature of the terminology used leads to enumerations, in which it is sometimes difficult to recognise what is additive and what appositional. There are many of these philological problems, which inevitably burden all Assyriological discussion.

If these points can be accepted as being inevitable, but of a secondary nature, there are more serious primary gaps in our knowledge. Especially the very restricted information on the taxation of animal husbandry must be mentioned again. Animals were in some respects easier to hide and thus less easy to tax than land and agriculture, but they must have been an important source of income and they were certainly taxed, even in the steppe of Northern Mesopotamia, as the occurrence of the title of *rab ṣibti* there indicates.

Of the products wool was of vital economic importance, linking animal husbandry and textile production. Producing a piece of textile for the institutional holder of rights is not entirely unknown in this period. The practice had a long tradition behind it, but the manner in which high quality textile was produced in our period remains undocumented. The importance of Mesopotamian textile production cannot be underrated, it provided the only important home produced item which could be widely exported. Its products, and the wool used, inevitably will have been taxed, but we are virtually uninformed on this point. In passing it should be noted that institutional herdsmen were constantly involved in semi-military police duties in the Neo-Babylonian period. It may be assumed that non-institutional herdsmen were also drawn into military and corvée obligations, where possible. That would not be specific to this period and it will also have applied to, for instance, fishermen. That many of these people had a tribal background is almost inevitable.

There is little information in our period regarding the taxation aspects of fisheries, beyond the bare fact that fisheries were leased, and therefore to all likelihood will have been incorporated in systems which had taxation aspects. The Ur III period is much better documented as far as revenues obtained from fisheries are concerned.

2. The role of agricultural land

What is clear, is that taxation and all forms of land holding were intimately linked. Apportioning or leasing of land by the government and the taxation of agriculture and its labour force are inseparable. At the beginning of the First Millennium much land was uncultivated, and royal policy, intent on recovery, used it to provide the remaining towns with a stable economic basis and to bring an increasing share of the population under effective administration. Corvée labour could be used for digging canals, providing water for the extension of cultivation, which was achieved by giving out land against service obligations or against short term leases, the conditions of which could be improved after a phase of reclamation during which nominal rents were asked. Both resulted in revenue for the government and were linked in their workings.

The main tax basis we can study consisted of land assigned by the king against service obligations, but, at the level which is documented, preferably to individuals in groups, and not to isolated persons. Though the link between obligations and land shared out is less explicit in the mainly urban *ḫanšû* environment than in the more ethnic and military world of the *ḫadrus*, there is enough evidence to regard the holders of *ḫanšû* land as subject to military obligations comparable to those of the members of the *ḫadrus*. A shared aspect of all land-for-service obligations is that these could be commuted into payments of silver. Though land-for-service arrangements were intended to obviate the need for payments in produce or silver by either of the parties concerned, the change over to payments in silver compelled the holders of these fiefs to produce goods which could be sold for silver, or to engage "specialists", who provided them with the silver against the use of their land. That requiring silver for tax payments compels the subject to produce for the market is a well-known general effect of manipulation of taxation in an agrarian context.

Agricultural land also lies at the basis of the Mesopotamian institutions. What was produced by the institutions, "palaces" and "temples", and was not required for the day to day running of affairs, was available for expenditure by the government. Those who worked in institutional agriculture had to part with the major part of the results of their work, that is: all but what was sufficient to stay alive, against a limited amount of additional security which the belonging to a large institution provided. But there are indications, especially in Sippar, that this system had come under pressure in our period and that at least some of the institutional dependants had obtained a contractual relationship with their masters. The relative scarcity of unfree institutional labour plays a role in this. A similar tendency can be observed in the Murašû texts.

3. Government services

It may be observed that payments for "government services" involved paying a share of the yield and another share will also have been required from products which had to be transported. This was again preferably payable in silver, which again in the end involved marketing and the middleman. It seems to be evident that also in Mesopotamia officials were often paid by those using their services, sometimes, perhaps, through the treasury. The Persian period possibly saw the development of special accounts for these purposes, the material from prebendal contexts is suggestive, and, at any rate in the Hellenistic period, the importance of silver may have increased. It is, however, certain, that not all payments claimed by the government for the service of officials went to those officials, already the Edict of Belsazzar implies as much.

We have tried to separate taxation called "costs" related to agricultural production from other costs, related to the later stages of handling products, which included transport, and to which taxation resulting from marketing should have belonged, if this stage were documented. If this separation is somewhat artificial, it is equally artificial to separate rent paid for the use of land and taxation. Payment for irrigation water, provided through canals of which the upkeep, as far as the main arteries were concerned, was in the care of the government, was in many cases an element of the rent paid for the land leased, to which extra percentages had to be added as a result of negotiations renewing the lease. The evidence for a direct tax on agricultural produce in the field is not strong, the *nisḫu ša māti*, reinstated here as a likely form of taxation, might be a candidate. The levy of *ešrû*, ostensibly a 10% tax benefiting the temples, seems to have been restricted to land (and goods) which were or had been in the hands of the sanctuaries, but this was not a universal form of taxation. When discussing "costs" we encountered, however, other types of levy, sometimes specifically mentioning the god Marduk, thus at least officially intended for his temple,[1] which may have been levied more generally, and not only on the estates of other gods.

4. The subject as a subject

What is notable, this must be stressed, is that we find no clear instances in which people were taxed because they were subjects. We do not see that a man was being called up simply because he was of the right age. But it is likely that from an early age onwards all male subjects belonged to an *eširtu*, "group of ten", which existed with certainty in the towns and on the estates of the gods. I would therefore not go so far as proposing that it was not possible to mobilise subjects as subjects. Mobilisation leaves traces of a financial nature: payments for substitutes or for equipment. The subject who serves and equips himself normally leaves no traces in the type of documentation available at present.

Military and civil corvée duties of the subject as a subject are difficult to distinguish from duties resulting from his holding specially assigned property, as the documentation on "land for service" systems predominates totally, and much of the terminology, *ṣāb šarri*, *urāšu*, is of a general nature.

5. The apparatus

The apparatus of government was not very elaborate, but we can safely assume the existence of a network of tax offices with extensions down to the more important villages. The *bit miksi* became the place where all sorts of property transactions had to be registered. It dealt ostensibly with all government income. It is clear that its officials used, as habitual, their own, private, personnel for the tasks involved. Though it cannot be much more than a suggestion, the possibility that the collectors were leaseholders of the rights concerned, should be left open. That payments for *ilku* or *urāšu* were collected by known capitalists, notably of the Egibi and related families, suggests that rent farm type arrangements may have existed, but the possibility that these families held properties for which they were collectively responsible should also be envisaged. It is possible that special personal arrangements had come into being in relation to the Babylonian corvée obligations in Susiana.

The leasing of institutional agricultural land, with its personnel and ploughs is well attested, as is the leasing of *ešru* income of the sanctuaries. In practice many of the more important government tenants will have acted as a kind of tax collector, a direct consequence of the fact that they passed on obligations put on themselves onto their own leaseholders, who belonged to the same lease-pyramid.

In practice increasing government power meant probably that collection was improved with the available apparatus, in our period especially through leasing. This implies, though it is for us nearly invisible,[2] a certain amount of rivalry between those

---

[1] Occasionally another god is mentioned, or mentioned with Marduk.

[2] But not completely, as some problems are illustrated, for instance, by the manner in which the lease of Gimillu ended in Uruk, TCL 13, 182.

bidding for the leases, a kind of market.[3] In general we can assume increasing government interference in the Persian period.

6. All taxation had a basis rooted in the past

Neither being paid for land in services, nor levying commodities from agricultural (and other) production can be regarded as something particularly original, and it had belonged to administrative routine in Mesopotamia since times immemorial. But all working systems of taxation can be expected to be systematised and extended over areas which were not subjected to it previously, both geographically and as to subject matter, if a government was strong enough and able to enlarge the area effectively administered.

When was the multiple based system of taxation in later Mesopotamia, as visible in the texts, created? If we could accept the first occurrence of a term as indicating, roughly, the moment of introduction, and if we could equally accept the fact that the overwhelming mass of tax documents originated in the Persian period as a valid support, that period without doubt would be seen as the creator of the system. But such a conclusion is inevitably wrong and not only because the prevailing terminology of the Persian period is prefigured in the scarcer, earlier, Chaldean material. The Neo-Babylonian kings possessed an apparatus which provided them with the means for huge public works, and they entertained armies which could operate effectively in the far west of the Mesopotamian world. That apparatus, no doubt, used all traditional means of obtaining what it required in a varied manner before it was inherited by the Persians. The inherited apparatus was expanded and systematised by the Persians, in which process Darius I is generally regarded as the organiser and administrator who brought the system to fruition. No doubt partially on account of the fact that Herodotus coloured his memory in a particular manner. Though not disinclined to regard Darius I as an accomplished administrator, I assume that there are reasons for the supposition that in Babylonia he, and his direct predecessors, used the existing structures.

The Persians took over a functioning system from the Chaldeans which had roots going back at least to Assyrian times and to tribal realities, a system, which would survive at least in part until the end of the Persian period. It would, however, be wrong to suppose that the system did not develop further after Darius. Whatever the truth behind Herodotus' Persian tribute, it cannot have been an unchanging entity.

7. The consequences of the taxation studied

Both the sharing out of property in land for service schemes and the conditions of the lease contracts caused a steady expansion of the amount of land under the plough. Taxation and leasing of land by the government cannot be separated. Both resulted in the fact that the government obtained huge amounts of agricultural produce, both of the staples and increasingly also of the specialised products mentioned in the Murašû documents. On top of that the surplus produced by the institutions was also available. In cases were this can be observed the middlemen preferred keeping the products and paid the dues they owned in silver. This may be regarded as an indication that a market for the products involved existed.

---

[3] The structure of the dialogue documents in which some of the important leases have come to our knowledge, automatically suggests in their phrasing a certain keenness on the part of the lessee to undertake the job, if he does not also manage to convey a certain feeling for the risks, as in TCL 13, 182. There is at least one Uruk lease where the person concerned brims over with enthusiasm about the information he is going to divulge and the benefits that will ensue: TCL 12, 57, 13 VIII Nbk 41.

The existence of the market created opportunities for extra taxation on the provisioning of the towns. The market will in itself have further increased taxation income. The yield of this type of taxation is difficult to estimate. If duties were collected per canal, per township passed and per trans-shipment, costs would grow exponentially. The instances in which the size of payments for this type of taxation is known with any precision provide divergent results: a *miksu* payment of "a *sūtu* in the kor", 3 1/3 % in an unpublished text mentioned by C. Wunsch, against a *kāru* of 1.2.0 on 13.0.0, in TCL 12, 85, just over 10% on top of what the owner received from the tenant, or if our calculations, above under *kāru,* are valid, 7% out of a total product of 20 kor. If amounts comparable to the *miksu* mentioned had to be paid on each movement of a shipment, it would increase prices rapidly, or rather, it would decrease the amount of the commodities available for sale by the producer and increase that available to the tax man and his superior. The net practical result in the market place would, probably, be limited, as the tax man would have had to dispose of what was collected and he probably had to give a rebate to his trader, as was the case in the Old Babylonian period. The trader would ask what the market could bear, or hoard. Texts from the Iddina-Marduk archive at least suggest that the tax man used the same channels to dispose of his goods as the producers did: through the same middleman. This situation would be unattractive for the producer and probably favour the urban middleman.

It should be noted that in the late Achaemenid period there was an increased diversity in the products planted and -we must add- included in the rents paid by tenants. The need to pay in silver will have contributed to the tendency to diversify agricultural production.

The general economic growth of the period presumably made taxation more acceptable, even though, in the Persian period, it meant that a share of the economic potential of Mesopotamia was siphoned off to the heartland of the empire, especially to Elam. This was a direct result of the loss of independence, which also entailed the loss of income from the earlier external possessions. Growth in a situation of peace had to compensate for these drawbacks.

Over all this should sound rather positive, but it depended to a large degree on the availability of virtually unrestricted amounts of land, as Mesopotamian irrigation inevitably caused, then as now, salinisation of the land used. In the Chaldeo-Achaemenid period we are, however, relatively spoken, still at the beginning of a new phase of the cycle.

A land-for-service system cannot work if the holder of the land is expected both to farm and to serve for the whole year. How the larger estates influenced general outcomes is another problem. We often cannot be certain whether payments were in lieu of obligations or additional to practical service. This is easily possible, for instance, in the form of payments for *urāšu*s for all sorts of specific requirements of the moment. Larger land holders would have found it easier to cope with these facts than small ones. The existence of a mixed system of "fixed" and "in lieu of" contributions is perhaps the best guess and that makes it again difficult for us to estimate the value of taxation for the government of the day.

8. The burden: an impossible quantification

All attempts at quantification are problematic. For a start, a serious problem is caused by the limited understanding of the practicalities of the flexible adaptation of the system of solid volume measures to government requirements. For the actual amounts paid this is of prime importance. Which measure was used is infrequently specified. We are still in a world where money as we know it, did not exist. The question of the supply of silver, which must have increased in the period studied, is equally intractable. Speculation on supplies deriving from Phoenician exploitation of Hispanic sources is possible, but the silver involved had to be earned by Babylonia in order to be able to forward it to the king. Contrary to what might be expected, the purity of the silver used as currency seems to have increased in the Achaemenid period. This may have increased the burden on the taxpayer, if this primarily meant that purer silver than that, that was actually current, was required. We remain virtually uninformed on this point.

In the end all estimates are little more than a form of -emphatically under-educated-speculation. Taxation of agricultural produce took the form of levies of costs and of duties, preferably on transport. Costs amounted to minimally 10%, but could imply, in institutional contexts, the planting of 20% more land, for which the costs in seed, fodder and labour had to be born completely by the lessee. It is noticeable that in Murašû context there is perhaps a tendency to move to "additional payments" of 20% on top of the rent, which, of course, had to be paid for in the end by the producers, the lowest layer in the lease hierarchy. If duties were levied on transit, we can assume that in total at least 30% of the products involved had to be relinquished, but that was perhaps only valid for commodities for the urban market. On top of that there was the *ešrû,* as the word suggests 10%, but often less and not levied generally. Perhaps what was consumed locally should be regarded as exempted, at least partially. This will have concerned a considerable proportion of the produce, since most of the population will have lived on the land. All this amounts, however, to little more than a very rough guess and it cannot serve as a basis for real quantification.

It all added up, however, for producers who also had to pay rent. But it would not have been completely crippling. The "rule" that roughly one third of the yield has to go to the owner of the land, another one third to the tenant, with the remainder for cultivation and related costs, cannot be applied, since it is only valid in low yield agriculture. It is difficult to mention a generally valid minimum, but there are indications of what was considered as "reasonable". The Edict of Belsazzar mentions a share in the yield for the owner of 12 kor per kor, 12:1 for him alone, which suggests the existence of a buffer. A tenant could, it may perhaps sound crude, survive on less than a third of what he produced.

Taxation in order to keep the cult of the gods provided seems to have depended, at least partially, on specific circumstances, but if it really was a patchwork of rights and obligations, its actual impact on the subject in general will be difficult for us to assess.

On present evidence it can only be suggested that what was demanded in taxes could represent roughly a third of agricultural production, and, to speculate further, from production in general, in which the importance of animal husbandry and also craft production, especially of textiles, must not be underestimated. The amount also had to cover local government costs, to which corvée labour or its equivalent in silver contributed, though the incidence and weight cannot be estimated realistically. The practical burden of service obligations will have depended greatly on the season in which they were required. Payments for work “in Elam” will have become automatic and pretty well continuous in the Persian period. Possibly the costs involved were additional to what was paid and required locally. It is also fairly certain that the burden of taxation was passed on downwards wherever possible.[4]

9. Social consequences

One of the purposes of (pre-modern) taxation is to confirm people in their (social) status, as subjects. The -for me- clearest instances of this phenomenon are the forms of

---

4 There are no signs of the structure of taxation being determined by a system of tax bands, which has the particular inequity of concentrating the pressure each time in the lower area of each band. Such tax bands were known in the later Parthian system of poll tax and may have had precursors.

taxation related to the delivery of flour, which is an intrinsic element of the land for service system and of the labour aspects of institutional agriculture. This has deep roots in Mesopotamian history. Its corollary is the delivery of (ordinary quality) textiles, already mentioned, which is not well attested in the Neo-Babylonian period, though it does occur and is expanded or replaced by an obligation to deliver skeins of linen thread and all the labour, also on the land, that that required, found in a number of later Achaemenid texts. We can assume that much of the labour that this type of taxation imposed fell on the female segment of society.

What is certain, is that in the land-for-service system the disappearance of the holder of a fief caused grave problems for his family, especially if the inheritor was a minor, in which equipment costs played an important additional role. This is a clear indication that serving also entailed indirect costs for land holders in such systems, though the loss of the breadwinner would have had serious consequences in any occupation.

There must almost inevitably have been practical time limits on the length of service and that will have made a conversion to payments in silver attractive for the authorities, especially in the case of duties undertaken outside the country. The subject may have avoided in this manner some of the indirect costs. But it remains difficult to distil a consistent pattern out of the amounts in silver paid by holders of fiefs according to the texts.

10. Herodotus' Persian tribute

Herodotus has the Persian king claim from Mesopotamia -which was more than the alluvium we are dealing with- 1000 talents of silver and 500 eunuchs. It is not clear whether these numbers were meant to include local expenditure or not. For some provinces certain special forms of local expenditure can be added to the amounts given, as they are specified separately, but not for Mesopotamia. What is mentioned, is probably to be seen as what had to leave the country. The eunuchs baffle us, we do not see them being bred, bought, prepared or delivered. We must leave this aside. But Herodotus is silent on the labour requirements "for Elam". We can not put a figure on this, but it probably was not a negligible burden. We find this requirement in virtually all our text groups, both institutional and private, from a whole range of places. This obligation probably was not included in the 1000 talents of silver, which the context suggests should be taken literally, implying for Mesopotamia a considerable amount of trade with other areas, through which the silver had to be obtained.

1000 talents represent 60.000 mina. We must try to envisage how these could be divided between types of income, and suggest five sources: payments by fief holders, income from arable agriculture, from date plantations, and from animal husbandry together with artisanal production, the last four should all include the institutional production surplus of the temples and possibly also the palace. But the many local expenses which needed to be covered must also be born in mind.

The theory that a bow fief annually paid one mina of silver has been mentioned. This theoretical one mina of silver per annum per fief is not particularly well-based, but may serve as a "notional sum". Perhaps we can accept that a kor of barley had a value of somewhat more than a shekel of silver, and that a kor of dates made a slightly lower price, which results in an assumed average of 1 *š* per kor. We can assume that roughly one third of agricultural production plus what the government in all its ramifications received as a landlord could be regarded as potentially contributing to the tribute, again minus local costs.

Using the one mina per bow criterion, 60.000 land holding bowmen would be needed to deliver the tribute. This is not realistic. Stolper has collected the names of sixty-odd *ḫadru*s near Nippur, but we cannot assume that that represents the whole number. We have little idea about the actual size of a *ḫadru*, possibly TÉBR no. 1 could be taken as roughly suggesting "some 25 to 30 men at most", a number never even approached by any of the groups of fief holders occurring in the Murašû archive.[5] 2000 fief holders seems to provide a good upper limit in the Nippur area, even though we will have to accept that none of the Murašû documents can give us an idea how many members a *ḫadru* had, as only those in difficulties will have come into contact with the Murašûs through their *šaknus*. Whether we can regard the situation in the Nippur area as exemplary for the whole of Southern Mesopotamia is questionable. What constitutes this "Nippur area" is also an open question, even so 60.000 fief holders or 30 "Nippurs" are unlikely to be achieved. Obtaining annually 15.000 mina of silver from this source seems to be rather optimistic.

For 15.000 mina of silver the one sekel/kor criterion would require 900.000 kor of barley and dates each, assuming that date plantations and arable each had to provide a quarter of the sum required. At the criteria used by the Edict of Belsazzar, one kor of date plantation is supposed to yield 40 kor of dates, and a kor of arable should yield 12 kor of barley, both for the landlord, to which we must not add the amounts for *gimru*, for they would be required locally. If we could speculate we would need the landowners share of 22.500 kor, 30.375 ha, just over 300 km^2, of date plantation and 75.000 kor of arable, equalling 101250 ha., a good 1010 km^2. In total this would mean the net yield of 1310 km^2, of date gardens and arable land.[6] The remaining quarter of the sum of 60.000 mina would have to come from other sources. The burden would inevitably be considerable, probably unrealistically so, certainly if we add the labour obligations in Elam. But it is, again, too early for effective quantification and we must avoid thinking in static terms. The practical value of this type of calculation is limited, it should, however open our eyes for what was possible. The result is, perhaps, a "not completely impossible", if the silver could be earned.

11. Final remarks

If we want to understand Mesopotamian society and its culture we will have to study what paid for the superstructure. We are only at the beginning. If we do not want to limit our interest in Ancient Mesopotamia to a collection of odd curiosities and outdated ideas or theories in the realms of religion or science, we must look for the solutions it applied to the problems of what was after all a relatively successful agricultural society.

Especially during Achaemenid rule all taxes answered to simpleton's general law of taxation: taxes only increase. In whatever system he happens to live the subject is powerless when confronted by a government, when it is accountable no less than when it is not. Perhaps even more so in the first case, because accountability is paralleled by insatiable claims on a share in a bounty deemed unlimited, which makes it even more difficult to master the natural greed for a share in the taxation bonanza. The overall growth of the economy during the Achaemenid period will have made the burden of taxation more bearable and we can conclude that in general government policy favoured agricultural expansion. Perhaps we are dealing with an economy which could only be sustained by growth. Is inability to stabilise in time a healthy sign? The question is of some current interest.

Only concerning agriculture, that is arable and date plantations in southern Mesopotamia, some sort of a general conclusion seems to be possible: the government could

---

[5] The next highest number is 18, in VS 6, 302.

[6] There is no possibility to compare these calculations in a meaningful fashion with the figures presented by E. Wirth, Agrargeographie des Irak, Hamburg 1962, p.42 Tabelle 2, especially not when 1913 and 1957 are compared.

claim up to about 30% of the production in rights and duties, additional was the rent of the land it gave out in leases and the surplus production of the temples and what we can call "the palace". On fully productive land that could be 33% of the harvest. On top of that came the rights to corvée labour, especially resulting from land held against service obligations, but these extended also, for instance over institutional land and over (some?) land held by townspeople. Varying, according to the nature of the relation between landholder and government, between 25 and 63% of the production of arable production could be claimed by the government, there where it governed. Much clarification of the practical meaning of this estimate is required.

TAXATION LITERATURE

Adams 1981	R. McC. Adams, Heartland of Cities, Surveys of Ancient Settlement and Land Use on the Central Floodplain of the Euphrates, Chicago and London, 1981.
Augapfel 1917	J. Augapfel, Babylonische Rechtsurkunden aus der Regierungszeit Artaxerxes I. und Darius II., Wien 1917.
Bongenaar 1997	A.C.V.M. Bongenaar, The Neo-Babylonian Ebabbar Temple at Sippar, its Administration and its Prosopography, Istanbul, 1997.
Cardascia 1951	G. Cardascia, Les Archives des Murašû, une famille d'hommes d'affaires babyloniens à l'époque perse (455-403 av. J.-C.), Paris, 1951.
Cardascia 1983	G. Cardascia, Le fief dans la Babylone Achemenide, Rec. Soc. J. Bodin, Les liens de vassalité et les immunités, Paris, 1983, p. 55-86.
Cocquerillat 1968	D. Cocquerillat, Palmeraies et Cultures de l'Eanna d'Uruk (559-520), ADFU 8, Berlin, 1968.
Dandamayev 1967	M.A. Dandamayev, Die Lehnsbeziehungen in Babylonien unter den ersten Achämeniden, in ed. G. Wiessner, Festschrift für Wilhelm Eilers, Wiesbaden, 1967, p. 37-42.
Dandamayev 1968	M.A. Dandamayev, Bagasarū gansabara, ed. M. Mayrhofer c.s, Studien zur Sprachwissenschaft und Kulturkunde, Gedenkschrift für Wilhelm Brandenstein, Innsbruck 1968, p. 235-239.
Dandamayev 2000	M.A. Dandamayev, Custom Dues in First-millennium Babylonia, AOAT 272, Gedenkschrift P. Calmeyer, Münster 2000, p. 215-222.
Donbaz-Stolper 1997	V. Donbaz and M.W. Stolper, Istanbul Murašû ṭexts, Istanbul, 1997. (Texts: Ist + no.)
Dosch 1993	G. Dosch, Zur Struktur der Gesellschaft des Königsreichs Arrapḫe, HSAO 5, 1993, Heidelberg.
Doty 1977	L.T. Doty, Cuneiform Archives from Hellenistic Uruk, Diss. Yale 1977.
van Driel 1987-8	G. van Driel, The Edict of Belšazzar, an alternative interpretation, JEOL 30, 1987-88, p. 60-64.
Joannès 1982	F. Joannès, Textes économiques de la Babylonie récente, Paris 1982.
Joannès 1989	F. Joannès, Archives de Borsippa, la Famille Ea-ilûta-bâni, Genève 1989.
Joannès-Lemaire 1996	F. Joannès et A. Lemaire, Contrats babyloniens d'époque achéménide du Bit-Abi-ram avec une épigraphe araméenne, RA 90, 1996, p. 41-60.
Jursa 1995	M. Jursa, Die Landwirtschaft in Sippar in neubabylonischer Zeit, AfO Beiheft 25, 1995.
Jursa 1998	M. Jursa, Der Tempelzehnt in Babylon vom siebenten bis zum dritten Jahrhundert v. Chr., AOAT 254, 1998.
Jursa 1999	M. Jursa, Das Archiv des Bēl-rēmanni, Istanbul, 1999.
Kraus 1958	F.R. Kraus, Ein Edikt des Königs Ammi-ṣaduqa von Babylon, Leiden, 1958.
Landsberger 1955	B. Landsberger, Remarks on the Archive of the Soldier Ubārum, JCS 9. 1955, p. 121-131; cf. JCS. 10, 1956, p.39.
MacGinnis 1998a	J. MacGinnis, BM 64707 and *rikis qabli* in the Ebabbara, WZKM 88, 1998, p. 177-182.
MacGinnis 1998b	J. MacGinnis, The Ordering of the House of Šamaš: texts from the management of the Neo-Babylonian Ebabbara, Iraq 60, 1998, p.207-217.
Oppenheim 1940	A.L. Oppenheim, *qabla rakāsu* and *qabla paṭāru*, OrNS 14, 1940, p. 239-241.
Peat 1983	J.A. Peat, *Ḫanšu* land and the *rab ḫanši*, Iraq 45, 1983, p. 124-127.

Peiser-Kohler 1890	F.E. Peiser und J. Kohler, Babylonische Verträge des Berliner Museums, Berlin, 1890. (Texts quoted as PV + number).
Postgate 1974	J.N. Postgate, Taxation and Conscription in the Assyrian Empire, Studia Pohl; Series Maior 3, Rome 1974.
Ries 1976	G. Ries, Die neubabylonischen Bodenpachtformulare, Berlin, 1976
Van der Spek 1986	R.J. Van der Spek, Grondbezit in het Seleucidische Rijk, Amsterdam, 1986.
San Nicolò 1953	M. San Nicolò, Ein Beitrag zu den Grunddienstbarkeiten im neubabylonischen Recht, Fs V. Arangio-Ruiz, Napoli 1953, p. 57-74.
Stolper 1977	M.W. Stolper, Three Iranian Loanwords in Late Babylonian Texts, in L.D. Levine and T. Cuyler Young jr., Mountains and Lowlands, Essays in the Archaeology of Greater Mesopotamia, BiMes 7, Malibu 1977, p. 251-266.
Stolper 1985	M.W. Stolper, Entrepreneurs and Empire, The Murašû Archive, the Murašû Firm, and Persian Rule in Babylonia, Istanbul 1985. (Texts: EE + no.)
Stolper 1988	M.W. Stolper, The *šaknu* of Nippur, JCS 40, 1988 p.127-155.
Stolper 1989	M.W. Stolper, Registration and Taxation of Slave Sales in Achaemenid Babylonia, ZA 79, 1989 p. 80-101.
Stolper 1994	M. Stolper, Militärkolonisten, RLA 8, 3/4, 1994, p.205-207.
Stolper 2000a	M.W. Stolper, No Harm done: on Late Achaemenid *pirku* Guarantees, in ed. J. Marzahn and H. Neumann, Assyriologica et Semitica, Festschrift J. Oelsner, AOAT 252, Münster 2000, p. 467-477.
Stolper 2000b	M.W. Stolper, Buildings on Bow Land and Encumbrances on Buildings, Gedenkschrift P. Calmeyer, AOAT 272, Münster 2000, p. 668-680.
Stolper 2001	M.W. Stolper, Fifth Century Nippur: texts of the Murašûs and from their surroundings, JCS 53, 2001, p. 83-132.
Thureau-Dangin 1924	F. Thureau-Dangin, La correspondance de Ḫammurapi avec Šamaš-ḫâṣir, RA 21, 1924, p. 1-58.
Waerzeggers 2001	C. Waerzeggers, Het archief van Marduk-rēmanni, I Studie van de familie Ṣāgit-ginê in Nieuwbabylonisch Sippar (548-484 v. Chr.) II De tabletten, Dissertatie, Gent, 2001. (Texts M.r. + no.)
Wunsch 1993	C. Wunsch, Die Urkunden des babylonischen Geschäftsmannes Iddin-Marduk, Zum Handel mit Naturalien im 6. Jahrhundert v. Chr. I und II, Groningen, 1993. (Texts: W, IM + no.)
Wunsch 2000a	Neubabylonische Geschäftsleute und ihre Beziehungen zu Palast- und Tempelverwaltungen: das Beispiel der Familie Egibi, in A.C.V.M. Bongenaar, Interdependency of Institutions and Private Entrepreneurs, MOS Studies 2, Istanbul 2000.
Wunsch 2000b	C. Wunsch, Das Egibi-Archiv, I, Die Felder und Gärten, Band I und II, Groningen 2000. (Texts: W, E I + no.)

SPECIAL ABBREVIATIONS

The Babylonian months are indicated by Roman numbers, I representing Nisan, etc.

A, L., and NBC + no.:	texts from published, in numerical order in Joannès 1998.
BM + no.	unless a special reference is given indicates texts in Jursa 1998.
EE + no.	texts in Stolper1985.
Ist + no.	texts in Donbaz-Stolper 1997.
M.r. + no.	texts in Waerzeggers 2001.
W, IM+ no.	texts in Wunsch 1993.
W, E I+no.	texts in Wunsch 2000b.

Abbreviated names

Names are regularly abbreviated, especially in summaries of rexts, after being given in full in the first instance in a text group

Always:

IM :	Iddin-Marduk Nur-Sin
MBU	Marduk-bēl-uṣur
MNA;	Marduk-nāṣir-apli s Itti-Marduk-balāṭu Egibi
M.r.	Marduk-rēmanni (s Bēl-uballiṭ Ṣāḫit-ginê)
NAI Sin-ili	Nabû-apal-iddina Sin-ili

Š(irik) s I(ddina) is the same person as Marduk-nāṣir-apli s Itti-Marduk-balāṭu Egibi

A POSTSCRIPT: THE FACTOR SILVER

The introduction insists that Mesopotamian society should be seen as both agrarian in character and cyclic in development, which will be to some no more than another instance of a dreary agrarian *longue durée* in which essentially nothing happens or evolves. That does not invalidate questioning why and how the various Mesopotamian cycles evolved, how human activities brought about the changes and effected development in the various stages of growth, which are as obvious as the periods of decline, which equally require explanation. We will not discuss here the possible role of what we can call "ethnic change", which was, possibly, in the ancient Near East in a sense also a permanent feature of the *longue durée*, perhaps providing in a sense a reserve labour force. But we must keep in mind, that, whatever is the case, the region moved inexorably towards larger political entities, a process finally disrupted only in the course of the Hellenistic period. The development from small, local, urban based political entities in the Third Millennium towards the increasingly centralised monarchy of the Achaemenid period took at the very least 2500 years, and it put urbanised Mesopotamia under considerable strain. The effects can be observed best in the middle years of the Old Babylonian period, when it seems to become clear that a single urban centre experienced considerable difficulties in controlling others with a similar structure.

For the long term developments we must depend on archaeology, which in the Mesopotamian South still means the Adams surveys and related work. For the details we must study the written documentation with its varying backgrounds, which presents itself to us, at least for the moment, in very period-specific guises, for which we are inadequately equipped, and which require the invention of concepts such as reciprocity and redistribution, private or institutional, household, patrimonial and patriarchal, and more, in various combinations in an attempt at comprehension. In reality all such props and stickers are part of a continuous groping, especially if the written word is studied, in which at least a part of the population, the non-sedentary and the tribal element, which is not of necessity the same, hardly figures. Agrarian Mesopotamia, in the various stages of the cycle which it passes through, can not be seen as something monolithic. The various phenomena observed must not be disconnected from their place in a stratified society, which, however, does not possess a uniform density.

A Mesopotamian institution, a palace or a temple, has much of the structure of a household, but it does not, even to its members, redistribute its holdings in a welfare state sense: it pays the lowest wages possible. A temple can be described as a household, but though dominated through his administrative apparatus by a king, it is problematic to regard the institution as an unrestricted royal patrimonial possession. At least since the Ur III period there are too many others with an established interest. Private exploitation and institutional ownership of assets, land and people, are often closely linked. There existed a market for all sorts of goods, but probably as yet no market economy. Household, as a kind of institution, is in a sense a misleading term when dealing with the "naked" nuclear family at the lower end of the social scala, sedentary or not. The size and intensity of the phenomenon to which the explicatory terminology is applied determines the practical meaning of both the phenomenon observed and the terminology used. If the gap between large and small becomes too wide the explanatory terminology used looses its contents. Important in Mesopotamia is the growth in size during separate steps in the successive cycles, which at least in a political sense, and probably also economically, is undeniable.

Here the main question must remain what the nature of change in Mesopotamian society was, other than the changes which were the direct consequence of alterations in the regional ecological situation. Typical of such "minor" changes are the inevitable effects of the application of irrigation, which causes salinisation and locally perhaps results in a cycle of some 60 to 70 years, difficult to observe in the written material, as most of our local documentation, in any case when of the required density, only covers shorter periods. Such changes are of limited importance, and could be answered in the past by a simple relocation of activities. That long term growth in political scale is here seen as one of the most notable observable changes in Mesopotamian society, will, perhaps, have become obvious. It will equally be clear that this development did not follow a straight line, and that it caused serious problems. Notably because growth of a political entity deprived other, similarly structured, entities not just of their power, but of their very function.

The increase in political scale meant also a change in the relation with the world outside Mesopotamia, which caused an important reversal in the status of Mesopotamian society: the land became a subject province in a much bigger construct.

One of the theses defended here is that the clerical elite played a crucial role in maintaining Mesopotamia as an urbanised society, effectively so because its structure spread membership widely. This is a development which acquired increasing momentum from the Ur III period onwards. An important fact is that the prebendal system could, if required, operate on a local, agrarian basis. Basically the offerings for the gods and the remuneration of the prebendaries were produced locally. Under pressure, this system possibly even could in essence function without silver. The fact must, however, not persuade us too easily that the prebendaries had no part in an economy in which silver became of increasing importance: the individuals we know best, especially in our late period, participated in a variety of economic activities, and they were also landholders. These activities could attract others.

The importance of our elusive silver within Mesopotamia becomes manifest when we study the relation between the subjects, both institutional and private, and (central) government. In a way an increasing role of silver changes the relationship between the rulers and the ruled. As an illustration F.R. Kraus' "Palastgeschäft" can serve: the government produces, and receives as taxation, agrarian products which it wants to exchange for something which it can hoard for longer periods than is possible for agrarian products. This asks for a market, a requirement which can be traced back to at least 2000 B.C. For the market to function there must be subjects capable of serving as buyers, creating a solvent demand.

A main difference with "modern" governments is probably that a modern government can better afford the permanent hole in its pocket, in which the invention of "money", something of which, with some "prudence", the value can be hollowed out at will, plays an important role. This represents a next step. Ancient governments had to create concrete reserves, and were worried about the lack of them.[1] The empty palace at Mari was a reason for apprehension. Spending the reserves is an indication of impending disaster. For instance the administratively attested handing over to his enemies of the Ur treasures by

[1] This does not mean that hoarding and withdrawing assets from circulation should be represented as something desirable in itself.

Ibbi-Sin is a clear sign. The merchant accounts from Umma suggest that the local administration collected silver (and gold), which would, we assume, appear on the account of the local ENSI with the king. The king of Persia hoarded silver supplied by Mesopotamia and other provinces, and we should notice silver of an increasing purity. In itself the fact is of interest, as it indicates that we must not regard this silver as money in our sense, but still as a generally accepted commodity, which could be exchanged for other commodities. The government has not yet made the important discovery that by turning silver, or gold, into coins, of which procedure it had to keep the monopoly, it could manipulate the value of its holdings in precious metal. The subject wisely continued to regard coined silver as something which had, at least, to be weighed, in Babylonia certainly into the Hellenistic period. No doubt purity was also watched. The noted increase in quality suggests that Gresham's law did not yet function, or, rather, that "money" had not yet come into being.

What makes silver an elusive commodity in Mesopotamia is not its absence or scarcity, but our lack of understanding concerning its origins. It was produced in areas outside Mesopotamia's military reach, though this aspect of the question anyhow could not play a role in the Achaemenid period. Mesopotamia had to earn what it required through trade. Only the Old-Assyrian texts make clear how this was done, but in a specific context. Here we are confronted by the "period specific" nature of our information. Are we allowed to generalise, using the known Old Assyrian example? Production of quality textiles, transit trade in essential commodities, for example tin, and participation in regional trade outside Mesopotamia? For most periods there is no information. But the fact that copper, though plentiful in Anatolia, is not brought to Mesopotamia indicates that foreign trade is also in a well-documented period a complicated affair.

If we are correct in suggesting that the silver we are dealing with cannot be regarded as money in our sense, we probably also must conclude that in a long term perspective the amount of silver in circulation, notwithstanding the known government inclination to hoard, increased, certainly when we compare the development of the price in silver of basic agricultural products like barley and dates. We must assume a steady supply of silver. The "elusive" applied to silver does not so much refer to the commodity itself, which, it would seem, was real enough, but to the manner in which a steady supply was secured. It played an increasing role in a growing economy.

Longue durée? Yes. An agrarian society? Yes, but all the same essential economic and social developments and considerable changes in content when "explanations" of the type "institutional" or "household" are applied. Also inevitably a growth of the area more intensively used by agrarian exploitation and to all likelihood an increasing importance as to volume and variety of goods of "the market", together with a greater role of silver. But not yet a market economy and "money". On its own the Ancient Near Eastern world managed to develop to this point. It certainly had changed since the third millennium.

REGISTER OF TEXTS USED

The texts are listed separately for the three separate parts of this study.
Arabic numbers indicate the page, roman number plus / followed by an arabic number indicates Chapter and footnote number.

1. Texts used in Part I: Merchants and the Problematic Market

II Texts used in Part II: Prebends

III Texts used in Part III: Taxation